HBJ SOCIAL STUDIES

THE WORLD
Past and Present

LANDMARK EDITION

Stephanie Abraham Hirsh, Ph.D.
GENERAL EDITOR

Phillip Bacon, Ph.D.
SENIOR EDITORIAL ADVISER

HBJ HARCOURT BRACE JOVANOVICH, PUBLISHERS
Orlando   San Diego   Chicago   Dallas

GENERAL EDITOR

Dr. Stephanie Abraham Hirsh is Director of Program and Staff Development for the Richardson Independent School District in Richardson, Texas. Dr. Hirsh has a B.S. degree from the University of Texas at Austin, an M.Ed. from North Texas State University, and a Ph.D. in Curriculum and Instruction from North Texas State University. In addition to her work within the school district, Dr. Hirsh has served as a consultant for social studies and staff development, has taught university courses, and has published numerous articles in several educational journals. Dr. Hirsh is a past president of the Texas Council for the Social Studies. She serves currently on the Executive Board of the Social Studies Supervisors Association and numerous committees for the National Council for the Social Studies.

SENIOR EDITORIAL ADVISER

Dr. Phillip Bacon is a professor Emeritus of Geography and Anthropology at the University of Houston. Dr. Bacon has also served on the faculties of Columbia University and the University of Washington. Formerly Dean of the Graduate School of Peabody College for Teachers at Vanderbilt University, Dr. Bacon began his career in education as a teacher of elementary and secondary social studies. He is the author or editor of more than 36 books, including the *Life Pictorial Atlas of the World*. For 18 years, Dr. Bacon served as a member of the Editorial Advisory Board of *World Book Encyclopedia*.

Among his numerous honors and awards, Dr. Bacon holds the distinguished titles of Fellow of the Explorers Club and Fellow of the Royal Geographic Society of Great Britain. He is a three-time recipient of the Teaching Excellence Award at the University of Houston. His biography appears in *Who's Who in America* and *American Men and Women in Science*.

Acknowledgments

For permission to reprint copyrighted material, grateful acknowledgment is made to the following sources:

Doubleday & Company, Inc.: "The Snake" by Kyoshi from *An Introduction to Haiku* by Harold G. Henderson. Copyright © 1958 by Harold G. Henderson.
Présence Africaine: From "Sebonwoma" by Christina Ama Ata Aidoo in *Présence Africaine*, Paris, No. 57 (1st Quarterly, 1966).

Printed in the United States of America.   ISBN 0-15-372906-6

SENIOR PROGRAM ADVISERS

John F. Barbini, Ed.D.
Assistant Superintendent
School District 54
Schaumberg, Illinois

Sister Marijon Binder
Global Concerns Center
Chicago, Illinois

Paul S. Hanson
Social Studies Supervisor
Dade County Public Schools
Miami, Florida

Cheryl Biles Moore
Director, Staff Development,
   Research and Evaluation
Orange County Department of Education
Costa Mesa, California

William D. Travis, Ed.D.
Curriculum Director
Pittsfield Public Schools
Pittsfield, Massachusetts

Donald P. Vetter
Supervisor of Social Studies
Carroll County Public Schools
Westminster, Maryland

Thomas Gregory Ward
Social Studies Specialist
Fairfax County Schools, Area II
Fairfax, Virginia

Alice Wells
Curriculum Consultant
Cartwright School District No. 83
Phoenix, Arizona

SENIOR CONTENT SPECIALISTS

Biliana Cicin-Sain, Ph.D.
Associate Professor of Political Science
University of California
Santa Barbara, California

Irving Cutler, Ph.D.
Chairman Emeritus, Geography Department
Chicago State University
Chicago, Illinois

Donald O. Schneider, Ph.D.
Professor and Head of
   Social Science Education
University of Georgia
Athens, Georgia

Wm. Doyle Smith, Ph.D.
Professor of Economics
University of Texas at El Paso
El Paso, Texas

Peter J. Stein, Ph.D.
Professor of Sociology
William Paterson College
Wayne, New Jersey

SKILLS DEVELOPMENT

H. Michael Hartoonian, Ph.D.
Supervisor of Social Studies Education
Wisconsin Department of Public Instruction
Madison, Wisconsin

CLASSROOM CONSULTANTS

Beverley A. Brezden
Newhart School
Mission Viejo, California

Marguerite L. Cherry
P.S. 270
Brooklyn, New York

Sue Hanauer
Balis Elementary School
Syosset, New York

Lucy Hatch
Region 14
Education Service Center
Abilene, Texas

Connie M. Lowe
Susquenita Elementary School
Duncannon, Pennsylvania

Mary N. Matthew
George Melcher Elementary School
Kansas City, Missouri

Marlene J. Morris
Flushing Jr. High
Flushing, Michigan

Robert Navarro
Doedyns Elementary School
San Juan, Texas

Fred W. Nelson
Pine Valley School
Wilmington, North Carolina

Esthyr Nipp
Roosevelt Elementary School
South St. Paul, Minnesota

Ronald Presl
Lincoln Elementary School
Merrill, Wisconsin

Jack Rudicil
Robert E. Lucas Intermediate School
Cincinnati, Ohio

Barbara Sanderson
Crawford Elementary School
Arcadia, Louisiana

Yvonne Sheek
Director of Elementary Education
Metropolitan School District of
   Perry Township
Indianapolis, Indiana

Betty Jo Siegrist
Thurston Middle School
Springfield, Oregon

Edith V. Spain
Kozminski Community Academy
Chicago, Illinois

Clara Irwin Traver
The Lovett Middle School
Atlanta, Georgia

Molly D. Vliet
Westlawn Elementary School
Falls Church, Virginia

Sharon Waicus
Buies Creek Elementary School
Buies Creek, North Carolina

Jessalyn H. Welch
Lake City Elementary School No. 2
Lake City, South Carolina

Janet E. Wilkins
North Palm Beach Elementary School
North Palm Beach, Florida

Marilyn T. Woodward
La Rose Elementary School
Memphis, Tennessee

Elizabeth Zanders
Franklin School
Summit, New Jersey

WRITER

Steven Warshaw
Emeryville, California

Contents

UNIT THREE   Africa, Past and Present   **255**

UNIT FIVE The Western Hemisphere, Past and Present 481

Maps and Globes

═══ Charts, Graphs, Diagrams, and Timelines ═══

xi

CITIZENS AND COUNTRIES OF THE WORLD

As you read this book, you will find out more about people around the world. You have learned about your important role as a citizen of your country. Now you will learn about the roles played by citizens of other countries. You will discover people's similarities and differences. You will find that despite differences in appearance, language, or lifestyle, people's basic needs of food, clothing, and shelter remain the same.

History and Culture

Many things contribute to the way people live. **History,** or what happened in the past, affects all people. Some beliefs and customs, or ways of doing things, have been passed from generation to generation. In this book you will read about people from the past and present, noting how they have, or have not, changed over time.

You also will compare how people dress and speak. You will explore people's customs and religious beliefs. Ways of dressing, speaking, acting, and believing make up a **culture.** Each human group, or **society,** has a culture that is unique in some way. In this book you will study cultures in five regions of the world.

Civilization

All societies have a culture. Not every group has created a **civilization** (siv•uh•luh•ZAY•shuhn), however. The word *civilization* basically means "city." If a society has created cities, it also has created a civilization.

To build cities, people must have tools and know how to use them. For example, they must be able to move large pieces of building materials. The word we use for this knowledge is **technology** (teck•NAWL•uh•jee).

To support a city, people must have an **economy** (ih•KAHN•uh•mee), or way of using resources to meet needs. They must be able to make, buy, sell, and trade to get what they need and want. In this book you will compare different economic systems—from the simple ones of the past to the more complex ones of today.

To survive and grow, cities need rules and people to enforce them. They need a **government** to make decisions and solve problems. You will discover that there are many different types of government in the world and that citizens' responsibilities to their government vary from one group to the next.

By tracing the building, and sometimes the destroying, of civilizations, you will note the progress that has been made in economy, government, art, and science. You will read how people developed science to understand and change their environment and art to express their feelings about life. Most of all, you will understand how much early civilizations have contributed to our modern world. You will discover the meaning of being a "citizen of the world."

1

USING YOUR TEXTBOOK

This book has special ways to help you learn about our world. From the table of contents you know that the book is divided into units and chapters. Within each chapter are numbered lessons.

Reading for a Purpose

Every lesson begins with a feature that will help prepare you to read the lesson. Notice that in this introduction some words like *history* and *culture* are darker than others. These words are printed in thick, dark type, called **boldface,** because they are important or new words. In the box at the beginning of each lesson you will find a list of all the boldfaced words.

Following the word list is a set of questions. The questions tell you what kind of information to look for as you read. When you have learned the important words and answered the questions, you should understand the ideas discussed in the lesson. You can check your understanding by answering the questions in the **Reading Check** at the end of the lesson.

The Glossary

Important new words are defined within the lessons where they first occur. Many of them are also defined in the **glossary** at the end of the book. Like a dictionary, the glossary lists words alphabetically. It gives the pronunciation of each word and a definition. It also tells you on what page of your book the word is first found.

The Index

Perhaps there will be a subject you would like to review. You may need to find the answer to a question at the end of a chapter or unit. How can you locate the subject in your book? One of the best ways is to find the subject listed in the **index.**

Important topics, words, people, and places are listed alphabetically in the index beginning on page R39. Each listing shows the page numbers where you can find information on any subject in the text or pictures.

The Atlas and Gazetteer

Because this book takes you to many countries in the world, knowing where places are located is very important. Many maps throughout the book will help you. These maps are listed on page x of the contents. For an overall view of the world there is an **atlas** at the end of the book. This atlas is a collection of maps that show the borders of every country in the world. The **gazetteer,** or geographic dictionary, includes the location of places shown on maps in this text. In addition there are reference tables of important world facts and figures.

Questions to Answer

1. How are units in this book divided?
2. Name two ways to find the definition of a new word in your book.
3. How might you find information on African explorers?
4. How is an atlas useful?

THE PLANET EARTH

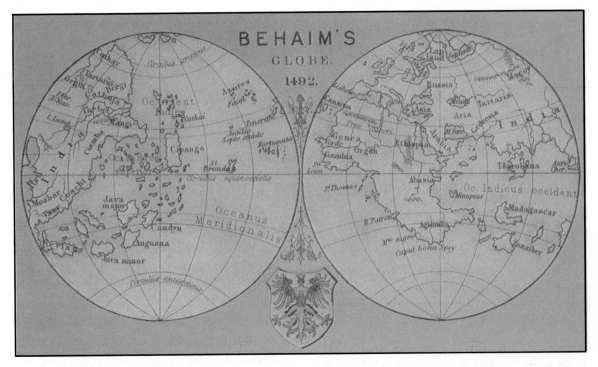

In 1492 a German explorer named Martin Behaim (BAY.hym) made the first globe we know about. It was a brightly painted model of the world. At that time, knowledge of the world's features was limited. Not until 1522 would anyone complete a journey around the world. Ferdinand Magellan's crew were the first sailors to make the trip. It took three years. More than 400 years later, the first American spacecraft, *Explorer I*, traveled around the entire planet in 114.7 minutes. Because of modern space equipment, we now have a truer sense of how our world appears in the vast universe.

Earth is the fifth-largest of the nine planets that circle the sun. Because of its distance from the sun, Earth has temperatures that are neither too hot nor too cold to support life. Life as we know it is also possible because of the air that surrounds the Earth. This air is called the **atmosphere.** In some places the atmosphere reaches 1,000 miles (1,600 km) into space. Yet the layer that supports life extends only about 10 miles (16 km) from Earth.

You know from looking at a globe that the Earth appears to be a **sphere,** or ball-shaped. Accurate measurements show that the Earth is not perfectly round, however. At the equator the Earth measures 24,901.55 miles (40,075.16 km) around. Measured from pole to pole, the Earth is slightly (42 miles/68 km) flatter.

The Earth weighs 6.6 sextillion (6,600,000,000,000,000,000,000) tons. This number is too large to understand, but it does tell you that the Earth is extremely heavy. Have you ever held a bowling ball? A bowling ball is heavy partly because it is not hollow. Like a bowling ball, the Earth is a solid mass. It is made of metal and rock.

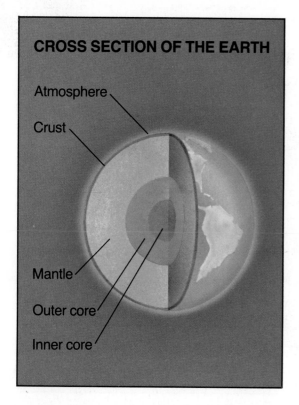

CROSS SECTION OF THE EARTH

Atmosphere

Crust

Mantle

Outer core

Inner core

Though no one has ever seen the center, or **core,** of the Earth, scientists believe that the **inner core** is made of iron and nickel. Surrounding the inner core is an **outer core** of hot, liquid iron and nickel. Between the core and the Earth's surface is a third layer, called the **mantle.** This layer of somewhat soft rock is the widest layer, measuring about 1,800 miles (2,900 km). The fourth, outermost layer is a thin layer of rock called the **crust.** It is about this continually changing crust that we know the most.

Land and Water

Looking down from space at Earth through the clouds, you can easily see the difference between land and water. The boundaries of continents seem carefully drawn into large stretches of water. Seven continents and many

islands make up about one-third of the Earth's surface. The other two-thirds is water—oceans, seas, rivers, lakes, and streams.

If you look more closely at the Earth's crust, various landforms become visible. Many landforms, such as mountains and canyons, have taken millions of years to develop. However, some changes in the land happen more quickly. Sudden shifts or splits in the Earth, called **earthquakes,** shatter human settlements.

Volcanoes are the result of another kind of change in the Earth's crust. Volcanoes form when melted rock, hot ashes, and gas force their way through cracks in the Earth. Sometimes these materials form a hill or a mountain shaped like a cone. Volcanoes may also surface in the oceans to form islands. Some volcanoes continue to erupt, while others grow cold and still.

Even as the Earth's crust is forming and changing, another process, called **erosion,** is taking place. Erosion is the gradual wearing down of rock by water, wind, or ice. Over long periods of time, mountains can become flat, or canyons can form where once there was flat land.

Learning about the physical features of the Earth and the way it changes from within and without is part of the science called **geography.**

Questions to Answer

1. What is the air that surrounds the Earth called?
2. We know most about which layer of the Earth?
3. Explain three ways that changes in the Earth's land occur.

GEOGRAPHIC DICTIONARY

basin a land area mostly surrounded by higher land

bay a small area of ocean partly surrounded by land

canal a waterway dug across land for transportation or irrigation

canyon a narrow valley with high, steep sides

cape a point of land that extends into a body of water

channel a narrow waterway connecting two bodies of water; the deepest part of a waterway

cliff a high, steep wall of rock

continent one of the Earth's seven main landmasses

delta a piece of land formed by silt built up at a river's mouth

divide a high ridge of land between areas with different river basins

fall line the point where a river forms a waterfall as it drops to lower land

fjord a narrow inlet of the sea between high, steep banks

foothill a low hill at the base of a mountain

glacier a large mass of slow-moving ice spread over a land surface

gulf a large area of ocean partly surrounded by land

harbor a sheltered area along a seacoast where ships can anchor

highland a region of hills, mountains, or plateaus

hill a small, raised part of the land, lower than a mountain

isthmus a narrow strip of land connecting two larger land areas

lowland a low, mostly level land area

marsh an area of low, wet land

mesa a flat-topped hill with steep sides, common in dry areas

mountain range a group or chain of mountains

mouth (of river) the place where a river or stream empties into a larger body of water

peak the pointed top of a mountain

peninsula land surrounded by water on three sides

plain a large area of flat or gently rolling land

plateau an area of high, flat land

port a city or place where ships arrive and depart

prairie a broad, grassy plains region

rain forest a woodland with rain much of the year and marked by a dense growth of trees and plants

reservoir a lake where a large water supply is stored

source (of river) the place where a stream or river begins

strait a narrow water passage between two larger bodies of water

stream a small body of flowing water

swamp low, wet land

tributary a river or stream that flows into another river

tundra a broad, treeless plain in a polar region

valley low land between mountains or hills

volcano a hill or mountain formed when melted rock is forced through the Earth's surface

Maps are a convenient way to study the geography of a region. At a glance you can find out about a region's size, its land and water features, and its location in relation to other regions.

There are many types of maps. In this book you will find **physical maps** and **political maps.** Physical maps show the Earth's landforms. Political maps identify countries, cities, and other people-made divisions in a region. Political maps show the **boundaries,** or borders, of nations or of areas within a nation, such as counties or states. These maps sometimes also show rivers and lakes.

Some maps have special purposes. They may show where people live or how much rain an area receives. They may show trade or transportation routes. Maps can show how something looked in the past or how it will appear in the future.

Although maps present a variety of information, the basic tools for reading maps are the same for all of them. Symbols used on a map are identified in a map's **legend,** or key. A compass symbol on a map (sometimes called a rose) indicates direction.

Scale

You can find actual distance between points on a map by using the **scale.** A scale gives you the number of miles or kilometers there are for each inch or centimeter on a map. Look at the maps of Texas. Using a straight-edge or piece of string, measure the distance between Dallas and Houston

on each map. Then use the scales to change the measurements to the actual distances. Are the distances the same?

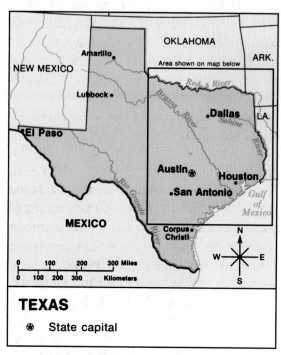

TEXAS

⊛ State capital

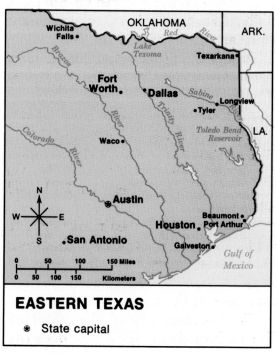

EASTERN TEXAS

⊛ State capital

6

Latitude and Longitude

Map makers draw lines on globes and maps to make places easier to find. The imaginary lines that go east and west around the Earth are called **lines of latitude,** or **parallels.** The most familiar line of latitude is the equator, which divides the Earth in half. Lands and waters north of the equator are in the Northern Hemisphere. Those to the south of the equator are in the Southern Hemisphere.

Lines of latitude are measured in **degrees.** The symbol for degrees is (°). Find the equator on Globe A to the right. It is labeled 0° (zero degrees). Parallels to the north of the equator are labeled *N*. Parallels to the south of the equator are labeled *S*. The number of degrees tells you how far north or south of the equator a place is. For example, the latitude of Philadelphia, Pennsylvania, is 40°N. Philadelphia is 40 degrees north of the equator. The latitude of the North Pole, the point that is the farthest north on Earth, is 90°N. The South Pole, which is the southernmost point, is 90°S.

Find Belo Horizonte, Brazil. How many degrees south of the equator is Belo Horizonte?

Most maps and globes do not show every line of latitude. This globe drawing shows every twentieth parallel. To find a city with a latitude of 30°N, you would look halfway between 20°N and 40°N.

Another set of lines runs north to south, from the North Pole to the South Pole. These lines are called **lines of longitude,** or **meridians.** All meridians meet at the poles.

The meridian labeled 0° is called the **Prime Meridian.** What city does the

Prime Meridian cross? The Eastern Hemisphere is east of the Prime Meridian. Everything to the west is in the Western Hemisphere. The line separating the hemispheres on the other side of the world is called the **International Date Line.** The line is exactly opposite the Prime Meridian, and it is labeled 180°.

Like latitude, longitude is measured in degrees. Lines of longitude are numbered east (*E*) and west (*W*) of the

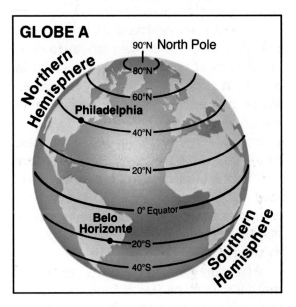

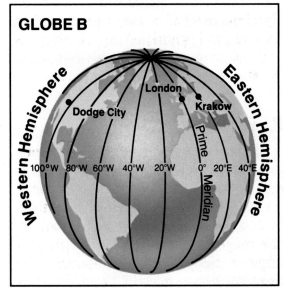

7

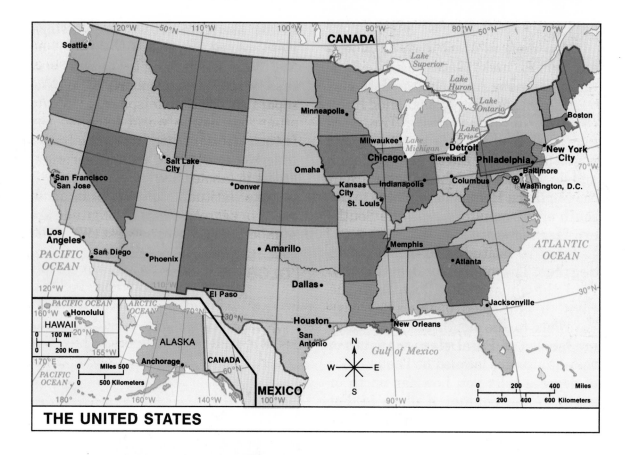

THE UNITED STATES

Prime Meridian. For example, Dodge City, Kansas, is near the meridian labeled 100°W. Dodge City is about 100 degrees west of the Prime Meridian. Now look at Globe B on page 7 and find Krakow, Poland. How is the meridian near Krakow labeled?

When lines of latitude and longitude are shown together on a map or globe, they form a **grid.** A grid is a pattern of crossing lines. A grid can help you locate places on a globe or map. Look at the map of the United States above. What city is located at about 35°N and 100°W?

You can use the system of latitude and longitude to locate a place on any marked map or globe. The United States always will fall between 25°N and 50°N and about 65°W and 125°W.

People and the Land

Geography is more than just the physical description of the world. Geography is also the study of people and how they relate to their surroundings, or **environment** (en•VY•ruhn•muhnt).

People live everywhere on Earth. They live on mountains, in deserts, and in forests. They live along rivers or near oceans. Wherever people live, they develop special relationships with their environment. They learn how to live in or change their environment to suit their needs.

Land formations and climate make the environment of one region different from another region. The type of environment affects how and where people live. Mild climate and good soil

8

Houses on stilts protect Brazilians against flooding in the Amazon Basin.

attract more people than do deserts or thick forests. People of the past usually settled near water, along coasts or near rivers. Such locations enabled farming, trading, and transportation.

The way land is used also affects the number of people in a region. Look at the map below. It shows which areas of the world have greater populations than others. In the United States, for example, more people live in the factory cities of the Great Lakes region than on the farmlands of the Great Plains. There are jobs for more people in cities than in areas where much of the land is farmed. In the People's Republic of China, on the other hand, most people are farmers. They live where the land is best for growing crops.

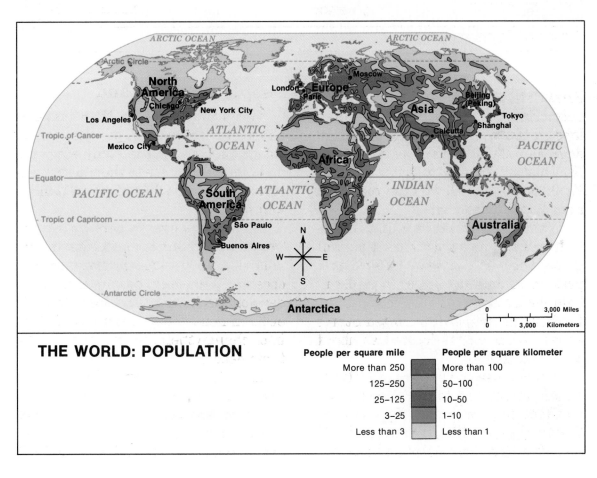

THE WORLD: POPULATION

People per square mile		People per square kilometer
More than 250		More than 100
125–250		50–100
25–125		10–50
3–25		1–10
Less than 3		Less than 1

Resources

The Earth provides many **natural resources** to help people supply their needs. Water, air, and sunlight are natural resources. Forests, minerals, and wildlife are also natural resources.

Resources affect how land is used. The map below shows how the world's land is being used today. You can compare land use maps and population maps to understand how environment influences the way people live.

Climate

You have read how different environments have different types of land and resources. Environments also have different annual weather patterns, or **climates.** If you were asked, how would you describe your weather? You might say that it is warm or cold or sunny or rainy. The climate of an area usually is identified by normal temperature ranges and average rainfall year after year. Many things influence the climate of a region.

Have you ever noticed that during different seasons of the year, the sun appears lower or higher in the sky? The Earth is tilted as it travels around the sun. The sun's rays, therefore, strike the Earth differently at different times of the year. For this reason, seasons come and go, and days are shorter in winter and longer in summer. The diagram on the next page shows how seasons change as the Earth moves around the sun.

The usual temperature of a region depends on how much direct sunlight that region receives during the year.

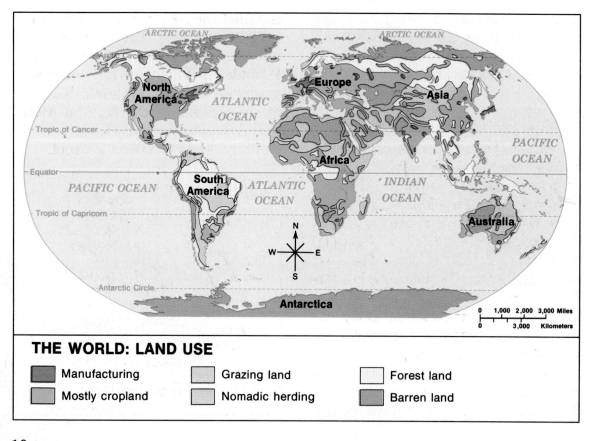

THE WORLD: LAND USE

Manufacturing · Grazing land · Forest land
Mostly cropland · Nomadic herding · Barren land

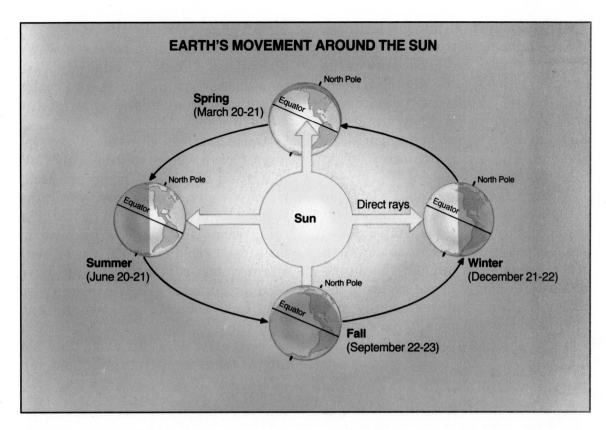

EARTH'S MOVEMENT AROUND THE SUN

Spring
(March 20-21)

North Pole
Equator

Summer
(June 20-21)

North Pole
Equator

Direct rays

Sun

Winter
(December 21-22)

North Pole
Equator

Fall
(September 22-23)

North Pole
Equator

To help us describe where the sun's rays hit the Earth, we use lines of latitude. Some latitudes receive more direct sunlight in a year than others.

Latitudes and Climate

Find the equator on the globe to the right. Twenty-three and one-half degrees north of the equator is the latitude called the **Tropic of Cancer.** The same distance south of the equator is the **Tropic of Capricorn.** Between these two latitudes are the **low latitudes,** or the **tropics.** The low latitudes receive more direct sunlight than other parts of the Earth. Temperatures in most places in the tropics are therefore warm all year.

The North and South poles are in the **high latitudes.** In the Northern Hemisphere the high-latitude region

is called the Arctic. A line of latitude called the **Arctic Circle** marks the beginning of this region. The high-latitude region of the Southern Hemisphere is called the Antarctic. It begins at the **Antarctic Circle.** The Arctic and Antarctic receive indirect or no sunlight. Their climates are cold.

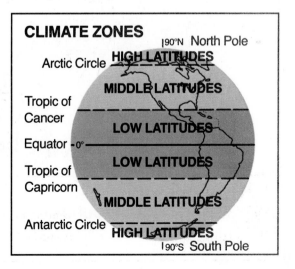

CLIMATE ZONES

90°N North Pole
HIGH LATITUDES
Arctic Circle
MIDDLE LATITUDES
Tropic of Cancer
LOW LATITUDES
Equator - 0°
LOW LATITUDES
Tropic of Capricorn
MIDDLE LATITUDES
Antarctic Circle
HIGH LATITUDES
90°S South Pole

11

Between the high and low latitudes are the **middle latitudes.** The United States, Canada, and Mexico are in the middle latitudes of the Northern Hemisphere. Middle-latitude climates are the most varied. They are generally cold in the winter and warm in the summer. These climates are referred to as **moderate** climates.

Other factors besides latitude influence climate. You know, for instance, that within the United States some areas are hotter or colder than other areas. The higher the land's **altitude,** or height above sea level, the colder the temperatures usually are. Mountain regions usually have colder climates than surrounding flatlands, for example.

Oceans and Climate

Nearness to large bodies of water also affects climate. Coastal lands are usually warmer in winter and cooler in summer than inland areas at the same latitudes.

Oceans affect climate in several ways. Ocean waters continuously flow in certain directions. There are great rivers of water, or **currents,** within the ocean. Ocean currents can be warm or cold. Warm currents flow from warm latitudes to cold latitudes. Areas near warm-water currents usually have warmer climates. The reverse is also true. Cold-water currents cool the land near them.

Warm or cold water alone does not affect land temperatures, however.

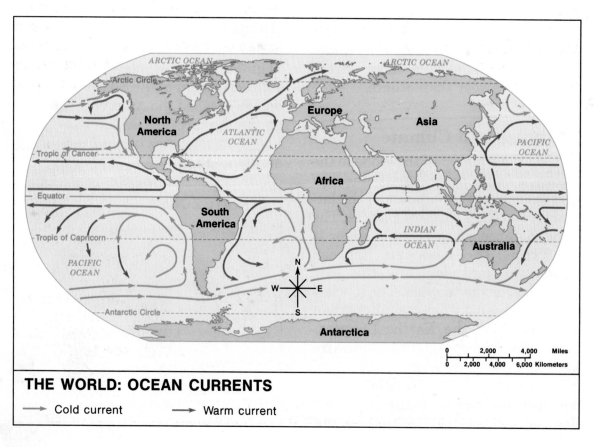

THE WORLD: OCEAN CURRENTS

→ Cold current   → Warm current

Winds blowing over the water are warmed or cooled by the currents. They carry the warm or cold air to the land.

You can see that many things affect the temperature of a region. Distance from the equator, altitude, and nearness to large bodies of water all affect temperature. Temperature in turn affects the amount of rainfall in an area.

Water and Air

To understand why rainfall occurs, you need to know how moist air reacts as it warms or cools. Look at the diagram below. It shows how heated water changes form and collects in the air. Then, as the warm, moist air rises and cools, the water falls back to the Earth as **precipitation.** Precipitation can take the form of rain, snow, sleet, hail, dew, or fog.

Because warm temperatures begin the rainmaking process, lower latitudes usually have wetter climates. The higher the latitude, normally, the less precipitation an area receives. Even in higher latitudes, though, wind, large bodies of water, and altitude may cause an increase in precipitation.

Wind and Climate

Our atmosphere is constantly moving as it presses against the Earth. You know already that air temperatures vary from place to place. In addition, warm air is lighter than cool air. When warm air and cool air meet, the heavier, cool air forces the warm air to rise. We call this air movement wind.

Wind is an important part of coastal climates. The temperature of the air above water is usually different from the air temperature above land. Warm and cool air constantly circulate along coasts. When wind carries warm air from the ocean across land, the warm air rises. This results in precipitation. Therefore, coastal areas near warm ocean currents receive large amounts of precipitation. The coast of the Pacific Northwest of the United States is a good example.

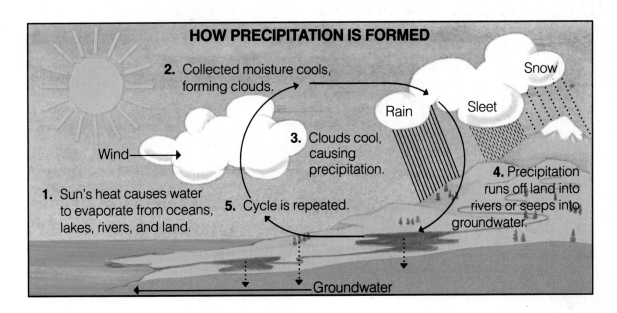

HOW PRECIPITATION IS FORMED

2. Collected moisture cools, forming clouds.

Snow

Rain

Sleet

3. Clouds cool, causing precipitation.

Wind

4. Precipitation runs off land into rivers or seeps into groundwater.

1. Sun's heat causes water to evaporate from oceans, lakes, rivers, and land.

5. Cycle is repeated.

Groundwater

Look again at the map of ocean currents on page 12. Notice that the southern part of the west coast of the United States lies along a cold ocean current. In this case warm winds usually blow from the land to the ocean. Precipitation occurs over the water, while the coastal land is hot and dry.

Wind also plays a part in the amount of precipitation that falls in mountainous areas. Warm, moist air rises up the side of a mountain, where it is cooled in the higher altitudes. The side of the mountain up which the wind blows receives more precipitation than the opposite side.

As you study the geography of different regions, remember that many things influence climate. Latitude, land formations, nearness to water, altitude, ocean currents, and wind affect temperature and precipitation.

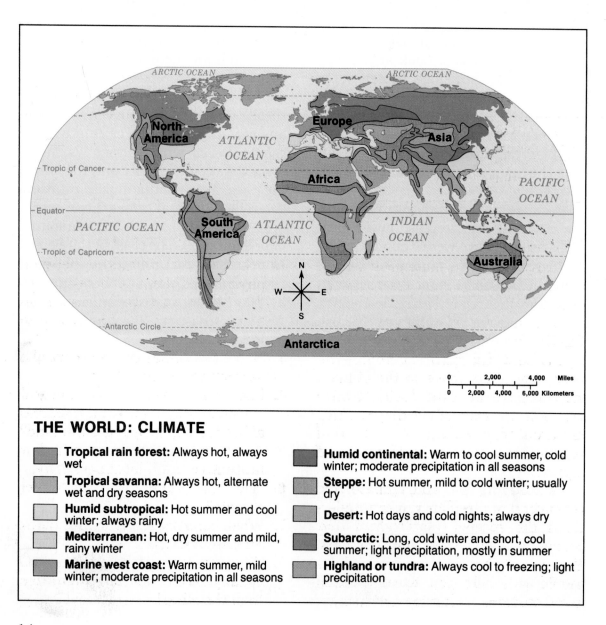

THE WORLD: CLIMATE

Tropical rain forest: Always hot, always wet

Tropical savanna: Always hot, alternate wet and dry seasons

Humid subtropical: Hot summer and cool winter; always rainy

Mediterranean: Hot, dry summer and mild, rainy winter

Marine west coast: Warm summer, mild winter; moderate precipitation in all seasons

Humid continental: Warm to cool summer, cold winter; moderate precipitation in all seasons

Steppe: Hot summer, mild to cold winter; usually dry

Desert: Hot days and cold nights; always dry

Subarctic: Long, cold winter and short, cool summer; light precipitation, mostly in summer

Highland or tundra: Always cool to freezing; light precipitation

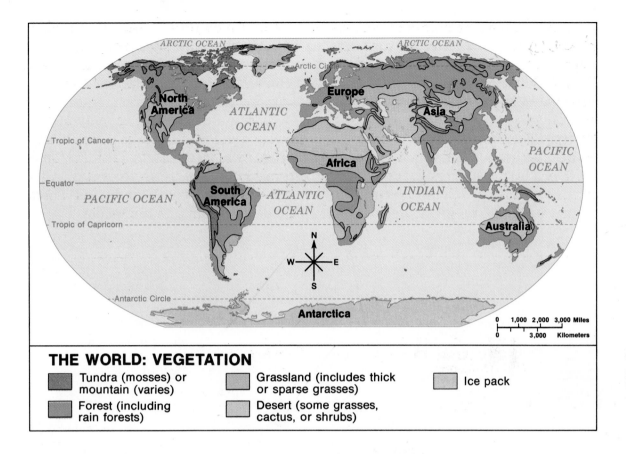

THE WORLD: VEGETATION

- ◼ Tundra (mosses) or mountain (varies)
- ◼ Forest (including rain forests)
- ◼ Grassland (includes thick or sparse grasses)
- ◻ Desert (some grasses, cactus, or shrubs)
- ◻ Ice pack

Vegetation

Many kinds of plants grow on the Earth. They range from desert shrubs to mountain forests. The natural plant life of an area is called its **vegetation.** The Earth's vegetation varies with the type of land and climate. Compare the vegetation map above to the climate map on page 14. Find Africa. Notice that a large part of northern Africa has a hot, dry climate. What kind of vegetation is shown in this part of Africa?

By studying the land, climate, and vegetation of a region you can understand the special relationships that people have with their environments. The geography of a region and its people will help you to understand world cultures, yesterday and today.

Questions to Answer

1. What is the difference between physical maps and political maps?
2. What helps you to find distances on a map or globe? What helps you to locate places?
3. Name two things that are part of a person's environment.
4. List six examples of natural resources. How do natural resources affect the way people use the land?
5. Are temperatures warmer in low latitudes or high latitudes? Why?
6. How do ocean currents affect climate?
7. What happens when warm, moist air rises and cools?
8. Why does one side of a mountain usually receive more precipitation than the other?

15

Key Dates and Events

About 8000 B.C.
Farming begins

About 4000 B.C.
Development of
Sumer begins

**About 3500–
3100 B.C.**
Cuneiform writing is
used in Mesopotamia

Menes unites
ancient Egypt

**About 3000–
1000 B.C.**
Bronze Age

**About 2700–
2200 B.C.**
Age of Pyramids

About 1800 B.C.
Hammurabi rules
Babylon, develops
a code of laws

About 1100 B.C.
Iron Age begins

About 539–519 B.C.
Persians conquer
Middle East

THE MIDDLE EAST, PAST AND PRESENT

The pyramids, temples, and tombs of ancient Egypt help us to understand a civilization that began more than 5,000 years ago. The temples of Abu Simbel are only a part of what has come down to us from early peoples of the Middle East. Their gifts to government, science, and religion have influenced much of the world.

The Middle East is that region of the world where the continents of Asia, Africa, and Europe meet. Important in the past, the Middle East is just as important today to Americans and to many other people and nations.

In this unit you will discover what gave this region its early start in history. You also will learn about the people and countries of the Middle East today.

A.D. **1798**	A.D. **1869**	A.D. **1922**	A.D. **1948**	A.D. **1960**	A.D. **1979**
Rosetta Stone is discovered	Suez Canal is opened	King Tutankhamen's tomb is uncovered	State of Israel is founded	OPEC is established	Israel and Egypt sign first peace treaty
				A.D. **1979** Revolution in Iran	

GEOGRAPHY OF THE MIDDLE EAST

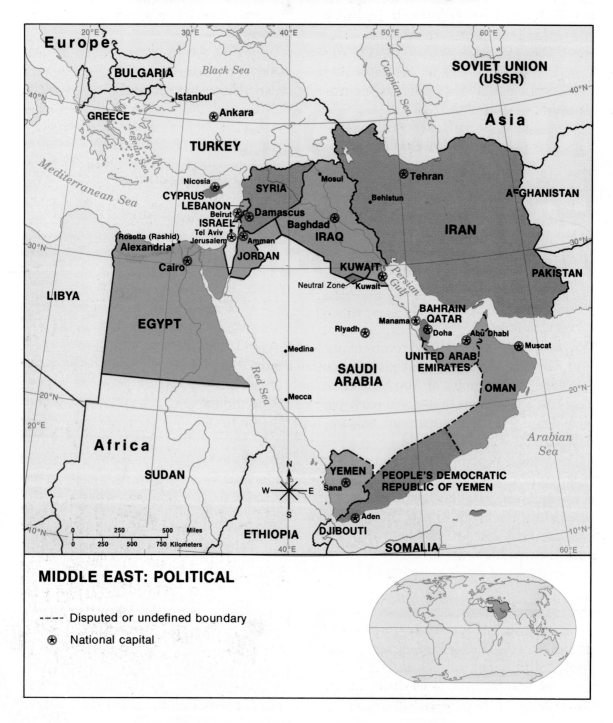

MIDDLE EAST: POLITICAL

---- Disputed or undefined boundary

⊛ National capital

Location

This region is named the Middle East because of its central location in the Eastern Hemisphere. It includes countries from three continents—Europe, Africa, and Asia. The Middle East is referred to in several ways. It is sometimes called the Mideast, Southwest Asia, or the Near East.

Seas, deserts, and mountains separate the Middle East from its neighbors in Africa, Europe, and Asia. To the north the Caspian Sea, the Caucasus (KAW·kuh·sus) Mountains, and the Black Sea lie between the Middle East and Europe. In the west the Mediterranean Sea separates it from Europe. The Red Sea lies between Africa and the Middle East. The Red Sea and the Persian Gulf empty into the Arabian Sea, which is the region's southern boundary.

In Africa, the region is bordered in the south by a desert called the Sahara. Sometimes the North African countries of Libya, Tunisia, Algeria, and Morocco are included in a discussion of the Middle East. However, in this unit only Egypt is discussed. Geographers do not always agree on the eastern boundaries of the Middle East either. Iran is the easternmost country we will consider.

The Land

Mountains make up about one-third of the land in the Middle East. These include the Zagros Mountains, the Taurus Mountains, and the Elburz Mountains. Mountains are found in Turkey, Iran, Syria, Lebanon, and Jordan. Several plateaus also cover wide areas of the Middle East. Parts of Saudi Arabia, Turkey, and Iran are large plateaus.

Deserts are common in the Middle East. Covered with rock, gravel, or sand, they may extend for long distances without interruption. Countries with large deserts include Egypt, Iran, Iraq, and Saudi Arabia.

Some deserts in the Middle East are surrounded by semidry plains called **steppes.** Though usually treeless, the steppes produce some grasses and thorny plants, which may supply food

Middle Eastern herders search for grazing land in the steppes of Iran.

for goats, sheep, or camels. There are steppes in Iran, Turkey, western Iraq, eastern Syria, Jordan, and Israel. Mountains, plateaus, deserts, and steppes cover so much of the Middle East that only a small amount of land remains for cities and farming.

Only about 7 percent of the land in the Middle East is suitable for farming. The greener, more productive land lies in the river valleys of the region.

There are fertile plains along the Nile River in Egypt and the Tigris and Euphrates rivers in Iraq. Fertile land is also found along the coasts of the Mediterranean Sea and the Black Sea.

The Climate

Much of the Middle East has a dry, or **arid** climate. Water is a limited resource. Precipitation occurs mainly

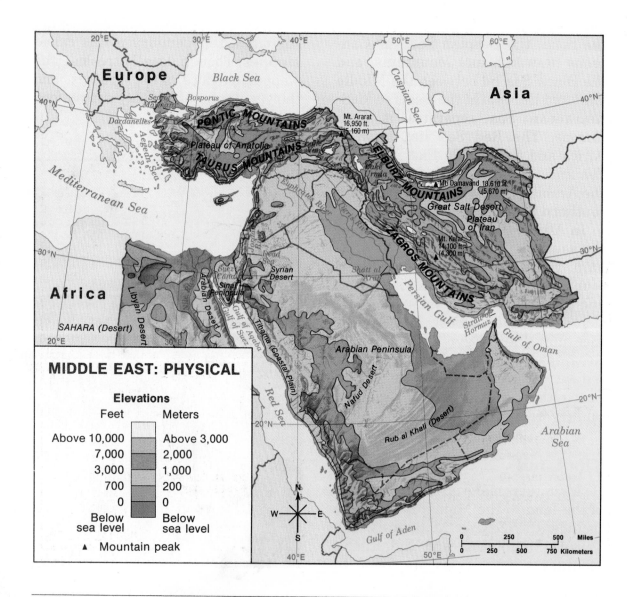

in the mountains. Water then flows from the mountains into the region's rivers. The map below shows that precipitation is greatest in the northern and mountainous parts of the Middle East, especially Turkey. Notice that Mediterranean coastal lands also have wetter climates than most other areas of the region.

In the mountains of the east and north, winter brings winds that freeze the land. On some of the high peaks storms howl throughout the winter, dropping the temperatures to well below freezing. Yet, at the same time, the lowlands and coastlands may be fairly warm.

In summer the temperatures soar in most of the Middle East. Choking heat withers plants and slows the activity of animals and humans. Spring and fall are the best times for people

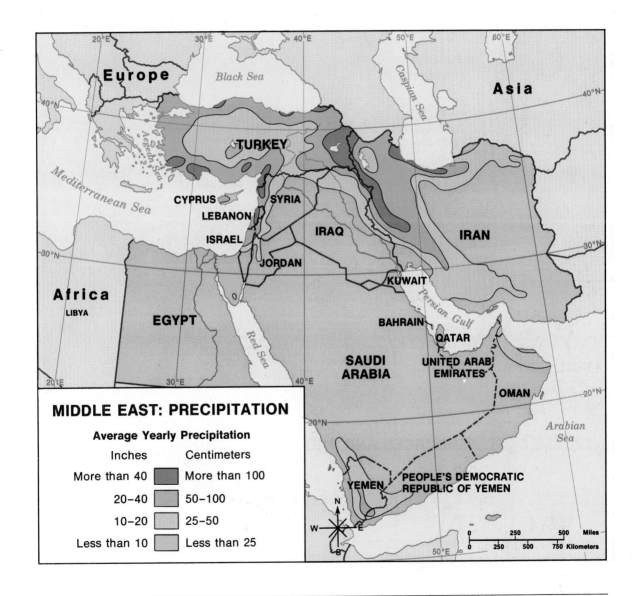

MIDDLE EAST: PRECIPITATION

Average Yearly Precipitation

Inches		Centimeters
More than 40		More than 100
20–40		50–100
10–20		25–50
Less than 10		Less than 25

in the Middle East. These are the times of fairs and holidays. The seacoasts and farming areas surge with activity during these pleasant months.

Resources

In the Middle East most people are involved in some kind of farming work. Yet, in many countries production is

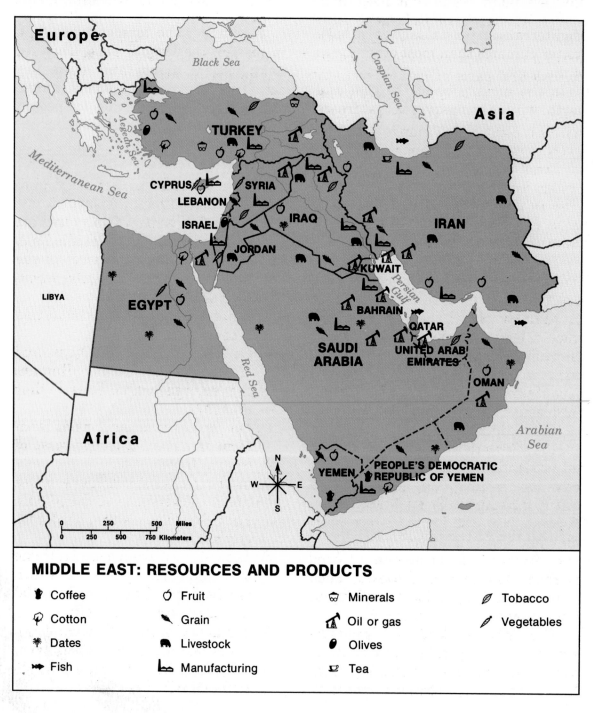

MIDDLE EAST: RESOURCES AND PRODUCTS

🍵 Coffee	🍐 Fruit	🦪 Minerals	🌿 Tobacco
🌱 Cotton	🌾 Grain	🛢️ Oil or gas	🥒 Vegetables
🌴 Dates	🐃 Livestock	● Olives	
🐟 Fish	🏭 Manufacturing	☕ Tea	

low. People are unable to grow all the food they need. A shortage of fresh water is the main problem.

To make up for this shortage, the farmers plant crops that need little water. Wheat, grown in large areas of Turkey, Syria, Lebanon, Jordan, Iran, and Israel, is one such crop. Farmers in Iraq and parts of Iran often plant barley because it is less likely to become diseased. In Turkey and Iran, with a cooler climate than in countries to the south, rye is a major crop.

Even though it requires more water, cotton is the most widespread crop in Egypt. Egyptians irrigate to grow cotton, which makes up almost two-thirds of its exports.

The Middle East is also well known for its fruits. Oranges, apricots, figs, peaches, and plums are among the main crops in Israel and Lebanon. Iraq produces a large date crop. Another fruit, the olive, is widely grown throughout the region. Its oil is burned as fuel and also is used as a substitute for animal fats, which are in short supply.

The Middle East provides an important resource to the world—oil. Today, oil production is the largest and most complex industry in some Middle Eastern countries. Saudi Arabia, Iran, Kuwait, Iraq, the United Arab Emirates, and Qatar pump between one-half and three-fourths of all the oil used outside this region. However, such countries as Turkey, Israel, and Egypt import oil to meet their needs.

The Middle East's oil industry employs many people. Tens of thousands of workers, including both laborers and highly trained scientists, find the oil and drill the wells. Other workers keep the oil flowing through pipelines that cross the desert sands. The pipelines end near the ocean, where the oil is loaded onto ocean steamers. Thus an enormous knot of tubes, meters, and gears combine with a network of ships. These ships link oil-producing countries with the rest of the world.

Geography Review

1. By what other names is the Middle Eastern region known?
2. Name four bodies of water that act as boundaries for the Middle East.
3. Name three large deserts in the Middle East and the country where each is located.
4. What are steppes? For what is this type of land useful?
5. Compare the lands of Egypt and Iraq on the physical map. How are the lands the same? How do they differ?
6. On the physical map, what landform is shown covering most of central Iran?
7. How does the Mediterranean Sea affect the climates of the Middle Eastern countries that border its shores?
8. Look at the map on page 21. Name two countries, parts of which receive more than 40 inches (100 cm) of precipitation yearly.
9. Name two Middle Eastern countries that have large deposits of oil.
10. Why is so little farming possible in the Middle East?

A Civilization Begins in Mesopotamia

Focus

The Middle East is often called the cradle of civilization. There, early civilizations began to grow, much as an infant grows—learning and developing its first skills in a cradle.

Records of life in the Middle East began when one group, the Sumerians (soo•MAIR•ee•uhnz), moved into a fertile river valley in what is now called Iraq. The first Sumerians were hunters. As they learned how to raise animals and how to plant and harvest crops, the Sumerians developed a civilization.

Look for these important words:

Key Words
- agriculture
- domesticate
- nomads
- obsidian
- oasis

Places
- Fertile Crescent
- Tigris River
- Euphrates River
- Mesopotamia
- Jericho

Look for answers to these questions:

1. Where is the Fertile Crescent and why is it important?
2. How did farming change the lives of early people in Mesopotamia?
3. What was life like in the farming villages of Mesopotamia?
4. How did early people get things they wanted but could not make or find in their own area?

1. THE FERTILE CRESCENT

It is difficult to imagine our lives without the wheel, without writing, and without numbers. Without these important inventions, life as we know it would be impossible. The inventors of these tools lived thousands of years ago. They lived in that section of the Middle East called the **Fertile Crescent.**

The Fertile Crescent starts on the eastern shore of the Mediterranean Sea. Then, like the shape of a quarter moon, the Fertile Crescent curves around the Syrian Desert, reaching south to the Persian Gulf. The Fertile Crescent is a rich food-growing area in a part of the world where most of the land is dry and unusable.

The richest land of the Fertile Crescent is the area between the **Tigris** (TY•gris) **River** and the **Euphrates** (yoo•FRAY•teez) **River.** Fed by winter snows and spring rains, streams plunge down the mountains of southern Turkey and western Iran. The streams pick up and carry soil as they flow toward the valley below. As a result, the valley is laced by streams and covered with good, black earth. In the valley the streams join either the Tigris or the Euphrates river system. The area between the Tigris and the Euphrates is named **Mesopotamia** (mes•uh•puh•TAY•mee•uh), which means "land between the rivers."

The First Farmers

Ten thousand years ago people lived by hunting and gathering the food they needed. They lived in small groups, moving often from place to place. They

25

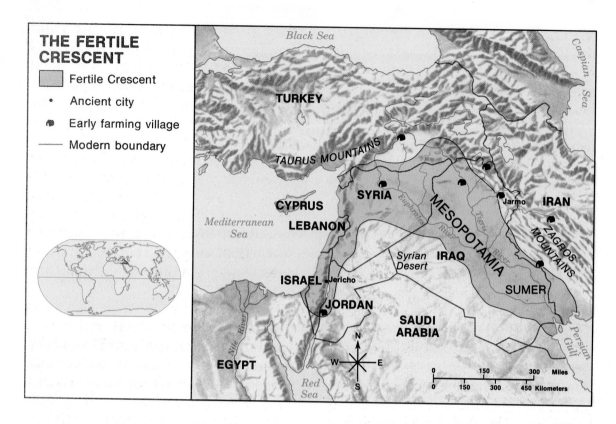

THE FERTILE CRESCENT

- Fertile Crescent
- • Ancient city
- Early farming village
- — Modern boundary

hunted animals and gathered wild fruits, nuts, roots, and grass seeds.

Gradually early people changed their way of life. They discovered how to grow crops and raise animals. They began to develop **agriculture** (AG•rih•kul•chuhr), or farming. No one knows why they changed. Perhaps there were fewer animals to hunt. Perhaps the population had grown so that new sources of food had to be found. Perhaps groups of people liked staying near a favorite watering spring and had to find a way to feed themselves.

Whatever the reasons, in many places in the Middle East people started farming and raising animals about 8000 B.C. This was an important change. People began to control their environment. They no longer were dependent on eating only what they could find and hunt. The change in

people's lives occurred as they learned to **domesticate** (duh•MES•tuh•kayt) plants and animals. *Domesticate* means to tame or to fit to the needs of people.

The first animal people learned to domesticate was probably the dog. Eventually people domesticated the wild sheep and goats that roamed the grassy foothills of the Taurus and Zagros mountains. People who depended mainly on animals for food became herders. These people were **nomads,** going with the animals from place to place to find pastures and water.

Wild grasses grew in the foothills where the sheep and goats roamed. These grasses included types of wheat and barley. In most hunting and gathering societies the women gathered while the men hunted. In summer women probably collected the ripe wild wheat. In time, they decided to grow their own wheat. They domesticated the wild grasses. They chose and grew grasses whose seeds were many and healthful.

Growing wheat, or any crop, means people must settle in one place. Planting and harvesting a crop takes many months. For this reason agriculture became the basis of village life and of civilization itself.

Farming Villages

Between about 8000 and 4000 B.C. people developed a way of life made possible by farming. During that time special tools and inventions were developed. Early villagers built walls and houses with bricks made of mud and straw. In outdoor brick ovens they baked bread made from wheat or barley flour. Later they used the ovens to bake pottery.

Clay pots were useless to nomads. They broke easily and were awkward to carry. As people settled, however, they made clay pots for storing water and for cooking. Like people in many societies, they wanted to show what they thought beautiful and important. When people made clay pots, they often decorated them. The pots were pleasant to look at as well as useful.

Unlike nomads, farmers did not have to move to find pastures for their animals. Farmers could keep animals in pens and feed them grain. By raising animals, the farmers further increased their food supply. From the wool of sheep and goats they spun thread and wove it into cloth.

Having learned to raise sheep and goats and to grow wheat and barley, the early farmers continued to develop a variety of foods. They learned to make barley into beer. Using native plants, they developed orchards of figs, apricots, almonds, pistachios, walnuts, dates, and olives. They raised lentils, chick peas, and fava beans. In some places they grew grapes. They domesticated herds of cattle, oxen, and donkeys. Cattle provided milk, meat, and

This water jug and bowl found in Turkey are almost 7,000 years old. By studying pottery closely, experts can learn about ancient life.

hides. Donkeys and oxen became beasts of burden, helping people transport themselves and their loads.

While farmers settled the rich valleys and plains of the rivers, nomads developed a life for themselves in the drier and hillier regions. Sometimes the nomads and farmers traded animals and food. Other times the nomads raided the farmers' land, seeking food for themselves and their herds.

Early people had long been traders. If the village farmers grew more wheat than they needed, they could trade the wheat for other goods. For example, they traded for **obsidian** (uhb•SID•ee•uhn), a black volcanic rock that was found in mountains far to the north and west. The razor-sharp obsidian was used as a cutting tool and for spear points. Polished slabs of obsidian were used as mirrors.

Jericho (JAIR•uh•koh), a city just north of the Dead Sea, was an important trading center as early as 8000 B.C. It was built in an **oasis,** a fertile place in the desert, where a gushing spring supported life for about 1,000 people. Jericho probably grew as an important stopover on an early trade route. For travelers crossing the desert, Jericho provided water and a place to rest.

The people of Jericho needed to defend their water and goods from nomads and robbers. To do so, they built thick walls around their city. Some of them were 20 feet (6.1 m) high and 6 feet (1.8 m) thick.

Although Jericho is the oldest city we know about, it did not last. After 6000 B.C. Jericho was abandoned for 1,000 years. Meanwhile, farming villages continued to dot the Fertile

Jericho's walls were built with crude stone tools nearly 10,000 years ago.

Crescent. Farmers began to settle the rich land of Mesopotamia. There, agriculture improved and villages grew into cities. In the history of these cities we may see how civilization advanced in the Middle East.

Reading Check

1. What is the Fertile Crescent?
2. What two major rivers flow through Mesopotamia?
3. How did domesticating animals and plants change people's lives?
4. How were the lives of nomads different from the lives of farmers in the Fertile Crescent?

Look for these important words:

Key Words
- city-states
- ziggurat
- division of labor
- surplus
- cuneiform

- stylus
- scribes

People
- Henry Rawlinson

Places
- Sumer
- Ur

Look for answers to these questions:

1. What useful things were invented by the Sumerians?
2. How were Mesopotamian cities governed?
3. What kinds of workers lived in Sumerian cities?
4. Why was writing important to Sumerians?

2. SUMER

By about 4000 B.C. the world's first civilization was beginning in southern Mesopotamia in the land of **Sumer.** For 3,000 years after that, Mesopotamian civilization was a source of inventions and ideas for neighboring lands. Many of those contributions remain with us today.

The early settlers of Sumer made a very important invention—the wheel. Before the wheel, early people probably moved heavy objects by placing them on logs that rolled. The first wheels may have been slices of tree trunks. The Sumerians made wheels by attaching planks together. Later they covered the rims with copper studs to make the wheels last longer.

The invention of the wheel made possible the wheeled cart. Wheeled carts were usable because the people of the Middle East had already domesticated animals that could pull heavy loads. If there had been no oxen to pull the lumbering carts, they might not

have been invented. Wheeled carts were very important in the development of Sumer.

Irrigation

Farmers who lived in the foothills depended on rainfall to water their crops. When farmers moved into the valley, they got water from the Tigris and Euphrates rivers to irrigate their crops. Yet the rivers were wild. At times they flooded the land, carrying away crops and villages. For the Sumerians a flood was the worst possible natural disaster. The loss of a year's harvest to floods meant starvation.

The Sumerians built canals and water-raising devices to water the fields in the dry summer. They built dikes to control the flooding waters of spring and to hold the water in lakes. They drained marshland to turn it into farmland. Thus, they learned to control the waters on which they depended.

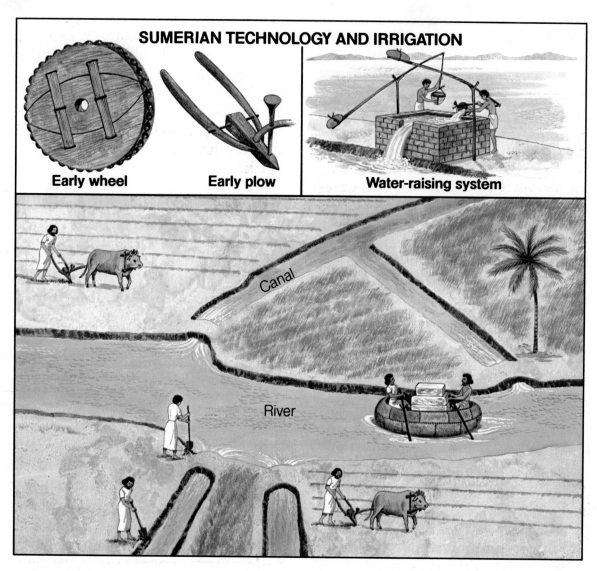

SUMERIAN TECHNOLOGY AND IRRIGATION

Early wheel

Early plow

Water-raising system

Canal

River

Getting water from the rivers and controlling the floods took large numbers of people. These people had to be organized so that each person did a necessary job. There had to be leaders who could make certain that the jobs were done correctly. This could be achieved only in an organized society.

The Growth of Cities

In Sumer, **city-states** made it possible to organize the building of dikes and canals. A city-state is made up of a city and the surrounding lands. Sumer had about 12 city-states. In early days each city was run by a group of citizens and a governor chosen by them. City leaders ruled the surrounding farmland and villages. They decided what work had to be done to keep the dikes and canals in repair.

However, the Sumerian city-states often warred on each other to protect or extend their boundaries. They also were attacked by nomadic and warlike peoples. In times of peril, the group of citizens and the governor could not always agree on a course of action. Often these people were farmers, not warriors.

As a way of providing the strong leadership needed for protection, the city-states gradually changed their system of government. Each city-state chose a king. Sumerians called the king "the big man." He ruled the city during peacetime and led soldiers in times of war. The king was concerned with every part of Sumerian life.

Within each city's walls were houses, temples, and a marketplace for trading. The most important building in the city was the main temple, called a **ziggurat** (ZIG•uh•rat). The Sumerians honored many gods. They believed that each city belonged to one of the gods. A ziggurat was built so that the god could visit Earth and oversee the city's welfare. The god's good will brought large harvests and peace. Disasters, the Sumerians thought, were a sign of the god's displeasure. Enlil, god of wind and air, was the father of the gods. Other important gods were Enki, the god of wisdom, and Ninhursag, mother of Earth.

The City of Ur

About 2000 B.C. the famous city of **Ur** probably had a population of more than 200,000 people. The streets of the city were narrow and winding. People lived in rectangular houses built around small courtyards. The houses of the richer people were often two stories high. These houses were built of brick and plaster. Reed mats and wool rugs lay on the floors. Furniture included low tables, high-backed chairs, and beds. There were baskets and chests made of both reeds and wood. A common household pet was the mongoose, a small animal that catches rats, mice, and snakes.

The people of Ur had many types of jobs. Some became skilled workers in copper, stone, pottery, weaving, or leather. Some became leaders and managers, skilled at directing the work of others. Some people became priests and priestesses. Others became traders, boat-builders, and merchants.

This kind of **division of labor** occurs when people do not have to spend most of their time growing or finding food. Agriculture provided a **surplus,** or extra supply, of food in Ur. Therefore, some people could spend their work hours doing other things that were valuable to the community.

ANCIENT MESOPOTAMIAN CITY-STATES

New Ideas and Inventions

The needs of Sumer's city-states led to more inventions. The need to build canals and to establish field boundaries led to a system of land measurement. The Sumerians developed a unit of land measurement they called *iqu.* Today we still use the *iqu,* but we call it the *acre.* The need to measure the grain harvest led to the development of the quart as a basic measurement.

The Sumerians developed a method of dividing time based on the number 60. We use their system to divide an hour into minutes and a minute into seconds. We also use their system to measure circles and angles.

Trade in Sumer led to another invention. Using reeds that grew along the river, the Sumerians invented large boats for carrying cargo. Eventually they added sails to the boats so that they could move more easily upstream. Sumerian traders returned to their cities with loads of wood, salt, precious stones, and metals.

The first metal to arrive was copper, which came from the area known today as Turkey. Copper beads were probably the first use of the metal. Later people made copper tools, such as ax heads and plowheads. By 3000 B.C. they were mixing copper with tin to make bronze. Bronze made stronger tools and weapons than pure copper. For the next 2,000 years bronze and copper were used to make most tools and weapons.

The Invention of Writing

The many activities of the Sumerians led to one of their greatest inventions—writing. With writing, history began. As people wrote, they preserved a record of their economic activities, their ideas, their feelings, their past, and their poems and stories. Until people began writing down their records and thoughts, there was no history, only prehistory. Everything we know about people in the time

The Sumerians used seals to sign and identify their possessions. The tag on the right was made by the cylinder-shaped seal on the left.

of prehistory is based on the things they left behind. With the invention of writing, people began to tell their own story in their own words.

Record keepers in Sumer marked picture symbols in pieces of clay. These pieces of clay were used as tags to label the contents and ownership of bags and baskets. With time the Sumerians developed a writing system called **cuneiform** (kyoo•NEE•uh•fawrm). *Cuneiform* means wedge-shaped, which describes the shape of the marks made on the clay.

The Sumerians used a **stylus,** a pointed reed instrument, to make marks in soft clay tablets. The clay tablets were then baked to make them hard. The people whose job it was to write were **scribes.** Scribes kept records, wrote letters for people, and copied down stories and songs.

Eventually cuneiform was forgotten, replaced by simpler ways of writing. Until recently no one could understand the "scratches" on the clay tablets. The record of ancient Sumer was a secret seemingly lost forever.

The person who unlocked that secret was **Henry Rawlinson.** Rawlinson, a British army officer, was sent to Iran in 1833 to help organize the Iranian army. On the face of a 1,700-foot (about 515-m) cliff near the town of Behistun he found mysterious inscriptions. Dangling from a rope 500 feet (about 150 m) above the ground, Rawlinson began to copy the inscriptions.

The inscriptions were written in three languages. It seemed to Rawlinson that whoever put the messages on the rock wanted to say the same thing in all three languages. He was right.

Trade agreements were recorded on cuneiform tablets like this one.

Knowing something of two of these languages, Rawlinson was able to translate the third. It was Sumerian writing. In this way he unlocked the secrets of cuneiform and of Sumerian civilization.

Since then people have been able to translate thousands of cuneiform tablets—only a part of the half-million tablets found so far. The cuneiform tablets that have been translated tell much about city life. They explain the thoughts of kings, of farmers, of traders, and of students. They tell that ancient people had many of the same concerns as people today.

Reading Check

1. Where did civilization first develop in the Middle East?
2. What is a city-state?
3. How does agriculture affect the division of labor?
4. How were the secrets of Sumerian civilization unlocked?

Ziggurats

In a Sumerian city, one structure was noticeable over all others. The ziggurat towered above the noisy city almost like a modern skyscraper. Reaching to the heavens, some ziggurats stood as tall as 70 feet (21.3 m).

In time, a ziggurat became more than a home for the gods. The Sumerians built smaller buildings around the base of the ziggurat. These buildings housed different kinds of community activities. There were workshops where craft workers made clothes and metal goods. There were temples in which priests performed religious ceremonies. The ziggurat and all its buildings were enclosed within walls. Great staircases led from one level of the ziggurat to the next. Trees and gardens on each level made pleasant, shady terraces through which to stroll and to look down upon the city.

A shrine stood on the highest level of the ziggurat. This is where Sumerian priests performed ceremonies in honor of the god for whom the ziggurat had been built. A statue of the god was kept in the shrine's innermost chamber.

Only the ruins of the lower levels of some ziggurats remain today. They reveal much about the people who built them. Sumerians had none of the tools or machinery that are used in construction today. They were careful builders, however. Brickmakers formed mud bricks that were all exactly the same size. After drying, the bricks were transported to the building site and set in place with bitumen (buh•TOO•muhn). Bitumen is a thick, sticky, black substance that is similar to the asphalt used today to pave roads. Reeds were braided together and used to bind the building in much the same way that builders today use steel cables. The Sumerians knew that this would help make their buildings strong.

Today visitors can climb the ruins of ancient ziggurats. They can look out over the desert where once were great cities. With mud as the most plentiful resource, it took master builders to raise such lasting monuments.

This golden bull's head is the front of a harp made by a Sumerian craft worker.

Stone figures were left to "pray" at the shrine when the worshippers themselves were absent.

The famous ziggurat of Ur was built to the moon god Nanna and showed the power of Ur's king. Notice the partly restored stairways.

Based on reports found on cuneiform tablets, artists and scholars can show how the ancient ziggurat at Ur was constructed.

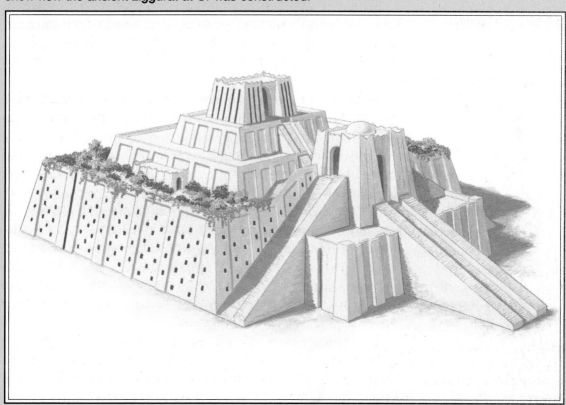

Look for these important words:

Key Words
- classes
- nobles

- commoners
- clients
- slaves

People
- Ur-Nammu

Look for answers to these questions:

1. How did each of the four groups of people that made up Sumerian society contribute to that society?
2. What role did women play in Sumer?
3. Why does a society need laws?
4. How were children educated in Sumer?

3. LIFE IN SUMER

Sumerian society was made up of different groups, or **classes.** This division took place because the work of some people was valued more than the work of others. Some people gained greater wealth or honors. The wealthiest class consisted of the **nobles.** Nobles included important priests and relatives of the king. The nobles and the temples owned much of the land.

Most people were **commoners.** Commoners were merchants, scribes, farmers, and skilled workers. Skilled workers included carpenters, potters, brickmakers, doctors, boatmen, and smiths. Commoners could both inherit and purchase land. Some commoners became quite wealthy by buying land. Even poor commoners usually owned farms or houses with gardens. The commoners who were skilled workers sold their goods in the marketplace. They received payment in other goods, such as grain, or in pieces of silver.

A third class of people in ancient Sumer was made up of **clients.** These were people who worked for nobles or for the temple. They often were given small plots of land to work but not to own. They were paid in food and wool.

The fourth class in Sumer was the **slaves.** Most slaves were prisoners of war. Some people were made slaves as punishment. Parents could sell their children into slavery. A person who was in debt could turn his family into slaves for as long as three years to pay off the debt. Slaves could buy their freedom if they could earn or borrow money. The free slave then became a commoner or a client.

The family was important in all classes. The father was the head of the family. Children were raised under the strict guidance of their parents. For example, parents decided who their children would marry.

The laws of Sumer allowed women to own property and start businesses or to act for their husbands, if necessary. Women sometimes held the most important religious positions,

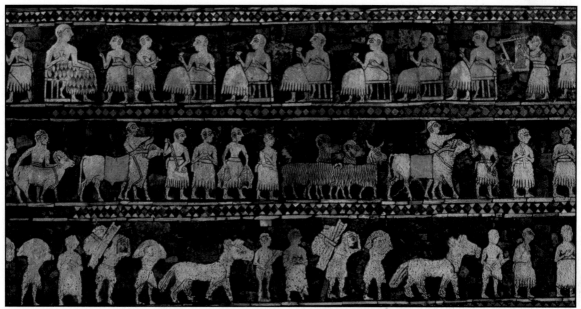

In a mosaic found at Ur, a king (top panel, seated left) and his officers enjoy a victory feast as conquered subjects bring gifts.

including that of chief priestess of the main temple. Most women, however, remained at home to care for their households.

The Importance of Laws

When thousands of people live together, laws are necessary to keep order and establish justice. By 2500 B.C. rulers were making laws to guide human behavior. One early law, for example, said that the punishment for theft was stoning. People threw stones, on which the crime had been written, until the wrongdoer lay dead.

Ur-Nammu, who became king of Ur in about 2050 B.C., established laws that were less harsh. Many of Ur-Nammu's laws used fines as punishment. Ur-Nammu was concerned with protecting the helpless. He made certain that "the orphan did not fall prey to the wealthy" and that "the widow did not fall prey to the powerful."

A Schoolboy's Day

It may be hard to imagine life as it was 4,000 years ago. The translations of the cuneiform tablets sometimes seem familiar, however. Let us imagine a schoolboy. His father might be a wealthy military officer or scribe because children of the poor did not go to school.

People with wealth sent their sons to school because knowing how to read and write was important. These skills were the keys to success in Sumerian society. Girls did not go to school. Sometimes they learned to read and write at home, however.

The Sumerian school day was long— from sunrise to sunset. Boys sat in groups of three and four on low brick benches. There they learned to write on clay tablets. They studied grammar and mathematics. They learned prayers to the gods, songs, and stories. They copied lessons repeatedly, memorizing as they wrote.

A strict master watches as Sumerian boys practice carving cylinders and writing on clay tablets. Writing was a valuable skill in Mesopotamia.

Long ago, one Sumerian wrote about his school day:

When I awoke early in the morning, I faced my mother and said to her, "Give me my lunch. I want to go to school." My mother gave me two rolls and I set out.

Discipline was harsh in Sumerian schools. If a student was late, the schoolmaster would beat him with a cane. The poor fellow had to endure several canings during the day. He was beaten for talking, for getting up without permission, or for having messy clothes. Some boys preferred not to go to school. In one tablet a scribe tells how upset he is because his son does not go to school but hangs around in the public square.

"Where did you go?" the father asks his son.
The son answers, "I did not go anywhere."
"If you did not go anywhere, why do you idle about?" the father asks.

The father then lectures his son about the importance of education:

You who wander about the public square, would you achieve success? Then seek out the past generations. Go to school, it will be of benefit to you.

The feelings of the father were expressed in a Sumerian riddle:

What is it that he whose eyes are not open enters it, and he whose eyes are wide open comes out of it?

The answer to this ancient riddle is a school.

Reading Check

1. What was the highest class of Sumerian society?
2. Name three types of jobs held by commoners.
3. How could slaves become free?
4. Why was education considered important in Sumer?

Look for these important words:

Key Words
- empire
- Code of Hammurabi
- chariots
- battering rams
- Persians

People
- Sargon of Akkad
- Hammurabi

Places
- Babylon
- Assyria
- Palestine

Look for answers to these questions:

1. How did the Sumerians get along with each other and with their neighbors?
2. Who were four groups of conquerors who at different times controlled Mesopotamia?
3. What kinds of laws were recorded by Hammurabi?
4. What change occurred in Sumer after the Persians conquered it?

4. A LINE OF CONQUERORS

Warfare constantly threatened the people of Sumer. People in the foothills and the nomads who lived on the edge of the Fertile Crescent envied the wealth of Sumer. Sumerian cities also were often at war with each other. There were no natural boundaries separating the various cities, and cities often fought for control of farmland or valuable water. The ancient histories are full of descriptions of one city conquering another and then being conquered itself.

The first important conqueror was **Sargon of Akkad.** By about 2300 B.C. Sargon had conquered much of the area surrounding Sumer. He then conquered Sumer itself and established an **empire.** An empire has many different peoples and places under one ruler. Sargon's empire lasted for about 200 years. When the empire was destroyed, the city-states became independent again.

This bronze head may be Sargon of Akkad.

39

About 1800 B.C. **Hammurabi** (hah‧moo‧RAH‧bee), king of the city-state of **Babylon** (BAB‧uh‧luhn), conquered and reunited Mesopotamia. Hammurabi worked tirelessly to develop the cities under his rule. Dictating to a scribe, he sent local officials hundreds of letters on clay tablets. These letters urged the construction of dikes, canals, temples, and roads.

The Code of Hammurabi

Hammurabi's fame is based chiefly on a code of law that he assembled. Tablets containing parts of the **Code of Hammurabi** still exist.

> To cause justice to prevail in the country
> To destroy the wicked and the evil,
> That the strong shall not injure the weak. . . .

With these statements, Hammurabi explained why he developed the code of laws. The code tells Babylonians to care for the sick, the poor, and the helpless. One part of the code is considered cruel today. It is the "eye-for-an-eye" law. This law says that whoever commits an injury should be punished in the same manner as that injury. For example, if a person broke someone else's arm in a fight, that person should be punished by having his own arm broken. Ur-Nammu's idea of using fines as punishment was forgotten.

Assyria

After the collapse of Hammurabi's empire, Mesopotamia was ruled by several different peoples. Then another great empire arose in Mesopotamia. This was **Assyria** (uh‧SIR‧ee‧uh). The land of the Assyrians was in northern Mesopotamia. For centuries the Assyrians had lived in the shadow either of Babylonia or of the warlike people in the mountains to the north. These warriors had learned to use **chariots,** carts drawn by horses.

In time the Assyrians also learned to make chariots and to use horses. They organized armies that included chariots, cavalry, bowmen, and lancers. With the armies went engineers with **battering rams,** heavy beams for breaking down city walls. Once the Assyrians became independent they began conquering their neighbors.

In 701 B.C. the Assyrian king, Sennacherib (suh‧NAK‧uhr‧ib), stormed **Palestine,** a part of the Fertile Crescent near the Mediterranean Sea. He captured 46 cities and seized more than 200,000 captives. In 689 B.C. he attacked and destroyed Babylon. Sennacherib bragged: "The city and houses, from its foundation to its top, I destroyed, I devastated, I burned with fire." After

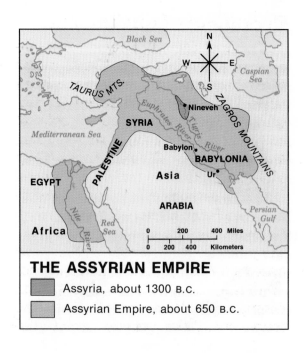

THE ASSYRIAN EMPIRE

Assyria, about 1300 B.C.

Assyrian Empire, about 650 B.C.

Riding wheeled chariots into battle, the warlike Assyrians overwhelmed their enemies. Many stone carvings illustrate their military strength.

destroying the city, he had canals dug from the Euphrates River and flooded the site. He wanted to turn the city, he said, into a meadow.

In time the mighty empire of the Assyrians was toppled by other peoples. Free of the Assyrians, Babylon again became the center of Mesopotamian culture.

Conquerors From the East

In about 539 B.C. Babylon was conquered by the **Persians.** The Persians came from east of the Zagros Mountains. They were unlike other conquerors of Mesopotamia. People of many cultures and languages had ruled Mesopotamia at different times. They all had adopted and continued the civilization established by the Sumerians. The Persians were different. They did not adopt Sumerian ways of life. They developed a system of writing based on their own language. Gradually the widespread use of cuneiform disappeared. When people could no longer read the ancient script, the civilization of Mesopotamia was truly dead, buried beneath the sands.

In 3,000 years the Mesopotamians had changed enormously. Using their natural surroundings—water, wheat, and clay—wandering herders began this civilization. They invented such tools as the wheel and the plow. They farmed the land and built cities. They developed mathematics. They recorded their laws.

Without their writing, of course, we would know little of the achievements of these early inventors and builders. Their written records have survived. With them we are able to piece together the history of their past.

Reading Check

1. What is an empire? Give two examples.
2. Who was Hammurabi? For what was he famous?
3. Why was the Assyrian army so powerful?
4. How did the early civilization of Mesopotamia disappear?

When you study geography, maps help you understand where places are. When you study history, **timelines** help you in much the same way. A timeline is a diagram of a certain period of time. Important events are marked on the timeline. By studying the timeline you can find out the year in which each event happened. You can see the order in which events happened. A timeline can also help you figure out how much time passed between two events.

World History on a Timeline

This horizontal timeline shows a period of time beginning with the history of ancient Sumer. The Sumerian civilization began about 6,000 years ago and lasted about 3,000 years.

We number years backward and forward from the time of Jesus Christ's birth. Christ's birthdate is shown for you on this timeline.

Notice that the years to the left of Christ's birthdate are B.C. dates. B.C. stands for "before Christ." Persia's conquest of Sumer was in 539 B.C., or 539 years before Christ's birth.

The *larger* the year B.C., the *earlier* the time in history. The date of Sumer's first farming villages, 5800 B.C., is larger than the date of Sumer's first cities, 3800 B.C. The date of the villages is thus earlier than the date of the cities.

The abbreviation **A.D.** is used to name years after the birth of Christ. A.D. stands for *anno Domini* (an•noh DAHM•uh•nee), a Latin phrase meaning "in the year of the Lord." Henry Rawlinson discovered Sumerian writing in A.D. 1833. This was 1,833 years after Christ's birth. Dates after Christ's birth are usually written without the abbreviation A.D. If you see a date such as 1833 with no abbreviation, you should assume it is an A.D. date.

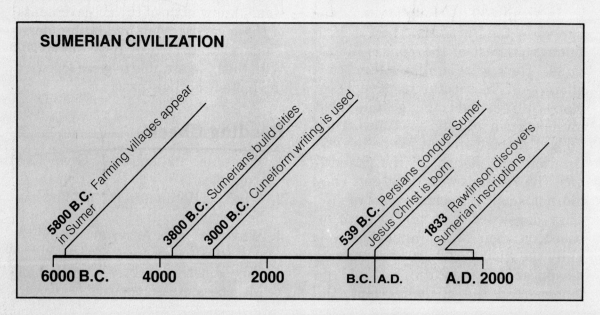

SUMERIAN CIVILIZATION

5800 B.C. Farming villages appear in Sumer

3800 B.C. Sumerians build cities

3000 B.C. Cuneiform writing is used

539 B.C. Persians conquer Sumer

Jesus Christ is born

1833 Rawlinson discovers Sumerian inscriptions

6000 B.C. | 4000 | 2000 | B.C. | A.D. | A.D. 2000

Centuries

A century is a period of 100 years. Look at the chart below. The year A.D. 25 is in the first century. This is because it is within the first 100 years. Therefore, the 400s are in the fifth century, the 1900s are in the twentieth century, and so on. We live in the twentieth century (nearly 2,000 years) after the birth of Christ. The name of a century is always one more than the number of hundreds in the year. The same is true for B.C. dates. The Persians conquered Sumer in 539 B.C. This was the sixth century B.C. Rawlinson discovered Sumerian inscriptions in 1833. In what century is 1833?

Years	Century Name
1–100	First century
101–200	Second century
201–300	Third century
301–400	Fourth century
401–500	Fifth century
501–600	Sixth century
601–700	Seventh century
701–800	Eighth century
801–900	Ninth century
901–1000	Tenth century
1001–1100	Eleventh century
1101–1200	Twelfth century
1201–1300	Thirteenth century
1301–1400	Fourteenth century
1401–1500	Fifteenth century
1501–1600	Sixteenth century
1601–1700	Seventeenth century
1701–1800	Eighteenth century
1801–1900	Nineteenth century
1901–2000	Twentieth century
2001–2100	Twenty-first century

Vertical Timelines

Now look at the timeline below. It shows the history of Sumer in more detail. This is a vertical timeline. It is read from top to bottom rather than from left to right. The earliest year is at the top, and the latest year is at the bottom. The earliest event is the forming of Sumer's farming villages. The next event, the building of Sumer's cities, appears below this, followed by Sargon of Akkad's conquest. What important event followed Sargon's conquest?

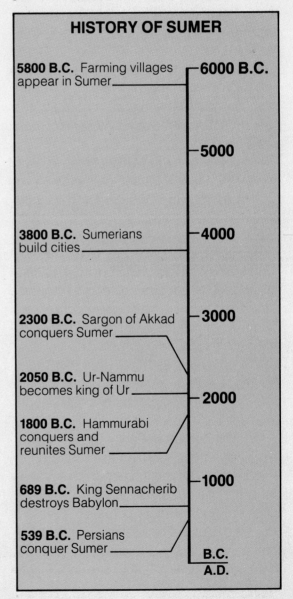

HISTORY OF SUMER

5800 B.C. Farming villages appear in Sumer

3800 B.C. Sumerians build cities

2300 B.C. Sargon of Akkad conquers Sumer

2050 B.C. Ur-Nammu becomes king of Ur

1800 B.C. Hammurabi conquers and reunites Sumer

689 B.C. King Sennacherib destroys Babylon

539 B.C. Persians conquer Sumer

6000 B.C.
5000
4000
3000
2000
1000
B.C.
A.D.

Finding Length of Time

You can use arithmetic to figure out how long ago an event happened. For an event with an A.D. date, you *subtract* the year of the event from the present year. For example, to find out how long ago Rawlinson discovered Sumerian writing, you would subtract 1833 from the present year. Let's say the year is 1988. The answer is 155. Thus, Rawlinson discovered Sumerian writing 155 years ago.

For an event that happened before the birth of Christ, you must *add* the present year and the year of the event. For example, the Persians conquered Sumer in 539 B.C. You add 539 and the present date to find out how much time has passed. Again, let's use 1988. The answer is 2,527. The Persians conquered ancient Sumer 2,527 years ago.

Look again at the vertical timeline. Find the date when Ur-Nammu became King of Ur. Would you add or subtract to find out how long ago this happened?

Using Approximate Dates

When people talk about events in the very distant past, they often use **approximate** dates. Approximate dates are close to the actual dates but are not exact. The first date on the Sumerian timeline does not mean that thousands of settlers suddenly flocked to Sumer in 5800 B.C. It means that people were settling in the area around that time.

To find out about how long ago something happened, you can use round numbers instead of exact numbers. This makes the arithmetic easier, and the date is usually close enough for most purposes. Find out how long ago the first settlers came to Sumer. First, round the present year to 2000. Then add 2,000 and 5,800. The first settlers arrived about 7,800 years ago.

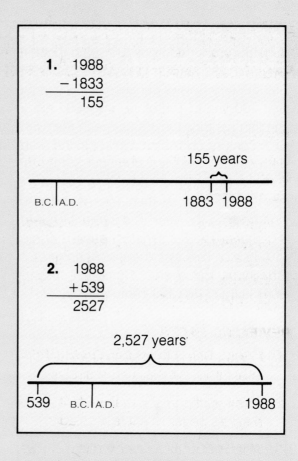

1.
$$\begin{array}{r} 1988 \\ -1833 \\ \hline 155 \end{array}$$

155 years

B.C. | A.D.   1883 1988

2.
$$\begin{array}{r} 1988 \\ +539 \\ \hline 2527 \end{array}$$

2,527 years

539   B.C. | A.D.   1988

CHECKING YOUR SKILLS

Use the timelines in the lesson to answer the following questions.

1. Do earlier dates appear to the left or the right on a horizontal timeline?

2. Which conqueror came first, Sargon or Sennacherib?

3. Writing came into use in Sumer around 3000 B.C. About how long ago was this? (Clue: Round the present year to 2000.)

4. The Code of Hammurabi may have been written between 1792 and 1750 B.C. In what century was that?

5. Approximately how much time passed between Hammurabi's rule and the destruction of Babylon? (Clue: Round 689 to 700.)

CHAPTER 1 REVIEW

USING WORDS

Explain the meaning of each of the words listed below. Then use each word in a complete sentence.

1. **agriculture**
2. **city-states**
3. **classes**
4. **cuneiform**
5. **division of labor**
6. **domesticate**
7. **empire**
8. **nomads**
9. **oasis**
10. **scribes**

REVIEWING FACTS

1. In what way is the Fertile Crescent different from the areas surrounding it?

2. What is the main reason that early peoples began to settle in villages?

3. What is the name of the earliest city we know about?

4. How did city-states meet the needs of Sumerians?

5. Why were ziggurats important in Sumer?

6. How was each of these inventions a response to a Sumerian problem?
   - a. wheel
   - b. pottery
   - c. dikes
   - d. measurement
   - e. boats

7. Which metals were important to ancient Sumerians? How were they used?

8. Name the four classes of Sumerian society and briefly describe each one.

9. How did Hammurabi's laws differ from Ur-Nammu's?

10. How were the Persians different from other conquerors in Mesopotamia?

THINKING CRITICALLY

1. Trade encouraged the invention of writing. Why might writing be needed in selling and shipping goods? For what reasons was writing important to Sumerian civilization? Why do you think the Sumerians wrote on clay tablets? How are ancient writings used today?

2. With Sumer's wealth came the constant threat of war. Why would other groups want to conquer the Sumerians? Why would city-states fight each other? As you answer these questions, consider Sumer's location and resources.

PRACTICING SKILLS

Timeline   Study the timeline below. Then answer the questions that follow.

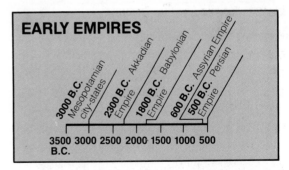

1. What kind of timeline is shown here?

2. How many years are represented?

3. What is the earliest empire shown?

4. About how many years passed between the Babylonian and Assyrian empires?

5. About how many years ago did the Persians rule in the Middle East?

Ancient Egyptians Bring Life to the Desert

Among the early cultures of the Middle East, the achievements of the Mesopotamians were matched by those of the ancient Egyptians. The Egyptians created an advanced civilization that lasted almost 3,000 years. Many of their monuments and ideas still exist.

Other important cultures of the Middle East were those of the Hebrews and the Persians. The Hebrews had lived both in Mesopotamia and in Egypt. The Persians conquered all the Middle East, forming a vast empire.

1. ANCIENT EGYPT

In the same centuries that Mesopotamian civilization was flourishing, another civilization was growing in Egypt. In its own region Egypt has long been called *Misr.* This word means "place of civilization and many people."

Egypt is in the northeast corner of Africa. In the north it faces the Mediterranean Sea. To the east beyond hills and mountains is the Red Sea. Throughout Egypt are dry, windswept deserts that cannot support much life. Egypt's inland area receives less than 1 inch (2.5 cm) of rainfall each year.

A narrow ribbon of fruitful land cut by a single river divides the desert lands of Egypt. This river, the **Nile,** flows north more than 4,000 miles (about 6,500 km) from the mountains to the Mediterranean Sea. The Nile is the world's longest river. Near the Mediterranean Sea the river widens into a fan-shaped **delta.** A delta is the deposit of rich soil left by a river where it empties into the sea. Deltas are often shaped like triangles.

The valley of the Nile River gave birth to one of the world's longest-lasting civilizations. There, ancient Egyptians practiced agriculture. They domesticated sheep, goats, cattle, and donkeys. Later they domesticated the honey bee.

Trade connected the peoples of Mesopotamia and early Egypt. Ideas passed back and forth that probably influenced each civilization. Like the Mesopotamians, the early Egyptians organized themselves into city-states. Egyptians, too, worked together to irrigate crops. However, as in early Mesopotamia, the Egyptian city-states also fought against each other for control of land and water.

47

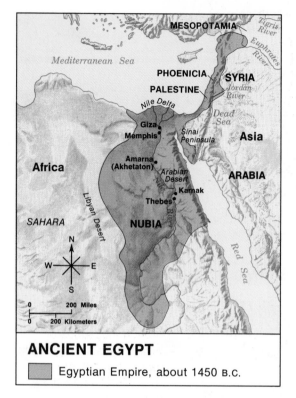

ANCIENT EGYPT

◼ Egyptian Empire, about 1450 B.C.

Although the early history of Egypt and Mesopotamia followed similar paths, the later Egyptians developed a unique civilization. The deserts, mountains, and seas on Egypt's borders helped protect this civilization. Egypt's geography allowed Egyptian civilization to develop fully, undisturbed by outside invaders.

The Importance of the Nile

Egyptians depended on the annual flooding of the Nile River. The Nile was more peaceful at floodtime than were the turbulent Tigris and Euphrates rivers. Every winter Egyptians watched patiently, seeing the stream move no faster than most people could run. Then, about April, rains in the mountains caused the waters to swell.

All Egyptians celebrated in June when the floods began. The rising water spilled over onto the land alongside the river. This was the beginning of the season called Inundation. The waters reached their peak during September and then began to leave the fields. The season of the returning waters was called Emergence. Emergence lasted until February. Drought, the third season, lasted from February to June.

During Emergence people trapped water in ponds to use later for irrigation. They also planted seeds in the fresh mud. During Drought they harvested the crops. During Inundation the farmers were free to work on building projects.

The Nile carried **silt,** fine bits of rock and soil, which it left behind during the annual floods. This rich black earth formed a strip 5 to 15 miles (about 8 to 24 km) wide on either side of the river. Thus each year the Nile brought the two things needed for agriculture: rich soil and water. Egypt, it was said, was the "gift of the Nile."

The lives of the Egyptians depended on the river's gift. When flooding was normal, the times were good. In the years when the flooding was below normal, less land was watered. There were fewer crops. Fewer crops meant starvation and bad times.

The early Egyptians developed sailboats to use on the Nile. The first boats were probably made of bound reeds, which grew abundantly in the marshes of the river. In time the Egyptians made their boats out of wood. In such boats the Egyptians traveled on the gentle Nile. The sails caught the winds from the north. These winds would send the boats against the current. Egyptians also sailed on the Mediterranean Sea.

The Nile River flows through thousands of miles of desert. Egyptians continue to depend on the fertile land along its banks.

The Nile River linked all Egyptians. The ease of travel on the Nile encouraged trading and contacts among the villages that dotted its shores. The Nile made it possible to unite Egypt into one country. The culture shared by people along the Nile formed the basis of Egyptian civilization.

The Pharaoh

The history of ancient Egypt begins with **Menes** (MEE•neez), a king of southern Egypt. Menes united Egypt about 3100 B.C. He built his capital at **Memphis,** a city near present-day Cairo. Menes is the first king we know about in Egypt.

Egypt's kings were called **pharaohs** (FAIR•ohz). The pharaoh had great power, but he was expected to rule fairly. Helping the pharaoh govern were many nobles and officials. They collected taxes, planned building projects, and enforced the pharaoh's laws.

Egyptians worshipped the pharaoh as a god. The pharaoh spent much time at religious ceremonies. As both political ruler and god, the pharaoh had complete control in Egypt.

Religious Beliefs

Religion was important in all parts of Egyptian life. Before Egypt was united, each village and town worshipped its own god or goddess. In time, the Egyptians organized these gods and goddesses into a family of gods.

The Egyptians identified their gods with animals. A god was often pictured as an animal. Sometimes the god had a person's body and an animal's head.

49

Much is known about the religion of ancient Egypt from *The Book of the Dead,* here showing an Egyptian official approaching Osiris's throne.

The first god recognized by all Egyptians was Re, the sun god. Other important gods included Hathor, goddess of love; Thoth, god of wisdom; and Anubis, judge of the dead. Hathor was often represented as a cow, Thoth as a dogheaded baboon, and Anubis as the wolflike jackal.

Two other important Egyptian gods were Osiris and Isis. Osiris, Egyptians believed, gave Egypt civilization. His jealous brother then killed him and scattered the parts of his body in the Nile. Isis, the wife of Osiris, gathered the parts and returned him to life.

Belief in life after death, as in the story of Osiris, was central to Egyptian life. The ancient Egyptians compared life to the Nile. The Nile may rise and retreat, but it continues to flow quietly forever. The Egyptians believed that if the body were preserved, then the soul would be able to continue its existence. Life after death, they thought, would be a continuation of the happy times on Earth.

The Egyptians developed ways of preserving bodies. They wrapped the bodies of their dead in linen. We call these wrapped bodies **mummies.** The Egyptians also buried their dead with the things they had used in this life and would probably need in the next life, too. In the dry climate of Egypt, mummies and their belongings lasted for thousands of years.

A Surplus of Food

By the time of Menes the Egyptians were so successful in agriculture that they produced a surplus of food almost every year. The Egyptians used this surplus, which included wheat, barley, and dates, for trade. Along the eastern Mediterranean coast they traded for cedar and pine timber to use for boats and furniture. Along the African coast, in present-day Somalia, they traded for ivory, ebony, and even pet monkeys. This trade brought luxury and wealth to Egypt.

For Egyptians the scarab, a kind of beetle, was a sign of good luck.

Arts and Crafts

The Egyptians became skilled workers of both copper and gold. They dug copper ore and turquoise from mines in the **Sinai Peninsula,** which lies between Egypt and Israel. They found a good supply of gold in the eastern desert.

The Egyptians had also learned to use the potter's wheel. In addition to potters, other skilled workers included carpenters, jewelry makers, linen weavers, and builders.

Love of Life

Throughout their history the ancient Egyptians showed a zest for life. They were playful people who liked good times and funny stories. Acrobats and musicians were popular. Early Egyptian paintings show children playing leapfrog and pet monkeys causing mischief.

The Egyptians liked to make themselves look beautiful. They carefully rubbed oils into their skin to protect it from the dry climate. Women wore cosmetics that gave their eyes an almond shape. Both men and women wore jewelry, whether simple strings of beads or fancy necklaces.

Egyptian Writing

We know the name of Menes because the Egyptians wrote it down. Egyptian writing developed about the same time that Menes unified Egypt. The Egyptians may have received the idea of writing from Mesopotamia. They developed their own system, however.

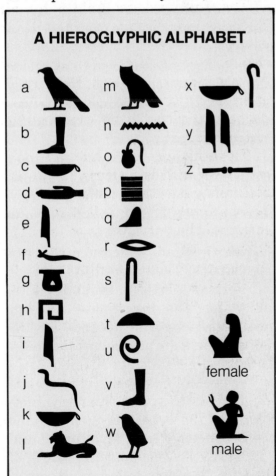

A HIEROGLYPHIC ALPHABET

51

Because the writing most often appeared on religious temples, it is called **hieroglyphics** (hy•ruh•GLIF•iks), or "sacred writing." Hieroglyphics started as a kind of picture writing, with pictures standing for ideas. In time the Egyptians added symbols that represented sounds.

As in Mesopotamia, scribes were among the most important persons in Egypt. Few others could write. Scribes were the officials, the tax collectors, and the engineers.

The Egyptians recorded their language in stone, on walls, and on paper. Paper was one of the great inventions of ancient Egypt. They created paper from **papyrus** (puh•PY•ruhs), reeds that grew in the swamps of the Nile River. Our word *paper* comes from the word *papyrus*.

To make paper, the Egyptians peeled the reeds into long strips. Next, they laid the strips close together, edges touching. Over these strips they added a crosswise layer of strips. Then they pressed the papyrus strips with stones until the two layers merged into one sheet of paper. They glued several sheets of paper together to make long rolls called **scrolls.**

The Egyptians sharpened reeds to use as pens. They dipped these reeds into ink made of soot, ground plants, and water. The dry climate of Egypt helped preserve the papyrus scrolls. Some of them are as easy to read today as they were in ancient times.

For several thousand years no one could read Egyptian hieroglyphics. Then in 1798 French armies invaded Egypt. One year later an officer found a large black stone near the mouth of the Nile. It is now called the **Rosetta**

The Rosetta Stone was carved in hieroglyphics, in late Egyptian, and in Greek.

Stone, after the name of the area where it was found. The message written on the stone's shiny surface was in three languages, including hieroglyphics. A Frenchman named Jean Francois Champollion finally translated the hieroglyphics in 1822. The ideas, thoughts, history, and secrets of ancient Egypt were unlocked for the modern world.

Reading Check

1. What are two ways that the Nile helped Egyptians?
2. Who was the first god recognized by all Egyptians?
3. How did the Egyptians make paper?
4. Why was the Rosetta Stone an important discovery?

Mummies

How do scientists and historians know so much about the ancient Egyptians? One way is by asking Ginger. Ginger is a 5,000-year-old Egyptian mummy who got his name from the reddish hair that is still on his head. He is now on display at the British Museum in London.

The ancient Egyptians used many different methods to mummify their dead. Early in Egyptian civilization, bodies were simply buried in the desert sand together with tools and pottery. The hot sand dried out the bodies and prevented them from decaying. Ginger was buried this way. Scientists studying him have found out how early Egyptians made the first mummies.

As time passed, Egyptians began to bury their dead in tombs. Without the drying effects of desert sand, bodies quickly decayed. To halt the decay, the Egyptians developed a process of **embalming**. They used their embalming method to preserve the bodies.

The embalming process took about 70 days. Embalmers first washed the body and brushed it with oils and spices. The brain was removed and sometimes thrown away because it was considered unimportant. The heart was kept in place because it was considered the source of intelligence. The lungs, liver, stomach, and intestines were removed, embalmed separately, and placed in special jars. Later, the jars were placed near the embalmed mummy. The remainder of the body was washed, oiled again, and filled with bundles of salt. The salt would dry the body in the same way as desert sand had dried mummies like Ginger. The body was then covered with more salt and left for 40 days.

The embalmers decorated the body with special dyes and adorned it with jewelry to make the mummy look as lifelike as possible. Then the mummy was wrapped in many layers of soft linen. An elaborate mask was placed on the head of the mummy. Then many more layers of linen were applied. Finally, the mummy was bound tightly, ready for the funeral ceremony and life ever after.

Mummy case

Inside of case

Look for these important words:

Key Words
- Old Kingdom
- Middle Kingdom
- New Kingdom
- Age of Pyramids
- architects
- peasants

- Great Sphinx
- obelisk

People
- Imhotep
- Hatshepsut
- Nefertiti
- Akhenaton

- Tutankhamen
- Howard Carter
- Ramses II

Places
- Giza
- Thebes

Look for answers to these questions:

1. How and why were the pyramids built?
2. What new idea did the pharaoh Akhenaton introduce?
3. What important discovery did Howard Carter make?

2. THE ACHIEVEMENTS OF ANCIENT EGYPT

The history of ancient Egypt is usually divided into three parts. They are the **Old Kingdom,** the **Middle Kingdom,** and the **New Kingdom.** The Old Kingdom is also known as the **Age of Pyramids,** for it was then that those awe-inspiring monuments were built.

The Old Kingdom

The Old Kingdom, or Age of Pyramids, dates from 2700 to 2200 B.C. The idea of the pyramid grew from the earlier brick tombs designed to protect and preserve the body. About 2700 B.C. **Imhotep** (im•HOH•tep), an adviser to the pharaoh, designed the first pyramid. For such a task, Imhotep was the first person to become famous without being a conqueror or king.

For years people puzzled over how the Egyptians built the pyramids. The stones used to build some pyramids weighed about 5,000 pounds (about 2,300 kg) each. At this time in their history the Egyptians did not have the wheel. Nor did they have levers to lift the stone blocks high, one on top of the other.

Some people now think they know how the pyramids were built. The huge blocks of stone were probably cut from cliffs using wooden wedges, stone hammers, and copper saws. The stones were put on wooden sleds. The sleds were pulled to nearby boats that took the stones to the building site. Again the sleds were pulled over the ground.

The pyramid builders built ramps of mud brick to the pyramid. As the pyramid grew higher, so did the ramps. Gangs of workers pulled the heavily loaded sleds up the ramps. It may not have been as hard as it sounds. If the clay ramps and road were kept wet, the sleds probably could be pulled quite easily. In one experiment, it was found

54

that a person could easily pull a one-ton (about 900-kg) block of stone over a wet path.

The designers, or **architects,** and engineers who planned the pyramids were probably scribes by training. They had important problems to solve. They had to make certain that the base of the pyramid was absolutely flat. Otherwise the pyramid might topple. They had to make certain that the base was square and that the angle of the walls was correct. According to Egyptian religious ideas, the pyramid had to face true north. To do so, the designers studied and charted the stars in the northern sky.

The very top of the pyramid was covered in gold. The gold caught the rays of the sun. The Egyptians believed that the shape of the pyramid was a sun ray in stone. The gold cap, they thought, reflected the eye of the sun god, Re. The golden-tipped pyramid was a ladder to the heavens. The Egyptians believed that the soul of the pharaoh could rise to the heavens on the sun rays. He could return to his body in the tomb the same way.

People used to think that only a system using thousands of slaves could have built the pyramids. In fact, the hundreds of thousands of workers who built the pyramids were probably **peasants,** poor people who lived on and farmed the land. During the season of Inundation they worked for the pharaoh. The pharaoh probably supplied the workers with such foods as wheat bread, beans, onions, and salt.

The Step Pyramid designed by Imhotep was the first great royal tomb. It was huge compared to earlier structures, but less than half the size of the largest pyramid in Egypt.

The Sphinx was worshipped by the Egyptians as a symbol of the sun god.

About 80 pyramids were built in the valley of **Giza** (GEE·zuh). The largest of these pyramids is called the Great Pyramid. It was built about 2600 B.C. as the tomb of the Pharaoh Khufu. This mighty pyramid looms 451 feet (137.5 m) high. Each of its four sides is 776 feet (236.5 m) long, and its base covers about 13 acres (5 ha). The pyramid contains 2,300,000 blocks of limestone. The stones are so finely cut that even today it is impossible to slip a sheet of paper between any two of them. The Great Pyramid probably took about 20 years to build.

Sharing the valley of Giza with the pyramids is the **Great Sphinx** (SFINGKS). This huge statue has the body of a lion and the head of a man.

The head is probably modeled after Pharaoh Khafre, whose pyramid tomb is nearby. The Sphinx stands 66 feet (20.1 m) high. Each of its forearms extends 187 feet (57 m).

The Middle Kingdom

From about 2050 to 1850 B.C. the Middle Kingdom saw a rise in the importance of the middle class in Egypt. The middle class was formed of those people who were neither nobles nor peasants. The members of the middle class were traders or had jobs in the pharaoh's government. Many were scribes. Members of the middle class owned their own land on which they built houses of mud brick. These houses were enclosed by high walls. Within the walls were courtyards, fish ponds, gardens, and animal pens. There were special buildings for grinding grain, baking bread, and cooking.

During the Middle Kingdom the capital of Egypt was **Thebes** (THEEBZ). Along the Nile River near Thebes, at Karnak, the pharaohs began to construct temples in honor of Amon, the chief god of Thebes.

During the Middle Kingdom the Egyptians conquered Nubia, the land to the south, and parts of the Fertile Crescent. Slaves from both Nubia and the Fertile Crescent became common in the households of the rich.

The Middle Kingdom came to an end when the Hyksos (HIK·sahs) gained control of northern Egypt. The Hyksos were nomads from the Fertile Crescent who had settled near the border of Egypt. Using horses and chariots, they easily defeated the pharaoh's army. Soon the Egyptians also learned to use

56

horses and chariots, and they chased the Hyksos from Egypt. Egypt then started another period of its history, the New Kingdom.

The New Kingdom

Trade had always been important to Egypt. With the New Kingdom, the Egyptians built an empire that included Syria, Palestine, and Nubia. Through both trade and conquest Egypt grew ever richer. The New Kingdom dated from about 1570 to 1090 B.C.

The Egyptians of the New Kingdom did not build pyramids. They buried their dead in more protected places, where grave robbers could not find them. Yet they continued to build massive monuments and temples. The Temple of Karnak contains the world's largest hall of columns. These columns, the first of their kind, are so broad at the top that 100 people can stand on any one of them.

A stone shaft called an **obelisk** (AHB•uh•lisk) stands near the Temple of Karnak. Made of a single piece of granite, it soars to almost 100 feet (about 30 m). Originally it was covered with a mixture of gold and silver. Hieroglyphics decorate the sides. A pharaoh named **Hatshepsut** (hat•SHEP•suht) had the obelisk made.

Hieroglyphics on Hatshepsut's obelisk celebrate her successes in trade.

Hatshepsut's rule was one of the most peaceful periods in Egyptian history.

Hatshepsut, the obelisk reports, sent ships south to find materials for her palace. She imported strange trees, perfumes, and jewels. With them, according to the obelisk, came "apes, monkeys, dogs, and the skins of the southern panther, and people of those lands and their children." The obelisk boasts that "never was brought the like of this for any ruler who has been since the beginning." Although it was unusual for a woman to become pharaoh, Hatshepsut was a powerful pharaoh who increased trade and promoted peace.

Akhenaton and Nefertiti

Like the Mesopotamians, the Egyptian people, led by their priests, worshiped many different gods. In 1379 B.C. a pharaoh who refused to believe in these many gods came to the throne.

The limestone head of Nefertiti was found in an artist's workroom at Amarna.

He was Amenhotep IV (ahm·uhn·HOH·tep). Amenhotep and his wife, **Nefertiti** (nef·ur·TEE·tee), urged the Egyptian people to worship only one god, the god Aton. Amenhotep changed his own name to **Akhenaton** (ah·kuh·NAH·tuhn), meaning the "servant of Aton." He moved his capital away from Thebes to Amarna, a site farther north. Then he ordered his officials into the temples of Egypt to destroy the images of the old gods.

This attack on the old gods angered the priests of Egypt. When Akhenaton died, the priests of the old religion picked a new pharaoh whom they could control.

The Boy Pharaoh

The pharaoh who was chosen to replace Akhenaton was a 9-year-old boy. The priests demanded that he take the name **Tutankhamen** (too·tang·KAHM·uhn) to honor the god of Thebes, whom the dead pharaoh had rejected. Tutankhamen died in 1352 B.C. at the age of 19.

We know about this young ruler because in 1922 **Howard Carter,** a British scientist, discovered his burial place. People promptly gave Tutankhamen the affectionate name "King Tut." They hailed Carter as a great discoverer.

Carter managed to trace the hidden passage through which Tutankhamen's body was carried into his tomb. The Egyptians kept such passages secret to prevent grave robbers from stealing the treasures in the tombs. As Carter peered through a drill hole into the tomb he had found, his companion asked what he saw. "Wonderful things!"

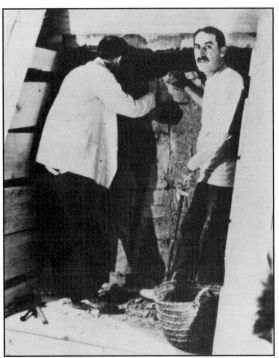

Carter's first glimpse into Tutankhamen's tomb led to ten years of further study.

Tutankhamen's solid-gold funeral mask shows how the boy-king may have looked.

The king's chair of carved wood is ornamented with symbols of eternal life.

The upper and lower portions of this perfume jar represent a united Egypt.

Carter exclaimed. He could see carved animals, statues, and the glint of gold.

In the four rooms of the tomb, Carter and his fellow scientists discovered a golden throne, white stone jars that had held perfumed oil, carved chests, gold-plated chariots, and boxes of preserved food. Everything was there that was needed to help Tutankhamen in the next life. In another chamber was Tutankhamen, buried in a solid-gold coffin weighing about 2,500 pounds (about 1,100 kg). The beauty and richness of the jewelry and gold work glittered in the light for the first time in more than 3,000 years.

Following Tutankhamen's rule, Egypt slowly began to lose its power. A series of wars took place between the Egyptians and other peoples of the Middle East. Egypt repeatedly fought for the lands now called Israel, Syria, and Turkey. Its enemies included the Hittites, fierce fighters whose empire centered in present-day Turkey and Syria. One strong pharaoh, **Ramses II,** made peace with the Hittites. For 67 years he ruled Egypt, briefly restoring its prosperity.

Then in 525 B.C. came an invader far stronger than any Egypt had faced. The Persian army, which had already seized most of the Middle East, overran Egypt.

The contributions of ancient Egyptians, however, were not forgotten. The Egyptians had made many important discoveries. As architects and mathematicians, the Egyptians planned and built some of the largest stone structures in the world. Egyptian doctors studied the human body. They carefully described diseases and their treatments. They even performed

Four images of Ramses II are carved into the cliff in front of his temple.

surgery. Other Egyptian scientists studied the stars and learned to keep track of time. From their records we know approximate dates for important events in their history. Finally, the Egyptians kept written records of their discoveries, using the language and paper they had invented.

Reading Check

1. What is another name for the Old Kingdom?
2. Which queen of Egypt became a pharaoh?
3. How was Ahkenaton different from other pharaohs?
4. Why were the passages into tombs kept secret by the Egyptians?

Look for these important words:

Key Words
- Hebrews
- Ten Commandments
- Old Testament
- tribute
- couriers

People
- Abraham
- Moses
- Saul
- David
- Solomon

- Cyrus
- Darius

Places
- Israel
- Jerusalem
- Persepolis

Look for answers to these questions:

1. What was different about the Hebrew religion, compared to other Middle Eastern religions of the time?
2. What nation was established by the Hebrews?
3. Why was the Persian army so successful?
4. How did Darius treat the people of his empire?

3. THE HEBREWS AND THE PERSIANS

Many cultures influenced the development of the Middle East. Two of these were the **Hebrews** and the Persians. Though a small group, the Hebrews were important in both the Fertile Crescent and ancient Egypt. The Persians held a large empire that included most of the lands of the Middle East.

The Hebrews

The Hebrews were the ancestors of the Jewish people. They trace their identity as a people to **Abraham.** Abraham, a citizen of Ur, left that city about 2000 B.C. As a leader of nomads, or possibly as a caravan leader, Abraham wandered over the Fertile Crescent to settle in Palestine.

Within several generations, the followers of Abraham traveled to Egypt to escape a famine. In Egypt they worked, possibly as slaves, for the pharaoh. About 1286 B.C. **Moses,** the leader of the Hebrews in Egypt, led his people back to their homeland in Palestine. On the way, according to the Bible, God gave Moses the **Ten Commandments.**

The Ten Commandments became the basis of the Hebrew religion and have influenced other religions as well. The First Commandment said that there should be only one god, whom the Hebrews called Yahweh (YAH•way). Their worship of only one god made the Hebrews different from other peoples of the Middle East.

After their return to Palestine, the Hebrews established their own nation. They called it **Israel.** Kings ruled Israel. The first king, **Saul,** established a strong state. He was followed by another strong leader, named **David.** David was also well known for songs

61

Bound for the land of Palestine, 600,000 Hebrews followed Moses
from Egypt. The land over which they traveled is now the Sinai Desert.

that he wrote, some of which are still read today.

In about 960 B.C. David's son **Solomon** became one of Israel's most famous rulers. He married a daughter of a pharaoh. Relations became friendly between the two countries. Peace and trade made the Hebrew kingdom strong and wealthy. Solomon used the wealth to build a magnificent temple in Israel's capital, **Jerusalem.**

Solomon was known for his wisdom. "Solomon's wisdom excelled the wisdom of all the children of the east country and all the wisdom of Egypt," says one part of the **Old Testament.** The Old Testament of the Bible contains the story and the literature of the Hebrews.

The ancient state of Israel lasted about 600 years. It was destroyed by the Babylonians in 587 B.C.

The Persians

Another important culture in the ancient Middle East was that of the Persians. The Persians lived on the

62

This stone head of the Persian King Cyrus was made about 600 B.C.

Plateau of Iran, a vast area stretching from the Zagros Mountains to India. Beginning with the conquest of Babylon in 539 B.C., the Persians spread their empire in all directions. Their vast and organized army seemed unbeatable.

The Persian army had masses of foot soldiers, some in bronze helmets, who carried shields and spears. The cavalry included men on horseback and on camels. The Persian war chariots had sharp knives attached to their wheels.

The Persians also acquired boats and the ability to fight at sea. Their energy and sheer numbers were overwhelming. Within 20 years the Persians had conquered lands from the Mediterranean to India.

The leader of the Persians was named **Cyrus.** Cyrus was kind to those who supported him, including the Hebrews. For them, he had the city of Jerusalem rebuilt.

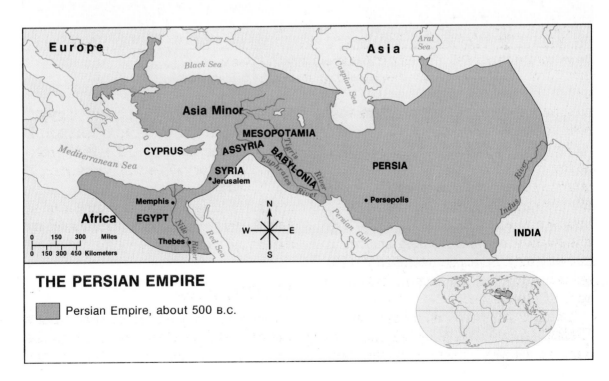

THE PERSIAN EMPIRE

Persian Empire, about 500 B.C.

Cyrus never lost a battle—except his last one. He led his armies to fight the people who lived near the Caspian Sea. Their ruler was Queen Tomyris (tuh•MY•ruhs). Angered at the Persian invasion of her lands, Queen Tomyris led her army against Cyrus. One historian wrote about the battle:

First the two armies stood apart and shot their arrows at each other. Then, when their quivers were empty, they closed and fought hand-to-hand with lances and daggers. And thus they continued fighting for a length of time, neither choosing to give ground.

In the end most of the Persians were killed, including Cyrus.

Darius (duh•RY•uhs) was the Persian king who developed ways to rule the vast empire conquered by Cyrus. Darius was successful because he let the many different peoples keep their own customs. Local officials were appointed to rule the empire fairly.

People conquered by the Persians were expected to send **tribute,** or annual payments. At **Persepolis** (pur•SEP•uh•luhs), the capital built by Darius, artists left a record in stone of the people paying tribute. There are Babylonians bringing livestock and

Decorating the staircase leading to the royal hall at Persepolis are stone carvings of people paying tribute to their Persian ruler.

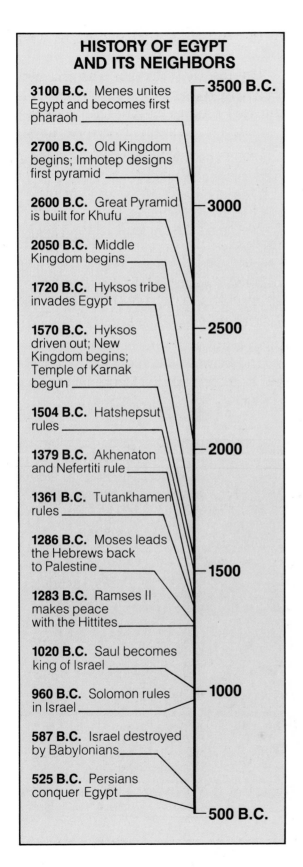

HISTORY OF EGYPT AND ITS NEIGHBORS

3500 B.C.

3100 B.C. Menes unites Egypt and becomes first pharaoh

2700 B.C. Old Kingdom begins; Imhotep designs first pyramid

3000

2600 B.C. Great Pyramid is built for Khufu

2050 B.C. Middle Kingdom begins

1720 B.C. Hyksos tribe invades Egypt

2500

1570 B.C. Hyksos driven out; New Kingdom begins; Temple of Karnak begun

1504 B.C. Hatshepsut rules

2000

1379 B.C. Akhenaton and Nefertiti rule

1361 B.C. Tutankhamen rules

1286 B.C. Moses leads the Hebrews back to Palestine

1500

1283 B.C. Ramses II makes peace with the Hittites

1020 B.C. Saul becomes king of Israel

960 B.C. Solomon rules in Israel

1000

587 B.C. Israel destroyed by Babylonians

525 B.C. Persians conquer Egypt

500 B.C.

fabric. The Assyrians, once so feared, are bringing hides of tanned leather. Greek people living in Asia are bringing cloth and dishes. Other peoples are shown bringing camels and horses. Indians carry containers of gold dust.

Darius faced a great problem: how to communicate with the parts of his widespread empire. To solve this problem, he established a pony-express system for delivering the mail. Riders called **couriers** galloped across the Persian Empire, changing horses at post stations.

Using couriers, information could travel 1,677 miles (2,698.3 km) in seven days—an unheard-of time. "There is nothing in the world that travels faster than these Persian couriers," wrote a famous historian. "Nothing stops these couriers from covering their allotted stages in the quickest possible time—neither snow, nor rain, nor heat, nor gloom of night."

The Persian Empire held power over most of the Middle East until it too was conquered by people from the west—the Greeks. Persian culture, however, continued to be important in Mesopotamia and Persia for a thousand years, until about A.D. 750.

Reading Check

1. The Hebrews are the ancestors of what group?
2. What did ancient Hebrews call their nation?
3. In what way was the Hebrew religion different from other Middle Eastern religions of the time?
4. How was Darius able to communicate with the different parts of the Persian Empire?

SKILLS FOR SUCCESS

USING RELIEF AND ELEVATION MAPS

It is not always easy to remember that the names on maps are real places. The smallest bend in a river, the roll of valleys and meadows, the peaks of mountains and hills—all are places that people must walk up, down, and around. A **relief map** gives us a bird's eye view of land. It uses lines or shading to show the heights and depths of the land.

The map on this page is a relief map of Egypt. Look at the key at the side of the map. On this map, shading indicates landforms above sea level, such as mountains, plateaus, and valleys. Find the west coast

of the Red Sea. The shading shows that the coast is mountainous.

Three mountains are shown on this map. Notice that they are marked with a ▲ sign. Two of these are Mount Katherine and Mount Sinai. What is the third?

The key also shows a line pattern that stands for a **depression.** A depression is a low area, such as a valley or canyon. Look for the Qattara Depression in the northwest corner of Egypt. This relief map shows that the land between the large, low-lying Qattara Depression and the Mediterranean Sea is hilly.

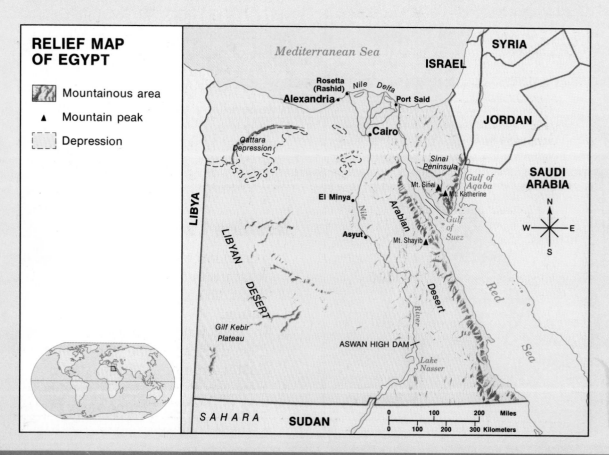

RELIEF MAP OF EGYPT

- Mountainous area
- ▲ Mountain peak
- Depression

ELEVATION MAPS

A landform's height above or below sea level is its **elevation.** A relief map does not tell how low the depression is or how high the hills and mountains are. To find the elevations of such features, you must look at an **elevation map.**

The five colors on the map below represent different elevations. Look at the map key. Yellow is used to show the highest parts of Egypt. These are mountains with an elevation higher than 7,000 feet (2,000 m) above sea level. The elevations of Egypt's highest mountains are given in both feet and meters. Find the mountain peaks shown on the map. Which mountain is the highest?

Now look at the orange area in the southwest corner of the map. This is the Gilf Kebir Plateau. As the map key shows, this area is from 3,000 to 7,000 feet (1,000 to

2,000 m) above sea level. The word *plateau* in the name tells you that the area is flat.

Find the tip of the Sinai Peninsula. This area is mountainous, but the map does not show this. It only tells you the area's elevation. What kind of map would tell you if an area is flat or mountainous?

You can use an elevation map to figure out in which direction a river flows. Water always flows from higher elevations to lower elevations. With the help of the map key you can see which part of a river is on high ground and which is on lower ground.

Look at the Nile River on this map. Most of the land around the southern part is pale green. The land around the northern part is a darker green. Which region of the Nile River valley is lower, the northern or the southern? In which direction does the Nile flow in Egypt?

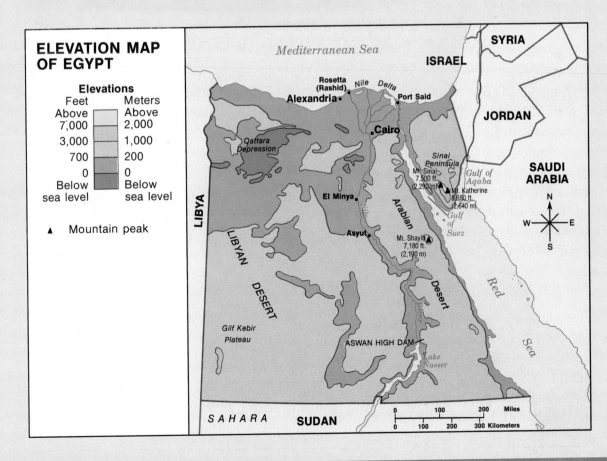

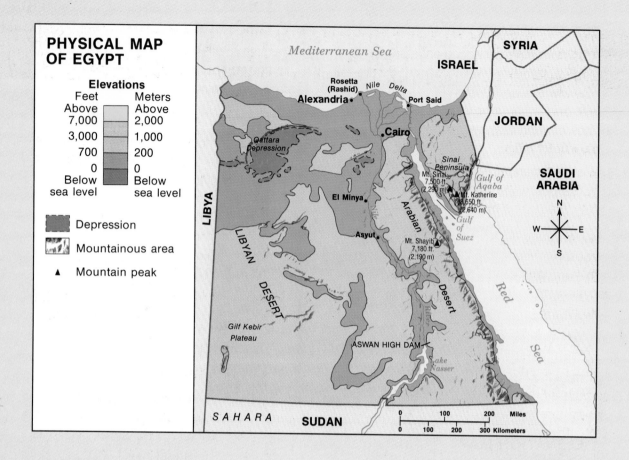

PHYSICAL MAP OF EGYPT

Elevations

Feet		Meters
Above 7,000		Above 2,000
3,000		1,000
700		200
0		0
Below sea level		Below sea level

Depression

Mountainous area

▲ Mountain peak

PHYSICAL MAPS

We call any map that shows the Earth's physical features, or landforms, a physical map. Relief and elevation often are combined on a physical map. What relief is shown on this map?

The physical maps in this book label such features as rivers, lakes, mountain ranges, plateaus, plains, peninsulas, and deserts. They also give the elevations of these features. What physical features are labeled on the map above?

Unlike the map on this page, many physical maps do not include political features, such as city names or state and national boundaries. To determine the physical features of a region in such cases, you would need both a political map and a physical map.

CHECKING YOUR SKILLS

Use the physical map to answer the following questions.

1. Find the border between Egypt and Sudan. Look at the land east of the Nile River. Is this land flat or mountainous?

2. Now look at the land west of the Nile. Is this land flat or mountainous?

3. Find Cairo on the map. What is the elevation of Cairo?

4. Are the lowest elevations found in northern or southern Egypt?

5. Based on the maps above, how would you describe Egypt's physical geography to someone who knows nothing about Egypt? Give as many details as you can.

CHAPTER 2 REVIEW

USING WORDS

Number your paper from 1 to 10. Use the words below to complete the sentences in the paragraphs that follow.

couriers
delta
hieroglyphics
mummies
papyrus

peasants
pharaohs
pyramids
silt
tribute

Toti-Shari looked out across the valley of Giza at the huge stone __(1)__ . She thought about all the __(2)__ who had been buried there, preserved as tightly-wrapped __(3)__ . With them were buried long scrolls of __(4)__ on which were written prayers in __(5)__ .

Toti-Shari also thought about how Egypt had changed. She heard her father tell about the messages that had been carried many miles by Persian __(6)__ . The messages commanded the Egyptians to pay __(7)__ to the conquerers.

The __(8)__ who were farming the Nile River __(9)__ were worried. The Nile's floods were late. If the river did not deposit __(10)__ this year, no crops could be sent to the new masters of Egypt.

REVIEWING FACTS

1. Why were boats with sails an important invention in Egypt?

2. Why did Egyptians preserve the dead?

3. How is Egypt's dry climate partly responsible for what we know about ancient Egyptians?

4. Tell whether these events occurred in the Old Kingdom, the Middle Kingdom, or the New Kingdom:

   a. Pyramids are built
   b. Middle class emerges
   c. Egyptians establish an empire
   d. Persian army conquers Egypt

5. Name three kings of Israel. In what part of the Bible can you read about them?

THINKING CRITICALLY

1. Think about the kinds of goods Egyptians traded. What kinds of resources were not available within Egypt? What did Egyptians find beautiful?

2. Darius thought it wise to let the conquered people in the Persian Empire keep their cultures. Do you think this was a good decision? Why or why not?

PRACTICING SKILLS

Relief and Elevation Maps   Use your skills lesson and the maps on pages 66–68 to answer the following questions.

1. What is the difference between a relief map and an elevation map?

2. What is the elevation where Lake Nasser flows into the Nile River?

3. What is the elevation of the Gilf Kebir Plateau?

4. What kind of map shows both relief and elevation?

World Paths Cross in the Middle East

Focus

In the ancient world in the Middle East was a center of civilization and trade. In recent times people have renewed their interest in trade with the Middle East because of its petroleum. The machines that drive the modern world depend upon this precious resource from which oil, gasoline, and plastics are made.

Today many countries in the Middle East suffer from religious disagreements and border disputes. Many countries are changing. Some people are unhappy with the changes. Other people want more changes. No one can understand these problems without first knowing about the way Middle Easterners live and what is important to them.

1. THE BIRTH OF ISLAM

Islam (is•LAHM) and **Christianity** are major religions of the world. Both have their roots in **Judaism** (JOOD•uh•iz•uhm), the faith of the Hebrews. Christianity has become the major religion in Europe and in the Western Hemisphere. Islam is the major religion in the Middle East, northern Africa, and parts of Asia.

Christianity started about 2,000 years ago in Palestine with the teachings of **Jesus Christ.** Jesus taught that God was a loving god. He taught that people on Earth should care for each other. "Do unto others as you would have them do unto you," Jesus urged.

Disciples (dis•EYE•puhlz), or followers, of Jesus carried his message of love and mercy far beyond Palestine and bound together people of different races, languages, and cultures. Christianity has had such a deep effect on the world that in the West events are dated from the birth of Jesus. The stories about Jesus and his disciples are contained in the **New Testament** of the Bible.

Six hundred years following the birth of Christianity, an Arab named **Muhammad** (moh•HAM•uhd) founded Islam. Muhammad lived in the Arabian trading town of **Mecca.** At the time of Muhammad's birth (about A.D. 570), most Arabs were nomads roaming the desert. Warfare was common among the various tribes. They believed in many gods. They had particular respect for a large black meteorite called the Black Stone. The sacred stone was kept in Mecca in a cube-shaped building called the **Kaaba** (KAH•buh).

As a young man Muhammad led camel caravans to Syria. There he heard of the one God worshipped by both Jews

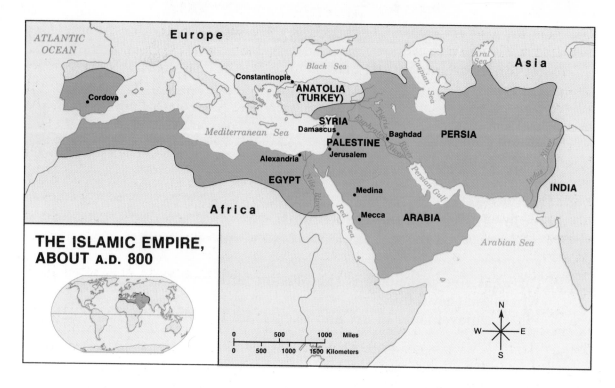

THE ISLAMIC EMPIRE,
ABOUT A.D. 800

and Christians. Muhammad came to believe that the Arabs should change their ways and believe in only one god, called Allah. He believed that the Arabs should show more mercy and kindness to one another.

Muhammad began to preach his ideas. His ideas were unpopular in Mecca. Muhammad and his followers were forced to flee to the nearby town of **Medina.** They supported themselves by raiding the caravans of their enemies in Mecca. This led to warfare. The followers of Muhammad fought fiercely. Soon they conquered Mecca itself. Muhammad ordered all the statues of gods destroyed. Only the Kaaba remained. The Kaaba, Muhammad said, was to be sacred. He declared Mecca a holy city.

Within a few short years the Arabs changed from warring nomads to conquerors. Islamic warriors conquered the Middle East from the Mediterranean

Sea to India. Within a few generations their empire ranged from Spain to the border of China. As Islam spread, a new culture developed that included parts of previous cultures and civilizations.

Beliefs of Islam

Islam means "submission to God." Muhammad named his followers **Muslims** (MUZ•luhms), which means "followers of Islam." To unite Muslims, Muhammad established strict rules. He recited these rules to an assistant. Since the Arabs had no paper, the assistant scratched them onto palm leaves, bark, and chips of pottery. Later these scraps were collected, copied, and bound into a book called the **Koran** (kuh•RAN).

The Koran is the holiest book in Muslim societies. Some Muslims memorize the entire volume. They consider the Koran to be their guide in all parts of life. The Koran contains the meaning of Islamic faith. The faith is based on five principles.

Believing in one god, Allah. With this principle of faith, the Arabs rejected the idea of many gods. They accepted Allah as their only god.

Praying five times a day to Allah. A Muslim must pray at sunrise, at noon, at midafternoon, at twilight, and at night. Muslims can pray wherever they are, but they should have a clean place to pray. For that reason prayer rugs are popular. Prayer rugs can be unrolled and placed anywhere. Muslims must always face Mecca when praying.

Giving alms, or gifts, to the poor. "Take care of the poor, the widows, and the orphans," Muhammad said. To do so, people are expected to share part of their wealth with those who are less fortunate.

Fasting during the holy month of Ramadan. During the ninth month of the Muslim year, people are not to drink or eat from dawn to dusk. Once night falls, Muslims can break their fast. At the end of Ramadan they often meet with families and friends in joyous festivity.

Visiting Mecca once during one's lifetime. Every Muslim is supposed to visit Mecca once to pay respect to the Kaaba and to hear the holy men of Islam speak.

The Koran also sets rules for daily life. It forbids the eating of pork and the drinking of alcohol. It forbids gambling. In addition, the Koran explains the roles of Muslim men and women. Men are considered superior to women. Women generally must keep themselves separate from men. Following

The writing on this page from the Koran is an important Islamic art form.

Some Muslim women cover themselves from head to foot when in public.

an old Islamic custom, many women hide their faces behind veils when they are outside their homes.

Some Middle Eastern countries, such as Egypt, Iraq, and Turkey, have relaxed the restrictions on women. Women may choose occupations other than that of wife and mother. For most Muslim men and women, however, the family remains the most important group. As in the past, the father makes the important decisions. He is the strict head of the family.

The Koran has had an important influence on the laws and government of Muslim countries. In many of these countries the laws of the nation are outgrowths of the rules of the Koran.

The Gifts of Islam

Like Christianity, Islam bound together people of different races and different languages. Islam has been the main culture of the Middle East since the seventh century. Outstanding achievements in art and science are part of the Muslim culture.

The best examples of Muslim art are in its sacred buildings, the **mosques** (MAHSKS). The basic form of a mosque is a dome on top of a square. A mosque may have one or more towers called **minarets** (min•uh•RETZ). Five times a day holy men announce the time of prayer from the minarets.

The meeting hall of the mosque can dazzle the eye with its wealth of detail

Minarets rise from the Great Mosque in Mecca. At the Mosque's center, Muslim worshippers from around the world gather at the Kaaba.

and decoration. The floors of the meeting hall may be covered in Persian rugs. These finely made rugs of rich colors can last several hundred years.

Islamic art in the mosque does not usually show people or animals. Instead it combines geometric patterns, the flowing forms of plants, and writing called **calligraphy** (kuh•LIG•ruh•fee). Calligraphy, an artistic form of writing, is considered the noblest art form. Muslims believe it makes the word of God visible to all.

Achievements in Science

The Muslims believed that to understand the world is to understand God. Mosques in such cities as Damascus, Baghdad, and Cairo became early centers of learning. Students journeyed there from all over the Islamic world.

Islamic scientists studied the skies. They charted the movements of the stars and planets. From these observations they developed the **astrolabe** (AS•truh•layb). The astrolabe was an instrument that helped sailors navigate by latitude. It also helped Muslims to locate the direction of Mecca at prayer time.

Medicine was important in Islamic culture. Muhammad had urged that Muslims take care of their sick. As early as A.D. 1155 a large teaching hospital was built as part of a mosque in Damascus. There the sick were treated and doctors were trained. The doctors of Islam advanced the understanding of the body and the treatment of illness. Later, the discoveries of these doctors became the principal source of knowledge for European doctors.

This thirteenth-century brass astrolabe was used for navigation. Notice the Islamic calligraphy on the outer circle.

In addition to their own discoveries, the Arab Muslims improved ideas that came from other places. For example, they added the symbol for zero to the system of numbers they had borrowed from India. They spread their system to other lands. The Arabic numbers we use today are based on that system.

Reading Check

1. Which two major religions of the world have roots in Judaism?
2. What is the Kaaba?
3. How did Islam spread from Arabia to other parts of the world?
4. Why was the astrolabe a useful invention?

Look for these important words:

Key Words
- Bedouins
- sheikh
- migrated
- textiles

Look for answers to these questions:
1. Why is farming difficult in the Middle East?
2. What type of life do the Bedouins lead?
3. How have cities in the Middle East been changing in recent years?
4. What kinds of work do people do in Middle Eastern cities?

2. THE PEOPLES OF THE MIDDLE EAST TODAY

Several different groups are part of the 200 million people living in the Middle East today. The people of Egypt, Saudia Arabia, Iraq, and Jordan are Arabic-speaking people. Other languages spoken in the Middle East are those of the Kurds, Israelis, Iranians, Turks, and Armenians.

Agriculture is the main occupation in most countries of the Middle East. Farming there is not an easy occupation, however. Ancient irrigation systems, built before the birth of Christ, still serve some parts of the region. Wooden plows are common. Progress is being made in a few countries, especially Turkey, Egypt, and Syria. In Israel farmers rely on modern farming methods to boost production.

The Bedouins

One group of people in the Middle East has a different way of life. These people, the **Bedouins** (BED•uh•wuhns), make up about 10 percent of the population in the Middle East. Bedouins are Arab nomads. For thousands of years they have made their homes on the desert edge or near an oasis.

Adapting to their land and climate, the Bedouins often live in villages when

In this Arab village, tools and farming methods have not changed for centuries.

Unloading a camel, a Bedouin prepares his camp for nightfall. The camel is his transportation and provides him with milk and cheese.

conditions are favorable. Then, when the spring rains produce grasses in the steppes, the Bedouins wander in search of food for their herds. Groups of nomads, each led by a **sheikh** (SHAYK), pack up and ride their camels to the grassy parts of the deserts.

Living in tents, the Bedouin families eat ground wheat mixed with mutton roasted over an open fire. In the evenings the father or grandfather may tell stories, recite poetry, or read from the Koran. The family sleeps, stretching themselves on long cushions scattered near the dying fire. Outside, a few men with rifles guard the camp.

Bedouins can be on the move for months. When the grasses have disappeared, either eaten by the sheep and goats or burned away by the sun, the nomads return to their villages.

Bedouins live in Saudi Arabia, Turkey, Syria, Israel, Jordan, Iraq, and Iran. Some of them live exactly as nomads have lived for centuries. Life is gradually changing for many others. The camel has been replaced by modern transportation. Some Bedouins have left their groups to work in cities or in oil fields. Others continue to herd animals but have given up their tents for more permanent shelters.

Though many fabrics are now factory-made, this Israeli craft worker uses an ancient method to spin textiles by hand.

Working in the City

Not all people in the Middle East live in deserts or on farms. In recent years many families have **migrated,** or moved, to the cities to find work. The cities have also grown because of a rising birth rate in the Middle East. The population of some cities has been rising at the rate of almost 3 percent a year. Cairo, the largest urban area in the Middle East, had about 2 million people during the 1950s. Today it has more than 10 million.

In Middle Eastern cities people work at many kinds of jobs. They produce leather goods, cotton, pottery, silver, and steel. In Syria and Egypt they make many kinds of **textiles.** Textiles are woven fabrics. The basements of many shops contain huge weaving looms, which are usually operated by women and children.

The Middle East is also well known for the production of fine handicrafts. Less than 300 years ago the whole world looked to this region for some of its best handmade copper, brass, silver, and pottery objects. The words *damask* and *muslin,* which refer to particular kinds of fabrics, are taken from the cities of Damascus and Mosul. Handmade goods can be found in many open-air markets throughout the Middle East.

Reading Check

1. What is the main occupation in the Middle East?
2. How does climate affect the lives of Bedouin nomads?
3. Why have cities grown so rapidly in the Middle East?
4. Name three jobs done by workers in Middle Eastern cities.

3. THREE NATIONS OF THE MIDDLE EAST

The people of the Middle East share an ancient history. Their nations also face similar problems: developing resources and adapting to change. Saudi Arabia, Egypt, and Israel are three of these countries whose people are facing these challenges.

The Kingdom of Saudi Arabia

Saudi Arabia occupies most of the Arabian Peninsula. It is the largest country in the Middle East. Deserts make much of the country a wasteland. With unbearable heat, little rainfall, and few streams, the barren land might appear useless. However, in 1932 the discovery of petroleum by American engineers made this land as desirable as any fertile valley.

Saudi Arabia sells more oil to foreign markets than any other country in the world. As a result, Saudi Arabia has great wealth. Many Saudi Arabians, however, live very simply. They farm or herd animals. They dress in long cotton robes. Their food consists of dairy products, fruits, vegetables, rice, and lamb. Tea and coffee are favorite drinks. Life in their villages is much the same as it has been for centuries.

Since the discovery of oil, some people have given up village life and moved to the cities to find work. A city such as **Riyadh** (ree•YAHD), the capital of Saudi Arabia, is evidence of a changing, more modern way of life.

During the 1960s and 1970s Saudi Arabia began to modernize. The government, then led by **King Faisal,** sponsored improvements in transportation and communication. Homes had electricity for the first time. Though they were not required to, boys and girls could attend separate, free schools. More people learned to read. Today, modern buildings and conveniences give Saudi Arabian cities the appearance of many other cities in the world. Yet some things, even in the cities, do not change.

Saudi Arabia is firmly committed to Islamic beliefs. As Muslims, Saudi Arabians strictly respect the religious and social customs of Islam. Daily prayers and fasts are observed. Men and women do not mix in public. Crimes are severely punished. A thief, for example, might lose a hand as punishment.

Although petroleum wealth has brought many improvements, it has also created some problems. The rapidly developing oil industry requires many skilled workers. Saudi Arabians cannot meet the demand. Therefore laborers from other countries are invited to live and work in Saudi Arabia. Saudi Arabians are thus exposed to people and ideas different from their own. Some Saudi Arabians believe that outside influences threaten the old ways. The government, as protector of the faith, discourages interference with long-held Muslim beliefs.

Combining the old ways of Islam and the new ways of the modern world has challenged the leaders of Saudi Arabia. Their goal is to educate the people and to build a modern culture based on the ideals of Islam.

Developers plan a new building in Riyadh, Saudi Arabia's capital. What evidence can you find of both old and new ways?

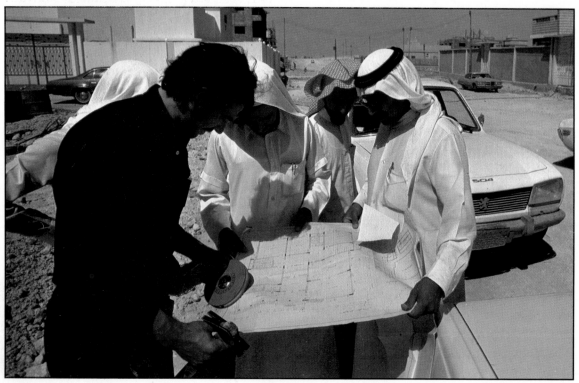

Middle Easterners trade goods and stories when they gather at bazaars like this one in Alexandria, Egypt.

The Arab Republic of Egypt

Egypt and Saudi Arabia are similar in many ways. Both countries are mostly desert. A majority of the people in both countries are Arabs and of the Muslim faith. Each of their governments is trying to build modern industries and to improve the lives of the people. In Egypt, however, there is no great wealth from oil to support rapid changes. In addition, Egypt has more people than any other Arab nation. Many of these people are poor, hungry, and unable to read or write.

As in ancient times, Egypt's population lives in villages along the Nile River. Peasants, called **fellahin** (fel•uh•HEEN), rent farmland from landlords. Every week families take their farm products to the village **bazaar,** or marketplace. Men wear long shirts called **galabiyah** (gal•uh•BEE•uh) and caps. Women put on jewelry and brightly colored dresses that hang to the ground. Many women cover their faces with veils. All are noisily buying, selling, and visiting with their neighbors. Perhaps some might discuss leaving their farms and trying new lives in the cities.

Egypt's capital, Cairo, is the largest city in Africa and the Middle East. Another city, **Alexandria,** also has experienced tremendous growth. Although both are modern cities, parts of Cairo and Alexandria are crowded and unclean. Both cities have problems feeding and providing housing and medical care for their ever-increasing populations.

Growing enough food is a problem in Egypt. Fertile land is limited.

Farming methods are out of date. Also, much of the land is used to grow a high-quality cotton, which is Egypt's largest trade good.

In 1953 **Gamal Abdel Nasser** (juh•MAHL uhb•DUHL NAH•sur) established a new government that is the basis of modern Egypt. Progress since then has been slow. Wars with Israel often interrupted Egypt's development. In 1979 President **Anwar Sadat** (ahn•WAHR suh•DAHT) persuaded Egyptians to stop the fighting and to put their energy into improving their country. Sadat was assassinated in 1981. His successor, **Hosni Mubarak** (HAHS•nee muh•BAHR•ak), has tried to carry out Sadat's plans for peace and economic development.

Education is emphasized in Egypt. Today all children between the ages of 6 and 15 are required to attend school. Students are also encouraged to attend universities in Egypt and other countries.

Egypt's leaders sometimes borrow money and materials to improve their economy. For example, in 1960 construction began on one of the world's largest dams, the **Aswan Dam.** Egypt hoped the dam would help to create more farmland and power for new industries. Egypt needed millions of dollars to pay for this huge project in the highlands of the Nile River. Nasser borrowed money from the Soviet Union.

The dam began to operate in 1968. This block of concrete, 361 feet (110 m) high and 2 miles (3.2 km) wide at the top, created a lake more than 300 miles (about 500 km) long. The Aswan Dam can store enough water to last the entire Nile Valley a full year. It controls floods and generates electricity. It has replaced outdated methods of irrigation.

Although it solved some problems, the dam also created others. It does not permit the waters of the Nile to carry as much soil into the valley as it did before. Therefore the land is not as fertile and cannot support as many crops.

In spite of its problems, Egypt's progress continues. The Egyptians take pride in the accomplishments of their past. Tourists from all over the world visit the monuments of that past. These visitors also observe Egyptians hard at work changing their deserts into industrial cities and more farmland. Egypt strives to set an example for other Arab nations.

Since the Aswan Dam opened in 1968, farmland in Egypt has increased.

Israel has almost tripled the amount of land used for farming since 1948. Modern machinery is used on most kibbutzim.

Israel

One country, Israel, is quite different from its Arab neighbors. Its people are Jews. Many of them came from other parts of the world to settle in the land of their religious ancestors. In 1948 Israel became an independent nation. Since then its pioneers have built and modernized cities and converted desert land into farms and orchards. Israel's factories and farms produce large quantities of goods for trade.

Israel lies on the eastern shore of the Mediterranean Sea. The **Jordan River** flows lengthwise along Israel's eastern border. Yet much of Israel is dry land or desert. Jews born in Israel call themselves **sabras** (SAHB•ruhz), after the prickly, sweet-centered cactus of the desert. The sabras and Jews who have come to settle in Israel have "made their desert bloom." These hardworking men and women use modern methods to irrigate the deserts and drain the marshes.

Some Israelis have developed large farms called **kibbutzim** (kib•uht•SEEM). Members of a kibbutz (kib•UHTS) live together and share the land and labor. Children on a kibbutz live apart from their parents in children's homes. They are grouped according to their ages. Parents visit them often when they are not working the farmland. All children between the ages of 5 and 14 must attend school.

Today there are fewer kibbutzim than in the past. More people are living on other types of farms called **moshavim** (moh•shuh•VEEM). On these cooperative farms families farm their own portions of land. The government provides moshav families with the supplies they need and later sells the families' crops. The land is most suitable for growing fruits, such as oranges and lemons. Israeli farms supply three-fourths of the food needs of Israel. Fruits and grains are also sent to other world markets.

In addition to food, Israel produces many manufactured goods for trade. Israelis make chemicals, machinery, plastics, and textiles. These goods are shipped from Israeli ports on the Mediterranean to all parts of the world. Manufactured goods are Israel's leading source of income, and the United States is its leading customer.

The factories for all these goods are located in Israel's major cities: **Tel Aviv** (tel•uh•VEEV), **Haifa** (HY•fuh), and Jerusalem. Many parts of these cities are quite modern. Tall buildings overlook busy streets. People leave their apartments and homes to work in factories and businesses. Stores and hotels serve the many tourists who visit the Holy Land.

Israel has overcome some of the problems challenging other Middle Eastern countries. Yet two large problems remain. Israel has not found peace with its Arab neighbors. Since its independence, Israel has always either been prepared to go to war or actually at war. Israel spends more money to maintain its armed forces than any other country.

The economy has suffered because so much money has gone for defense. There has been less money to spend on producing other goods. This forces Israelis to pay high prices for goods and services. Many Israelis question the wisdom of this policy.

Israelis have a democratic government. They elect representatives to

This picture of Golda Meir was taken in 1972 when she was Israel's leader.

the **Knesset** (KNES•et), or parliament. Israel's prime minister, who heads the government, is also elected. One of Israel's former prime ministers, **Golda Meir,** was once a schoolteacher in Milwaukee, Wisconsin. Golda Meir worked hard to build a strong nation. She was one of two women who signed Israel's Declaration of Independence in 1948.

Reading Check

1. What is Saudi Arabia's most important export?
2. How did Egypt try to solve its problem of enough farmland and electricity?
3. Name two types of farms found in Israel.
4. Why does Israel maintain a strong army?

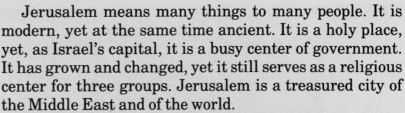

Jerusalem

Dome of the Rock

Jerusalem means many things to many people. It is modern, yet at the same time ancient. It is a holy place, yet, as Israel's capital, it is a busy center of government. It has grown and changed, yet it still serves as a religious center for three groups. Jerusalem is a treasured city of the Middle East and of the world.

Jerusalem contains many monuments of its history. People travel from all over the world to visit these monuments. Three monuments are especially popular. They represent the city's three main religious groups: Jews, Muslims, and Christians.

Church of the Holy Sepulcher

Many Jewish people gather every day in their capital city to pray at the **Wailing Wall.** This is the last remaining wall of the Jewish temple built by Solomon. Some of the stones of the wall are almost 3,000 years old. The Wailing Wall reminds the Jews of their long history in Jerusalem.

The golden-domed mosque called the **Dome of the Rock** is the monument that is sacred to Muslims. Completed around A.D. 691, it houses a great rock from which Muhammad is said to have made his night ride to heaven.

For Christians, Jerusalem is the city of Jesus Christ. They visit the places in Jerusalem where Jesus lived the last years of his life. On one such site now stands the **Church of the Holy Sepulcher** (SEP•uhl•kuhr).

Wailing Wall

Because so many people hold Jerusalem sacred, even the street signs reflect its mixed population. They are printed in Hebrew, Arabic, and English. Many people living in Jerusalem speak two or even all three of these languages. Today Arabs mainly occupy east Jerusalem and Jews live in the west part.

Jerusalem means many things to many people. It is modern, yet at the same time ancient. It is a holy place, yet it is a busy center of government. It has grown and changed, yet it still serves as a religious center for three groups. Jerusalem is a treasured city of the Middle East and of the world.

Look for these important words:

Key Words
- Zionism
- refugees
- Palestine Liberation Organization
- terrorism

- shahs
- fundamentalists

People
- Ayatollah Khomeini
- Saddam Hussein

Places
- Persian Gulf
- Suez Canal
- Dardanelles
- Lebanon
- Shatt al Arab estuary

Look for answers to these questions:

1. Why does war occur so often in the Middle East?
2. Which group leads the fight against Israel?
3. What causes conflict between Iran and Iraq?
4. How do actions in the Middle East affect the United States and the Soviet Union? How do those countries affect events in the Middle East?

4. PROBLEMS IN THE MIDDLE EAST

War has been a part of life in the Middle East for most of its long history. Conflicts continue for several reasons. With no natural boundaries to stop them, Middle Easterners fight for more land. Land can provide resources, such as petroleum. It also can feed growing populations. Some areas are important trade links.

A wide variety of people have settled the Middle East over the years. One group may believe strongly that their culture or religion is better than their neighbor's. Conflicts often arise from rival beliefs.

Trade and Defense

Middle Eastern resources, especially petroleum, are very important to world trade. All over the world countries depend on the oil produced in the Middle East. Control over the production and price of oil affects the economies of nations everywhere.

The Organization of Petroleum Exporting Countries (OPEC) was begun in 1960 to set the prices for oil and to control the amount produced and sold. The first members of OPEC were Iran, Venezuela, Saudi Arabia, Kuwait, and Iraq. Since then, other Middle Eastern nations have become members.

At the height of its power in the 1970s, OPEC's price increases shocked the world. Prices for oil doubled in one 6-month period. By the mid 1980s, however, OPEC could no longer control the price of oil. Nations, including the United States, began using less oil so that they would be less dependent on OPEC's oil. Also, new oil discoveries and increased oil production in non-OPEC countries forced OPEC to lower its prices in order to compete in the world market.

By refusing to cut oil production, OPEC members have had to accept lower prices for their oil. As a result, Middle Eastern nations have earned less income from their oil. This means that in future they may not have as much money to spend on projects to help their citizens. Oil, however, will continue to make the Middle East an important link in world trade.

The Middle East also is important because it borders major seas and oceans. Ships are used in trading. Goods travel across the world by ship. In addition, ships are important for defense. Warships are part of the strength of modern nations. Both for trade and defense ships must be able to move from sea to sea.

Several countries of the Middle East border on the **Persian Gulf,** a part of the Indian Ocean. Most Middle East oil travels through the Persian Gulf. Egypt controls the **Suez Canal,** the waterway that connects the Red Sea to the Mediterranean Sea.

Until the Suez Canal was built in 1869, ships had to make the long journey around Africa to go from Asian to Mediterranean ports. Turkey controls the **Dardanelles,** a waterway leading from the Black Sea to the Mediterranean. This is the easiest way for Soviet ships to reach the Mediterranean. The Soviet Union wants access to the warm-water ports of the Middle East. Most of its ports are frozen or ice-packed much of the year.

When the Suez Canal was completed, the shipping route between England and India was shortened by 6,000 miles (9,700 km).

The Arab-Israeli Problem

In recent years the major threat to peace in the Middle East has been disagreement between Israel and its Arab neighbors.

You may recall that the ancestors of the Jewish people had settled in Israel. They did not remain there, however. Conquerors attacked and chased them from their homeland. For centuries the Jews lived in all parts of the world, but they kept their culture alive. They held onto the memory of their ancient state in the land of Palestine. They believed that God had given them that land. Jewish leaders promoted the idea of a nation for Jews. This movement to reestablish a Jewish nation in Palestine was called **Zionism.**

After World War II, in which 6 million Jews were murdered by the Nazis, the world was ready to support the Zionist dream. In 1948 the state of Israel was established in Palestine. The Arab nations immediately declared war on the new nation and vowed to destroy it. Thousands of Arab Muslims who lived in Palestine also refused to accept the new state of Israel. They left, becoming **refugees.** Refugees are people who leave their homes to seek shelter and safety elsewhere.

Faced with Arab anger, Israel developed a strong and modern army. Time and again, Israel battled with the Arab nations.

The United States has tried to bring peace to the Middle East. In 1979 President Jimmy Carter invited President Anwar Sadat of Egypt and Prime Minister Menachem Begin (muh•NAHK•uhm BAY•gihn) of Israel to the United States to plan for peace. All three leaders signed an agreement, the Camp David Accords, to end warfare between Egypt and Israel.

Anwar Sadat, Jimmy Carter, and Menachem Begin sign the first formal peace agreement between Israel and an Arab country.

Opposition to Israel is led by the **Palestine Liberation Organization** (PLO). This group represents many Palestinian Arab refugees. For several generations these refugees have lived in neighboring Arab countries, always hoping to return to their homeland. Some members of the PLO try to bring attention to their problem through acts of **terrorism.** Terrorism is the use of violence and killing by a group to force a government to meet its demands.

People were shocked in 1972 when the PLO killed eleven Israeli athletes at the Olympics in Germany. Today terrorism threatens not only Israelis but the whole world. Bombings, kidnappings, and hijackings occur in the Middle east and Europe. World leaders agree it must be stopped. Israel and the United States have responded by attacking terrorist bases.

In 1982 Israel invaded its northern neighbor **Lebanon** to attack PLO bases that Israel felt were a threat. Most of the PLO were sent to other lands as a result. Israel withdrew in 1985, staying only in southern Lebanon to protect its own border. Yet, the problem of a home for Palestinians continues to prevent peace in the area.

The Iran-Iraq War

Iran is the modern name for Persia. Iraq is the nation that now occupies the land of Mesopotamia. Iran and Iraq disagree about their borders. Although both are Muslim countries, they also quarrel over religious viewpoints.

In the middle of the 1920s Iran started developing into a modern nation using new technology. Iran's **shahs,** or kings, wanted Iran to abandon its old ways. Women were given more equality, including the right to vote in 1963. New laws were based on French laws. In 1971 Riza Shah Pahlavi (rih•ZAH SHAH PAH•lah•vee) celebrated Iran's progress when he invited world leaders to observe the 2,500th anniversary of the Persian Empire.

Not all Iranians supported efforts to modernize. The new ways caused rapid social changes in Iran. European and American influences were everywhere. These included music, dress, and manufactured goods.

Many devout Muslims were upset. They were **fundamentalists** (fuhn•duh•MENT•uhl•uhsts). That means they wanted a return to the old ways of Islam. Their leader was the **Ayatollah Khomeini** (eye•uh•TOH•lah koh•MAY•nee).In 1979 these people led a revolution that forced the shah to leave.

Khomeini and the fundamentalist Muslims began to rule Iran according to Islamic law. One of the first laws they passed required women to wear veils in public. Foreign people and foreign ways were no longer welcome.

Khomeini's rule has emphasized strict enforcement of Islamic law.

Soon after the Iranian Revolution, war broke out between Iran and Iraq. One reason for the war was control of the **Shatt al Arab estuary.** An estuary is the place where the mouth of a river meets the sea. Water from the Tigris and Euphrates rivers flows through the Shatt al Arab estuary into the Persian Gulf. Control of the estuary means control of the entrance to the Persian Gulf. The border of Iran and Iraq is supposed to go down the middle of the estuary. However, each country wanted to control the whole estuary.

Another reason for the war was that the Ayatollah Khomeini did not approve of **Saddam Hussein** (suh•DAHM hoo•SAYN), the president of Iraq. Khomeini believed that Hussein was not a true Muslim. Khomeini called him an evil person because Hussein welcomed foreign technology and modern ways. Khomeini turned the war against Iraq into a holy war. He hoped to force Iraq to return to Islam's old ways. Today in every Muslim nation there are tensions between the old Islamic ways and modern ways.

Interests of World Powers

Both the Soviet Union and the United States have interests in the Middle East. The Soviet Union would like to build naval bases in Middle Eastern ports. To increase its influence, the Soviet Union has given money and military aid to such nations as Syria, Iraq, and Libya. In this way, it hopes to continue using these ports.

The United States wants to keep the Middle Eastern waterways open so that Arab oil will continue to be

Iraqi soldiers use weapons sold to their country by the Soviet Union.

available. To offset Soviet influence, the United States sells weapons to such nations as Israel, Egypt, and Saudi Arabia. It also gives economic assistance to Arab nations in hopes of remaining friendly with them.

Both the United States and the Soviet Union have worked to keep Middle Eastern conflicts from erupting into a world war. Peace may not come soon or easily to the Middle East, but Americans will continue to seek it in this troubled area.

Reading Check

1. Where is the Suez Canal? the Dardanelles? Why are they important?
2. What was the purpose of Zionism?
3. Which Muslim fundamentalist led the 1979 revolution in Iran?
4. Why are people concerned about war in the Middle East?

SKILLS FOR SUCCESS

USING GRAPHS

Suppose you are writing a report on the Middle East. You want to show the population of each nation in a brief, clear way. One way you might do this is by making a **graph.** A graph is a diagram for showing numbers. It makes a large amount of information easy to see and compare.

Reading Bar Graphs

Different kinds of graphs show information in different ways. **Bar graphs** use bars to show information. This bar graph gives the populations of five Middle Eastern countries listed at the bottom of the graph.

To find the population of Egypt, locate its bar on the graph. Now look from the top of the bar directly over to the number scale. The side of the graph lists populations in millions. For example, the number 5 means 5 million. The top of the bar for Egypt is between 45 and 50. This means that Egypt has between 45 million and 50 million people. The bar is closer to 45 than to 50. You can estimate that Egypt has about 47 million people. About how many people does Saudi Arabia have?

Bar graphs are especially useful for quick comparisons. Suppose you want to know which country has the smallest population. You look for the smallest bar because it shows the smallest population. What country has the smallest population? Which country has more people, Iraq or Iran?

The bars in this graph are vertical. Bar graphs may be horizontal, too. In a horizontal bar graph the bars go from left to right rather than from bottom to top.

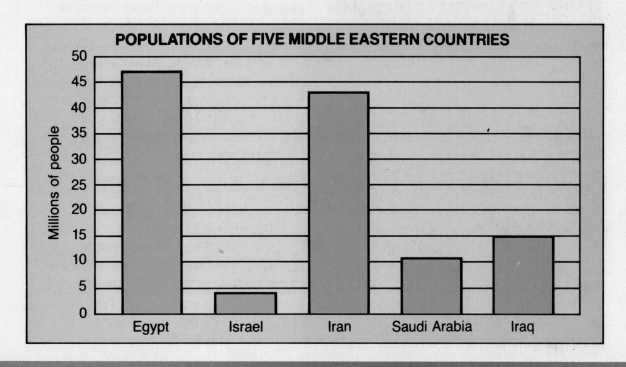

POPULATIONS OF FIVE MIDDLE EASTERN COUNTRIES

Millions of people

Egypt — Israel — Iran — Saudi Arabia — Iraq

Reading Picture Graphs

Picture graphs are another way to show information. Instead of bars, a picture graph uses symbols to show amounts.

This picture graph shows the number of producing oil wells in eight Middle Eastern countries. Find the key below the graph. It tells you that each symbol stands for 100 oil wells. There are 8 oil wells in the row for Syria. To find how many oil wells there are in Syria, multiply 8 by 100. Syria has about 800 producing oil wells.

Now look at the row for Turkey. There are 5 symbols and part of another. One symbol equals 100 oil wells. You know then that Turkey has more than 500 wells. Since only a small part of the eleventh symbol is shown, you can estimate that Turkey has a few more than 500 wells. In fact, it has 510.

You may have noticed that a picture graph can be harder to use than a bar graph. This is because you must use mathematics to find the amounts.

Reading Circle Graphs

A **circle graph,** often called a pie graph, divides information into parts. This circle graph represents known oil reserves throughout the world. Its parts are the amounts of oil found in six different areas of the world.

Notice that a percent is given in each part of the graph. Suppose you cut a giant pizza into 100 pieces. Those 100 pieces together equal the whole pizza, or 100 percent of it. Fifty pieces are one-half of the pizza, or 50 percent of it. Ten pieces are one-tenth of the pizza, or 10 percent of it.

Find the Middle East on the graph. The Middle East has about 57 percent of the Earth's oil. Its "slice" is close to 50 percent, or one-half, of the "pie."

Like other graphs, a circle graph can help you make comparisons. You can compare the parts to each other or to the whole. For example, two areas have about the same amount of oil. What areas are these?

To be useful, a circle graph should have only a few parts. If it has many parts, it becomes crowded and unclear.

PRODUCING OIL WELLS OF THE MIDDLE EAST	
Iran	𝅘𝅥 𝅘𝅥 𝅘𝅥 𝅘𝅥 𝅘𝅥 𝅘𝅥 𝅘𝅥
Kuwait	𝅘𝅥 𝅘𝅥 𝅘𝅥 𝅘𝅥 𝅘𝅥 𝅘𝅥 𝅘𝅥 𝅘𝅥 𝅘𝅥 𝅘𝅥 𝅘𝅥
Oman	𝅘𝅥 𝅘𝅥 𝅘𝅥 𝅘𝅥 𝅘𝅥 𝅘𝅥 𝅘𝅥
Syria	𝅘𝅥 𝅘𝅥 𝅘𝅥 𝅘𝅥 𝅘𝅥 𝅘𝅥 𝅘𝅥 𝅘𝅥
Turkey	𝅘𝅥 𝅘𝅥 𝅘𝅥 𝅘𝅥 𝅘𝅥
Abu Dhabi	𝅘𝅥 𝅘𝅥 𝅘𝅥
Qatar	𝅘𝅥 𝅘𝅥 𝅘𝅥
Bahrain	𝅘𝅥 𝅘𝅥 𝅘𝅥
𝅘𝅥 = 100 oil wells	

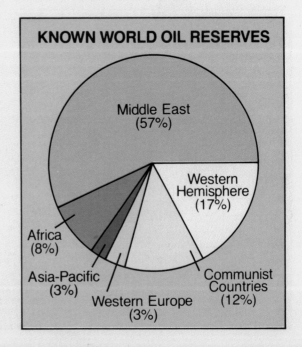

KNOWN WORLD OIL RESERVES

Middle East (57%)

Western Hemisphere (17%)

Africa (8%)

Asia-Pacific (3%)

Western Europe (3%)

Communist Countries (12%)

Reading Line Graphs

A **line graph** shows changes over time. Look at the graph below. It shows how much oil the United States used from 1972 to 1982.

Find 1976 at the bottom of the graph. Now go up the line until you come to the dot. The dot is between 17 and 18 on the number scale, at about 17½. This means that about 17½ million barrels of oil were used each day in the United States in 1976.

Next, find the dot for 1982. About how much oil was used each day in 1982? In which year was the most oil used?

A line connects all the dots on a line graph. Depending on the graph, the line may go up or down or stay at the same level. The line shows a **trend,** or the way something changes over time. On this graph the line goes steadily down after 1978. What do you think this means?

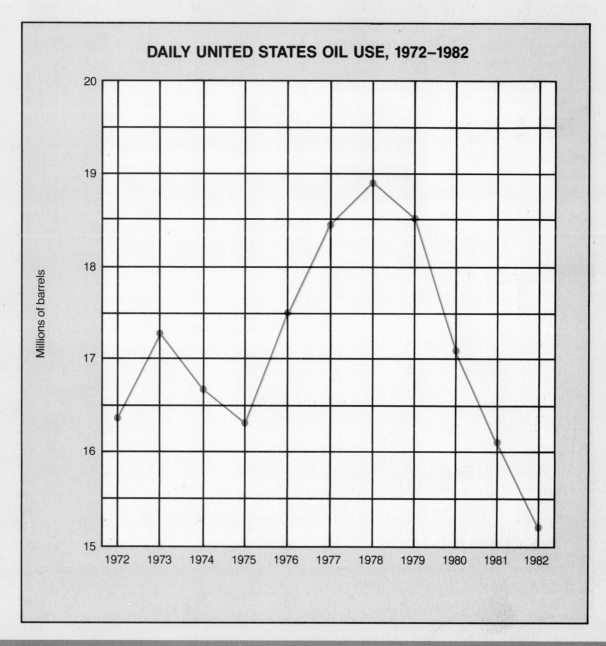

DAILY UNITED STATES OIL USE, 1972–1982

GRAPH A: WORLD OIL PRODUCTION

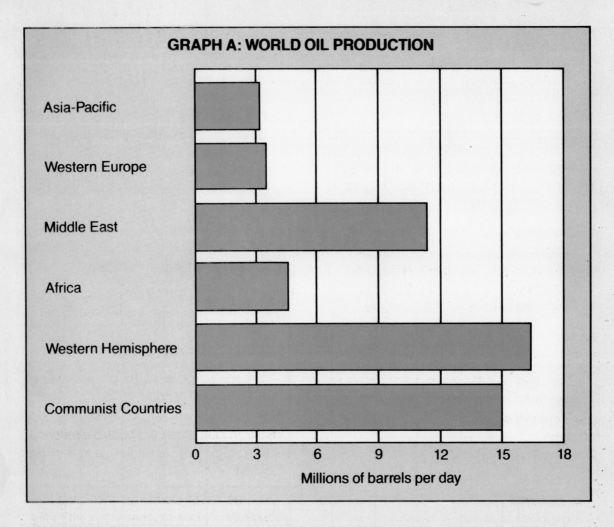

Asia-Pacific

Western Europe

Middle East

Africa

Western Hemisphere

Communist Countries

0   3   6   9   12   15   18

Millions of barrels per day

GRAPH B: SOURCES OF U.S. OIL

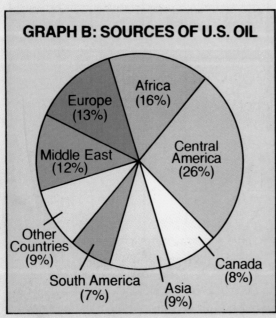

Africa (16%)

Europe (13%)

Central America (26%)

Middle East (12%)

Other Countries (9%)

South America (7%)

Asia (9%)

Canada (8%)

CHECKING YOUR SKILLS

Study the graphs on this page. Then answer the questions.

1. What kind of graph is graph A?

2. Which area produces the most oil? Which area produces the least oil?

3. About how much oil does the Middle East produce?

4. What kind of graph is graph B?

5. From what two regions does the United States get more than half of its oil?

6. What percent of the United States' oil comes from Canada?

CHAPTER 3 REVIEW

USING WORDS

Number your paper from 1 to 10. Write the letter of the definition that matches each of the words below.

1. **astrolabe**
2. **bazaar**
3. **calligraphy**
4. **disciples**
5. **fundamentalists**
6. **migrated**
7. **mosques**
8. **refugees**
9. **terrorism**
10. **textiles**

a. Muslim sacred buildings

b. Woven fabrics

c. People who leave their homes to seek shelter and safety elsewhere

d. People who wish to return to old or strict ways

e. A navigation instrument

f. Followers

g. A marketplace

h. Moved

i. Use of violence to force a government to meet demands

j. An artistic form of writing

REVIEWING FACTS

1. Which city is the "holy city" of Muslims?

2. Why is the Koran important to Muslims?

3. What are the five basic principles of Islam?

4. Give three examples of Muslims' past achievements.

5. What group of people have a way of life that is thousands of years old? How do they make their living?

6. How are Egypt and Saudi Arabia similar?

7. In what ways is Israel different from its neighbors?

8. Why do Palestinian Arabs oppose Israel?

9. Give two reasons for the disagreement between Iran and Iraq.

10. Why is it important for the United States to work for peace in the Middle East?

THINKING CRITICALLY

1. The people of ancient Egypt and the Fertile Crescent produced surplus food. Today these areas cannot produce enough food. What are possible reasons for this problem? How are these nations trying to solve it?

2. How are Islam, Judaism, and Christianity similar? How are they different? Why do you think people of one religion might disagree with people of another religion?

◯ PRACTICING SKILLS

Graphs Tell whether the following statements are true or false.

1. Bar graphs may be drawn either vertically or horizontally.

2. Picture graphs are easier to read than bar graphs.

3. Having many small parts in a circle graph makes it more useful.

4. Line graphs are best for showing trends over a period of time.

CLOSE-UP

KEEPING RECORDS

As you learn about cultures of the world, past or present, you will find that in some ways people have been much the same throughout history. They have all had to meet the same physical needs. They have needed food and water, homes and clothing, and health and safety. They have had similar emotional needs, too. They all have needed to work, to play, to love, and to be loved.

People of all times and places seem to have had another need as well—the need to reach beyond themselves. They have reached out to their families and friends by loving and sharing. They have reached out to others in their group by cooperating in work and government. They have reached out to the world around them by seeking to understand it through science. They have reached out to the mysteries and beauty of life through religion, literature, and art. They have reached beyond themselves by leaving records.

We in turn reach beyond ourselves when we study these records of the past. Records make it possible for us to know ancient people's thoughts, fears, hopes, and dreams. In a sense, records let these long-dead people "speak" to us.

Records were useful to their makers in many ways. They helped people carry on trade and business. They helped them plant crops at the right time and work together to construct strong, beautiful buildings. Records helped people govern themselves and obey the laws of their society. They let people pass on what they had learned so that life would be easier for their children. Above all, records let people say to the rest of the world, "We were here. We lived."

Oral Record Keeping

One of the oldest ways of keeping records is probably through spoken language. Parents taught their children through speech. Storytelling was one way of passing information from older to younger generations. The young people remembered this information and passed it on in their turn.

Ideas and records passed on through spoken language make up a people's **oral history.** In some societies certain people became experts in oral record keeping. Some ancient African kings, for example, had court officers called "rememberers." A rememberer knew the names and deeds of the king's ancestors. He was the keeper of the kingdom's history.

Artifacts as Clues

We do not know the oral history of the world's earliest peoples. They and their languages died out long ago. We do have other records of their lives, however. Some of these records are in the form of things that the people made. Tools, clothing, and other objects that people make and use are called **artifacts** (AHR·tuh·faktz). Ancient people left some artifacts behind when they moved. They buried other artifacts with their dead.

Archaeologists (ahr·kee·AHL·uh·jists), scientists who study people of the past, look closely at artifacts. Such objects show what people ate and how they gathered and prepared their food. They show how people dressed. They show what objects people shared to meet their needs. They give a great deal of other information about ancient people's day-to-day lives.

Artifacts also give clues about early people's feelings and beliefs. Painted pots, decorated clothes, and jewelry show that their makers cared about beauty, just like people of all other times. Artifacts that were buried with the dead suggest that some ancient peoples believed in a life to come.

Hunters living in France more than 12,000 years ago carved plants and animals on pieces of reindeer bone.

97

Telling Through Art

In most cases, artifacts were not intended to be records. Early people left more purposeful records in the form of pictures. Paintings in certain caves in France and Spain may be 20,000 years old. These paintings show lifelike animals and hunting scenes. They show that even so long ago, people looked carefully at their world and took the time and trouble to record what they saw.

Cave paintings were also found in a place called Tassili, in North Africa. They probably were made about 8,000 years ago. Today Tassili is part of the Sahara. When the paintings were made, however, the land must have been very different. The animals shown in the Tassili paintings are kinds that live in grasslands, not in deserts. Partly because of the record left in these paintings, we know that the Sahara was once a green and pleasant place.

When two boys followed their dog deep into a cave in France, they discovered these bulls, now the most famous example of prehistoric art.

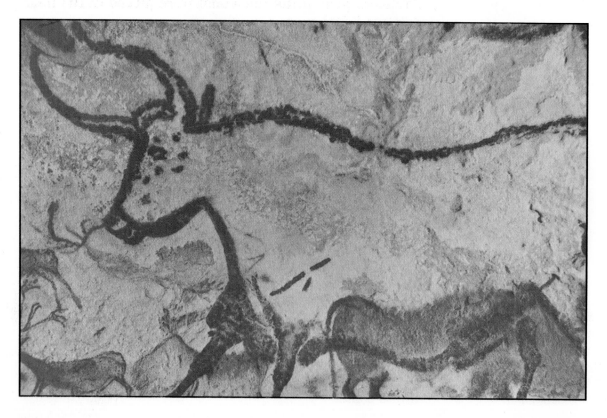

Art is a special form of record keeping. Through art people show things that are difficult to describe in words—the grace of an athlete, the robes of a king, or soldiers in battle. It includes all the hard-to-say ideas people have had about what is beautiful or terrible or glorious.

Ruins as Records

Some buildings, too, serve as a kind of record. Early farming peoples kept track of the seasons so they would know when to plant and harvest their crops. They found that certain positions of the sun, moon, and stars marked changes in the seasons. They used their knowledge to make outdoor structures that served as giant calendars.

One of the best known of these structures is in a field in Great Britain. People call this structure **Stonehenge.** It is a circle of huge stones, each weighing many tons. Archaeologists think the stones were placed in the field 4,000 to 5,000 years ago.

Little is known about the people who piled huge boulders to create Stonehenge, a monument whose purpose is still unclear.

On June 21, the sun reaches its highest point in the sky of the Northern Hemisphere. This is the beginning of summer. If someone stands in the middle of Stonehenge on that day, he or she will see the sun rise directly over a stone placed slightly apart from the rest. The sun or moon rises over other stones on other days that mark changes in the seasons.

American Indians also built giant calendars. The Mayas, an ancient people of Central America, built a temple called the **Caracol.** The rising sun and certain bright stars shine through its narrow windows on important days of the year. Some tribes of North America used small stones to make huge circles with spokes, called **medicine wheels.** Piles of stones on certain parts of the wheels could be used in sighting the positions of the sun, moon, and stars. From these ruins and others we have records of the architecture and science of early peoples.

The Caracol was used as an observatory by the Mayas. Its name means "snail," because a winding stairway leads to the observation windows.

Written Records

Most records we have from people of the past are in writing. Written records let ancient peoples speak to us more directly. These records are not always easy to understand, however. Different kinds of writing were invented in different times and places. Archaeologists often disagree about what ancient writings mean. Some of these writings cannot be read by anyone now living. They are like a secret code to which we have lost the key.

Important changes in record keeping were made after writing began. People started to write on paper or animal skin rather than on clay or stone tablets, for example. The printing press, invented about 1450, allowed many copies of records to be made. This invention made it worthwhile for growing numbers of people to learn to read and write. They could use the written records of others and make their own. People still used other forms of record keeping after they began to use writing. They did—and still do—leave records in their artifacts, art, and stories.

Modern Record Keeping

Today computers are making important changes in the ways people make, use, and store records. A person with a computer can send or receive records from distant parts of the world in seconds. Soon a whole encyclopedia may be stored on a disc smaller than a stone tablet that held one page of ancient writing. Computers have made the task of record keeping somewhat easier.

Like the people of the past, we use our records to reach beyond ourselves. Like them, we want to send messages about our lives to future generations. We have even sent records into space. A space probe called *Pioneer 10* carries a metal plate with pictures of humans and a diagram that shows where Earth is located. Other space probes carry phonograph records with music and natural sounds. These probes will travel to distant and unknown parts of space.

101

Perhaps other beings exist who will find these probes someday and learn about us from the records they carry.

All the ways of keeping records are the same in one important way. They store knowledge, just as one might store jewels or gold in a vault. Record keeping stores the knowledge of what people have done and learned so that other people can find this knowledge when they need it. Without record keeping almost everything people learn in their short lifetimes would be lost again and again. Each generation would have to reinvent the simplest tools and relearn the simplest skills.

Record keeping allows individuals to learn more, to compare, to plan—it allows people to think. Millions or billions of such records add up to human knowledge. From the earliest artifacts and cave paintings to the latest computer programs, the message of human records is the same. It says, "We were here. This is what we saw. This is what we did. The world is different because we lived."

How do you think computers are changing the way that we keep records?

UNIT 1 REVIEW

WORDS TO REMEMBER

Number your paper from 1 to 10. Complete the sentences below with the words from the following list.

agriculture   mosques
delta   nomads
domesticate   pharaohs
empire   silt
migrated   textiles

1. Early peoples developed _____ to meet their food needs.

2. People learned to _____ wild sheep and goats, adding to their food supply.

3. Wandering _____ sometimes raided the growing farming settlements in Mesopotamia.

4. The Persian _____ included most of the Middle East.

5. The _____ of Egypt were honored as gods.

6. The flooding Nile deposits _____ along its banks.

7. At the mouth of the Nile River farmers grow crops on a fertile _____.

8. Some Middle Easterners have _____ from farms and villages to the cities to find work.

9. Rows of workers sit at their looms busily weaving _____.

10. Five times a day Muslim holy men announce prayer time from the minarets of sacred _____.

FOCUS ON MAIN IDEAS

1. How is the geography of the Fertile Crescent different from the geography of other areas of the Middle East?

2. In what ways did early peoples control their environment to develop and improve agriculture?

3. Name four ancient Middle Eastern inventions or discoveries that have influenced our lives today.

4. Briefly describe how each of the following contributed to the growth of civilization:

   a. division of labor
   b. city-states
   c. laws
   d. writing

5. Why was the Egyptian civilization able to develop without interruption for so long?

6. In what ways was the Nile River important to the early Egyptians?

7. In what ways does Islam affect the daily lives of Muslims?

8. How is trade important in the Middle East today?

9. Identify several causes of war in the Middle East. Give examples from both past and present times.

10. Why is peace among the nations of the Middle East important to other nations of the world?

Imagine a meeting between an Iranian and an Iraqi, a Palestinian and an Israeli, or an American and a Russian. What might each want to say to the other about his or her hopes for the future of the Middle East? Write a brief conversation between one of these three pairs of people.

ACTIVITIES

1. **Research/Oral Report** Choose one of the famous people from this unit who interests you. Find out more about the person in a biography, an encyclopedia, or another reference book. Report your findings to the class.

2. **Research/Art** Mesopotamian and Egyptian art give many clues to the way people lived long ago. On your own or with others in your class, design a mural that could show future generations how people in your community live today.

3. **Reading/Current Events** Find and read magazine or newspaper articles that provide the most recent information on countries and events in the Middle East. Keep the following questions in mind: Do the disagreements mentioned in your book still exist? Have any governments changed leaders? Are there any new problems? You may wish to start a classroom scrapbook so that you can share information with your classmates.

SKILLS REVIEW

1. **Using Timelines** At one time stone and wood were used to make tools, utensils, and weapons. Then came the use of metals. The following timeline lists the names of metals used in the Middle East and the approximate times of their first known use. Use the timeline to answer the questions.

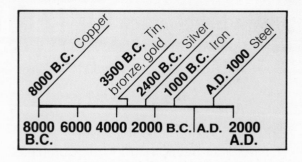

a. What was the first metal used in the Middle East?

b. Which metal was used first, silver or gold?

c. In what year was silver first used? In what century?

d. About how many years after copper was steel first used?

e. How long ago was bronze first used?

2. **Using Graphs** Arabic is one of the world's major languages. Spoken by more than 151 million people, it is the main language of the Middle East. The graph below shows five other languages used in the Middle East. Study the graph. Then answer the questions that follow.

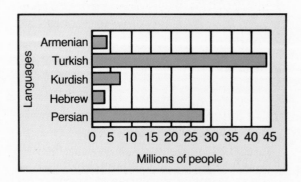

a. What kind of graph is this?

b. Which language shown here is spoken by the largest number of people?

c. Which language is spoken by the fewest people?

d. About how many people speak Persian?

YOUR WORLD

At the end of each unit in your book, you will find four activities. These activities will help you organize and remember what you have learned. The activities also will ask you to expand your knowledge of each region and its influence on your life.

MAKING A TIMELINE

1. With your class, begin a Timeline of the World. Keep in mind that throughout the school year you will be adding more information to the timeline. Choose important events mentioned in this unit, such as new inventions, the rise of empires, the achievements of famous people, and important current events. Add any other dates that interest you. Find or draw pictures to illustrate each event. Display the timeline so that you can glance at it as you continue your study of the world. It will help you to compare events in one area with what was happening somewhere else at the same time.

LEARNING ABOUT PEOPLE

2. Begin a notebook about different Cultures of the World. Pick one country in the Middle East that interests you. Gather information about its geography, history, and government. Draw a map in your notebook. Briefly describe the land, climate, and resources of the country. Make a timeline of its history. Identify the present leaders and type of government.

Next, collect pictures and articles about the country's people and their culture. You may have to draw your own pictures or write descriptions. Try to find someone to interview about the country and include that person's ideas in your notebook. Find out what the people of the country look like, how they live, how they earn money, what they like to do, and what they think is important.

EXPRESSING IDEAS

3. The designs of Islamic art can be seen in woven cloth and rugs from the Middle East. In buildings and homes there, floor tiles and wall coverings carry the geometric patterns that are popular in Middle Eastern art. Find and study examples of Islamic art. Create your own detailed design following the Middle Eastern style of repeated shapes and colors.

SHARING CULTURE

4. Many of our words in English are borrowed from other cultures. Match the English words below with their Arabic origins. Look in a dictionary for definitions of the words you do not know.

   1. cube   a. al-jabr
   2. tariff   b. kuth
   3. guitar   c. ka'ba
   4. algebra   d. ta'rifa
   5. taffeta   e. githar
   6. cotton   f. taftah

Key Dates and Events

800–500 B.C.
Archaic Age in
Greece

About 750 B.C.
Founding of Rome

About 460–430 B.C.
Golden Age of
Pericles

336 B.C.
Alexander the
Great becomes
King of Macedonia

27 B.C.–A.D. 14
Reign of Augustus
Caesar; Golden
Age of Rome

A.D. 500–1500
Middle Ages

A.D. 1095–1299
The Crusades

A.D. 1215
King John of
England signs
Magna Carta

A.D. 1400–1600
Renaissance in
Europe

EUROPE, PAST AND PRESENT

Two thousand years ago, Rome was the center of government for the Roman Empire, which stretched across much of Europe and parts of Africa and Asia. These ruins seen in Rome today were at that time buildings from which came decisions that affected much of the world. Millions of people who spoke many languages and worshipped many different gods were united by the military power and government of Rome. The Roman Empire included the lands of the ancient Greeks, from whom the Romans learned many things.

European civilization has its roots in ancient Greece and Rome. Later, during the Middle Ages, Europeans rediscovered the glories of their past. They made new advancements in religion, art, and government.

In this unit you will read about the early civilizations of Europe. You will also read how ideas, inventions, and wars changed Europeans' lives.

A.D. 1558–1603 Reign of Queen Elizabeth in England	A.D. 1782 James Watt invents steam engine; Industrial Revolution underway	A.D. 1789 French Revolution begins	A.D. 1914–1918 World War I A.D. 1917 Russian Revolution	A.D. 1939–1945 World War II	A.D. 1957 EEC (Common Market) established

GEOGRAPHY OF EUROPE

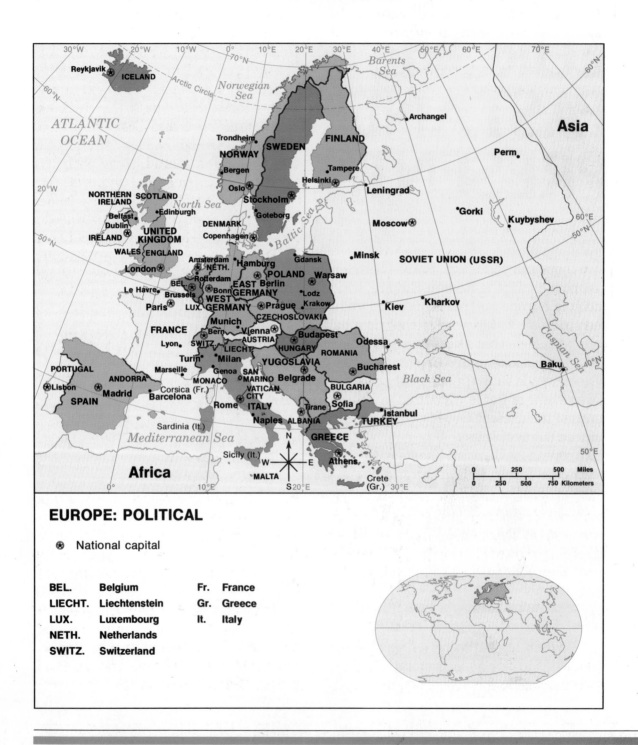

EUROPE: POLITICAL

⊛ National capital

BEL.	**Belgium**	**Fr.**	**France**
LIECHT.	**Liechtenstein**	**Gr.**	**Greece**
LUX.	**Luxembourg**	**It.**	**Italy**
NETH.	**Netherlands**		
SWITZ.	**Switzerland**		

Location

Europe is the second-smallest of the seven continents. As a continent, however, it is somewhat different from other major landmasses in the world. It is surrounded by water on only three sides. In this way it more closely resembles a peninsula. It is treated as a continent, though, because of its large size and because it differs greatly from its eastern neighbor, Asia.

Europe is bounded on the north by the Barents Sea and the Norwegian Sea. These seas blend with the icy waters of the Arctic Ocean. On the south, Europe is bounded by the warm waters of the Mediterranean and Black seas. The Ural (YOOR•uhl) Mountains in the Soviet Union mark the border between Europe and Asia. From the Urals Europe extends west to the Atlantic Ocean.

Four large peninsulas are part of the continent of Europe. The Balkan Peninsula, which includes Greece, and the Italian Peninsula lie in the Mediterranean. Europe's other two peninsulas are Iberia in the southwest and Scandinavia (skan•duh•NAY•vee•uh), which curves around the Baltic Sea in the far north. Spain and Portugal occupy the Iberian Peninsula. Norway and Sweden occupy the Scandinavian Peninsula. Denmark, another Scandinavian country, occupies its own, smaller peninsula called Jutland.

The Countries of Europe

There are 34 countries, including parts of Turkey and the Soviet Union, within Europe. Though most are small, European countries vary in size. Vatican City and Monaco are each less than one square mile (2.6 sq km). The European part of the Soviet Union, on the other hand, has ten times the land of the next-largest country, France.

The islands of Iceland and the United Kingdom are considered part of Europe. The United Kingdom, often called Great Britain, is located on two large islands known as the British Isles. England, Wales, and Scotland are on the bigger island. Northern Ireland is on the smaller island along with Ireland, which is an independent nation.

In this unit you will read about Western Europe and Eastern Europe. These terms refer mainly to political divisions. The countries of Eastern Europe include East Germany, Poland, Czechoslovakia (chek•uh•sloh•VAHK•ee•uh), Hungary, Yugoslavia (yoo•guh•SLAHV•ee•uh), Albania, Romania, and Bulgaria. Eastern Europe is strongly influenced by the government of the Soviet Union.

Most of the countries of Western Europe have governments that closely resemble our own. It is to the ancient lands of Western Europe that we trace our civilization. That is why we say that we belong to the Western world and have a Western culture.

There are other ways of dividing Europe into regions. Often you will see such terms as northern, central, and southern Europe. Countries are grouped into these regions based on their location, land, and climate. Northern Europe usually refers to the Scandinavian countries and Finland, parts of which reach north of the Arctic

Circle. This region also includes Iceland, the United Kingdom, Belgium, the Netherlands, and part of West Germany.

Southern Europe is made up of warmer countries on the three peninsulas that extend into the Mediterranean. The term central Europe refers to the remaining countries between northern and southern Europe. Although not as clearly defined as other regions, central Europe usually refers to Switzerland, Austria, Poland, Hungary, and Czechoslovakia. Parts of France and West Germany are also sometimes included.

The Land

Much of central Europe is a broad, fertile plain with some low hills. Many parts of northern and of southern Europe are hilly or mountainous.

A mountain range called the Pyrenees (PIR•uh•neez) isolates the Iberian Peninsula from the rest of Europe. It forms the border between France and Spain. Some of Europe's highest

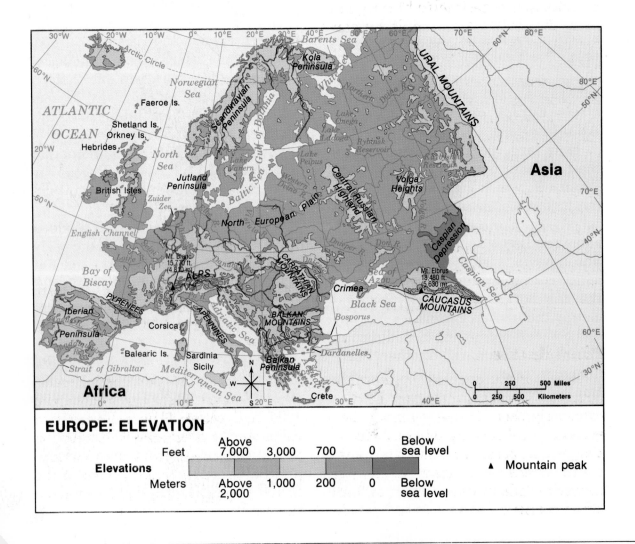

EUROPE: ELEVATION

Elevations						
Feet	Above 7,000	3,000	700	0	Below sea level	
Meters	Above 2,000	1,000	200	0	Below sea level	

▲ Mountain peak

mountains are in the ranges called the Alps. The Alps run through parts of France, Switzerland, Italy, and Austria. The Balkan Mountains cover most of the Balkan Peninsula. Europe's highest point is Mount Elbrus, in the Caucasus Mountains of southeastern Europe. Not far away is the Caspian Sea, Europe's lowest point.

In addition to the seas already mentioned, parts of Europe border the North Sea. The Baltic, North, and Norwegian seas surround the Scandinavian Peninsula. Along the coasts of Scandinavia, especially in Norway, are many **fjords** (FYORDZ). Fjords are narrow inlets of the sea between high, steep banks.

Large rivers empty into Europe's surrounding seas. They include the Loire (luh•WAHR) in France, the Rhine (RYN) in Germany, the Danube (DAN• yoob) in central and southeastern Europe, and the Volga (VAHL•guh) in the Soviet Union. The Volga is Europe's longest river. In addition, Europe has nearly 38,000 miles (about 61,000 km) of coastline. Because of Europe's many coasts, harbors, and rivers, Europeans have long been able to travel in and around their continent.

The Climate

Much of Europe has a moderate climate. Temperatures are neither extremely hot during summer nor extremely cold during winter. In addition, warm ocean currents and moist ocean winds give many European countries milder, wetter climates than other countries at the same latitude

Glaciers carved this fjord in Norway's coast long ago.

have. The United Kingdom, for example, has a warmer climate than Labrador, Canada, which is at about the same latitude.

Not all European countries have the same climate. In Southern Europe summers are hot and dry. Winters are mild and moist. This is sometimes called the **Mediterranean climate.** On the other hand, temperatures in Scandinavia and the northern parts of the Soviet Union are low during much of the year.

Precipitation varies somewhat within Europe. Most countries, however, average between 20 and 40 inches (about 50 and 100 cm) a year. Some countries, especially in northern Europe, receive precipitation throughout the year, while rainfall in southern Europe usually occurs only during winter months. The western side of Europe's mountains receives the most

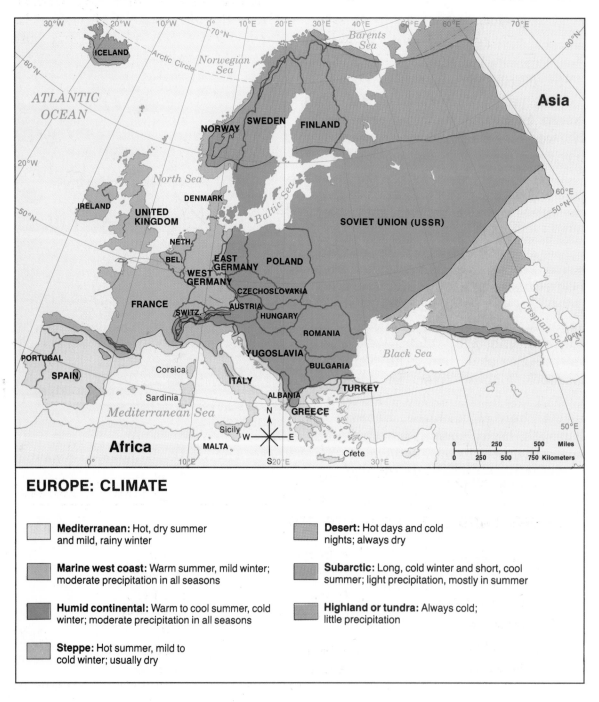

EUROPE: CLIMATE

Mediterranean: Hot, dry summer and mild, rainy winter

Marine west coast: Warm summer, mild winter; moderate precipitation in all seasons

Humid continental: Warm to cool summer, cold winter; moderate precipitation in all seasons

Steppe: Hot summer, mild to cold winter; usually dry

Desert: Hot days and cold nights; always dry

Subarctic: Long, cold winter and short, cool summer; light precipitation, mostly in summer

Highland or tundra: Always cold; little precipitation

precipitation. Meanwhile southeastern France has one of the driest climates.

Resources

Europe has a wide variety of natural resources. A broad band of coal lies under West Germany and other parts of central Europe. Many of Europe's industrial cities are located in that region. Large oil deposits have been found under the North Sea between Great Britain and Scandinavia. The Soviet Union has oil, uranium, and

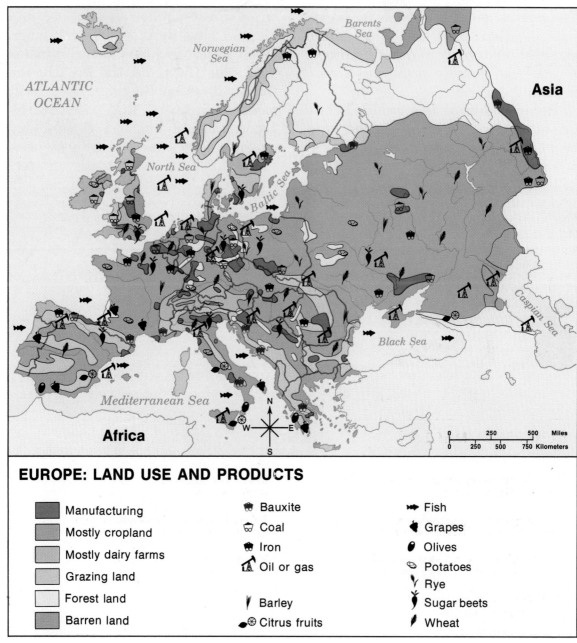

EUROPE: LAND USE AND PRODUCTS

■ Manufacturing	
■ Mostly cropland	
■ Mostly dairy farms	
□ Grazing land	
□ Forest land	
■ Barren land	

- Bauxite
- Coal
- Iron
- Oil or gas
- Barley
- Citrus fruits

- Fish
- Grapes
- Olives
- Potatoes
- Rye
- Sugar beets
- Wheat

iron. Europe's richest natural resources may be its fertile land and mild temperatures. They have allowed the continent to feed large numbers of people.

Europe's resources have contributed to its large population. When you divide the amount of land in Europe by the number of people living there, the result is about 170 people for every square mile (2.6 sq km). This is the **population density** of Europe. Europe is the most densely populated continent in the world.

Because Europe is a crowded continent, Europeans have learned how best to use what land they have. Little of the land is wasted. Farms run up hillsides and close to roads. Villages stand on mountain peaks as well as in plains and valleys. City buildings crowd against each other, and most streets and roads are narrow compared with those in the United States.

Europeans have learned which tasks are best suited for their special types of land. The Scandinavians with their large forests, mineral deposits, and harbors have developed fine lumber, fishing, and machine-producing industries. The Germans, the French, the Dutch, and the Belgians have built modern factories that use nearby deposits of iron and coal. Surrounded by their seas, the British have been successful in manufacturing and foreign trade. The Greeks, Italians, and

This mountain village is located in a valley in the Alps of northern Italy.

The buildings around this Amsterdam square are more than 500 years old.

Sturdy olive trees grow well in the dry, mountainous land of Greece.

Spanish use their sunny climates to grow olives, cork, grapes, and other crops that do well in warm areas with little rainfall.

European nations are close to one another. Extensive shipping and railroad systems that reach into every part of the continent bring French wines, Greek olives, Spanish leather, Irish linens and Dutch milk to every European country.

European trade extends beyond the continent, too. Ships arrive and depart regularly from Europe's main ports: Rotterdam, the Netherlands; Antwerp, Belgium; Leningrad, the Soviet Union; London, England; Le Havre, France; Hamburg, West Germany; Genoa, Italy; and Marseille, France.

The ships connect Europe with every country in the world.

The United States **imports,** or brings in, many European goods. Americans buy large amounts of European cars, clothes, furniture, and wines. In return the United States **exports,** or sends out, grain, machinery, tobacco, and electronic materials to European countries.

Geography Review

1. How is Europe like a peninsula?
2. Name six seas that border Europe.
3. What mountain range separates Europe from Asia?
4. Which two Asian countries have areas that are considered part of Europe?
5. Name the three peninsulas of southern Europe.
6. Look at the elevation map on page 110. How are Norway, Yugoslavia, and Greece similar?
7. How do ocean currents and winds affect the climate of Europe?
8. Find London on the political map on page 108. Then look at the climate map on page 112. What type of climate does London have?
9. Using the maps and the text, explain how Europe is able to feed large numbers of people. Describe how its fertile land and other natural resources have affected the population density of Europe.
10. Give two examples of goods imported by the United States from Europe. Give two examples of goods exported by the United States to Europe.

CHAPTER 4

Greece Introduces New Ideas

Focus

About 2,500 years ago the people of a small, rocky peninsula in southeastern Europe developed a civilization that helped to shape the rest of Europe's history. This was the civilization of ancient Greece.

The ancient Greeks introduced valuable new ideas. They said that citizens should be allowed to govern themselves. They made important discoveries in science. The Greeks also valued beauty and imagination. We still admire the art of the ancient Greeks.

Look for these important words:

Key Words
- isthmus
- Minoans
- Mycenaeans
- Dorians
- epics
- acropolis

- agora
- polis
- assembly
- Phoenicians

People
- Homer

Places
- Asia Minor
- Aegean Sea
- Peloponnesus
- Crete

Look for answers to these questions:

1. How did Greece's geography help shape its history?
2. What were the achievements of the early peoples who contributed to Greek civilization?
3. How was a Greek city-state organized?
4. What changes occurred in Greece during the Archaic Age?

1. THE DAWN OF GREECE

Greece occupies the southern part of the Balkan Peninsula. This peninsula curves slightly east toward a projecting part of the continent of Asia called **Asia Minor** or "Little Asia." Greece is separated from Asia by the island-dotted **Aegean** (ih•JEE•uhn) **Sea.**

Greece's history has been shaped by its mountains and the surrounding seas. Mountains cover three-fourths of the country, dividing it into small plains and narrow valleys. The mountains made travel in ancient Greece hard. As a result, people lived in small, independent settlements. Each settlement had its own government because no king or emperor could control a large area easily.

Greece's rugged landscape also made farming difficult. Its thin, rocky soil and rather dry climate could not provide food for large numbers of people.

Greek farmers grew olives, grapes, and some grain. They raised sheep, goats, pigs, and cattle. From these animals they could get wool for clothing and milk for cheese. Livestock was killed and eaten only on special occasions.

The lack of fertile farmland was one reason that the ancient Greeks eventually crossed the seas to set up distant colonies. Their colonies circled the Aegean Sea and extended along the coasts of the Mediterranean.

The Mediterranean Sea reaches far into the ragged Greek coasts. It almost divides the country in half. The southern half, called the **Peloponnesus** (pel•uh•puh•NEE•sus), is connected to the northern, or mainland, half by a small neck of land, or **isthmus** (IS•muhs). Greeks growing up near the sea became expert fishermen, sailors, and traders.

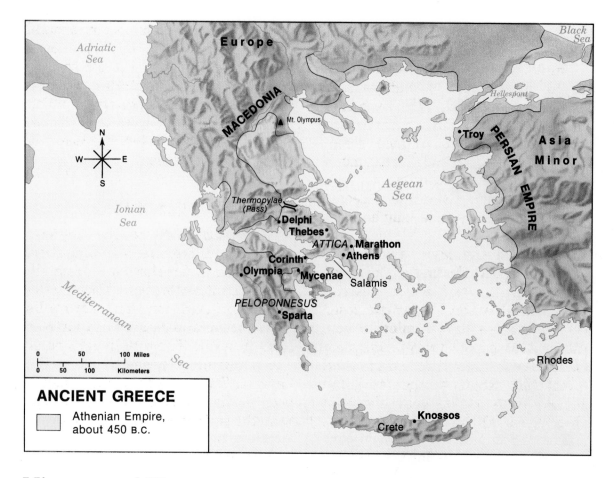

ANCIENT GREECE

Athenian Empire, about 450 B.C.

Minoans and Mycenaeans

Several groups of people contributed to ancient Greek civilization. The first of these groups was the **Minoans** (mi•NOH•unz). The Minoans lived on **Crete** (KREET), the large island that lies southeast of the Balkan Peninsula.

The Minoan civilization reached its peak between about 1750 and 1450 B.C. During that time the Minoans lived in well-built cities. Each city had a palace at its center. From their ruins, we know that Minoan palaces were several stories high and had dozens of rooms. They had water and sewage systems complete with flush toilets, bathtubs, and hot and cold running water. The rooms of the palaces were decorated with bright wall paintings.

They tell us much about the Minoan way of life.

The Minoans were sea merchants who traded with peoples of the Middle East. During the later days of their civilization, they also traded with the **Mycenaeans** (my•suh•NEE•auhnz), who lived in southern Greece.

At first the civilization of the Mycenaeans was less developed than that of the Minoans. The Mycenaeans learned quickly from their island neighbors, however. They adapted Minoan art to their own more forceful tastes. They changed the Minoan writing system to suit their own language, which was an early form of Greek. When the Minoan kingdom became weak, the warlike Mycenaeans conquered Crete. The

Mycenaeans occupied both Greece and Crete between about 1450 and 1100 B.C.

The Mycenaeans, in turn, were conquered by a fiercely independent people from the north called **Dorians.** After the Dorian invasion Greece seemed to fall into a deep sleep. Between about 1100 and 800 B.C. much of the previous civilization was lost. Overseas trade stopped. People returned to farming the land as their main way of life.

Long after the Mycenaean civilization had ended, the memory of it was preserved by the work of a blind Greek poet named **Homer.** Homer composed two long story-poems, or **epics** (EP·iks), both set in Mycenaean times. One poem about a great war was called the *Iliad* (IL·ee·uhd). Homer's other epic, the *Odyssey* (AHD·uh·see), tells about an adventurous hero on a long sea journey.

Homer composed his poems around 800 B.C. At that time the Mycenaeans were remembered only in old stories. Homer refined these stories to give a powerful picture of a society in which honor and courage were everything. Homer's epics are a lasting record of life in ancient Greece.

The Rise of City-States

After about 800 B.C. the people of Greece again organized communities. At first most Greeks lived in small, independent settlements. Each settlement centered on an **acropolis** (uh·KRAHP·uh·luhs), a walled fortress built on a hill. The settlement's ruler and a few other people lived in the fortress. The rest of the settlement's people moved inside the walls whenever the settlement was attacked.

This fresco, or painting on plaster, shows Minoan women attending a funeral on the island of Crete more than 3,000 years ago.

Slowly towns grew up around these fortresses. The towns had houses and temples and open-air markets. The marketplace was called an **agora** (AG•uh•ruh). People met in the agora to discuss the happenings of the day as well as to buy food and do other kinds of business.

Eventually the towns took nearby villages under their protection. A town and the farms and villages around it came to be called a **polis** (POH•lis), or city-state.

At first each polis was ruled by a king. In addition, the men of the polis met in an **assembly,** or lawmaking group, to discuss the government of the city. A council, usually made up of the oldest or wealthiest men in the polis, controlled the assembly. The assembly, the council, and the king all helped make decisions for the polis.

In Athens's agora, shoppers crowd around open stalls while politicians debate outside the Bouleuterion, meeting place of the Council of 500.

The Archaic Age

Beginning around Homer's time, the Greek people felt a new strength and energy. It was as though morning had come after a long night. This "morning," which lasted from about 800 to 500 B.C., is called the Archaic (ahr•KAY•ik) Age.

During the Archaic Age the Greeks regained the art of writing, which had been lost after Mycenaean times. The Greeks adopted their writing system from the sea-trading **Phoenicians** (fih•NIH•shuhnz), who lived in the Fertile Crescent in what is now Lebanon. Minoan and Mycenaean writing had used symbols to stand for syllables in words. Phoenician writing, and the writing system the Greeks made from it, used symbols to stand for single sounds instead.

The Greeks called the first letter of their sound-symbol list *alpha* (AL•fuh). The second letter was *beta* (BAYT•uh). Our word *alphabet* comes from the names of these Greek letters. However, the Greek alphabet contained more sound symbols than the alphabet we use today.

As the Greek city-states grew in power and population, their people looked more and more toward the sea. Greek trading ships carried olive oil, wine, wool, pottery, and other goods to lands around the Mediterranean. They returned with such necessities as iron ore and grain. The Greeks also set up colonies in what today is Asia Minor, Italy, France, Spain, and Russia, as well as on the many islands near Greece. The colonies provided space for an expanding population. In this way Greek civilization spread to other parts of Europe.

TRACING OUR ALPHABET		
Phoenician Letter	Greek Letter	Roman Letter
aleph	alpha	A
beth	beta	B
gimel	gamma	C
daleth	delta	D
he	epsilon	E
vav	digamma	F
zayin	zeta	Z
cheth	eta	H
teth	theta	
vod	iota	I
koph	kappa	K
lamed	lambda	L
mem	mu	M
nun	nu	N
samekh	xi	X
ayin	omicron	O
pe	pi	P
tsade	san	
qoph	koppa	Q
resh	rho	R
shin	sigma	S
tau	tau	T
	upsilon	V
	phi	
	chi	
	psi	
	omega	

Reading Check

1. Name two groups of people who contributed to ancient Greek civilization.
2. How did life in Greece change after the Dorian invasion?
3. Who composed the *Iliad* and the *Odyssey*?
4. From whom did the Greeks get their alphabet? How was Greek writing different from Minoan and Mycenaean writing?

Look for these important words:

Key Words
- ephors
- democracy
- demagogues

People
- Xerxes
- Pericles
- Socrates
- Aristotle
- Alexander the Great
- Philip

Places
- Athens
- Sparta
- Attica
- Marathon
- Salamis
- Macedonia

Look for answers to these questions:

1. How were governments and ways of life different in Sparta and Athens?
2. What was the outcome of the war between Greece and Persia? How did that outcome make the Greeks feel about themselves?
3. What were the achievements of Athens' Golden Age?
4. What happened to Greek civilization under Alexander the Great?

2. CLASSICAL GREECE

The ancient Greeks loved sports. Their ideal was "a sound mind in a sound body." People from all over Greece attended athletic contests, which were part of religious festivals. The most famous contest was the Olympic games. It was held every fourth summer to honor Zeus (ZOOS), the king of the gods. Each city-state sent its finest young men to take part in the Olympic games. The following story describes what an Olympic race may have been like during the fifth century B.C.

Victory and Honor

"I must control my breath," Miltiades (mil•TY•uh•deez) thought. He was nearing the end of the 3-mile foot race, and his heart was pounding violently. Behind him he could hear the steady beat of Lycurgus's (ly•KUHR•guh•suhz) feet on the path.

Miltiades came from the city-state of **Athens,** near the southeastern shore of mainland Greece. Lycurgus was from **Sparta,** an inland city-state in the Peloponnesus. Athens and Sparta were the most powerful city-states in Greece. They were also strong rivals. Miltiades and Lycurgus were running for the honor of their city-states.

Miltiades knew that whether he won or lost, his friends at home would crowd around him to talk about the race. Lycurgus, however, knew that he would be greeted with angry silence in Sparta should he lose.

As Lycurgus drew alongside Miltiades, the Spartan runner stumbled. Miltiades saw Lycurgus's grimace of pain. Lycurgus said nothing, however, and kept running. Just before the finish line, Lycurgus collapsed and Miltiades went on to win.

Before Miltiades was crowned with the victor's olive wreath, he went back to the fallen Lycurgus. "You ran well," Miltiades said. "You will win another race, I know." Lycurgus remained silent as two other Spartans carried him away.

The societies in which Miltiades and Lycurgus grew up were very different. Athens and Sparta represented opposite views of life during Greece's Classical Age, which lasted from about 500 to 400 B.C.

This vase picturing the goddess Athena was filled with oil and awarded to a winner of the games in Athens.

Sparta

Sparta was settled by Dorian warriors who defeated and enslaved everyone in their region. The slaves greatly outnumbered their Spartan masters, who sometimes treated the slaves harshly. Spartans lived in constant fear that the slaves would rebel. This fear, in part, caused Spartans to protect themselves by forming a military society. Spartan boys entered army training at the age of seven. Young Spartan men lived together in military camps. Only after age 30 were they allowed to have their own homes.

Spartan soldiers were proud of their obedience and self-discipline. In war they would fight even when wounded, wearing red clothing so that their wounds would not show. Spartan women, too, were strong and highly disciplined. They competed in such contests as wrestling and running.

Political power in Sparta was in the hands of a Council of Elders and five officials called **ephors** (EF•urz). Two kings assisted in governing, but their power was great only during wars. Sparta had an assembly, though it too had limited power. The most important task of Spartan government was to maintain a strong army.

Sparta's military state was successful in some ways. The Spartan army was the best in Greece. Sparta controlled a powerful group of city-states called the Peloponnesian League. However, Spartan society never let its people think for themselves. Spartans discouraged outsiders from moving into Sparta and spreading new ideas. Spartans themselves were not allowed to visit or trade with other regions. Life in Sparta changed very little as a result.

Athens

Athens was the chief city-state in **Attica** (AT•i•kuh), the southeastern part of the Greek mainland. Unlike Sparta, Athens allowed political freedom to its citizens. It required military service from its young men only during times of war.

Athenian government grew into the system called **democracy** (dih•MAHK•ruh•see), or rule by the people. A constitution provided rules for governing Athens. Every adult male Athenian became a citizen and a member of the city's assembly. Each assembly member had one vote. The assembly voted on every issue that was important to the city-state and elected its leaders. Athens also allowed trials by jury. Jury members decided what was fair by voting.

Not everyone participated in Athenian democracy. Only citizens could take part. Unlike Sparta, Athens encouraged outsiders to live in the city. Outsiders could not become citizens, however. Women also were not allowed to play a direct part in the government of Athens.

The group that gained the least from Athenian democracy helped to make it possible. That group was the slaves, who made up about a quarter of the population of Athens. Although better treated than Spartan slaves, they did most of the work in Athens. This left citizens free to spend their time on public affairs.

Athenian democracy, though limited, gave people the opportunity to make decisions for themselves. This kind of participation in government was a new idea that later became a model for other governments.

The Greeks and the Persians

About 490 B.C. Greece was attacked by the Persians. The Persian Empire, centered in the Middle East, included conquered Greek colonies in Asia Minor. The Persian king, Darius, next turned his armies toward the Greek mainland and Athens. He thought that conquering mainland Greece would be an easy task. Darius was surprised, indeed, when the Athenians met his army at the plain of **Marathon,** not far from Athens.

Although the Persians vastly outnumbered them, the Greeks fought so fiercely that they defeated Darius's men. The Athenian general sent the army's best runner, a man named Pheidippides (fy•DIP•ih•deez), back to Athens with the news. Pheidippides supposedly ran the entire distance without stopping. Then he gasped out the news of the victory and died of exhaustion. It is his great running feat that the 26.2-mile (42.2-km) marathon race of the modern Olympic games recalls.

Darius died soon after the defeat at Marathon. His son **Xerxes** (ZURK•seez) never forgot the blows that the Athenians had dealt his father. In 480 B.C. Xerxes sent a fighting force of about 200,000 soldiers and 800 ships against the Greeks. Although the city-states united against the Persians, the Greeks were badly outnumbered on land and on the sea. With cleverness and bravery, however, they finally defeated their powerful enemy.

In one of the first and greatest sea battles, Greek warships destroyed the Persian fleet near **Salamis** (SAL•uh•muhs). Xerxes had set up a throne on a hill overlooking the sea. He

Luring Persian ships into narrow channels between the coast and Salamis Island, Greeks split the enemy force into three parts. Unable to use their strong advantage in numbers, the Persians were defeated.

watched in rage and horror as more than 200 Persian ships were destroyed and 20,000 of his sailors died. The few captains who managed to save themselves and swim ashore Xerxes had beheaded.

The Greeks felt a tremendous pride after their defeat of Persia. This pride was especially strong in Athens, whose navy had played a major part in the victory. After the Persian Wars Athens entered a glorious time that was later called its Golden Age. This time lasted from about 460 to 430 B.C. Far-reaching Greek advancements occurred during this period.

The Golden Age of Pericles

The leader of Athens during its Golden Age was a wealthy noble named **Pericles** (PAIR•uh•kleez). Pericles was a popular leader who supported democracy. The Athenian assembly recognized Pericles' ability and usually followed his advice.

Pericles had great plans for Athens, and he achieved most of them. He kept the Athenian navy strong and encouraged sea trade. The city-states of Attica belonged to a group called the Delian League. Pericles strengthened the Delian League, expanding it into an Athenian-controlled empire.

Democracy in Athens reached its peak during the time of Pericles. About 40 times a year the assembly, numbering thousands of men, gathered on a hill near the city. In this open-air meeting they discussed and voted on the city's business. Any member could speak to the assembly.

THE ATHENIAN ACROPOLIS, ABOUT 400 B.C.

1. The Erechtheum (two-level temple dedicated to several gods)
2. The Sanctuary of Zeus
3. The Parthenon (main temple of the Acropolis)
4. The Bronze Statue of Athena (the work of Phidias)
5. The Propylaea (ceremonial gateway marking the only entrance from the steep slopes of the Acropolis)
6. The Temple of Athena Nike (guardian of Athens)

Pericles built the Parthenon as a monument to his city's victory over the Persians. A statue of Athena in ivory and gold stood inside.

A group called the Council of 500 drew up a list of matters to be discussed at each assembly meeting. Members of the assembly could add to or change the list if they wished. The council members were chosen from the assembly each year by the drawing of names from a bowl. Most other government posts, as well as the juries for court cases, also were filled this way. Almost every assembly member held public office at some time.

Pericles improved Athenian democracy by ordering that a small salary be paid to each juror or official during the time that person worked for the public. This salary made up for the money the man lost by taking time away from his regular job. It meant that poor citizens as well as rich ones could afford to hold office.

Pericles encouraged Athenians to excel in art, science, and thought as well as in politics. He had good reason to boast that "Athens is the school of Greece." Athenian ideas were an invisible cargo on the city's outward-bound merchant ships, too. These ideas inspired Greeks on nearby islands and in distant colonies.

Pericles hired the best artists to work on new public buildings for Athens. The grandest of these buildings was the Parthenon (PAHR•thuh•nahn). It was a temple honoring the city's patron goddess, Athena (uh•THEE•nuh). This building was a fitting monument to the majesty of Pericles' Athens.

127

Last Days of Classical Greece

By Pericles' time, Athens and Sparta were the most powerful city-states in Greece. Each had many allies and was eager to spread its way of life and government to as many other places as possible. War between them was unavoidable. In 431 B.C. Sparta attacked Athens, beginning the Peloponnesian War. The war lasted 27 years.

Athens was unlucky from the start. The city, crowded with refugees from Attica, was an easy target for a disease that swept through it in 430 B.C. One quarter of the Athenian army died. Pericles died a year later.

Without Pericles' wise leadership, the people of the assembly began to follow bad leaders called **demagogues** (DEM•uh•gahgz). These leaders made speeches that appealed to people's feelings instead of to their minds. By making false promises, the demagogues often persuaded the assembly to approve foolish or cruel actions.

Faced with starvation, Athens finally surrendered to Sparta in 404 B.C. Sparta set up a council of men to govern the city. The Athenians called these men the Thirty Tyrants. Self-government was restored to Athens later, but the true spirit of democracy was gone.

Great thinkers and teachers lived in Athens after the Peloponnesian War, but the city no longer supported them. One famous Greek teacher was **Socrates** (SAHK•ruh•teez), who taught by asking questions rather than lecturing. His pupils found the truth by

After the court ordered his death, Socrates swallowed poison made from the fruit of a hemlock plant. His death marked the end of Classical Greece.

Spear in hand, Alexander gallops into battle. This portrait is part of a larger work that shows Alexander's defeat of Darius III, the Persian king.

learning to think for themselves. Socrates called himself the city's "gadfly." As a fly bites a horse and makes it jump, Socrates tried to use criticism to "sting" Athens into recovering its earlier greatness. Such criticism would have been welcomed in Pericles' day. In 399 B.C., however, an Athenian court convicted Socrates of teaching dangerous ideas. Socrates was forced to end his life by drinking poison.

Alexander the Great

Another great teacher who lived after the Peloponnesian War was **Aristotle** (AIR•is•tah•tuhl). Aristotle taught in Athens for a while, but his most important pupil was not a Greek. He was a young prince of **Macedonia** (mas•uh•DOH•nee•uh) who later became known as **Alexander the Great.**

Macedonia lay to the north of Greece. Its people were related to the Greeks but were not as advanced. In 356 B.C. a sturdy, black-bearded man named **Philip** became their king. Philip had spent part of his boyhood in Greece and greatly admired Greek culture. He hired Aristotle to teach his son, Alexander.

Philip set out to conquer all of Greece. The Greeks were worn out from the fighting that had continued long

129

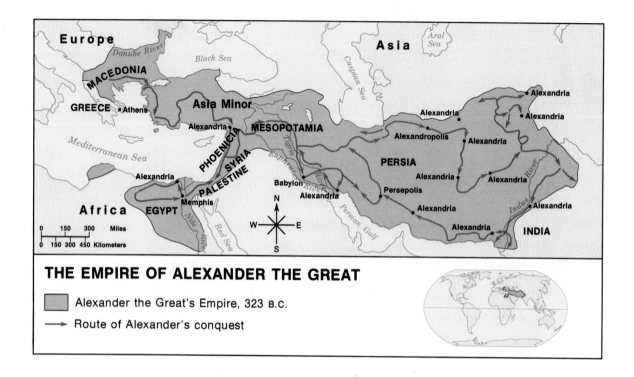

THE EMPIRE OF ALEXANDER THE GREAT

Alexander the Great's Empire, 323 B.C.

→ Route of Alexander's conquest

after the Peloponnesian War. They were no match for the well-trained Macedonian soldiers. By 338 B.C. Philip controlled most of Greece.

When Philip died in 336 B.C., Alexander, only 20 years old, took the Macedonian throne. He had an even larger dream than his father's. He wanted to rule the known world. In 13 years, this brilliant young man nearly achieved his goal.

Alexander began by conquering Greece's old enemy, Persia. Later, Phoenicia, Egypt, and parts of India fell to his hand. He established many cities in Asia and Africa.

Like his father, Alexander the Great admired Greek ideas. He spread Greek civilization to the lands he conquered. He also brought Asian ideas back to the Greek world.

Alexander died in 323 B.C. at the age of 33. His empire broke up quickly after his death. His generals divided it into three parts: Syria, Macedonia, and Egypt. In each area Greek ideas were combined with Asian ones to create a Hellenistic, or "Greeklike," civilization and culture.

The Hellenistic Age lasted from about 330 to 30 B.C. Important thinkers, writers, and artists lived during this time. However, the Hellenistic civilization as a whole never matched the achievements of classical Greece. The glory that had been Greece became a slowly fading memory.

Reading Check

1. Why were athletic contests important in ancient Greece?
2. What were the two most powerful city-states in Greece?
3. Who led Athens during its Golden Age?
4. How did Alexander the Great spread Greek civilization?

Look for these important words:

Key Words
- atoms
- philosophers
- tragedy
- comedy
- lyric poems

- fable
- architecture

People
- Democritus
- Hippocrates

- Herodotus
- Plato
- Sophocles
- Aristophanes
- Aesop
- Phidias

Look for answers to these questions:

1. What did the Greeks believe about their gods and goddesses?
2. What achievements did Greek scientists and thinkers make?
3. What achievements did Greeks make in drama, literature, and art?

3. THE ACHIEVEMENTS OF ANCIENT GREECE

In size, Greece is smaller than Florida. In spirit, however, few societies have matched Greece. Greek achievements in politics, art, drama, poetry, thought, and science have helped to shape Western civilization.

Religion

The ancient Greeks believed in many gods and goddesses. They imagined these gods and goddesses to be like humans only with much more power and physical perfection. The Greeks believed that if the gods were pleased, they would lend their support to human projects. If they became angry, they could make endless trouble. The Greeks offered prayers, gifts, and sacrifices to their gods. However, most Greeks did not live in fear of their gods and goddesses and often made them the subject of art, drama, and storytelling.

Many Greeks tried to learn more about the natural world and strongly encouraged the use of reason or thought. The Greeks' attitude toward nature and the world allowed them to take the first steps toward modern science.

Science and Philosophy

In ancient Greece, for the first time, people tried to find scientific ways to describe how the world worked. They carefully studied everything around them.

Some Greek thinkers tried to find out the nature of the basic matter of which the world was made. For example, **Democritus** (dih•MAHK•ruh•tus), who lived in Pericles' Athens, thought that everything was made of tiny particles, called **atoms.** Greeks also studied the stars and mathematics.

When beginning important projects, Greeks traveled to Delphi, where the gods were thought to give advice and tell the future.

Some Greeks studied human beings and their actions. **Hippocrates** (hih•PAHK•ruh•teez) studied the bodies of sick and healthy people. His studies showed how illnesses resulted from natural causes. He established rules, still followed today, for the proper conduct of physicians.

Other ancient Greeks studied history. **Herodotus** (huh•RAHD•uh•tuhs), often called the Father of History, wrote about the Persian War. He collected information from many people before he began to write. He reported events as fairly as he could and tried to explain what caused them.

Greeks who discussed the nature of ideas were known as **philosophers** (fih•LAHS•uh•fuhrz), or "lovers of wisdom." One of the greatest was **Plato** (PLAY•toh), a student of Socrates. Plato was disappointed in the lack of ability shown by the Athenian leaders of his time. He began to think about what it takes to be a great ruler. A ruler should be a good person, he decided, because good people understand everything. One can become a good person by studying hard and loving wisdom. Thus, Plato reasoned, philosophers would make the best rulers. Plato's ideas are still important today.

Drama and Poetry

Greek drama grew out of dances and songs at religious festivals honoring the god Dionysus. Actors in stiff masks performed plays on open-air stages. The audience sat on stone benches built into the sides of nearby hills.

132

The two main kinds of ancient Greek plays were the **tragedy** (TRAJ·uh·dee) and the **comedy** (KAHM·uh·dee). Tragedies were serious plays. They showed important actions of heroic people.

A main theme of Greek tragedies was that people's own actions often caused the troubles that befell them. Tragedies also showed people reacting bravely to troubles brought by the evil doings of others or by fate. **Sophocles** (SAHF·uh·cleez), a Greek playwright, wrote many of the most famous Greek tragedies.

Comedies told happy or humorous stories. Some showed happenings in everyday life. Others made fun of political leaders or ideas. The most famous Greek comedy writer was **Aristophanes** (ar·uh·STAHF·uh·neez). He lived in Athens during and after the Peloponnesian War.

Epic poems were written in Greece long after Homer's time. Greeks also wrote shorter poems called **lyric** (LIR·ik) **poems.** Lyric poems described the poets' feelings about other people or about the natural world. These poems usually were recited to the music of a Greek harp called a lyre.

Another popular form of Greek literature was the **fable.** Fables were

Epidaurus, 2,300 years old, is the ancient world's best-preserved theater. The softest stage whisper can be heard in each of its 14,000 seats.

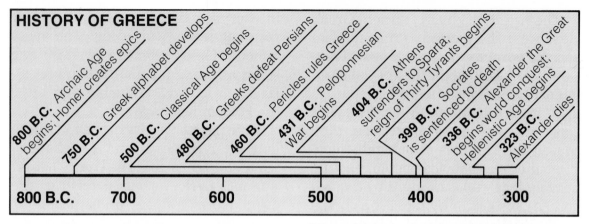

HISTORY OF GREECE

800 B.C. Archaic Age begins; Homer creates epics

750 B.C. Greek alphabet develops

500 B.C. Classical Age begins

480 B.C. Greeks defeat Persians

460 B.C. Pericles rules Greece

431 B.C. Peloponnesian War begins

404 B.C. Athens surrenders to Sparta; reign of Thirty Tyrants begins

399 B.C. Socrates is sentenced to death

336 B.C. Alexander the Great begins world conquest; Hellenistic Age begins

323 B.C. Alexander dies

800 B.C.   700   600   500   400   300

often animal stories that taught special lessons. **Aesop** (EE•sop) was a Greek storyteller whose fables are still enjoyed today.

Art and Architecture

Greek art combined a love of beauty with a careful study of the real world. Some Greek sculptures represented gods and goddesses. Others showed heroes or athletes at the height of their power and grace. One of the greatest Greek sculptors was **Phidias** (FID•ee•uhs). He made a statue of Athena covered in gold and ivory, which stood in the Parthenon.

Greek pottery was strikingly beautiful. It was often painted with orange and black glazes. Some Greek pottery showed religious processions or athletic contests. Other pottery pictured scenes of everyday life, such as boys in school, craft workers working in their shops, or women baking bread.

The greatest achievements of Greek **architecture,** or building style, are probably the Parthenon and other buildings built in Athens during Pericles' time. Temples in other parts of Greece are also famous. Many are made of the hard white stone called marble.

The Gifts of Ancient Greece

Of all our gifts from ancient Greece, perhaps the most valuable are ideas. The Greeks believed strongly in the value of wisdom. From an early age, Greeks were encouraged to study, to exercise, and to prepare to be good citizens. Greeks believed that every citizen had both the right and the duty to take part in public life. They felt it was important for people to take responsibility for their actions. The Greek spirit of democracy is shared by many people today.

The Greeks believed that people should learn as much as possible about the world. Their curiosity led to the growth of philosophy and science. A love of beauty led Greeks to create wondrous works of art. Greek achievements in art, science, and government were admired long after their time.

Reading Check

1. In what ways did gods and goddesses influence Greek life?
2. Who was Herodotus?
3. What method did Socrates use to teach his pupils?
4. What are the two main kinds of Greek plays?

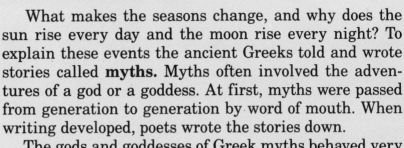

Gods and Goddesses

Zeus

What makes the seasons change, and why does the sun rise every day and the moon rise every night? To explain these events the ancient Greeks told and wrote stories called **myths.** Myths often involved the adventures of a god or a goddess. At first, myths were passed from generation to generation by word of mouth. When writing developed, poets wrote the stories down.

The gods and goddesses of Greek myths behaved very much like humans. They had special powers, but they also had very human jealousies, loves, and hatreds. In Greek myths the gods and goddesses argued like members of a loving but quarrelsome family. They were as often wicked and mischievous as they were good and helpful.

Artemis

Many gods and goddesses were said to live on Mount Olympus in northern Greece. Zeus was the king of the gods. He ruled with his queen, Hera. They had many children, including the twins Apollo, the god of the sun, and Artemis, the goddess of the moon. Some of their other children were Aphrodite (af•ruh•DY•tee), the goddess of love and beauty, and Ares, the god of war. The Greek myths also tell about Athena, the goddess of wisdom, who sprang armed and fully grown from Zeus's head.

Zeus had two brothers. Poseidon (puh•SY•duhn) ruled the seas and waters, and Hades ruled the underworld and the dead. Myths about them explained the reasons for the tides and what happened to people after death.

Athena

There were also two Earth gods living on Mount Olympus. They were different from the other gods because they could suffer lasting grief. They were Demeter (dih•MEET•uhr), goddess of growing things and the seasons, and Dionysus (dy•uh•NY•suhs), god of the grape and wine. One god acted as a messenger from the gods and goddesses on Mount Olympus to the mortals on Earth. He was Hermes, god of speakers, writers, and merchants.

The Greeks built many beautiful temples to honor their gods and goddesses. Later, when the Romans conquered Greece, they adopted the Greek gods and goddesses as their own, changing little but the names.

EXPLORING THE LIBRARY

Libraries are divided into fiction, nonfiction, and reference sections. Books of fiction are imaginary stories invented by their authors. *Wonderful Wizard of Oz* is a fiction book. It is a fanciful story about a visit to a make-believe land. Nonfiction books contain facts and information about real things. *Temple on a Hill* is a nonfiction book that describes the building of the Parthenon in ancient Athens.

Reference books are nonfiction books that contain collections of facts. Encyclopedias, dictionaries, atlases, and almanacs are reference books. They must be used in the library and cannot be checked out.

Libraries have special sections for **periodicals**—newspapers and magazines. Current issues usually are displayed on a rack, while older issues are stored away, sometimes on film. A librarian can assist you in locating all types of materials.

Wonderful Wizard of Oz	Temple on a Hill	The World Almanac
Baum	Rockwell	
F Ba	j938 Ro	R

Finding Books in the Library

The system many libraries use to organize books is the **Dewey decimal system.** Fiction books are arranged alphabetically by the authors' last names. Books by the same author are arranged alphabetically by title. The letter *F* on the spine of *Wonderful Wizard of Oz* tells you that it is a fiction book. The letters *Ba* are the first two letters in the author's last name, Baum.

Nonfiction books are arranged by their subject matter. Each book is given a **call number** according to its subject. Books about the same subject have the same call number and are placed together on the shelves. Notice that the call number on *Temple on a Hill* is j938. The *j* tells you that the book is a juvenile, or children's, book. The number 938 tells you where to look on the shelves for a book about ancient Greece. The *Ro* under the call number are the first two letters of Rockwell, the author's last name. All books with the same call number are arranged alphabetically by the author's last name.

The ten basic categories of nonfiction books and their call numbers are listed on the next page. A book about languages has a call number between 400 and 499. What kinds of books have call numbers between 500 and 599?

Within the broad subject categories of the Dewey decimal system are many related categories. Some of them are shown for you here. Once you have learned the range of numbers of the subject you need to find, you can easily locate all related materials in the same area of your library.

Dewey Decimal System

000–099	General information (encyclopedias, other reference books)
100–199	Philosophy (ideas about the meaning of life, psychology)
200–299	Religion (world religions, mythology)
300–399	Social Science (law, education, government, economics)
400–499	Language (dictionaries, grammars)
500–599	Pure Science (mathematics, astronomy, plants, animals)
600–699	Technology (medicine, agriculture, business, inventions)
700–799	Arts (sculpture, painting, music, photography, recreation)
800–899	Literature (novels, poetry, plays)
900–999	History (biographies, travel, geography)

Using the Card Catalog

To find a nonfiction book, you need to know its exact call number. The **card catalog** can give you the call number of any nonfiction book in the library. A card catalog is a file of cards that provides important information about every book in the library. There are three cards for each nonfiction book: a **title card,** an **author card,** and a **subject card.** Fiction books are listed only by title and author. All three types of cards are mixed together and kept in alphabetical order in the drawers of the card catalog.

Following are the three catalog cards for a nonfiction book. The title card gives the title of the book at the top of the card. The author's name is on the next line. In this example there are two authors, Shirley Glubok and Alfred Tamarin. The card lists the book's call number, 796.48, in the top left

Title Card

> 796.48
> G   Olympic games in ancient Greece.
>
> **Glubok, Shirley.** Written by Shirley Glubok and Alfred Tamarin. New York: Harper and Row, 1976.
> 116 p. illus.
>
> The authors describe a celebration of the games that might have taken place in ancient Greece.
>
> 1. Olympic Games

Author Card

> 796.48   **Glubok, Shirley**
> G   Olympic games in ancient Greece. Written by Shirley Glubok and Alfred Tamarin. New York: Harper and Row, 1976.
> 116 p. illus
>
> The authors describe a celebration of the games that might have taken place in ancient Greece.
>
> 1. Olympic Games   I. Title

Subject Card

> 796.48   OLYMPIC GAMES
> G
> **Glubok, Shirley**
> Olympic games in ancient Greece. Written by Shirley Glubok and Alfred Tamarin. New York: Harper and Row, 1976.
> 116 p. illus.
>
> The authors describe a celebration of the games that might have taken place in ancient Greece.
>
> I. Title

corner. The G means the author's last name starts with G.

The author card lists the name of the author at the top of the card. The title of the book comes next. The subject card has OLYMPIC GAMES at the top, because the book is about the Olympic games. Notice that the subject is printed in capital letters. The author's name and the title of the book follow the subject.

In addition to the call number, the author, and the title, each card lists the book's publisher and date of publication. The cards tell you the number of pages in the book and indicate if it is illustrated. Most cards also give a brief description of the book. The numbered items at the bottom of each card are other headings under which the book is listed.

Having three ways of finding a book in the card catalog can be very useful. Suppose you want to find a book on the Olympic games but do not know any titles or authors of books on the subject. You can look under OLYMPIC GAMES in the catalog for subject cards. Once you have found the call number for books about the Olympic games, you can go to that section of the library for books on the subject. You can also find other books by an author by looking under that author's name in the catalog.

Microfiche

Recently, many libraries have begun using a system called **microfiche** (MY•kroh•feesh), instead of a card catalog, to show you how to find a book. The microfiche is a sheet of film that lists, in alphabetical order, thousands of books. The sheets may be organized separately by title, author, and subject. Each listing has the same information as a card in a card catalog.

To use the microfiche system, you find the sheet you want by the guide words at the top. You then insert it into a microfiche reader, which is like an electric magnifying glass. By moving the locator, you can find the listing you want.

Some libraries now use computerized card catalogs. To use an on-line catalog, you send commands to a computer and the information will show up on the screen. Libraries in large cities and universities are likely to have computerized catalogs.

CHECKING YOUR SKILLS

Study the card below and answer the questions that follow.

j938	The lion in the gateway.
R	**Renault, Mary.** Written by Mary Renault. Edited by Walter Lord. Pictures by C. Walter Hodges. New York: Harper & Row, 1964. 196 p. illus.
	The author describes the heroic battles of the Greeks and Persians.
	1. Greece—History—Persian Wars, 500–499 B.C.

1. Is this an author card, a subject card, or a title card? Who wrote this book?

2. Would you find this card filed under *Renault, Greece,* or *Lion*?

3. What is the book's call number?

4. Is *The Lion in the Gateway* a fiction book, a nonfiction book, or a reference book?

5. Where else would you find a card for this book or for other books on the same subject?

USING WORDS

Explain the meaning of each of the words listed below. Then use each word in a complete sentence.

1. **agora**
2. **architecture**
3. **assembly**
4. **democracy**
5. **epics**
6. **fable**
7. **isthmus**
8. **philosophers**
9. **polis**
10. **tragedy**

REVIEWING FACTS

1. What two geographical features of the Balkan Peninsula have helped to shape Greece's history?

2. During what age did the Greeks begin to recover their civilization?

3. Why were the Spartans interested in a strong military?

4. How were Sparta and Athens different?

5. What event does the Olympic marathon race recall?

6. How were government decisions made in Athens during Pericles' time?

7. What war marked the end of Athenian power?

8. Which cultures combined to form the Hellenistic civilization? Who was responsible for its growth?

9. Name three famous Greeks and their contributions.

10. What long-lasting ideas did the ancient Greeks introduce?

THINKING CRITICALLY

1. The kind of democracy practiced in ancient Athens is called *direct democracy.* In this form of democracy, every citizen votes on every important issue. How is this different from the democracy practiced in the United States? Do you think direct democracy could work in the United States now? Why or why not?

2. Socrates said, "Know thyself." What do you think this means? This statement is only one example of the search for knowledge by some early Greeks. How do you think curiosity might contribute to great achievements?

3. Although Sparta eventually defeated Athens, Athenian contributions are better remembered and admired. Why do you think the Spartan way of life failed to have the lasting influence that Athenian culture had?

◯ PRACTICING SKILLS

The Dewey Decimal System Identify the range of Dewey decimal system numbers (page 137) within which you would find each of the following nonfiction books.

1. *Modern Sculpture and the Greek Influence*

2. *The Life of Alexander the Great*

3. *The Greek Alphabet*

4. *How to Grow Olives*

5. *The World Book Encyclopedia*

Rome Governs an Empire

Focus

About 2,700 years ago a group of farmers set up a village on the bank of a river in Italy. The village grew into a city that became the center of government for lands on three continents. The city's name was Rome.

The civilization of ancient Rome lasted about 1,000 years. It left buildings and roads throughout Europe. Under its rule people learned Roman skills, the Roman language, and Roman law. A unified Roman government created a long-lasting peace that allowed European civilization to grow.

Look for these important words:

Key Words
- Latins
- Etruscans
- republic
- consuls
- patricians
- plebeians
- tribunes

- veto
- Twelve Tables
- dictator

People
- Hannibal
- Pompey
- Julius Caesar

Places
- Sicily
- Alps
- Apennines
- Tiber River
- Carthage
- Gaul

Look for answers to these questions:

1. What legends did the Romans tell about the beginning of their city?
2. How was the Roman Republic governed?
3. Which empires did the Roman Republic conquer?
4. How did Julius Caesar gain control of Rome? What changes did he make?

1. THE ROMAN REPUBLIC

Italy is the middle peninsula of southern Europe. Like the Balkan Peninsula, it extends into the Mediterranean Sea. Italy's shape reminds many people of a high-heeled boot. Southwest of the boot, like a giant soccer ball, lies the island of **Sicily** (SIS•uh•lee). From there it is less than 100 miles (about 160 km) across the Mediterranean to the coast of North Africa.

Like Greece, much of Italy is covered by hills and mountains. The high mountain ranges called the **Alps** stretch across the northern border of the country. Another range, the **Apennines** (AP•uh•nynz), runs south through Italy. Italy has some fertile flatlands, mostly in the north. With more tillable soil and fewer good harbors than Greece, the first Italians stayed close to home, developing their own land.

On the banks of the **Tiber** (TY•bur) **River,** about halfway up the "shin" of Italy near the western coast, a village appeared about 2,700 years ago. Its strong, independent farmers were the first residents of what would later become the city of Rome.

The Founding of Rome

A prince of Troy named Aeneas (i•NEE•us) fought in the Trojan War, the war about which Homer composed his epic poem, the *Iliad*. When Troy was captured by the Greeks, Aeneas and his followers had to search for a new home. After much traveling, they came to Italy. They settled on the plain where the city of Rome later grew up.

ANCIENT ITALY, ABOUT 600 B.C.

Europe

ALPS

Po River

Arno R.

ETRUSCANS

APENNINES

Tiber R.

Corsica

Rome

LATINS

Adriatic Sea

Sardinia

Tyrrhenian Sea

GREECE

Mediterranean Sea

Sicily

GREEKS

Carthage

Africa

N
W   E
S

0   75   150   Miles
0   75 150 225 Kilometers

The story of Aeneas was only one of the legends the Romans told about the beginning of their city. Another legend said Rome was begun by twin brothers named Romulus (RAHM•yoo•lus) and Remus (REE•mus). These brothers, the legend said, were abandoned on the bank of the Tiber when they were babies. Their lives were saved by a mother wolf. The Romans believed that Romulus went on to found the city that was named for him.

The legend of Romulus and Remus tells something important about the Romans. Like the twins who grew up in the wilderness, ancient Romans were proud of their power to survive on their own. The Romans' courage and self-reliance helped them build a rich and far-reaching civilization. The story also shows the Romans' faith in their own future. Romulus is supposed to have said, "Proclaim to the Romans it is heaven's will that my Rome shall be the capital of the world." The ancient Romans believed in this idea, whether or not they actually believed the story.

The real beginnings of Rome were not as dramatic as the legends. The **Latins** (LAT•inz) were one of the many groups in Italy. They established a farming village on the Tiber River around 750 B.C. At about this same time, the people called **Etruscans** (ih•TRUS•kuhnz) lived alongside the Latins in central Italy. The Etruscans were sea traders. They traded with the Greeks, who had established colonies in Sicily and southern Italy. They also traded with the kingdoms of Asia and with the peoples of northern Africa.

Between about 600 and 500 B.C. Etruscan kings ruled early Rome. They provided a link between the Greeks and the Latins. They introduced Greek customs and ideas. They also introduced ideas from Asia and the Middle East. These different cultures became important to the developing Roman civilization.

This miniature chariot found in a tomb shows Etruscan skill in metalwork.

The Birth of the Republic

During the Etruscan rule, Rome grew into a walled city spread on and around seven hills. Although the Etruscans had contributed much to the culture of Rome, Romans were dissatisfied with the harsh rule of Etruscan kings. In 509 B.C. the Romans drove the Etruscans out of the city and set up their own government.

The Romans decided that they did not want to be ruled by kings. Instead, they formed a **republic.** A republic is a form of government led by elected officials. Like Athens, the Roman Republic had an assembly of citizens. Instead of making government decisions themselves, however, the Roman assembly elected representatives to make these decisions for them. The Romans called their council of representatives the Senate. Two officials from the Senate, called **consuls** (KAHN.sulz), were elected each year. The consuls held supreme power over Rome.

Some Roman citizens had more power in government than others. The noble families of Rome were called the **patricians** (puh.TRISH.uhnz). Their ancestors were the city's first settlers. The common people of Rome were the **plebeians** (plih.BEE.uhnz). Like the patricians, the plebeians were Roman citizens. They had to pay taxes and serve in the army. However, they could not become senators or consuls. This high honor was reserved for those of noble birth.

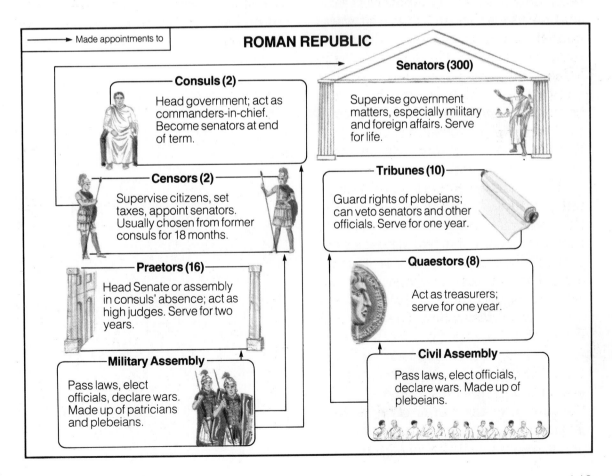

ROMAN REPUBLIC

→ Made appointments to

Senators (300)
Supervise government matters, especially military and foreign affairs. Serve for life.

Consuls (2)
Head government; act as commanders-in-chief. Become senators at end of term.

Censors (2)
Supervise citizens, set taxes, appoint senators. Usually chosen from former consuls for 18 months.

Tribunes (10)
Guard rights of plebeians; can veto senators and other officials. Serve for one year.

Praetors (16)
Head Senate or assembly in consuls' absence; act as high judges. Serve for two years.

Quaestors (8)
Act as treasurers; serve for one year.

Military Assembly
Pass laws, elect officials, declare wars. Made up of patricians and plebeians.

Civil Assembly
Pass laws, elect officials, declare wars. Made up of plebeians.

Beginning early in the fifth century B.C., the plebeians demanded more rights. They won the right to have their own assembly. Each year it elected ten officials called **tribunes** (TRIB•yoonz). The tribunes attended Senate meetings. If the Senate passed a law that seemed harmful to the plebeians, the tribunes could stop passage of the law by saying "**veto**" (VEE•toh). This Latin word means "I forbid."

Around 450 B.C. the demands of the plebeians led to the writing of the first Roman code of law. The code was called the **Twelve Tables.** It was engraved on bronze tablets that were posted in Rome's main square. Writing down the laws helped make sure that they would be applied equally to patricians and plebeians. The Twelve Tables were the basis for Roman codes of law that were to follow.

Growth of the Republic

After the Romans drove out the Etruscan kings and set up the Republic, they began taking over new land in Italy. The Roman army was very successful. It conquered the Etruscans and other peoples in central Italy. By 265 B.C. Rome controlled nearly all of Italy.

As Rome's power grew, it came into conflict with powerful lands around the Mediterranean. The strongest of these lands was **Carthage** (KAHR•thij). Carthage was a city-state in North Africa that had been settled by the Phoenicians. Both Carthage and Rome had settlements on the island of Sicily. Both were interested in controlling the growing Mediterranean sea trade. Both had strong defenses. Rome had a well-trained army, while the strength of Carthage lay in its navy.

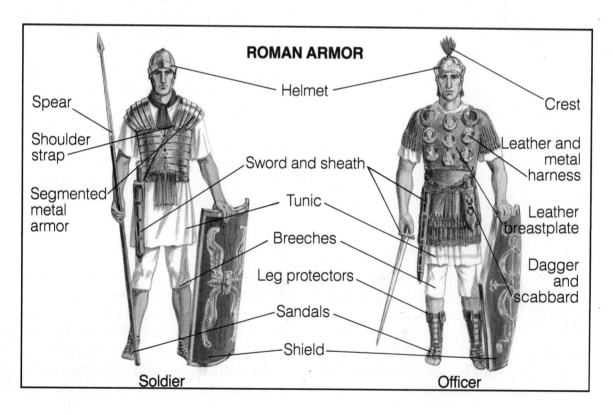

ROMAN ARMOR

Helmet

Spear

Shoulder strap

Segmented metal armor

Sword and sheath

Tunic

Breeches

Leg protectors

Sandals

Shield

Crest

Leather and metal harness

Leather breastplate

Dagger and scabbard

Soldier

Officer

Hannibal builds a pier and launches his war elephants on rafts to cross the Rhone River. On the opposite bank, enemy troops await his army.

Rome fought three wars with Carthage between 264 and 146 B.C. These wars were called the Punic (PYOO•nik) Wars, after the Roman name for the Phoenicians. During the first war, Rome's newly built navy defeated the experienced fleet from Carthage. In the peace settlement Romans forced Carthage to give up Sicily.

In the second Punic War, a young general from Carthage nearly captured Rome itself. His name was **Hannibal** (HAN•uh•buhl). Instead of attacking by sea, Hannibal came by land from the north. He led his army, including a number of war elephants, in a daring and difficult journey across the Alps. Hannibal fought in Italy for 15 years. He was then recalled to Carthage to fight off a Roman invasion. Hannibal was defeated there in 202 B.C. Fifty-eight years later, Rome destroyed Carthage in the final war.

You may recall that following the death of Alexander the Great, his empire broke into three pieces. One part was in Syria. One was in Alexander's homeland, Macedonia. One was in Egypt. Rome fought with and conquered each of these empires in turn. The reputation of the Roman army spread far. Even today military students discuss the methods of famous Roman generals. The following story shows how a Roman soldier might have felt before going to war.

Honor for Rome

Marcus looked once more around the walls of his home. He knew it might be the last time he would see them. Today he was leaving with the Roman army on its long journey to Macedonia.

In a space in one wall stood the shrine to the family's household god.

Marcus's father had just finished placing offerings on the shrine and praying for Marcus's safe return.

"I hope I can bring honor to our family and to Rome," Marcus told his parents.

"I know you will," they replied. "You are strong and well disciplined, as a Roman should be."

"But what about the Macedonians' long spears?" Marcus's younger brother asked in a worried tone. "How can your army's swords ever get past them?"

"We can move more swiftly than they, and we are better trained," Marcus reassured him. "Others have already felt the power of our swords. Soon Macedonia will, too. No one stands against Rome for long!"

Marcus was proud of his ability as a Roman soldier. His training included vigorous exercise. Roman soldiers could march up to 24 miles a day, sometimes carrying as much as 60 pounds of food and equipment. Marcus also practiced the art of using sword and shield. With his fellow soldiers, he drilled in various formations used by the army to march, attack, and protect itself. Marcus and his family knew that a Roman soldier must be prepared to serve and to die, if necessary, for his homeland.

Julius Caesar

By 44 B.C. Rome controlled not only Italy but large parts of what is now Spain, France, and Greece. It also controlled land in North Africa, the Middle East, and western Asia Minor.

The Romans divided their empire into provinces and appointed a Roman governor over each. They did not try to change the religions or customs of the conquered peoples. They ruled their territories firmly but not harshly. Supported by Roman troops, the governors collected taxes and encouraged trade with Rome. Rome also protected its possessions against other invaders. For this reason, many defenseless peoples, hoping to become more secure and prosperous, welcomed the Romans. Others, of course, fiercely resisted invasion, refusing to give up their independence.

During this first century B.C., the leaders of patrician families competed for power and high government positions. They sought the support of the common people by promising to give them land or to help in other ways.

In the early days of the Republic, a law had been passed saying that one leader could be given total power in Rome only during a war or military emergency. This kind of ruler was called a **dictator.** A dictator was supposed to give up his power after the danger was over. Now, however, men began ruling Rome as dictators even when there was no war. They ruled until rivals overthrew or killed them.

Two military leaders, **Pompey** (PAHM•pee) and **Julius Caesar** (JOO•lee•us SEE•zur), became rivals for power. Pompey was a consul in Rome. Caesar was governor of the rich province of **Gaul** (GAWL), which included most of what is now France. In 49 B.C. the Senate, which supported Pompey, ordered Caesar to return to Rome. Caesar, knowing that he would probably be killed if he came by himself, brought an army with him. Pompey fled, first to Greece and then to Egypt, where an assassin killed him.

Twenty-three dagger thrusts from the senators of Rome left Caesar dead at the foot of Pompey's statue.

Caesar took control of Rome. He promised its war-weary people a return to honest, peaceful government. He promised land to the landless and grain to those who were hungry. He promised jobs to the city's poor. He was able to keep some of these promises.

In addition to his other reforms, Julius Caesar redesigned the calendar. His calendar, which was used for centuries, is closely related to the one we use today. The month of July is named after Julius Caesar.

A number of Roman nobles, including some men who had been Caesar's friends, did not trust him. They feared he would make himself king. Claiming that they were restoring liberty to the Roman people, they killed Julius Caesar in 44 B.C.

Reading Check

1. How was the form of government of the Roman Republic different from Greek democracy?
2. With which North African city-state did Rome fight three wars?
3. How did leadership of the Republic change during times of war?
4. Who was the governor of Gaul who took control of Rome?

147

Look for these important words:

Key Words
- civil war
- aqueducts
- *Pax Romana*
- legions

People
- Augustus Caesar
- Constantine
- Justinian

Places
- Constantinople
- Byzantine Empire

Look for answers to these questions:

1. Why was the reign of Augustus called the Golden Age of Rome?
2. How did people in the Roman Empire benefit from Rome's government?
3. Why did the Roman Empire's power decline?
4. How and where was Roman civilization preserved after the fall of Rome?

2. THE ROMAN EMPIRE

With Caesar gone, the Roman Republic came to an end. Caesar's followers and enemies quarreled violently with each other. **Civil war,** war among opposing groups of citizens, broke out once more. However, the winners of this war proved strong enough to bind Roman lands together. They were led by Octavian (ahk•TAY•vee•uhn), Caesar's grandnephew and adopted son. Caesar had chosen Octavian as his heir when Octavian was 19 years old. Over a period of 17 years Octavian defeated all opposition to his rule. In 27 B.C. he became head of the Roman Empire.

Augustus Caesar

Octavian ruled Rome and all the lands under its control for 41 years. He took the title **Augustus** (aw•GUS•tus) **Caesar.** Augustus means "respected one." After his death, Augustus was worshipped as a god.

Augustus was the first emperor of Rome, but he did not call himself emperor. He held only offices that had existed in the Roman Republic. Yet, he held these offices year after year and held several of them at one time. He also controlled the Roman armies. Every soldier swore loyalty to him alone.

Augustus brought peace and good government to Rome. He carefully chose people to fill government jobs. Some jobs were given to trusted freedmen or to slaves from his household. Some were held by merchants and other businesspeople. Augustus made sure that lands throughout the empire were run by experienced governors and that taxes were fair.

THE CITY OF ROME, ABOUT A.D. 350

1. Aqueduct of Nero
2. Aurelian Wall
3. Baths of Caracalla
4. Basilica of Maxentius
5. Temple of Venus and Roma
6. Arch of Constantine
7. Colosseum
8. Temple of Claudius
9. Temple of Jupiter Victor
10. Palace of Septimus Severus
11. Circus Maximus
12. Tiber River

Augustus made improvements in Rome itself. He once said, "I found Rome brick and left it marble." Among the new buildings he ordered built were government offices, public baths, and libraries. These building projects provided jobs for the city's people while making Rome more beautiful.

Augustus also encouraged literature and art. Some of Rome's finest literature was written during his time. Later, Romans referred to the reign of Augustus Caesar, which lasted from 27 B.C. to A.D. 14, as the "Golden Age of Rome."

The *Pax Romana*

Unlike Augustus, the emperors who followed him made no secret of their complete power. The Senate did not dare to argue with them. Some emperors used their power wisely. Others were foolish and cruel. The system of Roman government was so strong, however, that it worked fairly well even during the reigns of bad emperors.

Under the emperor Trajan (TRAY·jun), around A.D. 117, the Roman Empire reached its greatest size. It measured about 2½ million square miles (about 6½ million sq km). It extended from Britain and Spain through what is now France, southern Germany, and the Balkan lands. The empire reached into Asia as far as the Caspian Sea. It included most of the Middle East and North Africa as far south as the Sahara.

Taxes and trade from the many lands of the empire made Rome incredibly rich. In return, Rome gave many benefits to the lands it governed. It gave them new public buildings and great water-carrying systems called aqueducts (AK·wuh·dukts). Rome also provided 50,000 miles (80,000 km) of paved, well-kept roads. Soldiers and traders alike traveled along these roads. So did the carriers of a postal service, first set up by Augustus.

Rome's greatest gift to the people of its empire was the **Pax Romana** (PAKS roh·MAH·nah), or "Peace of Rome." This peace, which began with the reign of Augustus, lasted over 200 years in most parts of the empire. The powerful Roman army maintained the *Pax Romana*. This well-trained, professional army was divided into large units called **legions** (LEE·junz). Each legion might have as many as 6,000 soldiers. Forts manned by Roman soldiers protected the provinces from the attacks of tribes who lived in the wild lands beyond the empire.

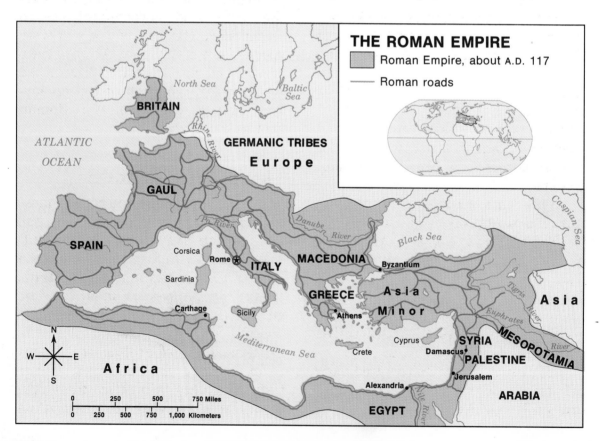

THE ROMAN EMPIRE

- Roman Empire, about A.D. 117
- Roman roads

The Pont du Gard, the greatest of all Roman aqueducts, was built at Nimes in southern France. Along the top level of its arches, water is carried 180 feet (54 m) above the river.

The Fall of Rome

As the Roman Empire grew larger, it became harder to control. Many of the empire's citizens had never seen Rome. They felt little loyalty to it. Interest in holding the empire together declined even in the city of Rome itself. Because so many emperors governed badly, the Romans lost their respect for the emperors and for the Roman Empire.

In the time of the emperor Marcus Aurelius (aw•REE•lee•us), about A.D. 170, the Roman Empire began to feel strong pressure against its borders. Invaders from the north attacked Gaul and Spain. The Persian Empire tried to conquer Roman lands in Asia. African people called Berbers (BUR•burz) raided Roman lands in North Africa.

Defending the empire required more and more soldiers and weapons. Governing it required more and better government officials. Rising costs for the army and government caused rising taxes. The price of food and other goods also rose sharply. Attacks from outside, rising taxes and prices, bad government, and lack of citizen loyalty helped to cause the Roman Empire's collapse.

The Survival of Rome

The Romans were tolerant of most religions. Christianity, however, was one religion they tried to stamp out. The Christians refused to worship the Roman emperor as a god. Christians criticized much about Roman life. The emperors mistreated the Christians because they were afraid that the Christians would rebel against them.

In spite of mistreatment, Christians continued to practice their religion. Christianity spread through the

151

empire. In A.D. 312, a Roman emperor named **Constantine** (KAHN•stuhn•teen) became a Christian. Forty-three years later Christianity became the state religion of Rome.

Constantine established a new capital for the Roman Empire. He chose the city of Byzantium (bih•ZAN•tee•uhm), in Asia Minor. He hoped this city would be safe from the invaders who were attacking Rome. Later Byzantium became known by a new name: **Constantinople** (kahn•stan•tuh•NOH•puhl), the city of Constantine. Constantinople became the official capital of the Roman Empire in A.D. 330.

Every year, the attacking bands of northern invaders came closer to Rome. Finally, in A.D. 410, a group called the Visigoths (VIZ•uh•gahths) overran the city. In A.D. 476 a German chief named Odoacer (oh•doh•AY•sur) made himself emperor of Rome. He was the first emperor to come from outside the empire.

The city of Rome lived on, but it no longer had much power. The empire broke up into small kingdoms. Rome remained an important religious center, however, for it was the headquarters of the Roman Catholic Church.

Roman civilization survived for centuries in the eastern empire that Constantine had ruled. This empire was called the **Byzantine** (BIZ•uhn•teen) **Empire**. It covered Greece, the Balkan lands, and Asia Minor. The Byzantine Empire lasted until 1453.

The people of the Byzantine Empire thought of themselves as Romans. They wanted to remember the greatness of Rome. They patterned their homes and other buildings after those in Rome. Around A.D. 530 a Byzantine emperor

This Byzantine mosaic of Justinian is at Ravenna, an ancient Roman city.

named **Justinian** (jus•TIN•ee•un) ordered the writing of a law code that preserved and added to the old Roman codes. Over the years, however, the Byzantine Empire mixed Roman culture with the cultures of Greece and Asia. The civilization of ancient Rome gradually disappeared.

Reading Check

1. During whose rule did Rome's Golden Age occur?
2. How did the *Pax Romana* affect life in the Roman Empire?
3. Why were the Roman army and its leaders important?
4. Which city became the capital of the empire ruled by Constantine?

152

Look for these important words:

Key Words	People	Places
• atrium	• Cicero	• Forum
• census	• Vergil	• Colosseum
• Romance languages		• Baths of Caracalla
• concrete		• Pantheon

Look for answers to these questions:

1. What was daily life like in ancient Rome?
2. How have Roman achievements in law and government affected the Western world today?
3. What did the Romans achieve in language, literature, and art?
4. What examples of Roman building and engineering exist today?

3. THE ROMAN WAY OF LIFE

The republic and empire of ancient Rome lasted about 1,000 years. Rome's influence on Europe lasted far longer than that. Roman building methods, Roman ideas about government and law, and words from the Roman language, Latin, are still important in the Western world.

The Streets of Rome

Ancient Rome had many things we would recognize today. It had take-out food, multistoried apartment buildings, and recreation centers. It also had air pollution, crowded streets, and unemployment.

The **Forum** was Rome's main square. In its center was the Golden Milestone, the point from which all roads began and were measured. There, too, was the meeting place of the Roman Senate, along with other government buildings, temples, and shops. Senators, priests, and businesspeople strolled in the Forum and discussed the events of the day.

Romans also gathered at the public baths. These huge building complexes had different rooms for hot baths, cold baths, and massages. They had libraries, gymnasiums, halls for lectures and entertainments, and many shops.

Shops also lined the streets of Rome. Some sold raw meat and vegetables. Some had food that was cooked and ready to eat. Craft workers sold sandals, cloth, and pottery. Booksellers had copies of the latest books written on scrolls of Egyptian papyrus. Roman shopkeepers sold many goods from Egypt, Spain, and other distant parts of the empire.

Home and Family Life

Poorer Romans lived in apartment buildings several stories high. A whole family often lived in one or two rooms. Terrible fires sometimes swept through these crowded buildings.

The home of a wealthy Roman was built around an inner courtyard called an **atrium** (AY·tree·um). The home's outside walls had no windows. A home included bedrooms, slaves' quarters, and a large hall.

Roman life centered around the family. The father held authority over the family. According to Roman law, he had the power of life and death over his wife and children. In fact, however, women in Rome had more freedom than women in ancient Greece. They entertained guests with their husbands. They often helped in business. Slaves did the housework in many homes.

Girls as well as boys in wealthy Roman families received an elementary education from slave teachers, who were often Greeks. Between the ages of 12 and 18, boys went to school to learn Greek and Latin literature, history, geography, and other subjects. Girls were educated at home. Many girls received training in music, literature, and philosophy as well as in household management. Children from poor families also were educated during their early years. However, they did not receive a higher education. Boys usually went to work after age 12.

On holidays Roman families might attend public ceremonies honoring the "great gods." The Roman gods and goddesses were nearly the same as the Greek ones, but they had different names. Other spirits were also important to Romans. The father of each family made frequent offerings to the household spirits and the spirits of the family's ancestors. The Romans believed that these spirits protected their homes. Roman emperors also were worshipped as gods.

Law and Government

Many laws of Europe and the United States can be traced to the written collections or codes of Roman law. Roman law said, for example, that a person is innocent until proved guilty. It also said that during a trial people cannot be forced to speak against themselves.

The Roman Republic helped develop the idea of representative government. Rome was too large to be governed by gatherings of all its citizens as Athens had been. Instead, citizens chose officials to make decisions for them.

Augustus and the emperors who followed him appointed people to carry out the system of Roman government throughout the empire. At its best, this system placed government in the hands of intelligent, carefully trained people. The governors of Roman provinces were responsible for the fair treatment under Roman law of citizens and noncitizens alike. In order to control taxes, these governors were also responsible for taking a **census,** or population count.

Language and the Arts

The Romans spread the Latin language to all parts of their empire. Latin became the basis for modern French, Spanish, and Italian. These Latin-based languages are called the **Romance languages.** Latin also contributed

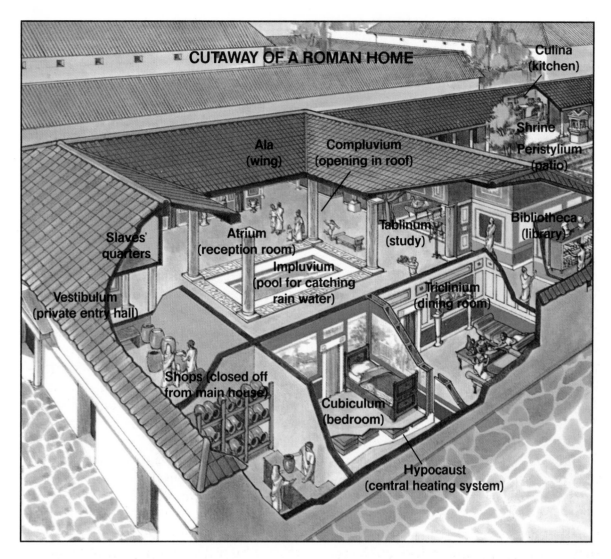

CUTAWAY OF A ROMAN HOME

Culina (kitchen)

Shrine

Peristylium (patio)

Ala (wing)

Compluvium (opening in roof)

Bibliotheca (library)

Tablinum (study)

Slaves' quarters

Atrium (reception room)

Impluvium (pool for catching rain water)

Triclinium (dining room)

Vestibulum (private entry hall)

Shops (closed off from main house)

Cubiculum (bedroom)

Hypocaust (central heating system)

many words to English, German, and other European languages that are not Romance languages.

You may recall that the Greeks borrowed their alphabet from the Phoenicians. This Greek alphabet was then borrowed and changed by the Romans. Today we use the alphabet of the ancient Romans with the addition of *J, U,* and *W.*

Roman writers carefully recorded the history and manners of their own day and of previous times. One such writer, **Cicero** (SIS•uh•roh), is read and quoted today. His letters, speeches, and poems told about Roman life during the Republic. Roman writing often imitated Greek literature. A Roman poet named **Vergil** (VUR•juhl), for example, wrote an epic similar to those of Homer. Vergil's poem, the *Aeneid* (ih•NEE•uhd), tells the legend of the founding of Rome by Aeneas.

Roman art also imitated Greek art. Roman art, however, was more lifelike. It showed portraits of actual men and women rather than of gods and goddesses. While Greek art emphasized beauty and perfection, Roman art showed people as they really looked.

Buildings and Engineering

Some of Rome's best achievements were in the construction of buildings. The ruins of huge structures such as the **Colosseum** (kahl•uh•SEE•um) and the **Baths of Caracalla** (kahr•uh•KAL•uh) can be seen in Rome today. Wherever the Romans went, they built. Ruins of their buildings are found all over Europe from Great Britain to Turkey.

The Romans learned the use of the arch from the Etruscans. The Romans used crossed arches to support huge half-spheres, or domes. One of the largest domed Roman buildings is the **Pantheon** (PAN•thee•ahn), a temple for all the gods and goddesses.

Long, straight roads connected most parts of the Roman Empire. These roads allowed the quick movement of Roman legions throughout the empire. Most Roman roads were sloped on each side so that water would drain off the roads. Roman roads provided not only good transportation routes but also jobs. Many people were needed to build and repair them. These roads were among Rome's greatest engineering feats.

Roman sewers and aqueducts also were very well constructed. Roman roads and buildings were often made of **concrete.** Concrete is made from sand or gravel bound together with cement. This Roman invention is still widely used in building.

Light pours through the opening in the dome of the Pantheon, built in A.D. 125.

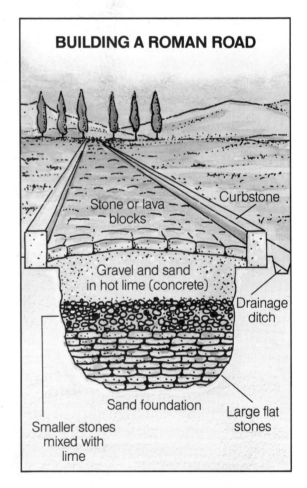

BUILDING A ROMAN ROAD

Stone or lava blocks

Curbstone

Gravel and sand in hot lime (concrete)

Drainage ditch

Sand foundation

Smaller stones mixed with lime

Large flat stones

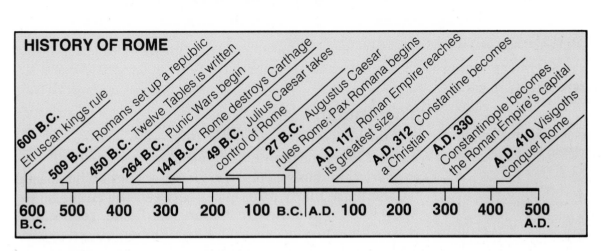

HISTORY OF ROME

600 B.C. Etruscan kings rule

509 B.C. Romans set up a republic

450 B.C. Twelve Tables is written

264 B.C. Punic Wars begin

144 B.C. Rome destroys Carthage

49 B.C. Julius Caesar takes control of Rome

27 B.C. Augustus Caesar rules Rome; Pax Romana begins

A.D. 117 Roman Empire reaches its greatest size

A.D. 312 Constantine becomes a Christian

A.D. 330 Constantinople becomes the Roman Empire's capital

A.D. 410 Visigoths conquer Rome

600 B.C. | 500 | 400 | 300 | 200 | 100 | B.C. | A.D. | 100 | 200 | 300 | 400 | 500 A.D.

The Gifts of Ancient Rome

The imaginative Greeks explored and questioned almost everything in heaven and on Earth. They loved to argue. They wanted to find out hidden truths. The early Romans were a more practical people. They believed in a few simple values: justice, honesty, valor, loyalty to family and to Rome. They wanted to set up a dependable system for living and governing. They succeeded amazingly well.

The Romans preserved and spread the ideas of Greek and other cultures to distant parts of Europe. Roman roads, Roman trade, and, above all, Roman peace allowed people, goods, and ideas to move freely over an enormous area.

Long after Rome's empire collapsed, Europe went on using Roman customs and writing forms of the Roman language. Roman ideas of fair law and dependable government worked deep into European culture.

The Appian Way was the first of many paved roads extending from Rome.

Reading Check

1. What kinds of activities occurred in the Roman Forum?
2. How was the lifestyle of wealthy people different from the lifestyle of poor people in Rome?
3. What is the name for languages based on Latin?
4. What substance was used in the construction of Roman roads and buildings?

157

The Roman Circus

Hurry, hurry, hurry! See the greatest show in the ancient Roman Empire! See charioteers race to the finish in chariots of many colors! See gladiators fight wild beasts!

There are many differences between the circus as we know it today and the circus of ancient Rome. Yet because it was built around an arena, the Roman circus is generally considered the forerunner of modern circuses.

The Roman circus was mainly a race course. Charioteers raced chariots pulled by two, three, and sometimes four highly trained horses. Charioteers were honored much like our superstar athletes of today. Many earned as much or more money in one year as Roman senators.

The Roman circuses were huge sports arenas. The *Circus Maximus,* for example, held as many as 385,000 people. It was about 20 times the size of an American football field and had 80 doorways. Julius Caesar had Circus Maximus built for the enjoyment of all the people of Rome. A Roman political figure could increase his popularity if he proposed building a sports arena for the people. Admission to the Circus Maximus was free.

Another arena called the Colosseum was slightly different from the circus. The Colosseum was a smaller structure but was capable of housing and producing spectacular events for about 50,000 people. The public had to pay for admission to the Colosseum. For a few *sesterces* (pennies), Romans could see trained fighters called **gladiators** (GLAD•ee•ayt•uhrz) fighting each other or fighting such wild animals as lions, leopards, and tigers. Sometimes the floor of the Colosseum was flooded so that water sports and boat pageants could be held.

Roman charioteers

By A.D. 300 the Romans had as many as 175 holidays a year. On those days, government offices and most businesses were closed. A good portion of the population would attend the games at the Circus Maximus or the Colosseum. Late in Rome's history its emperors thought that the people would remain content and peaceful if they were given two things—bread and circuses.

Beneath the Colosseum's floor are dozens of small rooms where wild animals or gladiators were housed before a contest.

Though much of its shell has been damaged by lightning and earthquakes, the Colosseum remains one of Rome's most impressive structures.

SKILLS FOR SUCCESS

Special sources of information exist to help you find out about many different subjects. You may recall that such reference books are found in most libraries. Knowing which reference books to use and how they are organized can help you locate specific information easily.

Using Encyclopedias

An encyclopedia contains articles, or **entries,** on thousands of subjects. The entries are arranged alphabetically. Some encyclopedias have all entries in a single volume, but most encyclopedias are made up of 20 or more numbered or lettered volumes. Often you can find basic information by looking up a subject in the proper volume. For example, an article on the Roman ruler Julius Caesar would appear in the volume marked *C-Ch* because the first letter of Caesar comes between *C* and *Ch* alphabetically. People are listed alphabetically by their last names.

Sometimes the information you need appears in several articles. Suppose you want to learn about structures built by the ancient Romans. To locate these entries, you should use the encyclopedia **index.** The index usually appears in the final volume of the encyclopedia. Look at the following index listings.

> **Rome, Ancient**
> *See also* Roman Empire *in this index*
> *Art and architecture*
>   Arch **A:555**
>   Colosseum **Ci:684**
>   Pantheon **P:111**

Entries are listed alphabetically in the index. In this example related subjects are listed under the general heading *Rome, Ancient. Art and architecture* is the first related subject. Look at the listings for this subject. For each listing the letters before the colon tell you which volume to find. (In some encyclopedia indexes, a volume number is used instead of a letter.) The number after the colon tells on which page in the volume the article appears. For example, an article on the *arch* in Roman architecture begins on page 555 of Volume A. Where would you look to find out about the Colosseum of Rome?

The general entry for the subject of ancient Rome contains a **cross-reference.** A cross-reference tells you where to look in the index for related information. In this example the entry says to look under *Roman Empire* for more information.

An encyclopedia helps this student prepare her social studies report.

Using Almanacs

Encyclopedias take years to write and publish, so they are not always good sources of up-to-date information. If you need to know the current population of the city of Rome, for instance, you should look in an almanac rather than in an encyclopedia. Almanacs are collections of current facts and figures. Most almanacs are published every year.

General almanacs contain population figures for cities and countries throughout the world. They give production figures for major crops, amounts of rainfall in previous years, and names of world leaders. Some almanacs even have color drawings of flags of all nations.

Entries in an almanac are not arranged in alphabetical order. You must use the **general index** to find on which page an entry appears. In an almanac the general index is often at the front, like a table of contents. Here is part of an almanac index.

Italy **550-551**, 605, 727, 733, 738, 739	
Cities (population) 550, 605-606	
Earthquakes (1980) 919	
Petroleum production 130	

Almanacs list many interesting facts.

The first line in the example tells you the pages where Italy is mentioned. The first page numbers given are usually where the main body of information about Italy can be found. In this case, a summary of facts about Italy is on pages 550 and 551. Suppose you want to know whether the earthquake in 1980 affected buildings in Rome. The general index tells you that you can look on page 919 to find out. On which page would you find information on petroleum production in Italy?

Using Periodicals

Articles about current events can be found in periodicals. Newspapers and magazines usually appear daily, weekly, or monthly. They contain articles on a variety of subjects. For example, a magazine or newspaper article might give you information about which Roman ruins are being restored this year. A periodical usually has a table of contents that lists page numbers for the articles it contains.

When you need to know which magazine has an article on the subject in which you are interested, the **Readers' Guide to**

Periodicals have current information.

Periodical Literature can help you. It lists magazine articles by subject. It gives the name and issue date of every magazine that has an article on a particular subject. It also gives page numbers of each article. Look at the *Readers' Guide* listing below.

```
ROME (city)          Antiquities
Saving Italy's ruins from ruin.
P. Hofmann. il Art News 80:78-85 Mr '81
```

Entries are listed alphabetically by subject. In this example the subject listing is *Rome*. The listing tells you the name of the article, "Saving Italy's Ruins from Ruin," and the author, P. Hofmann. The article appeared in the magazine titled *Art News*. The volume number is 80, and the article is on pages 78 to 85. The date of publication is March, 1981. The *il* in the entry means illustrated.

Other Sources of Information

Two other sources of information are dictionaries and atlases. There are special dictionaries of sports, music, biographies, foreign languages, and other subjects. Since entries are arranged alphabetically, you must know what you are looking for.

Atlases give details about world geography.

Atlases are collections of maps. For example, **political atlases** contain maps showing boundaries of counties, states, or nations. **Geographic atlases** contain maps showing such geographical features as population, rainfall, natural resources, industries, roads, and railways. **Historical atlases** contain maps that show the world at different times in the past. Map titles in an atlas are listed in its table of contents. You can look in the index of an atlas to find the location of a city, river, or other feature. Since boundaries and names may change, it is important to check the copyright date of an atlas to be sure that it is current.

A good place to get information on a country is from its **consulate,** or foreign office. For example, you could write to the Italian Consulate in New York City and ask for information about ancient Roman structures in Italy. Most nations have one or more consulates in the United States. A telephone directory of a large city may be able to give you addresses of foreign consulates, or you can request help from a librarian.

CHECKING YOUR SKILLS

Where would you look to find the following information?

1. How the ancient Romans constructed roads.

2. The amount of rain that fell on Rome last year.

3. How to get permission from the Italian government to visit Italy as a tourist.

4. An important discovery about ancient Rome made two months ago.

5. How to say *hotel* in Italian.

6. The boundaries of the Roman Empire in A.D. 117.

CHAPTER 5 REVIEW

USING WORDS

Use the words below to complete the sentences in the paragraphs that follow.

consuls   patricians   tribunes
dictator   plebeians   Twelve Tables
Forum   republic   veto
legions

The Roman __(1)__ was a form of representative government. Two classes of people participated. The __(2)__ were wealthy nobles. From the Senate they chose two __(3)__ to lead the government. The __(4)__ were commoners. Although they appointed __(5)__ to represent them, they had less influence in government. In times of war the Romans followed only one leader, called a __(6)__ .

Government officials met regularly in buildings located in the Roman __(7)__ . There, too, were posted the __(8)__ , which stated the laws that applied to all Roman citizens. When laws were being decided, a tribune could protest a law by shouting, "__(9)__ ." Laws adopted by Rome were enforced in the provinces by __(10)__ of Roman soldiers.

REVIEWING FACTS

1. Which two groups from central Italy developed the city of Rome?

2. In what ways did the plebeians improve their rights as Roman citizens?

3. How were the lands of the Roman Empire governed?

4. Why was Julius Caesar killed?

5. What benefits did Rome give to people in the empire?

6. Give three reasons for the collapse of the Roman Empire.

7. What two important changes did Constantine make?

8. How was Rome like cities of today?

9. Which culture did Roman writers and artists often imitate?

10. What evidence of Roman culture is found today?

THINKING CRITICALLY

1. Discuss as many ways as you can think of that roads contributed to the success of the Roman Empire. What forms of transportation are important today?

2. During the *Pax Romana* Rome reached the peak of its development. How do you think peace contributed to Rome's development?

⬤ PRACTICING SKILLS

Reference Books   Pompeii was an ancient Italian city buried after an eruption of the volcano Vesuvius. Name three different kinds of reference books that might help you prepare a report on Pompeii or volcanoes. Briefly describe the purpose of each reference book. The skills lesson on pages 160–162 will help you.

The Middle Ages Brings Changes to Europe

The fall of the Roman Empire marked the end of the ancient Western world. Europe changed greatly over the next thousand years. At first, with no central government to keep the peace, West Europeans huddled in farms and villages. They tried simply to stay alive. Later as new ways of governing, farming, and making war replaced old ways, Europeans began to set up powerful kingdoms. Cities grew in importance. Religion and trade reached new heights. Today we call this period from about 500 to 1500 the **Middle Ages.**

Look for these important words:

Key Words
- Germanic tribes
- chieftains
- Pope
- scholars
- Vikings

- plunder
- shrines
- Turks
- crusaders
- Crusades

People
- Charlemagne
- Pope Urban II

Places
- Holy Roman Empire

Look for answers to these questions:

1. What peoples from northern Europe took over the Roman Empire?
2. Why is Charlemagne considered a great ruler?
3. Who were the Vikings?
4. How did the Crusades change European thinking?

1. A TIME OF WARS

By the beginning of the sixth century, peoples from northern Europe had taken over the Roman Empire. Because many of these groups began in or near what is now Germany, they are called the **Germanic** (jer•MAN•ik) **tribes.** Five Germanic tribes controlled most of Europe.

The Visigoths (VIZ•uh•gahths), who had conquered Rome, held most of the Iberian Peninsula, where Spain now is located. The Vandals controlled North Africa and the large Mediterranean islands. The Ostrogoths (AHS•truh•gahths) had taken over most of Italy and the western Balkans. The Saxons conquered the southern part of what is now England. The Franks controlled much of the Roman province of Gaul, now France and western Germany.

The Germanic tribes did not govern these large areas as single countries. Each tribe had many leaders, called **chieftains.** Each chieftain ruled only as much land as his warriors could defend. The Germanic tribes spread fear and destruction at first. Gradually, however, they learned the ways of their more civilized neighbors. Chieftains often preserved or imitated Roman forms of government. Many Germanic people became Christians. They brought new life to the lands of a dying empire.

Charlemagne

The man who came closest to recreating the Roman Empire during the early Middle Ages looked every bit the king he was. In a time when most warriors were a little over 5 feet (1.5 m) tall, he was 6 feet 4 inches (1.9 m). His broad shoulders and straight posture seemed to show his strong will.

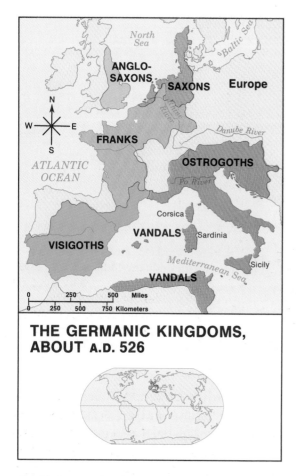

THE GERMANIC KINGDOMS, ABOUT A.D. 526

The king's name was **Charlemagne** (SHAHR·luh·mayn). The name means "Charles the Great." In 768 he became king of the Franks, the tribe that gave France its name. Later, Charlemagne conquered large parts of Germany and Italy.

Charlemagne had close ties with the leader of the Roman Catholic Church, the **Pope.** Both Charlemagne and his father had helped popes defend Rome. In 800 Pope Leo III crowned Charlemagne as the head of lands later called the **Holy Roman Empire** and gave him the title of "Augustus."

In Charlemagne's time, very few people could read and write. Most of those who could were priests. A few were **scholars,** or learned people, who worked for kings or nobles. Charlemagne respected learning. He encouraged scholars from all over Europe to come to his court. He set up schools for his nobles and their sons. He urged

On Christmas Day in A.D. 800, Charlemagne became "Emperor of the West." He united most of Western Europe for the first time in 400 years.

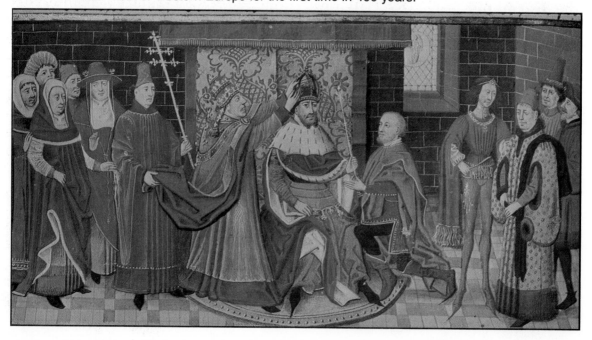

166

This sleek Viking ship is similar to those that raided European coasts. Used for the burial of a ninth-century Norwegian queen, the vessel still shows its detailed carvings.

priests throughout his empire to teach "all those who with God's help are able to learn."

Charlemagne had a strong desire to rule fairly. He dictated many letters to his nobles, giving them instructions about government, law, religion, education, and trade. He sent royal messengers to find out how well his government was working. Charlemagne also traveled around his lands to make sure his people were treated justly.

Once or twice a year Charlemagne met with his major officials. Spring meetings called the Fields of May became famous. They were festivals for Charlemagne's followers. In a pasture filled with flowers, Charlemagne set up a small city of tents and consulted with his officials. In his concern for strong, wise government, Charlemagne was like Augustus, the emperor of Rome. Charlemagne's peaceful rule was the high point of the early Middle Ages.

The Vikings

Before Charlemagne's death in 814, fierce warriors called **Vikings** (VY. kingz) threatened the security of his empire. The Vikings came from the north, from Norway, Sweden, and Denmark.

At first the Vikings were interested mostly in **plunder,** or goods taken by force. They sailed along coasts and far up European rivers in their dragon-headed ships. Wearing leather helmets, the Vikings carried double-edged swords and round shields. These sailors were so tough that they slept on the open decks of their ships even in the freezing storms of the North Sea.

When the Vikings arrived at a town, they usually attacked its church first. They took religious objects made of gold and silver. Then they raided the homes of the townspeople and the outlying farms. Europeans often said this prayer before going to sleep: "From the fury of the Northmen, O Lord, deliver us!"

By the middle of the tenth century, raids became fewer as the Vikings developed other interests. Some Vikings became traders, sailing as far as Constantinople and what is now Russia. They contributed a knowledge of trade routes and sailing to the people they met. Some Vikings were explorers. They sailed to North America about 500 years before Christopher Columbus. Other Vikings became colonists, setting up farms and towns in the countries they formerly had attacked. Many of them became Christians.

The Vikings, like the Germanic tribes before them, became part of Europe's settled communities. The Vikings both enriched and were absorbed by the lands they raided.

The Crusades

Pope Urban II stared in amazement at the crowd in the town square of Clermont, France, one day in 1095. He saw far more people than he had expected. Not just nobles and armed warriors, but common people, too—men, women, and children—had gathered to hear his words.

Pope Urban spoke to the crowd about the city of Jerusalem and other Christian **shrines,** or holy places, in the Middle East. Many Christians had journeyed to these sacred sites. Now Jerusalem and the other holy places were in the hands of the Muslim **Turks.**

The Turks were a mountain people who had been slaves of the Arabs until about the year 1000. Then they began to rebel. Soon they managed to capture

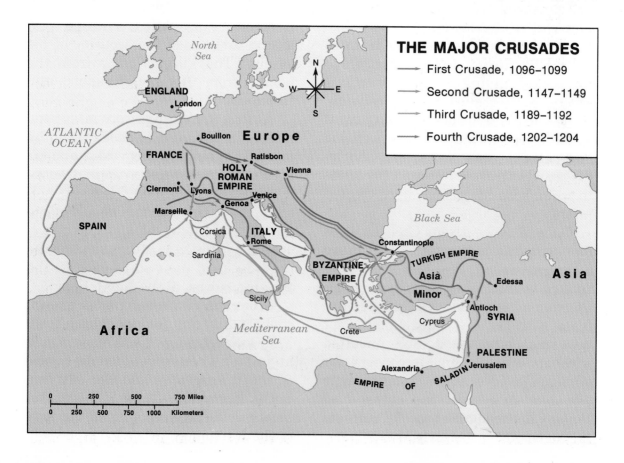

In the Children's Crusade, 30,000 children marched to France's coast.
Later, betrayed by ships' captains, they were sold at slave markets.

the entire Arab Empire, including Jerusalem. In that holy city they neglected ancient shrines and prevented Christians from visiting them. The Turks often robbed or even killed Christian visitors.

Jerusalem, Urban said, must be freed from the Turks. The Christian empire of Byzantium also needed help in fighting these "unbelievers." Who would go to war for this holy cause?

"God wills it! God wills it!" thousands of voices shouted. Noble and peasant alike vowed on the spot to rescue Jerusalem and Byzantium from the Turks. The excited volunteers tore strips of cloth from their cloaks. They pinned the cloth strips to their tunics in the shape of a cross. Because these people "took the cross" as their sign,

they were called **crusaders** (kroo. SAYD.urz). The wars they fought were called **Crusades.**

There were eight major Crusades between 1095 and 1291. Some Crusades were People's Crusades. Whole families left their homes and set out for the Middle East. Not only French but also English, German, and Italian crusaders marched to battle. Even two armies of children took up arms and set out for the Holy Land in what became known as the Children's Crusades. Most of these children died of hunger and sickness or were captured and sold into slavery before they ever saw Jerusalem.

The skilled warriors of the larger Crusades had better luck. They captured Jerusalem in 1099 and held

Crusaders stormed Jerusalem's walls in 1099. Paved streets and comfortable homes were new to the Europeans, who came from simple villages.

it until 1187. They also took other Middle Eastern lands away from the Muslims. In the thirteenth century, however, the Muslims reclaimed these lands.

The Crusades changed European thinking even more than they changed Middle Eastern land ownership. Some crusaders gained a new respect for the Muslims. They found that the best of the Muslim leaders were civilized, educated men. The crusaders even developed a taste for many parts of Muslim culture. Crusaders learned to season their food with Eastern spices. They began to dress in silk clothing.

When they returned home, taking Eastern goods with them, a demand for such goods grew in Europe. This demand encouraged the growth of trade, which helped cities to grow.

Reading Check

1. What groups took over most of Europe after the fall of the Roman Empire?
2. Which king's rule was the high point of the early Middle Ages?
3. Why did Europeans fear the Vikings?
4. Why were the Crusades fought?

Look for these important words:

Key Words
- feudalism
- vassals
- fiefs

- serfs
- manor
- knights

- page
- squire
- chivalry

Look for answers to these questions:

1. How did people gain protection from danger in the Middle Ages?
2. How did peasants live during the Middle Ages?
3. How did nobles live during the Middle Ages?
4. How were noble warriors of the Middle Ages trained?

2. LIFE ON FARM AND MANOR

Most people in the first half of the Middle Ages lived in constant danger of attack by Vikings, bandits, or warriors from neighboring kingdoms. Because of this danger, a system grew up in which strong people protected weaker ones. In return for this protection, the weaker people gave loyalty, farm labor, and military service. The following story shows how a farmer may have felt about this system.

Loyalty and Protection

Kneeling, Boniface (BAHN•uh•fuhs) clasped his hands as if in prayer. He looked up at the lord who stood over him. The lord was dressed in a fine purple jacket, black knee breeches, and leather slippers. Boniface wore a loose tunic. He placed his clasped hands inside the lord's open palms. Next, placing his right hand on a Bible, Boniface said, "Whatever in life I do, I swear to be thy man. Thou art my lord."

The lord gave Boniface a clod of earth. The earth represented Boniface's small farm. When Boniface swore his oath, he gave the ownership of the farm to the lord in return for the lord's protection. By giving Boniface the clod of earth, the lord granted him the right to farm the land. The lord now owned the land, but Boniface thought this was a small price to pay for security. He knew that he, his wife, and their two children would be safer as part of a larger, stronger group.

When Boniface returned home, his wife and children were waiting anxiously. "Things will be different now," Boniface promised them. "I have sworn for the lord. Let Vikings or bandits come. We will be ready!"

Feudalism

The system of loyalties and protections in the Middle Ages was called **feudalism** (FYOOD•uhl•izm). It began

171

around 800 and lasted until about 1300. Feudalism can be pictured as a pyramid. Everyone owed loyalty and service to a king, who was at the top of the pyramid.

Below the king came powerful noble families, who controlled most of the land. Lesser nobles, called **vassals,** owed loyalty to the more powerful nobles. In return for military service, the nobles and kings gave the vassals gifts of land. These lands were called **fiefs** (FEEFS).

At the bottom of the pyramid were the peasants, who farmed the land. Some owned their small farms. Many others were **serfs,** who lived and worked on land belonging to nobles or to the Church. Serfs were treated only slightly better than slaves. Their lord could not sell them or give them to someone else, but the serfs were not free. They had to stay on the land all their lives, no matter which lord owned the land.

Life in a Village

Most villages in the Middle Ages were very small. About 200 or 300 people, mainly peasants, lived in each village. Villages were located on a **manor** (MAN•uhr), a large estate or farm belonging to a noble family. Most villagers never traveled from the manor.

The only two large buildings on most medieval manors were the manor house, where the lord and his family lived, and the church. A village usually included the homes of peasants, a mill, barns, fields, and a pasture for the villagers' livestock. Woods often surrounded a village and its lands.

Peasants lived in small cottages made of mud and straw plastered over a timber frame. The roof was made of hay twisted into bundles. The floors were dirt. There were usually two windows covered with oiled paper. The cottages were dark inside and smoky from cooking fires.

Villagers made almost everything they needed. Women wove cloth and sewed. Blacksmiths made farm tools and weapons. Carpenters built houses and furniture. Being able to make or trade for the things they needed, villagers seldom left the manor. Most peasants never traveled more than a short distance in their lifetimes.

Beginning around Charlemagne's time, new farming methods and tools helped villagers grow more food. The kind of plow the Romans had used was not strong enough to turn the heavy

FEUDAL SOCIETY

King

Powerful nobles

Loyalty and military aid

Land and protection

Lesser nobles (vassals)

Labor

Protection

Serfs

West field

Manor house

Common pasture

Church

Mill field

Village

Mill

South field

Meadow

A FEUDAL MANOR

soil of northern Europe. Now, however, farmers began to use an iron-tipped plow that dug deeply into the earth. Pulled by oxen, these new plows turned up rich soil over much larger areas of land. More land could be planted and harvested.

Instead of planting their fields the same way each year, farmers learned to divide their fields into three parts. They planted one part with wheat or other grain crops. They planted a second part with peas or beans. They left the third part unplanted.

Each year the planting in the fields was changed. The previous year's unplanted field was planted with wheat. The wheat field was planted with peas. The pea field was left empty. In this way the soil would not wear out.

Holidays were almost the only relief that the peasants had from their hard work. The biggest holidays came at key points in the seasons. There was Christmas in midwinter, for example, and Easter in spring. During the holidays the villagers sang, danced, or played a game something like football. Often the lord gave a great feast to which all the villagers were invited.

Manor and Castle

During most of the Middle Ages, nobles' manor houses were not much more comfortable than the cottages of serfs. Dogs pawed through dirty straw on the floors of the great hall. Cold drafts blew in through glassless windows.

During a raid, people went to their lords for protection. Bodiam castle was built in England in 1386 to resist French attacks.

If a lord lived in an area that was raided often, he might build a castle as well as a manor house. The central part of the castle was a thick-walled tower called the keep. People could store supplies in the keep and live there for months if necessary. An open courtyard lay outside the keep. The lord's warriors and their horses stayed there. Villagers could run to this courtyard if the village was attacked.

A high wall surrounded the keep and courtyard. Outside the wall was a deep, water-filled ditch called a moat. If the castle's defenders wanted to let someone in, they lowered a drawbridge.

Nobles led a richer life after the eleventh century. Wealthy families began to enjoy fine goods from the east. They dressed in silks, furs, and cloth embroidered with gold thread. They had great feasts. In fine weather they went hunting or boating.

Knights

Armored horsemen called **knights** became important in warfare after the middle of the eighth century. The training of knights was a major part of the lives of nobles. At the age of seven, a noble's son went to the home of another noble to begin training. First he became a **page.** He carried messages and waited on the lord's table. He learned to ride, to hunt with a falcon, and to use small swords.

At about age 15, the page became a **squire.** The squire was the servant of a knight at the lord's court. He helped the knight put on his armor. He took care of the knight's horse and weapons. In return, the knight taught him advanced fighting skills.

The squire became a knight at about age 21. He promised to fight for his lord, defend the Christian Church, and protect anyone who needed his help. In a special ceremony the lord tapped him on the shoulder with a sword. The young man was then a knight.

Knights became less useful in war during the late Middle Ages. Their armor became so heavy that they could not move easily. Trained foot soldiers fighting with spearlike pikes, crossbows, and powerful longbows easily defeated them.

Knights remained an important part of the nobility's social life, however. They fought fake battles at entertainments called tournaments (TOOR·nuh·munts). Nobles also enjoyed songs, poems, and stories about knights. The knights in the stories followed certain rules for honorable behavior. These rules were called the code of **chivalry** (SHIV·uhl·ree).

The code of chivalry said that knights should protect and honor women. Women in the Middle Ages were treated as helpless beings. They were simply possessions of their fathers or their husbands. Even noblewomen had few rights and little control over their lives.

Reading Check

1. What was the name of the system of loyalties that governed people in the Middle Ages?
2. Who ranked highest in Middle Age society? Who ranked lowest?
3. How did farming methods change during the Middle Ages?
4. How did the role of knights change during the late Middle Ages?

Armor

Soldiers, fighters, and knights during the Middle Ages wore many different kinds of armor. At first, armor consisted of specially treated leather worn on the legs, chest, and arms. It offered some protection but was no defense against blows from heavy metal swords.

Later, leather armor was combined with **chain mail.** Chain mail was a type of armor made of small loops of iron or steel. A suit of chain mail resembled a long shirt that was slit up the middle. In that way a soldier's legs could move while still being protected. While chain mail was almost as flexible as cloth or leather, it was also heavy. It was, however, effective against swords.

As time went on, another kind of metal armor replaced leather and chain mail. This armor fit the shape of a knight's body. Movable joints were fastened to the armor at the elbows, knees, hips, and ankles. This let the limbs move as they would normally. A horse and knight fully covered in metal armor acted as the "armored tank" of the Middle Ages.

Although this heavy metal armor could protect a mounted knight from the weapons of foot soldiers, it was awkward to wear. Sometimes armor weighed as much as 100 pounds (about 45 kg). Once a knight, with the help of his squires, completed the difficult task of putting the armor on, a device similar to a crane was needed to lift the knight onto his horse. If a heavily armored knight was knocked off his horse, he lay sprawled on the ground like a turtle on its back, helpless to turn over or defend himself.

Armor was very expensive and took a long time to make. Only the richest of knights and kings could afford to have a suit of armor. In some cases, the armor was only worn in ceremonies so that a knight could display his power, wealth, and strength. By the early 1400s, the armored knight had become too heavy, too slow, too expensive to equip, and too easy to defeat.

This French suit of armor is made of gold-covered steel and weighs 77 pounds (35 kg). It was worn in about 1600.

Look for these important words:

Key Words
- monks
- monasteries
- nuns
- convents

- clergy
- parchment
- Romanesque
- cathedrals
- Gothic

Places
- Paris
- Chartres

Look for answers to these questions:
1. What contributions did the Christian Church make to life in the Middle Ages?
2. What role did the Christian Church play in European politics?
3. How did different groups in a town contribute to building a large church?

3. THE CHURCH IN THE MIDDLE AGES

Every morning, noon, and evening, church bells rang over the villages of Europe. They summoned people to prayer. The bells became a way to tell people when to worship and when to work. They rang in a different way and much longer on Sunday or when there was an attack. If enemies were sighted, the bells called families in the distant fields to safety behind the walls of the manor.

The unity of Europe under the Roman Empire was replaced during the Middle Ages by a wider unity under the Christian Church. The idea of "Christendom" (KRIS•uhn•duhm)—the community of all Christians—was very important to the people of the time.

Monks, Nuns, and Priests

Christian unity was spread by men and women who gave their lives to religion. The religious life attracted people during the Middle Ages for different reasons. The Church was the only place where someone could get an education, for example. It was also one of the few places in which a peasant might escape a dreary life and even rise to power.

Some religious workers lived together in special communities. The men who did so were called **monks.** Their communities were **monasteries** (MAHN• uh•stair•eez). The women, who were called **nuns,** lived in **convents** (KAHN• vuhnts). Together with other religious workers monks and nuns made up the **clergy.**

A monastery or convent was like a small village. It had workshops, flower and vegetable gardens, pens for livestock, and places for sleeping, eating, and praying. Monasteries and convents often owned surrounding lands farmed by peasants and serfs just as feudal lords did.

177

This gold-ornamented prayer book was given to a duchess in 1345.

helpers lived among villagers and took care of the local churches.

The Christian Church of the Middle Ages was a worldly power as well as a religious power. It could crown kings, as Pope Leo III did with Charlemagne. It could send men to war, as Pope Urban II did when he started the first Crusade. High church officials often owned as much land as the richest noble families.

Sometimes church leaders and kings or nobles helped each other. Sometimes they were bitter rivals. In addition, Church leaders in Rome frequently disagreed with those in Constantinople. These rivalries weakened the Christian unity that the monks, nuns, and priests tried to maintain.

Monks kept many carefully-copied books safe from looting by invaders.

Many monasteries and convents had libraries and places for making books. Workers copied books by hand onto **parchment,** a paperlike material made from sheepskin. They decorated the pages with tiny paintings. Copying a book of average length took three or four months. The Bible might take a year or more. Most books copied by monks and nuns were religious works. However, they also preserved some Greek and Roman writings.

Monks and nuns helped their neighbors in many ways. Some ran hospitals or orphanages. Some gave travelers food and a place to sleep. Some taught school. Some left their communities and spread the Christian religion to distant lands. Not all religious workers lived in their own communities, however. Priests and their

Throughout Europe, towns competed to raise the tallest, grandest cathedrals. Some people spent their entire lives working to complete the projects.

Cathedrals

Because religion was so important to the people of the Middle Ages, most art dealt with religious subjects. The best art decorated the churches themselves.

During the eleventh and twelfth centuries, churches were built in a style of architecture called **Romanesque** (roh•muh•NESK). Romanesque churches had round-topped arches like those in Roman buildings. The thick walls and small windows of these churches made them seem dark inside. However, they were often beautifully decorated with paintings and gold objects covered with jewels.

New wealth, religious devotion, and town pride contributed to the building of great churches called **cathedrals** (kuh•THEE•druhlz). Many thirteenth-century cathedrals were built in a new

Marketplace, shelter, fairground, and place of worship, Chartres Cathedral and its vicinity was the center of town life in the Middle Ages.

style, called **Gothic** (GAHTH•ik). The arches in a Gothic cathedral were pointed on top rather than rounded. New ways of supporting the cathedral's heavy roof left large parts of its walls open for glass windows. Large, triple doors welcomed passersby.

Gothic cathedrals such as those in **Paris** and **Chartres** (SHAHRT), France, may be the finest achievements of art in the Middle Ages. The cathedrals' tall stone towers and pointed arches reach toward the sky like praying hands. Their stained-glass windows show stories from the Bible in jewellike reds, blues, and golds. Wood and stone carvings decorate every space.

Building a cathedral took many years. Almost everyone in town worked on it. The best architects and artists designed it. Nobles and rich merchants helped pay for it. Poor people gave their labor. They made long trips to the building site with carts and wheelbarrows loaded with stone. When the cathedral was finished, the whole town took pride in it.

Reading Check

1. How were church bells used in the Middle Ages?
2. List three services provided by members of religious communities during the Middle Ages.
3. With whom did Church leaders in Rome sometimes disagree?
4. What were the two main styles of architecture used in building churches during the Middle Ages?

Look for these important words:

Key Words
- charter
- guilds
- apprentice
- journeyman

- master
- plague
- nation-states
- Magna Carta

People
- King John

Places
- Flanders

Look for answers to these questions:

1. How did improvements in trade lead to the growth of cities in the late Middle Ages?
2. How were craft workers trained in the cities?
3. How did government change in Europe in the late Middle Ages?

4. THE GROWTH OF CITIES

Very little travel or long-distance trade took place during the early Middle Ages. The old Roman roads were in disrepair and overrun by bandits. People usually could not spare enough goods for trade. When they did trade, it was by direct exchange of goods. The coins of the Roman Empire had gone out of use.

Many towns that had prospered in Roman times were nearly deserted during the early Middle Ages. Almost everyone had to live on farms in order to grow enough food. Around the year 1000 the economy began to improve. People grew more food. Travel became safer. By the thirteenth century coins were used again. Large fairs in the countryside attracted many people who came to sell and to trade their wares.

As merchants traveled more, groups of them began to look for safe places on or near their trade routes to spend the winters. They chose spots that had castles for defense. Villages favored by the merchants grew into towns. Slowly the towns grew into cities.

Many people besides merchants were eager to live in the new towns. Craft workers came hoping to find a wider market for their skills. Serfs came, too, fleeing from the hard life of the manor. A law of that time said that a serf who escaped and managed to live hidden in a town for a year and a day was free of all feudal duties.

At first, each town was controlled by the lord who owned the land on which it sat. As merchants grew more powerful, however, they demanded the right to govern their own towns. They forced the lords to give them a document called a **charter.** A charter granted a town the right to self-government.

Townspeople elected officials to a council. The town council taxed trade and provided services for the poor, sick, and homeless. Every town also had its own laws, which were strictly enforced.

181

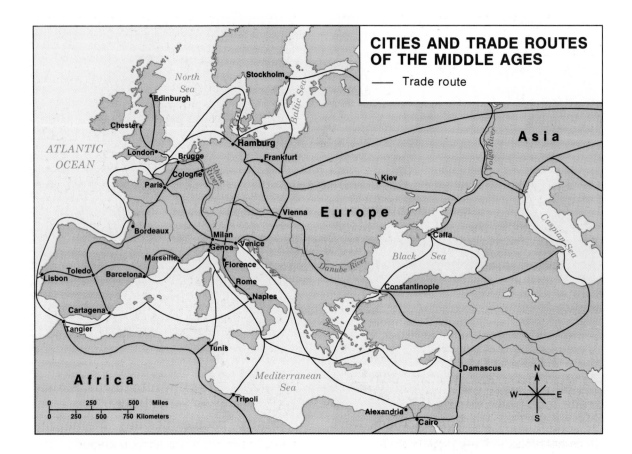

CITIES AND TRADE ROUTES OF THE MIDDLE AGES

— Trade route

Life in a City

Most cities in the late Middle Ages were crowded, unhealthy places. Rickety wooden buildings rose several stories above narrow streets full of people, animals, and garbage.

Even so, life in the city could be exciting. In one part of the city, the sounds of hammering filled the air and the skeleton of a half-finished cathedral rose against the sky. In another part, students strolled, talking about law or medicine with their teachers. In the marketplace, shopkeepers sold wool cloth from **Flanders.** Flanders was a small country that included parts of what is now France, Belgium, and the Netherlands. Shops in the marketplace also contained leather goods from Spain and spices and silks from the east.

In these growing cities people opened their eyes and ears to the products and ideas of the world.

Above all, the city of the thirteenth century belonged to the merchants. They became a new "middle class" between nobles and peasants. Many merchants were actually richer than most nobles. The richest merchants usually formed the town council that governed the city.

Merchants often formed groups called **guilds** (GILDZ). A merchant's guild helped protect its members when they were traveling. It bargained with local lords about rents and taxes.

Later, craft workers also organized guilds. A large city was likely to have guilds for bakers, weavers, glassblowers, and many other craft workers. The

At dawn, bakers prepare loaves of bread
to be sold in the village.

A tailor and his assistants busily fit a
customer with a new gown.

Some medicines in this druggist's shop
came from Africa, Arabia, and China.

In a cabinetmaker's workshop, a woman
spins and a child gathers wood chips.

guilds set the prices that their members could charge. Guild inspectors made sure members' work met certain standards of quality. Workers had to belong to the guilds in order to practice their crafts in the city.

Craft guilds also trained new workers. A young person began as an **apprentice** (uh•PREN•tis) in a master's shop. Like pages in a noble's court, apprentices ran errands and did chores. Meanwhile they learned the skills of their trade.

An apprentice had to stay in the same shop for a certain number of years. Then he became a **journeyman,** or day worker. He could hire himself out to other shops for daily wages. As a journeyman he learned advanced skills.

Finally the journeyman became a **master.** He produced a fine work that showed all he had learned. The guild had to approve this "masterwork"

before the craft worker could set up a shop.

Guilds helped to ensure quality work. They also gave people a chance to succeed through ability rather than wealth or parentage. However, they discouraged their members from competing or looking for better ways to do things. Toward the end of the Middle Ages, many craftspeople broke free of the guilds.

Another kind of guild grew into a new place of learning—the university. Guilds of students and teachers began to appear in the twelfth century. At first, students heard lectures in town squares, in rented rooms, and even in sheds. Later, universities had their own buildings. The universities were part of a new feeling about learning. As in ancient Greece, the idea that people should explore the world of knowledge became popular.

The University of Paris, founded in the twelfth century, was supported by the Church. Here, students listen as a lecturer reads aloud.

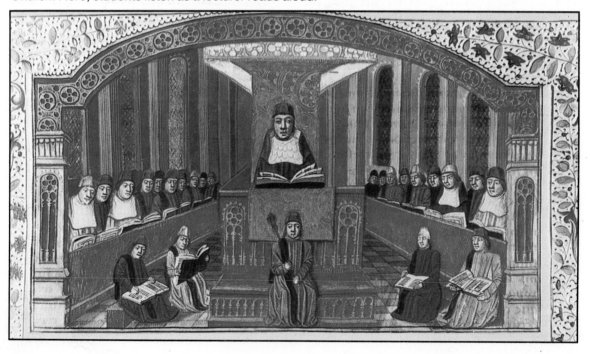

NAMES AND OCCUPATIONS

Cooper   Weaver   Carpenter   Miller

Baker   Mason   Smith   Archer

Disaster and Change

In the fourteenth century, disaster struck the thriving society of Europe. A widespread sickness called the **plague** (PLAYG), or "Black Death," appeared in the late 1340s. So many people died of the plague that their bodies had to be hauled away in carts and buried in mass graves. The plague killed between one-fourth and one-half of the people in Europe.

The few farm workers who survived the plague realized that their skills were greatly needed. They demanded the right to leave their land and go where they would be paid the most. They insisted on fairer treatment from the nobles who controlled their lives. Sometimes they emphasized their demands with bloody revolts.

Some people became dissatisfied with the Church as well as with feudal society. Competition for power between kings and Church leaders shocked many people. Others were frightened because the Church had not been able to stop the plague.

The Rise of Nation-States

Governments were changing, too. Beginning in the twelfth century, strong kings began to take power away from the nobles, especially in England, France, and Spain. **Nation-states** began appearing in many parts of Europe. Each nation-state had a strong central government with a single ruler. Sometimes the ruler had to share power with a governing body representing the people. Each nation-state had a system of written laws, paid government officials, and a permanent army.

The people of each nation-state began to think of themselves as members of a single country. They usually shared the same language and culture. They felt pride in their nation. They would go to war to defend its honor or to prove its superiority.

Merchants and other members of the middle class supported the governments of the nation-states. They needed peace and strong government so they could safely carry on trade. The rulers of the nation-states, in turn, usually

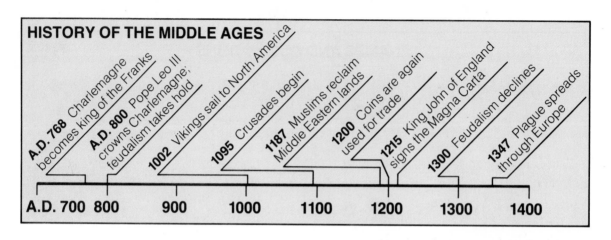

HISTORY OF THE MIDDLE AGES

A.D. 768 Charlemagne becomes king of the Franks

A.D. 800 Pope Leo III crowns Charlemagne; feudalism takes hold

1002 Vikings sail to North America

1095 Crusades begin

1187 Muslims reclaim Middle Eastern lands

1200 Coins are again used for trade

1215 King John of England signs the Magna Carta

1300 Feudalism declines

1347 Plague spreads through Europe

A.D. 700 800   900   1000   1100   1200   1300   1400

encouraged the merchants. They needed the money that taxes on trade and business brought.

Naturally, the nobles resisted their loss of power. In England, for example, they found ways to limit the king's growing power. They outlined these limits in the English document called

English nobles watch as King John unwillingly signs the Magna Carta.

the **Magna Carta** (MAG•nuh KAHR•tuh), or "Great Charter." Powerful nobles forced **King John** to sign this English document in 1215. The nobles were interested only in protecting their own rights. However, some parts of the Magna Carta became the basis of laws that protected the rights of everyone down to the lowliest peasant. One part, for example, established the right to trial by jury. The Magna Carta stated that everyone, including the king, was governed by the laws of the land.

The Middle Ages was a time of great change in Europe. Cities and new kinds of government arose during this time. Toward its end, the Middle Ages gave birth to ideas, inventions, and forms of society that would shape the modern world. You will read more about these changes in the next chapter.

Reading Check

1. Why did trade decrease during the early Middle Ages?
2. What group formed the middle class of growing cities?
3. What sickness struck Europe in the late 1340s?
4. How did people feel about their nation-states?

SKILLS FOR SUCCESS

NOTE TAKING AND OUTLINING

Note taking and outlining are ways of organizing and remembering information. Both can help you prepare for giving speeches, writing stories or reports, or studying for tests. When you take notes on something you are reading or discussing in class, you become more familiar with the subject. Writing down and organizing ideas helps you understand as well as remember what you hear or read. As you study to take a test, to give a speech, or to write a report, you can use notes or an outline to review important points quickly.

Suppose you are writing a report on the Magna Carta. As you do your research, you should take notes about the information you need for your report. Read the paragraphs below.

The Magna Carta

The Magna Carta contains 63 articles. Though it chiefly benefited the nobles, some rights were granted to the Church and to the rising middle class. Peasants, who formed 80 percent of the population, were largely ignored.

Many articles were promises of King John to his people. Others were to make sure the king kept his promises.

One important article said, "No freeman shall be . . . imprisoned, . . . outlawed, or exiled, . . . nor will we . . . prosecute him, except by the lawful judgment of his peers or by the law of the land." This was the basis for our due process of law and trial by jury. In King John's time there was no trial by jury in criminal cases.

Another article said, "No scutage nor aid shall be levied in our kingdom, unless by the common consent of our kingdom."

This meant the king could not levy taxes without the consent of his nobles. Later, representatives of all the people had to approve taxes.

Now read the notes taken on the information above.

> *The Magna Carta*
> 1. 63 articles benefiting nobles, Church, and middle class – peasants ignored
> 2. Promises of King John to people – articles to make sure he kept promises
> 3. No one punished except by judgment of equals or by law – basis of due process and trial by jury – not like that then
> 4. No taxes without consent of nobles – later representatives of all people had to approve

The notes review the main ideas from the paragraphs. The first note describes who benefited, and who did not, from the 63 articles. The third describes one of the king's promises. What was it?

Notes are usually written in words or phrases rather than in well-constructed sentences. They should say only enough to help you remember what you need to know for your report. Notes should be in a form that makes them easy to use. Notes for reports can be made on note cards with one card for each topic. Cards make it easier to put your notes in order when you begin writing the report.

Sometimes rough notes on main ideas are not enough. If you find graphs or charts that give useful information on the subject you are researching, it is a good idea to copy them exactly. You may want to include some of them in your report.

It is also important to write down the sources you use for a report. On the back of each card you should note the author, the name of the book or magazine, the publisher and date of publication, and the name and page numbers of the articles you use. These notes can help you to prove your facts or to remember where you found your information. If you find your notes are unclear, you will know which source to check.

Outlines

Once you have finished taking notes for your report, you should arrange them in a sensible order. One way to do this is to make an **outline,** or list of the main points of a subject. Read the following outline of the material at the beginning of this lesson.

THE MAGNA CARTA

I. Sixty-three articles
  A. Benefits chiefly for nobles
    1. Some rights for Church
    2. Some rights for middle class
  B. Peasants largely ignored
II. Promises of king to people
  A. No punishment except by judgment of equals or law
    1. Basis for due process
    2. Basis for trial by jury
  B. No trial by jury for criminals then
III. Guarantee of king keeping promises
  A. No taxes without consent of nobles
  B. No taxes without consent of representatives of all people later

---

Notice that this outline uses words and phrases to focus on important information from the paragraphs at the beginning of this lesson. Some formal outlines use complete sentences. There are different styles you can

use to make an outline. You should follow the style selected by your teacher or the one found in your language arts book.

All outlines follow some basic rules. Related information is grouped together under a **main topic** or idea. The main idea is labeled with a Roman numeral. For example, the first main topic in the sample outline is "sixty-three articles." It is labeled with the Roman numeral I. **Subtopics** are listed under the main topics. A subtopic is less-important information that supports the main idea. For example, under Roman numeral I the subtopics tell how people were affected by the document. Subtopics are labeled with capital letters. Suptopics also may have **supporting details,** which are numbered with Arabic numerals.

Outlines are good guides for writing reports. An outline recalls the most important information in a logical order. As you use an outline to write your report, you can fill in the details under each topic.

CHECKING YOUR SKILLS

Use the sample outline to answer the following questions.

1. Where would you look to find who received some benefits from the Magna Carta?

2. What is the second main idea in this outline?

3. How many subtopics are listed under II? What are they?

4. What detail might you fill in under subtopic I.B. when writing a report?

5. Look again at the paragraphs at the beginning of this lesson. What other detail could you list under II.A., *no punishment except by judgment of equals or law?*

USING WORDS

Write the letter of the definition that matches each of the words below.

1. **apprentice**
2. **charter**
3. **chivalry**
4. **clergy**
5. **crusaders**
6. **feudalism**
7. **guilds**
8. **nation-states**
9. **plague**
10. **serfs**

a. A code of honorable behavior for knights
b. Widespread sickness
c. The system of protection and loyalty during the Middle Ages
d. A document granting the right to self-government
e. Organized groups of merchants or craft workers
f. Peasants bound to land belonging to nobles or the Church
g. A beginning worker in a craft guild
h. People who used the cross as their sign while fighting Muslim Turks
i. Systems of central government uniting people with similar cultures
j. Religious workers

REVIEWING FACTS

1. How did Charlemagne improve education and government in his empire?

2. What effect did the Crusades have on European trade?

3. Put these groups in order of importance: vassals, nobles, kings, serfs.

4. How did people living on a manor provide for their needs?

5. Describe how each of the following parts of a castle was used: keep, courtyard, moat, drawbridge.

6. Why were people attracted to the religious life during the Middle Ages?

7. What were the great churches of the Middle Ages called? Who helped to build them?

8. What changes during the Middle Ages made the growth of cities possible and improved the economy?

9. List three responsibilities of the craft guilds.

10. What document limited the power of English kings?

THINKING CRITICALLY

1. Describe the training of a knight and of a craft worker. In what ways were these two kinds of training alike? How are some people today trained for jobs?

2. Manors, monasteries, and convents were self-sufficient during the Middle Ages. *Self-sufficient* means that people grew or made everything they needed to live. What are the advantages and the disadvantages of this way of living?

◯ PRACTICING SKILLS

Outlining Choose one of the following sections from this chapter: "The Vikings," "Knights," "Cathedrals." Make an outline of the important information.

CHAPTER 7

The Renaissance Begins the Modern World

Toward the end of the Middle Ages, Europeans changed many of their ideas. They became more interested in studying the world around them. Their art became more true to life. They began governing themselves in new ways and exploring new lands.

We call this period between about 1400 and 1600 the **Renaissance** (REN•uh•sahns), which means "rebirth." Europeans wanted to revive the glory of ancient Greece and Rome. In part, they succeeded. More importantly, the Renaissance marked the beginning of many ideas that led the way toward the modern age.

Look for these important words:

Key Words
- patrons
- perspective
- mercenaries
- alliances

People
- Medici family
- Giotto
- Leonardo da Vinci

- Michelangelo Buonarroti

Places
- Florence

Look for answers to these questions:

1. What wealthy group supported art and education in Italy during the Renaissance?
2. What new ways of thinking about the world arose in Italy?
3. In what ways did the style of art change?
4. How did warfare and international politics change around the end of the Italian Renaissance?

1. THE RENAISSANCE IN ITALY

The Renaissance came to different parts of Europe in different ways and at different times. It came first to Italy in the fourteenth century.

Italy's position on the Mediterranean gave it an advantage in the sea trade between Europe and the Middle East. Although many cities built during the Roman Empire disappeared during the Middle Ages, such cities as Naples, Genoa, and Venice became wealthy centers of trade. With trade came new ideas, which may explain why the Renaissance began in Italy.

The Italian City-States

Italy during the Renaissance was divided into several independent city-states. Like the ancient Greeks, the people of the Italian city-states believed that it was a citizen's duty to take part in public life. Several city-states had constitutions and elected governments. The real power in most city-states, however, was held by families of rich "merchant princes."

Florence, a city-state on the Arno River, was where many Renaissance ideas began. Florence was controlled by the **Medici** (MED•uh•chee) **family.** The Medicis were bankers. They and other "merchant princes" held courts, or social gatherings. People at their courts were expected to have excellent manners, wide-ranging educations, and skills in many fields.

The "princes" themselves often had many talents. For example, Lorenzo de Medici was not only a shrewd banker and a clever politician but also a scholar and a poet. His many accomplishments earned him the title "Lorenzo the Magnificent."

ITALIAN CITY–STATES, ABOUT 1494

— Boundary of Holy Roman Empire

Learning to read was important to the culture of the Renaissance.

Families like the Medicis were **patrons** (PAY•truhnz) of the arts. *Patron* comes from the Latin word for "father." Wealthy patrons paid artists generously to create paintings and sculptures. They paid writers and educators to work at their courts. Their money and encouragement made the masterpieces of Renaissance art possible.

Learning About the World

The merchants of Italy were practical in business and had strong views about the importance of education. They made sure their sons could read, write, and do arithmetic. These skills, as well as the study of law, were needed in business. The merchants also wanted their children to study the writings of ancient Greeks and Romans. The practical thinking of the Romans and the Greeks' love of beauty strongly appealed to the Renaissance merchants.

Love of ancient Greek and Roman culture played a major part in the Renaissance. Scholars eagerly studied all the old manuscripts they could find. The finding of a "new" manuscript caused excitement. Writers and artists often imitated Greek and Roman works.

Practical ideas in everyday life and interest in the past combined in a new way of thinking about the world. After the hard times of the Middle Ages, people awakened to a more interesting life. They wanted to learn about and enjoy nature. Like the ancient Greeks, they felt that each individual person was important.

These new ideas appeared first in literature. During the Renaissance, writers chose many different subjects about which to write. They chose to write in the languages of their own countries rather than in Latin. Some works were serious; others were humorous.

A New Kind of Art

Renaissance artists were encouraged to create new kinds of art. Merchant patrons wanted art that showed the same joy in human beauty and life's pleasures that they felt. The art they bought was lifelike. It was more like the art of Greece and Rome than like the art of the early Middle Ages.

The people in Renaissance art are real human beings of flesh and blood. They show individual feelings. Even the backgrounds of Renaissance art looked real for the first time. Renaissance artists studied **perspective** (pur•SPEK•tiv), or the differences in the way things look when they are close to a person and when they are far away. The artists painted in a way that showed these differences. As a result, their paintings seem to have depth.

The first painter of this new style of art was called **Giotto** (JAHT•oh). Giotto lived in Florence in the early fourteenth century. People in his religious paintings show real feeling in their faces. Their bodies look solid. The backgrounds of his paintings are beginning to show perspective.

There was an explosion of great art in Italy during the fifteenth and early sixteenth centuries. One of the finest

This painting by Giotto shows a sleeping man who is visited by an angel. Notice the lifelike, human quality of the two shepherds who approach him.

artists of this time was **Leonardo da Vinci** (lee•uh•NAHR•do duh VIN•chee). People have been trying to guess the secret behind the mysterious smile of his *Mona Lisa* ever since he painted it around 1505. His *Last Supper,* though faded, shows clearly the different feelings of Christ and his disciples.

Da Vinci was the perfect "Renaissance man," skilled in many fields. He was a scientist and inventor as well as an artist. He made notes and drawings of everything he saw. He drew plants, animals, and bones and muscles of the human body. He invented clever machines for warfare. He even designed imitation wings that he hoped would let a person fly like a bird.

Michelangelo Buonarroti (my•kuhl•AN•juh•loh bwahn•uh•RAHT•ee) of Florence was one of the great artists of all time. He was a sculptor, a painter, and an architect. His famous statue of David shows the hero of the Bible story of David and Goliath. His figure of Moses is equally famous. Both sculptures have dignity and power like the finest Greek statues.

Michelangelo also designed the dome of St. Peter's Church in Rome. Nearby, his paintings cover the whole ceiling of the Sistine (SIS•teen) Chapel. The Christian Church, like the merchant princes, acted as a patron of the arts. Some of the finest Renaissance art is found in the churches of Europe.

Leonardo da Vinci's *Mona Lisa* is known as a model of Renaissance beauty.

Michelangelo helped to design the dome of St. Peter's Church in Rome.

Michelangelo's *Moses*, who appears ready to rise from his chair, shows the emotion and power that the great sculptor could create from stone.

The Invasion of Italy

When French troops invaded Italy in 1494, the Italians were completely surprised. Italy had not been attacked from outside for almost 200 years. Even the Italian city-states had kept an uneasy peace with each other for more than 40 years.

The French did little damage during their invasion, and they went home the following year. Unfortunately for Italy, however, they soon returned, followed by the Spanish. Later, the soldiers of the Holy Roman Empire invaded as well. The rulers of these regions were trying to enforce old claims to parts of Italy. Italy became a battleground for more than 50 years.

At the time of these invasions, warfare was changing in important ways. Cannons and crude handguns began to play a part in European battles in the second half of the fourteenth century. They were often used during the Renaissance. Foot soldiers were taking the place of soldiers on horseback. They served for pay, not out of loyalty. Such hired soldiers were called **mercenaries** (MUR•suh•nayr•eez).

International politics was changing, too. Countries began to form **alliances,** agreements to help each

The French attacked Italy in 1494 with iron cannonballs and highly trained armies. The Italians responded with new, stronger fortifications.

other keep rival countries from gaining too much power. These alliances kept the "balance of power."

The invasions of Italy meant the end of the city-states' political power. The discovery of new routes to Asia and the Americas by Spanish and Portuguese explorers in the 1490s meant a sharp decline in the Italians' trading wealth. Because of the decline in trade, it was more difficult for artists and scholars to find wealthy patrons.

The Renaissance did not come suddenly to a halt in Italy. Despite the decline in power, Italy's masters continued to produce great works. However, in the sixteenth century, leadership in art and ideas passed to other parts of Europe.

Reading Check

1. Which family ruled Florence during the Renaissance?
2. Which ancient cultures played a major part in the Renaissance?
3. Why is Leonardo da Vinci considered the perfect Renaissance man?
4. How did warfare change during the Renaissance?

Ancient sundial

English clock

Portrait clock

Early Clocks

"Woe to the blackfaced clock which woke me," wrote a Welsh poet around 1335. Perhaps you feel the same way about the clock that wakes you. Yet, imagine what your life would be like without time-telling devices. You can schedule your time today because of an advancement in technology that took place about 700 years ago—the development of the mechanical clock.

There were many different kinds of devices for telling time before the invention of the mechanical clock. There were hourglasses, water clocks, sundials, and special candles and oil lamps. As the candle or oil lamp slowly burned, it reached certain markings for the hours. None of these devices, however, was exact in its measurement of time.

European society became more complex as people moved from small villages and farms to large cities. People needed to know when to rise, when to go to work, when to stop working, and when they should go to sleep. The chiming of the bells from the local tower clocks helped them to keep track of time and organize their lives.

Each large town and city had its own clock tower that tolled the hours by the ringing of bells. The bells not only let people know the time of day but also called them to prayer and to important town meetings. More important, the bells alerted them to danger if an enemy was approaching.

After a while people began to want clocks in their homes. At first, only the rich could afford them. Those clocks were large and sometimes so elaborate that it was difficult for anyone besides the clockmaker to read them. Clocks became such a symbol of importance that some kings had their portraits painted on the faces.

One very early clock given to Charlemagne by the King of Persia was made of inlaid gold and had 12 doors. Each door opened at the correct hour and out rolled the corresponding number of small silver balls. When it was 12 o'clock, 12 miniature horsemen emerged and shut all the other doors.

Look for these important words:

Key Words
- printing press
- movable type
- heresy
- Reformation
- Moors
- monarchs
- heir

People
- Johann Gutenberg
- Martin Luther
- Philip II
- Henry VIII
- Elizabeth Tudor
- William Shakespeare
- Joan of Arc

Places
- Wittenberg
- Low Countries

Look for answers to these questions:

1. How was the Renaissance elsewhere in Europe like the Renaissance in Italy? How was it different?
2. What enabled more books to spread throughout Europe?
3. What led to major changes in the Christian Church?
4. Under whose reign did England reach its height during the Renaissance?

2. THE RENAISSANCE ELSEWHERE IN EUROPE

Visitors to Italy spread Renaissance ideas to the rest of Europe. The Renaissance in other parts of Europe, however, had a stronger religious base than it had in Italy. People learned Greek and Latin so that they could read the Bible, not the works of Homer or Cicero. Sixteenth-century Europe saw the founding of new forms of Christianity and the fighting of bitter religious wars.

Most thinkers of Renaissance Europe agreed with the Italians on certain points. They felt that life on Earth was important. They felt that people had both the ability and the right to think for themselves. This interest in learning led to new inventions. In turn, new inventions led to the spreading of knowledge, which sparked an even wider interest in learning.

Gutenberg's Printing Press

Renaissance ideas spread through Europe with the help of an invention from Germany. During the fourteenth century the wood-block method of printing was used. The words and pictures on each page of a book were carved on a block of wood. The block was then inked and stamped onto paper. The whole block had to be carved over if anything needed to be changed.

Around 1450 a German named **Johann Gutenberg** (YO•hahn GOOT•uhn•burg) invented a better way of printing. Instead of wood blocks, Gutenberg's **printing press** used small pieces of metal. Each piece had a single alphabet letter. The metal pieces could be placed in trays to form lines of print. **Movable type,** as it was called, could be used over and over.

At an early press, printers ink type (right) and print pages (left). In the rear, pieces of type are formed into words and set in pages.

Bookmaking further improved with the introduction of paper to Europe. Muslims had learned about making paper from the Chinese. They then introduced the method to Europeans. Printing on paper was quicker and less expensive than writing by hand on parchment.

Not too long after Gutenberg made the first one, printing presses were being built all over Europe. People no longer had to be rich or belong to the Church in order to have books. The printing press allowed the Bible, the Greek and Roman classics, and the works of Renaissance writers to spread throughout Europe.

Luther and the Reformation

In a public square in the German town of **Wittenberg** (WIT•uhn•burg), a priest was beating a drum. "God's forgiveness is yours!" he cried. Then he held out a box and asked for money. Another priest stood in the audience. His name was **Martin Luther.** The year was 1517.

Luther had seen something similar when he had visited Rome six years earlier. The idea that forgiveness could be bought with money had shocked him then. It shocked him now.

The next day, Martin Luther nailed some pieces of paper to the door of the church in Wittenberg. They contained 95 complaints against the Church of Rome. Luther offered to debate Germany's religious leaders on these ideas.

A Church court quickly put Luther on trial. It convicted him of denying the beliefs of the Church, a crime called **heresy** (HAIR•uh•see). Later the Holy Roman Emperor, Charles V, put Luther on trial as well. In both trials, Luther explained that he did not want to harm

199

On trial at Worms, Germany, Luther is asked to deny his beliefs. His books piled nearby, he delivers his refusal and is condemned by Charles V.

the Church. He wanted only to correct its weaknesses. However, he refused to deny or change any of his ideas.

Charles V issued an order forbidding any citizen of the empire to give Luther food or shelter. A German prince defied the order and gave Luther a place to live. From this safe shelter, Luther wrote constantly. He said that people could find their way to God through their own faith.

Luther also said that people should read the Bible themselves rather than letting priests interpret it for them. To aid people in this task, Luther translated the Bible into German. He used the printing press to spread his German Bible and other writings to large numbers of people. His ideas eventually led to the formation of the Lutheran Church.

Many Germans became Lutherans. When certain German princes protested attempts to stamp out the new religion, they became known as "Protestants." Later, that name was used for churches that did not acknowledge the Pope as their religious leader. The Protestant religious movement was called the **Reformation** (ref•uhr•MAY•shuhn) because it began as an attempt to reform the Roman Catholic Church. The Reformation spread to many parts of Europe.

The Roman Catholic Church remained powerful in Spain, Portugal, France, Italy, Ireland, and most of Eastern Europe. England, Scotland, Germany, Scandinavia, and the Netherlands became largely Protestant. Religious rivalry led to many wars during the Renaissance.

Spain and Portugal

During the Middle Ages, most of the Iberian Peninsula was controlled by Muslim people called **Moors.** Toward the end of this time Christian armies began driving the Moors out of the peninsula.

Ferdinand of Aragon (AR•uh•gahn) and Isabella of Castile (kas•TEEL) were next in line for the thrones of their large Spanish kingdoms. After their marriage in 1469, they united most of Spain under their joint rule. They drove out the last of the Moors in 1492.

In that same year Ferdinand and Isabella sent an Italian explorer, Christopher Columbus, to look for a new sea route to the rich lands of India. As you know, Columbus instead reached the "New World" of the Americas. Soon after that, explorers from Spain's neighbor, Portugal, sailed around Africa to reach India. Silver and gold from the Americas made Spain incredibly rich. Trade with Asia did the same for Portugal.

The Spanish kings spent most of their money on wars as they tried to

A Flemish tapestry shows Isabella and Ferdinand with their richly dressed court. Such tapestries hung on castle walls to keep out cold drafts, and, since there were few windows, to provide scenery.

gain power in other parts of Europe. Most of their efforts failed. In 1588 **Philip II** of Spain planned an invasion of England. He was angered by English attacks on Spanish ships. He also wanted to force Protestant England to rejoin the Catholic Church.

Philip built a huge fleet of ships to carry soldiers to England. He called this fleet the Armada (ahr•MAH•duh).

He was sure that nothing could conquer it. The English heard about the Armada, however, and prepared for it. Fast-moving English ships attacked the Spanish fleet as it neared their shores. The English sank many Spanish ships. A tremendous storm finished the Armada's destruction. Only half of Spain's 130 ships returned home. As a result, Spain was weakened while

Elizabeth I launched a fleet of ships and crews of expert sailors against the Spanish Armada. Victory brought new confidence to the British.

England proved itself a powerful nation. In addition, England began to challenge Spain for the wealth of the Americas.

The Elizabethan Age

The Tudors (TOO·durz) were the ruling **monarchs,** or kings and queens, in England during the Renaissance. The first Tudor king, Henry VII, took power in 1485. His rule ended a long period of civil war. Henry VII was followed to the throne by his son, **Henry VIII.** Henry VIII was handsome, intelligent, and popular. He loved hunting and other sports, music, and poetry.

In 1534 Henry established a new kind of Protestant Church. He made himself its leader. Unlike Luther, Henry acted for selfish reasons. He wanted to take over the lands and riches that the Catholic Church owned in England. He also wanted to divorce his wife and remarry, an action which the Pope would not permit.

Henry was able to make his break with the Pope because most of the English people supported him. The Pope seemed more like a foreign king than a spiritual leader to them. They did not want the Pope to own English land and take English tax money.

Henry VIII married six times. He did so partly because he wanted a male **heir** (AIR). An heir is one who inherits, or receives, possessions or a social position after the death of a parent. Henry had two daughters, Mary and Elizabeth. However, he did not think the English people would accept a queen. He was afraid civil war would break out again after his death if he did not leave a son on the throne.

Court artist Hans Holbein, who was famous for his strong and lifelike portraits, painted Henry VIII in 1540.

Henry finally had a son named Edward. Edward died, however, soon after Henry did. Edward's oldest sister, Mary, then became queen. Mary was a devoted Catholic. She ordered the deaths of many nobles who would not rejoin the Catholic Church. The English called her "Bloody Mary."

Mary died in 1558, and **Elizabeth Tudor** took the throne. A shrewd and intelligent woman, Elizabeth I was even more popular with the English people than her father had been. She never lost that popularity. Elizabeth restored her father's church, the Church of England. Unlike Mary, she usually did not punish people whose religion was different from her own.

The Renaissance reached its height in England during Elizabeth's rule. She made herself the center of a glittering court. She wore elaborate dresses, stiff

203

with lace and jewels. She attended plays and balls. She listened as men read poems about her and paid her compliments, though she never married.

Some of England's finest poetry and drama was written during Elizabeth's rule. England's most famous playwright, **William Shakespeare,** lived during this time. His plays appealed to noble and commoner alike and are still popular today.

Elizabeth surrounded herself with wise government leaders as well as brilliant poets. Often her own decisions proved wisest of all. She encouraged trade, business, and exploration. Sir Francis Drake and other bold sailors claimed land in the Americas for her. They brought her a share of the wealth that Spain was gaining there.

Elizabeth ruled England for 45 years. She was a better leader than most of the country's kings had been. England gained steadily in wealth and power during her rule. For centuries afterward, English people looked back on Elizabeth's time as a "Golden Age."

France and the Low Countries

Between 1337 and 1453 England and France fought the Hundred Years' War. Most of the fighting was in France. In 1429 a peasant girl, **Joan of Arc,** said that heavenly voices told her to drive the English out of France. An inspired army followed her to victory in many battles. After her death the English were defeated. France became a powerful nation-state.

Elizabeth I brought peace and unity to England. This portrait was done in 1575.

At age sixteen, Joan of Arc put on a suit of armor and went to war for France.

At this shipyard in Rotterdam, the Netherlands, the Dutch built warships to fight the Spanish and to protect their sea trade.

After France invaded Italy in 1494, Italian Renaissance artists inspired the French. French kings and queens encouraged Renaissance fashions in art and architecture. After the Reformation France, like its neighbors, was torn by fighting between Catholics and Protestants. These civil wars continued until the late 1500s.

The lands between France and Germany were called the **Low Countries** because they were almost at sea level. They became part of the Holy Roman Empire in 1477. Later, large numbers of their people became Protestants. The Holy Roman Emperor, who was Catholic, punished these people. The punishments became worse when the emperor's son, Philip II of Spain, took over the rule of the Low Countries.

At last, in 1566, the northern provinces of the Low Countries rebelled against Philip. They had to fight for almost a century before they gained their independence in 1648. Their land became the Netherlands. The southern regions remained loyal to Spain. They later became Belgium.

Even while the Dutch people were fighting for their freedom, their skill in trade and business was making them rich. Dutch-built ships carried their own goods and those of others through European waters and beyond.

Reading Check

1. What invention helped spread Renaissance ideas in Europe?
2. How did Protestants get their name?
3. Why did Henry VIII establish a new church in England?
4. Which English monarch's reign was remembered as a "Golden Age"?

205

Look for these important words:

Key Words
- heliocentric
- telescope
- gravity

People
- Nicholas Copernicus
- Galileo
- Isaac Newton

Look for answers to these questions:

1. What new idea did Nicholas Copernicus propose, and how was it proved?
2. For what do we remember Isaac Newton?
3. What principle does the scientific method state?

3. THE BEGINNING OF MODERN SCIENCE

As European countries were establishing their identities during the Renaissance, nations formed or were strengthened. Religions spread their influence. Art flourished. European power was growing and moving to other parts of the world.

During this period, too, Europeans sought new knowledge of the world around them. For the first time since the days of Greece and Rome, people were interested in science.

One of the greatest Renaissance scientists was a Polish thinker named **Nicholas Copernicus** (koh•PUR•ni•kus). In 1543 a book he wrote was published. It said the Earth traveled around the sun. This new idea went against both Church teachings and popular beliefs. Most people at the time believed that the Earth was the center of the heavens. In time, however, Copernicus' **heliocentric** (hee•lee•oh•SEN•trik), or sun-centered, idea was accepted.

Other scientific advancements followed. In the early 1600s an Italian named **Galileo** (gal•lih•LEE•oh) learned about a Dutch invention that used glass lenses to make distant objects appear nearer. Working at home, he turned this invention into a larger device that could

Motioning skyward, Galileo explains his ideas to a doubtful listener.

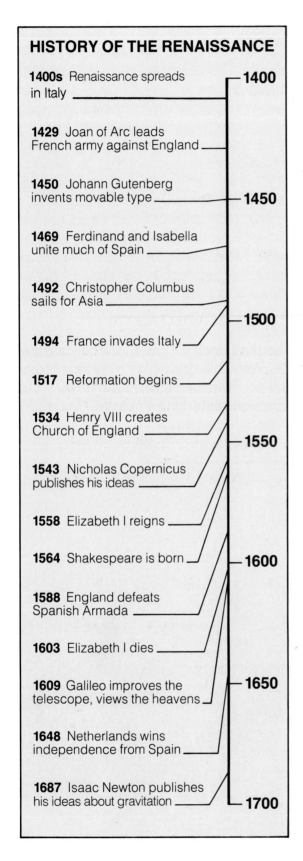

HISTORY OF THE RENAISSANCE

1400s Renaissance spreads in Italy — **1400**

1429 Joan of Arc leads French army against England

1450 Johann Gutenberg invents movable type — **1450**

1469 Ferdinand and Isabella unite much of Spain

1492 Christopher Columbus sails for Asia

— **1500**

1494 France invades Italy

1517 Reformation begins

1534 Henry VIII creates Church of England

— **1550**

1543 Nicholas Copernicus publishes his ideas

1558 Elizabeth I reigns

1564 Shakespeare is born — **1600**

1588 England defeats Spanish Armada

1603 Elizabeth I dies

1609 Galileo improves the telescope, views the heavens — **1650**

1648 Netherlands wins independence from Spain

1687 Isaac Newton publishes his ideas about gravitation — **1700**

magnify objects in space. Thus Galileo has been credited with improving the **telescope.** What Galileo saw through his telescope helped prove the ideas of Copernicus.

The discoveries of Copernicus and Galileo inspired an English scholar named **Isaac Newton.** In 1687 Newton published a book to explain why people and objects do not fall off the Earth as it moves. He proved that objects are held to the Earth by a force, called **gravity.** He said that this same force kept the planets circling the sun.

Newton and other scientists of his time developed what is now called the "scientific method." This method states that no idea should be accepted as true unless it is thoroughly tested. Many people complimented Newton on his work and his method. He said, "If I have been able to see farther than others, it is because I have stood on the shoulders of giants."

Copernicus, Galileo, and Newton were not the only scientists to make advances. Scholars studying medicine and mathematics made important breakthroughs, too. Scientific discoveries during the Renaissance, like Renaissance ideas about government, education, religion, and art, helped shape the world we know today.

Reading Check

1. How did the ideas of Copernicus differ from popular beliefs of his time?
2. Who improved the telescope?
3. What force keeps people and objects from falling off the Earth?
4. What is meant by the "scientific method"?

COMPARING MAPS

One way to learn about history is to study **historical maps.** Historical maps show how the world looked in the past. By comparing historical maps, you can trace some of the changes in a nation's history. You can discover how boundaries have changed or what different names have been given to a particular area.

Many atlases and history books contain historical maps. Usually the title or key of a historical map tells you what year or years are represented.

The maps that follow show Europe at four different times in history. As you look at the maps, read their titles and notice the year given for each. Look at the key for Map A,

the Roman Empire about A.D. 117. The brown areas on the map show lands governed by the Roman Empire. The green areas indicate lands controlled by other groups.

By 1200 another empire had risen to power. Find Rome on Map B. It is within an area called the Papal States. These were lands that belonged to the Catholic Church, headed by the Pope. The Papal States are colored pink on this map. According to the key, pink is used to show the countries in the Holy Roman Empire. You can see that the Papal States were part of the Holy Roman Empire. Look at the key again. Notice that England controlled parts of two other countries. What were they?

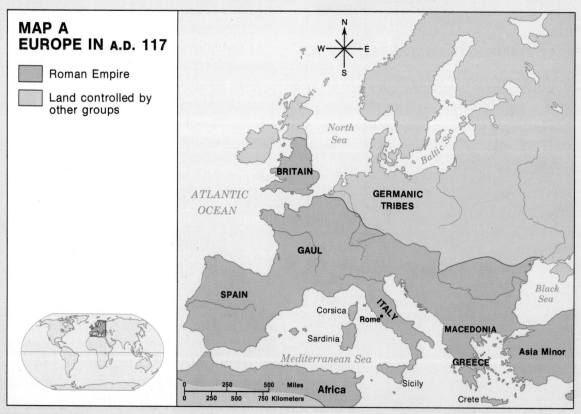

MAP A
EUROPE IN A.D. 117

- Roman Empire
- Land controlled by other groups

N W E S

North Sea

Baltic Sea

BRITAIN

ATLANTIC OCEAN

GERMANIC TRIBES

GAUL

SPAIN

Corsica

Rome

Sardinia

ITALY

MACEDONIA

Black Sea

Asia Minor

Mediterranean Sea

GREECE

Africa

Sicily

Crete

0   250   500   Miles
0   250   500   750 Kilometers

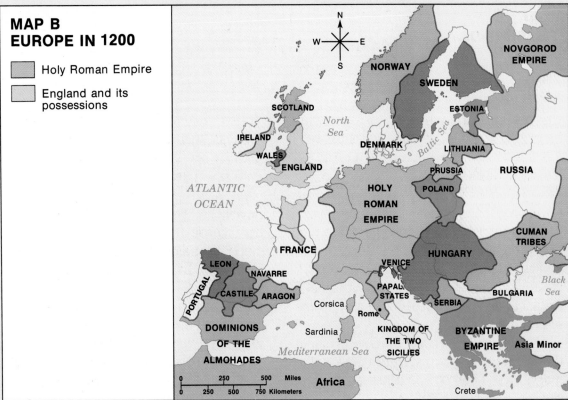

MAP B
EUROPE IN 1200

Holy Roman Empire

England and its possessions

NORWAY

SWEDEN

NOVGOROD EMPIRE

ESTONIA

SCOTLAND

North Sea

Baltic Sea

IRELAND

DENMARK

LITHUANIA

WALES

ENGLAND

PRUSSIA

RUSSIA

POLAND

ATLANTIC OCEAN

HOLY ROMAN EMPIRE

CUMAN TRIBES

FRANCE

VENICE

HUNGARY

LEON

NAVARRE

PAPAL STATES

Black Sea

PORTUGAL

CASTILE

ARAGON

Corsica

SERBIA

BULGARIA

Rome

DOMINIONS

Sardinia

KINGDOM OF THE TWO SICILIES

BYZANTINE EMPIRE

Asia Minor

OF THE

ALMOHADES

Mediterranean Sea

Africa

Crete

| 0 | 250 | 500 | Miles |
| 0 | 250 | 500 | 750 Kilometers |

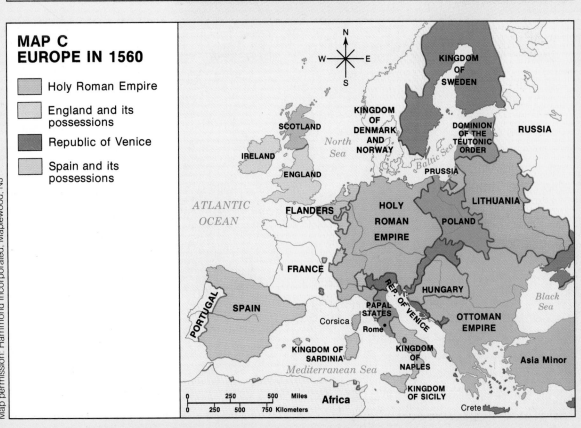

MAP C
EUROPE IN 1560

Holy Roman Empire

England and its possessions

Republic of Venice

Spain and its possessions

KINGDOM OF SWEDEN

SCOTLAND

North Sea

DOMINION OF THE TEUTONIC ORDER

RUSSIA

IRELAND

KINGDOM OF DENMARK AND NORWAY

Baltic Sea

PRUSSIA

ENGLAND

LITHUANIA

ATLANTIC OCEAN

FLANDERS

HOLY ROMAN EMPIRE

POLAND

FRANCE

REP. OF VENICE

HUNGARY

PORTUGAL

SPAIN

PAPAL STATES

Corsica

OTTOMAN EMPIRE

Black Sea

Rome

KINGDOM OF SARDINIA

KINGDOM OF NAPLES

Asia Minor

Mediterranean Sea

KINGDOM OF SICILY

Africa

Crete

| 0 | 250 | 500 | Miles |
| 0 | 250 | 500 | 750 Kilometers |

Map permission: Hammond Incorporated, Maplewood, NJ

MAP D PRESENT-DAY EUROPE

BEL.	Belgium
LIECHT.	Liechtenstein
LUX.	Luxembourg
NETH.	Netherlands
SWITZ.	Switzerland
Fr.	France
Gr.	Greece
It.	Italy

Look at Map C. It shows Europe in about 1560. The Holy Roman Empire still controlled most of the same areas it had controlled in 1200. Notice, though, that the Papal States had become independent. Look at the area just north of the Papal States on Map B and Map C. Map C shows a new region, the Republic of Venice.

Compare France as it appears on Map B to France on Map C. What country had lost its lands in France by 1560?

Look at Map D and read its title. Find Greece on Map D. Now look at the same area on the other maps. Notice the different empires that have controlled Greece. Each conquering group had an influence on the lives and culture of the Greeks. This is one of the reasons that a culture changes over the centuries. Often you can use historical maps to trace cultural change.

CHECKING YOUR SKILLS

Use the maps and keys to answer the following questions.

1. Which map shows Ireland, Wales, and England united under the same rule? What year does this map show?

2. On which maps are Norway and Denmark separate countries? What years do these maps represent?

3. Find Vatican City on Map D. Vatican City is a small independent area inside the city of Rome. It is owned and controlled by the Catholic Church. It is all that remains of a region that was part of the Holy Roman Empire in A.D. 1200. What was the former name of this region?

4. Name three countries today that were once part of the Holy Roman Empire.

USING WORDS

Explain the meaning of each of the words listed below. Then use each word in a complete sentence.

1. **alliances**
2. **gravity**
3. **heir**
4. **heliocentric**
5. **heresy**
6. **mercenaries**
7. **monarchs**
8. **patrons**
9. **perspective**
10. **Reformation**

REVIEWING FACTS

1. Why did the Renaissance appear first in Italy?

2. How did "merchant princes" contribute to the growth of Renaissance Europe?

3. How did the cultures of ancient Greece and Rome influence the Renaissance?

4. In what ways was Renaissance art more true to life than art of the early Middle Ages?

5. What one man of the Renaissance was an artist, scientist, and inventor?

6. What caused Renaissance leadership to pass from Italy to the rest of Europe?

7. How did the Reformation affect the countries of Europe?

8. Which monarchs united Spain?

9. In what ways did Elizabeth I improve the wealth and power of England?

10. How did the discoveries of Copernicus, Galileo, and Newton contribute to our knowledge of the planets?

THINKING CRITICALLY

1. The Renaissance is sometimes called the Age of Exploration. France, England, Portugal, and Spain explored newly discovered lands. How were religious thinkers, artists, scientists, and inventors involved in exploration of a different kind?

2. How did the use of paper, movable type, and languages other than Latin help change Europe during the Renaissance? What new forms of communication have had similar effects in recent times?

3. Think about the monarchies of the Renaissance. Often they were concerned with religious struggles and wars among their countries. How do you think the monarchs were able to pay for their rich courts and these wars?

○ PRACTICING SKILLS

Historical Maps Use your skills lesson and the maps on pages 208–210 to answer the following questions.

1. Name four European countries that once belonged to the Roman Empire.

2. What country was formed by the joining of Leon, Castille, Navarre, and Aragon?

3. Who controlled Hungary in 1560?

4. How did Lithuania change from 1200 to 1560?

5. Find Portugal on Maps B, C, and D. What can you tell about the boundary of Portugal from these maps?

Europeans Adjust to New Ideas

Focus

Europe has produced changes that have shaped the entire modern world. From Europe also has come a series of wars and revolutions that have bathed that continent—and half the globe—in human blood.

Many of the most important changes began in one of four European countries. They are Great Britain, France, Germany, and the Soviet Union. These four countries play leading roles in Europe today.

Look for these important words:

Key Words
- Industrial Revolution
- flying shuttle
- spinning jenny
- crop rotation

People
- James Watt
- John Kay
- James Hargreaves
- Charles "Turnip" Townshend

Look for answers to these questions:

1. How did Great Britain's use of resources change during the Industrial Revolution?
2. How did the Industrial Revolution change the British textile industry?
3. What changes occurred in farming and transportation?
4. What problems in cities were caused by the Industrial Revolution?

1. GREAT BRITAIN'S INDUSTRIAL REVOLUTION

In the eighteenth century the invention of new machines and the discovery of new sources of power in Great Britain brought changes that caused the **Industrial Revolution.** The Industrial Revolution changed the way people worked, lived, and traveled, both in Great Britain and in other parts of the world to which it spread.

The Machine Age

The Industrial Revolution came first to Great Britain partly because of the country's large resources of iron and coal. New ways of using these resources were invented in the eighteenth century. Iron was used to make machine parts. Coal was burned to produce the energy that ran the machines.

In many machines, burning coal provided energy by turning water into steam. The steam pushed against certain parts of the machine and made them move. The kind of steam engine used in many machines of the Industrial Revolution was invented by **James Watt** in 1782. This invention was part of an explosion in technology in Great Britain. The invention of new kinds of machines increased at an amazing pace.

Most new machines in the early part of the Industrial Revolution were made for the textile industry. Before the middle of the eighteenth century, families made cloth by hand in their homes. First, they spun raw cotton and wool into threads. Next, the workers would weave the thread into cloth on large wooden looms. Making cloth by hand was a slow process. New methods were needed to make enough material for a growing population.

213

INDUSTRIAL INVENTORS AND INVENTIONS

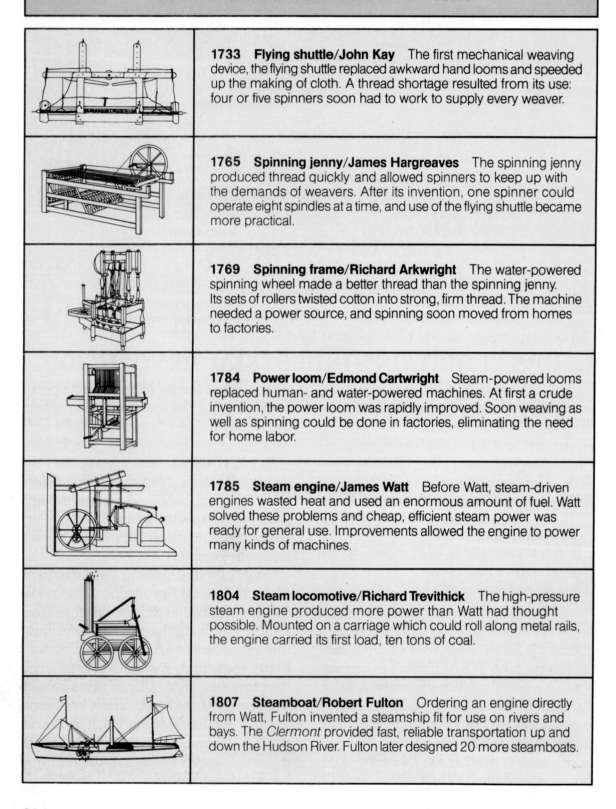

1733 Flying shuttle/John Kay The first mechanical weaving device, the flying shuttle replaced awkward hand looms and speeded up the making of cloth. A thread shortage resulted from its use: four or five spinners soon had to work to supply every weaver.

1765 Spinning jenny/James Hargreaves The spinning jenny produced thread quickly and allowed spinners to keep up with the demands of weavers. After its invention, one spinner could operate eight spindles at a time, and use of the flying shuttle became more practical.

1769 Spinning frame/Richard Arkwright The water-powered spinning wheel made a better thread than the spinning jenny. Its sets of rollers twisted cotton into strong, firm thread. The machine needed a power source, and spinning soon moved from homes to factories.

1784 Power loom/Edmond Cartwright Steam-powered looms replaced human- and water-powered machines. At first a crude invention, the power loom was rapidly improved. Soon weaving as well as spinning could be done in factories, eliminating the need for home labor.

1785 Steam engine/James Watt Before Watt, steam-driven engines wasted heat and used an enormous amount of fuel. Watt solved these problems and cheap, efficient steam power was ready for general use. Improvements allowed the engine to power many kinds of machines.

1804 Steam locomotive/Richard Trevithick The high-pressure steam engine produced more power than Watt had thought possible. Mounted on a carriage which could roll along metal rails, the engine carried its first load, ten tons of coal.

1807 Steamboat/Robert Fulton Ordering an engine directly from Watt, Fulton invented a steamship fit for use on rivers and bays. The *Clermont* provided fast, reliable transportation up and down the Hudson River. Fulton later designed 20 more steamboats.

This picture shows a steam-powered coal mine in the 1700s. Coal supplied the energy for factories that sprang up in the English countryside.

One new machine that helped to increase production was called the **flying shuttle.** Invented by **John Kay** in 1733, this machine could weave cloth twice as fast as the wooden looms. In 1765 **James Hargreaves** invented the **spinning jenny.** The spinning jenny could spin thread a thousand times faster than a spinning wheel. Now enough thread could be spun to supply the weaving machines.

New machines such as the spinning jenny and the flying shuttle changed the way people worked. The machines were too expensive for single families to own. They were too big to fit in cottages. The machines had to be placed in factories.

The new machines needed water as a source of power. Therefore factories were located near streams. Each factory employed many workers. Cities grew up around the factories as more people came there to work. After Watt perfected the steam engine, industries and cities also grew up in the coal-producing areas of Great Britain.

Some people moved to the cities because of changes happening in farm life at the beginning of the Industrial Revolution. New machines and new ways of farming created an agricultural revolution. Plows were built so that broken parts could be easily replaced. This made it possible to cultivate more land. Farmers experimented with less wasteful ways of planting seeds. Instead of tossing the seeds on top of the soil, farmers planted them in neat rows. This made it easier to control life-choking weeds.

The system of **crop rotation** used on farms today was invented by **Charles "Turnip" Townshend** in

1732. Rather than leaving some fields empty, Townshend found that soil would stay fertile if the farmer periodically changed the kind of crop being planted. By alternate planting of such crops as turnips and clover, all farmland could be productive. New farming methods let people grow more crops and raise more animals for meat and wool.

The new methods worked best on large farms, however. People with small farms often could not afford the new methods. They had to sell their land and look for work elsewhere. This, in turn, provided more workers for the factories.

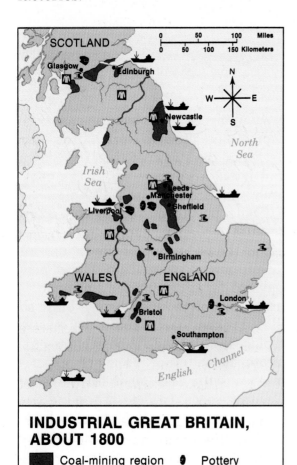

INDUSTRIAL GREAT BRITAIN, ABOUT 1800

- ■ Coal-mining region
- Cottons
- Ironworks
- Pottery
- Shipbuilding
- Woolens

More Changes

As more cloth and food were produced, people needed better ways to move them from place to place. New methods of transportation became an important part of the Industrial Revolution. Canals connected rivers with one another. Steamboats and steamships greatly increased the speed of water travel. New methods of road building made travel by land smoother, safer, and more efficient. Railroad trains, pulled by steam locomotives, carried goods and passengers on land.

The changes brought by the Industrial Revolution were both bad and good. On one hand, life in an industrial city was difficult. The swelling population was crowded into carelessly constructed buildings. Fires swept easily through these neighborhoods. Street dirt and garbage and unclean living areas fostered the spread of disease. Illnesses claimed the lives of many, especially children.

Working conditions in factories also were miserable. Wages were very low and factory workers had to work 12 hours or more every day except Sunday. These workers included women and young children, who were paid even less than the low salaries of other workers. Some children were deformed or crippled by unsafe machines. Dust and fumes in the air made many workers sick.

Not only the air inside the factories but also outside air became unbreathable. The coal that burned in the factories filled the skies over the cities with black smoke.

On the other hand, people's lives gradually improved as a result of the Industrial Revolution. A strong

After a day of heavy factory work, orphans and young children came home to the streets of London's rapidly growing slums.

middle class of businesspeople lessened the gap between rich and poor. There were more opportunities for people to advance and lead comfortable lives. Even poor people could afford to eat meat more often and have better clothes.

The Industrial Revolution made Great Britain the "workshop of the world." The revolution soon spread to other parts of Europe and to North America.

Reading Check

1. Which two natural resources were used in new ways during the Industrial Revolution?
2. For what industry were most machines made during the early part of the Industrial Revolution?
3. Describe three changes in farming methods that caused an agricultural revolution.
4. How did transportation improve during the Industrial Revolution?

Look for these important words:

Key Words
- aristocrats
- divine right
- fraternity
- reign
- Battle of Waterloo

People
- Louis XVI
- Marie Antoinette
- Napoleon Bonaparte

Places
- Versailles
- Bastille

Look for answers to these questions:

1. Why were French peasants dissatisfied with their lives during the eighteenth century?
2. What event started the French Revolution?
3. Who was the successful general who became emperor of the French Empire? What led to his final defeat?

2. THE FRENCH REVOLUTION AND NAPOLEON

Much of France is fertile, level farmland. Rivers provide water for farming and transportation. In spite of France's natural resources, most of its people led miserable lives in the eighteenth century. The improvements in farming and industry that had begun in Great Britain had hardly reached France. Poor people in French cities were often hungry. Most French peasants were bound to the land as serfs, as their ancestors had been. Only the **aristocrats** (uh•RIS•tuh•kratz), or nobles, led comfortable lives.

The French monarchy believed in the **divine right** of kings. *Divine right* meant that the kings' authority to rule came from God and could not be questioned. Some people in France did not agree. They knew that a revolution in England had changed the English monarchy during the seventeenth century. Afterwards English kings and queens had their power limited by Parliament, which represented both nobles and the common people. The American Revolution served as another example of people gaining new rights for themselves. The French people wanted the kind of freedom that people in North America had gained.

The French Revolution

In July 1789 King **Louis XVI** moved soldiers into Paris. Recent events had made it seem that there might be trouble. The people complained loudly about a careless king and his costly court. Because of a poor wheat crop, bread was hard to get and expensive. The French people were angry that their taxes paid for luxuries at the palace while the poor of France were starving. Leaders of these people stirred them to action.

In **Versailles** (vair•SY), where the king lived, a group called the National Assembly was trying to change the French government. The National Assembly represented the common people of France. The National Assembly could only advise the king, however, not command him. Even so, the French people hoped that the National Assembly could persuade the king to make badly needed changes.

A group of people who had gathered in Paris were not willing to wait, however. "To the Bastille! To the Bastille!" they shouted. The **Bastille** (bas•TEEL) was a grim prison-fortress in the city. A large supply of weapons was kept there. Parisians stormed the Bastille on July 14, 1789. They killed the guards, released the prisoners, and took the stored guns. Then they tore the fortress apart. The French Revolution had begun.

King Louis XVI tried to restore order. To show his concern he appeared in a hat bearing the new revolutionary colors—red, white, and blue. He promised that the soldiers in Paris would be sent away.

Promises were not enough. A mob, most of whom were women, marched to Versailles on October 5. They shouted their revolutionary slogan, "Liberty, equality, fraternity!" **Fraternity** (fruh•TUR•nuh•tee) means brotherhood and sisterhood. The mob seized the royal

The angry mob prepares to behead the Bastille's governor, who surrendered moments before. Their victory sparked revolts across France.

Marie Antoinette, Louis XVI, and their pleasure-loving nobles entertain a favorite court visitor, the plainly dressed Benjamin Franklin.

family and brought them back to Paris. "We have the baker, the baker's wife, and the baker's little boy," they sang. "Now we shall have bread!"

The National Assembly began writing a constitution for France in 1791. It said that the king might keep his throne but must obey the will of the people. Many French people did not trust the king, however. They demanded an end to the **reign,** or rule, of Louis XVI. Some people even called for his execution. Fiery speeches and newspaper articles by revolutionary leaders stirred the people's anger.

The most violent leaders became the strongest. They executed Louis XVI in January 1793. Many other executions followed, including that of the queen, **Marie Antoinette** (an•twuh•NET). No aristocrat or anyone even suspected of sympathizing with the old way of life was safe. The years of 1793 and 1794 were long remembered as the Reign of Terror.

At last, however, the people became tired of bloodshed. They wanted peace and order in France. A new constitution was written in 1795, which declared France a republic.

Napoleon

Several rulers of Europe, alarmed that the bloodshed of the French Revolution might spread to their own lands, went to war with the new republic. The leaders of the French Republic gave a high post in the army to a young man named **Napoleon Bonaparte** (nuh‧ POH‧lee‧uhn BOH‧nuh‧part).

Napoleon was a military genius who planned his operations carefully. He worked or fought for many hours without resting. Above all, he inspired men to fight for him. He led the French army to victory after victory.

Napoleon's ambitions were as boundless as his talent. In November 1799 he seized control of the French government. He crowned himself Emperor of the French in 1804. He extended his empire into parts of what is now Italy, Germany, Belgium, and the Netherlands. He set up kingdoms in Spain and Egypt. Napoleon became one of the most powerful men in European history.

Napoleon, mounted on a white charger, leads the French army across the Alps. Boulders beneath him bear the names of Charlemagne and Hannibal. The artist, Jacques Louis David, did this to show that Napoleon was as great as these two famous warriors.

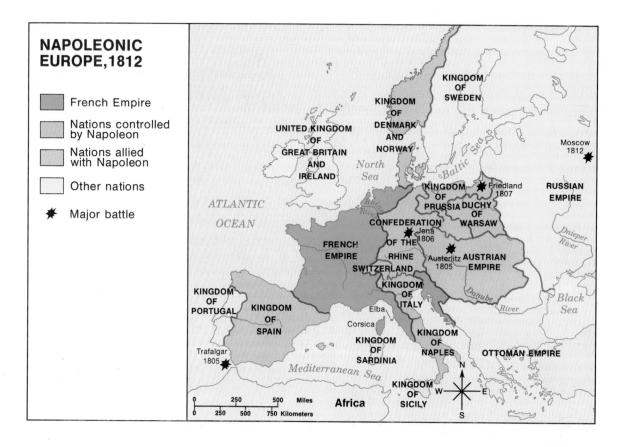

NAPOLEONIC EUROPE, 1812

- French Empire
- Nations controlled by Napoleon
- Nations allied with Napoleon
- Other nations
- ✸ Major battle

KINGDOM OF SWEDEN
KINGDOM OF DENMARK AND NORWAY
UNITED KINGDOM OF GREAT BRITAIN AND IRELAND
North Sea
Baltic Sea
Moscow 1812 ✸
RUSSIAN EMPIRE
ATLANTIC OCEAN
KINGDOM OF PRUSSIA
Friedland 1807 ✸
DUCHY OF WARSAW
CONFEDERATION OF THE RHINE
Jena 1806 ✸
Dnieper River
FRENCH EMPIRE
SWITZERLAND
Austerlitz 1805 ✸
AUSTRIAN EMPIRE
Danube River
Black Sea
KINGDOM OF PORTUGAL
KINGDOM OF SPAIN
KINGDOM OF ITALY
Elba
Corsica
KINGDOM OF SARDINIA
KINGDOM OF NAPLES
OTTOMAN EMPIRE
Trafalgar 1805 ✸
Mediterranean Sea
Africa
KINGDOM OF SICILY

0 250 500 Miles
0 250 500 750 Kilometers

Napoleon was busy at home, too. He restored peace inside France. He set up a stable central government and the Bank of France. He oversaw the writing of a new law code, the Napoleonic Code. This code granted some of the freedoms fought for during the revolution and is the basis for French law today. Napoleon, however, ruled with an iron fist, allowing no opposition.

Napoleon's battles were not always successful. When he provoked war with Great Britain in 1803, he was defeated by the British navy. In 1812 he tried to conquer Russia. Most of his men died of cold and hunger during the fierce Russian winter. Other defeats followed that one. Napoleon's ambitions were becoming costly for France.

Finally, in 1815 forces from Great Britain and other European countries defeated Napoleon at the **Battle of Waterloo.** He was sent away from France to the island of St. Helena. After his death in 1821, many people remembered him as a hero. A Second Empire under the rule of Napoleon's nephew was one of several forms of government that France tried before it became the republic it is today.

Reading Check

1. What fortress did the people of Paris destroy on July 14, 1789?
2. How did the National Assembly try to change the French government in 1791?
3. What happened in France during the Reign of Terror?
4. Why did European rulers declare war on the French Republic?

Modern Kings and Queens

Charles and Diana, Prince and Princess of Wales

The official announcement came on February 24, 1981: Charles, Prince of Wales, would marry Lady Diana Spencer on July 29. The future king of England had chosen his future queen. Not only the people of Great Britain but also well-wishers of other nations greeted the news with cheers and anticipation.

Everyone wanted to be a part of the excitement. Stories and photographs filled magazines and newspapers. Key rings, T-shirts, and every other imaginable souvenir lined shelves and shop counters. When the wedding day finally arrived, people all over the world knew, and in a sense took part. Satellites transmitted live television coverage of the event to every corner of the Earth.

Queen Margrethe of Denmark

The royal wedding put many people to work. It became as much an industry for England as it was an event in the history of the royal families of Europe. What about those royal families? Does royalty still exist? Who are the modern kings and queens?

Though most countries in the world are no longer governed by kings and queens, members of royal families still have important positions in their countries. Queen Margrethe of Denmark, for example, considers her role as queen an important job. She is a representative of her country and the person to whom the people of Denmark can look for guidance. Beatrix, Queen of the Netherlands, feels much the same way. As a working mother, she divides her time between serving her country and raising her three children.

King Juan Carlos of Spain

Today many princes, dukes, princesses, lords, and ladies have jobs and lead lives similar to people who have no titles. Prince Tomohito of Mikasa, a member of the royal family of Japan, is a successful journalist. In France, the Duke of Orleans publishes an art magazine while his brother, Prince Thibaut, runs an art gallery. Some kings, such as King Carl XVI of Sweden, even pay income tax. Even though most kings and queens have little power, there is still much public interest in royal families.

Look for these important words:

Key Words
- kaiser
- nationalism
- Central Powers
- Allies
- Treaty of Versailles
- Nazi

- depression
- chancellor
- Axis Powers

People
- Francis Ferdinand
- Adolf Hitler

Places
- Prussia
- Serbia
- West Germany
- East Germany

Look for answers to these questions:

1. How was World War I made possible by the "second Industrial Revolution"?
2. What troubles in Germany helped Adolf Hitler rise to power?
3. What happened to Germany after its defeat in World War II?

3. GERMANY AND THE WORLD WARS

At the time of Napoleon's death, the land we now call Germany was made up of many separate states. One of these states, **Prussia** (PRUSH.uh), became stronger than the others. The German states were united under the leadership of the king, or **kaiser** (KY.zur), of Prussia in 1871. They became the nation of Germany.

A wave of new inventions created a "second Industrial Revolution" at the end of the nineteenth century. People built machines made of steel rather than iron. Factories became larger than ever. Electricity replaced steam as a source of power. Germany was a leader in many of these changes.

New forms of transportation and communication "shrank the globe." Goods and people traveled more quickly in trains, steamships, automobiles, and airplanes. The telegraph sent messages faster than anyone could travel. These new inventions changed European affairs into world affairs. Unfortunately, they also helped to change European wars into world wars.

World War I

World War I began in 1914 after the assassination of an Austrian Archduke named **Francis Ferdinand.** Austria-Hungary blamed a small rival nation called **Serbia.** The quarrel caused by the assassination spread quickly to involve most of Europe. One reason it spread so rapidly was because of the alliances between many European countries. Their leaders had signed treaties to come to each other's aid in case of war.

Another reason war broke out so quickly was that a strong feeling of **nationalism,** or patriotic pride, had developed in most European countries. People were proud of their culture and history. Their countries had become independent nations. Each nation felt it had to prove it was stronger than the others. Nationalism was especially strong in Germany.

The warring powers arranged themselves into two groups. The **Central Powers** were Germany, Bulgaria, Austria-Hungary, and Turkey. The other group, the **Allies,** was made up of Russia, France, Great Britain, Italy, Belgium, Serbia, Montenegro (mahn•tuh•NEE•groh), and Japan. After German submarines sank several American ships in 1917, the United States entered the war on the side of the Allies. The conflict truly became a world war.

Many people thought the war would be over quickly. However, it lasted for more than four years. Some 65 million soldiers fought in it. At least 9 million of them died. Terrible weapons such as machine guns, poison gas, and tanks were used for the first time in this war. The war was fought not only on the land and sea but also under the sea in submarines and in the air with blimps and airplanes.

The Allies defeated the Central Powers in 1918. The peace treaty that ended the war was called the **Treaty of Versailles.** It was especially harsh toward Germany because Germany had supplied most of the soldiers and weapons for the Central Powers. It took away German lands both in Europe and elsewhere. It severely limited the number of soldiers and weapons the German government could have. It

World War I machine gunners wear masks to protect themselves from poison gas. New weapons made warfare deadlier than ever before.

ordered Germany to pay a huge sum of money to the Allies as a war debt.

Although victory went to the Allies, Great Britain, France, and Germany all lost in World War I. They lost, among other things, thousands upon thousands of young people who would have provided the leadership for their countries in the 1930s and 1940s.

The Rise of Adolf Hitler

After World War I Germany became a republic. This republic, like other European countries in the 1920s and early 1930s, faced many problems. For example, German money had become almost worthless. People had to use wheelbarrows full of banknotes to buy a loaf of bread. There was little money to repair the war damage to homes and businesses. Jobs were hard to find.

Many Germans were unhappy with the government during these difficult times. They were also angry about the Treaty of Versailles, which they blamed for many of their troubles. They wished a strong leader would make Germany powerful again. Some thought they had found that leader in a man named **Adolf Hitler.**

In 1920 Hitler organized a political party called the **Nazi** (NAHT•see) party. At first the Nazi party was small. Beginning in 1929, however, a world-wide **depression,** or slowdown in business, brought even more misery to Germany. Large numbers of German people listened to Hitler's screaming speeches. His fierce nationalism, with its claim that the Germans were a "super race," appealed to many. Businesspeople liked his promise to rebuild Germany's finances and industry.

Millions listened as Hitler promised war as the solution to Germany's problems.

In the early 1930s Hitler's Nazis won many seats in the German legislature, the Reichstag (RYKS•tahg). Using this new political strength, Hitler persuaded Germany's president to make him **chancellor,** or prime minister, in 1933. Hitler then asked the Reichstag to give him complete control of the government. Packed with Nazi supporters, the Reichstag agreed.

World War II and After

Hitler tightened his grip on Germany. He made the Nazi party the only legal political party. He set up secret police to spy on German citizens. He spread misleading stories to persuade Germans to think what he wanted them to think. Hitler convinced many people in Germany that their troubles were caused by the Jewish people. He passed laws that took away Jewish citizens' rights and property.

Meanwhile, Hitler prepared Germany for war. He took over Austria in 1938. In 1939 he invaded Czechoslovakia. When Hitler's armies marched into Poland in that same year, other European powers declared war on Germany. World War II had begun.

Italy and Japan fought on the same side as Germany during the war. These three powers were called the **Axis Powers.** The countries fighting against the Axis Powers were called the **Allies,** as they had been in World War I. The Allies included Great Britain, France, and most of the other countries of Europe.

During the war Hitler and his Nazis forced the Jews from all over Europe into prisons called concentration camps. People who opposed the Nazis also were sent to these camps. Millions of men, women, and children were executed in "death camps" or died there under terrible conditions.

In June 1941, after being invaded by Germany, the Soviet Union entered the war on the side of the Allies. On December 7, 1941, Japanese planes bombed Pearl Harbor, Hawaii. The following day the United States declared war against Japan. Within several days the United States was also at war with the other Axis Powers.

Adolph Hitler's powerful, well-trained armies, with their tanks and dive bombers, had easily conquered the smaller nations that they invaded. They took over France. They severely damaged Great Britain and the Soviet

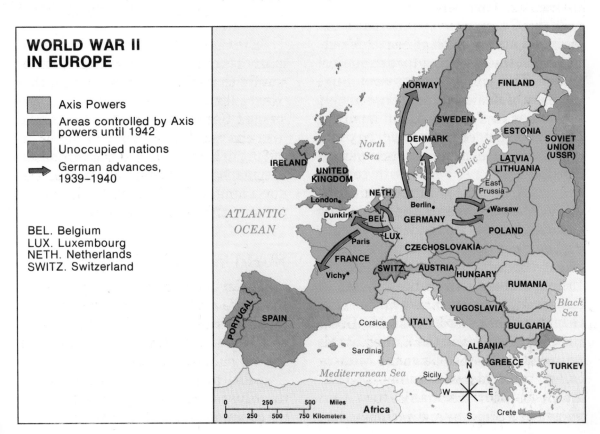

WORLD WAR II IN EUROPE

- Axis Powers
- Areas controlled by Axis powers until 1942
- Unoccupied nations
- German advances, 1939–1940

BEL. Belgium
LUX. Luxembourg
NETH. Netherlands
SWITZ. Switzerland

In 1961 the Soviets built the Berlin Wall to prevent East Germans from moving to freedom in West Berlin. Berlin lies within East Germany.

Union, but they were unable to conquer these countries. The Germans also marched across much of North Africa.

At last the war began to turn against Hitler. The United States sent huge numbers of soldiers and supplies to help the Allies in Europe. Allied bombing attacks weakened Germany. The countries that Germany had conquered were freed one by one. Faced with certain defeat, Hitler killed himself in April 1945. A few days later, the remaining German leaders surrendered.

The four most powerful Allies—Great Britain, France, the Soviet Union, and the United States—set up temporary governments over parts of Germany. The parts controlled by Great Britain, France, and the United States reunited in 1949 to form the country called the Federal Republic of Germany, or **West Germany.** West Germany has a democratic government like those of most other Western European countries.

The Soviet Union refused to let its part of the German territory rejoin the rest of Germany. That territory is now **East Germany,** or the German Democratic Republic. It has a government like that of the Soviet Union. The reuniting of Germany is a dream of many Germans, but it is unlikely to come true for a long time, if ever.

Reading Check

1. What were the countries fighting against Germany in World Wars I and II called?
2. How was Germany punished following its defeat in World War I?
3. What was the name of Hitler's political party?
4. Why is Germany divided into two countries today?

228

Look for these important words:

Key Words
- socialism
- communism
- czar
- Bolsheviks

- soviet
- collective farms

People
- Karl Marx
- Nicholas II

- Lenin
- Joseph Stalin

Places
- Siberia
- Moscow

Look for answers to these questions:

1. What solution to the problem of poverty did Karl Marx propose?
2. What form of government was established in Russia after the Russian Revolution?
3. How did Joseph Stalin make changes in industry and farming?
4. How has the government of the Soviet Union affected the governments of other Eastern European countries?

4. THE SOVIET UNION AND COMMUNISM

The Union of Soviet Socialist Republics (USSR), usually called the Soviet Union, is the world's largest country. It stretches across large parts of Europe and Asia, covering about one-sixth of the world's land area. It is about two and one-half times the size of the United States.

The European part of the Soviet Union is mostly hills and plains. Much of it is good farmland. The eastern, or Asian, part of the Soviet Union is more mountainous and thinly settled. The largest region in the eastern part of the Soviet Union is **Siberia.** Huge reserves of coal, iron ore, copper, oil, and natural gas from Siberia have helped the Soviet Union grow into a great industrial power in the twentieth century.

Soviet planning has given special attention to industrial projects in Siberia.

The following labels appear on the map:

ARCTIC OCEAN

THE SOVIET UNION
⊛ National capital
⊛ Republic capital

Karl Marx

The government of the Soviet Union is based in part on the ideas of a German named **Karl Marx.** Marx described some of these ideas in a book called the *Communist Manifesto,* published in 1848.

Marx was troubled by the poverty in early industrial Europe. He believed the solution was to share wealth more equally. Marx thought that workers, not wealthy businesspeople, should own all farms and factories.

"Workers of the world, unite!" Marx said. The workers were sure to win in a struggle with the business owners, he thought. The workers would then set up a society in which all property would be owned by the government. Under this system, called **socialism,** the government would make sure that people got everything they needed. Marx believed that once everything was divided equally there would be no separate classes of people.

Followers of Marx took his ideas to many European countries. Some groups wanted to use violence to bring about change. Government leaders often tried to outlaw these groups. In Russia, however, a form of Marx's system was adopted after a successful revolution. The system was called **communism,** a name that is drawn from the word *community.* Today the communist governments of Eastern European countries are strongly influenced by the Soviet Union. It has been developing its form of communism since the early 1900s.

230

The Russian Revolution

In the 1800s most Russians lived just as Europeans had in the Middle Ages. European history—the Renaissance, the Reformation, the Industrial Revolution—had touched the Russian people only slightly, if at all. The nobles and the king, or **czar** (ZAHR), held all the wealth and power. The government of the czar did little or nothing to help the many serfs, poor peasants, and low-paid factory workers.

World War I made the problems of the Russians even worse. Millions of people were killed. Food was in short supply. Russians blamed the czar, **Nicholas II,** for the poverty and starvation. In March 1917, the Russian people rebelled. Workers all over the country refused to work. Even the army withdrew its support of the government. The people demanded that the czar give up his throne. The following year Nicholas and all his family were executed.

During the revolution different groups in Russia struggled for power. The most violent of the groups, the **Bolsheviks** (BOL•shuh•viks), finally won. The leader of the Bolsheviks was **Lenin** (LEN•in). Lenin wanted a communist government. He was certain that communism would replace all other systems throughout the world.

In November 1917, Lenin and the Bolsheviks seized control of the government. They made the Communist party the only legal political party in Russia. They destroyed groups that disagreed with them. The Communists arrested or killed religious leaders, businesspeople, and anyone who

This painting by Ilya Repin shows the costly wedding of Czar Nicholas. Much of what the Czar did, including his marriage, was criticized by the Russian people.

231

The Kremlin, headquarters of the Soviet government, was the ancient capital of Russia. Cathedrals and palaces stand inside its walls.

opposed their government. The government of ruthless czars had been replaced with yet another harsh government.

Under Lenin, **Moscow** became the new capital of Russia. In 1922 the name of the country was changed to the Union of Soviet Socialist Republics. The word **soviet** referred to workers' councils that operated factories, businesses, and farms for the government. Above them all was a Supreme Soviet, headed by Lenin himself.

Although Lenin established a strong government, he was unable to make great improvements in the lives of the Soviet people. A bloody civil war made conditions even worse. The Communists of the Soviet Union were called Reds, for that was the chief color of their flag. Those Russians who opposed them were called Whites. The Red and White armies battled each other brutally between 1918 and 1920, leaving the country in ruins. The Soviet Union was still in a desperate position when Lenin died in 1924.

Joseph Stalin

After Lenin's death, his followers competed for control of the government. The winner was **Joseph Stalin** (STAH.lin). Stalin means "steel." It was a well-chosen name, one that he selected for himself. Upon taking control Stalin was determined to strengthen the Soviet Union quickly. He had everyone enroll in defense organizations where they raised flags, sang Russian songs, and saluted statues and pictures.

Stalin believed that his most important job was to make the Soviet Union a world power. To gain strength, he declared, the Soviet Union would have to build up its industries. To do this, it had to buy machinery from the West. It had to pay for this machinery with food, the only thing of value that the Soviet Union produced. However, the Soviet Union needed most of the crops to feed its people.

Food production would have to be increased. Thus Stalin ordered that small farms be combined into giant **collective farms.** Stalin's secret police killed hundreds of thousands of small farmers who opposed him. He forced the peasants to work on the farms.

Stalin placed all farming and industry under state control. He laid out the country's path to modernization in stages called Five-Year Plans. Each Five-Year Plan set goals higher than the one before. Stalin ordered that huge factories be built and that people be trained to work in them. By the

Soviet steel mills operated at top speed in the 1940s. War-weary workers labored to meet the goals of the government's five-year plan.

beginning of World War II, he had made Russia a world leader in industry.

Under Stalin's government most people had food and jobs, but few of them enjoyed the comforts of life. Soviet citizens had no more voice in their government than the people of Hitler's Germany did. A few Soviet citizens complained: Why were students taught never to question their government? Why could people not say what they pleased? Why did life have to be so hard?

Stalin responded by killing or imprisoning the people who complained. He sent countless millions of people into slave labor camps. It is estimated that at least 30 million Soviet citizens died as Stalin's prisoners. His police spied on, arrested, and often tortured anyone suspected of opposing him. The arrested citizens rarely had the right to a trial. Stalin said that his wishes must be carried out because the country was in a new kind of war. In this war, his government was seeking to spread communism.

The Cold War

After World War II the Allies set up temporary governments in some countries that had been overrun by the Germans. Countries governed by Great Britain, France, or the United States became independent again in a few years. The Soviet Union, however, refused to give up the Eastern European countries it controlled. Stalin made some of these countries part of

In 1945 the Allied victors of World War II met in Yalta, Russia, to discuss Europe's future. From left to right they are Churchill, Roosevelt, and Stalin.

After a 1980 strike by workers, the Polish government briefly tolerated Solidarity, a labor organization independent of the Communist party.

the USSR. He helped form communist governments in the others, establishing a kind of Soviet empire. Thus Europe became divided into two camps, one communist, the other democratic.

Most countries in Eastern Europe today have communist governments. The Soviet Union sends soldiers and weapons any time rebellions threaten these governments. Eastern European countries with communist governments include Poland, Czechoslovakia, Hungary, Albania, Bulgaria, East Germany, Romania, and Yugoslavia. Many people in these countries are not happy. Uprisings in Hungary, Czechoslovakia, and Poland have shown that the people would prefer something other than a communist government.

Joseph Stalin died in 1953. Since then, recent Soviet leaders have used some of his ideas and rejected others. As a result, relations between communist countries and democratic ones have been poor. The high level of tension between the two groups of countries is known as the Cold War. Although the Cold War continues, in the last few years efforts have been made to seek understanding and deal peacefully with each other.

Reading Check

1. Who wrote the book called the *Communist Manifesto?*
2. Which Communist group took over the Russian government after the revolution?
3. How did Lenin and Stalin deal with people who opposed them?
4. Why was it important for Stalin to increase food production in the Soviet Union?

5. EUROPE TODAY

Wars brought many hardships to Europeans during the twentieth century. Most countries, however, have recovered and are strong once more. In most of Western Europe industries are again efficient sources of manufactured goods. European farms are among the most productive on Earth. As a result, most Western Europeans enjoy prosperity.

Europe's large population is crowded into a small continent divided into many nations. Since World War II many of these nations have cooperated to solve their common problems. They have formed trade associations and have worked together in science, finance, transportation, and defense.

International Organizations

To improve trade and to compete with such countries as Japan and the United States, Western European countries joined together to form the European Economic Community (EEC). The EEC or **Common Market,** as it is called, was established in 1957. Its original members were France, Belgium, Luxembourg, the Netherlands, Italy, and West Germany. Denmark, Great Britain, and Ireland voted to join in 1973. Greece joined in 1981 and Spain in 1986.

The Soviet Union and the Eastern European communist countries, except Yugoslavia and Albania, also have an international economic organization. It is called the Council for Mutual Economic Assistance **(COMECON).** Non-European members include Cuba, Mongolia, and Vietnam. The Soviet Union is the main producer and buyer in COMECON.

As in other parts of the world, European countries have suffered from

Of the many organizations dividing the West and the communist world, NATO is one of the most powerful. NATO headquarters are in Brussels, Belgium.

inflation. Inflation is a constant increase in the price of goods and services. **Unemployment** also has been a problem. There are not enough jobs for Europe's large population. The Common Market promotes an easier flow of money and workers from country to country. Prices of European goods sold in Common Market countries are kept lower than those of goods from other continents. This encourages Europeans to buy their own products, which in turn keeps many Europeans employed.

European countries cooperate in the development of sources of energy as well as in trade. Except for the Soviet Union, most European countries have only small reserves of oil and natural gas. Coal and hydroelectric power run most factories and heat homes. Coal burning creates air pollution, however. European countries, therefore, import expensive oil or turn to other energy sources. Europe has been building many nuclear plants to add to their energy sources. The Common Market seeks better use of both coal and nuclear power.

Finally, Europeans are cooperating in matters of defense. Most nations of Western Europe have joined with the United States and Canada in a defense organization called the **North Atlantic Treaty Organization,** or NATO. NATO was formed in 1949 and is now headquartered in **Brussels,** Belgium. The purpose of this organization is to protect member countries from attack. The members of NATO have agreed that an armed attack on any of them will be considered an attack on all. They have given each other financial and military help to maintain a strong defense.

The countries of Eastern Europe formed their own defense organization. Because they met regularly in **Warsaw,** the capital of Poland, they became known as the **Warsaw Pact**

Automobiles, an important West German product, are assembled by workers.

Sheep raised in England provide wool for the manufacture of fine cloth.

Grapes grown in the French province of Champagne are among the world's finest.

Cod, sardines, and tuna are three kinds of fish caught off of Portugal's coast.

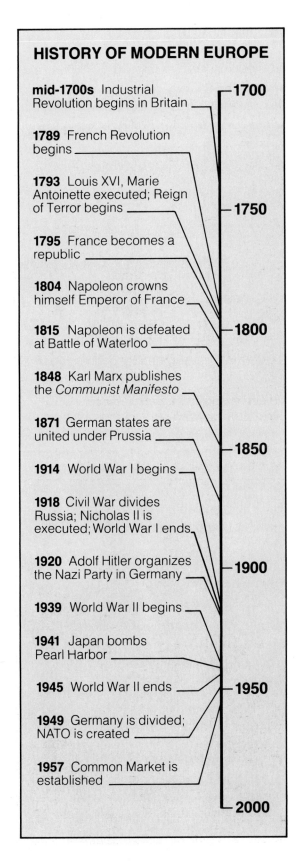

HISTORY OF MODERN EUROPE

mid-1700s Industrial Revolution begins in Britain ⎯⎯ **1700**

1789 French Revolution begins ⎯⎯

1793 Louis XVI, Marie Antoinette executed; Reign of Terror begins ⎯⎯ **1750**

1795 France becomes a republic ⎯⎯

1804 Napoleon crowns himself Emperor of France ⎯⎯

1815 Napoleon is defeated at Battle of Waterloo ⎯⎯ **1800**

1848 Karl Marx publishes the *Communist Manifesto* ⎯⎯

1871 German states are united under Prussia ⎯⎯

1914 World War I begins ⎯⎯ **1850**

1918 Civil War divides Russia; Nicholas II is executed; World War I ends ⎯⎯

1920 Adolf Hitler organizes the Nazi Party in Germany ⎯⎯ **1900**

1939 World War II begins ⎯⎯

1941 Japan bombs Pearl Harbor ⎯⎯

1945 World War II ends ⎯⎯ **1950**

1949 Germany is divided; NATO is created ⎯⎯

1957 Common Market is established ⎯⎯

⎯⎯ **2000**

nations. Led by the Soviet Union, they announced that they, too, would combine their forces and weapons to defend themselves.

Europe's Changing Role

For hundreds of years Europe led the world in both political power and achievements in art and science. European countries today do not have quite so much political power as they did during earlier centuries. World leadership has passed largely to the United States, the Soviet Union, and China. However, Europeans still make important contributions to science, art, politics, and trade.

Europeans are proud of their different cultures, languages, and lifestyles. They know that they have a common **heritage.** Their heritage is the wealth of ideas that have passed down through their history. The European heritage began with the achievements of ancient Greece and Rome. It includes the artistic and cultural gifts of the Middle Ages and the Renaissance. Memories of this heritage help Europeans work together to meet the challenges they face today.

Reading Check

1. What is another name for the European Economic Community?
2. Why are Europeans seeking energy sources to replace coal?
3. What is the name of the Western European defense organization? the Eastern European defense organization?
4. How is Europe's role in the world different today than during its past?

One of the most common questions asked by children and adults is "Why?" Almost every event is the result of something that happened before or the reason for something that follows. We call this relationship between events **cause and effect.** A cause is an action that leads to an event. An effect is the event brought about by an action.

Suppose you are pouring a glass of milk. You knock over the glass and milk spills on the floor. How would you explain the puddle of milk on the floor? You could say that knocking the glass over was the cause. The spilled milk is the effect. One way to identify cause and effect is to remember that the cause is *why* it happened. The effect is *what* happened.

Here are some examples of causes and effects. In each pair, tell which is the cause and which is the effect.

The ground gets wet.
It rains all day.

Lumberjacks saw through a tree trunk.
The tree falls.

The walnut cracks.
You hit a walnut with a hammer.

Some cause-and-effect relationships are easy to recognize. Often a cause will be stated, followed immediately by the effect. However, you cannot assume that causes and effects always follow in order. To help find causes and effects, you can look for word clues. Words and phrases such as *because, as a result of, since, brought about,* and *therefore* are some of the clues that

signal cause and effect. Notice the word clues in the following examples.

The road was closed *because* it needed repairs.
As a result of bad weather, the game was canceled.
Marty won first place in the speech contest. *Therefore,* she will compete in the statewide contest.

Even with word clues, cause-and-effect relationships may not be easy to find. An event may have more than one cause or effect, and these may not be obvious. For example, suppose that you have started a vegetable garden. After a rain shower, the plants begin to grow. In this case the rain seems to be the cause, but there are other causes as well. You planted the seeds at the right time of year, and you added fertilizer. The plants might not have grown unless you had done these things.

Flow Charts

History is a series of events. Often the results of one event become the causes of later events. One way to show a series of events is by using a **flow chart.** Study the following example.

Europe was covered with forests in the early Middle Ages. For many centuries wood was used for building almost everything. It was used for heating and cooking. Later, it provided fuel for making iron. As populations grew, forests were cleared to make room for farms. Fewer trees meant less wood. Wood became more and more expensive.

By the 1600s many people could not afford to heat their homes with wood. Although mining was difficult and dangerous, people began to use coal for fuel.

Beginning in the 1700s, the steam engine helped bring coal to the surface and pump water out of the mines. Coal had to be carried from the mines to villages and towns. Horses, which were used to haul goods over land, were slow and expensive. The steam locomotive, invented in the early 1800s, became a faster and cheaper way to transport coal.

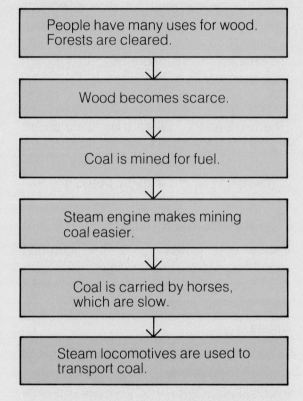

People have many uses for wood. Forests are cleared.

↓

Wood becomes scarce.

↓

Coal is mined for fuel.

↓

Steam engine makes mining coal easier.

↓

Coal is carried by horses, which are slow.

↓

Steam locomotives are used to transport coal.

Because forests were cleared, there was less wood. Wood became expensive. This effect became the cause of another event. What was the event? In turn, the use of coal produced other effects. The heavy use of wood began a chain of events that eventually led to the invention of the steam engine and railroads. The flow chart helps you to see how one cause leads to an effect, which then becomes the cause of another effect.

CHECKING YOUR SKILLS

Read the paragraphs below and answer the questions that follow.

New inventions brought about the Industrial Revolution. In fact, some people have said that during that time the most important invention was the act of inventing. One very useful invention was the steam engine. Human strength and horsepower were limited. Windmills depended on wind power. Water mills used the power of flowing water. However, the machines powered by wind and water had to remain in one place. Steam power was less limited. Because it used heat, steam power could be used anywhere that a good supply of water was available and a fire could be built.

The engines developed by James Watt used steam power to force wheels to turn regularly. Since these wheels could be driven automatically, they could run for long periods of time. Unlike humans or animals, steam engines never got tired. As a result, businesspeople all over Great Britain bought steam engines to power their newly invented machinery. Powered by steam, weaving machines in a factory could produce many times more cloth products than hand weavers could. The machine-made object had arrived.

1. What caused the Industrial Revolution?

2. List three clues that signal cause-and-effect relationships in the preceding paragraphs.

3. Why was steam power less limited than other sources previously used?

4. What advantages did steam engines have over humans and animals?

5. What effect did steam engines have on the way products were made in Great Britain?

CHAPTER 8 REVIEW

USING WORDS

Explain the meaning of each of the words listed below. Then use each word in a complete sentence.

1. **aristocrats**
2. **communism**
3. **depression**
4. **divine right**
5. **heritage**
6. **Industrial Revolution**
7. **inflation**
8. **nationalism**
9. **reign**
10. **socialism**

REVIEWING FACTS

1. How were most goods made in Great Britain before the Industrial Revolution?

2. Name two machines that helped increase cloth production in Great Britain.

3. What caused cities to grow and develop during the Industrial Revolution?

4. Which two countries had revolutions that inspired the French to question the divine right of their monarchy?

5. How did Napoleon help restore order in France?

6. What were two reasons that an international quarrel became a world war in 1914?

7. How were the Russian and French revolutions alike? How were they different?

8. What methods did Stalin's government use to modernize the Soviet Union?

9. What two groups of countries are waging a Cold War?

10. Name two important European international organizations and describe their purposes.

THINKING CRITICALLY

1. Some people say that new inventions are causing a "third Industrial Revolution" today. Why might they think that? What inventions might be causing such a revolution?

2. Napoleon, Hitler, and Stalin were powerful leaders. What conditions seem likely to allow such rulers to seize power? What are the dangers of allowing one person to have complete control?

PRACTICING SKILLS

Cause and Effect Read the following lists. Then match each cause with its effect. (You may have to refer to your text to match them correctly.)

Cause

1. King Louis XVI ignores the problems of French peasants.
2. A person from Serbia assassinates Archduke Ferdinand.
3. Russian peasants and soldiers rebel.
4. The Japanese attack Pearl Harbor, Hawaii.

Effect

a. The United States enters World War II.
b. World War I begins.
c. Nicholas II gives up his throne.
d. An angry mob attacks the Bastille.

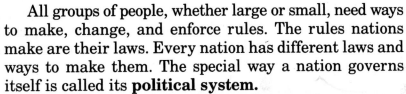

CLOSE-UP

COMPARING POLITICAL SYSTEMS

Augustus Caesar

All groups of people, whether large or small, need ways to make, change, and enforce rules. The rules nations make are their laws. Every nation has different laws and ways to make them. The special way a nation governs itself is called its **political system.**

Throughout history people have developed many types of political systems. Among the ancient Egyptians a pharaoh held most of the power. Some pharaohs were better than others and ruled wisely and fairly. Yet, fair or not, the pharaoh's word was always the law.

In ancient Greece there was no single ruler. Each city had its own government. For some of these governments the power to rule came from all the citizens of the city. This type of political system was very different from the one in ancient Egypt.

There are many ways to study political systems and to see how they differ. One important question to ask is *How much power does the government have?* In some modern countries the government either owns or controls all land, buildings, schools, and newspapers. It can make laws affecting every part of its citizens' lives. The government can decide what work people do, what is taught in schools, and what is written in newspapers. Such a system of government is called **totalitarianism** (toh‧tal‧uh‧TAIR‧ee‧uh‧niz‧uhm). The government has *total* authority.

In other nations, the people govern themselves. Through voting they choose representatives to make laws for them. They have constitutions that guarantee certain rights. Their government cannot make laws that harm these rights. These nations have democratic governments.

243

You may remember that the ancient Greeks gave the world the idea of democracy and the word itself. In Greek, *demos* means "the people" and *kratos* means "rule." A democracy is rule by the people.

Greek democracy was a *pure* democracy. Everyone who was a citizen could meet to make laws. Today most nations have too many people for this type of democracy. As in ancient Rome, citizens elect representatives to make laws and decisions for them. A government of this type is a representative democracy or **republic.** Another question we can ask about a political system is *Who governs?* Is it a single person, a small group, or many people?

Monarchy

A government ruled by a king or queen is a monarchy. The word *monarchy* means "rule by one." A king or queen is born into power and usually rules for life. One example is the English monarchy.

England nearly always has been ruled by a king or queen. Elizabeth I reigned from 1558 until 1603. She was one of England's most famous monarchs. Queen Elizabeth did not rule alone, however. Parliament helped make the nation's laws. The most powerful members of Parliament were nobles chosen by the queen. The English queen shared power with Parliament, but no one doubted who really ruled England. Queen Elizabeth could keep England at peace or declare war. She could reward friends and punish enemies. Queen Elizabeth I had almost unlimited power.

In modern times, the monarchies in Great Britain and many other countries have given way to different political systems. These nations no longer believe that their leaders are born to rule. In Great Britain Parliament is the lawmaking body. The prime minister is the chief leader.

Great Britain continues to have monarchs, but they no longer rule. They may attend ceremonies and perform other public duties. Queen Elizabeth II reigns in Great Britain today. She is an important symbol of its history and glory.

Elizabeth II

244

Dictatorship

Dictators have existed since the days of ancient Rome. The word *dictator* means "one who gives orders." Like kings or queens, a dictator is a leader who rules alone. A dictator, however, is not born into power. Often a dictator seizes control by the violent overthrow of the government. Powerful groups in the country support the rule of this leader. This type of government is called a **dictatorship.**

Because dictators often force their way to power, their rule may be unpopular with some people. They may have to use force to keep their power. They often can keep power only by destroying enemies. They cannot allow public criticism. Therefore, dictators also control what kind of information is printed or broadcast to the people. Depending on how powerful they are, dictators may rule for only a short time—months or even weeks—or for life.

Libyan soldiers

LIBYA'S DICTATORSHIP Libya was a colony of Italy from the early 1900s until World War II. This country in North Africa then became a monarchy. In 1969 a group of army officers overthrew King Idris and took power. The leader of this revolt was Colonel Moammar El-Gadhafi (moh•AHM•ahr el•guh•DAH•fee). Since the 1969 revolt Gadhafi has ruled Libya. His government has **absolute,** or complete, control of all of Libya's affairs.

Gadhafi rules Libya as a dictator. He allows no one to challenge his decisions. Anyone who disagrees with Gadhafi can be jailed or executed without trial. He controls the armed forces, the press, and important government committees. He also controls the Libyan economy.

Libya's oil wealth has brought some prosperity to the country in recent years. However, the people have had no voice in their government. There have been no elections in Libya since 1969. Libyans have no influence over how their country's oil wealth is spent. The threat of force prevents Libyans from attempting to make any changes or even from expressing their opinions. Gadhafi, not the people, rules in Libya.

245

Czar Nicholas and his family

Oligarchy

Most modern dictatorships have a small group that controls the government. The leaders in the group may be nobles who own much of the nation's wealth. Sometimes the group is a political party.

Such a government is called an **oligarchy** (AWL‧uh‧gahr‧kee), which means "rule by a few." An oligarchy may have a leader or premier (prih‧MEER). The leader, however, does not rule alone. In the Soviet Union, for example, the premier needs the support of the Communist party.

SOVIET DICTATORSHIP Generations of czars and World War I had brought great poverty to Russia. When the Communist party came to power in 1917, it wanted to form a new kind of government. The Communists used violence to install their government. Total control allowed them to develop the government quickly. The Communists seized ownership of all property. Workers were ordered to factories and large state-owned farms.

Today the Soviets believe they have made progress. Soviet citizens have better medical care, housing, and education. The government allows individuals to make some decisions, especially in their work places. The Soviet Union has become a major world power.

Soviet power, however, still comes from the Communist party. Although only about 6 percent of the Soviet people are party members, the Communist party continues to control every part of people's lives. The State plans the economy. It chooses what goods will be produced and who will make them. It controls the press and punishes those who disagree.

All government officials must be members of the Communist party. They can decide who is allowed to join the party. The majority of Soviet citizens do not take part in the important decisions that affect their lives. Soviet citizens vote during elections, sometimes in very large numbers. Yet, there is only one carefully controlled party for whom to vote.

Lenin, the "Father of Communist Russia"

Democracy

In democratic nations, the people have opportunities to participate fully in their government. They freely choose representatives to promote their points of view. They can criticize when their government acts in a way that they consider unacceptable.

Most democratic governments are republics. The power in a republic comes from its citizens whose political freedoms are protected by law.

White House

Capitol Building

Supreme Court

THE UNITED STATES   The United States is the oldest large republic in the world today. Times have changed, but the basic ideas of American democracy have not. People in the United States govern themselves. They do so by voting, speaking out, seeking public office, and joining political groups. They can vote for anyone they wish. To stay in office, government leaders must listen to voters. In these ways, the government shares power with the American people.

The Constitution of the United States guarantees the right of each individual over age 18 to take part in government. The government cannot take this right away. For their part, citizens in a democracy have the responsibility to participate in government.

Through the years, the Constitution has remained the basis of American government. It states the important rights in which Americans believe. All law in the United States is based on the Constitution. In addition, the Constitution describes how the national government is organized. It provides ways to make, change, and enforce the laws of the United States.

The national government only has certain powers. The Constitution gives all other powers to the states and the people. This makes the United States a **federal republic,** or union of states. The federal government decides matters that affect all the states or the people as a whole. Individual states are responsible for local government. For example, each state controls its own schools, highways, and law enforcement.

247

THE BRANCHES OF THE UNITED STATES GOVERNMENT

• Can overide a veto

• May veto proposed laws

EXECUTIVE BRANCH
The President

- Recommends laws
- Heads armed forces
- Manages the government

LEGISLATIVE BRANCH
The Congress

House of Representatives   Senate

- Passes taxes
- Makes new laws

• May rule a President's actions unconstitutional

• Appoints judges

Voters

• May change size of Supreme Court

• Decides on constitutionality of laws

JUDICIAL BRANCH
The Supreme Court and other Federal Courts

- Judges fairness of laws
- Settles disputes between states

 System of checks & balances

The United States government is divided into three separate branches: the **executive,** the **legislative,** and the **judicial.** Each of these branches has certain responsibilities.

The executive branch manages the government. It enforces the nation's laws. As executive, the President is head of many departments that manage the nation's money and resources. The President is commander in chief of the military and the chief of foreign affairs. The President can recommend laws and can veto proposed laws.

The legislative branch, Congress, is responsible for lawmaking. It is divided into two groups, or houses: the Senate and the House of Representatives. Each state has two senators. The number of representatives a state has depends on the size of its population. Voters in each state elect members of Congress.

The judicial branch decides if laws have been broken or if they are unfair. The Supreme Court is the highest court in the land. Nine judges, or **justices,** are appointed by the President for life. They review laws to find out if Constitutional rights are being violated. The Supreme Court also settles disputes between states or between a state and the federal government.

This system of sharing power in the government is known as **checks and balances.** The power of government is *balanced* among the three branches. The Constitution also provides ways to *check*, or control, each branch from becoming too powerful. Each branch is given some of the powers that the others have. For instance, Congress passes laws, but the Supreme Court can declare a law unconstitutional. The President may veto a law, but Congress can vote to override, or set aside, the veto.

As you have seen, government in the United States is shared by the federal government, the states, and the people. Unlike a dictatorship, the American system of government prevents any one leader or group from gaining too much power. At voting places, in political parties and groups, in city and state governments, and in the federal government, millions of Americans are involved in governing America. When people are free to take part in government, they can protect their rights.

Voting in the United States

249

Advantages and Disadvantages

A U.S. political convention

The U.S. Congress in session

You have looked at four types of political systems. Only one of these is a democracy. Democracies are outnumbered even among modern nations. Why is this so?

History gives some reasons. Most nations have had monarchies in the past. When a monarch is just, rule by one person has certain advantages. A monarch rules for life. A long rule can bring order and stability to the nation. People know what to expect for the future. Many citizens feel secure under a strong leader who makes all decisions.

Even so, a nation is always in danger when one person or group has too much power. Leaders who do not have to answer to their people can become cruel and unjust. They can take away their citizens' rights and punish enemies harshly.

In time, the people may become angry and their anger may build into violence. In some cases, revolutions result. The French Revolution in 1789 was one example. While the king and the nobles lived in luxury, many French peasants went hungry. During the revolution, the king and many nobles were killed.

Change in a democracy is much slower and usually peaceful. Many people from all parts of society make decisions together. Citizens and leaders alike must work within the law. They often disagree with each other. Arriving at a decision with which the majority of people agree takes time. During that time leaders can change, which makes long-range planning difficult. These things mean a government may be slow to act. In the case of an emergency, slow reaction might be a disadvantage. However, it also means a government will make fewer reckless decisions. The decisions it makes will have a better chance of working over the years.

The people in a democracy have choices. This may well be the most important benefit of this system. In dictatorships, people have very few choices. In democracies all citizens have political freedom and are expected to use it. It is this idea that separates democracy from all other political systems.

UNIT 2 REVIEW

Words to Remember

Number your paper from 1 to 10. Complete the sentences below with the words from the following list.

communism　　　**nationalism**
democracy　　　**patrons**
dictator　　　　**philosophers**
feudalism　　　**republic**
heresy　　　　**serfs**

1. A system of _____ in Athens allowed all citizens to vote on the decisions that governed them.

2. Greek _____, like Socrates, encouraged people to think for themselves and to seek truth.

3. The early Romans established a _____, which was governed by the Roman Senate.

4. The absolute rule of a Roman _____ usually ended when he was overthrown or killed.

5. The Middle Ages was a time when noble and peasant were bound together under a system called _____.

6. Feudal _____ could not leave the land to look for work.

7. Renaissance artists often lived at the courts of _____.

8. For his attacks on the Church of Rome, Luther was accused of _____.

9. Feelings of _____ in Europe helped to cause World Wars I and II.

10. The nondemocratic form of government in the Soviet Union is called _____.

Focus on Main Ideas

1. How was democracy in ancient Greece different from democracy in the United States today?

2. Name three ways that ancient Greece has affected your life.

3. Why was Rome so successful at governing a large empire?

4. List four reasons for the fall of Rome.

5. How did life change throughout Europe's countryside after the fall of Rome?

6. What contributed to the growth of nation-states in Europe at the end of the Middle Ages?

7. Europeans in the Renaissance thought of their time as a "rebirth." Why did they feel that way?

8. How did each of the following change during the Renaissance?
   a. art
   b. government
   c. religion
   d. science

9. List at least two advantages and two disadvantages of the Industrial Revolution.

10. How did World Wars I and II affect the spread of communism in Europe?

The English Bill of Rights was written in 1689. This document served as a way of transferring much of the power of the monarch to a freely elected Parliament. Thus a major step was taken to guarantee the rights of the individual. Read the following excerpts from the English Bill of Rights. Think about how they influenced the writers of our own Bill of Rights. Then write one or two paragraphs explaining this influence.

> The freedom of speech and debates or proceedings in Parliament ought not to be ... questioned in any court or place out of Parliament.

> Excessive bail ought not to be required, nor excessive fines imposed, nor cruel and unusual punishments inflicted. . . .

ACTIVITIES

1. **Research/Art** Imagine you are traveling through Europe's history in a "time machine." Draw one or more postcards to send to your friends in the twentieth century. On each postcard, show an event from one of the historical periods covered in this unit. Title and date the backs of the postcards. Then describe briefly your impressions of each event.

2. **Research/Technology** Investigate the invention of something you use at home or at school. Find out who invented the object, when it was invented, and what older invention it improved or replaced.

3. **Research/Current Events** Find and read current magazine or newspaper articles on countries and events in Europe. Choose one country to research or collect articles on different countries. Organize the articles by topic for your class scrapbook. Topics could include government and foreign affairs, economy and trade, and people and places.

SKILLS REVIEW

1. **Using the Library** Identify each of the following terms and explain its usefulness.
   a. almanac
   b. atlas
   c. card catalog
   d. Dewey decimal system
   e. encyclopedia
   f. index
   g. librarian
   h. outline
   i. periodical
   j. *Readers' Guide to Periodical Literature*

2. **Finding Cause and Effect** Skim Chapters 4 through 7 in this unit. Find two examples from each chapter that state cause-and-effect relationships. The clue words given on page 240 may help you.

3. **Note Taking and Outlining** Reread pages 247 and 249. As you read, take notes. Use your notes to develop an outline entitled "Democracy." Then use your outline to write two or three short paragraphs restating the information.

4. **Using Historical Maps** Use your skills lesson and the maps on pages 208–210 to answer the following questions.
   a. How can you tell what time period a historical map represents?
   b. The Roman Empire had become the lesser Byzantine Empire by 1200. At that time which empire controlled central Europe?
   c. How did Poland change between 1200 and 1560? What small country occupied the northeast corner of what is today Poland?
   d. How can historical maps help to explain cultural influence in a region?

YOUR WORLD

MAKING A TIMELINE

1. Add to the Timeline of the World that you began in Unit 1. The first European entry should show the Minoan civilization about 1750 B.C. Mark on the timeline such periods as the Golden Age of Greece, the *Pax Romana,* the Middle Ages, and the Renaissance. Make a list of important events and their dates from your text. The timeline in each chapter will help you locate information. When you have finished, compare what was happening in Europe and in the Middle East during the same periods of time. For example, what was happening in Europe during the time that the Persians built their empire?

LEARNING ABOUT PEOPLE

2. Continue your notebook on Cultures of the World. Pick one European country to research. Organize information about that country in the same way as you did for the Middle East. In addition, include a section describing with words or art the symbols of the country, such as flags, stamps, coins, mottoes or slogans, anthems, costumes, and national holidays. Write to a consulate or an embassy representing the country in the United States. (A librarian can help you find the address.) Ask the consulate or embassy for materials that will help you find out more about their country. Another source of information is a travel agency that has brochures about places that people visit.

EXPRESSING IDEAS

3. Most European countries have heroes about whom legends or myths have been written. Choose heroes/heroines from the following list and find and read stories about them in your library.

   Athena (Greece)
   Romulus and Remus (Italy)
   Sigurd (Norway)
   King Arthur (Great Britain)
   Robin Hood (Great Britain)
   Siegfried (Germany)
   Roland (France)
   Countess Jeanne of
       Montfort (France)
   El Cid (Spain)

4. Invent a modern hero. Write a story describing an adventure for your hero.

SHARING CULTURE

Many European immigrants have settled in the United States. Some examples include Norwegians in North Dakota, Swedes in Minnesota, Germans and Dutch in Pennsylvania, Polish in Illinois, Scots in North Carolina, French in Louisiana, and Italians in New York.

5. Find out what Europeans have settled in or near your area. Make a list of the ways you share their culture. The list might include special kinds of food, types of clothing, sports and games, common words or phrases, names of streets and towns, and celebrations.

UNIT THREE

AFRICA, PAST AND PRESENT

One thousand years ago, wealthy African empires attracted traders from Europe and Asia. Since then Africa has undergone great changes. Today farming villages, such as this one in the Republic of Mali, look out over land long ago marked by important trade routes. Rural villages as well as busy cities are the homes for many different African cultures.

In many parts of Africa people are leading new lives as citizens of growing independent nations. At the same time they are discovering the glories of their past. The rich resources of these countries and their growing voice in international politics make them important to the United States and the rest of the world.

In this unit, you will read about the achievements of early Africans. You will also find out about the changes that Europeans brought to Africa and the many challenges that Africans face today.

About A.D. 1500–1880 African slave trade making iron tools	A.D. 1652 First Dutch settle in South Africa	About A.D. 1795 Europeans begin to explore the African interior	A.D. 1884 Berlin meeting to divide Africa among European powers	A.D. 1957 Ghana gains independence	A.D. 1963 Organization of African Unity is founded

GEOGRAPHY OF AFRICA

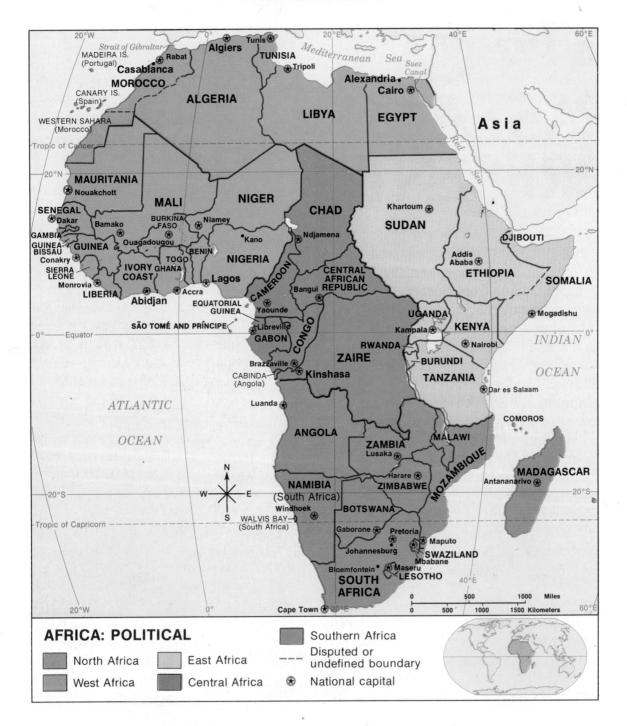

AFRICA: POLITICAL

- North Africa
- West Africa
- East Africa
- Central Africa
- Southern Africa
- - - - Disputed or undefined boundary
- ⊛ National capital

Location

Africa is a giant among continents, the second-largest in the world. It is three times the size of its northern neighbor, Europe.

Africa is separated from Europe by the Mediterranean Sea. At one point the two continents are separated by a narrow waterway, or **strait,** 32 miles (51 km) wide. The Strait of Gibraltar (jih•BRAWL•tuhr), as it is called, connects the Mediterranean Sea with the Atlantic Ocean, which lies along Africa's west coast.

In the northeast the Suez Canal connects the Mediterranean Sea and the Red Sea, which separates Africa from the Middle East. The rest of Africa's east coast lies along the Indian Ocean.

Regions of Africa

Geographers usually divide the continent of Africa into five regions, each with its own characteristics. Look at the key on your political map of Africa to find these regions.

All the countries of **North Africa** border the Mediterranean Sea. North Africa extends south through the Sahara. **West Africa** stretches from the southern Sahara to the Gulf of Guinea (GIN•ee). It reaches eastward as far as Lake Chad. **Central Africa** includes the countries of Chad in the north and Zaire (zah•IR) in the south. It extends from the Atlantic Ocean to Sudan and the large lakes along Zaire's eastern border.

Notice on your map that the country of Somalia (soh•MAHL•ee•uh) juts into the Indian Ocean. This area of land forms what is known as the **Horn of Africa.** It is shaped like the tusk of a rhinoceros and is part of the region called **East Africa.** Tanzania (tan•zuh•NEE•uh) is the southernmost country of East Africa.

Southern Africa includes the rest of the continent south to its tip. The tip is called the **Cape of Good Hope.** As you are reading your text, do not confuse the region of Southern Africa with the country of South Africa.

The Land

Africa is a land of great variety. Parts of the continent are rolling grassland, while other parts are desert or thick forest. Much of Africa is a high, flat area of land, or plateau. The plateau is a little higher in the east and south. Near the tip of Southern Africa, the plateau rises to a high ridge, ending in steep cliffs along the coast.

Africa has few high mountains or deep valleys. Most of Africa's mountains are found in the eastern and southeastern parts of the continent. They include the Ethiopian Highlands and the Drakensberg Mountains. A fairly low range of mountains, called the Atlas Mountains, is in the northwestern part of Africa. The highest mountain in Africa is Mount Kilimanjaro (kil•uh•mahn•JAH•roh) in Tanzania. It is 19,340 feet (5,894.8 m) high.

Some of Africa's lowest points are in the Great Rift Valley, which stretches about 3,500 miles (5,600 km) north and south through eastern Africa. Lake Victoria, Africa's largest lake, and Lake

Tanganyika (tan•guhn•YEE•kuh) also are located in the valley.

Several deserts cover wide areas of Africa. The Libyan and Nubian deserts in the northeast and the Kalahari (kahl•uh•HAHR•ee) Desert in the south are three examples. The Sahara is the largest desert in Africa. A dry plain called the **Sahel** (SAH•hel) lies south of the Sahara. The Sahara and the Sahel extend across northern Africa.

South of the Sahel lies a broad, grassy plain or **savanna** (suh•VAN•uh), which stretches across much of West Africa. Coarse grass and a few stunted trees cover the savanna. Savannas also are found in Southern Africa, where they are called **velds** (VELTS), a Dutch word meaning fields.

Great rivers course through African lands. These rivers include the Niger (NY•juhr), the Senegal (sen•uh•GAHL), the Gambia, and the Volta of West Africa. The Nile River is North Africa's most important river. The longest river in Central Africa is the Zaire, or Congo.

Southern Africa's major rivers are the Zambezi (zam•BEE•zee), the Orange, and the Limpopo. The Zambezi River

A huge sand dune shades this oasis, a small fertile area in the dry Sahara.

Giraffes, the tallest of mammals, roam the savanna at the foot of Mt. Kilimanjaro.

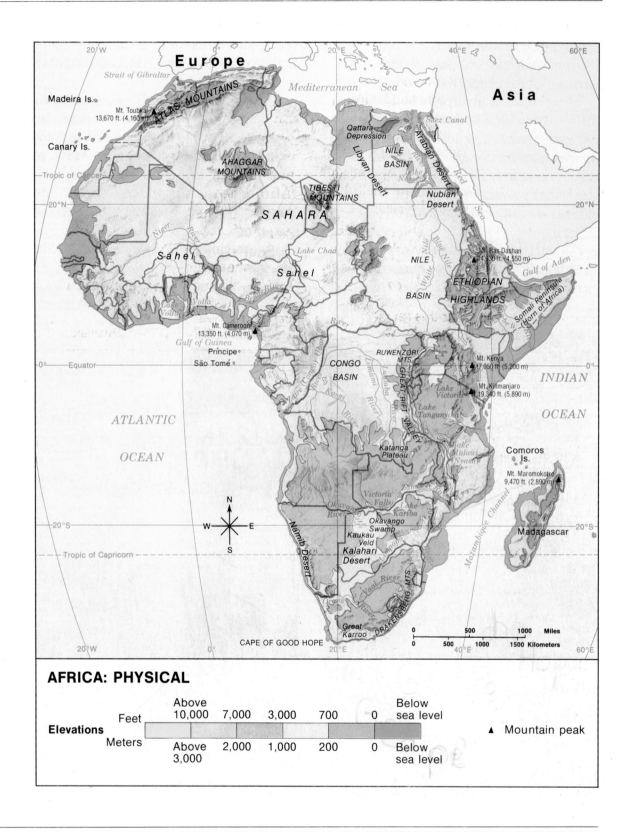

AFRICA: PHYSICAL

Elevations

	Above				Below
Feet	10,000	7,000	3,000	700	0	sea level

	Above				Below
Meters	3,000	2,000	1,000	200	0	sea level

▲ Mountain peak

forms the border between Zambia and Zimbabwe (zim•BAH•bway). At one point the river drops 355 feet (108.2 m) in Africa's largest waterfall, Victoria Falls.

Waterfalls and rapids make travel difficult for long stretches on many of Africa's rivers. Large modern vessels cannot use these waterways. However, the rivers are important sources of electrical power.

The Climate

Africa's climate is as varied as its land. The climate of the North African coast is like that of other Mediterranean regions, with mild winters and moderate amounts of rainfall. The barren, dry Sahara separates this fertile northern strip from the savanna. The savanna has a rainy season and a dry season. The temperatures during both seasons are hot.

Much of Africa lies in the tropics on both sides of the equator. Some of the wettest places in the world cover West Africa's southern coast and most of Central Africa. This steamy land, with its tall trees that block the sunlight, is called a **rain forest.** Rain falls there almost all year around, often averaging more than 100 inches (about 254 cm) per year.

The coast of Southern Africa and the highlands around East Africa's lakes have mild climates. The good climates of these areas have always attracted visitors and settlers.

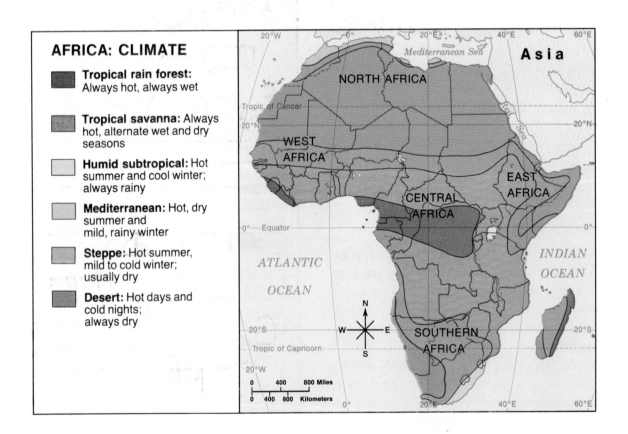

AFRICA: CLIMATE

Tropical rain forest: Always hot, always wet

Tropical savanna: Always hot, alternate wet and dry seasons

Humid subtropical: Hot summer and cool winter; always rainy

Mediterranean: Hot, dry summer and mild, rainy winter

Steppe: Hot summer, mild to cold winter; usually dry

Desert: Hot days and cold nights; always dry

Tall trees in this rain forest in Burkina Faso remain green all year long.

Southern Africa provides most of the world's gold and diamonds. From there also come huge amounts of cobalt, a metal stronger than iron. Cobalt is used to make other metals.

Other parts of Africa supply such important metals as copper and manganese (MANG•guh•neez). Manganese is used to strengthen steel. Gabon and South Africa have uranium (yoo•RAY•nee•uhm) deposits. Uranium is used to make atomic fuels.

Finally, most of the world's supply of such rare metals as platinum and chromium come from Africa. Platinum, which is even more precious than gold, is used in jewelry. Chromium is

It is the different amounts of rainfall in Africa and not the different temperatures that determine the landscape. Notice that there is a pattern to Africa's land and climate. As you move either north or south from the equator, rainfall decreases gradually. Tropical forests give way to grasslands and then to deserts.

Resources

The rich mineral wealth under Africa's soil has brought many traders to the continent. Today these natural resources provide the means by which African nations are developing their lands.

Algeria and Libya in North Africa and Nigeria in West Africa have rich deposits of petroleum and natural gas.

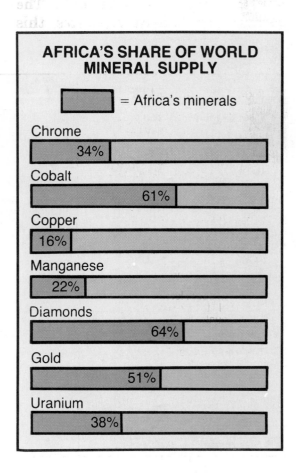

AFRICA'S SHARE OF WORLD MINERAL SUPPLY

= Africa's minerals

Chrome
34%

Cobalt
61%

Copper
16%

Manganese
22%

Diamonds
64%

Gold
51%

Uranium
38%

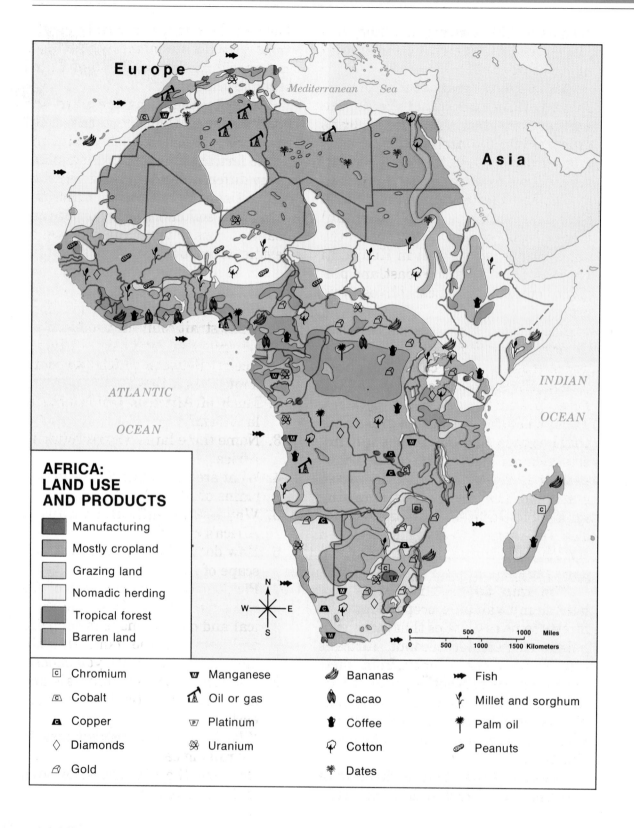

AFRICA: LAND USE AND PRODUCTS

Manufacturing
Mostly cropland
Grazing land
Nomadic herding
Tropical forest
Barren land

c Chromium	w Manganese	Bananas	Fish
c Cobalt	Oil or gas	Cacao	Millet and sorghum
c Copper	P Platinum	Coffee	Palm oil
◇ Diamonds	Uranium	Cotton	Peanuts
Gold		Dates	

Europe

Mediterranean Sea

Asia

Red Sea

ATLANTIC OCEAN

INDIAN OCEAN

N
W E
S

0	500	1000	Miles
0	500	1000	1500 Kilometers

used as a shiny coating on other metals. You can find it on car bumpers and in stainless steel.

Although minerals are important, Africa's farm crops and herds are among its greatest resources. Africans grow food for themselves and for cash crops to use in trade. They cultivate all types of land to produce what they need.

The best farming and grazing is in East and Southern Africa. Plentiful crops of tobacco and corn grow in the velds. Coffee grows well in Kenya. In North Africa the fertile coastland provides crops of grapes, olives, and oranges.

The people of the savanna herd cattle or raise grain crops, such as **millet** and a tropical grass called **sorghum** (SAWR•guhm). They also grow groundnuts (peanuts) and sweet potatoes. Though not as suitable, the grasslands that lie north and south of the rain forests also are used for farming. However, the insect pest called the **tsetse** (TSET•see) **fly** makes cattle raising impossible in most of Central Africa. The fly carries sleeping sickness, a serious disease that kills both people and cattle.

The rain forests themselves produce many valuable crops. From the forests come cash crops that include oil palms, rubber, and coconut. Africans also harvest the timber from their hardwood trees. Another type of tree in West Africa supplies more than half of the world's **cacao** (kuh•KAY•oh). Chocolate is made from the beans of this tree.

Because of the climate, farming in and near the forestlands is difficult. The soil there is not naturally fertile. To prepare it for planting, Africans use an old method of farming called **slash and burn.**

First, farmers clear the trees and brush from the land. Next, they burn the trees and mix the ashes with the soil to fertilize it. Later, farmers plant many different kinds of crops together in the fields. After several years the exhausted soil can no longer produce healthy crops. Farmers then move to new fields and begin again.

Geography Review

1. What strait connects the Mediterranean Sea and the Atlantic Ocean? Between which two continents does it flow?
2. Much of Africa is which type of landform?
3. Name three large deserts found in Africa.
4. What are two names for the grassy plains of Africa?
5. Why is travel difficult on many of Africa's rivers?
6. How does rainfall affect the landscape of Africa?
7. Pick one country from each of Africa's five regions. Use your physical and climate maps to compare and contrast the land and climate of the countries you choose.
8. List five important minerals and an African country that supplies each.
9. Why is Central Africa unsuitable for raising cattle?
10. Describe the old slash-and-burn method of farming.

Ancient Africans Build Empires

Africa has a long history. Ancient Egyptians developed Africa's first important civilization. It was not the only one, however. Between the tenth and sixteenth centuries A.D., powerful empires appeared in other parts of Africa. Many of these empires lay in the grasslands of West Africa.

Some African empires became world famous. Their rulers ate from golden dishes and had thousands of servants. Traders and scholars from distant lands visited them. These empires had well-organized governments and trade.

Look for these important words:

Key Words
- isolates
- sub-Saharan

- Nok
- Soninkes
- barter

Places
- Nigeria

Look for answers to these questions:

1. What important discovery did people of the Nok culture make, and how did it change their lives?
2. Why did large populations develop in West Africa?
3. Who were the traders who came to West Africa? What did they find?

1. WEST AFRICAN BEGINNINGS

You may recall that North Africa gave rise to the ancient civilization of Egypt, beginning almost 5,000 years ago. However, the Sahara **isolates,** or separates, most of Africa from Egypt and other lands in North Africa. Thus, the history of **sub-Saharan** Africa, or Africa south of the Sahara, has followed a path different from that of North African countries.

West Africa has had its own peoples and cultures for thousands of years. Many of those people came from the north when, beginning in about 3000 B.C., the Sahara changed from a green and fertile land into the desert it is now.

The Nok Culture

Around 300 B.C. some of West Africa's people made an important discovery: how to heat and shape iron. The earliest known West African ironmakers were a people we call the **Nok** culture. They lived from about 900 B.C. to A.D. 200 in what is now northern **Nigeria** (ny•JIR•ee•uh). They may have been the first people in sub-Saharan Africa to use iron.

This clay head was sculpted by a Nok artist more than two thousand years ago.

265

Iron changed the lives of the Nok people as it did for every people who discovered its secret. With iron-pointed spears, a people could hunt more effectively than their neighbors who had only stone or bronze weapons. They could defend themselves from wild animals better. Iron tools meant more food. People could clear land and raise crops more easily with iron axes and hoes.

During Africa's early history, populations grew large in West Africa. The soil of the savanna was fertile and could provide food for increasing numbers of people. The people could settle in large, permanent communities. Travel on the savanna was also easier. Groups of people were not cut off from each other by lakes, forests, or mountains. They could spread into new lands. The Noks and other iron-using peoples spread throughout West Africa and beyond.

The ancient ironworking methods used by the Nok are still practiced today.

The Soninkes

West Africa had rich resources that drew outsiders to it. Elephants with tusks of valuable ivory roamed its forestlands. Gold glittered in its riverbeds and could be mined in great quantity.

From earliest times, traders came to West Africa in search of these valuable resources. Most came from North Africa or the Middle East. They crossed the Sahara on the backs of camels—the "ships of the desert."

By about A.D. 700 more traders were coming across the Sahara to West Africa than ever before. Most were Muslims. These Muslim traders were eager to visit the grasslands of West Africa, which they called *Bilad as-Sudan,* "the land of the blacks." The reason for their eagerness showed in another name they sometimes gave the same place: "the land of gold."

Most of the Muslim traders never saw the forests and river valleys in the southern part of West Africa, where the gold came from. They never saw the people of those areas, who had learned to mine and crush the gold-bearing ore by hand to extract an amazing amount of valuable metal. The traders came only as far as the savanna south of the Sahara. This region became the center of trade for the goods of North Africa and the gold from the rain forest.

The Muslim traders found prosperous farming communities in the West African grasslands. The people in these communities were called the **Soninkes** (suhn•IN•kays). Mud or brick walls circled the Soninke towns, with their clusters of round houses. Green fields of millet, rice, and sorghum surrounded the towns. An irrigation

Peoples of West Africa met their needs with a well-organized barter system. Here, Soninkes trade along the Niger River.

system of dikes and earthen dams watered the fields.

The Muslim traders quickly learned that the Soninkes were as good at trading as they were at farming. The Soninkes had a long history of trading with each other. Villagers who lived near rivers traded dried fish for the grain of farmers who lived inland, for example. This trade of one kind of goods for another without the use of money is called **barter.**

As trade with the Muslims increased, the Soninkes learned how to barter to their own advantage. They found that if they joined together, they could control the trade. The trading efforts of these enterprising people lay at the root of the first West African grassland empire.

Reading Check

1. Why did sub-Saharan Africa develop differently from North Africa?
2. Who were the earliest known iron-makers in West Africa?
3. Who were the traders who came to West Africa? From where did they come?
4. How did the Soninkes make their living in West Africa?

Look for these important words:

Key Words
- scarce
- tariff
- monopoly

Places
- Ghana
- Kumbi

Look for answers to these questions:

1. What people founded the empire of Ghana?
2. What was the most important business in West African cities?
3. How did the kings of Ghana control its wealth?

2. THE FIRST WEST AFRICAN EMPIRE

Land that could feed large numbers of people and allow them to travel freely helped to make large empires possible in the grasslands of West Africa. Trade, and the resources that supported that trade, helped such empires to prosper. The first great West African empire became known to the world by a title its rulers took, that of **Ghana** (GAHN·uh) or "war chief." Its own people called it *Aoukar* (ah·oo·KAHR).

The empire of Ghana began growing around A.D. 700. Its founders, the Soninkes, had bows and arrows and sharp iron-tipped spears. These weapons, which most of their neighbors did not have, helped the Soninkes control a large territory. Horses could carry a king's messengers or soldiers swiftly across the savanna. This ease of travel also helped West African rulers conquer and hold together large empires.

The land claimed by the Soninkes lay between the Senegal and upper Niger rivers. At its height, around A.D. 1000, the empire of Ghana included more than 100,000 square miles (about 161,000 sq km). It spread eastward as far as Lake Chad.

Hundreds of traders crossed the Sahara to visit Ghana each year. Let us look at what one journey might have been like.

Salt for Gold

Hussein (hoo·SAYN) drew his protective white headdress closer around his neck. He sang a quiet little song to the rhythm of the camel beneath him. Smiling, Hussein looked ahead and behind him. The camel caravan stretched in both directions almost as far as he could see.

The 50 men in the caravan were led by Hussein's father, a trader from the North African town of Fez. They had been traveling for ten weeks. Guided by the stars at night and the wind and sun during the day, they headed southward, always southward, toward the gold of Ghana.

Desert-traveling nomads still use camel caravans to transport salt. Today, they might trade their cargo for grain, sugar, tea, or cotton.

Most of the camels' backs were weighed down by blocks of salt. The people of Ghana would pay dearly for salt, Hussein knew. There was plenty of salt here in the desert, but salt was in short supply in West Africa. He could use some salt now, Hussein thought. He had been sweating during the long afternoon ride, and he felt weak. The salt would help him regain his strength.

With relief Hussein noticed that his father, who was on the lead camel, was slowing. That meant they were coming to an oasis, where they could unload some salt and get fresh water. Then they would sleep under the cooling palms.

At the oasis, after they had watered their camels, Hussein strolled with his father beyond the well. His father pointed to the distant horizon. There, for the first time, they could see a dark line. It meant they had reached the edge of the desert at last.

Kumbi

The capital of Ghana was called **Kumbi** (KOOM•bee). Many caravans came to Kumbi, for that thriving city of 15,000 people lay on the most important trade route in the western Sahara. The Arab traders would not stay in Kumbi itself. They and the other Muslim visitors had their own town 6 miles (9.7 km) away from Kumbi. There they built houses of stone, in the North African style, instead of using the clay, thatch, and wood that the people of Ghana preferred.

The markets of Kumbi were swollen with goods. Arab traders unloaded swords, glass cups, woolen gowns, and copper plates, as well as salt blocks, from their camels. They traded these goods for gold, ivory tusks, and cotton cloth. They also had another cargo in mind: slaves. For centuries the Arabs had been buying slaves in sub-Saharan Africa and selling them in the north. African slaves had been in Mediterranean lands since Roman times.

Kumbi was not the only large city in Ghana. Audaghost, Walata, and other cities lay on important trade routes. Some of these routes were near the Atlantic coast. Others crossed the central part of the Sahara. The trading of salt for gold was the most important business in all those cities, though many other goods were bartered as well. Salt was **scarce** in Ghana. Scarce means there was not enough salt to meet the demand. This made it as valuable as gold, which was plentiful. Salt was used to season foods. Because the body needs salt, it was also important for good health.

When salt was rare and valuable, this Saharan oasis made merchants and rulers rich. Today, though salt made in factories is commonly available, thousands of tons are mined here each year.

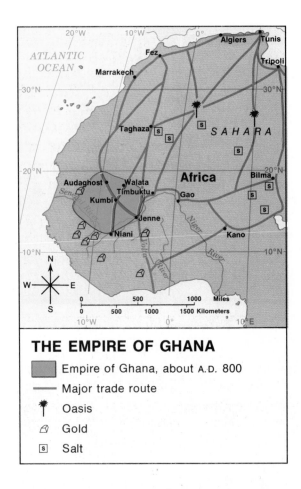

THE EMPIRE OF GHANA

■ Empire of Ghana, about A.D. 800

— Major trade route

✹ Oasis

⌂ Gold

ⓢ Salt

Controlling Trade

The kings of Ghana were incredibly rich. When the king held court, one traveler wrote, he was guarded by young men carrying shields of gold and gold-handled swords. The princes of his kingdom stood by him, wearing gold ornaments in their hair. Even the king's guard dogs had collars of gold.

The wealth of Ghana came from trade and taxes. The people of the West African grasslands were in an ideal position to control the trade between the Saharan traders and the forest people to the south. To control trade a ruler also had to control most of the land through which it passed. Any ruler who taxed that trade grew rich. Traders bringing salt or other goods into Ghana had to pay a **tariff,** or tax to the king. Any trader taking goods out of the kingdom had to pay another tariff. Chiefs of the different lands in Ghana's empire also had to pay taxes or give goods to the king.

These tariffs paid for more than golden dog collars. They supported the police and judges who carried out the laws of the king's government and kept the peace. They also fed the 200,000 soldiers that the king would gather in time of war.

The wealthy kings of Ghana had a **monopoly** on gold. A monopoly is complete control or ownership. All the best pieces of gold brought from the south had to be given to the king. He decided how much of it would be sold. In that way, he could control the price.

The rulers of Ghana kept peace in their land for hundreds of years. In the middle of the eleventh century, however, an army from North Africa came across the western Sahara. It conquered many cities in Ghana. Rebels inside the empire attacked other cities. By 1087 nearly all of Ghana's power was gone. A new, stronger West African empire soon rose in its place.

Reading Check

1. By what two names was the first West African empire called?
2. Why were the Soninkes able to control their lands?
3. Name the two most important goods that were traded in the cities of Ghana.
4. How was the wealth from tariffs used?

271

Look for these important words:

Key Words
- pilgrimage
- mansa
- Mandinkas
- Songhais
- standing army

People
- Kankan Musa
- Ibn Battuta
- Askia Muhammad

Places
- Mali
- Timbuktu
- Jenne
- Gao

Look for answers to these questions:

1. In what ways were Mali and Songhai like Ghana?
2. What did the Muslims teach the people of Mali?
3. How did Askia Muhammad govern his empire?

3. MALI AND SONGHAI

At a clap of the emperor's hands, eight laborers stooped to raise the ebony throne on which he sat. At another clap they moved eastward while the emperor, dressed in vivid silks and jewels, waved to his cheering subjects.

They had a long way to go; the journey would take months. This emperor, whose name was **Kankan Musa** (KAN•kuhn MOO•suh), was making a **pilgrimage** (PIL•gruh•mij), a visit to the holy city of Mecca in Arabia.

As the emperor, with his party of thousands of men and women, progressed through the Middle East, all who saw him were stunned. His servants glittered in their fine clothing. His warriors carried golden spears. He gave rich presents to almost everyone he met along the way.

Mali

Kankan Musa was the **mansa,** or emperor, of **Mali,** the second great West African grassland empire. By the time Mansa Musa made his pilgrimage to Mecca in 1324, Mali controlled the land that had belonged to ancient Ghana and much more besides. It was the second-largest empire in the world.

The people who founded Mali were called the **Mandinkas** (man•DING•kuhs). They were related to the Soninkes of Ghana. Their fertile homeland, Kangaba (kuhn•GAH•buh), lay on the upper Niger River. It had been one of many small kingdoms or states under the control of Ghana.

Many of the Mandinkas were traders. They played active parts in the business that made Ghana rich. When the empire of Ghana weakened, the Mandinkas had their chance to seize power. Beginning about 1235, Mali conquered most of the lands that had belonged to Ghana.

Like the wealth of Ghana, the riches of Mali came mostly from the trade between the Saharan caravans to the north and the forest kingdoms to the south. Because Mali controlled more

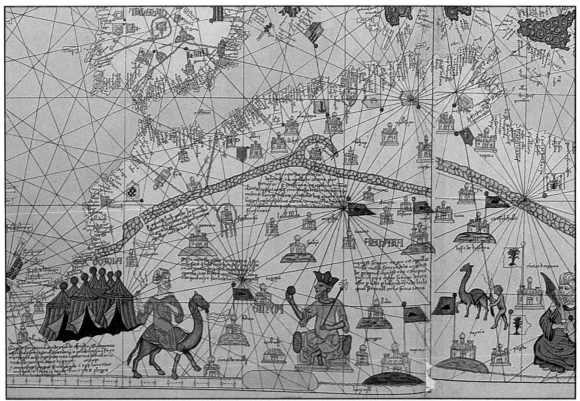

Under Mansa Musa, Mali extended its trading empire over large parts of western Africa. This kingdom was a peaceful and orderly land.

land than Ghana had, its wealth was even greater. Also, the demand for West African products had grown since Ghana's time. Europe, as well as North Africa and the Middle East, wanted West African gold.

A system of good laws made Mali an unusually peaceful place to live. **Ibn Battuta** (IHB·uhn bah·TOO·tah), a Muslim who wrote about Mali a little after Mansa Musa's time, said that its people hated injustice more than any others he had seen. He said that a traveler in Mali was as safe from thieves and bandits as a person who stayed at home.

Mansa Musa and other Mali emperors encouraged their people to adopt Muslim ways. Muslim traders showed Mali traders how to use money and credit instead of barter. Muslim scholars taught people in the Mali government how to read and write. Cities such as **Timbuktu** (tim·buk·TOO) and **Jenne** (juh·NAY) became important centers for law and study as well as for crafts and trade.

Not all of Mali's people welcomed these new ideas. Only a small number of them became Muslims. Most of those who did were involved in trade or government and lived in the cities. The people of the countryside kept their old religion and way of life.

Often the old and the new ways conflicted with each other. Slowly, the people of Mali learned to combine them in a civilization that was uniquely their own. They spread ideas from this civilization to many parts of Africa.

This mosque, made of sun-baked earth and timber, rises above the city of Jenne. It looks much the same today as it did 700 years ago.

Unfortunately, many of the emperors who followed Mansa Musa were less strong and wise than he. They were not able to hold the lands he had gained. Mali's fame lived on long after Mansa Musa's time, but its real power slowly declined.

Songhai

As Mali's strength faded, that of another people was growing. These people were the **Songhais** (SONG·hys). At first they farmed and fished along the Volta River. Later they took over the town of **Gao** (GOW), on the Niger. Gao lay on an important trade route for the Saharan merchants.

Beginning in 1464 the Songhais began conquering lands that belonged to Mali. They took over important trading centers such as Timbuktu and Jenne. The new empire of Songhai became even larger and more powerful than Mali had been.

Askia Muhammad (uh·SKEE·uh mo·HAM·uhd) was the most famous Songhai emperor. Like Mansa Musa, he combined African and Muslim ideas in new ways that made his empire strong. He supported a large university in Timbuktu and paid the scholars who studied there.

Askia Muhammad controlled his empire by dividing it into provinces, each with its own governor. Askia Muhammad chose these governors himself instead of letting the people of the provinces select them. He made sure that the governors were loyal only to him.

Askia Muhammad kept an army of paid, full-time soldiers. This kind of army, called a **standing army,** was another new idea. In Mali and Ghana, emperors had called people from the countryside to be soldiers in time of war. In peacetime these people did other work. However, Askia Muhammad realized that the soldiers in a professional army could be carefully trained. They would be able to ride and use weapons better than part-time soldiers could. Professional soldiers also could be called on more quickly to stop rebellion inside the empire or attacks from outside. Askia Muhammad also had a navy that sailed war canoes on the Niger River.

Askia Muhammad's new ways of governing kept the Songhai Empire strong during his time. As had happened in Mali, however, most of the rulers who followed him were weaker. Outsiders envied the wealth of the Songhai Empire. They waited for their chance to seize it.

In 1591 the ruler of Morocco, in North Africa, decided that the right time had come. He sent an army of 4,000 soldiers across the desert to attack Songhai. These soldiers were

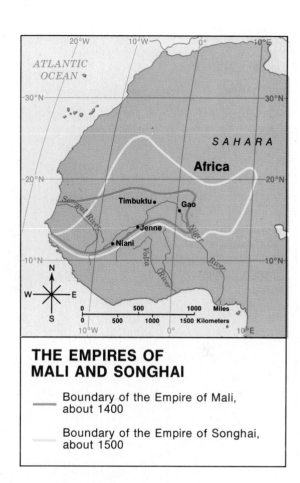

THE EMPIRES OF MALI AND SONGHAI

—— Boundary of the Empire of Mali, about 1400

—— Boundary of the Empire of Songhai, about 1500

even better trained than Songhai's army. They also had guns, including a few cannons. The warriors of Songhai had never seen anything like these weapons. The army from Morocco won battle after battle, and the Songhai Empire quickly came to an end.

Reading Check

1. Which Mali emperor made a famous pilgrimage? Why?
2. Which groups of people in Mali adopted the Muslim religion?
3. Which West African city contained a large university?
4. What are two advantages of a standing army?

HIGHLIGHT
Timbuktu

Heinrich Barth, the first European to keep a record of his travels in central Africa, drew this picture of his 1853 arrival at Timbuktu.

The story of Timbuktu began around A.D. 1000. Then it was merely a well and a sand dune. There travelers could stop for water on their way to the Niger River from the Sahara. Because of its location, Timbuktu became a valuable marketplace. It was said that as many as 25,000 camels passed through Timbuktu in a year.

By the sixteenth century, Timbuktu had grown into a city of many thousands of people. This was the time when Timbuktu reached its height as a center of learning and culture. The city's university and libraries were well known. Scholars from Arabia, Egypt, and Morocco traveled there to study and to teach. One traveler wrote:

> In Timbuktu there are numerous judges, doctors, and clerics, all receiving good salaries from the king. He pays great respect to men of learning. There is a big demand for books in manuscript, imported from Barbary [North Africa]. More profit is made from the book trade than from any other line of business.

Sadly, the great city of Timbuktu also attracted greedy invaders from the north. As they fought among themselves for power, the city declined. Its great books were lost and many of its buildings demolished. In 1893, when the French army entered a ruined Timbuktu, its population had dwindled to 6,000. Today Timbuktu exists as a small town in the country of Mali. Its university is gone. Travelers can find the famous city only in their imaginations.

I would like to go
 where
In days of old
  The Aged
  Sharp-eyed
  Hardknuckled
  Sages of our race
Kept in silent grove
  and dark,
  The sacred Lore…

Christina Ama Ata Aidoo

Look for these important words:

Key Words	Places
• Edo	• Benin
• oba	• Kanem-Bornu

Look for answers to these questions:

1. What empires existed in ancient Africa besides those of the West African grasslands?
2. What were the achievements of Benin?
3. What was life like in African cultures that did not form empires?

4. OTHER AFRICAN CULTURES

Ghana, Mali, and Songhai were the largest empires in early sub-Saharan Africa. They were not the only ones, however. The rain forest of the West African coast, for example, contained the empire of **Benin** (be•NEEN). The kingdom of **Kanem-Bornu** (KAHN•uhm BOR•noo) grew up in the central grasslands around Lake Chad. It lasted longer than the Songhai Empire, and at times it was more powerful.

Cities along East Africa's coast grew as rich from trade by sea as the grassland empires did from trade across the desert. In southeastern Africa, the people of the Monomotapa Empire built the great stone fortress of Zimbabwe. Powerful kingdoms flourished in other parts of Africa, too.

Benin: A Forest Empire

By the middle of the sixteenth century, Benin was the largest of several West African forest kingdoms. Visitors from Europe marveled at its great capital city, also called Benin. One visitor praised the capital's broad streets and clean, well-built houses. Another said that the king's palace, with its many apartments and galleries, was as big as a whole town.

The **Edo** people of Benin lived near the mouth of the Niger River in what is now southern Nigeria. They were well located for trade both by land and by sea. The merchants of Benin traded cotton cloth, pepper, and animal skins for copper, fine clothes, and other goods made in North Africa and beyond.

Benin was famous for its art, especially its metal sculptures of brass or bronze. Many brass plaques decorated the palace of Benin's king, or **oba.** The plaques pictured the glories of Benin's past. They also showed daily life.

Benin was like the grassland empires in some ways and was different in others. Unlike Mali and Songhai, Benin was not shaped by Muslim ideas. Benin's people kept their own religion. Even so, the obas of Benin governed in many of the same ways that the grassland rulers did. They, too, developed a

Portraits of royalty were cast in bronze by Benin's highly trained artists.

strong government to control trade. Benin, like Songhai, had many governors who were responsible to the king. It had a single system of laws, with judges, police, and other officials to enforce them.

Africans Without Empires

Visitors could easily admire Africa's trading empires with their broad-streeted cities and gold-bedecked kings. However, many African peoples never formed large empires. They lived in small villages or wandered in groups from place to place. Outsiders often did not understand that these peoples, too, had valuable achievements.

Many African peoples were farmers. They raised millet, rice, yams, bananas, and other crops. Some were herders, driving their cattle from one feeding ground to another. Some peoples were both farmers and herders. A few others lived on what they could hunt and gather. All these peoples were skilled at surviving in harsh environments. They invented ways of farming and caring for animals. Their methods have been used successfully in other tropical countries.

African gold miners worked out useful tropical mining techniques, too. They found the gold and dug it out of the earth. They crushed it and melted it down in earthen furnaces. Then they let it harden in clay molds, which they designed. All of this the miners accomplished without the use of machinery.

To outsiders who did not learn about their ways, African societies sometimes seemed to have no laws, leaders, or government. This was far from true. Complicated rules, often very wise ones, governed these peoples' lives. The "leaderless" societies often had many leaders. Those leaders might be the wisest or most experienced people in the village. In other cases, everyone in a village might have to agree on important decisions.

In the arts, in farming, in government and law, and in other fields as well, the achievements of Africa's peoples have been significant.

Reading Check

1. Why were the Edo people well located for trade?
2. For what was Benin especially famous?
3. What crops were grown by farmers in Africa's tropical climate?
4. How did "leaderless" societies in Africa make decisions?

SKILLS FOR SUCCESS

EVALUATING INFORMATION

We get information from many sources, such as television, radio, newspapers, encyclopedias, and almanacs. To understand information, we must **evaluate** it. To evaluate information is to decide whether or not we can trust it.

One kind of information is **fact.** A fact can be proved to be true. Take the statement, "Few people in Nigeria own telephones." You can check **statistics** to prove whether this statement is true. Statistics are facts presented as numbers. In this case, you could look in an almanac or another reference book to find out the number of telephones in Nigeria.

Look at the table below.

AVERAGE NUMBER OF PEOPLE PER TELEPHONE	
Country	People per Telephone
Nigeria	572
Cameroon	366
Liberia	282
Ivory Coast	104
United States	1.76

This table shows the average number of people per telephone. The table shows that few people own telephones in Nigeria. There is only one telephone for every 572 people. In contrast, there is almost one telephone for every person in the United States. When a statement can be proved with statistics, you can assume that it is probably true. Now use the table to decide if this statement is correct: "Nigeria has more people per telephone than Cameroon."

Some kinds of information cannot be proven easily. **Anthropologists** are scientists who study cultures. Their research comes from historical information, observations, and interviews. To learn all they can, many actually live among the groups they study. Based on these sources, anthropologists form an **opinion.** An opinion is someone's belief or judgment.

Consider this statement:

Anthropologists believe that ancestors of the Berbers were the first settlers in North Africa.

The word *believe* tells you that the statement is an opinion. Often a writer identifies an opinion by using certain clue words and terms. Some other clues are *think, probably, it is estimated,* and *in the opinion of.*

You may remember that archaeologists study ancient cultures. They find and study ancient buildings, tools, and other artifacts to learn something about the people who made and used them. For example, near Jos, in what is now Nigeria, archaeologists have found stone tools and grains of millet. Through special testing they have come to believe that the Nok people lived there from about 900 B.C. to A.D. 200. The archaeologists have discovered clay heads in the area. From this evidence, they think that the Noks were farmers who had enough leisure time to be artists as well.

Scientists gather as much information or evidence as they can before they form their opinions. If a large number of these people agree, the information may very well be true. This does not mean it is a fact, however. It is an opinion based on evidence.

Statements about the future are also opinions. It is impossible to state a fact about something that has not happened yet. Here is an example: "Africa will be producing more oil than North America by the year 2000." Notice that this statement sounds like a fact. Yet, no one can know for certain what will happen in the year 2000. Read the sentence again. How could you change it so it will express what *may* happen?

Other clues can help you evaluate the truth of statements. Some statements include words like *fantastic, terrible,* and *best.* These words express strong feelings and tell you that the writer is giving a personal opinion about something.

The writer may express a strong opinion because he or she wants you to share it. A strong opinion may help convince you. Read the following sentences about Mansa Musa,.

The king was extremely generous with his gold and delighted many with his dazzling riches.

The king was horribly wasteful with his gold and shocked many with his showy riches.

Both sentences contain the idea that Mansa Musa displayed great wealth. The writers' feelings are quite different, however. The first sentence might have been written by someone who is loyal to the king. The writer may have wanted others to support the king. He might have lived in the palace and been afraid to criticize the king, or perhaps he had received some of the gold himself. Who might have written the second sentence?

Both writers took the same information and then expressed different opinions about it. They probably had quite different reasons for doing so. When evaluating opinions, you should always consider *why* someone might have these opinions.

Occasionally an opinion that at first seems doubtful will turn out to be sensible. Alexander Graham Bell, for example, believed that the telephone could be valuable for public use. Some people considered Bell a *crackpot,* a person whose ideas seem to make little sense. They soon found out, however, that Bell's idea was quite useful. Sometimes a different opinion can open our minds to new things.

When evaluating information it is always useful to recognize the difference between fact and opinion. A fact can be proved to be true. An opinion is a feeling or judgment. Some opinions are based on limited evidence and cannot be proved completely. Others are based on wishes and dreams. Opinions about the future cannot be proved because no one knows what will happen. Remember that people may sometimes state opinions as if they were facts. You must listen and read carefully to separate fact from opinion.

CHECKING YOUR SKILLS

On a sheet of paper, write whether each sentence below is a fact or an opinion. If a fact includes a statistic, write the word *statistic* after the word *fact.*

1. Soon the poor elephant will be completely extinct in Africa.

2. Southern Mali's average rainfall is about 40–60 inches (about 100–150 cm) a year.

3. The Moors are people of mixed Arab and Berber ancestry who live in the northwestern Sahara.

4. Dakar, the capital of Senegal, had a population of 978,553 in 1980.

5. Desert nomads would have a better life if they moved to wetter areas.

CHAPTER 9 REVIEW

USING WORDS

Explain the meaning of each of the words listed below. Then use each word in a complete sentence.

1. **barter**
2. **monopoly**
3. **pilgrimage**
4. **scarce**
5. **tariff**

REVIEWING FACTS

1. In what ways did iron working improve the lives of the Nok people?

2. How did the geography of West Africa encourage population growth?

3. What attracted Muslim traders to West Africa?

4. Why was salt considered a valuable trade good in ancient Ghana?

5. How did the kings of Ghana get their wealth?

6. How did Muslims influence the people of Mali?

7. What methods did Askia Muhammad use to make Songhai a strong empire?

8. Why were the soldiers who were sent from Morocco able to defeat the Songhai army?

9. How was Benin like the empires of Mali and Songhai? How was it different?

10. What were some achievements of the Africans who did not form empires?

THINKING CRITICALLY

1. Gold is a precious metal and continues to be valuable. Do you think you could trade salt for gold today? Why or why not? What are some other things people consider valuable? What determines how valuable something is?

2. Strong leaders, such as Kankan Musa and Askia Muhammad, helped develop important empires in West Africa. Do you think ancient empires depended on the strong leadership of one person? Why or why not?

3. We do not know as much about early sub-Saharan cultures as about some others in the Middle East and Europe. One reason is that these African cultures did not record their history. How do scientists today form opinions about how sub-Saharan Africans lived long ago?

◯ PRACTICING SKILLS

Fact and Opinion   Identify each of the following statements as a fact or an opinion.

1. West Africa borders on the Atlantic Ocean.

2. Many West Africans have probably never seen the ocean.

3. The Niger River is the third-longest river in Africa.

4. In 1979 Ghana produced 241 tons (219 T) of gold.

5. The Sahara may someday spread over the West African savanna.

Europeans Come to Africa

Focus

During their early history, the civilizations of sub-Saharan Africa had little direct contact with Europeans. The Europeans called Africa the "dark continent." In their minds it was a vast, dangerous land. Most Europeans did not understand African peoples.

In the sixteenth century, explorers and traders from Europe visited Africa. They were followed by settlers. The Europeans brought many changes to Africa. Some of these changes were harmful. Europeans disrupted African ways of life and took over African land. At the same time, Africans learned new ways of life and new skills from the Europeans.

Look for these important words:

Key Words	People	Places
• plantain	• Vasco da Gama	• Quelimane
• taro	• Henry the Navigator	• Indonesia
• dhows	• Bartholomeu Dias	• Kilwa
• Swahili		

Look for answers to these questions:

1. What lands sent traders to East Africa?
2. Why was Prince Henry the Navigator interested in exploration of the African coast?
3. Why were the Portuguese unwelcome in East Africa?

1. THE FIRST EUROPEANS

Newcomers are always amazed at their first sight of Kenya (KEEN·yuh) in East Africa. A beach of white sand glitters under the tropical sun. Beyond it tall coconut palms wave against the sky. The green slopes of Mount Kenya tower in the distance. This is one of the most inviting coasts in the world.

Because of its good harbors, East Africa has always been a gateway to the African continent. Sea trade along Africa's eastern coast has a long history.

East Coast Traders

In 1498 a fleet of four ships sailed into **Quelimane** (kel·uh·MAHN·uh), a town on Africa's southeastern coast. The ships were from the small European country of Portugal. Their captain was named **Vasco da Gama.** Da Gama was the first European to sail up the East African coast.

Da Gama might have expected the people of Quelimane to be amazed to see him. If he did, he was disappointed.

The people often saw big ships like his. In fact, ships from foreign lands had been visiting East Africa for more than a thousand years.

Some of the earliest visitors to East Africa were from the Asian islands of **Indonesia** (in·duh·NEE·zhuh). They began sailing across the Indian Ocean to East Africa about A.D. 300. The Indonesians brought some of their native plants with them. These plants included the yam, a kind of banana called **plantain** (PLAN·tin), and the **taro** (TAH·roh), whose starchy roots could be eaten. The plants grew well in Africa and became important sources of food.

Large triangular-sailed boats called **dhows** (DOWZ) brought many Arab traders to East African ports. Like the Arabs who rode the "ships of the desert" to West Africa, these traders wanted ivory, coconuts, animal skins, and gold. Some also wanted slaves, whom they took back to the Middle East. In return the Africans wanted cloth, spices, glassware, and iron tools.

283

The dhow shown here is the same kind of craft that was used in ancient times to carry trade goods between Africa, India, and China.

Some of the Arab traders stayed in the growing coastal cities. They married African women and raised families there. By A.D. 900 a language and culture that was part African and part Arab grew up along the coast. Both the language and the people were called **Swahili** (swah•HEE•lee). Most Swahilis were Muslims, but they also kept African beliefs.

Some of the vessels in Swahili harbors came from India and China. Swahili traders also visited those distant lands. Ambassadors from the Kenyan city of Malindi (mah•LEEN•dee) went to China in 1415. They brought a unique present that amazed the Chinese emperor: a magnificent giraffe.

One of the richest Swahili trading cities was **Kilwa.** Kilwa was on a little island just off the coast of modern Tanzania. Visitors admired Kilwa's tall houses of coral stone. They marveled at the rich clothing of its merchants, who combined ornaments of African gold with silks from India and China. The profits of trade were visible everywhere.

Vasco da Gama visited the Swahili cities peacefully, but other Portuguese did not. In 1505 a large Portuguese fleet attacked Kilwa, robbed it, and burned it to the ground. The attack surprised the unsuspecting Africans.

The Portuguese

The Portuguese were the first Europeans to explore and trade with sub-Saharan Africa. They began by sailing south along Africa's western coast. By the time of Vasco da Gama's voyage, Europeans had been visiting West Africa for about 50 years.

The Portuguese explorations began because of one man. He was Prince **Henry the Navigator,** son of King John I of Portugal. Prince Henry did not explore Africa, but he hired men who did. Beginning about 1419, he paid mapmakers to make new maps of the area. He paid navigators to improve such instruments as the compass and the astrolabe. He paid ship designers to make new ships that could sail into the wind. He paid brave men to sail in those ships.

Prince Henry had good reasons for encouraging exploration of the African coast. Like other countries of Europe, Portugal wanted to buy spices and other goods from Asia. At that time, however, it could do so only from the Muslims of the Middle East. The Muslims charged high prices for their trading services. If Prince Henry's men could find a way to sail around Africa to India, they could buy Asian goods at their sources. The Portuguese would no longer have to pay the Muslims. In fact, Portugal might gain control of the Asian trade and grow rich itself.

Prince Henry died in 1460, but his dream lived on. In 1488 a Portuguese captain named **Bartholomeu Dias** (bahr•too•loo•MAY•oo DEE•ahs) became the first European to sail around the southern tip of Africa. Following Dias, Vasco da Gama sailed even farther to the coast of East Africa. Da Gama then sailed on to India, achieving Prince Henry's goal.

The Portuguese came to Africa to explore and stayed to trade. Sometimes the trade was peaceful. Portuguese ambassadors paid friendly visits to the courts of Mali, Benin, and Kongo, which was in Central Africa. In other places, especially along Africa's eastern coast, the Portuguese took what

Henry was the patron of navigation.

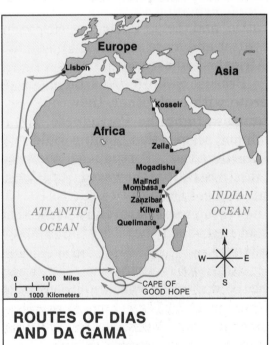

ROUTES OF DIAS AND DA GAMA

→ Dias, 1487–1488

→ Da Gama, 1497–1498

• Major East African trading city

285

From this fort at Luanda, the Portuguese organized slave raids and wars against local tribes. They met with strong resistance, but eventually destroyed most of the civilizations of Angola and the nearby Kongo kingdom.

they wanted by force. Sometimes they killed everyone in a town, even the cattle and pets. Their attacks were swifter and more violent than any the Africans had ever seen.

Because Swahili cities did not cooperate with each other, they could not unite to fight the Portuguese. For a while it seemed that nothing could stop the invaders. Portuguese violence finally backfired, however. By attacking and destroying cities such as Kilwa, the Portuguese destroyed the trade that had flourished there for hundreds of years.

Meanwhile, during the second half of the sixteenth century, other European nations followed the Portuguese into Africa. The Spanish, English, French, and Dutch were soon competing with the Portuguese for Africa's riches.

The Portuguese tried to protect their position in Africa by building forts along the coasts. They did not have enough soldiers to defend their forts, however. Furthermore, when other European nations attacked Portuguese forts and trading posts, they were often helped by the Africans, who hated Portuguese cruelty. By 1650 the Portuguese had lost most of their early advantage over other Europeans in Africa.

Reading Check

1. Who was the first European to sail up the coast of East Africa? From which European country did he come?
2. Which two groups combined to form the Swahili culture?
3. How did Prince Henry the Navigator encourage exploration?
4. Why did Africans help the Europeans who attacked Portuguese forts?

HIGHLIGHT

Swahili

There is an old Swahili saying that reads *Maji ya kifuu ni bahari ya chungu* (MAH•jee YAH kih•FU•oo NEE bah•HAH•ree YAH CHUNG•oo). In English, the proverb means: "The water in an empty coconut shell is like the sea to an ant." This saying means that what seems small to one person is actually very important to another. Swahili may not seem like an important language to speakers of English, but it is actually one of the 12 most important languages in the world. It is spoken by more than 35 million people in East Africa.

Karibu (kah•REE•boo) means "welcome" in Swahili. If you traveled to the countries of Tanzania and Kenya, where Swahili is the official language, your hosts would greet you by saying *karibu*. Swahili is spoken in the People's Republic of the Congo, Zaire, Zambia, Mozambique, Somalia, Rwanda, Burundi, and Malawi.

Schule (SHOO•lay) means "school" in Swahili. Though the Swahili letters look the same as English letters, the Swahili language has no *Q* or *X* sounds. Therefore, there are 24 letters in the Swahili alphabet instead of 26 as in English.

Uzuri (oo•ZOO•ree) means "beauty" in Swahili. The Swahili language is as beautiful and varied as the countries in which it is spoken. Swahili has borrowed from the languages of people who came to East Africa, such as the Arabs and the Portuguese. It has a large vocabulary and many different ways of saying things. For example, there are more than five different ways to say *building*. The choice of the correct word depends on whether the building is ugly or beautiful. The word may change again to mean inside, outside, or around the building.

Because Swahili is widely used in many countries, more than 60 newspapers and journals are printed in Swahili. Many books have been published in Swahili, including the Bible, which was first printed in Swahili in 1891.

Rafiki (rah•FEE•kee) means "friend" in Swahili. To help nations remain friends, people study each other's languages so that they can communicate clearly.

Only one-quarter of Africans living south of the Sahara can read and write.

Governments are now trying to build more schools. This one is in Zaire.

Look for these important words:

Key Words
- thatching
- racism

Places
- Zanzibar

Look for answers to these questions:

1. For what purposes did Europeans want African slaves?
2. How did Europeans' feelings about the slave trade change near the end of the eighteenth century?
3. How did the slave trade harm the different groups involved in it?

2. THE SLAVE TRADE

When Europeans first traded in Africa, they bought gold, ivory, pepper, and tortoiseshell. Soon, however, European traders became interested in another trade: slaves.

Slaves had been taken out of Africa from earliest times. The Africans themselves used slaves. African rulers sold criminals and prisoners of war into slavery. Until the sixteenth century, however, the slave trade in Africa had not been large. Then suddenly there was a new demand for slaves—not just thousands, but millions of them.

The New World

While Portuguese explorers were finding their way around Africa to India, other explorers from Spain also were looking for a passage to India. Crossing from one hemisphere to another, they claimed lands in what they called the New World. Other European countries soon followed them. They established settlements in North, Central, and South America.

European settlers mined the mineral wealth of the Americas. They also started huge farms or plantations in tropical areas of the New World. They grew sugar cane, pineapples, cotton, tobacco, and coffee on the plantations.

Advertisements like this were published in parts of the Americas in the 1700s.

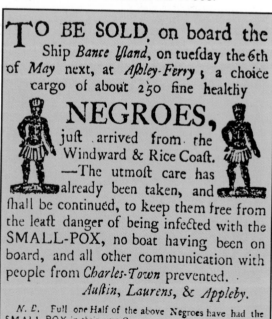

TO BE SOLD, on board the Ship *Bance Island*, on tuesday the 6th of *May* next, at *Ashley-Ferry*; a choice cargo of about 250 fine healthy NEGROES, just arrived from the Windward & Rice Coast. —The utmost care has already been taken, and shall be continued, to keep them free from the least danger of being infected with the SMALL-POX, no boat having been on board, and all other communication with people from *Charles-Town* prevented.

Austin, Laurens, & Appleby.

N. B. Full one Half of the above Negroes have had the SMALL-POX in their own Country.

Driven by a European master, Africans on a Caribbean island plantation haul sugar cane from the fields to make molasses.

The mines and plantations needed many workers. Few Europeans were willing or able to work in tropical climates. Africans, however, were experts at tropical farming and mining. As slaves, they would not have to be paid. For these reasons, mine and plantation owners in the Americas demanded ever-growing numbers of African slaves.

The West African Slave Trade

The Portuguese began the West African slave trade. Later, other European and African nations took part in it as well. Most slaves came from West Africa. Slave catchers tore them from their families and marched them to the coast. After being sold, the slaves were jammed into small ships. As many as one in six died on the long voyage across the Atlantic. Many more died from forced labor in the New World.

By the late eighteenth century, as many as 70,000 slaves were being taken from West Africa each year. A total of about 12 million West Africans were sold during the years of the slave trade. Almost that many more captives died before being sold.

Many Europeans' feelings about the slave trade began to change toward the end of the eighteenth century. In Great Britain, for example, religious leaders pointed out the cruelty and injustice of the slave trade.

In 1807 the British government forbade its citizens to take part in the slave trade. France did the same in 1818. At first, slave traders paid little attention to the new laws. However, the British sent well-armed ships to West Africa to enforce the laws. At the same time,

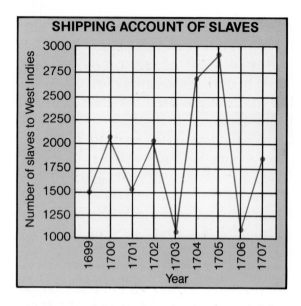

SHIPPING ACCOUNT OF SLAVES

Number of slaves to West Indies / Year

the need for new slaves in the Americas was lessening. The West African slave trade finally stopped about 1870.

The East African Slave Trade

Slaves had been traded in East Africa since before the time of Christ. However, the selling of East African slaves to Europeans became important only after 1750. By then, huge numbers of slaves had been kidnapped from West Africa for more than 200 years.

The East African slave trade brought new wealth to the Swahili cities that had been nearly destroyed by the Portuguese. Arabs had helped the Swahilis drive out the Portuguese. They had stayed to reap the profits of the slave trade for themselves.

Much of the East African slave trade took place in the island city of **Zanzibar** (ZAN•zuh•bahr). The slaves usually came from the lands around the lakes in East Africa. For millions of such people, slavery happened suddenly. Here is one example of how a capture might have taken place.

Kidnapped

Mbuku (em•BOO•koo) lived at the foot of Mount Kenya. He had just taken a wife. Now, like any other proud Kikuyu (kih•KOO•yoo) bridegroom, he prepared to build a hut for her.

Kikuyu men built separate huts for their wives. When doing so, they called on their neighbors for help. All of Mbuku's neighbors promised to be there. Some offered to bring long branches to be used as supporting poles. Others said they would come with twine made of soft wood. Many of the women told Mbuku they would bring meat, beans, and a drink made of sugar cane.

It was a Kikuyu custom that huts had to be built in a single day so that evil spirits would have no time to enter them. Mbuku's male neighbors worked hard, singing as they dug holes for the outer wall. They put up the framework and moved aside for the women. The women were experts at **thatching,** or arranging reeds and straw on a roof to shed rain. The men feasted together and sang to the women as the work went on, teasing them for being slow.

"You men," the women sang back. "You lack the most important art in building, namely, thatching. A wall and an empty roof cannot protect you from heavy rain, nor from burning sun."

The day went on joyously. Towards dusk the hut was almost done when, it turned out, the women needed more thatch.

"I will go for it," Mbuku laughed.

He went into the forest. Suddenly, without warning, Mbuku was surrounded by people from an enemy village. He tried to run as a net was thrown over him. No amount of struggling would free him. He thought sadly about his new wife and home.

The African slave traders took Mbuku to join their other captives. There were at least 25 men, women, and children. The slaves' wrists were tied by leather thongs to yokes resting across their shoulders. A rope linked each slave to the one behind him. This device enabled three traders to control all the captives. Mbuku would work the rest of his life as a slave on an Indian tea plantation.

Results of the Slave Trade

The Zanzibar traders sent some slaves to the Americas. Many others were sold in Asia and North Africa. Some slaves worked on plantations in Zanzibar itself or on other islands off the East African coast. By 1840 tens of thousands of slaves were being taken from East Africa each year.

As in West Africa, pressure from Britain and other European countries finally brought the East African slave trade to an end. In 1873 the ruler of Zanzibar promised Britain that he would end the slave trade in his city. The East African slave trade was dead by 1880.

In East Africa and West Africa the slave trade harmed everyone involved in it. The slaves themselves suffered the most. The people left behind in Africa suffered, too. In some places, so many slaves were taken that the land was left almost empty. Few young people were left to herd the cattle or plow the fields. The slave trade disrupted the Africans' economy and their whole way of life.

Even the Europeans involved in the slave trade suffered from it in a way. To take part in this terrible traffic in human beings, they had to harden themselves. They had to think of Africans as not quite human. Slave traders and slave owners began to think they were better than the people who labored for them. This feeling of superiority, called **racism,** caused much trouble for both Africans and Europeans.

Traders yoked their captives and marched them to markets on Africa's coast.

Reading Check

1. Why did the demand for slaves increase?
2. Which European country was the first to pass laws forbidding the slave trade?
3. In which city did most of the East African slave trade take place?
4. How did the slave trade affect African farming and herding?

Look for these important words:

Key Words
- missionary
- prejudices
- imperialism

People
- David Livingstone

Places
- Liberia
- Ethiopia

Look for answers to these questions:

1. Why did Europeans want to explore the unknown lands of Africa?
2. How and why did European traders gain control of Africa?
3. What problems did the division of Africa cause for Africans?

3. EXPLORERS AND CONQUERORS

On December 13, 1855, a group of travelers appeared on the top of a hill overlooking the Zambesi River in the country now called Zambia. One member of the party, a Scottish doctor, wrote this report:

The plain below us had more large game on it than anywhere else I had seen in Africa. Hundreds of buffaloes and zebras grazed on the open spaces, and there stood lordly elephants feeding majestically, nothing moving apparently but the proboscis [trunk]. I wished that I had been able to take a photograph of a scene so seldom beheld, and which is destined, as guns increase, to pass away from earth. When we descended, we found all the animals remarkably tame. The elephants stood beneath the trees, fanning themselves with their large ears, as if they did not see us at 200 or 300 yards' distance. The number of animals was quite astonishing.

The Explorers

The Scottish doctor who described the African countryside was **David Livingstone.** Beginning in 1841, Dr. Livingstone spent a quarter of a century exploring Africa and helping its people. Wherever he went, he treated the sick. He also acted as a Christian **missionary** (MISH•uhn•air•ee). Missionaries are people who are sent out to teach about their religion.

Dr. Livingstone kept a journal of his experiences. In his journal he described the beauties of Africa and its people. Dr. Livingstone's journal became a best seller when it was published.

Dr. Livingstone was one of the Europeans who began to explore Africa's unknown interior in the second half of the nineteenth century. Most Europeans who came to Africa earlier had stayed on the coasts. Now, brave men and women, such as Heinrich Barth, Rene Caillie (ruh•NAY kah•EE),

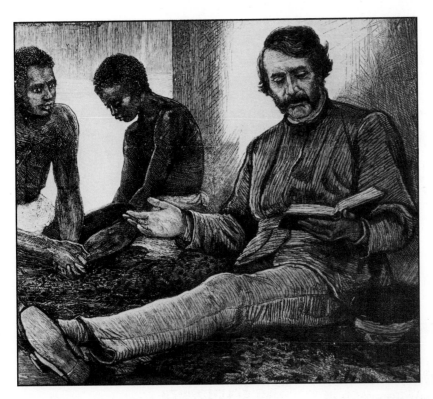

Dr. David Livingstone, a Scottish explorer, worked to stop the slave trade and to convert Africans to Christianity. Here, he reads the Bible to his native guides.

and Mary Kingsley, followed Africa's rivers, climbed its mountains, and lived in its remote villages.

Explorers came to Africa for different reasons. Some explorers were driven by scientific curiosity. Some loved adventure or wanted fame. Others, like Dr. Livingstone, were missionaries. They converted many Africans to Christianity.

Some explorers, including Dr. Livingstone, admired and respected the Africans. Many other Europeans had **prejudices** (PREJ•uh•dis•uhz) about the African people. A prejudice is a belief that is not supported by facts. These Europeans believed Africans had no culture and no history. The Europeans thought they were helping the Africans by teaching them Western ways. Prejudices kept many Europeans from recognizing the accomplishments of the African people.

Africa Divided

Most Europeans who followed in the explorers' footsteps came for trade. Europe was in the midst of its Industrial Revolution. Europeans wanted resources from Africa, including rubber, timber, palm oil, and metals. In return, they hoped Africans would buy European goods.

European trade in Africa quickly became big business. Traders organized themselves into large companies. These companies put pressure on European governments to take over the lands through which their trade passed.

In the 1870s Britain, France, and other European countries began to build empires to protect their trade. This practice of empire building was called **imperialism** (im•PIR•ee•uhl•iz•uhm). European countries believed that they had not only the right but also the duty to spread their government to as

British soldiers and missionaries discuss terms for peace with African leaders after a fierce battle in 1879.

many places as they could. Countries competed with each other to add more foreign lands to their empires.

This competition took place in Africa, too, until 1884. At that time representatives of 14 nations met in Berlin, Germany, to work out a way to divide Africa among the major European countries. Each country got the parts of the continent in which it had the most settlements and trading posts. One important group, however, had not even been invited to this meeting. Europeans never considered letting Africans have a say in what happened to their land.

Because exploration of the interior was very difficult, the new boundary lines on the map of Africa showed how little Europeans knew or cared about Africans. Some boundaries split the land of a single African group sharing the same language and culture. Some boundaries placed groups who had been at war with each other for centuries under the same government.

After 1884 the Europeans built new towns and settlements in the parts of Africa they had been given. Sometimes they tricked African leaders into signing away the rights to a group's land. Sometimes they sent soldiers to take control of the land by force. Except for **Liberia** (ly•BIR•ee•uh) and **Ethiopia** (ee•thee•OH•pee•uh), all of Africa "belonged" to European governments by 1900. For the next 50 years, Europeans controlled the lives of African peoples.

Reading Check

1. What Scottish doctor explored Africa and wrote about his travels?
2. Give three reasons why explorers traveled to Africa.
3. What important group was not invited to the 1884 Berlin meeting about Africa?
4. How did the new boundary lines drawn by Europeans affect the African people?

Look for these important words:

Key Words
- indirect rule
- direct rule
- League of Nations

Places
- Nairobi

Look for answers to these questions:

1. What forms of government did the Europeans use in ruling Africa during the colonial period?
2. How did European rule change African economy and work life?
3. What improvements did Europeans bring to Africa?

4. AFRICAN COLONIES

The nations of Europe kept control of Africa for almost 100 years. During that time they introduced tremendous changes to the continent. Some of these changes were helpful. Most of the changes eventually led Africans to reject European control.

Colonial Government

European countries ruled their African colonies in different ways. Some colonies, such as the British ones in West Africa, were governed by **indirect rule.** The Africans in these colonies were allowed to keep some of their own leaders and their old forms of government.

African officials were usually left alone to run local affairs. Decisions affecting the whole colony, however, were made by Europeans. These were passed along through the African leaders. Although Africans participated in government, Europeans had authority over what happened in the colonies.

Other colonies were governed by **direct rule.** Many French colonies were governed in this way. Under direct rule, all the officials of the colony were chosen by the European government. Officials were almost always Europeans.

The history of the East African country now called Tanzania shows the differences in the ways European powers treated their African colonies. This land was given to Germany at the 1884 meeting in Berlin. Both the Swahili people of the coast and the other groups in the interior fought fiercely against the German takeover of their land. The Germans answered them by burning villages and destroying crops so that the people would starve. Between 1905 and 1908 the Germans killed more than 100,000 East Africans.

Germany lost its African colonies after its defeat in World War I. The **League of Nations,** a forerunner of the United Nations, gave Germany's East African colony to Great Britain. The League gave Great Britain an order to manage this land for the Africans until local governments could be restored.

The British agreed to the League's terms. They gave the colony an African name, Tanganyika. As a step toward allowing the Africans a part in the colony's government, the British set up councils that had both African and European members. These councils managed most of Tanganyika's local affairs. The British managed its national and foreign affairs. The councils had limited power, but they were a beginning.

Using African Resources

Europeans changed African economy and work life as much as they changed African government. To gain resources for their growing industries, the Europeans built mines, factories, and plantations in Africa. Just as they had in the New World, the Europeans needed millions of Africans to work on these projects.

Some European powers forced Africans to work for them as if the Africans were slaves. Others accomplished the same thing in a more indirect way. They said that every African family had to pay a tax. To get money to pay the tax, African men had to work on the plantations or in the factories. The men were away from home for months or even years at a time. Usually they were not allowed to bring their wives and children with them. This type of labor destroyed many African villages and families.

The Europeans also changed the kinds of crops that African farmers grew. Usually farmers grew only what they needed for food. The Europeans wanted the Africans to grow crops that could be sold overseas. Such crops included cacao, rubber, oil palms, and coconuts. Sometimes these cash crops used up land that was needed for food.

Effects of Colonial Rule

Europeans brought some improvements to Africa. They introduced new food crops from South America, including corn, cassava, and sweet potatoes. They brought better medical

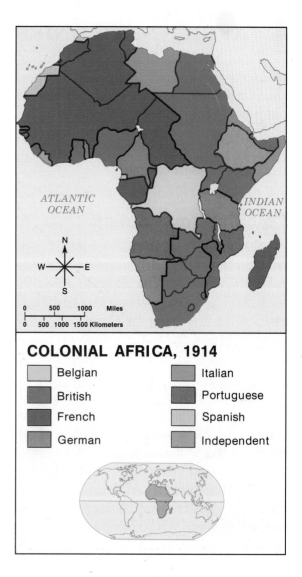

COLONIAL AFRICA, 1914

Belgian	Italian
British	Portuguese
French	Spanish
German	Independent

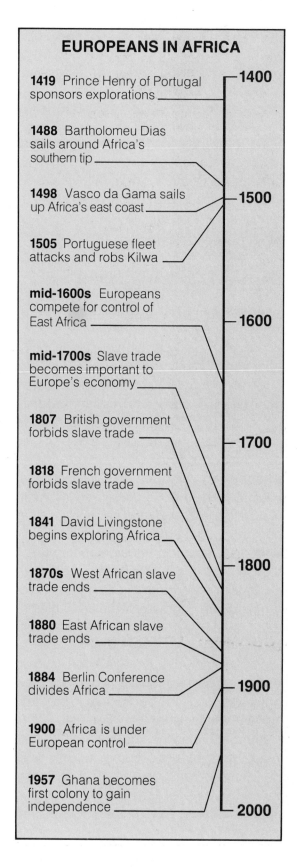

EUROPEANS IN AFRICA

1419 Prince Henry of Portugal sponsors explorations — 1400

1488 Bartholomeu Dias sails around Africa's southern tip —

1498 Vasco da Gama sails up Africa's east coast — 1500

1505 Portuguese fleet attacks and robs Kilwa —

mid-1600s Europeans compete for control of East Africa — 1600

mid-1700s Slave trade becomes important to Europe's economy —

1807 British government forbids slave trade — 1700

1818 French government forbids slave trade —

1841 David Livingstone begins exploring Africa —

1870s West African slave trade ends — 1800

1880 East African slave trade ends —

1884 Berlin Conference divides Africa — 1900

1900 Africa is under European control —

1957 Ghana becomes first colony to gain independence — 2000

care. Sometimes they brought peace to lands torn by war.

Europeans established schools for the Africans. At first most schools were run by missionaries. Later the governments sponsored the schools. Most Africans learned only a little reading, writing, and arithmetic in school. Some of them, however, learned new ways of farming, manufacturing, and government that were helpful when their countries later became independent.

Europeans brought the beginnings of modern science and technology to Africa. For example, in Kenya the British ordered the building of a railroad from the port of Mombasa to Lake Victoria in the west. Cities, such as **Nairobi** (ny•ROH•bee), grew up near the railway line. Modern industries developed, supplying jobs for many people.

Such changes, however, often interfered with the Africans' way of life, which had worked well for thousands of years. Many Africans could not adjust to the rapid changes that the Europeans brought. Most colonial governments gave the Africans very little help in learning to deal with the changes. As a result, African nations faced many problems when they finally freed themselves from European rule.

Reading Check

1. Which kind of colonial rule let Africans keep some of their own leaders?
2. What international group gave Germany's East African colony to Britain after World War I?
3. How did Europeans change the way Africans worked?
4. How did Europeans change farming in Africa?

SKILLS FOR SUCCESS

READING PRIMARY AND SECONDARY SOURCES

You may recall that anthropologists and archaeologists are scientists who study people and places of the past. They form opinions about past cultures based on evidence they discover. Another person who studies and writes about the past is called a **historian.** A historian gathers many different kinds of information. Then, as if assembling a giant puzzle, the historian pieces together past events. The information in this textbook about the people, places, and events of the past is the work of many historians.

We rely on historians to help explain the past. How, then, do historians find out about things that happened long ago? You may remember that much of our knowledge of ancient civilizations in the Middle East came from clay tablets and stone-carved hieroglyphics. Greeks and Romans also kept records. Throughout history people have recorded their ideas and achievements.

There are many sources of information about the past. Readers need to be careful, however, that their sources of information are trustworthy.

Primary Sources

One important source of information comes from people who observe and record events at the time that these events happen. This kind of information is called a **primary source.** Primary sources can be letters, diaries or journals, autobiographies, paintings, maps, newspapers, or photographs. Look again at Dr. Livingstone's journal on page 292. Is this a primary source?

Dr. Livingstone's journal is a primary source of information about Africa in 1855. It describes what he saw at that time. Several years later, a writer named Henry Stanley was sent to Africa by the *New York Herald Tribune* to search for Dr. Livingstone. Stanley searched for more than seven months and wrote articles about his explorations. His articles also are primary sources about Africa in the late 1800s. Maps drawn by African explorers are yet another primary source. All are records of people's observations at a particular time in history.

Often primary sources include people's impressions or opinions. This information is not always strictly factual. Sometimes people who are actually involved in the events they record may not be aware of everything that is happening. Also, someone writing about a popular or powerful person might put in information that would compliment rather than offend that person.

Primary sources, therefore, not only tell about people and events but may also show the writer's feelings at the time. The historian's job is to compare all the available primary sources and separate the facts from the opinions.

Primary sources can be interesting to read because they can add a personal feeling to the past. In your text you read that African slaves were crowded into ships where many died. To find out more details about the hardships of such a journey, read the following passage from an autobiography written by Olaudah Equiano (OL•uh•dah eh•kwee•AH•noh). It is a primary source from a former African slave.

The first object which saluted my eyes when I arrived on the coast was the sea, and a slave ship, which was then riding at anchor and waiting for its cargo. These filled me with astonishment, which was soon converted into terror when I was carried on board. I was immediately handled and tossed up to see if I were sound by some of the crew; and I was now persuaded that I had gotten into a world of bad spirits, and that they were going to kill me. When I looked round the ship, too, and saw a large furnace of copper boiling, and a multitude of black people of every description chained together, every one of their countenances [faces] expressing dejection and sorrow, I no longer doubted of my fate; and, quite overpowered with horror and anguish, I fell motionless on the deck and fainted.

I was soon put down under the decks, and there I received such a salutation in my nostrils as I had never experienced in my life; so that, with the loathsomeness of the stench and crying together, I became so sick and low that I was not able to eat, nor had I the least desire to taste anything. I now wished for the last friend, death, to relieve me; but soon, to my grief, two of the white men offered me eatables; and, on my refusing to eat, one of them held me fast by the hands and laid me across, I think, the windlass, and tied my feet, while the other flogged [whipped] me severely.

I had never experienced anything of this kind before, and although not being used to the water, I naturally feared that element the first time I saw it, yet, nevertheless, could I have got over the nettings, I would have jumped over the side, but I could not; and, besides, the crew used to watch us very closely who were not chained down to the decks lest we should leap into the water.

At last, when the ship we were in had got in all her cargo...we were all put under deck, so that we could not see how they managed the vessel. The closeness of the place and the heat of the climate, added to the number in the ship, which was so crowded that each had scarcely room to turn himself, almost suffocated us. This produced copious perspirations, so that the air soon became unfit for respiration, from a variety of loathsome smells, and brought on a sickness among the slaves, of which many died.

One day they [the crew] had taken a number of fishes; and when they had killed and satisfied themselves with as many as they thought fit, to our astonishment who were on deck, rather than give any of them to us to eat, as we expected, they tossed the remaining fish into the sea again, although we begged and prayed for some as well as we

This diagram instructed captains of slave ships to crowd their holds with human cargo. One out of six Africans died on the ships.

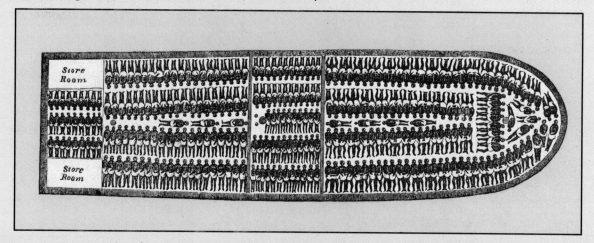

could, but in vain; and some of my countrymen, being pressed by hunger, took an opportunity, when they thought no one saw them, of trying to get a little privately. But they were discovered, and the attempt procured them some very severe floggings. One day, when we had a smooth sea and moderate wind, two of my wearied countrymen who were chained together (I was near them at the time), preferring death to such a life of misery, somehow made through the nettings and jumped into the sea. Immediately, another quite dejected fellow, who, on account of his illness, was suffered to be out of irons, also followed their example; and I believe many more would very soon have done the same if they had not been prevented by the ship's crew, who were instantly alarmed. Those of us that were the most active were in a moment put down under the deck, and there was such a noise and confusion among the people of the ship, as I never heard before, to stop her and get the boat out to go after the slaves. However, two of the wretches were drowned, but they got the other, and afterward flogged him unmercifully for thus attempting to prefer death to slavery.

Secondary Sources

A description or interpretation of events after they have happened is called a **secondary source.** Secondary sources can be textbooks, magazine articles, or anything that describes or shows something from the past. These sources are created by people who have not witnessed the events but who must rely on someone else's evidence.

Basil Davidson is a British writer. His interest in African history has led him to write a number of books on that subject. Davidson's careful research has earned him a reputation as a reliable historian. His books, which were written in modern times about the distant past, are secondary sources.

When writing about the empires of West Africa, for example, Davidson relied on many sources of information. He studied the reports of such early travelers to West Africa as Leo Africanus and Ibn Battuta. Much of what they observed and recorded is used as primary sources.

The following passage is a secondary source taken from Basil Davidson's *History of West Africa.*

The slave trade was generally very bad for the peoples of Africa. But it was bad in different ways at different places. It was worst of all for the victims themselves. Once delivered to the captains of European and American ships, they were stripped, branded, and pushed into airless underdecks, crushed together, often chained by hand and foot. Like this they crossed the Atlantic in harsh weeks of sailing. Perhaps as many as one in every six captives died on their voyage across the ocean.

We use secondary sources because they are convenient references. A historian has already done the difficult job of researching and summarizing information.

CHECKING YOUR SKILLS

1. Name four examples of primary sources.

2. Compare the primary and secondary sources you just read. What clues might tell you which was the primary source?

3. Find a fact in the secondary source that is supported by a description in the primary source.

4. Which source do you think is more interesting? Which do you think is easier to understand?

5. Which type of source would be used most often by a historian? by a sixth-grade student?

CHAPTER 10 REVIEW

USING WORDS

Number your paper from 1 to 5. Write the letter of the definition that matches each of the words below.

1. **imperialism**   4. **racism**
2. **missionary**   5. **Swahili**
3. **prejudices**

a. A culture and a language of Africa

b. A feeling of superiority

c. One who is sent out to teach religion

d. Beliefs that are not supported by facts

e. A practice of empire building

REVIEWING FACTS

1. Name two groups of traders who visited the East African coast before the Portuguese arrived.

2. Why were the Portuguese eager to sail around Africa?

3. What effect did the Portuguese have on the people and cities of East Africa?

4. For what type of work were African slaves used?

5. Who controlled the slave trade in East Africa?

6. How was the slave trade ended?

7. Why were Europeans interested in building empires in Africa?

8. Why did representatives of European nations meet in Berlin, Germany, in 1884?

9. What was the difference between direct rule and indirect rule in African colonies?

10. How did Europeans change Africa during the colonial period?

THINKING CRITICALLY

1. European explorers also explored and settled in North and South America. There, too, they met unfamiliar native cultures. How do you think the treatment of Indians in the Americas may have been similar to the treatment of Africans?

2. Which type of colonial government, *direct* or *indirect*, do you think was more successful? Why do you think so?

⬤ PRACTICING SKILLS

Primary/Secondary Sources

Identify each of the following as either a primary or secondary source.

1. *The Flame Trees of Thika*, Elspeth Huxley's autobiography describing her childhood in East Africa.

2. *Colonial Conquest of Africa*, Robin McKown's history of European imperialism in Africa.

3. Cantino chart of 1502, a map of Portuguese stops in East Africa.

4. *Travels in the Interior Districts of Africa*, Mungo Park's observations from a trip he made to Africa in the 1800s.

5. *First Book of Africa*, Langston Hughes' history of Africa for young students.

Africans Build New Nations

Focus

Most countries in Africa have gained their independence from Europe since World War II. The new nations of Africa face many challenges and problems. In many parts of Africa poor soil and too much or too little rainfall make farming difficult. In richer countries cities are growing quickly. Some cities are terribly overcrowded.

Africans belong to hundreds of very different groups, each with its own language and culture. For many groups, learning to work together in their new countries has been a slow process. However, Africans today are trying to meet their challenges by combining newly learned technology with the strengths of age-old African cultures.

Look for these important words:

Key Words
- descendants
- language families
- Mbutis
- pygmies
- Fulanis

- Hausa
- Kikuyus

People
- Jomo Kenyatta

Places
- Madagascar
- Ituri Forest

Look for answers to these questions:

1. What different groups of people live in Africa?
2. How do Africans earn their living?
3. What old ways of life do some Africans still follow?

1. THE PEOPLES OF AFRICA

About 11 percent of the world's population—some 502.5 million people—live in Africa. Most of them are crowded into West Africa, the fertile lands around the East African lakes, and parts of the African coasts. Few Africans live in the deserts or rain forests.

Africans belong to many different groups. Often these groups differ in the way they look. Some, like the slender, cattle-herding Masai (mah•SY) of northern East Africa, are tall. Others, such as the Bushmen of the Kalahari Desert, are short. Berbers of Morocco may have pale skins, brown or reddish hair, and green eyes. Most West Africans and the Somalis (soh•MAH•leez) of East Africa, on the other hand, have very dark skins.

Some Africans look different from others because their ancestors came from outside Africa. Arabs settled in North Africa and on the East African coast. People whose ancestors came from Indonesia live on the large East African island of **Madagascar** (mad•uh•GAS•kuhr). Many **descendants,** or children and grandchildren, of European settlers have remained in South Africa and some East African countries. All these groups and their descendants have added to the rich variety of the African people.

In Africa there are more than 1,000 different languages spoken. These languages can be grouped into **language families,** or groups of similar languages. Many Africans speak two or more languages. A large number, especially in North and East Africa, speak Arabic. Many speak Swahili. Some Africans speak French, English, or some other European language.

Africans differ as much in their way of life as they do in appearance or language. A growing number of Africans live in cities and work in government or in business. Other Africans work in factories or mines. However, most African people, perhaps 80 percent, are farmers or herders.

This Berber boy's ancestors have lived in northern Africa since prehistoric times.

Gathering food is a daily job for the Mbutis. This man may be pounding nuts or roots.

In Africa today many groups maintain the lifestyle and customs of their ancestors. Here are three examples of African peoples who still follow old ways of life.

The Mbutis

The **Ituri** (ih•TUR•ee) **Forest** of northeastern Zaire is the home of the **Mbutis** (em•BOOT•eez). Most of these 150,000 light-brown-skinned people are 4½-feet (1.4-m) tall. They are often called **pygmies.** *Pygmy* is a Greek word meaning "dwarf." They live as they have for thousands of years.

The Mbuti people say the forest is their "mother and father," because it gives them everything they need. It provides bark for cloth, saplings for making the frames of temporary homes, and large, waterproof leaves for roofing. Mbuti women and children gather mushrooms, nuts, fruits, berries, and roots as they walk through the forest. The men hunt with short spears or poisoned arrows. Sometimes several families work together in a hunt. The women and children chase animals into large nets that the men hold. The men kill the animals with their spears.

The Mbutis are nomads. They start a new camp every month or so. Each traveling band is made of 20 or 30 families. The band has no leaders. When a decision must be made, everyone in the band talks the matter over until all are satisfied.

Today, the Mbutis' way of life is threatened. More and more of their forest is being cut down to make way for farming and mining. Government attempts to teach them farming have had little success. When taken away from their forest, many Ituri Mbutis die.

The Fulanis

About six million **Fulanis** (FOO.lah.neez) live in the grasslands of West Africa. They are tall, graceful people with light-copper skins. They may be descended from Berber groups of North Africa.

There are two groups of Fulanis. One group is the "town Fulanis." They are devout Muslims. Long ago, in a religious war, they conquered the **Hausa** (HOW.suh) farmers of the grasslands and ruled over them. Many town Fulanis have intermarried with their Hausa neighbors. Often they are powerful figures in the villages where they live.

The other group of Fulanis is the "cattle Fulanis." Like the Mbutis, the cattle Fulanis are nomads. In the wet season they take their herds north, away from the tsetse flies. In the dry season they move south, digging deep wells or seeking water holes for their animals.

Cattle are everything to the cattle Fulanis. Fulani boys sing to their herds as they guard them. The Fulanis give their cattle names and treat them almost like members of the family.

Droughts in the grasslands and sickness among their herds have been hard on the cattle Fulanis in recent years. Many have had to give up their

These Fulani women, watering their cattle at a well in Niger, follow nomadic customs practiced by their ancestors for thousands of years.

Nairobi, which means "cold water," was a stopping place for cattle herders when Kenya joined the British Empire in 1895. Today, Kenya's capital is a busy city with modern buildings.

nomadic ways. They have settled down with their Fulani cousins and the Hausas in the towns.

The Kikuyus

The **Kikuyus** are the largest group in Kenya. More than 2 million Kikuyus live in the fertile highlands near the foot of Mount Kenya.

In a Kikuyu village, people's positions depend on their ages. The young men are the warriors. They marry while they belong to this age group. After they have their first children, they become junior counselors. Finally they become elders, respected by everyone in the village. The women also belong to different age groups that usually indicate whether or not they are single, married, or widowed.

The Kikuyus are farmers. Land is as important to them as cattle are to the Fulanis. Kikuyus inherit land from their fathers. Both men and women work on it, raising millet, beans, and sweet potatoes. They also raise cash crops, such as coffee, sugar, and tea.

Many Kikuyus today have left their farms and moved to Kenya's cities. Some have taken an active role in their government. **Jomo Kenyatta** (JOH∙moh ken∙YAHT∙uh), Kenya's first president, was a Kikuyu.

Reading Check

1. How do physical appearances differ among some Africans?
2. Why do the Mbuti people think of the forest as their mother and father?
3. What is the most important thing to nomadic Fulanis?
4. What determines the positions people have in a Kikuyu village?

306

Look for these important words:

Key Words
- Boers
- Afrikaners
- apartheid
- policy

- Bantustans
- Ibos
- Yorubas
- seceded
- hydroelectric

People
- Helen Suzman

Places
- Biafra

Look for answers to these questions:

1. What caused Africans to begin demanding their independence?
2. What problems does South Africa's separation of races cause?
3. Why has Nigeria suffered from conflict and civil war?
4. How has Kenya's government tried to gain wealth for the country's people?

2. THREE NATIONS OF AFRICA

In 1911 two African countries, Liberia and Ethiopia, were independent of European rule. Today, there are 51 independent nations in Africa. Most of these countries have gained independence only during the last 25 years.

Although many Africans had always resisted European rule, organized efforts did not occur until the early 1900s. Several things led Africans to increase their demands for independence. During World Wars I and II some Africans went to Europe to fight. There they learned new skills and were exposed to different ways of life. They took new ideas back to Africa. After World War II European powers freed colonies in Asia and elsewhere. African leaders insisted that their countries be set free as well.

Often reluctantly, the European powers let their African colonies go. In 1957 Great Britain's Gold Coast colony won its independence. The new African nation adopted the name *Ghana,* recalling the former great empire of West Africa. One by one, other African nations followed in Ghana's footsteps.

Recent history has taken different paths in different parts of Africa. What is happening in three countries—the Republic of South Africa, Nigeria, and Kenya—will help explain some problems facing Africa today and some ways Africans are solving these problems.

The Republic of South Africa

The Republic of South Africa is the only country in Africa still ruled by people of European descent. Europeans came to South Africa in far greater numbers than to any other African country. They were attracted by South Africa's mild climate and fertile farmland. People of European descent now

307

make up about 18 percent of South Africa's population. This white population has played a major role in the country's recent history.

Two different groups of Europeans settled in South Africa. The Dutch came first. They set up a trading base in South Africa in 1652. Dutch settlers in South Africa called themselves **Boers** (BORZ), which means "farmers." Later they came to think of themselves as **Afrikaners** (af·rih·KAHN·erz). They spoke their own language, Afrikaans.

The British were the other important group of Europeans who came to South Africa. They first appeared in 1795. The Afrikaners and the British often did not get along. In 1899 these two groups fought for control of South Africa. The British won the war, but the Afrikaner point of view has remained strongest in South Africa.

Both the British and the Afrikaners had racist ideas about the black Africans whose land they controlled. The ideas of the Afrikaners were more extreme, however. They felt that different races should come in contact with each other as little as possible. This feeling grew into a strong belief called **apartheid** (uh·PAHRT·hayt), a word meaning "apartness." After an Afrikaner government took control of the Republic of South Africa in 1948, apartheid became the official **policy,** or plan of action, in the country.

Life for black South Africans under apartheid is hard. They can own land

South African police are prepared to enforce government policy.

South African Archbishop Desmond Tutu speaks against apartheid in his country.

Helen Suzman's work has led to growing opposition to South Africa's policies.

and govern themselves only within **Bantustans** (BAN•too•STANZ). Bantustans are homelands in the countryside set up strictly for black Africans. Outside the Bantustans, they cannot eat in the same restaurants, go to the same schools, ride in the same buses, or be treated in the same hospitals as white people. They are paid less than one-tenth as much as whites for the same work.

Black South Africans, and some white ones, protest the injustice of apartheid. One white who does so is **Helen Suzman.** She was born in South Africa. In 1953 she became the only member of her political party to criticize the government. As a member of Parliament she cast the only vote against an act permitting the government to hold blacks without trial. Often her life was threatened, but Helen Suzman stood firm.

For speaking out despite the dangers to herself, Suzman won the Human Rights Award of the United Nations in 1978. "If I were black," she pointed out, "I might not have lived to accept this award." Other protest leaders have been imprisoned, exiled, or even killed.

Many countries, as well as the United Nations, are protesting against apartheid. Some people are demanding an end to trade with South Africa until the apartheid policy is changed. However, South Africa has deposits of useful minerals, some of which can be found nowhere else. Thus, cutting off trade with South Africa is not easy.

The South African government has attempted to make some changes in its policies. Leaders, such as Archbishop Desmond Tutu and Zulu Chief Gatsha Buthelezi (boo•tuh•LAY•zee), continue their work to influence the government to make more changes.

Nigeria

Nigeria is a land of contrasts. Thick rain forests and mangrove swamps extend to the sea along its southern coast. A strip of hilly woodland separates the rain forest from the broad grassland plains to the north.

Over 200 separate groups live in Nigeria, which has the largest population in Africa. The main groups are the **Ibos** (EE•bohz) of the southeast, the **Yorubas** (YAWR•uh•buhz) of the southwest, and the Hausas and Fulanis of the northern grasslands. These groups are proud peoples who controlled large empires in the past. Conflict among Nigeria's many groups has been the country's biggest problem.

Nigeria won independence from Great Britain peacefully in 1960. At first it had an elected government. However, in 1966 the Nigerian army took control of the country. First, leaders from one group ruled, then leaders from another took over.

In 1967 the Ibo people **seceded,** or separated, from Nigeria. They tried to set up their own country, **Biafra** (bee•AF•ruh). The resulting civil war lasted more than two years. A million people died, mostly from hunger, before the Biafrans surrendered.

Today, Nigeria is ruled by a military government. It continues to be a deeply troubled country. The civil war left bad feelings as well as physical damage to towns and factories. Nigeria suffers from lack of food, housing, and jobs for its 89 million people, especially those crowded into its cities. Once its oil reserves are used up, it will not be able to rely on oil exports for most of its money.

Nigeria, however, is using some of its oil money to help its people. It is trying to improve its farming methods so that there will be enough food. It has set up **hydroelectric** projects to make electricity from waterpower. It wants to build enough schools so that all Nigerians can have free primary education. If Nigeria continues to spend its income wisely, it can improve life for its people.

Kenya

Many people call Kenya the most beautiful country in Africa. The land around Lake Victoria and the highlands below snow-capped Mount Kenya are green and fertile. Like South Africa, Kenya has a pleasant climate that attracted many European settlers. Most of these settlers were British. Before its independence Kenya, too, was a British colony.

Kenya had far fewer white settlers than South Africa, however. The settlers wanted to keep control of Kenya's government, but they were not able to do so. Kenya's black citizens demanded self-government and became independent of Great Britain in 1963. Jomo Kenyatta, who had led the independence movement, became the new republic's first president.

Kenya does not have Nigeria's oil money or the minerals and industry of South Africa. However, its government has remained fairly strong, and its economy has grown steadily.

Oil, Nigeria's most important resource, adds billions of dollars to its economy.

Elephants, once widely hunted for their ivory, are now protected by law in Kenya's game reserves.

Farming is the main occupation in Kenya. The government of Kenya has encouraged farmers to join together in cooperatives. By working together farmers can share expensive, modern machinery. They can use the machines to cultivate large areas of land.

Kenya's government also has helped its economy by encouraging tourism. More tourists come to Kenya than to any other African country except Egypt. They are eager to visit Kenya's beautiful lakes and mountains. They are also fascinated by its lions, antelopes, and other wildlife. Large areas of land in Kenya have been set aside as wildlife parks. More than 500,000 people visit these parks each year.

Kenya does have some of the same problems that other African nations have. Most of Kenya's people are poor and uneducated. Many, especially in the cities, cannot find jobs. As in Nigeria and other African countries, rivalries between group leaders have shaken the government. There are more than 40 different groups in Kenya, including the Masai and the Kikuyu.

When Jomo Kenyatta was in power, he tried to unite Kenya's people with the Swahili slogan *harambi* (hah. RAHM.bee), which means "pulling together." If Kenya's people do pull together, they have a good chance of solving the problems they face.

Reading Check

1. Which African country was the first to win its independence?
2. Who are the Afrikaners?
3. Why are the many different groups living in Nigeria one of its biggest problems?
4. Why are farmers in Kenya encouraged to farm cooperatively?

311

Diamonds

Diamonds! The word brings to mind brilliantly sparkling stones worth fortunes. Perhaps it brings to mind diamonds of different colors, such as the beautiful blue Hope diamond. This famous diamond is on display at the Smithsonian Institution in Washington, D.C.

Another famous diamond, the Eureka diamond, was probably the first diamond discovered in South Africa. A small boy and his sister who were looking for interesting stones found the diamond in 1868 on the banks of the Orange River. They showed the stone to a man who recognized its worth. He passed the word that diamonds had been discovered in South Africa. A "New Rush" began, similar to the 1849 Gold Rush in California. A few people became very rich because of their diamond finds.

Diamond mine

Diamonds are one of the hardest naturally formed minerals on Earth. The only mineral hard enough to scratch a diamond is another diamond. Perfect diamonds are used for jewelry. Imperfect diamonds that cannot be sold as gems have numerous industrial uses. Because they are hard, diamonds are used to drill through rock. This makes them valuable to the oil industry. They are also used on special saws that cut rock and metal and in most phonograph needles.

Uncut diamond

Diamonds are formed in the earth from carbon. It takes millions of years and tremendous pressure and heat for the earth to form a diamond. Although some diamonds are found on the surface, most are mined in the same way as some metals. Miners dig deep in the earth to find them.

Diamonds are found in many colors. Some are transparent, or clear; others are not. Diamonds used for gems are usually clear. Pale-blue diamonds are the best but most are slightly yellow. Industrial diamonds are gray or brown and cloudy in appearance.

Hope diamond

Sixty-four percent of the world's diamonds are mined in Africa, many in South Africa. Because they are precious stones and difficult to mine, diamonds command high prices. Diamonds are therefore an important part of the economy of South Africa, providing many jobs.

Look for answers to these questions:
1. What problems do African countries face today?
2. How are African countries trying to solve their problems?
3. How are Africans showing new pride in themselves and their land?
4. Why are events in Africa important to the rest of the world?

3. AFRICA TODAY AND TOMORROW

African nations today face many challenges. Some are problems that Africans have always had, such as poor soil and disease. Other problems have become worse in recent years. They include drought and overpopulation.

Africa is caught between old and new ways. African leaders have learned that farming and herding alone can no longer feed their people or allow them to compete in the world marketplace. At the same time, few African countries have machines for industry or people who know how to run them.

Poor transportation within Africa is another problem. The Europeans who designed most of Africa's roads and railroads were concerned only with getting cash crops or minerals from the interior to the coast. As a result, few roads or railroads connect countries within Africa. Often railroads use different widths of track, so they cannot easily be connected.

Many Africans moved to the cities in the years after World War II. Some were trying to get away from hunger in the countryside. Some came because they needed money to pay taxes or buy things for their families. Others hoped to get good jobs and become rich. Whatever their hopes, they were usually disappointed. There were not enough jobs, houses, or food for these millions of new arrivals. Unplanned, unhealthy "tin-can towns" grew up around the edges of most African cities.

Quarrelling among countries has been one of Africa's greatest problems. More and more African governments are recognizing the need to cooperate with one another, however. Thus, the **Organization of African Unity** (OAU), founded in 1963, has representatives from most of Africa's countries. The OAU meets yearly to plan cooperative projects, such as the building of roads and railways across Africa.

313

Disagreement inside African countries is also an important problem. It has caused one African government after another to be overthrown. Outsiders have sometimes criticized the African governments for this unsteadiness. Those outsiders forget that new governments often go through difficult times of adjustment before they reach their final forms.

Hope for the Future

African governments today are trying to blend the old with the new. They hope to combine new technology with the love of the land and the cooperative spirit that have been such important parts of Africa in the past.

Money from the sale of newly discovered minerals is giving many African governments the chance to carry out development programs. Some use the money for schools and hospitals. Some build new factories and train workers to run them. Others start hydroelectric or irrigation projects.

Africans today are feeling a new pride in themselves and their land in spite of their problems. Modern African artists and writers are both preserving and adding to their heritage. African governments accept aid and ideas from countries outside the continent, but they try to avoid close ties with those countries. They want to succeed on their own. They hope never to return to a situation in which outsiders control African life.

The world today is watching Africa closely. The African nations have resources that are valuable to everyone. Actions taken by African governments can affect international trade.

Irrigation of dry land is a major goal of many African nations.

Africans know that the years ahead will not be easy ones. They have learned, often painfully, that solving their problems will not be easy. Even painful learning can bring growth, however. The determination of the African people will help them build united, prosperous nations.

Reading Check

1. List three problems challenging African nations today.
2. How have African cities changed since World War II?
3. What group meets yearly to plan cooperative projects?
4. Why do African governments try to avoid close ties with non-African countries?

SKILLS FOR SUCCESS

USING POPULATION MAPS

Population maps show where people live or do not live. Most such maps also show **population density,** or how many people live on one square mile or one square kilometer of land. To find population density you need to know both the size of the land area and the number of people living there.

Population density can be shown on maps in several ways. One way is with colors. Look at the key on the population map of Africa. The key tells you that the colors on the map stand for different population densities. On the map key the color yellow stands for the least crowded areas. Red stands for the most crowded areas. Each color tells you how many people live in one square mile (2.6 sq km).

Read the map key and find the areas on the map that have less than 1 person per square mile (2.6 sq km). One of these areas is the Sahara, the desert stretching east to west across northern Africa.

Comparing a population map to a physical map or vegetation map will help you understand why some places are more populated than others. Find the large area in southwestern Africa with a density of less than 1 person per square mile (2.6 sq km). Then locate the same area on the physical map on page 259. What kind of land is this?

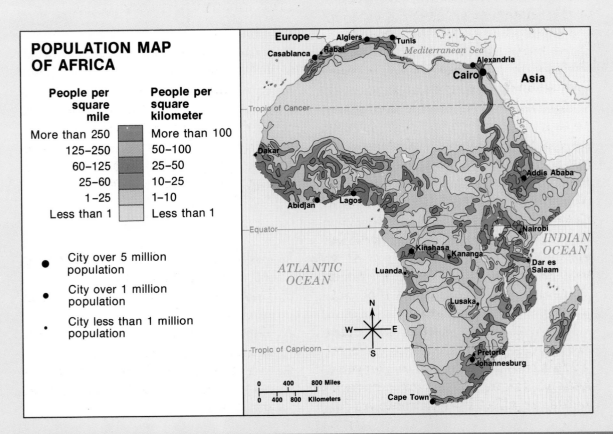

POPULATION MAP OF AFRICA

People per square mile		People per square kilometer
More than 250		More than 100
125–250		50–100
60–125		25–50
25–60		10–25
1–25		1–10
Less than 1		Less than 1

- City over 5 million population
- City over 1 million population
- City less than 1 million population

Next, find the northeast corner of Africa on the population map. Here the Nile River flows through Egypt into the Mediterranean Sea. What color is shown at the mouth of the Nile? Checking the key, you will see that this region is heavily populated. Dense populations usually mean urban areas. Near the mouth of the Nile, for example, is the city of Cairo. What other Egyptian city is located at the mouth of the Nile?

The populations of the cities on the map also are given. Different-sized dots represent these populations. The largest dot stands for a population of more than 5 million people. The next-sized dot represents cities of a million or more people. What is the symbol for cities with less than a million people?

Notice that these symbols do not give you the exact populations of the cities. They do enable you to compare the sizes of the cities, however. Find the matching dot for Cairo on the map key. How large is the population of Cairo?

Cartograms

You know that people are not evenly spread throughout the world. Some areas are nearly empty, while other areas are overcrowded. Small countries or continents may have larger populations than large countries or continents. One interesting way to show population is to use a special map called a **cartogram.** Cartograms are used to show statistics geographically.

This cartogram shows what countries of the world would look like if everyone occupied the same amount of land. On such a map you can quickly compare populations around the world.

The cartogram does *not* provide the number of people in an area. By making countries larger or smaller, the cartogram

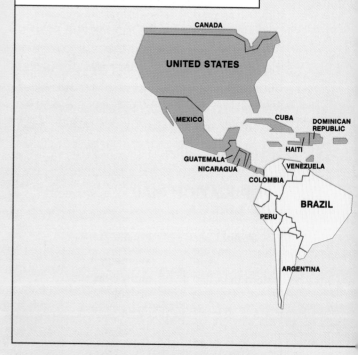

POPULATION CARTOGRAM OF THE WORLD

AFG.	Afghanistan
BEL.	Belgium
BULG.	Bulgaria
CZECH.	Czechoslovakia
E. GER.	East Germany
HUNG.	Hungary
ROM.	Romania
UG.	Uganda
YUGO.	Yugoslavia

shows only how one country compares with another in terms of population size. For example, on this cartogram the size of India indicates that it has a larger population than all of Africa.

Locate Australia and Japan on a map or globe. Notice that Australia has a much larger land area than Japan. According to the cartogram, however, which of these countries has the larger population?

CHECKING YOUR SKILLS

Use the population map and the cartogram in this lesson to answer the following questions.

1. What color on the map represents a density of 125 to 250 people per square mile (2.6 sq km)?

2. Look at the northwest and southeast coasts of Africa. Are their population densities high or low? What reason might you give for their density?

3. Name three cities with populations of more than one million people.

4. Which country in Africa has the largest population?

5. Which continent has a larger population, Europe or Africa?

CHAPTER 11 REVIEW

USING WORDS

Explain the meaning of each of the words listed below. Then use each word in a complete sentence.

1. **apartheid**
2. **descendants**
3. **hydroelectric**
4. **policy**
5. **seceded**

REVIEWING FACTS

1. Name three groups of people from other countries who came to settle in Africa.

2. What is a language family?

3. How do most Africans make their living?

4. Name three groups of Africans who still follow old ways of life.

5. What led Africans to demand independence in the twentieth century?

6. What are some hardships that black South Africans face under the system of apartheid?

7. Why is it difficult to persuade the South African government to change its policy?

8. Which country has the largest population in Africa?

9. What has Kenya's government done to help the country's economy?

10. List three things that Africans are doing to develop their countries.

THINKING CRITICALLY

1. How might the country boundaries set up in Africa by the Europeans during the colonial period have helped to cause the disagreements that trouble Africa today?

2. You have read how Africans are solving their problems and developing their countries. They have built schools, hospitals, factories, and dams. Discuss how each of these can help to improve people's lives. Why might some of these improvements be difficult to make? Suppose you belong to an African group that has lived in the same way for hundreds of years. How might you react to attempts to change the way you live or work?

○ PRACTICING SKILLS

Population Map   Use the population map of Africa on page 315 and your skills lesson to answer the following questions.

1. What two things must you know to find the population density of an area?

2. Which color on the map indicates a density of 1 to 25 people per square mile (2.6 sq km)? Would areas of this color be crowded or uncrowded?

3. Parts of West and East Africa have dense populations. How would a physical map help to explain why?

4. Name a city in North Africa with a population of less than one million people.

5. Which city is larger, Addis Ababa or Nairobi?

CLOSE-UP

THE UNITED NATIONS: FAILURES AND SUCCESSES

Flags of many different countries wave in front of the United Nations Building in New York City.

It is spring of 1945 and World War II is nearly over. Allied armies—the Americans, the British, the Soviets—have begun their final push to defeat Nazi Germany. On the other side of the world, American generals are preparing their big attack on Japan. No one believes that Germany or Japan will surrender without a terrible fight. Many more lives will be lost.

Representatives of 50 nations have come together in San Francisco, California, on April 25, 1945. They have gathered to think beyond the war. They have come to plan for peace. World War II will leave many nations in ruins. Millions of people will be homeless. The leaders of the United States, Great Britain, China, and the Soviet Union hope to prevent this. The previous fall, they had gathered at Dumbarton Oaks, an estate near Washington, D.C. There they began to make plans for an organization of nations that would bring peace to the war-torn world. Now, in San Francisco, they and other nations would continue to plan the **United Nations** (UN).

The San Francisco meeting concluded successfully. The **Charter,** or constitution, of the United Nations was signed on June 26, 1945. The purpose of the UN, it said, is "to save succeeding generations from the scourge [punishment] of war." The Charter set up a congress of nations that works to keep the peace. If any nation is attacked, it can come to the UN for help.

A second main purpose of the UN is cooperation among all nations to solve world problems. The war caused great destruction. The United Nations helped the defeated to rebuild. It continues to help the starving and the homeless.

319

The Structure of the UN

Most of the nations that formed the UN believed in democratic government. A main idea of democracy is that power should be shared. This idea can be found in the structure of the United Nations. There is a leader, or executive, called the Secretary General. The Security Council, a kind of senate, gives power to the strongest nations. The General Assembly, somewhat like our House of Representatives, gives a balancing power to the other nations. There is a judicial branch, the World Court, which is designed to settle problems of law among nations. Under the direction of the Economic and Social Council, smaller agencies carry out special tasks.

THE SECURITY COUNCIL   The Security Council is given the responsibility for keeping peace. The five great powers—the United States, Great Britain, France, the Soviet Union, and the People's Republic of China—are permanent members. These five members have to agree on important matters that come before the Security Council. Any of the **Big Five** can veto a Security Council decision. When even one nation vetoes a proposal, the UN cannot take action.

Also on the Security Council are ten members from other nations. They are chosen for two-year terms. The Security Council thus has fifteen members to settle conflicts. If nine agree—the Big Five plus four others—the Council can offer a peace plan. All UN members have promised to obey these decisions. The Security Council can ask members to punish nations that refuse to cooperate with decisions made by the UN.

A session of the United Nations General Assembly meets.

THE GENERAL ASSEMBLY   Today the General Assembly of the UN has 159 members, one representative from each member nation. Like the Security Council, the General Assembly meets at UN Headquarters in New York City. The members of the General Assembly can discuss questions of peace. They can, if a majority agrees, recommend actions to the Security Council. However, the Assembly cannot take direct action on its own.

The Secretary General is Javier Pérez de Cuéllar of Peru.

The General Assembly also elects members to the other UN bodies. It assigns committees to study problems and receives their reports. Its debates and decisions are widely reported in newspapers and on television. Such debates can have great influence on world opinion.

THE SECRETARY GENERAL   The Secretary General is the chief officer of the UN. The General Assembly appoints the Secretary General after receiving the Security Council's suggestion. The Secretary General may call on the UN to discuss any conflicts or problems. The Secretary General speaks for all member nations and therefore has influence as a world leader.

THE WORLD COURT   The International Court of Justice, or the World Court, meets at The Hague (HAYG), in the Netherlands. Fifteen judges form the World Court. When nations have a dispute over treaties or rights, the World Court can make a decision. UN members are supposed to follow its decisions.

THE ECONOMIC AND SOCIAL COUNCIL   The Economic and Social Council of the UN directs more than 250 special agencies. These agencies have special tasks. Some lend money to poor nations to build industries. Some help countries train skilled workers. Some give advice to farmers. Others are designed to help the world's children by supplying food, clothing, and medical care. Still other UN agencies help spread scientific information and work to wipe out disease. All the agencies work in some way to help member nations improve the lives of their people.

A representative from an African nation presents his views.

The UN's Problems

The nations that founded the UN were sure about its most important job: to keep the peace. They were convinced that the Security Council could do this job. Representatives from the five most powerful nations sit on the Security Council. With these powers in agreement, the council's decisions can have force.

321

Danish soldiers keep
peace in Egypt in 1956.

The burned jeep in the
background is a reminder
of recent fighting.

The charter gives the Security Council real power. If one nation refuses to agree to a peace plan, the Security Council can recommend that member nations stop doing business with that nation. Goods and services can be cut off. After that, the council has the power to call for armed action. Each UN member agrees to contribute soldiers and equipment for the UN peace-keeping force.

In the beginning, the UN succeeded in settling some disputes. When Soviet troops refused to leave northern Iran in 1946, the Security Council quickly took action. At its first meeting, it judged that the Soviet troops were violating the UN charter. Under UN pressure, the Soviet troops withdrew.

The UN can work when the Security Council agrees. It cannot work when problems arise and its members disagree, which is, unfortunately, most of the time. During the 1940s the Soviet Union and the large democracies were united to fight the Nazis and to form the UN. Shortly after the war, their interests went in opposite directions. Cases that came before the Security Council developed a pattern. Four of the Big Five would agree. The Soviet Union would disagree and veto any plan for a settlement. Since the charter said all the Big Five had to agree, the Security Council was unable to act.

In 1950 the UN passed a rule that allowed the General Assembly to discuss threats to peace if the Security Council could not act. The assembly can talk about a conflict and vote to send observers to study the problem. It can urge the parties to talk. Sometimes, as when the Soviet Union invaded Afghanistan in 1979, the General Assembly condemns an invasion. Only the Security Council can send peace-keeping forces to a troubled area, however.

Often the decisions of the General Assembly have little effect on nations at war. Nevertheless, the assembly has become more important in recent years. Because most nations of the world have a voice in the assembly, they have a place to speak out and be heard by the world community. The assembly's debates and votes sometimes reflect, and sometimes shape, the ideas of many different people around the world. No nation wants to have its actions criticized before millions of people.

322

When the UN began in 1945, the General Assembly had 50 members. Since 1946, the world has changed. More than 100 new nations are now members. Many of these nations are very small, and many are not democracies. Their leaders often oppose American interests. The new UN members can outvote the older democracies in the General Assembly. For this reason many Americans have complained about the UN recently. They say the UN no longer serves democracy's purpose.

Similar complaints have been made about paying for the UN. The United States has always paid the largest share of UN expenses. The main UN buildings are in New York City. The city's costs for providing police and other services for the UN are great. Many nations, such as the Soviet Union, pay less than their share. This again causes some Americans to complain that the United States pays most for the UN and gets little in return.

UN Successes

The founders of the UN made peace its main goal and helping people its second goal. The UN has often met this second goal. UN agencies in almost every part of the world have helped people to help themselves. UN workers have taught people how to use modern tools, helped them to buy and use modern equipment, and shown them how to share or trade the goods they produce.

The **United Nations Children's Fund** (UNICEF) began by feeding children in the war-torn cities of Europe after World War II. It has continued to help starving children in many countries. UNICEF has helped many nations develop dairy industries for the first time. In India, for example, UNICEF helped build cooperative dairies that supply much-needed milk to children.

One of these cooperative dairies is Amul Dairy, about 200 miles (about 322 km) north of the city of Bombay. The dairy milks water buffalo and turns half of the milk into powdered milk or cheese for sale. The other half goes to city milk stations in Bombay. There needy children get free milk.

This emblem represents UNICEF.

UNICEF also cooperated with the **World Health Organization** (WHO) to help develop a modern health system in Zaire. Zaire had been a colony of Belgium until 1960. Most doctors and nurses were Belgian. When the Belgians left, the government of Zaire had few doctors of its own. It called on the UN for help. By 1970 WHO had helped Zaire train more than 200 doctors. With UNICEF's aid, Zaire built special centers for mother-and-child care. Medical schools and hospitals were built in cities. A hospital boat with modern equipment traveled along the Congo River to serve Zairians there. WHO aided Zairian health workers to fight widespread diseases, such as smallpox, leprosy (LEP·ruh·see), and polio. In a short time, Zaire had an effective health program.

The World Health Organization has done similar work elsewhere. It has spread modern health news worldwide. It has begun vaccination programs in nation after nation. These efforts have worked to control malaria, tuberculosis, smallpox, and other serious diseases.

Cooperation in education and science is the job of another large agency, UNESCO. UNESCO is the **UN Educational, Scientific, and Cultural Organization.** In a fast-changing world, information is an important tool. UNESCO's main service is to spread information. It calls meetings on new developments in science and education. It publishes books that give all nations the chance to learn about new developments such as computers or space travel. UNESCO programs help many nations send their students to study in foreign countries. Students and professors learn each other's customs, needs, and problems.

In its 40 years the UN has failed in some ways and succeeded in others. It has failed mainly in its first job of keeping the peace. Although there have been no world wars, through the years large and small conflicts have taken many lives. Few have been settled by the UN.

At its second task the UN has succeeded very well. Millions of refugees have received direct aid. Millions more have received the benefits of UN programs. Nations have been helped to build modern ways of life in record time. People from different countries have met, studied and worked together, and learned from each other.

Lack of reading skills is a worldwide concern. Here, through a UNESCO program, Ethiopians learn to read and write.

WORDS TO REMEMBER

Number your paper from 1 to 10. Complete the sentences below with the words from the following list.

apartheid	monopoly
barter	prejudices
descendants	racism
imperialism	scarce
missionary	tariff

1. The Soninkes learned to _____ for the goods they needed from other traders.

2. Some trade goods, such as salt, were _____, in the savanna.

3. Ancient rulers of Ghana had a _____ on the gold trade.

4. To support early grassland empires, a _____ on trade goods was collected.

5. Dr. David Livingstone was a _____ who lived, worked, and preached in Africa.

6. Without a true understanding of African peoples, Europeans often formed _____ against them.

7. A policy of _____ spurred Europeans to set up colonies in Africa to protect their trade interests.

8. Because of _____ some Europeans believed Africans did not deserve to be treated equally.

9. The _____ of European settlers continue to live on their lands.

10. Many nations have protested the South African policy of _____.

FOCUS ON MAIN IDEAS

1. Why did large empires appear in West Africa more often than in other parts of the continent?

2. Which group of people crossed the Sahara to trade in West Africa? How did they influence the people of the savanna?

3. What enabled the Portuguese to explore the coasts of Africa?

4. Explain the effects of the slave trade on each of the following groups:

   a. slave traders
   b. plantation owners
   c. Europeans
   d. Africans

5. How did the Industrial Revolution in Europe influence the colonization of Africa?

6. What were two types of colonial government in Africa? How were they different?

7. What were some of the main effects of colonization on African ways of life?

8. How is the government of the Republic of South Africa different from other African governments?

9. Name four problems Africans face today. What are African governments doing to solve their problems?

10. Why are countries outside of Africa interested in the events taking place in African countries today?

"Drought is the biggest problem facing Africa today." Consider the effects of drought on Africa's human population, animal population, and economy. Then write a paragraph telling why you agree or disagree with this opinion.

ACTIVITIES

1. **Research/Art** Art is an important part of African culture. Look at books in the library that show masks, statues, or other kinds of African art. Cloth weavings or paintings on cloth are also good examples. Make a drawing or painting that uses African ideas or designs.

2. **Research/Oral Report** Choose an animal, a bird, a plant, a tree, or a flower native to Africa. Prepare an oral report describing your choice. Point out its unique qualities. Tell if it or anything similar is found in other parts of the world.

3. **Research/Current Events** Collect newspaper and magazine articles about Africa and put them in a class scrapbook. Organize your articles by region (North, West, Central, East, and Southern). Notice if a particular region or country appears in the news more often than another. Find out if boundaries or governments have changed recently.

SKILLS REVIEW

1. **Evaluating Information** On a separate sheet of paper, identify each of the following statements as a fact or an opinion.

   a. About three-fourths of sub-Saharan adults cannot read or write.
   b. Africa was probably the home of the first people on Earth.
   c. Vasco da Gama was the first European to sail around Africa to Asia.
   d. More than half of the world's cacao is produced in Africa.
   e. Algeria, Libya, and Nigeria are the leading producers of oil in Africa.
   f. We Africans believe that big changes will ruin our way of life.
   g. Africa has the most beautiful landscapes in the world.
   h. Most Africans live in rural areas.
   i. Africa has more nations than any other continent.
   j. It will probably take some time for African economies to become fully developed.

2. **Using a Cartogram** Use the cartogram in your skills lesson on pages 316–317 to answer the following questions about Africa. A globe or a political map (see page 256) will help you answer questions *b* through *e*.

   a. How does the cartogram show differences in the populations of African nations?
   b. Name a country in Africa with a large population. Name a country in Africa with a small population.
   c. Which country is larger in size, Ghana or Mali? Which has more people?
   d. Which country is larger in size, Angola or Uganda? Which country has more people?
   e. Which country is larger in size, Tunisia or Libya? Which country has more people?

YOUR WORLD

MAKING A TIMELINE

1. From early Nok ironmakers to modern African nations, you have covered 2,200 years of African history. Pick out the most important events to add to your Timeline of the World. As you add these dates to those for ancient civilizations in North Africa, you can see a long and varied history. Compare developments in Africa with events in the other areas.

LEARNING ABOUT PEOPLE

2. Pick one of the following groups to discuss in your notebook on Cultures of the World.

Amhara	Hausa	Nuba
Ashanti	Ibo	Nuer
Berber	Kikuyu	Somali
Bushman	Malagasy	Tuareg
Dogon	Mbuti	Yoruba
Fulani	Masai	Zulu

Find out where the group's ancestors lived and to what other peoples it is related. Describe where and how the people of the group live and what they eat. Draw a picture showing the way they dress and their ornaments and hair styles. Include information about the way the group is organized. Are there group leaders or different classes? What roles do men, women, and children play in their family and their community? What special beliefs distinguish these people?

EXPRESSING IDEAS

3. Read the following proverbs from various parts of Africa. In your own words, describe the message being offered.

He who does not listen to an elder's advice comes to grief. (Swahili)

Do not tell the man who is carrying you that he stinks. (Sierra Leone)

Do not make a dress for the baby before the child is born. (Tanzania)

He who hunts two rats, catches none. (Uganda)

Do not call to a dog with a whip in your hand. (Republic of South Africa)

No one tests the depth of a river with both feet. (Ghana)

SHARING CULTURE

4. Listed below are eight black Americans and the occupations for which they are known. Choose one of the people listed and prepare a short biography. Read your biography to the class.

Marian Anderson	Singer
Dr. Ralph Bunche	Diplomat
Charles Drew	Physician
Alex Haley	Writer
Matthew Henson	Explorer
Barbara Jordan	Politician
Garrett A. Morgan	Inventor
Jackie Robinson	Athlete

Key Dates and Events

About 2500 B.C.
Farming along the
Indus River

About 1500 B.C.
Aryans conquer
northern India

About 1122–256 B.C.
Chou dynasty
in China

660 B.C.
Japan's first
emperor

214 B.C.
Great Wall of
China built

About A.D. 320–500
Golden Age of
India

A.D. 618–906
Golden Age in
China under T'ang
dynasty

About A.D. 800–1854
Feudal Japan

ASIA, PAST AND PRESENT

The art and architecture of the Chinese remind us of the power and achievements of Asian civilizations. These civilizations have dominated Asia for thousands of years and have contributed much to the Western world. They have attracted explorers and would-be conquerors many times, but they have survived. Today, more than half the world's people still feel their influence.

In this unit you will read about India, China, and Japan. You also will learn about smaller nations in Southeast Asia, including Indonesia, the Philippines, and Thailand. You will discover that in some parts of Asia very little has changed through the centuries. You will see that in other Asian countries, where great changes have occurred, people continue to value their ancient cultures.

A.D. 1275 Marco Polo visits China	A.D. 1600 British East India Company formed in India	A.D. 1854 Commodore Perry visits Japan	A.D. 1949 Communists take control of mainland China	A.D. 1941 Japan bombs Pearl Harbor	A.D. 1978 The United States recognizes the government of communist China
		A.D. 1915–1947 Gandhi leads India to independence			

GEOGRAPHY OF ASIA

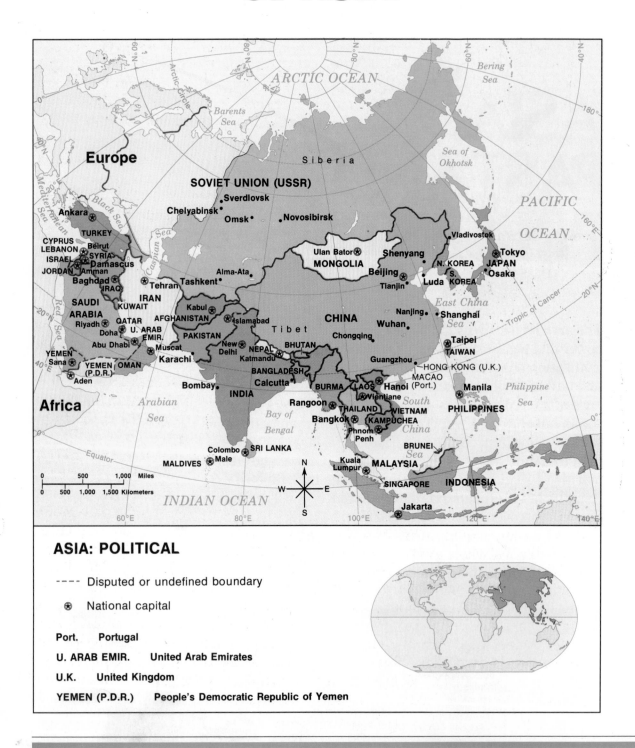

ASIA: POLITICAL

- - - - Disputed or undefined boundary

⊛ National capital

Port.   Portugal

U. ARAB EMIR.   United Arab Emirates

U.K.   United Kingdom

YEMEN (P.D.R.)   People's Democratic Republic of Yemen

Location

Asia is the world's largest continent. It is larger than North and South America combined. From the Mediterranean Sea in the west to the Pacific Ocean in the east, Asia extends about 6,000 miles (9,654 km). From the northern tip of Siberia to the southern tip of Southeast Asia is nearly the same distance. You may remember that Asia shares its landmass with Europe. Often the entire area is called **Eurasia.**

The lands of Asia border three oceans. They are the Indian Ocean in the south, the Pacific Ocean in the east, and the Arctic Ocean in the north. These oceans form broad seas or bays along Asia's coasts. In the south lie the Arabian Sea and the Bay of Bengal. To the east are the Bering Sea, the Sea of Okhotsk (oh•KAHTSK), the Sea of Japan, the Yellow Sea, the East China Sea, and the South China Sea. Within these coastal waters are thousands of islands that are also part of Asia. The nations of Japan, the Philippines, and Indonesia are the largest of the island groups.

Regions of Asia

Asia can be divided into six regions. Two of these regions have been discussed elsewhere in your book. The countries of Southwest Asia are included in Unit 1 on the Middle East. Unit 2 discusses the Soviet Union, which occupies North Asia.

The remaining four regions are South Asia, Central Asia, East Asia, and Southeast Asia. South Asia includes Afghanistan, Pakistan, Nepal, Bhutan, Bangladesh, India, and Sri Lanka. Central Asia refers to the area where the Soviet Union, China, and Mongolia meet. Central Asia includes Tibet, which is part of China.

East Asia contains the nations of Japan, North Korea, South Korea, Taiwan, and the eastern parts of China. Southeast Asia is made up of the Indochina peninsula and the islands that extend like stepping stones to the southeast.

Southeast Asia includes Thailand, Laos, Burma, Kampuchea (Cambodia), Vietnam, Malaysia, Indonesia, Singapore, the Philippines, and Brunei. In all, 40 countries belong to the continent of Asia.

The Land

The countries of Asia contain nearly every type of land known on Earth. In the far north are vast areas of arctic **tundra.** Tundra are cold, treeless plains whose subsoil is permanently frozen. Just south of the tundra is the **taiga** (TY•guh), or forest.

Mountains and plateaus cover about three-fourths of Asia's total land area. The Ural Mountains form Asia's western boundary. Most of Asia's mountains are centered in an area called the **Pamir** (puh•MIR) **Knot.** Often referred to as the "roof of the world," the Pamir Knot is located where Pakistan, Afghanistan, China, and the Soviet Union meet. From this central knot, Asia's mountains extend west into Turkey, northeast toward Siberia, and southeast into India, China, and Southeast Asia.

The highest spot in the world, Mount Everest, and the lowest place, the shores of the Dead Sea, are both in Asia. Mount Everest towers 29,030 feet (8,850 m) above sea level, while the Dead Sea lies 1,299 feet (396 m) below sea level.

Mount Everest and others of the world's highest peaks are in the Himalaya (him•uh•LAY•uh) Mountains. They form the border between Nepal and Tibet. Many of Asia's rivers begin in the Himalayas and the Plateau of Tibet and flow across plains to the sea. In South Asia the Indus, Ganges (GAN•jeez), and Brahmaputra (brahm•uh•POO•truh) rivers flow through Pakistan, India, and Bangladesh. The Mekong (MAY•KAWNG), the Irrawaddy (ir•uh•WAHD•ee), and the Salween (SAL•ween) are important rivers of Southeast Asia.

The longest river in Asia is the Chang Jiang. It flows 3,915 miles (6,299 km) from the Tibetan Plateau into the East China Sea. China's other major rivers include the Xi Jiang (SHEE JANG) and Huang He. With the exception of the Amur River, which forms part of the border between the Soviet Union and China, the main rivers of North Asia empty into the Arctic Ocean. These very long rivers include the Yenisey, the Ob, and the Lena.

Large areas of Asia are without rivers. The largest desert in Asia is the Gobi. The Gobi stretches across most of Mongolia and part of China.

Cool-weather crops grow in a Nepalese valley below Mount Everest.

Here the Chang Jiang winds through a gorge in a mountainous region in China.

West of the Gobi, covering the southern part of the Soviet Union and northwest China, are the steppes of Central Asia. The poor land and dry climate of this region make it hard to live there. Enough precipitation falls in parts of this region, however, to allow some grain farming. Drier parts of the steppes with their short grasses are better suited for grazing.

Although Asia is a huge landmass, much of the land is not used by people. The chapters in this unit will focus on the areas of Asia that have supported large populations: India, China, Japan, and Southeast Asia.

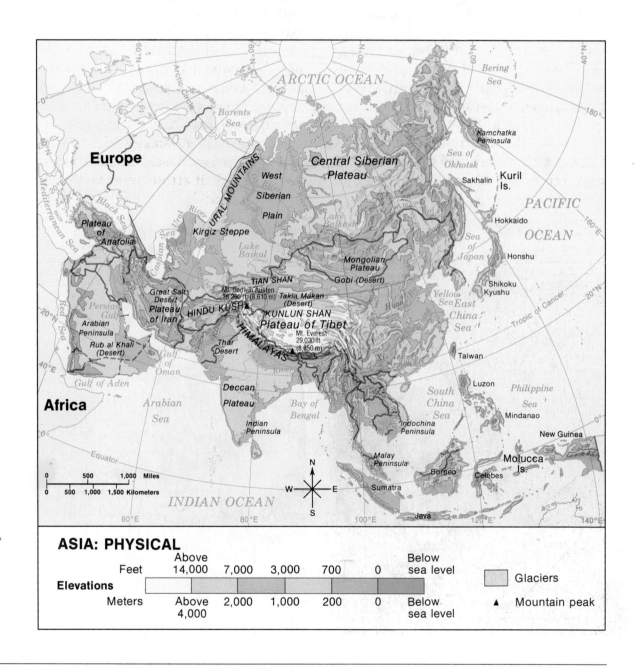

ASIA: PHYSICAL

Elevations	Above 14,000	7,000	3,000	700	0	Below sea level		
Feet							Glaciers	
Meters	Above 4,000	2,000	1,000	200	0	Below sea level	▲	Mountain peak

The Climate

Because Asia stretches from the arctic to the equator, its climates vary greatly. Most of Siberia, in North Asia, has a **subarctic** climate. Winters are long and cold. Summers are cool. In parts of this region the land is frozen year round.

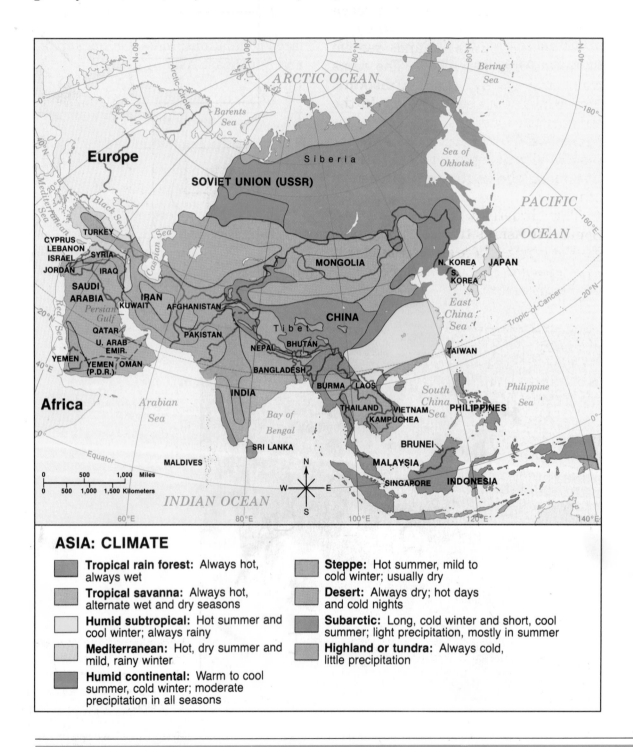

ASIA: CLIMATE

Tropical rain forest: Always hot, always wet

Tropical savanna: Always hot, alternate wet and dry seasons

Humid subtropical: Hot summer and cool winter; always rainy

Mediterranean: Hot, dry summer and mild, rainy winter

Humid continental: Warm to cool summer, cold winter; moderate precipitation in all seasons

Steppe: Hot summer, mild to cold winter; usually dry

Desert: Always dry; hot days and cold nights

Subarctic: Long, cold winter and short, cool summer; light precipitation, mostly in summer

Highland or tundra: Always cold, little precipitation

High mountains keep moist ocean air from entering much of Central Asia. Little rain falls on the steppes, plateaus, and deserts. Summers can blaze, while winter temperatures can reach as low as 40°F below zero (−40°C).

By contrast, coastal lands receive large amounts of rainfall. The rains come and go with the **monsoons.** Monsoons are seasonal winds. In the summer they bring rain that drenches farmlands. Such monsoon rains are one reason why so many of Asia's people live along the southern and eastern coasts.

The climate of South Asia and Southeast Asia is tropical. Because of the heavy rains there and on the islands in the Pacific, much of the land is covered by rain forests.

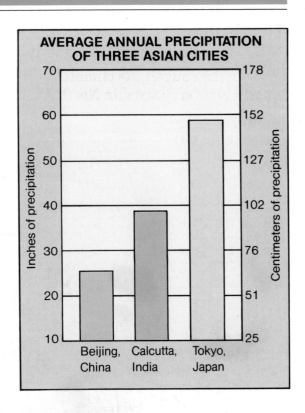

AVERAGE ANNUAL PRECIPITATION OF THREE ASIAN CITIES

Work elephants in Asia are taught by skilled trainers. Here, the elephants use both tusks and trunks to lift teakwood logs.

Resources

Between the arctic tundra and the rain forests of the south, Asia's resources are numerous. Sixty percent of the world's coal is in Asia. Much of it is in China and India. Besides coal, the arctic tundra of Siberia contains large oil and natural gas deposits. India,

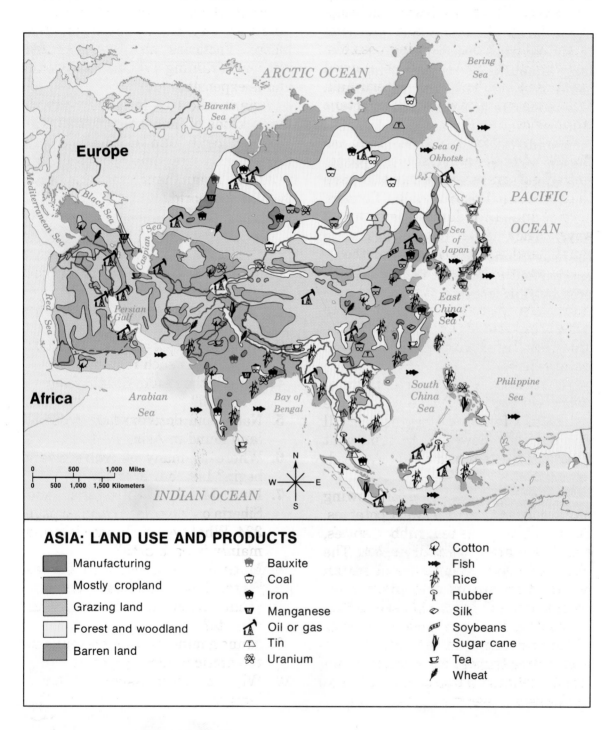

ASIA: LAND USE AND PRODUCTS

■ Manufacturing	
Mostly cropland	
Grazing land	
Forest and woodland	
Barren land	

Bauxite	Cotton
Coal	Fish
Iron	Rice
Manganese	Rubber
Oil or gas	Silk
Tin	Soybeans
Uranium	Sugar cane
	Tea
	Wheat

China, and the Soviet Union all have uranium deposits. Large tin reserves exist in Southeast Asia.

Rivers are another of Asia's many resources. Water, delivered in huge amounts by its rivers and monsoon rains, makes Asian farming possible. A plentiful water supply has allowed farmers in southern and eastern Asia to develop one of their most important crops—rice.

Rice grows best in fields that are flooded when the rice plants are young. These fields are called **paddies.** To keep their paddies flooded, Asian farmers have changed the landscape in many ways. They have developed dikes, canals, and other irrigation methods. To increase available farmland, they have learned ways to farm their hillsides. Rice farming has also led to widespread use of the water buffalo, a kind of ox that can draw plows through watery fields.

Agriculture is an important part of Asian economies. Two out of three Asians are farmers. They are not all rice farmers, however. In somewhat drier areas wheat and cotton are leading crops.

Tropical areas are good for growing fruits, vegetables, and sweet potatoes. Such cash crops as tea, rubber, spices, and fibers are grown for export. The fibers of hemp, bamboo, and rattan plants often are used to make rope, rugs, and many kinds of baskets. Basket weaving is a large industry in parts of tropical Asia. In addition to the plants already mentioned, tropical rain forests contain palm trees and rare hardwoods as well as rubber trees.

Many Asian countries are building factories. Industrialization, however, has been difficult. Some countries lack the resources that provide power to run factories. Such countries often cannot afford to buy those resources elsewhere. Factories also need skilled workers. Training workers takes time and is expensive.

Asians who live in cities work in many kinds of industries. They manufacture cloth and clothing. Many Asians also are employed as craft workers. Asian handicrafts are sold around the world.

Geography Review

1. Asia is a part of what larger landmass?
2. Which three oceans border the continent of Asia?
3. Name four regions of Asia and two countries in each region.
4. What is the Pamir Knot? Where is it located?
5. Name and describe four types of land found in Asia.
6. Where do many of Asia's rivers begin? List four examples.
7. Find Malaysia, Mongolia, and Siberia on the climate map on page 334. What type of climate is found mainly in each area?
8. Much of the midwestern United States has a moderate climate. What part of China has a similar climate?
9. Name a mineral resource found in the arctic tundra of Siberia.
10. What do most Asians do for a living?

Cultures Mix in India

Focus

India is the world's largest democracy. It produces atomic energy, and its industries are among the fastest growing in the world. Even so, India is underdeveloped. Near modern factories, farmers still scratch a living from small plots of land, using tools invented thousands of years ago. This contrast in lifestyles exists in a nation that once was one of the world's wealthiest.

During its long history, many different peoples came to India. They came from Europe, the Middle East, and other parts of Asia. Some people came to trade. Others came to settle. All left their mark on Indian culture.

Look for these important words:

Key Words

- subcontinent
- Dravidians

Places

- Hindu Kush
- Deccan Plateau

- Thar Desert
- Punjab

Look for answers to these questions:

1. How has the land of the Indian peninsula affected the human settlement of the area?
2. What type of climate does India have?
3. On what feature of India's climate do Indian farmers depend?

1. A PENINSULA IN SOUTH ASIA

Jutting out from the south of Asia like a huge triangle is the Indian peninsula. It is bordered by the Arabian Sea, the Indian Ocean, and the Bay of Bengal. The nation of India occupies about three-fourths of the peninsula. Pakistan, Nepal, Bhutan, and Bangladesh share the landmass with India. So large is the Indian peninsula that it often is called a **subcontinent,** which means a large part of a continent.

Mountains, plains, and plateaus form the Indian peninsula. In the north are the Himalaya Mountains. Stretching for about 1,500 miles (2,414 km) across India's northern border, the Himalayas join the **Hindu Kush** to form a wall of mountains between the peninsula and the rest of Asia.

South of the mountains are large plains, watered by the Indus, Ganges, and Brahmaputra rivers. It is on these fertile plains that most of the people of the subcontinent have settled. Farmers there grow rice, wheat, cotton, and tea on the northern plains.

Still farther south is the **Deccan** (DEK•uhn) **Plateau.** It is ringed by a triangle of hills and mountains north, east, and west. Descendants of India's most ancient people, the **Dravidians** (druh•VID•ee•uhnz), live in this southern part of India. The soil there is good for growing peas, beans, and cotton.

Adding to the variety of India's landscape are a desert and tropical rain forests. The huge **Thar Desert,** also called the Great Indian Desert, forms India's northwest border. Along the southwest coast, tropical rain forests are home to elephants and cobras. Coffee and rubber are important products.

Wind and Rain

Most of India lies between the Tropic of Cancer and the equator. As in other tropical climates, temperatures in India are warm or hot throughout the year. The mountain barriers in the north prevent cold air from passing into India. India has two separate seasons, a dry season and a wet season.

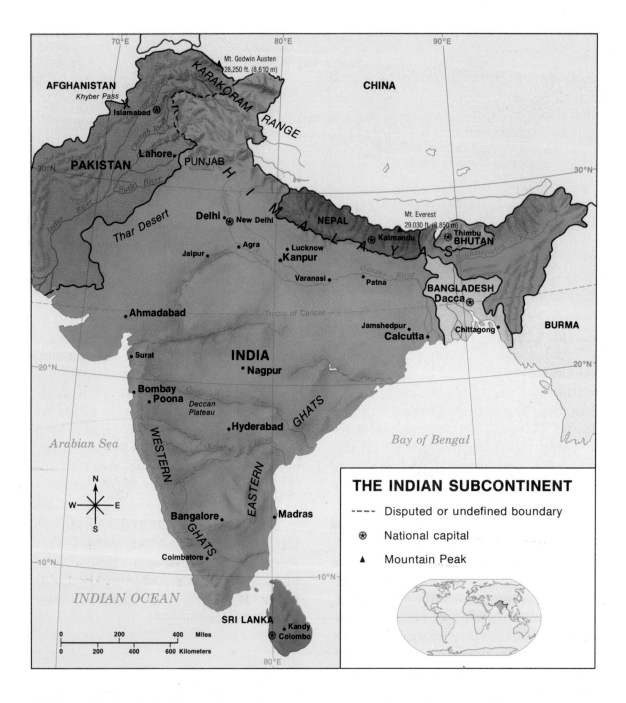

THE INDIAN SUBCONTINENT

---- Disputed or undefined boundary

⊛ National capital

▲ Mountain Peak

Seasonal winds have the biggest influence on the climate of India. Dry winter monsoons blow across the land from the northeast, beginning around October. By March the winter winds have completely dried and cracked the land. Then, for about three months before the next monsoon, the weather is very hot. During this hot season, temperatures in much of India rise to an average of over 90°F (32.2°C).

The summer monsoons come in June. Roaring in from the Indian Ocean to the south, the moisture-filled winds bring heavy rains from June to September. This rainy season gives many

During the dry season, the land is brown, crops die, and the air is heavy with dust.

Six weeks of rain have turned the dry land into fields of green, growing crops.

parts of India more than 80 inches (about 200 cm) of rain a year.

The heavy monsoon rains have always been important to Indian farmers. When the monsoons come, the hot, baked soil is flooded. Crops grow rapidly. Some years the monsoons are late. At times they may not come at all, causing hard times for farmers and their crops.

India is rich in such resources as coal and iron ore. These have added to India's wealth in the past and now contribute to India's modern industries. Mainly, however, India is a farming country. With more usable farm land than any other Asian country, India has always depended on its farms.

Some of the most fertile land is in the **Punjab** (puhn•JAHB) region. This wheat-growing area of northwest India and Pakistan is irrigated by the Indus River. It was in this area, too, that India's history began.

Reading Check

1. Why is the Indian peninsula called a subcontinent?
2. Name four countries that share the Indian peninsula with India.
3. What are the Indian peninsula's three major rivers?
4. How do the mountain ranges that border northern India affect its climate?

341

Asian Elephants

Elephants are found in Africa and in Asia. The Asian elephant, however, is different from the African elephant. Unlike most African elephants, the Asian elephant can be domesticated.

Tamed elephants can act as work animals, like horses and oxen do. In some Asian countries, such as India, Sri Lanka, and Burma, elephants are very important because of the work they do. They are trained to haul loads as light as bundles of straw or as heavy as logs.

Elephants often use their trunks in the work they do. The elephant's trunk is actually its upper lip and nose combined. It contains more than 40,000 muscles. With its trunk an elephant can pour water and dust over itself, care for its young, and sniff out food and water. An elephant can smell water up to 3 miles (about 5 km) away. This is very important since it needs to drink 30 to 40 gallons (about 115 to 150 L) of water every day.

It is believed that an elephant never forgets. The elephant's reputation for good memory probably comes from the fact that some elephants, especially Asian females, are easy to train. They learn very quickly and do not forget what they have learned. The intelligence of the elephant makes it a popular circus performer. In India the elephant-headed god Ganesh is the god of intelligence. This shows the respect held for the animal's cunning.

Elephants have been charming, gentle companions to nobles and common people alike. In some countries where elephants are used as work animals, they are sometimes given the job of minding children. King Henry II of France had an elephant, as did Queen Elizabeth I of England. These animals were often the main attraction at parties.

Because their tusks have been used to make precious objects of ivory, many elephants have been killed by hunters. As a result, the elephant is in danger of disappearing from the Earth forever. In many places in Africa and Asia, however, elephants are now protected from hunters by law.

Royal elephant

Ganesh

Ancient seal

Look for these important words:

Key Words
- Aryans
- Sanskrit
- caste
- untouchables
- Hinduism
- Hindus
- reincarnation

- Vedas
- Buddhism
- rajas

People
- Gautama
- Buddha
- Chandragupta Maurya

- Asoka
- Kalidasa
- Aryabhata

Places
- Harappa
- Mohenjo-Daro
- Khyber Pass
- New Delhi

Look for answers to these questions:

1. How did the Aryans influence Indian culture?
2. What are some beliefs of Hinduism?
3. Who was Buddha and what did he teach?
4. What advances were made during India's Golden Age?

2. THE FIRST CIVILIZATIONS

Like the civilizations of Sumer and ancient Egypt, India's first civilization arose on the flood plain of a great river. By 2500 B.C., along the Indus River, Indian farmers were growing enough crops to support large cities.

In recent times, archaeologists have uncovered the remains of two of these cities, **Harappa** (huh•RAP•uh) and **Mohenjo-Daro** (moh•HEN•joh DAHR•oh). The cities show that ancient Indians built walled communities complete with plumbing. These ancient Indians had a written language that is not totally understood today. The ruins of Harappa and Mohenjo-Daro include fine cups and vases of bronze, silver, copper, and lead. Coins show that the ancient Indians traded with people living as far away as Persia.

We know that the Indian people have one of the oldest civilizations in the world. We do not know, however, exactly why this early civilization disappeared. Some scientists believe that a flood of the Indus River scattered and weakened the people. Others believe they were conquered. Whatever the cause, the early civilization of the Indus Valley disappeared.

The bull, a symbol of strength, is shown on this seal found at Mohenjo-Daro.

343

The Aryans

About 1500 B.C. powerful warriors appeared in northern India. They crossed through such high mountain passes as the **Khyber** (KY•bur) **Pass** between what are now Afghanistan and Pakistan. The warriors had been nomadic herders in Central Asia. They called themselves **Aryans** (AR•ee•uhnz). With swift, horse-drawn chariots the Aryans conquered the lands of the Indus River valley.

The Aryans heavily influenced Indian culture. They introduced their language, **Sanskrit,** which is the basis for many Indian languages today. Aryans divided their own society into separate classes: the priests, the warriors, and the common people. In India the Aryans added a fourth and lower group for the conquered Indians.

The Caste System

In time, the Aryan social system became the basis for India's **caste** system. A *caste* was an unchanging group within Indian society. A person born to one caste could never change castes or mix with members of other castes. Caste members lived, ate, married, and worked within their own group.

The highest group was the *Brahman* (BRAHM•un) caste of priests and scholars. Next came the *Kshatriya* (kuh•SHAH•tree•uh), or ruling caste. Warriors were also included in this group. Third was the *Vaisya* (VYSH•yuh), or merchant-and-farmer caste. Last was the *Sudra* (SOO•druh) caste of laborers, craft workers, and servants.

Below all castes was a group called the **untouchables.** Untouchables were not allowed to belong to organized

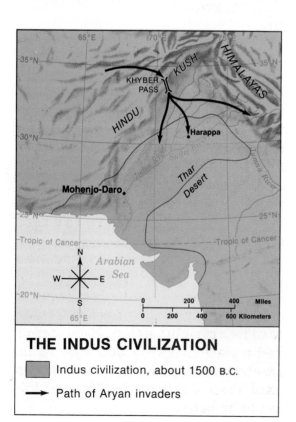

THE INDUS CIVILIZATION

◼ Indus civilization, about 1500 B.C.

→ Path of Aryan invaders

Though illegal, castes still exist. Here an untouchable sweeps the street.

For Hindus, the Ganges is the most sacred of all rivers. Millions travel there to bathe and become purified. Some travel there to die.

society. They carried garbage and did all the lowly tasks. Even the shadow of an untouchable could not fall upon a higher caste person. Absolutely no contact was permitted.

Hinduism

Hinduism is the oldest of the world's religions still practiced today. There are many gods and goddesses in Hinduism and many different ways of worshipping. **Hindus,** or believers in Hinduism, have always been considerate of each other's beliefs.

A central belief of Hinduism is that people live many lives until they reach spiritual perfection. This belief that the soul lives on after death and then returns to life in a new body is called **reincarnation.**

Brahman priests encouraged Hindus to accept and to follow the rules of the caste into which they were born. If they humbly performed the duties of their caste, they might be rewarded by being born into a higher caste in the next life. If they neglected their duties and did not live a good life, they might return in a lower form, perhaps as a bug or a worm. Hindus believed that every living creature had a soul.

For over a thousand years Brahman priests used reincarnation and their interpretations of the **Vedas,** books of sacred writings, to give a sense of order to India's complex society. Each person had a place in society and a job to do. No change was possible. If this life was hard, there was hope that the next life would be better.

A New Way

To many Indians, the life of a Hindu seemed harsh and difficult. In the sixth century B.C. a new religion sprang up in India. It was started by an Indian prince named **Gautama** (GAW·tuh·muh). His followers called him **Buddha** (BUHD·uh), which means "the enlightened one." The new religion, called **Buddhism** (BUHD·izm), eventually spread to much of Asia.

Unlike the Hindu priests in their temples, Prince Gautama taught in a park that was a deer refuge. He did not believe in caste. He spoke in common language for all to understand. "There are two ends that the seeker must avoid," he said, "the pursuit of pleasure and the pursuit of pain."

Here, the Buddha sits upon a lotus flower, which is the symbol of life.

Prince Gautama himself had spent his early life in pleasure. His royal father gave him everything and shielded him from suffering. Later, as a wandering beggar, Gautama made himself suffer much pain. Both these goals were wrong, he said. In their place Gautama suggested another way. He believed that people should seek human love and friendship, the joy of knowledge, and calmness of mind.

Neither Buddha nor his followers in the deer park organized a central church. They did not write sacred books like the Hindu Vedas. Their goal was to set an example for others. They did so through unselfishness and peaceful behavior in the monasteries, where many of them lived.

A Buddhist Empire

Several centuries passed before Buddhism really took hold in India. During that time India was a divided land. Dozens of Hindu princes called **rajas** (RAH·juhz) ruled over small kingdoms that were rich in foods, jewels, and precious metals. This wealth attracted outside invaders. From Persia came warriors to conquer the northwest. Then came the Greeks, led by Alexander the Great.

When Alexander died in 323 B.C., an Indian leader drove the remaining Greeks out of India. That leader, **Chandragupta Maurya** (chuhn·druh· GUP·tuh MOW·ree·uh), then became the first king to unite India under one rule. With his reign began a period of prosperity.

When Chandragupta's grandson **Asoka** (uh·SOH·kuh) became king about 255 B.C., Buddhism reached its peak in India. As a young man, Asoka was no lover of peace. He used armed force to conquer lands for his new empire. The bloodshed, however, suddenly turned him against all violence. He became a Buddhist and refused to eat meat or to hunt and kill animals. His influence led many Indians to adopt peaceful ways and vegetarian food.

Asoka used his energies to improve life for his people. His new roads had shade trees and wells for travelers. Along highways he placed stone pillars carved with words of Buddhist wisdom. He sent Buddhist missionaries to carry their ideas to China, Japan, Korea, Vietnam, and elsewhere throughout Asia. So fair and peaceful was Asoka's reign that one historian called him "the greatest and noblest ruler India has known."

After Asoka's death in 232 B.C. Hindu priests restored the caste laws. It was not long before Hindu leaders were again firmly in control of India. The ideas of Buddhism faded away. However, Buddhism continued to grow and influence other areas of Asia.

The Golden Age of India

In the fourth century A.D., India entered its Golden Age. The arts and sciences flowered. **Kalidasa** (kah•lee• DAH•sah), an author known as India's Shakespeare, wrote his plays at this time. Indian architects and sculptors developed styles of art that became models for Hindu temples and sculpture. Indian farmers grew cotton that craft workers made into fine cloth. Indian merchants traded these and other crafts with China, Southeast Asia, and European lands as well.

Krishna, shown with blue skin in this painting of the 1700s, is a Hindu god.

Gods and sacred animals of Hindu legend are carved on this Indian temple.

It was in science that India made perhaps the most astonishing advances. Indian scientists developed the idea that matter is made of tiny molecules. Indian mathematicians used the idea of *zero* for the first time. Borrowed by

More than 1,500 years old, this shiny iron pillar reminds us of India's achievements.

Arab traders, the Indian number system eventually became the basis for our own. An Indian scientist named **Aryabhata** (AHR•yuh•BUT•uh) wrote that the Earth was round and that it spun constantly. Indian metal workers learned how to shape iron that did not rust. A pillar made of this iron now stands near India's capital, **New Delhi** (DEL•ee). Its surface is still unrusted.

Other sciences made surprising advances during the Golden Age. Indian doctors discovered ways to set broken bones properly and to help mothers give birth safely. Doctors also could repair damage to faces. Like some surgeons today, they borrowed skin from other parts of the body to mend ears and noses.

Many of these ideas were carried to other lands by traders. Arab merchants brought Indian spices, cloth, carpets, and jewelry westward. They carried Indian books and ideas to the Roman Empire and later to the new European nations and Africa. Stories of the fabulous wealth and learning of Indian courts reached many different parts of the world.

Reading Check

1. Along which river did the first Indian people build their cities?
2. Name the four castes of Indian society. What group did not belong to organized society?
3. What two religions influenced ancient Indian cultures? Which of the two religions later became more important in other parts of Asia?
4. How did the advances made during the Golden Age of India spread to other parts of the world?

Look for these important words:

Key Words	People	Places
• sultans	• Akbar	• Taj Mahal
• Moguls	• Shah Jahan	• Calcutta
• British East India Company		• Bombay
		• Madras

Look for answers to these questions:

1. What problems were caused by the arrival of Muslims in India?
2. How did India change during the Mogul Empire?
3. How did the British take control of India?
4. What changes did the British bring to India?

3. FOREIGN RULE

By A.D. 500 India's wealth attracted invaders once more. In different waves they came to rob and then rule India for more than a thousand years. The first were Huns from Central Asia. Then Arabs came to trade and stayed to seize land. As followers of Islam, they brought Muslim beliefs to India for the first time.

In about A.D. 1200 other Muslims followed. This time they were fierce Muslim warriors from Turkish kingdoms in what is now Afghanistan. Plunging down from the north, they attacked Indian cities everywhere. Their leaders, or **sultans,** set up kingdoms throughout the northern plains and some parts of the south.

With the sultans in power, Hindus and Muslims had to live together. They could not always do so peacefully. The Muslim sultans placed special taxes on non-Muslims. This caused bad feelings among Hindus.

In religious matters, too, Hindus and Muslims did not agree. Hindus, for example, believed in many gods, while Muslims believed in only one. Hindus believed in many rebirths. Muslims believed in only one life.

In addition, Hindus had long based their society on caste, with Brahmans superior to all others. Muslims said all people were equal regardless of class. Hindus respected all forms of life, including animals. Cows were especially honored. They were allowed to roam through cities untouched. Muslims ate beef and saw no reason not to slaughter cows.

These different ideas often caused problems. Still, the Muslim sultans brought some order to India. With Delhi as their capital they maintained some unity. Meanwhile, in the villages the people continued their Hindu customs. Perhaps they knew that sooner or later, new invaders would come.

The Moguls

About A.D. 1500 new invaders, called **Moguls** (MOH•guhlz), did arrive. Again they were Muslim warriors, this time from Central Asia. They swept through Afghanistan and the Khyber Pass to conquer the sultans in northern India. Then the Moguls continued southward, spreading their empire over nearly the whole of India.

The greatest of the Mogul emperors was **Akbar** (AK•buhr), who ruled from A.D. 1556 to 1605. Unlike the sultans, Akbar did not try to force Hindus to become Muslims. He said that he was ruler of both Hindus and Muslims equally. He stopped the destruction of Hindu temples. He also ended the unfair taxation of Hindus. All his subjects paid the same taxes and could worship as they chose. His land reforms helped farmers make the best use of their land.

Under Akbar India became more prosperous than ever. A united India put aside fighting between religious groups or rival princes. Merchants were encouraged to expand trade with both China and Europe. Akbar and the emperors who followed him became some of the richest rulers on Earth. Their courts attracted scholars and poets. Akbar's grandson, **Shah Jahan** (SHAH juh•HAHN), built one of India's most famous monuments, the **Taj Mahal** (TAJ muh•HAHL).

Unfortunately, other emperors were not so skilled as Akbar was at keeping Hindus and Muslims at peace. Soon, wars between Hindus and Muslims broke out. More importantly, a new wave of invaders from Europe was soon to come by sea.

Akbar, shown here with his son and grandson, ruled India at almost the same time as Elizabeth I ruled England.

The British in India

You may recall that in the late 1400s Europeans had wanted to break Muslim control over Asian trade. After Portuguese navigators found a way to sail around Africa, other nations tried to get a share of the shipping trade. It was the British who became the clear winners in India.

Great Britain's first successes in India were a result of the work of private merchants. In 1600 Queen Elizabeth I allowed these merchants to form the **British East India Company.** The company built trading posts along India's coast. Merchants

Look for these important words:

Key Words
- nonviolent action
- Mahatma

- harijans
- boycott
- satyagraha

People
- Mohandas Gandhi
- Jawaharlal Nehru

Look for answers to these questions:

1. What experiences shaped Mohandas Gandhi's political beliefs?
2. What way of gaining political change did Gandhi suggest?
3. How and when did India gain its independence?
4. What disagreement divided India at the time of its independence?

4. INDIA AS A NATION

Late in the nineteenth century, a group of Indian leaders declared that India was able to run its own government. The leaders did not agree about how to do this. Some wanted a modern industrial state. Others wanted India to return to village life. Still others wanted rule by a Muslim government. They were united on only one idea—they all wanted the British to leave.

Even after Indian troops helped Great Britain in World War I, the British refused to set a date for Indian freedom. Many Indians took action. They placed bombs in British offices, clubs, and trains. They attacked British soldiers. These attacks added confusion at a time when India was suffering from other problems. Unemployment, sickness, and hunger were widespread. In the middle of this confusion, the Indian people increasingly turned to a single leader: **Mohandas Gandhi** (MOH•han•dahs GAHN•dee).

Mahatma Gandhi

During his lifetime, Gandhi showed no outward sign of importance. Being shy, he always had difficulty speaking to crowds. At the end he was frail and bent, unable to walk without a cane. When he died at age 78, his only possessions were some eating utensils, a pen, and a spinning wheel.

Gandhi left his people something more important than speeches or possessions, though. He left a major idea. It called for people to gain justice without physically attacking their enemies. Gandhi suggested **nonviolent action** as a way of political change.

His background helped Gandhi to develop this idea. He came from a large, loving family. Especially important was his mother. Very religious, Mrs. Gandhi told her son all the ancient Hindu stories. She urged him to respect all forms of life and to avoid bringing harm to anyone or anything.

To boycott the hated British salt tax, Gandhi led thousands of followers to the coast. There he showed Indians how to take salt from the sea.

When Gandhi came to choose a profession, these ideas affected him. Should he become a doctor? No, he thought, a doctor might have to operate on and thus possibly harm those he cared for. One of his older brothers suggested that he go to England and study law.

When he returned to India with his English clothes and a law degree, Gandhi was still too shy to appear in court. Some fellow lawyers rescued him by sending him to South Africa on business. This trip changed Gandhi's life. As soon as he arrived in South Africa, conductors threw him off a train for refusing to ride in a separate "colored" section. The night Gandhi spent shivering in a cold station gave a new purpose to his life. He would combine his knowledge of law with his wish to help his suffering people.

Gandhi set aside his English suits. He began to wear Indian clothing again to show he was proud to be an Indian. He spoke to groups of Indians in South Africa about human rights. He urged them to work to change the laws that kept them servants to the whites.

Gandhi suffered greatly for his actions. He refused to hate, however, or to urge his followers to fight. Feelings of race hatred could not be ended by violence, he believed. When people in India heard of Gandhi's work, they began to call him the **Mahatma** (mah. HAHT.muh), which means "holy one" or "great teacher."

By 1915 Gandhi was back in India, leading the groups that were opposed to the British. Most people, especially the poor, followed him. He took the side of the untouchables at the very bottom of the caste system. Gandhi began to call them by a new name—the **harijans** (HAR.uh.jahnz), which means "children of god." He said the *harijans* had been blessed by their suffering.

354

With millions of people behind him, Gandhi developed peaceful methods to fight the British. He led his followers in many nonviolent actions. Thousands would stop work for a day or two even though they had to go without pay. Millions of Gandhi's supporters would **boycott,** or refuse to buy, British goods. Sometimes Gandhi and his followers would sit down in factories or in the middle of streets. Women would even lie along railroad tracks to stop trains. By halting traffic and business the Indians harmed the British in a nonviolent way.

Gandhi and his followers often were beaten or jailed. Even in prison, however, Gandhi had effect as a leader. He wrote, or prayed, or went on long hunger strikes to unite his followers. The whole world came to know what Gandhi called **satyagraha** (SUT•yuh•gruh•huh), or "truth force."

Indian Independence

By the end of World War II, the British realized they would have to leave India. In 1947 they passed governing power to **Jawaharlal Nehru** (juh•WAH•huhr•lahl NAY•roo). With Gandhi's support, Nehru would be India's first prime minister. India had once again come under the control of the Indian people.

Fighting was not over, however. India's Muslims had split with Hindu leaders over the type of government India should have. Muslims began to flee northward to where most other Muslims lived. As these refugees left the south, they both attacked and were attacked by Hindus. The fighting and riots left thousands dead.

Jawaharlal Nehru wanted to unite India, and to create a modern, highly industrialized, and peaceful nation.

When the new conflict ended, there were two nations on the Indian subcontinent. One, called Pakistan, held the northwest and northeast corners of the land. Its people and government were mainly Muslims. The rest of India, about 80 per cent Hindu, began the country's first democratic government with Nehru as leader.

The same fight that divided India produced another victim. An assassin who blamed Gandhi for the division of India shot him to death. The whole world mourned the death of India's great leader.

Reading Check

1. Who led India's peaceful fight for independence?
2. How did the Mahatma feel about the untouchables?
3. When did India gain independence?
4. Why did India split into two countries?

Look for these important words:

Key Words
- extended family
- bullocks

- pesticides
- neutral

People
- Indira Gandhi

Look for answers to these questions:

1. How were Prime Minister Nehru's plans for India different from Gandhi's?
2. What is life like in the cities and villages of modern India?
3. How has the Indian government tried to help India's people?
4. What is India's relationship with other nations?

5. INDIA TODAY

Before Gandhi died, he had planned for India's future. He thought the Indian people would do best if they went back to small businesses and the old village way of life. Villagers could raise their own food. India's weavers could again learn to spin and weave in their cottages. In this way Gandhi believed India's large population could compete with modern industries.

Prime Minister Nehru disagreed with Gandhi. He wanted to develop India in the way of European nations. He said, "She [India] has to come out of her shell and take full part in the life and activities of the modern age."

With Gandhi gone, Nehru's plan was adopted. Indians created new factories, highways, mines, and railroads. The cities of Bombay, Delhi, and Calcutta grew to many millions of people. Modern buildings shot up everywhere. Many people began to live in much the same style as Europeans.

This rapid growth has led India to become one of Asia's largest industrial nations. Rapid growth also has caused problems for India. As millions of villagers continue to move to the cities to find work, urban areas are more crowded than ever. Many factory workers today live jammed into small apartments. They must walk or ride bicycles many miles to their jobs. Many cannot find jobs at all. For such city dwellers, life is hard. Some put up flimsy shacks. Others live in the streets with no homes at all. Poverty and sickness are widespread.

The Indian government has spent much money to improve the cities. Homes and apartments have been built. However, some Indians think that more housing attracts even more people from the villages. The cities only get more crowded. They agree with Gandhi, who said, "Go to the villages. That is India, therein lies the soul of India."

Modern apartment buildings make room for newcomers to Bombay. Still, thousands of Indians live in slums and have no water or electricity.

Cattle, sacred to Hindus, roam freely in many areas of Indian cities. The twisted streets are too narrow for cars, so many Indians ride bicycles.

Most Indian marriages are still arranged by the parents of the bride and groom.

Home industries such as spinning cotton thread provide families with income.

Village Life

Today nearly 80 percent of India's more than 700 million people live in villages. A typical village contains a few hundred households. Each household forms what is often called the **extended family.** Such a family might include the wives and children of two brothers, a grandmother, and an aunt or uncle. Another brother may live in the nearest city, working in a factory. He will send most of his salary home to help the family. As many as 30 close relatives may live together and support each other in one household.

Indian villages are much the same as they have always been. Farming families may own a few acres of rice paddy or cotton field. Other families may be carpenters, weavers, or potters. These workers do the same caste jobs that their fathers did. In return for their work, they are usually paid in goods, not money.

Three or four old Brahman families may own land, which they do not farm. They earn their living by renting the land to tenant farmers, who give them a share of the crop. The job of a Brahman is to teach at a small school and perform religious services. As payment, they receive food from farmers and services from craft workers.

In most places farmers work in the old way. They plow their fields with wooden plows pulled by oxen called **bullocks.** They sow the seed and then pray for the monsoons. Some farmers have learned to use fertilizers, new seed, and **pesticides** provided by the government. Pesticides are chemicals used to kill insects. This increases farmers' crops, but their profit stays small because pesticides are expensive.

Barefoot and using an old-fashioned wooden plow, a village farmer drives his oxen through the soil of an Indian field.

Many farmers hope that the government will start irrigation projects. With extra water they could farm more vegetables in the winter season. They could earn cash to buy some of the goods they need.

India's government has made many attempts to solve the problems of its nation of villagers. It has sent experts to teach farmers better farming methods. It has allowed foreign companies to build fertilizer factories in India. It has introduced modern farm machinery to replace animal power. It has passed laws to do away with the caste system.

Still, many villagers cling to the old ways. Most continue to live according to caste rules. They say this at least provides everyone with a job and a sense of belonging. Many also refuse to eat wheat grown in other countries or new types of rice grown with fertilizers. As for machines, most do not work well on small plots of land. Gasoline is too expensive. The old ways seem to work best.

Facing the Future

The tasks ahead for India's government are difficult. Population continues to grow, putting greater demands on the food supply. India's many new industries need power. Even with new dams for water power and new atomic power plants, more is needed.

While trying to meet these and other needs, India's leaders have tried to keep India **neutral.** A neutral country does not take sides in the disagreements of other countries. India has accepted aid from both communist and democratic nations. India's leaders have refused to take sides in the struggle between the Soviet Union and the United States. Nor does India want to risk offending its powerful neighbor, China.

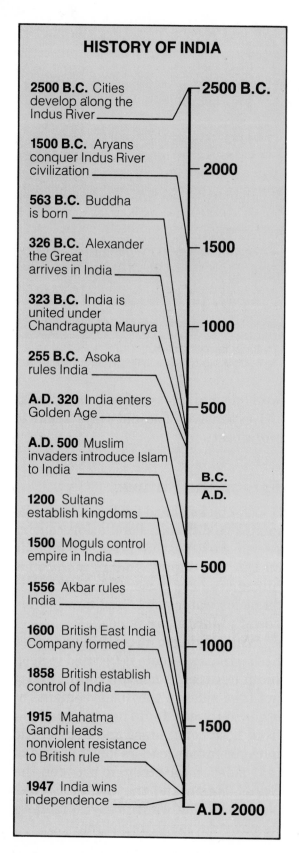

HISTORY OF INDIA

2500 B.C. Cities develop along the Indus River — **2500 B.C.**

1500 B.C. Aryans conquer Indus River civilization — **2000**

563 B.C. Buddha is born —

326 B.C. Alexander the Great arrives in India — **1500**

323 B.C. India is united under Chandragupta Maurya — **1000**

255 B.C. Asoka rules India —

A.D. 320 India enters Golden Age — **500**

A.D. 500 Muslim invaders introduce Islam to India — **B.C. / A.D.**

1200 Sultans establish kingdoms —

1500 Moguls control empire in India — **500**

1556 Akbar rules India —

1600 British East India Company formed — **1000**

1858 British establish control of India —

1915 Mahatma Gandhi leads nonviolent resistance to British rule — **1500**

1947 India wins independence — **A.D. 2000**

Rajiv Gandhi has continued the policies begun by his mother, Indira Gandhi.

Nehru's daughter, **Indira Gandhi,** became prime minister in 1966 and continued to keep India neutral until her death in 1984. Her son Rajiv took her place and works to help solve problems of food, energy, and population growth. His challenge is to persuade all Indians to pull together as a nation. New ideas spread slowly among people who speak 14 major languages and about a thousand forms of those languages. Almost two-thirds of these people cannot read or write *any* language. India's success depends on Indians working together to plan their future.

Reading Check

1. How has rapid growth created problems for India?
2. Do most of India's people live in cities or in villages?
3. Explain two ways that the Indian government is trying to help village farmers.
4. Who became prime minister of India in 1966?

SKILLS FOR SUCCESS

USING CULTURAL MAPS

Within a region and even within a country peoples vary greatly. Their cultures have been shaped by a history of movement and mixing or one of isolation. The culture of a people includes their languages and religions. The languages and religions in a geographic region can be shown on a **cultural map.** The cultural maps in this lesson use colors and symbols to identify languages and religions in Asian countries.

This map shows the main religions of the Indian subcontinent. The map key lists the religions. Look at Pakistan. Most of it is colored green. The map key tells you that green stands for Islam. Since most of Pakistan is colored green, Islam is its main religion. This does not mean there are no other religions in Pakistan. It means that Islam is the religion of a majority (more than half) of the people there.

Look at the yellow area in northwestern India. The key tells you that Islam and Hinduism are the major religions in this area. Patches of India on this map are colored blue. There are a number of religions there, none of them practiced by a majority. Most of India is colored purple. What is the main religion of India?

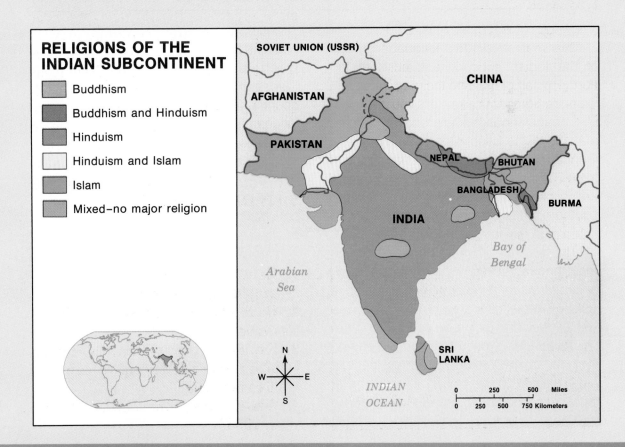

RELIGIONS OF THE INDIAN SUBCONTINENT

- Buddhism
- Buddhism and Hinduism
- Hinduism
- Hinduism and Islam
- Islam
- Mixed—no major religion

SOVIET UNION (USSR)

CHINA

AFGHANISTAN

PAKISTAN

NEPAL

BHUTAN

BANGLADESH

BURMA

INDIA

Bay of Bengal

Arabian Sea

SRI LANKA

INDIAN OCEAN

N
W—E
S

| 0 | 250 | 500 | Miles |
| 0 | 250 | 500 | 750 Kilometers |

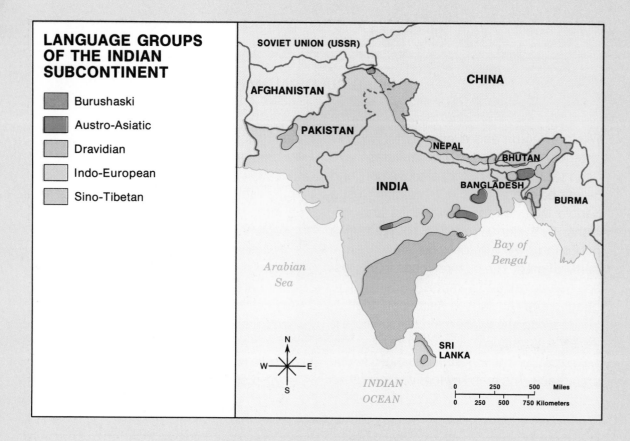

LANGUAGE GROUPS OF THE INDIAN SUBCONTINENT

- Burushaski
- Austro-Asiatic
- Dravidian
- Indo-European
- Sino-Tibetan

SOVIET UNION (USSR)

AFGHANISTAN

CHINA

PAKISTAN

NEPAL

BHUTAN

INDIA

BANGLADESH

BURMA

Arabian Sea

Bay of Bengal

N W E S

SRI LANKA

INDIAN OCEAN

| 0 | 250 | 500 | Miles |

| 0 | 250 | 500 | 750 Kilometers |

This map shows five language groups of the Indian subcontinent. Look at the northern half of India on the map. Most of it is colored green. The key tells you that Indo-European languages are spoken by the majority of the people there. One of these languages, **Hindi,** is the official language of India. Other languages, including English, are spoken by fewer people there. Find southern India. What major language group is found in this part of India?

The map on the next page shows the main languages and religions of Asia. Each color stands for a major language group in Asia. Find the pink area on the map. The key tells you that pink represents Sino-Tibetan languages. Notice that some areas on the map are colored brown. People in these areas have languages that belong to smaller language groups that are not identified on this map.

Next, find the Soviet Union and the light green areas in it. The key tells you that Indo-European languages are spoken in this country. These are Armenian and Slavic languages, primarily Russian. Name another language group in the Soviet Union.

Look again at the map of India above. Find the area showing the Burushaski language group. Notice that this language is not shown on the map of Asia. On a map of a large area, it is often difficult to show details and small areas.

The major religions of each area on the map are shown by symbols. Each symbol is placed in the middle of the area where that particular religion is mainly practiced. Look at Japan. The symbol 丹 tells you that the major religions in Japan are Shintoism and Buddhism.

Now look at the northern part of the Soviet Union. What does ⬙ tell you?

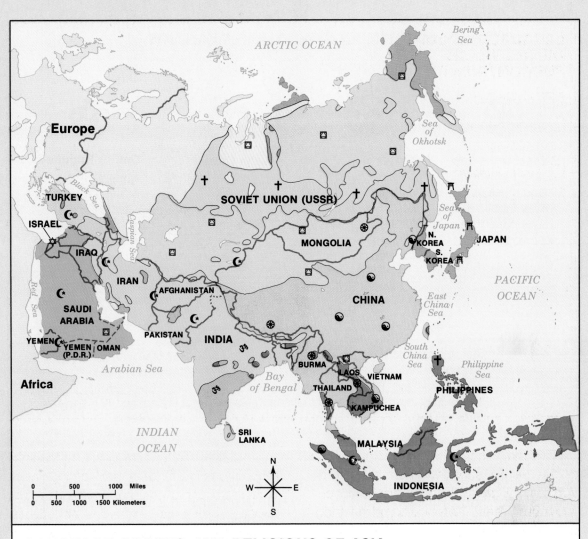

LANGUAGE GROUPS AND RELIGIONS OF ASIA

Languages

☐	Altaic
☐	Austro-Asiatic
☐	Dravidian
☐	Indo-European
☐	Semitic
☐	Sino-Tibetan
☐	Uralic
☐	Other

Religions

❋	Buddhism
☯	Chinese religions (Confucianism, Taoism, and Buddhism combined)
†	Christianity
ॐ	Hinduism
☪	Islam
⛩	Japanese religions (Shintoism and Buddhism combined)
✡	Judaism
▨	Mixed—no major religion

MAP SYMBOLS AND THEIR MEANINGS

Wheel of the Law
Spokes of wheel stand for steps of Noble Eightfold Path in Buddhist teachings

Yin-yang
Chinese symbol: dark and light areas stand for opposite forces of the universe; circle is their harmony and unity

Latin Cross
Associated with Jesus Christ, founder of Christianity

Om, or Brahma-Atman
Written form of *om*, a sacred Hindu word for the highest Hindu god

Star and Crescent
Ancient sacred symbols of the Middle East, birthplace of Islam

Torii ("gateway")
Japanese symbol: stands for the gateway that separates a holy place from the outside world

Star of David
Associated with King David, a king of the ancient Jewish people

CHECKING YOUR SKILLS

Use the map of Asia to answer these questions.

1. What is the main religion of the Philippines?

2. Name four countries where people practice Buddhism.

3. What is the main language group in Mongolia?

4. A large part of one country is populated by followers of Islam who speak Dravidian languages. In which country do these people live?

5. Do all Chinese people speak the same group of languages? What information on the map supports your answer?

6. In addition to Islam what religions are practiced in Indonesia?

7. In which country of Southwest Asia is Judaism practiced?

8. What is the main language group of the Arabian peninsula?

9. What are the major religions practiced in Japan?

10. Name the main language group and the main religion found in each of the following countries:

   a. Malaysia
   b. Iran
   c. Yemen
   d. Turkey
   e. Kampuchea

CHAPTER 12 REVIEW

USING WORDS

Explain the meaning of each of the words listed below. Then use each word in a complete sentence.

1. **boycott**
2. **bullocks**
3. **caste**
4. **neutral**
5. **nonviolent action**
6. **rajas**
7. **reincarnation**
8. **subcontinent**
9. **sultans**
10. **untouchables**

REVIEWING FACTS

1. Why are summer monsoons important to India's farmers?

2. How was India's first civilization similar to those of Sumer and ancient Egypt?

3. What change did the Aryans bring to Indian society?

4. What are some major beliefs of the Hindu religion?

5. What did Prince Gautama teach his followers?

6. Name three advances that took place during India's Golden Age.

7. Identify three differences between Muslims and Hindus.

8. What attracted the British merchants to India? How were they able to gain control?

9. How did Gandhi and his followers "fight" the British?

10. What are three problems facing India today?

THINKING CRITICALLY

1. The caste system continues to influence life in Indian villages. Why might people living in villages cling to the caste system more than people who live in the cities? How does the caste system affect the choices young people can make about their future?

2. Indian families are usually large and often include members of the extended family. What might be the advantages of having many relatives living together?

3. Ancient African and European civilizations traded with India. Muslims and, later, Europeans controlled India's resources. How do you think these contacts affected the development of India? How does India protect itself today from too much foreign influence?

PRACTICING SKILLS

Cultural Map Use the maps and your skills lesson on pages 361–364 to answer the following questions.

1. Which language group of the Indian subcontinent is not shown on the map of Asia?

2. How many language groups are shown in Sri Lanka? Name them.

3. What is the main religion of Pakistan? of India?

4. What is the major religion of Indonesia?

5. What is the main religion found in Burma and Thailand?

China Withstands Many Changes

China is called the oldest continuous civilization in the world. China began at about the same time as the ancient civilizations of Mesopotamia, Egypt, and the Indus Valley. These civilizations broke down and were replaced by new ones. Chinese civilization was never replaced by anything. From its earliest days, it has remained Chinese in language and culture.

This is not to say that China has been untouched by change. It has been changed again and again by forces from outside and from within. Yet, China has absorbed these changes. The China of 3,500 years ago and the China of today are more alike than different.

Look for these important words:

Places
- Mongolia
- China Proper
- Shanghai
- Beijing

Look for answers to these questions:

1. What are the four main regions of China Proper?
2. How are the climates of these four regions different?
3. How are the Chinese developing their country today?

1. THE GEOGRAPHY OF CHINA

China lies between the Himalaya Mountains in Central Asia and the Pacific Ocean. China is the third-largest country in the world. Mountains, deserts, and plateaus cover two-thirds of its land. From lofty peaks in the west, mountain ranges extend eastward like fingers. Between these mountains are river basins. It is within these river basins that most of China's people live.

North of China lie the high plateaus of **Mongolia.** From this area come dry, cold winds that give northern China its severe winters. The lack of rain makes much of northwest China suitable only for nomadic herders.

To the east of China is the Pacific Ocean. From here come the tropical summer rainstorms. Driven by monsoons, the heavy rains make rice farming possible in much of southern China. The monsoons also may cause flooding of China's major rivers. The Chinese have long had to deal with terrible floods that have brought death to millions. One river, the Huang He, has been responsible for so many deaths that it is called "China's Sorrow."

China Proper

For centuries natural boundaries prevented outsiders from interfering in China's growth. Shut off by mountains, deserts, and seas, the Chinese people developed a unique culture. Their land, however, has not made this an easy task. Most of it is too dry, mountainous, or windswept. Therefore, the Chinese have clustered in four main areas that make up only one-third of their land. The areas are the North China Plain, the Chang Jiang valley, the Sichuan (SEECH. WAHN) Basin, and the Guangzhou (GWAHN.JOH) Delta. Together these areas are called **China Proper.**

Rivers are the key to China Proper. The Huang He, the Chang Jiang, and the Xi Jiang enrich the land with their floods. Early Chinese settled in the fertile valleys and deltas of these rivers.

Population

The Chinese make up the largest population on Earth. More than a billion people live in China, or about one

367

The Forbidden City, home of China's ancient emperors, was considered a holy place. No one outside the royal court ever entered its gates.

CHINA

----- Disputed or undefined boundary

⊛ National capital

⌇⌇⌇ The Great Wall of China

Buses crawl through Shanghai's crowds on Sunday, which is a shopping day.

The Chinese have tended rice fields with simple tools for thousands of years.

of every five human beings. China has many large cities. With almost 12 million people, **Shanghai** is one of the largest cities in the world. **Beijing,** China's capital, has over nine million people. Eighty percent of the Chinese, however, live on farms or in villages. This enormous Chinese population includes great variety. People in one region may differ in customs, appearance, and spoken language from those in other regions.

Climate

Climate also varies among the regions. The North China Plain, for example, enjoys pleasant, dry summers. However, it suffers from high winds that blow from the deserts. These winds often carry clouds of dust that are deposited along the banks of the Huang He. Like the American Great Plains, the North China Plain is well suited for crops that require little water, such as wheat.

The Chang Jiang valley receives much more rain than the north. Tropical storms in summer sweep in from the sea. They bring water to the farms. Farmers in this region grow rice, often two crops a year.

Farther west on the Chang Jiang is a high, hilly region known as the Sichuan Basin. Sichuan means "four rivers," named after four tributaries of the Chang Jiang. The area also is called the Red Basin, which refers to

EXAMPLES OF CHANGES IN CHINESE SPELLING			
People		Places	
Pinyin	Old Spelling	Pinyin	Old Spelling
Jiang Kai-shek	Chiang Kai-shek	Beijing	Peking
Kongzi	Confucius	Chang Jiang	Yangtze
Mao Zedong	Mao Tse-tung	Chongqing	Chungking
Qin Shi Huangdi	Jin Shih Huang Ti	Guangzhou	Canton
Sun Zhong shan	Sun Yat-sen	Hangzhou	Hangchou
Tang (dynasty)	T'ang	Huang He	Huang Ho
Yin (dynasty)	Shang	Jiangxi	Kiangsi
Zhou (dynasty)	Chou	Meng gu	Mongolia
		Nanjing	Nanking
		Qingdao	Tsingtao
		Sichuan	Szechuan
		Taibei	Taipei
		Tianjin	Tientsin
		Xi Jiang	Hsi Chiang
		Xizang	Tibet
		Xuzhou	Suchow
		Zhengzhou	Chengchou

the red sandstone that lies under the region's rich topsoil.

Since it is about 2,000 feet (about 600 m) above sea level, the Sichuan Basin has a drier climate than the Chang Jiang valley. Fertile land and a mild climate make the Sichuan Basin a highly productive agricultural region. Such crops as rice, millet, wheat, and cotton do well during the area's long growing season.

Far to the south is the Guangzhou Delta. It is a tropical area crossed by the Xi Jiang. Rice and fish are among the most important products of this area. Its deepwater harbor makes the Guangzhou district a major shipping center as well.

From their first settlements beside the rivers, the Chinese have spread out to occupy more of their land. Today they are working to develop their country. Irrigation and new fertilizers are helping to cultivate parts of the dry western lands. Modern highways connect distant areas with the east. Modern industries have arisen to take advantage of China's large deposits of coal, oil, and other minerals. From about 20 deepwater harbors, the Chinese have increased their growing trade with other nations. They import fertilizer, metals, and machinery and export tea, silk, and oil.

Reading Check

1. Why do most of China's people live on only one-third of their land?
2. Name China's three main rivers.
3. In which of China's major areas does wheat grow?
4. Why is the Chang Jiang valley suitable for growing rice?

Two Ways to Spell Chinese

Before the twentieth century, the Chinese language did not have an alphabet. Writers of Chinese wrote by making small drawings that represented ideas or objects. When Chinese was first written down, there were as many as 10,000 drawings. Today there are about 3,000 that are commonly used. However, it still takes a long time and much practice to learn to read and write Chinese.

More people speak Chinese than any other language in the world. There are many forms of Chinese, however. In order for China to modernize, its people needed to be able to understand each other. To make that job easier, in 1956 the leaders of China introduced an alphabet called **pinyin.** The word *pinyin* means "spell sounds."

The pinyin alphabet is made up of 25 letters that are similar to English letters. The pinyin alphabet has no *V.* Once introduced, pinyin changed the way Chinese words were spelled by speakers of other languages. For example, Peking, the capital city of China, was changed to Beijing (BAY-JING) in the new pinyin alphabet. The new spelling more closely represents its true sound in Chinese.

Pinyin is meant not to replace the old Chinese form of writing, but to be used with it. The pinyin alphabet is better for some uses, such as introducing scientific words into Chinese. There are some uses for which the Chinese drawings are superior, however. A story or poem can be more expressive when read in old-style Chinese. Just imagine being able to see pictures of a story while you are reading the story!

For example, the Chinese drawings that stand for the word *China* are a combination of two characters, one that means "center" and one that means "country." Together these express the idea that China is the center of the world. The two drawings for the United States of America are 美, which means "beautiful," and 國, which means "country." To read the Chinese drawings that represent the United States of America, you would know it is a beautiful country.

Learning to write

Drawing words

Chinese students

Look for these important words:

Key Words
- dynasty
- pictographs
- character
- Mandarins

- Mandate of Heaven
- jade
- civil service
- porcelain

People
- Confucius
- Li Po

Places
- Chung-Kuo

Look for answers to these questions:

1. What were four important ruling groups of ancient China?
2. What kind of writing system do the Chinese have, and how did it develop?
3. What belief caused the Chinese to support or rebel against their rulers?
4. How did Confucius influence the ancient Chinese?

2. THE ANCIENT CHINESE

Chinese legends claim that China had a civilization long before any other people did. They say that the Chinese invented calendars, coins, canoes, and chariots. There is no proof that these legends are true. There is proof, however, that the Chinese built a very early civilization near the Huang He and the Chang Jiang. The ancient Chinese probably began to develop their civilization at about the same time that river valley civilizations began in the Middle East and India.

The ancient Chinese named their land **Chung-Kuo,** which means "Middle Kingdom." They believed that they were at the center of the world. They thought that others, such as the nomads who lived to the north of them, were uncivilized. From early in their history the Chinese considered themselves leaders among Asian peoples.

The Yin Dynasty

From its early civilization until the beginning of the twentieth century, China was ruled by one **dynasty** (DY•nuh•stee) after another. A dynasty is a ruling family that passes control from one generation to the next. The first recorded dynasty appeared about 1766 B.C. It was called the Yin dynasty. The Yin kings expanded China to include all the land between Mongolia and the Pacific Ocean.

The Yin kings established customs, some of which have lasted in China ever since. The Yin style of building is seen in China today. The Yin method of using vast numbers of workers to build public works, such as canals and bridges, also was copied for many years.

The majority of people of the Yin period were farmers. They grew millet,

372

The characters on these 2,500-year-old bones are like those of modern Chinese.

the cracks. The fortune tellers believed that the pattern would give answers to their questions.

Ancient bone drawings formed the basis of China's written language. The drawings, called **pictographs,** were combined to make countless words. For example, the Chinese word for "movie" is given by a drawing that means "electric shadows."

Chinese differs from English because it developed without an alphabet to represent sounds. Instead, each Chinese word, or **character,** has a different form. Students must learn thousands of characters to read and write Chinese well.

The difficulty of writing Chinese has had an important effect on China's history. Only the rich could afford time to learn to read and write. Since all government officials had to read and write, farmers and laborers rarely qualified for these jobs. It was mainly wealthy, educated Chinese who ran the government.

raised chickens and pigs, and cultivated silkworms for silk cloth. For all these occupations they depended upon the events of nature, such as regular rains. To understand weather patterns better, the ancient Chinese studied nature. They tried to predict the weather.

This desire to predict events led not only to science but also to a form of writing. Fortune tellers scratched pictures of such things as the sun or animals on animal bones or turtle shells. The fortune tellers asked questions about rain or drought. Then they heated the bones. When the bones cracked, the fortune tellers looked at the pattern of

electric shadows

Scholarly officials oversaw Chinese government for thousands of years.

The Chinese people supported each new ruler because of what they called the **Mandate of Heaven.** They believed that the king or emperor who gained power had been selected by heaven to lead. When a ruler's control was weak or if disasters occurred, the people said the ruler had lost the Mandate of Heaven. Then they rebelled against him.

The Zhou Dynasty

A dynasty called the Zhou (JOH) was China's longest-lived dynasty. It lasted from about 1122 to 256 B.C. The founders of this dynasty headed a group of nomads who lived in the western mountains near the source of the Huang He. They had reached China just as the use of iron was spreading. The nomads hammered this metal into tools for farming. They used powerful iron weapons to overthrow the Yin kings.

Offerings to the gods were placed in this bronze container from the Zhou dynasty.

These government officials in China were called **Mandarins.** The Mandarins passed laws to protect their wealth. They wore lengthy robes to set themselves apart from common people. They grew very long fingernails to show they did not work with their hands. They alone advised China's rulers.

The Mandate of Heaven

After the Yin kings, 24 dynasties ruled China. One dynasty lasted more than eight centuries. Another lasted only 15 years. The change from one dynasty to another usually meant rebellion and violence.

The Zhou rulers introduced lasting changes to China. They developed a feudal system like the one developed in Europe more than 1,500 years later. Their nobles received land from Zhou rulers and divided it into smaller units for single families. Several families would then work together under bonds of loyalty and affection. The families owed loyalty to the lord, who in turn owed his support to the king.

The Zhou kings appointed inspectors who made sure that the nobles treated the people well. The government supported the sick and the aged. The inspectors used income from taxes to build public works for all. At a time before Rome was built, China under Zhou rulers had irrigation systems, dams, and highways. China grew and prospered under the Zhou rulers.

The Ideas of Confucius

By about 500 B.C. attacks by northern nomads, striking out of Central Asia, began to weaken the Zhou government. Armies and nobles fought among themselves. China fell into what is now called the Warring States Period. During this time people forgot the rules by which they had lived for hundreds of years. Bandits roamed the country, burning farms and cities. No government had the power to protect the people.

When this troubled period began, Chinese people turned to their wisest philosophers for guidance. The most important of these was a teacher named **Confucius** (kuhn•FYOO•shuhs).

Born in 551 B.C., Confucius witnessed the breakdown of the feudal government. He began to think about the more secure times of the past. Why, he wondered, were past leaders so respected? He decided that it was because they had a sense of order. They seemed to understand how every person should behave.

The Chinese word *qen* became the center of Confucius's teachings. *Qen* refers to the kindness and love each human should have for all others and for nature. The person who develops *qen* becomes superior. This did not mean, as it did in feudal times, that the superior person had to be of noble birth. Confucius stressed education. Any person, rich or poor, could become superior by learning.

An early ink drawing shows Confucius, the wandering philosopher whose teachings came to rule Chinese life.

When Confucius talked about rulers, he used the same ideas. The superior ruler sets the example for the people, as a parent does. "To govern is to set things right," said Confucius. The successful ruler begins by learning to act correctly. If a leader rules badly, the people have a right to revolt.

Confucius believed that a good society is like a family in which all members know their place and act responsibly. Children respect parents, parents respect officials, and officials respect rulers. Nor can any person act alone. Each person must take part in family, village, and government. The family was most important. Families lived and worked together. Older family members were especially honored.

The ideas of Confucius spread widely among the Chinese. Their actions were guided by the five virtues of Confucius: charity, kindness, hard work, good faith, and courtesy. Confucius said: "What you do not want done to yourself, do not unto others."

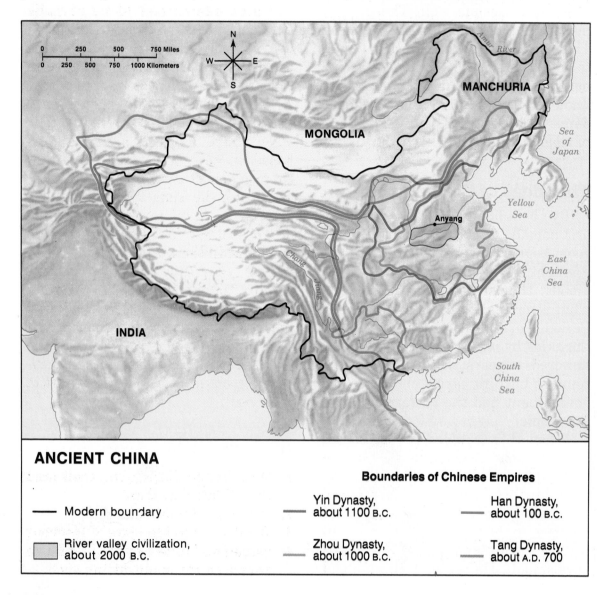

ANCIENT CHINA

Boundaries of Chinese Empires

—— Modern boundary

River valley civilization, about 2000 B.C.

—— Yin Dynasty, about 1100 B.C.

—— Zhou Dynasty, about 1000 B.C.

—— Han Dynasty, about 100 B.C.

—— Tang Dynasty, about A.D. 700

More Dynasties

China's advances under the Yin and Zhou dynasties left a heritage that lasted for thousands of years. First, the development of language unified the Chinese people, enabling them to build their civilization. Second, the members of Chinese families learned to work closely together, helping each other whenever possible. Third, a strong central government was established. These were the keys to China's long-lasting civilization.

During the Han dynasty, between 202 B.C. and A.D. 220, China grew into a powerful empire. Overland trade began between China and Europe. Han dynasty silk, spices, wood carvings, and a precious stone called **jade** reached as far as Rome. Scholars who trained according to Confucius's ideas ran the government with great skill. During the Han period the Chinese invented paper. Writers recorded the history of China. During this time Buddhism spread from India to China.

A Golden Age

China entered its Golden Age under the Tang dynasty between A.D. 618 and 906. The Tang emperors developed an examination system for government officials that was used for centuries. This system established a **civil service.** In the civil service system, government officials were selected based on their qualifications rather than on noble birth.

During the Tang dynasty the arts prospered. Chinese **porcelain,** a type of clay pottery, was considered to be the finest in the world. Poetry written during the Tang dynasty became equally famous. One well-known poet, **Li Po,** wrote, "I desire to select and transmit the old, so that its splendor will last a thousand ages." Thus the Chinese continued to develop their civilization based on the achievements of their past.

Found in a Chinese tomb, this glazed earthenware figure of a Tang dynasty lion dates back to the eighth century.

Reading Check

1. Why did the Chinese call their land the Middle Kingdom?
2. Who were the Mandarins?
3. What was the Mandate of Heaven?
4. Name two Chinese dynasties and an advancement made during each.

Look for these important words:

Key Words	People	Places
• junks	• Shi Huangdi	• Grand Canal
• Manchus	• Marco Polo	• Orient
• opium	• Kublai Khan	• Macao
• Nationalists	• Genghis Khan	• Manchuria
• warlords	• Sun Zhong shan	• Taiwan
	• Jiang Kai-shek	

Look for answers to these questions:

1. Who built the Great Wall of China, and why?
2. How did Marco Polo's discoveries in China affect Europeans?
3. How did foreign influence spread in China under the Manchus?
4. What group led the Chinese rebellion against the Manchus?

3. CHANGE FROM THE OUTSIDE

In the north of China is a wall. It is unlike any other wall in the world. Twenty-five feet (8 m) high with 40-foot (12-m) towers, it winds more than 1,500 miles (2,414 km) from east to west. It is wide enough for wagons to pass each other in opposite directions.

A Chinese emperor, **Shi Huangdi** (SHIR HWANGTEE), started the Great Wall in 214 B.C. He used more than 100,000 workers to build it, hoping to end the constant invasions by northern nomads. Other emperors improved the wall for the same reason—to protect China's civilization from outsiders.

Marco Polo

The Great Wall was one of the marvels that impressed an Italian visitor to China in A.D. 1275. **Marco Polo** was one of the first Europeans to spend much time in China. He was amazed by what he saw there.

While Europe was still in the Middle Ages, the Chinese had a brilliant and well-organized empire. Chinese cities such as Beijing bustled with trade and art. Polo learned that the Chinese had a mail service. More than 200,000 riders on horseback delivered letters along the Great Wall. Chinese boats called **junks** carried goods about 1,000 miles (1,600 km) along the **Grand Canal,** which linked Beijing with Hangzhou. It had been built 600 years earlier.

Marco Polo also commented on other Chinese inventions, such as gunpowder and the compass. He marveled that the Chinese were using paper money. It was far easier to use than the

A great water festival celebrated the Grand Canal's completion in the seventh century. Today, junks and barges still travel its length.

heavy metal coins of Europe. Chinese houses were heated with coal. In some areas the Chinese used coal to heat bath water at a time when few Europeans ever bathed.

China's emperor, a Mongol named **Kublai Khan** (KOO•bluh KAHN), held court in a palace filled with gold, jewels, and silks. According to Polo, the building was so large that the dining room could hold 6,000 guests. The palace was decorated with paintings and sculptures of dragons, birds, horses, and lions.

All this especially surprised Marco Polo. He knew that only a short time before, the Mongols had been rough nomads in Central Asia. Kublai Khan's grandfather, **Genghis** (JENG•guhs) **Khan,** had led an army of Mongol nomads through the Great Wall to conquer North China. They were an example, however, of how the Chinese have always civilized even their conquerors. Rulers might change, but the values of Chinese civilization would survive.

Marco Polo's reports of his Chinese adventures were at first not believed. Later, however, Polo's book sparked European interest in China. As a result, traders sought routes to the east, or

Amazed by Marco Polo's descriptions, Europeans of the 1300s tried to picture how the Orient might look. In a painting from the *Book of Marvels,* an artist has imagined Beijing's splendor and its strangeness.

the **Orient,** as it was called. By 1514 the Portuguese had made their first landing. In 1557 they set up a trading post in the port of **Macao** (muh•KOW), near Guangzhou. In general, China's rulers, who were now known as the Ming dynasty, kept the Europeans in a few port cities. To them China was still the center of the Earth and they had no need for Europeans.

The Manchus

By the 1800s new invaders from **Manchuria,** known as **Manchus,** had taken control of China. While some of the early Manchu leaders ruled China well, later emperors weakened. In addition China faced increasing problems from drought and famine. The Chinese lost faith in their rulers.

Meanwhile European nations grew more powerful. They insisted that China allow them to trade freely in China. The British especially wanted the right to sell their Indian **opium** to China's laborers. With the huge profit from this dangerous drug, the British could buy Chinese tea.

The Manchus at first tried to stop the opium trade. When the British declared war, the Manchu leaders gave in. They signed treaties giving not only the British but also the French and the Americans special trading rights in China. Each nation then set up trading posts in China. Foreign merchants refused to respect Chinese laws or to pay Chinese taxes. They hired Chinese laborers at low pay to work in factories they owned.

All these abuses led to rebellions inside China. Each time British and American support helped the Manchus control the rebels. Throughout this violent period, the last Manchu rulers were spending government money on themselves. Meanwhile China's people suffered. Millions starved or died in famines and floods or from spreading diseases. The Manchu government grew weaker.

In 1894 the Japanese declared war on China. They seized the Chinese island of Formosa, which later became known as **Taiwan.** By that time China was controlled by more than British, French, and Americans. Germans, Russians, and Japanese were ruling parts of the land, too. China was totally overrun by foreigners.

Chinese Nationalism

Believing that the Manchus had lost the Mandate of Heaven, the Chinese people began to support a group called the **Nationalists.** Fighting in many parts of China, the Nationalists pledged to free China from foreign rule. The leader of this political party was a doctor named **Sun Zhong shan.** By 1912 his followers had driven out the last of the Manchu rulers, and Sun Zhong shan became president of China. His goal was to make China a republic.

The Boxers, fierce warriors who claimed they couldn't be harmed by bullets, used cannons and dynamite to try to drive foreigners from China in 1900.

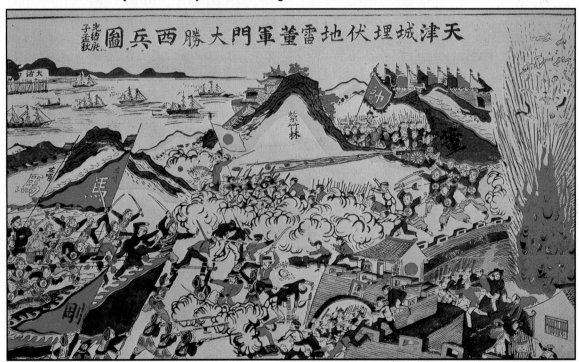

Jiang Kai-shek, in military dress, visits a school. One goal of the Nationalist government was to improve China's educational system.

The new government did not succeed in unifying China. During the last days of Manchu rule, small armies had arisen in many parts of China. They had divided the land among themselves. Led by bandit chiefs called **warlords,** these groups threatened the weak government. At the same time, foreign governments continued to own most of China's resources.

When Sun Zhong shan died in 1925, a young general named **Jiang Kai-shek** (jee•ANG KY•SHEK) took control of the Nationalist party. The Western powers supported him, for he promised to protect their interests in China. Jiang Kai-shek also had the support of the wealthy Chinese landlords.

Jiang Kai-shek successfully led a large army to rid the nation of its warlords. Later he commanded the army in battle against the Japanese, who invaded China again in 1937. The Japanese invasion of China was the beginning of World War II in Asia.

From 1925 until after World War II, Jiang Kai-shek also fought a group of Chinese who called themselves Communists. After more than 20 years of war, it was the Communists who triumphed.

Reading Check

1. Why was the Great Wall built?
2. Name three things that amazed Marco Polo in China.
3. Why did the Chinese rebel against the Manchus?
4. Who were Sun Zhong shan and Jiang Kai-shek, and what did they try to do?

Look for these important words:

Key Words
- Long March
- communes
- Great Leap Forward
- Red Guards
- Cultural Revolution

- Four Modernizations
- quotas

People
- Mao Zedong

Places
- People's Republic of China

Look for answers to these questions:

1. How did Mao Zedong gain control of China?
2. What changes did Mao make in China?
3. How did the Cultural Revolution affect China?
4. How has China's attitude toward the West changed in recent years?

4. THE COMMUNISTS: CHANGE FROM WITHIN

Jiang Kai-shek hoped to build a strong nation with the help of business leaders and foreign allies. China's Communists opposed Jiang Kai-shek. Like Communists everywhere, they hoped to win support from factory workers. In cities such as Shanghai, they led workers in revolt against the government. The revolution was unsuccessful until one communist leader named **Mao Zedong** proposed another plan. He knew that most of China's people were peasants. Mao Zedong would try to win them over to revolution and communism.

Mao Zedong

As a youth, Mao lived like millions of other Chinese peasants. His family shared a plain, mud-walled house with another family. Difficult problems threatened their village. Landlords squeezed all the extra money they could out of the peasants. Troops shot into a mob begging for rice. Outlaw bands demanded that whole villages pay them ransom.

During this time, Mao's family learned to depend only on itself. No government would help them. On its land the family raised rice and pigs. Mao fed the animals, carried fertilizer to the fields, and planted rice seedlings in the flooded soil. Mao was not interested in farming, however. He yearned to continue his education. Mao's family was more prosperous than most peasant families. Mao felt his family could run the farm without his help. Against protests from his father, Mao left home to go to school.

While in school, Mao wrote political articles. It seemed to him that China's government should do more for its suffering people. A new hero was needed,

Mao moved with communist troops across the countryside of the Shanxi province in 1947. The Nationalist army, better equipped but discouraged, later surrendered to Mao's popular forces.

someone like Sun Zhong shan, who would throw out the foreigners and help the poor.

Mao believed that the peasants together should own their resources. In 1921 he helped to form the Chinese Communist party. He urged the nation to accept a communist form of government. In taking this view, Mao directly opposed Jiang Kai-shek. Unlike Mao, Jiang believed strongly in China's old ways—individual ownership of property and the order and duty taught by Confucius. Mao began to build an army.

The Communist Revolution

Slowly Mao's followers won the support of millions of Chinese peasants. While other armies had often stolen their food and property, Mao's army helped the peasants to plant and to harvest crops. In the areas that they

controlled, they took land away from landowners and shared it among the peasants.

Jiang's forces were victorious at first. In 1927 they destroyed communist forces in Shanghai. In 1934 the Nationalist army surrounded communist troops in southeast China. About 100,000 people managed to escape. They marched 6,000 miles (9,654 km) with Mao to safe mountain caves in the northwest. Only 8,000 survived what became known as the **Long March.**

After World War II, however, Mao became stronger. More and more peasants joined his army, while others supplied it with food, clothing, and weapons. Mao's army took control of the countryside. Jiang's weakening army concentrated in the cities. Jiang had lost the support of the peasants, however. The Nationalist government showed no concern for the poor, while government officials grew rich.

In October 1949, Mao established a communist government in China, with Beijing as its capital. He called it the **People's Republic of China.** Jiang and his supporters fled to the island of Taiwan and set up a government there. Both governments claimed to be the official rulers of the Chinese. Actually, Mao and his followers ruled China. Jiang ruled a small island off China's coast.

Communism in China

As head of the new government, Mao was looked upon by many with the same awe as the emperors of the past. Mao wanted this support because he wanted to change more than China's government. He wanted to change the people themselves. The result, Mao believed, would be a better China and a better world.

China became a communist state. Mao divided the country into small districts. In each one the people ran the factories and farms in which they worked. However, the central government really controlled each district. Anyone who disagreed with the communist program was punished, imprisoned, or put to death. Many millions of Chinese were killed.

With this control, the new government tried to solve many of the problems that had troubled China in the past. Teams of laborers cut roads over high mountains and built needed flood-control projects. With help from the Soviet Union the Chinese rebuilt war-torn factories and farms. In spite of a growing population, the Chinese began to produce enough food to prevent famine. The government supplied everyone with housing, simple clothing, and medical care.

Chinese women clean the streets in a modern part of Beijing. New apartment buildings make room for the city's large population, but housing is still in great demand.

Modern machinery like the "walking tractor" makes farming easier in some parts of China. Older, ox-driven plows are also in use.

Though Mao's government solved some problems, it also created many new ones. Mao seemed to believe that the millions of Chinese peasants could do anything if they were united. He was wrong. Peasants had long waited to get land of their own. Instead, many were settled on **communes,** government-run farming communities with shared housing and work. Most communes failed to produce as much as the government had planned.

In 1958 Mao ordered the Chinese people to produce steel in furnaces in their backyards. This command was part of a program called the **Great Leap Forward.** If it worked, Mao believed, China would soon overtake other nations in steel production. The peasants were not able to produce much steel in their small furnaces. Like many

others, this experiment of Mao's proved to be a mistake.

Other communist leaders used more proven ways of planning. They offered workers and peasants extra rewards for good production. During the early 1960s Mao attacked these methods as a return to the old China. He said that many government officials were becoming privileged like the old Mandarins. Moreover, Mao disliked any criticism of his rule. To block his opponents, he called on his followers in the army and among students. The students formed a group called the **Red Guards.**

The Cultural Revolution

Beginning in 1966 the Red Guards attacked any signs of old beliefs in China. They destroyed temples and family altars. They beat and often murdered people suspected of opposing Mao. They severely criticized anyone who accepted the ideas of Confucius. Only the thoughts of Mao were acceptable. On buildings and bridges the Red Guards raised pictures of Mao several stories high.

The attack on old beliefs in China was called the **Cultural Revolution.** While it went on, progress in China nearly stopped. Schools were closed because the Red Guards forced teachers to go to work beside peasants in the fields. Most research was halted and some factories closed. Many officials were removed from their jobs and publicly shamed.

Students, many of whom wore Red Guard uniforms, recited Mao's teachings.

A fatherly portrait of Mao decorated Tien-An-Men Square in Beijing, the capital.

The Cultural Revolution lessened Mao's popularity among the Chinese. It harmed innocent people and tried to destroy Chinese ways that had outlived many different rulers. Soon after Mao's death in 1976 the Chinese began to attack his reputation. In 1980 the Chinese government announced that the nation owed much to Mao but that his mistakes had been costly.

China Today

Many Chinese peasants and workers remember the harsh times before 1949. Few seem to want to go back. Under communism the Chinese people have more food, housing, and industries. However, life for most Chinese today is still difficult. Poverty and overcrowding continue to be major problems in China.

China's government still believes it can solve China's problems by controlling people's lives. The Chinese have little choice in the work they do or where they live. Education is available to more people, but it is also under government control. Because China's population is still growing, leaders have taken steps to control it. Families are urged to have only one child and must receive permission to have another.

Although China now has atomic weapons, modern buildings, and new farming methods, the Chinese know that they are far behind the world's leading industrial countries. China's industry started late. For this reason, China's leaders have realized that their system would benefit from American, European, and Japanese ideas.

In the late 1960s China hinted that it wanted new allies and trading partners in the West. A Chinese ping-pong team toured the United States. Suddenly American artists and scholars were welcomed in China. Within a few years formal government contacts began. 1972 saw the first visit of an American President, Richard Nixon, to China.

In 1978 President Jimmy Carter announced that the United States would recognize the Chinese communist government as China's legal

Silk spinning, women's work since ancient times, is still an important industry. Much factory-made Chinese silk is exported to the United States.

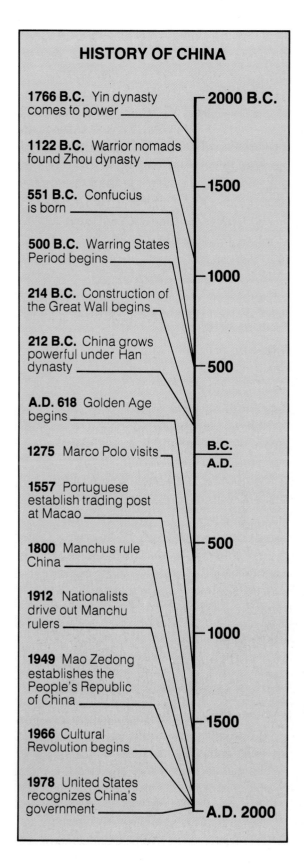

HISTORY OF CHINA

1766 B.C.	Yin dynasty comes to power
1122 B.C.	Warrior nomads found Zhou dynasty
551 B.C.	Confucius is born
500 B.C.	Warring States Period begins
214 B.C.	Construction of the Great Wall begins
212 B.C.	China grows powerful under Han dynasty
A.D. 618	Golden Age begins
1275	Marco Polo visits
1557	Portuguese establish trading post at Macao
1800	Manchus rule China
1912	Nationalists drive out Manchu rulers
1949	Mao Zedong establishes the People's Republic of China
1966	Cultural Revolution begins
1978	United States recognizes China's government

government. Before then, the United States had dealt only with the government in Taiwan. The new relationship has brought many changes to Chinese life.

China and the United States have increased their trading. Americans are interested in China's resources, especially petroleum. With over a billion people, China is a promising market for American goods. The Chinese, for their part, buy American machines and appliances, surplus grains, and new technology such as computers.

China has begun a program called **Four Modernizations.** They hope to modernize agriculture, industry, defense, and science and technology. Under this program the government sets **quotas,** or required amounts, of goods to be produced. Farmers and factory managers can then sell any extra goods and keep the money for themselves or their factory. In this way, the government hopes to encourage growth in the economy. No one knows how these changes will affect the future. However, it seems that China is trying hard to regain its influence.

Reading Check

1. From which group of people did Mao Zedong hope to win support?
2. After leaving mainland China, where did Jiang Kai-shek set up his government?
3. What caused Mao Zedong's loss of popularity? Why?
4. How has the relationship between the United States and the People's Republic of China changed since the 1960s?

389

The Parts of a Newspaper

Modern newspapers have a number of parts, or sections. The news sections have stories about local, national, and international events. The editorial section has articles that give opinions about news events. Also in the editorial section are letters from readers. The classified ads list such things as job offerings, houses for sale or rent, and lost and found articles. Other sections may include entertainment, travel, food, and comics.

Newspaper Articles

Read this article. It is a **news article,** one of the three main kinds of newspaper articles.

BRADSHAW ELECTED MAYOR
By JUDY WARREN
CHAMBERVILLE

Chamberville's spirited campaign for mayor ended in a narrow victory for Alice Bradshaw last night. With 99 percent of all precincts reporting, Supervisor Bradshaw's total stood at 40,381 to Mayor Farnold's 39,998. At her rally at Lincoln Hotel, Bradshaw promised "to work for all of Chamberville's citizens."

A news article reports current events in local areas, in the nation, and around the world. A news article tells the facts about an event. The **headline** is the title of the article. It briefly tells what happened. Often the headline is followed by a **byline,** the writer's name. Also following the headline is

a **dateline,** which indicates where the article originated. The first sentence or paragraph, which is called the **lead,** states the important facts of the article. This allows readers to find out the important facts quickly. What is the headline of the story you just read? What fact does the lead sentence state?

Feature Articles

A **feature article** entertains readers or gives background information about stories in the news. Features often are written to report the effects of news events or to appeal in some way to readers' emotions. A feature on the election might discuss delays in voting caused by broken machines.

Feature articles may include facts, but they are written more like a story than a news article. Features may be about the main news stories or about such topics as sports, fashion, or science. A feature in the entertainment section might tell how a new movie was made or what a popular actor is like.

Editorials

The third type of article is the **editorial.**

A VICTORY FOR CHAMBERVILLE

Chamberville is fortunate to have Alice Bradshaw as its mayor. Bradshaw showed good sense as city supervisor. As head of the budget committee, she saved our city millions of dollars. The other supervisors say they respect her abilities. We think she will be fair to all of our citizens. We feel that she will make Chamberville a better place to live.

An editorial gives someone's opinion about some item of news. In an editorial the writer usually speaks for the owners of the newspaper. The writer often says "we think" or "we believe." The editorial "we" stands for the newspaper's owners or managers.

Political Cartoons

Along with editorials, many newspapers publish **political cartoons.** These are drawings that show cartoonists' opinions about political issues and events. Political cartoonists usually express their opinions through humor. Look at the cartoon below. Notice the title of the speech in President Reagan's hands. As commander in chief, the President is responsible for the nation's defense. What kind of defense is President Reagan suggesting in this cartoon?

To appreciate the cartoon, you need to be able to recognize the "team of experts." They are characters from two popular movies. The robots are Artoo-Detoo (R2-D2) and See-Threepio (C-3P0), characters in the movie *Star Wars*. The space creature on the right is E.T. (the Extra-Terrestrial) from the movie of the same name.

The cartoonist used these make-believe characters as symbols. He believed that the new defense plan was like a science fiction movie, mostly imaginary.

Because the United States is a democracy, its citizens have the right to express political opinions like this one. An effective political cartoon can help people understand a particular viewpoint. With a single drawing and a few well-chosen words, a political cartoonist can influence the way people feel about an issue.

CHECKING YOUR SKILLS

Study the political cartoon above carefully and read the description that follows.

A Chinese man is leaning out a door in the Great Wall. He wants to get rid of twelve tons of "little red books." The books contain the teachings of Mao Zedong, the former leader of China, who did not believe in the free market system. The Chinese man is asking the man from the free market system to help him exchange these books for something more useful or valuable.

Write answers to these questions about the second cartoon. You may want to reread pages 386–389 of your textbook for background information.

1. What country do you think the truck represents? What makes you think so?

2. Why do you think the cartoonist chose a wall as a symbol for China?

3. The Chinese man represents China's new government. Why do you think he wants to sell the little red books?

4. What do you think this cartoon is saying about the Chinese leaders' changing attitude toward the free market system?

CHAPTER 13 REVIEW

USING WORDS

Copy the sentences below. Replace each underlined definition with the correct word from the following list.

civil service   **dynasty**
communes   **Mandate of Heaven**
Cultural Revolution

1. For nearly 4,000 years the Chinese culture lasted through one ruling family after another.

2. The qualified government officials helped maintain a strong central government.

3. The Chinese people changed rulers when they thought those rulers had lost the right to rule.

4. Under communism the Chinese population was divided into communities with shared housing and work controlled by the government.

5. The Red Guards tried to wipe out opposition to Mao Zedong during the attacks on old beliefs in China.

REVIEWING FACTS

1. Name the four fertile areas where most of China's people live.

2. In what ways did Confucius think people could become superior?

3. What group pledged to free China from foreign rule?

4. How were Mao Zedong's ideas different from the ideas of Jiang Kai-shek?

5. How did Mao Zedong want to change the Chinese people?

THINKING CRITICALLY

1. Early civilizations in Mesopotamia and China grew up in fertile farm areas that were surrounded by less rich lands. Attacks from nomads in these poorer lands led the farming peoples to unite. Explain how and why this might have happened.

2. The Chinese people were attracted to the teachings of Confucius during the Warring States Period. Why do you think they were influenced by new ideas at that time?

3. New leaders often try to stamp out the ideas of the past. Mao Zedong tried to do this to the ideas of Confucius. Why do you think this is so?

⭘ PRACTICING SKILLS

Newspapers   Use your community newspaper or another newspaper in your library to do the following:

1. List the sections that make up your local newspaper. Describe what is included in each section.

2. Find examples of the three types of newspaper articles—news, feature, and editorial.

3. Choose a political cartoon from your newspaper. Explain what you think the cartoonist is trying to say.

The Japanese Invite Challenges

Focus

Of all the Asian nations, only one is a fully modern industrial state. Japan is one of the world's leading producers of steel, automobiles, and electronics. Japan's success is remarkable considering its geography and history. This island nation is separate from the Asian landmass with few resources for industry.

In the mid 1800s Japan ended a long isolation. It modernized swiftly. In the 1900s it began to use military might to seize Asian lands with raw materials. Japan's military expansion ended in total defeat in World War II. Thereafter, hardworking Japanese rebuilt their nation. Today, this prosperous democracy competes successfully in the world marketplace.

Look for these important words:

Key Words
- archipelago
- terrace
- bonsai

Places
- Honshu
- Mount Fuji
- Tokyo
- Kanto Plain

Look for answers to these questions:

1. Where do most of Japan's people live?
2. Why is farming difficult in Japan?
3. On what resources do the Japanese depend?

1. AN ISLAND COUNTRY IN THE PACIFIC

The islands of Japan lie in a broad arc off the Asian mainland. The southern end of the arc is about 100 miles (161 km) from the peninsula of Korea. The center of the arc encloses the Sea of Japan. The northern part of the arc ends near the southeastern coast and islands of the Soviet Union.

Japan's numerous islands form a long chain, or **archipelago** (ar•kuh•PEL•uh•go). They are so closely linked that some of them seem joined just beneath the sea. Long ago volcanoes thrust these islands out of the Pacific Ocean. Today, earthquakes and some active volcanoes continue to affect where and how the Japanese live.

Japan's people live mainly on the coasts of the four major islands. The largest and most important island is **Honshu** (HAHN•shoo). The other three islands are Kyushu (kee•OO•shoo), Shikoku (shee•KOH•koo), and Hokkaido (hoh•KY•doh).

Japan's major islands stretch from 30°N to 45°N. On a globe, this is about the same latitude as the East Coast of the United States between northern Florida and Maine. For that reason, Japan has a similar range of climate. Snow and cold winters occur in the far north. The southernmost islands have near-tropical summers. Warm ocean currents make the climate in much of Japan unusually even, however. As in other parts of Asia, monsoons bring abundant rainfall to Japan. Most areas receive more than 40 inches (about 100 cm) of precipitation each year.

Using the Land

Mild climate and good rainfall normally mean rich farmland. In Japan, however, more than three-fourths of the land is covered by hills and mountains such as snow-capped **Mount Fuji** (FOO•jee). Though this makes Japan very beautiful, it means that less than 25 percent of its land can be farmed. Only the hard work of Japanese farmers makes up for the limited farmland. Every bit of land that can grow rice or other crops is used.

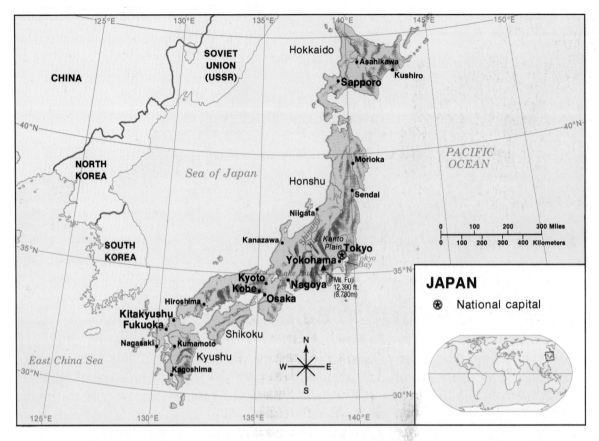

Terraced rice fields are found in many parts of Japan. These are on Kyushu.

Farmers in Japan **terrace** hillsides to prevent erosion and to make extra farmland. Terraces are like stairways. The soil along a hill is leveled in steps and held in place by earth-and-rock walls. This prevents water from running too swiftly down the hill. The farmers also regularly add nutrients to enrich the soil. By conserving water that runs off the mountains, they can usually do without irrigation systems.

The Japanese use their forests and fishing areas well. More than half the land is tree covered, giving Japan a leading timber industry. The Japanese protect their forests. They would rather import timber than reduce the number of trees on their land.

Along the long coast are hundreds of fishing villages. Small ships set out regularly to fish nearby waters. Much

Japan's "bullet train," a high-speed electric express, races past snow-capped Mount Fuji at 150 miles an hour (about 250 km/h).

larger ones sail out into distant oceans to catch more fish. These ships are called "floating factories" because the fish is prepared for market aboard them. Along with being a popular food, fish is the main source of protein for Japan. It leads all other countries in the size of its catches.

More than either farming or fishing, Japan's manufacturing has become its leading source of income. Factories have grown up in two main areas. The largest of these is located between **Tokyo,** the capital, and Yokohama (yoh•kuh•HAHM•uh), the main port. This area is called the **Kanto Plain.** It is one of several coastal plains on which most Japanese people live. The second-largest industrial area lies between the cities of Kobe (KOH•bee) and Osaka. Fast trains link Japanese cities.

A view of the city from a skyscraper shows Tokyo's severe overcrowding.

After a day of crowds and noise, the Japanese may return to homes designed to create a sense of quiet and privacy. At night, bedding is unfolded onto the floor.

A Crowded Land

The Japanese people have trained themselves to waste as little as possible. By planning carefully, they use all their available materials and space. This is necessary because the country is densely populated. Japan's population of almost 120 million is more than half that of the United States. Yet, Japan has less land than the state of California. Moreover, most Japanese live on only a small part of their land, an area about the size of South Carolina or Maine.

Over the years the Japanese have developed artistic ways to use the space they have. So that houses do not take up valuable land, they are usually built small. Japanese-style homes have sliding screens for inside walls. The screens allow small rooms to open into larger areas when needed.

Walls also open onto miniature outside gardens. The Japanese design these in a way that seems to copy the larger landscape. **Bonsai** (bohn•SY), the art of growing miniature trees and plants, adds to this effect. In this way, the Japanese stay close to the beauty of nature, which is so important to their culture. The simple styles of Japanese homes and gardens are often copied in other parts of the world.

Reading Check

1. Name Japan's four main islands.
2. How does terracing help Japanese farmers?
3. What is Japan's leading source of income?
4. How have the Japanese adapted their homes to suit the crowded environment?

398

Look for these important words:

Key Words
- Ainu
- jomon
- Malays
- typhoons
- Shinto

- kami
- clan

People
- Jimmu
- Murasaki Shikibu

Places
- Nara
- Heian-kyo

Look for answers to these questions:

1. What groups contributed to the civilization of early Japan?
2. How did the beliefs of Shinto affect Japanese culture?
3. What ideas and customs did Japan borrow from China?
4. How did Japanese government change after the seventh century A.D.?

2. EARLY CIVILIZATION

Many thousands of years ago, land bridges connected Japan with the Asian mainland. This let people migrate to Japan from what is now Korea in the south and from Siberia in the north. After some time the Earth changed. The land bridges were submerged, isolating the islands of Japan and their inhabitants from the rest of Asia.

One early group in Japan was the **Ainu** (EYE•noo), who probably came from northern Asia. They were short with white skin and round faces. Originally they lived all over Japan, but new settlers gradually pushed them to the northern-most islands.

Another group of arrivals, from southern Asia, were probably the ancestors of today's Japanese. This group takes its name from the design on its pottery. The pottery was decorated with marks made by coiled ropes called **jomon.** The people of this Jomon Period had no writing. However, they told stories that have been repeated in Japan ever since.

Clay figures imprinted with coiled rope patterns were made in the Jomon Period.

399

Other people helped settle Japan, too. Nomadic hunters came from Mongolia. Southern Chinese brought the knowledge of rice growing. **Malays,** seafarers from the South Pacific, brought the art of fishing. All these groups helped to shape the Japanese people.

The Japanese call their country *Nihon* or *Nippon,* meaning "land of the rising sun." According to their stories, the descendant of a sun goddess was the first emperor of Japan. To his own name, **Jimmu,** he added the word *Tenno,* which means "born of heaven." This reminded his people that the emperor's ancestor was a goddess. Since Jimmu's reign in 660 B.C., Japan's many emperors are thought to have inherited his power in an unbroken line. In parts of Japan today there are people who believe that the emperor and nation are sacred.

The Beginning of Japanese Culture

The first Japanese were spared invasions from neighboring countries. Stormy seas and fierce hurricanes called **typhoons** shielded them from outside harm. These same winds and seas, however, discouraged them from sailing overseas themselves. The Japanese limited their travels to the four main islands. Alone, they developed loyal feelings for their land that would shape their culture for centuries.

In *The Great Wave*, a woodblock print by the artist Hokusai, simple, powerful shapes illustrate Japanese respect for the sea.

Shinto beliefs honor and protect the land. Places of worship, often found in wooded areas, blend into and reflect their natural surroundings.

A special religion was part of this culture. It was called **Shinto,** or "way of the gods." As farmers and hunters, the early Japanese had a great respect for nature. Their religion said that spirits called **kami** (KAHM•ee) lived in all natural things, such as stones, trees, and animals. These *kami* were worshiped and offered gifts.

To practice Shinto, individuals would concentrate on a part of nature, such as a cherry blossom. Often they would gaze into a small shrine dedicated to their ancestors. The shrine included a mirror that was thought to contain the spirits of the past and of the land.

Shinto also said that each family had its own protective *kami*. This encouraged people to unite around the family or a group of related families called a **clan.** Individuals were not considered

so important. People were expected to pledge their loyalty to families, clans, and the rulers of these groups.

The Influence of China

By the fourth century A.D. Japanese clans that often had fought among themselves began to unite. Ever larger groups gathered together under strong leaders and the authority of the emperor. One reason for this move toward unity was China. Japanese merchants had developed a growing trade with China. In China they found beautiful cities, highways, and a well-organized government able to keep peace. Though it took time, the Japanese were ready to adopt some of China's ways.

You may recall that Buddhism had spread from India to China and then to China's neighbor, Korea. In the sixth century A.D. these Buddhists came to Japan. With them they carried many parts of Chinese civilization. They introduced books written in Chinese. They brought the Chinese arts of painting and sculpture. They also brought Chinese ideas in law, style of dress, architecture, and manners. The Japanese willingly accepted Chinese ideas. For about two centuries they imitated the Chinese almost completely. Chinese law codes were taken over nearly word for word.

Eventually the Japanese made the imported ways their own. They used China's written language to represent the sounds of their own speech. Clan leaders, not civil servants as in China, ran the government. The Japanese adapted Chinese art and architecture to fit their own needs and tastes.

Even Chinese philosophies were molded to suit the Japanese. In China, for example, Buddhist monks lived in isolation from society. In Japan, however, Buddhists took an active part in society and government. Sometimes they became leaders in business or advisers to the emperor.

The ideas of Confucius also blended into Japanese culture. In China, if the emperor ruled badly, the people were urged to rebel. In Japan, however, the ideas of Confucius combined with Shinto to increase the power of fathers and clan leaders. Fathers had complete control over their families. Clan

The Kamakura Buddha, still visited by millions of worshippers, is more than 800 years old. Its temple was washed away by a tidal wave.

The Heian Shrine, modeled after an eighth-century emperor's palace, was built in 1895 to celebrate the city's eleven-hundredth anniversary. Heian-kyo is now named Kyoto.

leaders demanded full loyalty from their subjects. Under no conditions could the people rebel.

Unity in Japan

During the seventh century A.D. loyalty to fathers and clan leaders spread to the emperor. Long looked upon as the descendant of gods, the emperor had never been a political leader. People had always accepted the authority of clan leaders. However, differences between clans often led to civil wars.

Finally the emperor took control. In A.D. 710 he formed a central government and built his capital at **Nara.** For the first time in its history, Japan was united under its emperor. In A.D. 794 the capital was moved to **Heian-kyo** (HAY•AHN KYOH), or Kyoto. However, this unity continued for 300 years.

Japanese culture grew during this time. An important example was a new Japanese form of writing. Instead of trying to fit Chinese characters to Japanese words, the new system used characters to represent Japanese syllables. Japanese could now be written with more freedom. Writers began to create a lasting literature.

Japanese women at the emperor's court wrote some of the finest works. **Murasaki Shikibu** (MOO•RAH•SAH•KEE SHY•KY•BOO) wrote the world's first novel, called *The Tale of Genji* (GEN•jee). It is an imaginary story about a Japanese prince. Written around the beginning of the eleventh century, the book beautifully describes Japanese life at that time. *The Tale of Genji* has since taken its place as a masterpiece of world literature.

Reading Check

1. From what areas did the people now called Japanese migrate?
2. How did typhoons affect the development of Japanese culture?
3. How did parts of Chinese civilization come to Japan?
4. Before Japan united under the emperor in A.D. 710, who had authority over the Japanese people?

403

3. FEUDALISM AND THE SHOGUN

Although Japan had no contact with feudal Europe, the Japanese developed a similar form of government. It began with the weakening power of Japanese emperors during the ninth century A.D. To pay for their courts, the emperors had called upon farmers to raise food and pay taxes. The emperors gave land to the farmers who pledged support.

The emperors also gave huge areas of land to nobles and clan leaders. Some warlike clan leaders gathered large numbers of people under their control. In time a few became more powerful than the nobles, and even the emperor. At last, one clan leader, **Minamoto Yoritomo** (MIH·NAH·MOH·TOH YOH·RIH·TOH·MOH), set up a military government. He persuaded the emperor to give him the title **shogun,** which means "leading general." He kept the emperor on the throne but allowed him little political control.

Yoritomo and the shoguns who followed organized the government in a military way. A council of warriors met regularly to learn the shogun's wishes.

Minamoto Yoritomo's system of military rule lasted for nearly seven centuries.

They directed a group of officials, including military governors and tax collectors. At the bottom of Japanese society were the peasants laboring on their farms. They grew the food that permitted leaders and warriors to live without working. As taxes rose, the peasants lost ownership of most of their land.

Because the shogun's council met in the city of **Kamakura** (kahm•uh•KUR• uh), this part of Japanese history is called the Kamakura Shogunate. It lasted almost 150 years, ending in 1333. Japanese art and trade advanced during the Kamakura Shogunate. Buddhists helped in this development.

A new form of Buddhism called **Zen Buddhism** became popular in Japan. Zen taught its followers to concentrate totally on whatever they did. This teaching extended to the warriors. Like European knights, these warriors, called **samurai** (SAM•uh•ry), were duty-bound to their nobles.

With Zen concentration, the samurai could swing a long, heavy, two-handed sword. They could send an arrow to its mark from the back of a galloping horse. Many samurai also wrote poetry or mastered other arts. The samurai became an important class in Japanese society.

Invasion by Sea

With all the warriors who owed him loyalty, the shogun at Kamakura had great power. He was not safe from all threats, however. Rivals often plotted to overthrow a shogun, which led to civil war. Pirates struck at ships in the Sea of Japan. Even more dangerous was the threat from the ruler of China.

This photograph, taken when the samurai no longer held power, shows the weapons once carried by these warriors.

The Mongol emperor named Kublai Khan controlled China. Having conquered the mainland, he demanded that Japan surrender too. When the Japanese refused, the Mongol forces prepared to invade Japan.

In 1274 more than 30,000 Mongol warriors arrived in 150 ships. Although the fierce Mongol army was better equipped, neither side won the first battle. That night a typhoon swept in from the sea, crushing the Mongol ships. The Japanese called the storm a **kamikaze** (kah•mih•KAH•zee), or "divine wind."

Later a second Mongol army, five times the size of the first, was also destroyed by a kamikaze. The Japanese became certain that their religious beliefs had saved them. Many thought that invasion of Japan was impossible.

Europeans and Christianity

Safe on their islands, the Japanese knew little or nothing of Europe or its technology. Japanese samurai were expert sword handlers and archers but had no rifles. In 1543 Portuguese sailors became the first Europeans to arrive in Japan. A few local lords, or **daimyo** (DY•myoh), bought rifles from them. The new weapons added greatly to the daimyos' power.

Encouraged by this trade, the Portuguese sent trading ships regularly to Japan. Also to Japan came a Jesuit priest, **Francis Xavier** (ZAY•vee•ur). This famous missionary taught the Japanese about Christianity. Before long, Portuguese and Spanish priests had converted hundreds of thousands of Japanese to Christianity.

Jesuit Francis Xavier dreamed of making Japan the first Christian nation in Asia.

Serious conflicts soon arose, however. The Christian priests would not accept Japan's older religions. They told people to give up their old ways and practice Christianity alone. This angered many Japanese, but the priests were allowed to remain in Japan.

Then, in 1596 the Japanese government changed its attitude toward Christians. An incident in the life of one daimyo contributed to the government's decision.

Into a small harbor sailed a Spanish ship in need of repairs. The daimyo explained that according to Japanese law, the ship was now his property. To save himself, the Spanish captain explained that his king was more powerful than even the shogun.

"First," he said, "the king sends missionaries. They convert people to Christianity. Next, the king sends ships with soldiers and weapons. With the help of the Christians, soldiers bring a new government to the land."

When the shogun heard this, he decided to protect Japan from invasion. New Christian missionaries were forbidden to enter Japan. The next shogun, **Tokugawa Ieyasu** (TOH•KUH•GAH•WUH EE•uh•YAH•soo), carried this rule even further. He wanted the benefits of increased trade with foreigners while banning Christianity. He forced Christian missionaries to leave Japan and executed those who did not. Trading with foreigners was confined to the port of **Nagasaki** (nahg•uh•SAHK•ee).

In the 1630s Ieyasu's grandson, now shogun, completed Japan's isolation. The Japanese were forbidden to leave their islands, and all contact with foreigners was prohibited. By 1639, Japan was closed to outsiders.

A detail from a painted screen shows subjects of feudal Kyoto bowing in the streets as a member of the Tokugawa family leaves the castle.

Tokugawa Feudalism

Cut off from outside influence, Japan further developed its own form of feudalism. The people were completely organized. Shogun controlled daimyo, daimyo controlled officials, and officials controlled peasants. Everyone had to obey.

Tokugawa officials dealt harshly with lawbreakers. Whoever failed to obey their rules faced punishment by stern samurai. Filled with pride, the samurai strode about cities and villages. By law, they had the right to behead anyone who even neglected to bow to them.

The samurai code of behavior was called the **bushido** (BOO•shee•doh), or "way of the warrior." It commanded the samurai to be always ready to fight. Samurai worked hard and exercised daily. Above all, they owed their first duty to their lords.

The people of Japan were given the same kind of instruction. Duty to Japan and their lords came first. Government officials raised large signs in every village. The signs informed the people how to behave. "Work hard!" they often declared. In times of drought they might say, "Eat less rice!"

Most Japanese peasants lived in small villages. They occupied thatched huts whose walls were made of mud and reeds. They heated their homes with small charcoal cooking stoves.

407

Beds were simple pads that lay on the earth. Peasants felt strong loyalty to the nobles, even though the nobles might demand great sacrifice.

In both peasant and noble families the father was the guardian of the family's all-important reputation. To protect the family name, he needed complete obedience from all members. Any Japanese father would have been shamed if he discovered disloyalty to him in his family. A family's reputation for hard work and good behavior lasted for many generations.

Women's roles in the family were also important. Early in their lives they looked forward to marriage. Once married, they usually became the managers of the family. Many found time to do creative tasks. Those married to wealthy lords learned the arts

Floating world art sometimes showed rich entertainments and court life. Here, a graceful princess steps from her carriage.

of landscape painting or poetry. Peasant women often wove cloth to make fabrics.

Japan's Merchants

Japanese culture continued to grow under the strict feudal system. Merchants became important. Living mostly in large cities, they sold food, clothing, jewelry, and weapons. They organized associations to control prices and credit. Many merchants gained power over the samurai to whom they had lent money at high costs. The merchants also persuaded the government to end the old barter system and introduce a standard form of money. A dependable form of money made more trade easier.

The new wealth of the merchants helped the arts. Merchants bought fine paintings and prints for which Japan has been famous ever since. The famous prints known as the *ukiyo-e* (yoo•kee•oh•YAY), or "floating world," developed at this time. They have this name because their images seem very graceful while picturing common scenes of fish peddlers, sailors, or servants.

Poets and playwrights also developed new art forms. One of these, the **haiku** (HY•KOO), is a poem that has exactly seventeen syllables, such as:

A snake! Though it passes,
eyes that had glared at me
stay in the grasses.

Another new form of literature was the **Kabuki** (kah•BOO•kee) play. Actors spoke and sang of real kinds of events in the lives of people. The brilliant costumes, scenery, and lively actions attracted large audiences.

In Kabuki dramas, common people often daringly outwitted those above them. The plays offered a colorful escape from strictly-governed everyday life.

In trade, art, and peaceful government, Japan grew rich during the long period of Tokugawa rule. Its very success, however, began to break Japanese society apart. The old feudal forms no longer fit so well. Many of the peasants were squeezed for profits by the merchants and were starving. Some nobles thought of entering trade themselves. The samurai were unhappy as well. In a society at peace and more interested in business, these feudal warriors were no longer needed.

By the middle of the nineteenth century, Japan was the only major nation clinging to a feudal system. By the 1850s Europe and the United States were building large industries. Feudal lords and ladies, with their castles and their knights, no longer had great power in any major country except Japan.

Reading Check

1. What helped the Japanese defeat the Mongol invasions?
2. Who were the first Europeans to visit Japan? What changes did they introduce?
3. What was the samurai code of behavior called? How did it influence Japanese life?
4. The growth in importance of which class of people brought feudalism to an end in Japan?

The Tea Ceremony

Leave your shoes at the door, bow, and enter on your knees this quiet room. This is the room of *cha-no-yu* (CHAH•NOH•YOO), the Japanese tea ceremony. Whether in sixteenth century feudal Japan or in a twentieth century tea house, the ceremony is the same.

Each step of the tea ceremony is very important. A solemn, respectful manner must be maintained at all times. It is polite to admire the way the tea master conducts the ceremony. It is impolite to say anything more. Courtesy and silence help the host and guests enjoy the peaceful atmosphere.

First, the guests kneel on the floor on woven straw mats called **tatami** (tah•TAHM•ee). Before beginning the tea-making process, the tea master will probably serve sweet cakes called **kashi** (KAH•shee). Next, the tea master will take great care in preparing the tea. The master knows that this is the most important part of the Japanese tea ceremony.

One of two kinds of tea is served: **koicha** (KOH•ee•chah), thick tea, or **usucha** (OOS•uh•chah), thin tea. For whichever kind of tea is being made, the tea master measures the needed amount of special powdered tea into the bowl. Water, heated to just the right temperature, is then poured into the bowl. It takes many years of practice to perform the tea ceremony properly. The tea master must know exactly when the tea is ready to be served.

The tea is poured into bowls and handed to the guests. Slowly and carefully the tea master performs this step. If the tea tastes the way it should, it is not too hot, not too cold, and not too bitter. If it is light green with just a hint of froth at the top, then the tea master of this ceremony has been successful.

The tea ceremony is part of the culture of Japan. Special rooms or buildings are used to practice the ceremony. The importance of this ceremony does not rest alone in a good cup of tea. Rather, the Japanese respect the simplicity and delicate beauty of this ancient custom.

Tea whisk

Brewing tea

17th century teapot

Look for these important words:

Key Words
- Meiji
- seppuku
- atomic bomb

People
- Matthew C. Perry
- Mutsuhito
- Hirohito

Places
- Pearl Harbor
- Hiroshima

Look for answers to these questions:

1. What was the result of Commodore Perry's visit to Japan?
2. What changes occurred in Japan during the Meiji period?
3. Why did Japan begin a series of military campaigns?
4. How did Japanese soldiers' feelings about the emperor affect their actions?

4. INDUSTRIAL JAPAN

During the nineteenth century the Japanese could see that conditions were changing all around them. European ships sailed regularly past their islands to China. The governments of Europe had forced China to grant them trading privileges. It seemed certain that Japan, though isolated, would one day become part of this change.

At last that day arrived. In 1853 some Japanese, who were fishing in Tokyo Bay, spotted the smoke of four enormous black steamships out at sea. The ships were commanded by Commodore **Matthew C. Perry** of the American navy. Under orders from the President of the United States, Perry had come to discuss future relations with the Japanese.

Perry explained that the United States wanted to begin trading with Japanese merchants. Also, the United States wanted to use the Japanese islands as a naval depot for refueling American steamships. Americans were concerned, too, with protection for sailors, who sometimes were shipwrecked during storms in Japanese waters. Perry said he would return later for Japan's answer.

In 1854 Perry appeared again with a larger force of 10 ships and 2,000 troops. Impressed by the strength of the American fleet, the Japanese signed a treaty granting American requests. Trade began between Japan and the United States. European countries soon followed the United States in this trade.

The reopening of Japanese ports to foreign trade marked the end of feudal Japan, samurai, and the rule of the shogun. Once again the Japanese united in support of their emperor. Although only fourteen, **Mutsuhito** (MOO•TSOO•HEE•TOH) represented all the people. In 1868 he made Edo the official capital and renamed it Tokyo. He

411

Steaming into Tokyo Bay, Perry threatened to block supply routes to the capital if the Japanese would not allow trading to begin.

then reformed his government. In 1889 Japan adopted its first constitution.

Mutsuhito's reign became known as the **Meiji** (MAY•JEE) period. During it, the Japanese made major changes. Once refusing to learn from outsiders, now they adopted every modern method to catch up with leading industrial nations. The country built its first public schools, libraries, newspapers, and steamships. Factories sprang up rapidly. The nation's slogan became "rich country, strong arms." Japan's leaders were determined not to let European nations capture Japan as they had China. Everyone had to contribute to the strength of the country.

Military Conquest

As Japan entered the twentieth century, it faced some problems as a developing industrial country. Its population had grown rapidly and needed more space. Moreover, Japan had few resources to supply its new industries. While European powers had colonies in Asia from which to get resources, Japan had none.

The Japanese began a campaign to expand. In a successful war against China, Japan gained control of the island of Formosa and the southern tip of Manchuria, which they were forced to return. Japan also wanted to control Korea. This led to war with Russia.

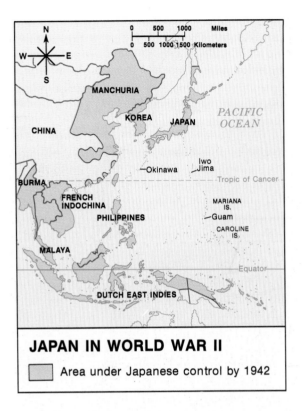

JAPAN IN WORLD WAR II

☐ Area under Japanese control by 1942

With its possessions under attack, the United States entered World War II. It declared war on Japan and its allies, Germany and Italy.

At first the Japanese were successful. British, French, Dutch, and American colonies fell under Japanese attacks. Among the conquered lands were Malaya, Indonesia, the Philippines, French Indochina, Thailand, Burma, and much of China. Japan's armies reached India before they could be stopped. Its navy won victory after victory in the Pacific.

The old warrior code seemed to give the Japanese forces uncommon courage. Their sense of duty to their emperor, **Hirohito** (HEAR•OH•HEE•TOH), made them willing to undergo any hardship in battle. One event in Hirohito's childhood helps to explain this loyalty.

The world thought that mighty Russia would crush Japan. The war proved otherwise. The Japanese army smashed Russian forces in Manchuria, while its navy defeated the Russian fleet near Korea. From this victory, Japan learned that it might defeat other nations in its region.

Many Japanese leaders urged a more peaceful policy. However, Japanese military leaders became ever more powerful. They believed that materials and markets were becoming scarcer and that Japan had to expand or face ruin. Again the Japanese struck. They seized Manchuria in 1931. Six years later they attacked China itself.

The final stage of Japan's long military campaign began on December 7, 1941. On that day Japanese planes sank or heavily damaged many of the American ships at **Pearl Harbor** in Hawaii.

Training a Prince

As a boy, Hirohito attended classes in a famous building called the Peers' School. Only the future leaders of Japan could attend it. These children of nobles were expected to work harder and to train themselves longer than any other students. Hirohito had to become the strongest possible leader of Japan.

The head of the school, a general named Nogi, had become a military hero when Hirohito was three years old. General Nogi had led the Japanese army to victory over Russia. Like the other students in the Peers' School, Hirohito had great respect for General Nogi.

"What is your fondest wish?" the general often asked the students at assemblies.

"To die for the emperor!" the students called back together.

In 1912 Hirohito's grandfather, the emperor Mutsuhito, died. After the emperor's death, General Nogi went to Prince Hirohito. He addressed the twelve-year-old boy who would one day become the emperor:

Please remember that my physical presence is not necessary for me to be with you in your work. I shall always be watching you, and your welfare will always be my concern. Work hard, for your own sake and for the sake of Japan.

The emperor was buried in an impressive funeral. Thousands of uniformed soldiers and sailors appeared before a horse-drawn casket in which the body lay. Most people, including Hirohito and other children, lined the streets. As the cannons boomed a last salute to the emperor, General Nogi and his wife knelt before a Shinto shrine in their apartment. Hearing the sound of the cannons, General Nogi and his wife took their own lives.

Throughout history the Japanese have believed strongly in personal loyalty. People were taught to make any sacrifice for their families. The emperor deserved the greatest sacrifices. He was the head of the family of Japanese people. Therefore, when Emperor Mutsuhito died, his favorite general committed **seppuku** (seh•POO•koo), killing himself with a sword. By doing so, General Nogi was honoring the emperor. The general's wife also committed seppuku to prove loyalty both to her husband and to her ruler.

Almost all Japanese felt the same sense of loyalty to Hirohito and to Japan during World War II. Eventually,

Paper birds inside this monument *Girl of 1,000 Cranes,* honor the dead of Hiroshima.

though, Japan's military leaders led the nation to terrible defeat, the first in its history. Nearly every city of size was destroyed. Worst hit were **Hiroshima** (hear•uh•SHEE•muh) and Nagasaki. American bombers in 1945 leveled these two cities with a weapon never used before nor since—the **atomic bomb.** The Japanese surrendered.

Reading Check

1. Who was the American naval officer sent to propose trade with Japan?
2. Name two reasons that Japan began its military conquests.
3. What event prompted the United States to enter World War II?
4. How did the Japanese feel about their emperors?

414

Look for these important words:

Key Words
- traditions
- kimono

- geta
- sumo
- judo

People
- Douglas MacArthur

Look for answers to these questions:

1. How did the Japanese help their country rebuild after its defeat in World War II? How did the United States help Japan rebuild?
2. What problems has Japan's rapid industrial growth caused for Japan and for other countries?
3. How has Japanese life changed since the end of World War II? What values and ways of behaving remain the same?

5. MODERN JAPAN

In 1946 Japan appeared to be a ruined nation that could never recover. An American army under General **Douglas MacArthur** occupied the land. Emperor Hirohito had to announce publicly that he was not a god. Military leaders were put on trial. The leaders of huge companies lost their positions, and the companies were divided. Many people in the cities roamed the countryside in search of food. Japan's economy was shattered.

Japan made a miraculous recovery, however. It left behind its empire and the military. It turned instead to democracy and to developing its business strength. The United States made loans to help Japan rebuild. The resource that Japan used was its most proven one—a united people willing to work and save for the good of Japan.

The savings of individual Japanese supplied money to Japanese banks. Japan's new leaders used this money with courage and boldness. They worked in cooperation with the government to rebuild Japan's damaged factories. They modeled their new industries after the best the world had and then improved them. They trained people to work in the industries.

Using resources from overseas, factory workers processed them into well-made products. Their steel industry began to compete with the world leaders, the United States and the Soviet Union. Cameras, stereos, television sets, and calculators streamed off modern assembly lines. By the 1970s Japan was the world's third ranking industrial power. It led all nations in shipbuilding. In the 1980s its automobile industry became the largest in the world.

Today the Japanese people have a prosperous economy. Their major cities of Yokohama, Osaka, and Nagoya each have populations of more than two

415

Thousands of brand-new automobiles, ready to be exported around the world, stretch across a loading area at one of Japan's ports.

PRODUCTION OF GOODS IN JAPAN, 1974-1984

Bicycles — Cameras — Color Televisions

Millions of goods

1974 1975 1976 1977 1978 1979 1980 1981 1982 1983 1984

Japanese workers use magnifying lenses to do detailed industrial work.

Regular exercise breaks for the workers are scheduled by many companies.

million. Tokyo has almost 12 million people. These cities are filled with modern buildings, busy subways, and automobiles. Within its borders, Japan has more universities than Western Europe.

Working in Japan

Employment is high and very secure in Japan. Companies supply more than jobs. They provide workers with social activities, group vacations, and sometimes housing. Workers are loyal and take pride in their products. Many put in extra hours to learn new skills.

Japan has not reached its level of success without problems. In such countries as the United States, people have started to worry about Japanese competition. Americans who buy Japanese automobiles do not buy American ones. If automakers must close their factories, Americans lose jobs. In such cases governments can charge high taxes on Japanese goods, making them more expensive. This could harm Japanese trade.

Problems of rapid industrial growth, such as pollution, crowding, inflation, and the need for more oil, have caused some Japanese to question the country's direction. Some people are trying to persuade the government to return Japan to older ways and values.

Others say that such Japanese values as loyalty, hard work, cooperation, and the ability to organize are still at work in modern industries. They point out that many Japanese companies are spending money to clean up the environment. With these virtues, they say, the Japanese can overcome any problems.

417

Living in Japan

You have read how the Japanese borrowed their ancient culture from China. Later they used ideas from Europe and the United States to modernize their country. After World War II the Japanese again joined together to rebuild Japan. Throughout their history the Japanese have adapted quickly and fully to changes in their lives. At the same time they have kept many of their **traditions.** Traditions are customs or beliefs that have been passed from one generation to the next.

Today, Japan is a blend of Eastern and Western ways. For the most part, Japanese have adopted Western clothing styles. Only on special occasions does a woman wear a long, belted robe, called a **kimono** (kuh.MOH.nuh), and wooden sandals, called **geta** (GET.AH).

Many homes and apartments in Japan's cities have Western-style furniture and modern conveniences. Japanese-style homes are very simple. Traditional homes with their sliding screens have little furniture. Families eat at low tables and sleep on quilts on the floor.

While lifestyles may be shifting in Japan, many ways of behaving remain the same. Japanese are extremely polite. One example of this is that they bow each time they greet strangers. The love of nature and the respect for elders found in the ancient Shinto religion are also continuing traditions in Japan.

Family life has changed in some ways since World War II. Industrial expansion has meant more jobs and more people moving to the cities. Both

Many homes, like the one shown here, are furnished entirely in a Western style. Often, Western and Japanese comforts are combined.

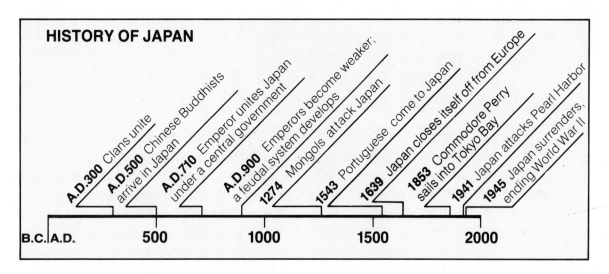

HISTORY OF JAPAN

A.D.300 Clans unite

A.D.500 Chinese Buddhists arrive in Japan

A.D.710 Emperor unites Japan under a central government

A.D.900 Emperors become weaker; a feudal system develops

1274 Mongols attack Japan

1543 Portuguese come to Japan

1639 Japan closes itself off from Europe

1853 Commodore Perry sails into Tokyo Bay

1941 Japan attacks Pearl Harbor

1945 Japan surrenders, ending World War II

B.C. | A.D.   500   1000   1500   2000

men and women now work outside the home. Laws have been passed to give women equal opportunities. Parents and children share family responsibilities. Though families are generally smaller, older relatives may still live with their families.

The ancient traditions of Japan are respected still. Here, Shinto worshippers pause to offer prayers at a shrine.

The Japanese people are proud of their ancient arts. Scroll painting, flower arranging, architecture, music, dance, and theater preserve many traditions of Japanese culture. The Japanese also enjoy many forms of recreation. Baseball and golf are popular. Side by side with these sports are the traditional sports of **sumo** and **judo,** two forms of wrestling.

In business, family, and recreation, the Japanese combine what they consider the best of new and old ideas. Their accomplishments in the last 40 years indicate the success of this combination. Their achievements also have inspired many other Asians to work hard in developing their countries.

Reading Check

1. Which general commanded the American army of occupation in Japan?
2. How did Japanese savings help industrial growth?
3. Name one industry in which Japan has led other nations.
4. How can Japanese competition with other countries cause problems?

419

READING WIND AND OCEAN CURRENT MAPS

During World War II the Japanese released thousands of bomb-carrying balloons. To design the balloon-bomb project, the Japanese studied maps of **prevailing winds.** Prevailing winds are winds that generally blow in one direction. The prevailing winds that blow from the west to the east in the middle latitudes are called westerly winds or **westerlies.** The Japanese hoped the westerlies would carry the balloon-bombs to North America.

The Japanese hopes were realized. About 1,000 such bombs did indeed drop in North America. The Americans and Canadians, however, remained quiet about it. Thinking the balloon project was a failure, the Japanese stopped it.

The westerlies are a part of great circular movements of air. The maps on the next page show the patterns of this air movement in the Northern Hemisphere over the Pacific Ocean.

Use one of the maps to follow the westerlies from Japan to the United States. Continue following the movement of air. Notice that it begins to sweep east near 30°N. At this point the winds get a new name—the **trade winds.** Ship captains sailing across the Pacific quickly learned to catch the trade winds as the fastest course east.

Ships sailing near the equator, however, found themselves in the **doldrums.** The doldrums are very light, shifting winds near the equator. On the wind maps the doldrums appear as broken lines. The weather in the doldrums can vary between calms, with no wind at all, to squalls, which are sudden, violent storms.

Another area of calm winds is located around the Tropic of Capricorn and the Tropic of Cancer. These areas are called the **horse latitudes.** No one knows exactly why. One story is that many horses died on sailing ships stuck in the calm winds. Another story is that sailors thought weather in the horse latitudes to be unpredictable, like a skittish horse.

The Effect of Winds on Climate

The patterns of prevailing winds affect climate. Look at the map of prevailing winds for January. Notice that the prevailing winds have arrows showing that they move from northeastern Asia south to Japan.

Look at the wind map for July. Where do Japan's prevailing winds come from in the summer? Would you expect these winds to be cold or warm? Why?

In both summer and winter the winds bring precipitation to Japan. In winter the dry arctic winds pick up moisture from the Sea of Japan and then drop it as rain or snow. In summer winds from the southeast bring warm, moist air. These winds are monsoons. The rain they bring is sometimes called the "plum rain" because it begins when the plums ripen.

Ocean Currents

Like prevailing winds, ocean currents affect climate. In addition, prevailing winds affect ocean currents. Compare the ocean current map with a prevailing wind map. Notice that ocean currents and prevailing winds

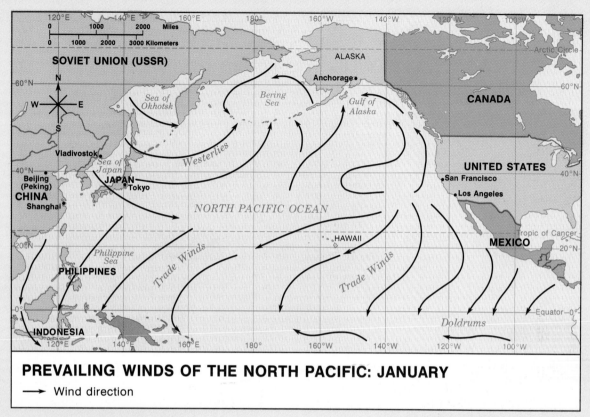

PREVAILING WINDS OF THE NORTH PACIFIC: JANUARY

→ Wind direction

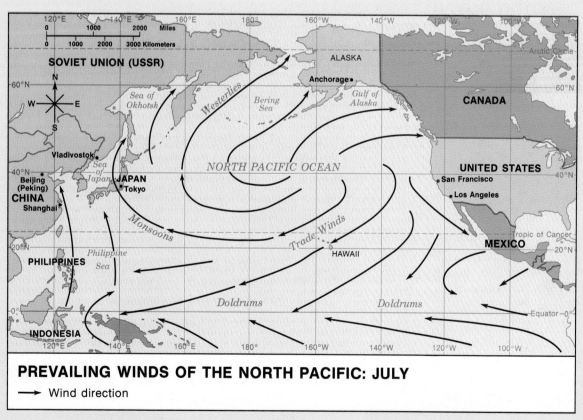

PREVAILING WINDS OF THE NORTH PACIFIC: JULY

→ Wind direction

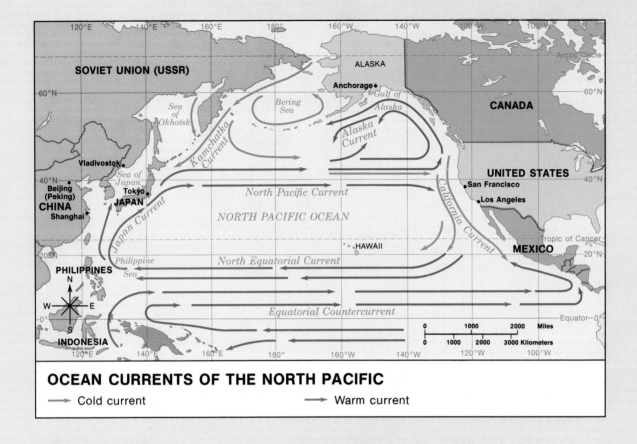

OCEAN CURRENTS OF THE NORTH PACIFIC

→ Cold current   → Warm current

often follow the same patterns, circular movements caused by the spinning Earth.

In the Northern Hemisphere ocean currents that come from the north are cold. Those that come from the south are warm. On the map, cold currents are shown in blue, and warm currents in red.

The Japan Current, also called the Kuro-shio (koor•oh•SHEE•oh) Current, flows north from the Philippine Sea. This current has a warming effect on much of Japan.

On the ocean current map you can see a cold current sweeping past the north-eastern parts of Japan. This is the Kamchatka (kam•CHAHT•kuh) Current. The parts of Japan near the Kamchatka Current are generally colder than areas affected by the Japan Current. When the warm air over the Japan Current meets the cold Kamchatka Current, fog is produced.

CHECKING YOUR SKILLS

Use the maps of winds and ocean currents to answer the following questions.

1. Is the North Pacific Current warm or cold?

2. Imagine you find a corked bottle bobbing in the ocean near Tokyo. Is it more likely that the bottle came from the Philippines or from Alaska? Why?

3. Would it be easier to sail from Hawaii to Japan in summer or in winter? Why?

4. What are the prevailing winds called at the middle latitudes? at the low latitudes? at the equator?

5. Compare the Pacific coast of Asia with the Pacific coast of North America at 40°N. Would the Asian coast generally be colder or warmer in winter than the North American coast? Why?

CHAPTER 14 REVIEW

USING WORDS

Use five or more of the words listed below to write a paragraph about Japan.

archipelago	samurai
bushido	Shinto
clan	shogun
daimyo	traditions
kami	typhoons

REVIEWING FACTS

1. What method do Japanese farmers use to prevent erosion and to increase their farmland? Describe how it works.

2. How does the Shinto religion encourage a love of nature and a respect for ancestors?

3. How did China influence Japan?

4. How was the feudal government of Minamoto Yoritomo organized?

5. What role did the Samurai play in Japan?

6. Why did the Japanese decide to close Japan to all outsiders in the 1630s?

7. How did the new merchant class affect the development of Japan?

8. Why was Commodore Perry sent to Japan?

9. What was the Japanese slogan during the Meiji period?

10. Give three examples of problems facing Japan because of rapid industrial growth.

THINKING CRITICALLY

1. The actions of modern nations can often be explained by their past histories. What parts of Japanese history and culture might explain the country's military adventures in the twentieth century? What might explain its return to more peaceful ways?

2. Countries often borrow ideas from other cultures. How did Japan's borrowing differ from simple copying? What traditions have been preserved?

3. The Japanese respect each other's privacy. How might the size of their population contribute to that attitude?

◯ PRACTICING SKILLS

Wind and Ocean Currents Use the maps and your skills lesson on pages 420–422 to answer these questions.

1. Would a sailing ship going from the United States to Japan in July make better time sailing at 40°N or 25°N? Why?

2. Would you likely find more fog along the Pacific coast of the United States or off the coast of China? Why?

3. Do cold currents or warm currents circulate through the Sea of Japan?

4. If you threw a corked bottle in the water off Hawaii, would it more likely travel east or west? Why?

5. Why do wind and ocean currents follow a circular pattern?

Asians Blend Old and New

Focus

Nearly a third of the Earth's land and more than half its people—this is the continent of Asia. In this unit, you have now read about three Asian countries. They are important countries, but they are only part of Asia.

In this chapter you will read more about Asia's lands and the types of people who live there. You will learn about three countries in Southeast Asia—Thailand, Indonesia, and the Philippines. Each country shares similar tasks with other developing Asian countries.

Look for these important words:

Key Words
- yaks
- malas
- Minangkabaus

People
- Dalai Lama

Places
- Indochina
- Plateau of Tibet
- Sumatra

Look for answers to these questions:

1. For what reasons is there such a wide variety of peoples in Asia?
2. What different ways of life do Asians follow?
3. What traditional ways of living can be found among the nomads of Tibet? among the Minangkabaus of Sumatra?

1. DIFFERENCES AMONG ASIANS

Asia contains 2.9 billion people. This is more than half the total population of the world. The nations of China and India alone make up more than a third of the world's people. In Indonesia and Bangladesh, some rural areas have more than 1,300 persons per square mile (2.6 sq km). In the United States, by comparison, the population density is 64 persons per square mile (2.6 sq km). Asian countries are among the most densely populated on Earth. Overpopulation is a problem for many Asian nations.

Except in a few countries, such as Japan, the great mass of Asians live mainly in small villages. The villages are located on the 10 percent of Asia's land that can produce crops. These areas are mainly in southern and eastern Asia.

With such a huge population, Asia has a variety of people. Asians differ in the way they look, the languages they speak, and the customs they follow.

Dravidians in south India have very dark skins and speak a different language from the lighter-skinned northern Indians. The Ainu of northern Japan seem unrelated not only to most Japanese but also to all other Asians. Certain groups in the hills of Laos, Burma, and Vietnam consider themselves much different from most other Southeast Asians.

Human groups have been moving and mixing on the Asian continent for many centuries. From plains near Europe have come groups to invade India. From Arab countries have come traders, many of whom stayed. Mongols from the central part of Asia continually invaded China. Meanwhile, the Chinese have for centuries moved south and east onto the peninsula called **Indochina** and the nearby islands.

Broad patterns of settlement can be found in Asia. From India west toward Afghanistan, Asia contains many people who resemble Europeans. Their

425

This Ainu woodworker belongs to a small tribe, which was one of the first to occupy the Japanese islands.

Descendants of Genghis Khan's powerful warriors, Mongolian people today keep many of their ancestors' traditions.

ancestors were Aryans who invaded the Indian peninsula 4,000 years ago.

East of India, people are more typically Asiatic. These people are the most numerous of all Asians. Their skin color is usually brownish-ivory. Their hair is straight and black. An inward fold of the upper eyelid is a common feature of most East Asians.

Finally, in outlying parts of India and Southeast Asia live darker-skinned people, whose hair may be curly. Their eyes have no inward folds. Many scientists believe they descend from the earliest inhabitants of Asia.

Asia is a rich mixture of peoples and ways of life. Here are two examples of Asian peoples who still follow traditional ways of life.

Nomads of Tibet

The **Plateau of Tibet** is the highest inhabited land on Earth. There are cities, such as Lhasa (LAHS•uh), in the lower plains. The higher plains and pastures, however, have always been home to nomads. Tibetan nomads are herders. Like many herders, they often need to find fresh grasslands for their herds of sheep, goats, ponies, and **yaks.** Yaks are a kind of long-haired cattle. Living in movable tents made of black yak hair, herders move with the seasons. In summer they drive their herds to pastures nearly 3 miles (about 5 km) high. In winter, snow and cold weather force them to return to lower valleys for grass. Many groups move at least three times a year.

Most Tibetan nomads live in small groups in five or six tents. Some larger groups have as many as 80 tents. Usually one family lives in each tent. The men tend the herds, train pack animals, and sometimes hunt. The women milk the yaks, make butter and cheese from yak milk, and collect fuel. They weave cloth and sew sheepskin clothing.

The herd is the nomads' most important possession. It provides food, clothing, housing, and products to trade. Tibetans drink their tea mixed with yak butter. Demand for the butter is therefore great. Nomads trade butter and also meat with other Tibetans. In return they get barley, tea, cloth, and tools. This trading usually takes place just after the fall harvest, when the nomads set up their winter camp.

Free to move whenever they choose, the nomads are a proud and independent people. They own their own herds.

They are skilled at riding ponies and at guiding travelers through difficult mountain passes. Their rugged life makes them fearsome warriors. A few, in fact, live as bandits who raid the herds of others.

Fall is a favorite time of year for the nomads. With everyone together, it is the season to arrange marriages. Parties and entertainments often last through the night. In cross-country races on their ponies, some nomads win prize cattle. Others simply show off their great skill at riding.

Like many people of Tibet, the nomads are Buddhists. Many braid their hair in multiples of nine, a sacred number. They wear the Buddhist **malas** (MAH•luhz), or prayer beads, around their necks. Many nomads send their sons to Buddhist monasteries to live as monks. This is considered a high honor among Tibetans.

Nomads herd yak in the treeless plateaus of Tibet. Yaks meet many of the nomads' needs. Yak chips provide the only fuel obtainable in these northern highlands.

427

Once most Tibetans were nomads. Then in 1950 a great change swept over Tibet. The People's Republic of China claimed Tibet as part of its territory. Its troops forced the Tibetan government to accept Chinese control. By 1959 all resistance was crushed. Tibet's leader, the **Dalai Lama** (dah•LEE LAH•muh), fled to India with thousands of followers. Many nomads also fled to camps in nearby Nepal. The Chinese closed Tibet to outsiders and tried to change it over to communist ways.

Today Tibet is much changed. Old cultural ways have been replaced by modern organization. Yet, reports say that in many places the nomads refuse to change. They carry on their old ways of life, herding and trading. No one is sure if they can do this for very long. Many of those who fled, however, still plan to return and take up the old ways again. For them, it is the only way.

The Dalai Lama now travels around the world, preaching to his followers.

The Minangkabaus

Sumatra is the westernmost island of Indonesia. It is a tropical land of rain forests, mountains, and swamps. Many different groups live on Sumatra. The **Minangkabaus** (mee•NAHNG•kuh•bowz) are the largest group. They live in villages in western Sumatra near the cities of Bukittinggi (boo•kuh•TING•jee) and Padang.

The name *Minangkabau* has an important part in the people's history. It means "triumphant water buffalo" and refers to an ancient legend. To save their land from an invading prince, the Minangkabaus proposed a fight to the death between their baby buffalo and the prince's giant champion buffalo.

The Minangkabaus secretly fitted the baby buffalo with sharp iron horns. The smaller animal won and the Minangkabaus were saved. In thanks, the people renamed their land after the baby buffalo.

The Minangkabaus also declared that the roofs of all houses should take the shape of buffalo horns. Such houses can still be seen. The pointed "horns" are really the sharpened ends of long poles. These poles raise the houses about 6 feet (about 2 m) off the ground. Houses with large families may have many such horns. Each represents a single family's own space within the house.

The Minangkabaus have been Muslims since the fourteenth century, when Arab traders brought their religion to Sumatra. This has not changed a very important tradition, however. Women have always been the owners of Minangkabau property. Women own the houses and name their children after

Though they are Muslims, the Minangkabaus have kept their tradition of passing property through women. This Minangkabau home shows the customary horned roof.

the mother's family. When a girl marries, she remains in her family's house. It is headed by a woman. Her husband visits her but lives in his own mother's house. Women and uncles, not fathers, care for the children.

The Minangkabaus have traditionally been farmers. Their terraced rice fields cover the hillsides near their villages. Abundant rainfall and irrigation provide water for the growing rice. An important part of each village is the community storage house for rice. The Minangkabaus raise tobacco, cinnamon, and several kinds of vegetables. They are expert woodcarvers and weavers.

In recent years some Minangkabaus have left their homeland. Many people migrated to nearby Malaysia. Some worked in the tin mines, while others worked at farming or set up stores. Men, especially, are likely to travel. Often they become very successful in business or politics. The Minangkabaus say that their way of life is one reason for the men's success. Without the usual roles of homeowner and father, Minangkabau men have more freedom to seek their fame.

Today, some of the Minangkabau ways have changed. Men may take their wives with them to other cities. Many traditional villages remain, however. Shared houses run by families of women still can be found. On holidays a favorite form of entertainment is still the water buffalo fights. Similar to bullfights, these matches continue to celebrate the legendary victory of the baby water buffalo.

Reading Check

1. Why do people in western Asia resemble Europeans?
2. In what ways do Tibetan nomads use the yak?
3. To where did many Tibetans flee in 1959?
4. What is unusual about the Minangkabau people?

Look for these important words:

Key Words
- humid
- bamboo
- raw materials

Places
- Chao Phraya
- Bali
- Malay Peninsula

Look for answers to these questions:

1. Which nations occupy the peninsula of Southeast Asia?
2. How have outside nations influenced Southeast Asia?
3. What problems have Southeast Asian nations faced since they gained independence?

2. SOUTHEAST ASIA

Several small nations make up the peninsula of Southeast Asia. They include Burma, Thailand, Laos, Kampuchea (kam•puh•CHEE•uh), Vietnam, and Malaysia. The island nations of Singapore, Indonesia, Brunei (BROO•ny), and the Philippines are also part of Southeast Asia.

Lying near the equator, most of Southeast Asia is hot and **humid,** or wet. Rainfall in many areas reaches more than 100 inches (about 3 m) a year. There are many rain forests that contain rare hardwoods as well as palm and rubber trees. **Bamboo,** a tall, strong, grasslike plant, also is plentiful. Spices, such as pepper and cinnamon, are important crops. Along such rivers as the Mekong, the Irrawaddy, and the **Chao Phraya** (CHOW PRY•uh) in Thailand, Southeast Asians grow large rice crops. Rice is the basic food of Southeast Asia and a major export.

Southeast Asia has long been a crossroads of peoples and cultures. From the earliest times Chinese have migrated south to mix with native peoples. Vietnam and Thailand especially have been influenced by Chinese ways of life.

Indian traders also have been coming to the peninsula and the islands since before the time of Christ. Their culture left lasting marks. Hindu practices are still followed on the Indonesian island of **Bali** (BAHL•ee). Buddhism became the major religion of Burma and Thailand. Muslim traders from India brought their religion to Malaysia, Indonesia, and parts of the Philippines.

Colonies in Southeast Asia

Beginning in the 1500s Western nations gained colonies in Southeast Asia. Led by the Portuguese, they came first for the precious spices of the "Indies." Spain later sent missionaries to convert the Philippines. Dutch traders won control of the islands of Indonesia. During the nineteenth century,

430

the English occupied Burma and the **Malay Peninsula,** which contains Malaysia and part of Thailand. The French took over much of Vietnam and Kampuchea. Everywhere the Europeans set up plantations, where natives worked for low wages. **Raw materials** went back to Europe to be turned into finished goods. Raw materials are natural resources, such as wood, that can be made into useful products. Southeast Asian cities, such as Singapore, became centers of European culture.

Japan was the next nation to invade Southeast Asia. In search of raw materials for its growing industries, Japan in the 1930s began its campaign to take over the South Pacific. During World War II its armies conquered the Philippines, Indonesia, and most of Southeast Asia as far west as Burma. At first, many national leaders welcomed the Japanese for freeing Asia from European rule. Soon, however, most people realized that the Japanese military brought harsh rule. Many Southeast Asians joined the fight against Japan.

Once they had helped defeat the Japanese, nation after nation demanded freedom. Some nations succeeded quickly. The Philippines gained independence from the United States in 1946. Burma became free of England in 1948. In some places more fighting was necessary. Four years of war were needed to free Indonesia from the Dutch. It took many years of bloodshed before France agreed to an independent Vietnam in 1954.

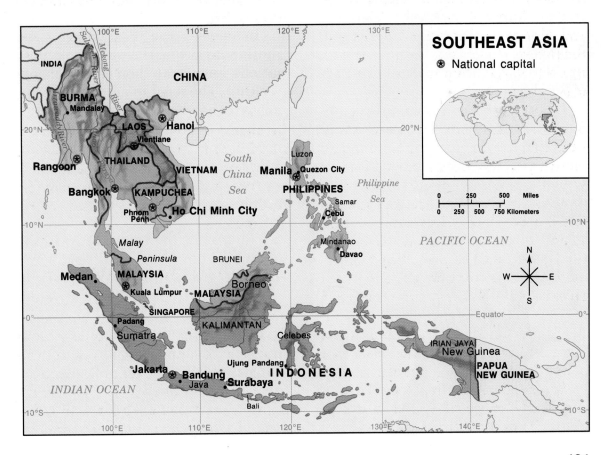

Southeast Asia Today

Independence has not meant the end of trouble for most Southeast Asian nations. Industrial development has been slow. Large populations require numerous resources. The political power in many nations rests in the hands of single rulers. Often they are generals who have seized power. Southeast Asians have little control over their governments.

One reason for military rule is that Southeast Asia continues to be an area of struggle between the major powers.

Fighting continues between communists and noncommunists in Kampuchea.

Following Vietnam's independence from France, communists fought to gain control of the country. The long conflict involved thousands of United States troops and eventually spilled over into neighboring Cambodia. The United States was helping South Vietnam fight communist North Vietnam. As the fight continued, opposition to American involvement grew in the United States. American forces withdrew in 1973.

Today all of Vietnam is under communist rule, while fighting continues in communist-controlled Cambodia, now known as Kampuchea. Soviet-backed Vietnamese communists fight against the Chinese-backed Kampucheans. Millions of peasants have been killed or left homeless. Thousands have fled these war-torn countries.

Communists also have been active in Indonesia, the Philippines, and Thailand. So far, the rulers of these nations have kept their governments working. The need to prepare for war, however, has used valuable resources that most nations need for development. Meanwhile, many people live in poverty.

Reading Check

1. What plants and crops grow in the humid climate of Southeast Asia?
2. Name two cultures that strongly influenced the people of Southeast Asia.
3. Why were Europeans and Japanese interested in colonizing Southeast Asia?
4. How was the United States involved in the political struggles in Southeast Asia?

432

Bamboo, the Magic Grass

It has been called the most useful plant that grows on the Earth. It is a kind of grass. It bends like grass, but it can be as strong as steel. Some kinds grow so fast that, if you are patient, you can watch them grow almost 2 inches (5.1 cm) per hour. No other plant in the world grows more quickly. No other plant in the world has so many uses for animals and people alike. No other grass is like bamboo.

Bamboo is made up of strong hollow stalks called culms. The outside of a culm is strong and shiny. It can be carved on, like the bark of a tree. Along the culm are joints called nodes. These help to give bamboo stalks their strength. Bamboo can be very small, or it can grow to be 120 feet (36.6 m) high and 12 inches (30.5 cm) wide.

The young bamboo shoot, or sprout, can be boiled and eaten. It is a favorite food, especially of the Chinese. Some other parts of the bamboo are used as medicine. Prepared in special ways, bamboo parts are used to cure fever, prickly heat, coughs, and other ailments.

There is one creature on Earth who enjoys bamboo perhaps even more than people do. That is the panda. Pandas love to eat bamboo, every part of it. They will devour the hard, stringy culms as well as the young, tender shoots.

Bamboo's uses in construction are an example of its flexible strength and durability. Some strong kinds of bamboo are used to reinforce concrete the way steel cables are used in large buildings in the United States. As a material for scaffolds, bamboo is much more useful than steel because it is flexible. Bamboo scaffolds on tall buildings, fastened together with tied strips of bamboo, have been known to withstand powerful typhoons.

Bamboo is especially common in Asian countries. It is used to build cradles. It is used to make paper and as a pleasing food. It is made into walking canes and is used in funeral ceremonies. Bamboo plays a part in Asian life from cradle to coffin.

Bamboo grove

Giant panda

Bamboo flutes
(instruments)

Look for these important words:

Key Words
- teak
- klongs
- betjaks
- wayang kulit
- dwarf rice
- barrios
- protectorate

- abaca
- martial law

People
- King Mongkut
- Anna Leonowens
- Prem Tinsulanonda
- Rama IX

- Sukarno
- General Suharto
- Ferdinand Marcos

Places
- Bangkok
- Jakarta
- Manila

Look for answers to these questions:

1. How are the countries of Thailand, Indonesia, and the Philippines alike? How are they different?
2. What outside cultures have influenced each of these nations?
3. What problems does each of these nations face?

3. THREE NATIONS OF SOUTHEAST ASIA

The people of Thailand, Indonesia, and the Philippines are developing modern, secure nations. In some ways these nations are similar. In other ways there are striking differences.

Thailand

Thailand is a small country located in the heart of the Southeast Asian peninsula. It is a land of mountain forests and rivers. The climate is tropical, with average temperatures of 75° F (23.9° C). Colorful plants and fruits thrive in this country where tigers, panthers, and monkeys roam.

Most of Thailand's people live on a large central plain watered by the Chao Phraya River. The capital city, **Bangkok,** is located on this river. Rice farming is the main occupation on the central plain. To the north are rich forests of **teak,** still harvested by elephants. Teak is a hard wood often used to build ships or fine furniture. To the south, on the Malay Peninsula, rubber plantations and tin mines provide much of Thailand's exports.

The name *Thailand* means "land of the free." This is a reminder that the country has been independent since the fourteenth century, when it was called Siam (sy•AM). While nearby nations became European colonies, Siam in the 1600s cast out all foreigners and forbade contact with outsiders. Not until the 1850s did **King Mongkut** (Rama IV) reopen Siam to Western influence. He introduced Western science. He signed treaties of trade with France, Great Britain, and the United States. He hired an Englishwoman, **Anna**

434

Leonowens, to teach his children. A book called *Anna and the King of Siam* tells of her adventures.

King Mongkut's heirs continued to change Siam. In 1932 Siam adopted a constitution. Two houses of parliament began to share rule with the king. A prime minister became chief of state. In 1939 the country's name became Thailand.

The Peoples of Thailand

Many of Thailand's almost 52 million people are descendants of southern Chinese who were driven from China by Kublai Khan, the Mongol ruler. They settled in Thailand in the twelfth century.

More recent immigrants from China also play a major role in modern Thailand. They make up about half the population of Bangkok, and they control much of Thailand's trade.

In addition, such groups as the Meos and the Karens live in the northern mountains. They maintain ancient languages, customs, and ways of life. Their ancestors are believed to be the original peoples of Thailand.

Like many other Asian nations, Thailand is mainly a rural country. Most of its people are rice farmers and live in villages. Some raise other crops such as sugar cane, cotton, and tobacco. Vegetables and tropical fruit, such as mangoes and bananas, are also important crops.

Years of difficult training prepared this woman to perform a Thai dance.

This woman is from the Meo tribe, a rugged and independent people.

435

In some parts of Thailand, klong markets are the only source of fresh vegetables.

Bangkok's Chinatown is a busy area crowded with people and cars.

Some of Thailand's crops get to market by waterways. Rivers and canals called **klongs** lace the countryside as well as the city of Bangkok. Houseboats line the rivers, while smaller boats fill the canals. Floating markets filled with vegetables are a common sight.

Thailand's Resources

In recent years Thailand's leaders have been developing more industry. Some factories produce cement, lumber, and textiles. Most industry, however, involves such farm products as rice and rubber. Even the important cotton and silk industries still use mostly hand labor.

Except for the tin mines in the south, Thailand's rich mineral resources remain largely undeveloped. Yet, Thailand is one of Southeast Asia's most prosperous countries. Farmers grow enough rice to export large quantities to its main trading partner, Japan. New highways and railroads are replacing crowded klongs. Goods are transported in larger quantities and more quickly.

During the 1970s Thailand was struck with such problems as rising prices and threats of war. The continuing conflict in neighboring Kampuchea spilled into Thailand's territory. Vietnamese at times invaded Thai villages. This armed threat from nearby Communists caused Thailand to spend extra money on arms.

These problems led to dissatisfaction with the government, which changed several times. Today, Thailand's problems rest on the shoulders of a general, **Prem Tinsulanonda** (TIN•soo•lah•nohnd). Along with the much respected king, **Rama IX,** Prime Minister Prem is working to improve the lives of the country's rural poor. Many farmers have received land from the government.

Bangkok needs improvements, too. It is more than 200 years old and terribly crowded. Traffic congestion is only one of the resulting problems. Increased use of water from city wells is lowering the land. Bangkok is slowly sinking. The government plans to build new cities to make more room for Thailand's population. Many nations hope that Thailand's tradition of national unity will set an example for other developing Asian countries.

Indonesia

The nation of Indonesia includes 13,500 islands that stretch more than 3,000 miles (4,827 km) from east to west. They form the world's largest archipelago. The major islands are Java, Sumatra, Kalimantan (part of Borneo), Irian Jaya (IR•ee•ahn JAH•yuh), part of New Guinea, and Celebes (SEL•uh•beez), also called Sulawesi (soo•luh•WAY•see).

The islands of Indonesia are all on the equator or slightly south of it. This means that Indonesia has a hot climate and abundant rainfall year round. The rain forests of Indonesia are home to the only orangutans (oh•RANG•uh•tanz) left on Earth. On another small island, Komodo, scientists discovered a unique lizard. Called the Komodo dragon, it often grows to a length of more than 10 feet (about 3 m).

Java is Indonesia's most important island. The capital, **Jakarta** (juh•KAHRT•uh), is there. It is the main trading and travel center of Indonesia. Modern buildings line its wide boulevards. During business hours, the streets are crowded with a noisy mix of cars, trucks, bicycles, motorcycles, and **betjaks.** Betjaks are three-wheeled cabs powered by bicycle drivers.

There are other cities on Java, but much of the land is rural. Farming villages surrounded by rice fields share the island with mountains and rain

Mild-mannered orangutans nest in the trees of Indonesia's rain forests.

Betjak drivers hoping for customers wait on the crowded streets of Jakarta.

forests. There are more than 100 volcanoes on Java. One-third of them are active and 18 have recently erupted. The people both fear and depend on these volcanoes, for it is volcanic ash that enriches the soil. The most fertile rice fields are clustered around volcanic mountains.

The Peoples of Indonesia

Indonesia has 169 million people. It is the third-most populous nation in Asia, after China and India. This large population is not spread evenly. Two-thirds of the Indonesians live on the island of Java. This gives some parts of Java one of the highest population densities in the world—1,500 people per square mile (2.6 sq km).

Indonesians are descended from the Malays, who came from Asia's

mainland around 2500 B.C. Indian traders began to come to the islands around 500 B.C. They introduced Indian culture and religion. Other Indian influences are visible in two famous ruins on Java. Borobudur (bohr•oh•boo•DOOR) is a stone monument dating from the eighth century A.D. It is the largest Buddhist retreat in the world. Not far away is Prambanan (prahm•BAHN•ahn), a ninth-century Hindu temple group.

Hindu influence is also strong in Indonesia's famous theater form, **wayang kulit,** or shadow play. Often lasting all night, these plays enchant Indonesian villagers everywhere. A single puppeteer moves leather figures behind a lighted cloth screen. The figures form shadows on the screen. The shadow figures represent characters from ancient Indian epics, such as the *Ramayana.* Many traditional

The great Hindu shrine at Prambanan is surrounded by 124 miniature temples.

Sharp-jointed puppets like this one perform in Indonesian shadow plays.

In addition to spices and coffee, rubber became an important Indonesian product in the early 1900s. Here, an Indonesian taps a tree to get the milky latex from which rubber is made.

Indonesian ideas, such as respect for authority, are expressed in the shadow plays.

Arab traders from India were the next group to leave a lasting mark in Indonesia. They brought the religion of Islam. Ninety percent of Indonesia's people now practice this religion. Though mixed with older Indonesian beliefs in nature spirits, Muslim ceremonies and duties are central in village life.

From a Colony to a Nation

Indonesia's spices, mainly pepper and cinnamon, later attracted Europeans to these "Spice Islands." In 1597 the Dutch defeated other European traders and took control of the islands. Later the islands became known as the Dutch East Indies. This colony provided the Dutch a wealth of spices and coffee for more than 300 years. Only after World War II and four years of fighting did Indonesia become an independent nation. In 1949 the Indonesian leader **Sukarno** (soo•KAR•noh) became the first president of the republic.

Indonesia's independence has not been without problems. A few wealthy families live rich lives. Yet, nearly half of Indonesia's villagers have no land and live in poverty. In the 1960s this inequality led to a communist uprising. When the Indonesian Communist party tried to set up a communist state in 1965, a military leader, **General Suharto** (soo•HAR•toh), took control.

Suharto crushed the Communists and became president in 1967. Since then Indonesians have worked to improve their country. Large oil resources and an increase in the demand for rubber and coffee have also contributed to Indonesia's profitable trade.

Another recent improvement has come in farming. Many Indonesians have begun to use a new type of rice called **dwarf rice.** Dwarf rice is a sturdy rice that grows quickly and produces a large crop. It has doubled the crop production of farmers who can afford it. It has resulted in prosperity for other villagers, too. Landowners can hire more labor. They can afford to hire workers to build new homes.

Perhaps most importantly, Indonesia's population growth has slowed for the first time in many years. Fewer villagers are leaving their homes to live in crowded cities. Some city-dwellers are returning to live in their villages. Thus far, Indonesia has experienced success as a developing industrial nation. It is one of the most prosperous countries in Southeast Asia.

The Philippines

The nation of the Philippines seems in many ways typical of Southeast Asia. It is an archipelago of more than 7,000 islands running north to south in the Pacific Ocean. Its climate is tropical, with rain much of the year. Typhoons often strike. Most islands are mountainous and forest covered. Rice fields cover the plains and many terraced hills.

The people of the Philippines are mostly Malayan villagers who live on the largest islands: Luzon, Cebu, Leyte (LAHT•ee), and Mindanao (min•duh•NAH•oh). As elsewhere in Southeast Asia, the hills and distant villages are home to darker-skinned groups descended from the original peoples. In contrast to these villages are modern cities, such as **Manila,** the capital city.

Western Influence

Some major differences set the Philippines apart from other Southeast Asian countries. Most Filipinos have Spanish names. One well-known president, for example, was **Ferdinand Marcos.** Most Filipinos speak not only native languages such as Tagalog (tah•GAH•lahg) but also Spanish and English. Roman Catholicism is the main religion. Instead of Oriental temples, Spanish-style churches are found in villages and cities.

A Tasaday scrapes pulp from a wild palm, the small tribe's major food source.

Throughout the Philippines, too, American culture is felt. Pop music plays over radios. American movies play in theaters. Children in villages called **barrios** (BAR•ree•ohz) read American comic books. Many people even wear American-style clothing.

Philippine history helps to explain this Western influence. In 1521 the Spanish explorer Ferdinand Magellan landed on the island of Samar. He claimed the islands for Spain. Within a short time Spanish troops had conquered the islands. They renamed them *Las Felipinas,* the Philippines, after the Spanish King Philip II. The Philippines remained a Spanish colony for 333 years. Spanish priests converted most Filipinos to Catholicism and established Spanish customs on most islands.

An American Protectorate

In 1896 the Philippine people revolted against the Spanish. At the same time the United States was fighting a war with the Spanish over Cuba. The American navy in the Pacific joined the Filipinos and helped them defeat the Spanish by 1898. The Filipinos then claimed independence.

The United States, however, decided that the islands were not yet ready for self-government. After defeating the Philippine nationalists, the United States made the islands an American **protectorate.** A protectorate is a territory protected and controlled by another country. Only after the end of World War II in 1946 did the Philippines gain complete independence.

American rule had a strong effect on the Philippines. To prepare the

The Roxas Boulevard stretches along Manila Bay, passing modern buildings, restaurants, homes of wealthy Manilans and the United States embassy.

Public schools provide four years of free education for Philippine children.

Other important crops are sugar, coconuts, bananas, and **abaca** (ab•uh•KAW), a valuable hemp used to make rope.

As in other parts of Asia, dwarf rice has made larger crops possible. Many Philippine farmers have not been able to use these new grains, however. In the Philippines much of the farmland belongs to landlords, who receive one-fourth of the crop as rent. This means that the tenant farmers who work the land often make no profit. They cannot afford to pay for chemicals and fertilizers needed for the new grains. The landowners get wealthier while the farmers become poorer.

Landless farmers in the Philippines, therefore, became dissatisfied with their government. Some joined groups who were fighting the government. In 1972 President Marcos declared **martial law,** or rule by the military. He brutally stopped opposition to his power.

Early in 1986 the people of the Philippines forced Marcos to give up his presidency and to flee the country. A new government is now faced with such problems as poverty and unemployment. The future prosperity of the Philippines will depend on the success of this new government.

Reading Check

1. What does the name *Thailand* mean? What does the name tell you about its history?
2. How have volcanoes affected agriculture in Indonesia?
3. What is dwarf rice?
4. In what ways have the Spanish and the Americans influenced the Philippines?

people for self-rule, Americans set up schools and universities everywhere. Today more than 88 percent of Filipinos can read and write. There are more than 40 universities in the country.

The American model influenced government and business, too. The Philippines has a two-house legislature and an elected president. The number of factories has increased. Thousands of miles of highways link the island towns and cities. Unlike most Asian nations, the Philippines has a fairly large middle class.

Farming in the Philippines

Rich soil and plentiful rainfall make farming the main business in the Philippines. Rice is the most important crop.

SKILLS FOR SUCCESS

USING GREAT CIRCLES

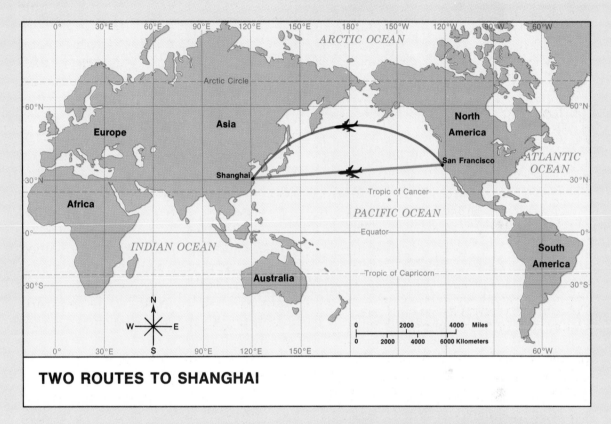

TWO ROUTES TO SHANGHAI

Two planes are flying from San Francisco, California, to Shanghai, China. This map shows their routes. The red route extends from the west coast of the United States south of Alaska to the east coast of the Soviet Union. The green route stretches across the Pacific Ocean south of Japan. Which plane is taking the shorter route?

On a flat map like this one, the straight route looks shorter. A flat map, however, does not show the world as it really is. An airplane has to fly around the curved surface of the Earth. To measure these routes accurately, you must use a globe.

Find San Francisco and Shanghai on a globe. Use a piece of string to measure the shortest route between them. (It will cross Alaska, the USSR, and North Korea.) Lay another piece of string along the route that was straight on the flat map. Compare the two strings. You will see that the route that follows the curve of the Earth is shorter than the straight route on the flat map.

Next, look at Globe A on the next page. Notice that the curved route is part of a complete circle around the globe. This circle is called a **great circle.** The shortest distance between two places on a globe is always on a great circle.

A great circle divides the Earth into two halves. The equator (Globe B) is one great circle. It goes around the middle of the Earth,

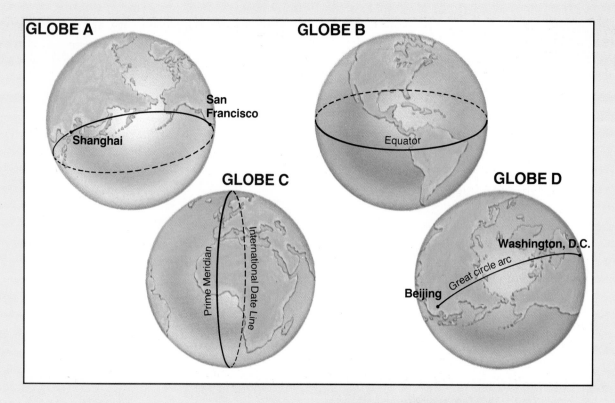

GLOBE A

San Francisco

Shanghai

GLOBE B

Equator

GLOBE C

Prime Meridian

International Date Line

GLOBE D

Washington, D.C.

Great circle arc

Beijing

dividing it into the Northern and Southern hemispheres. Another great circle (Globe C) is formed by the prime meridian (0° longitude) and the International Date Line (180° longitude). It divides the Earth into Eastern and Western hemispheres. All other meridians form great circles, too. In fact, *any* line that divides the Earth in half is a great circle. The line can run in any direction.

Look at Globe D. Two dots appear on this great circle. One marks Washington, D.C.; the other marks Beijing, the capital of China. The part of the great circle between these two cities is called a **great circle arc.** An *arc* is part of a circle. A great circle arc is the shortest distance between two places.

On your globe, find the shortest route between Washington, D.C., and Beijing. Does it follow the same arc as on Globe D?

Great circles are important to pilots and navigators. They help determine the shortest routes between places. Following great circle routes saves time and fuel.

CHECKING YOUR SKILLS

Use a globe and a piece of string to answer the following questions.

1. A ship travels from San Diego, California, stops in Honolulu, Hawaii, and then goes on to Tokyo, Japan. Is this a great circle route?

2. You are traveling from Paris, France, to Bombay, India. Is the shortest route over land or sea?

3. Is the shortest route between New York City, New York, and Beijing, China, across Europe or over the North Pole?

4. Should a plane flying between Washington, D.C., and Moscow refuel in Iceland or in Greece if it is to make the shorter trip?

5. Do any lines of latitude, or parallels, form great circles? Think carefully before you explain your answer.

CHAPTER 15 REVIEW

USING WORDS

Number your paper from 1 to 5. Write the letter of the definition that matches each of the words below.

1. **humid**
2. **martial law**
3. **protectorate**
4. **raw materials**
5. **yaks**

a. long-haired cattle
b. wet
c. natural resources that can be made into useful products
d. territory protected by another country
e. rule by military law

REVIEWING FACTS

1. Why is there such a wide variety of people in Asia?

2. What happened to the nomads of Tibet?

3. Which European nation colonized each of the following countries?

   a. Burma   b. Vietnam   c. Indonesia

4. Why do many Southeast Asian nations have military rulers?

5. Which group of immigrants controls most of Thailand's trade?

6. Communist fighting in which neighboring country has caused problems in Thailand?

7. What island has the highest population density in the world? Of which nation is it a part?

8. What has contributed to Indonesia's profitable trade?

9. List two ways that the Philippines is similar to other Southeast Asian nations. List two ways in which it is different.

10. Why were farmers in the Philippines dissatisfied with their government?

THINKING CRITICALLY

1. Suppose you were part of a large group of people who had to leave Europe and settle in Asia. In which region would you settle? What way of life would you prefer to follow? Explain your choice.

2. Some people have predicted that Southeast and East Asia will become the fastest-growing regions in the world. On what do you think the economic success of these areas will depend?

⬤ PRACTICING SKILLS

Great Circles   Use a globe and the skills lesson on pages 443–444 to tell if the following statements are true or false.

1. The shortest distance between any two points on Earth is always a straight line.

2. All meridians form great circles.

3. The great circle route between Chicago and Moscow crosses the country of Greenland.

4. A plane flying the shortest distance between Anchorage and Los Angeles would fly over western Canada.

CHAPTER 16

Pacific Nations Blend Europe with Asia

Focus

People often think of Australia and New Zealand as branches of Great Britain transplanted to the Pacific Ocean. Most people are of British ancestry, and their customs reflect this heritage.

These two Southern Hemisphere nations, however, have a physical environment very different from Great Britain's. As a result, Australians and New Zealanders have created cultures uniquely their own. Today, they value their British heritage while adapting to the Asian-Pacific community in which they play important parts.

Look for these important words:

Key Words
- coral
- stations
- outback
- bauxite

Places
- Oceania
- Great Dividing Range
- Great Barrier Reef
- Sydney
- Murray river system
- Auckland
- Canterbury Plain

Look for answers to these questions:

1. What are Australia's three regions? What are New Zealand's two main islands?
2. Describe the land, climate, and resources of Australia's three regions and New Zealand's two islands.
3. Where do most Australians live?

1. THE LANDS "DOWN UNDER"

In the south and central Pacific Ocean, there are thousands of islands. Together these islands are called **Oceania.** Some are so small they look like dots on a map, while one is so large it is the seventh continent.

Sometimes called the "island continent," Australia is the smallest of the world's continents but the sixth-largest nation. Its area is a little less than that of the continental United States excluding Alaska. It is the only continent covered by a single nation.

Australia lies south and east of Asia, with the Indian Ocean off its western and southern coasts. The Arafura and Coral seas are to the north, and the Pacific Ocean to the east. Its nearest neighbor to the north is the island of New Guinea, containing Irian Jaya, a part of Indonesia, and Papua New Guinea. Its other large neighbor

is New Zealand (about the size of Colorado), which consists mainly of two islands about 1,200 miles (1,950 km) to the southeast.

Most of Australia is hot and dry. Over two-thirds of the country receives less than 20 inches (50 cm) of rain a year, and temperatures over 100°F (38°C) are common in its central deserts. The coastal areas, particularly in the southeast and southwest, have a more moderate climate.

Australia is mostly a land of plains. The few mountain ranges it has are located just inland from the eastern and western coasts, but erosion has flattened most of the rest of the land. Australia's six states and two territories can be divided into three geographical regions: the Eastern Highlands, the Central Lowlands, and the Western Plateau.

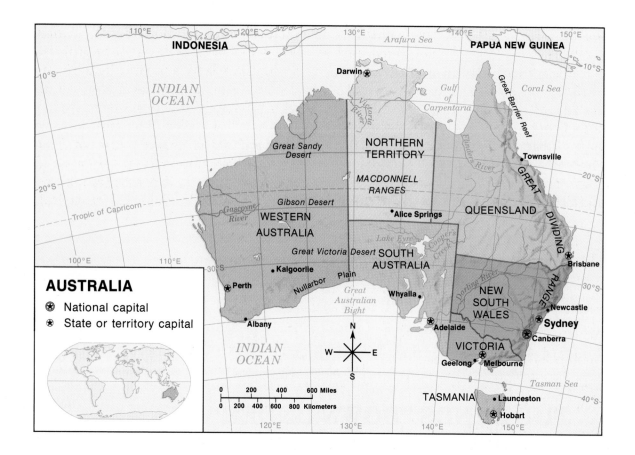

AUSTRALIA
⊛ National capital
⊛ State or territory capital

The Eastern Highlands

The Eastern Highlands have the most varied geography and climate, and also by far the largest population, of Australia's three regions. Four of Australia's six states share this third of the country. The coastal area, which contains the nation's largest cities, is separated from the interior by the **Great Dividing Range.** Land west of these mountains is much drier than that of the coast.

Queensland, in the north, is Australia's second-largest state. Its northern coast has a hot, humid climate in which tropical rain forests mix with plantations growing sugar cane and pineapples.

Just off Queensland's east coast lies the **Great Barrier Reef,** one of the natural wonders of the world. This 1,200-mile (1,950-km) underwater structure is made of over 300 kinds of **coral.** Coral is formed by the skeletons of millions of tiny sea animals. Colorful tropical fish thrive along the reef, which contains more life per square inch than any other place on Earth.

Brisbane, Queensland's capital, is near the state's southern coast. Sunny beaches just south of this area are called the Gold Coast. In southwestern Queensland are large sheep and cattle ranches, called **stations.** Parts of the interior are also rich in minerals such as copper and uranium.

South of Queensland lies New South Wales, Australia's oldest state. Its capital, **Sydney,** is Australia's oldest and largest city. Melbourne, the second-largest city, is the capital of Victoria, a state in the southern part of the Eastern Highlands.

Many landowners in New South Wales and Victoria raise both sheep and wheat, Australia's largest grain crop. Their land is irrigated by the **Murray river system,** Australia's main river system. The continent's highest mountains are also located in Victoria and in New South Wales. Minerals found in these mountains include silver, lead, and zinc. In addition, it was in the mountains of New South Wales that gold was first discovered.

About 150 miles (244 km) south of Victoria is the island state of Tasmania. Tasmania is mountainous and has many forests. It is also famous for its apple orchards. Hobart is its capital.

Colonies of small fish live among the varied formations of vividly colored coral on the Great Barrier Reef. The living coral attaches itself to the skeletons of dead coral and traps the food on which the fish feed.

The Central Lowlands

Australia's first British settlers lived on the east coast. They thought of the land west of the Great Dividing Range as "out back" of the mountains. The central part of Australia is still called the **outback.** The northern and southern coastal areas of the outback contain good grazing land, but most of central Australia is desert. Its red sands are scattered with stones, scrubby bushes, and tufts of spiky grass. Parts of this low central plain are covered by dry salt "lakes" such as Lake Eyre, the lowest place on the continent. It is 52 feet (16 m) below sea level.

West of Lake Eyre, in the Great Victoria Desert, temperatures can climb as high as 127°F (53°C). The discovery of opals there has led miners to adapt to their environment in an unusual way. To escape the summer heat, the residents of tiny Coober Pedy live entirely underground!

The Central Lowlands are divided into two parts, the state of South Australia and the Northern Territory. Parts of the northern coast, including the area near Darwin, the territory capital, are hot and humid. This area contains **bauxite** (BAWK•syt), the mineral from which aluminum is made. Australia is one of the world's major producers of bauxite.

Southeastern South Australia has a more moderate climate than the rest of the Central Lowlands. Farms and orchards are found near the state capital, Adelaide.

Rising more than 1,000 feet (305 m) from the desert floor, Ayers Rock is the world's largest monolith (single block of stone). The Rock is more than 2 miles (3.2 km) long and 1 mile (1.6 km) wide.

An Australian family enjoys a day in Kings Park overlooking the Swan River and the skyline of Perth. Perth has one of the most pleasant climates in Australia.

The Western Plateau

The land rises again in the western part of Australia, though much of it remains relatively flat. This Western Plateau takes up more than half the continent. It includes parts of the Northern Territory and South Australia, as well as all of Western Australia, the country's largest state. Like the Central Lowlands, most of the interior of the Western Plateau is desert.

Mountains separate the coast of Western Australia from the interior. The mountains are not as tall or as continuous as in the east, however. Huge reserves of iron ore and gold have been found in the western mountains.

Most of Western Australia's people live in its capital, Perth, on the southwestern coast. Like Sydney and Melbourne, Perth is famous for its parks and beaches and for its warm, pleasant climate.

New Zealand's Two Islands

People on New Zealand's two main islands are always within 80 miles (130 km) of the Pacific's cooling breezes. They enjoy a moderate climate of cool summers and mild winters. Unlike Australia, New Zealand has adequate rainfall and no deserts.

Many mountains on North Island, including some around New Zealand's largest city, **Auckland,** are extinct volcanoes. Active volcanoes on North Island include those at Rotorua (roh•toh•ROO•uh).

Much of North Island's eastern half is pastureland and farmland. Sheep, which provide New Zealand's main exports of meat and wool, can be seen everywhere. Dairy cattle are also common. Wellington, the country's capital and second-largest city, is on the southern tip of North Island.

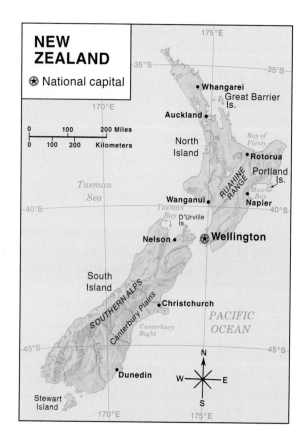

Auckland, with harbors on two sides, reflects New Zealanders' preference for living in single-family homes rather than highrise apartments.

452

From South Island's Canterbury Plain rise New Zealand's mountains. Here shepherds and dogs tend a flock of sheep.

South Island has higher mountains and a cooler climate than North Island. The heavily forested Southern Alps lie along South Island's western side. The beautiful mountain scenery, as well as hiking, skiing, and fishing, attracts many tourists. Just as in Scandinavia thousands of miles to the northwest, parts of the western coastline are cut by fjords carved by glaciers long ago. Other glaciers still move down the mountains, and the many rivers provide hydroelectric power.

Sheep and cattle stations and wheat farms fill **Canterbury Plain** on the eastern side of South Island. This is the largest area of flat land in New Zealand. South Island's largest city is Christchurch, on the northeastern coast.

Reading Check

1. Why do you think most Australians live on the country's east coast?
2. What is the land like in most of central and western Australia?
3. What important resources have been found in Western Australia's mountains?
4. What are New Zealand's two main exports?

HIGHLIGHT

Kangaroo with joey

Koala

Amazing Animals "Down Under"

Most animals native to Australia and New Zealand are found nowhere else on Earth. Many of these animals are marsupials (mahr•SOO•pee•uhls). Female marsupials carry their babies in pouches on their bodies.

The biggest Australian marsupial is the kangaroo, which may grow to be 7 feet (2 m) tall. The kangaroo usually stands upright on its big hind feet, using its long tail for balance. The powerful feet let it leap up to 27 feet (8 m) at a time. Kangaroos eat grass and brush on the Australian plains. Baby kangaroos are called joeys. Wallabies and wallaroos are small kinds of kangaroos.

The koala (kuh•WAHL•uh) is another Australian marsupial. This small, shy animal looks like a teddy bear. Its name means "I don't drink." In fact, koalas get all the moisture they need by eating leaves of the tall eucalyptus (yoo•kuh•LIP•tuhs) trees in which they live.

The platypus (PLAT•uh•puhs) is a very strange creature, combining features of mammals, birds, and reptiles. It has a broad, soft bill and webbed feet like a duck and a beaverlike tail. It has soft fur like a mammal, yet it hatches its young from eggs. It lives in streams and eats insects and small water creatures.

New Zealand's national bird is the kiwi (KEE•wee). It has a long, narrow bill and stubby wings. The kiwi lives in a burrow, or hole in the ground, and cannot fly. The female kiwi lays a single huge egg. Then the male sits on the egg until it hatches.

In Australia, the male emu (EE•myoo) also takes care of the eggs. He even takes care of the chicks after they have hatched. The emu is one of the world's largest birds, growing up to 5 feet (1.5 m) tall. Like the kiwi, the emu cannot fly. It can, however, run as fast as a horse in full gallop. Emus live on the grass, fruit, and insects found in the interior of Australia.

Many other strange animals live "down under," as well. It is truly an amazing natural "zoo"!

Platypus

Kiwi

Look for these important words:

Key Words
- Aborigines
- Maoris
- pas
- transportation
- Treaty of Waitangi
- commonwealth

People
- Abel Tasman
- James Cook
- Matthew Flinders
- Edward Gibbon Wakefield

Places
- New Holland
- Nullarbor Plain
- Canberra

Look for answers to these questions:

1. How were Australia and New Zealand settled by Europeans?
2. How did Australia and New Zealand become independent nations?
3. How did Australia and New Zealand change after World War II?

2. BRITISH OUTPOSTS IN THE PACIFIC

The **Aborigines** (ab·uh·RIJ·uh·neez) are Australia's dark-skinned natives. They probably arrived from Southeast Asia more than 10,000 years ago—and perhaps even as much as 50,000 years ago. They hunted with boomerangs and woomeras (WOO·muhr·uhs), or spearthrowers. Women and children gathered seeds and edible plants. The Aborigines developed many ways of finding water and adapting to their harsh environment.

The **Maoris** (MOW·reez), New Zealand's natives, arrived much later than the Aborigines. These tall, brown-skinned people are Polynesians, like natives of Hawaii and other Pacific islands. Maori legends say that around A.D. 1300 seven large canoes carried their people from Tahiti to New Zealand. On North Island they built fortified villages called **pas.**

Boomerangs in this dream painting show how Aborigines used art to pray to the gods for help in hunting.

British naval man and explorer, Captain James Cook studies his maps. For more than ten years he charted the lands of the South Pacific Ocean. He was awarded a medal for the healthy conditions on board his ships.

The Unknown Southern Land

The Dutch were the first Europeans to visit Australia. In the early seventeenth century, several Dutch explorers sailed along the west coast of Australia, which they called **New Holland.** Most were looking for new trade routes to Asia. In 1642 **Abel Tasman** discovered the island named after him and then sailed east, finding New Zealand. A second voyage in 1644 took Tasman along the northern coast of Australia.

Tasman was seeking *Terra Australis Incognita,* the "unknown southern land." Egyptian, Greek, and Incan legends had told of this land, and a vague outline of it had appeared on some maps from the Middle Ages.

A century later, in 1769, the great British explorer, Captain **James Cook,** rediscovered New Zealand. He then sailed north along the east coast of Australia, landing at Botany Bay. Here Cook saw the Aborigines, who first confronted, then ran away from, the newcomers. Cook described the land as having an "agreeable variety of hills, ridges, valleys, and large plains."

Convict Colonies

Cook claimed the entire eastern coast in the name of King George III, calling the colony New South Wales. After the American Revolution, the British needed a new place to send convicts sentenced to **transportation,** or serving time in a distant colony. New South Wales seemed a likely spot.

The first shipload of convicts, with their military guards, provisions, and livestock, landed on the east coast in 1788. They established a settlement there, calling it Sydney.

At first the settlement struggled to survive. Supply ships did not arrive, the convicts were not skilled at farming or manual labor, crops failed, and famine set in. As the colony eventually became better established, some of the military guards and other free settlers started farms and the wool industry. The convicts had to work for the free settlers until they finished serving their sentences. Many convicts then remained in Australia to start farms or businesses of their own.

Desert Sands, Golden Rocks

The boldest Australians soon set out to see how far their land extended. **Matthew Flinders,** a naval officer, began sailing around and charting the continent in 1801. He recommended calling the whole land Australia. In 1813 a young farmer named Gregory Blaxland crossed the Great Dividing Range west of Sydney. He found wide, fertile plains beyond. Soon sheep and cattle stations grew up in this new territory. In the mid 1820s Great Britain took possession of the west coast and opened it up for settlement. Fearing rival claims to the land, the British claimed the whole continent in 1829.

By 1803 Sydney was thriving. Livestock had been imported from India, and farmers planted crops, such as cotton and hemp, to see what grew best. Aborigines, carrying woomeras, stayed a safe distance from the activity.

"The people are perfectly mad and are flocking in their hundreds," wrote one miner who braved the outback to search for gold.

The interior, however, remained a mystery. As settlers traveled further inland, they found that the outback grew drier and drier until it became desert. Midcentury explorers risked, and often lost, their lives trying to learn the extent of the "vast and dreary desert of the interior." Edward Eyre traveled from Adelaide to the southwestern coast across the **Nullarbor Plain** in 1841. A team led by Robert Burke and William Wills crossed the continent's "red, dead heart" from south to north in 1860. Burke and Wills died from illness and starvation on the difficult journey back to Melbourne. In 1862 John McDouall Stuart became the first person to reach the geographical center of the continent during his successful round trip between the south and north coasts.

Meanwhile, a sheepshearer named Edward Hargraves had decided to try his luck in the California gold rush. He noticed that the gold-bearing rocks there looked a lot like rocks he had seen in New South Wales. He returned to Australia and began prospecting near Bathurst in 1851. Gold! Australia now had its own gold rush. During the next 20 years gold fields were discovered all over the continent and on Tasmania.

People came from Europe, North America, Africa, and Asia to work the gold fields, and Australia's population tripled in just ten years. One by one, the major settlements grew large and prosperous enough to separate from New South Wales. By 1859, five of Australia's six states were separate, largely self-governing colonies.

The Struggle for New Zealand

In the 1820s a few Australian convicts escaped and made their way to New Zealand. British and American whaling crews often stopped there, too. Some of these people decided to stay. They tried to take land from the Maoris by force. Unlike the Australian Aborigines, who usually retreated from colonial settlements, the Maoris fought back. Great Britain finally had to send soldiers to bring peace.

In 1840 five hundred of North Island's Maoris signed the **Treaty of Waitangi** (WY•tahn•gee) with the British. The Maoris promised loyalty to the British. In return, Great Britain promised to protect them and their lands.

In the meantime, **Edward Gibbon Wakefield** had established the New Zealand Company with the idea of creating a colony of middle-class people. Everyone would enjoy a high standard of living, with prosperity guaranteed. The first settlement was at Wellington. New Zealand was a part of New South Wales at first, but it became a separate colony in 1841.

The promises of the Treaty of Waitangi were not kept. Again settlers tried to drive the Maoris from their lands, and again the Maoris resisted. Fighting broke out on a large scale in the 1860s. In the end, the Maoris were defeated. Their defeat, and the discovery of gold in 1861, opened New Zealand to more and more settlers.

The signing of the Treaty of Waitangi took place February 6, 1840, the day New Zealand became part of the British Empire. This painting shows Tamati Waka Nene, one of the Maori chiefs who signed the treaty.

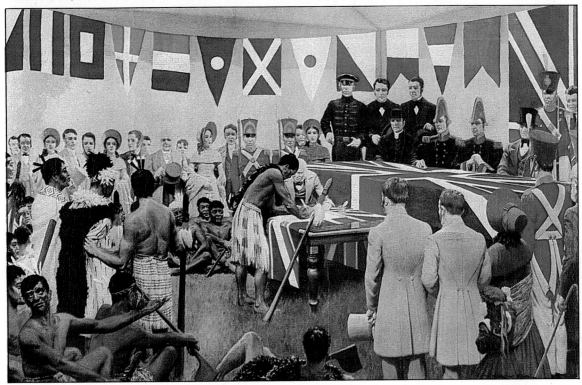

On its completion in 1927, Parliament House in Canberra was opened by the Duke and Duchess of York, who later became King George VI and Queen Elizabeth of Great Britain.

Unity and Independence

At first the Australian colonies did not get along very well with each other. For example, they often set up protective tariffs that taxed each other's goods. Even so, by the beginning of the 1900s, they began to see benefits in uniting. Germany and France had colonies on nearby Pacific islands. The Australians feared that if they did not have a strong national defense, these countries might stake claims on the Australian continent as well.

In 1901 the six Australian states decided to unite under one centralized government. The form of government they chose to create was a **commonwealth,** or a group of states with common ties and interests. They kept the two-house parliamentary form of government used in Great Britain. However, their constitution was modeled after that of the United States. The Australians built a new city, **Canberra,** to be the commonwealth's capital. Canberra occupies its own small territory, just like Washington, D.C.

New Zealand had had its own constitution since 1852 but did not become self-governing until 1907. In contrast to Australia, New Zealand has a one-house lawmaking body. Even though Australia and New Zealand were both nations now, they were still possessions of Great Britain.

The Twentieth Century

When Great Britain went to war with Germany in 1914, Australia promised to help "to the last man and the last shilling." The ANZACs (Australia–New Zealand Army Corps) fought bravely in many battles.

Like other nations, Australia and New Zealand had a postwar boom in the 1920s and a depression in the 1930s. Unemployment rose as prices for the countries' farm products fell.

Japan took over many Pacific islands before and during World War II. Fearing an invasion, Australians and New Zealanders helped the United States drive the Japanese from the lands they had conquered.

Soon after World War II, both Australia and New Zealand became fully independent members of the Commonwealth of Nations. They still give their loyalty to the British monarch, but they make all their own decisions in government.

After World War II Australia encouraged more people to move there. "Populate or perish" became its slogan. Australia turned first to the British Isles and then to the rest of Europe. Greeks, Italians, and other southern Europeans flocked to Australia during this time. All worked for a stronger, more prosperous nation.

In the last 40 years Australia and New Zealand have looked to the United States rather than to Great Britain as their major trade and defense partner. The three countries signed the ANZUS mutual defense treaty in 1951. The United States has now withdrawn from its defense partnership with New Zealand because of that nation's opposition to nuclear-powered ships and weapons. However, the United States maintains several bases in Australia. They are important links in our worldwide defense communications system.

In the 1960s Australia experienced a mineral boom far greater than the gold rush a hundred years earlier. Much of the country's economy still took its traditional "ride on the sheep's back," but some of it began to be built on "rock"—minerals such as iron, copper, and uranium.

Cities and industries grew as mineral wealth developed. Labor unions, always strong in Australia and New Zealand, won even more benefits for workers. Today both governments provide health care and fill many other human needs directly.

Reading Check

1. Who were the natives of Australia and New Zealand? How did they react to newcomers to their lands?
2. What kinds of Europeans first settled in Australia?
3. Who signed the Treaty of Waitangi? What did each side promise?
4. What country became the main trade and defense partner of Australia and New Zealand after World War II?

461

Look for these important words:

Key Words
- mustering
- primary products
- unfavorable balance of trade

Look for answers to these questions:

1. What groups of people live in Australia and New Zealand?
2. What is life like in the cities and in the country?
3. What are the major industries of Australia and New Zealand?
4. What challenges do Australia and New Zealand face today?

3.   AUSTRALIA AND NEW ZEALAND TODAY

Today Australia and New Zealand are both peaceful, highly productive countries. They have abundant natural resources. Their standards of living are among the highest in the world. Yet, like other nations, they do have problems and face challenges to their future.

The People

There are about 15,500,000 people in Australia and 3,500,000 in New Zealand, most of whom are of British descent. A small percentage of "Aussies" and "Kiwis," as Australians and New Zealanders are called, come from other European countries. Another small percentage come from the Western Hemisphere and Asia. Most Asians arrived after 1973, when Australia eased its immigration policy and began accepting nonwhite immigrants. The number of Asians in both countries is likely to increase, perhaps greatly, in the future.

Relatively few native people remain in either country. The Maoris have been more successful than the Aborigines at gaining equal rights and becoming part of mainstream society. Today, 1 out of 12 New Zealanders is a Maori. Maoris have four representatives in New Zealand's 92-member law-making body.

"Good day, mate!" (G'dy, myt!) is a typical greeting down under, where everyone's your mate, or friend. Aussies and Kiwis are open, friendly, and relaxed. They pride themselves on their independence. They share the same rugged, pioneering spirit as the people who pushed west in the United States in the nineteenth century.

"Cityside" Life

Eighty-five percent of Australians and 83 percent of New Zealanders live in or near the countries' major cities. Most people own their own home, so suburbs have sprung up around the larger cities. Sydney, for example, is very proud of being a modern, fast-paced "big city." People in other Australian and New Zealand cities live at a quieter, slower pace. New Zealand cities look like villages in England.

Aussies and Kiwis are energetic, hard-working people. However, their leisure time is especially important, and they spend it outdoors as much as possible. Swimming, fishing, riding, surfing, sailing, and skiing are very popular. So are professional sports such as rugby, Australian football, cricket, tennis, and horse racing. Less athletic activities might include strolling through the cities' many parks or attending concerts in places like Sydney's famous opera house.

Life in the Country

A large sheep or cattle station in the outback may be thousands of acres in size. Stations in New Zealand are smaller, but neighbors can still be miles away. People keep in touch by using radios and airplanes. Station children often go to school by two-way radio. Radios can also be used to call a "flying doctor" if someone on an isolated station gets sick. There are landing strips on many large stations, and ranchers often own planes.

Modern skyscrapers, the arch of Harbor Bridge, and the "sails" of the opera house highlight this panoramic view of today's Sydney.

463

Each year a station's mob, or herd, of sheep or cattle must be rounded up, counted, and marked. This **mustering** is done by ringers or jackaroos, as Australian cowboys are called. Just as in the United States, today's mustering is more often done with jeeps and planes than with horses and dogs. After mustering, sheep being raised for wool are sheared. Other sheep and cattle are carried to market in "trains" of huge trucks.

New Zealand and the more fertile parts of Australia also have farms. In Australia, farmers share with ranchers the dangers of drought, flood, and brush fires. Having enough water is a constant worry.

Miners, too, must live in the outback. Many make their home in the desert. Some mining towns are modern; others look like towns from America's Old West. People there have to depend on the supply train for all their necessities.

Large trucks form "trains" to take cattle from the outback to markets in the cities. Australia produces more than 1.5 million metric tons of beef a year.

Inspectors check and grade the quality of wool. New Zealand's wool is among the finest quality in the world.

The Economy

Historically, Australia and New Zealand traded mostly with each other and with Great Britain. When Great Britain joined the European Common Market in 1973, however, Australia and New Zealand had to find other trading partners. Today their main trading partners are the United States and Japan. Australia's valuable minerals provide raw materials for Japanese industry. Asian countries also buy meat and grain from these Pacific "breadbaskets."

Industries in Australia and New Zealand include iron and steel, food processing, cloth, paper, automobiles, and chemicals. Many products of these industries are used in the countries themselves. Manufactured products also account for about 20 percent of Australia's export income.

Most exports of Australia and New Zealand are **primary products.** Primary products come from the land rather than from industry. Minerals, which account for about 30 percent of Australia's export income, are primary products. Farming and ranching, each of which provides another 20 percent of Australia's export income, are also primary products. Almost all of New Zealand's exports are agricultural products.

At a geothermal power plant near Rotorua, geysers are harnessed to produce electricity for residents of North Island.

Facing the Future

Prices of primary products tend to change more quickly than prices of manufactured goods. In the late 1970s and early 1980s Australia's and New Zealand's economies suffered due to their dependence on the export of primary products. Australia had a period of drought that decreased the amount of agricultural goods it could export.

New Zealand was affected by the rise in oil prices at this time, as well as by a decrease in the demand for its primary products in the international market. The result was that the income from its exports was less than the cost of its imports. Such a situation is known as an **unfavorable balance of trade.** The result for both nations was high inflation and unemployment.

Since then, both countries have increased their productivity. They export more manufactured goods so that there is less chance of these problems happening in the future. As a result, the economies of both nations have improved.

Another issue that has created problems for the two nations is that of racial discrimination. The Aborigines have not adapted well to the urban, industrialized life of modern Australia. While some work with the livestock on stations, others have had difficulty finding jobs in the cities. Many Aborigines live in settlements similar

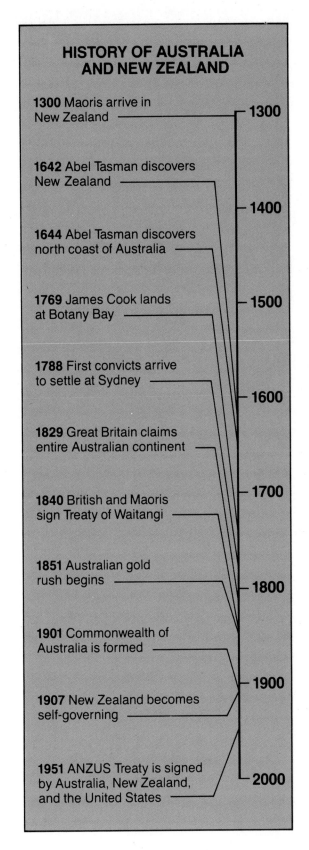

HISTORY OF AUSTRALIA AND NEW ZEALAND

1300 Maoris arrive in New Zealand

1642 Abel Tasman discovers New Zealand

1644 Abel Tasman discovers north coast of Australia

1769 James Cook lands at Botany Bay

1788 First convicts arrive to settle at Sydney

1829 Great Britain claims entire Australian continent

1840 British and Maoris sign Treaty of Waitangi

1851 Australian gold rush begins

1901 Commonwealth of Australia is formed

1907 New Zealand becomes self-governing

1951 ANZUS Treaty is signed by Australia, New Zealand, and the United States

1300 — 1400 — 1500 — 1600 — 1700 — 1800 — 1900 — 2000

to Indian reservations in the United States. These people have a much lower standard of living than other Australians. A greater appreciation of the contributions of Aborigines to Australia's history and culture, however, gives hope of a better life for Aborigines in the future.

In New Zealand, Maoris and other Pacific islanders have moved into the cities, creating racial tensions as these new residents compete for jobs. New Zealanders are now working to lessen these tensions.

In the past, Australia and New Zealand were isolated from other countries. They were free to preserve their unique way of life. Today, however, isolation is no longer possible. These "European lands in an Asian sea" are now learning how to get along with their recent immigrants and with their neighbors in matters of trade and defense. They are changing their attitudes and accepting their roles as members of a larger Asian-Pacific community. Finding the best ways to do this is probably the biggest challenge these countries face.

Reading Check

1. From what group are most Australians and New Zealanders descended?
2. Where do most Australians and New Zealanders live?
3. What kinds of primary products provide most of Australia's and New Zealand's export income?
4. What are the greatest challenges facing Australia and New Zealand today?

SKILLS FOR SUCCESS

ANALYZING GENERAL STATEMENTS

When you read about people or places and their history, you often have to think about what you are reading and evaluate it. Information and ideas may be presented in a variety of ways. For example, the first group of sentences below might appear in an article about Australia, while the second group might be found in an article about New Zealand's animals. How are the sentences different?

> About 15,500,000 people live in Australia.
> Australia has too few people.
> Most Australians live in cities.

> Two types of bat are the only land mammals native to New Zealand.
> New Zealand has very few different kinds of animals.
> Most of New Zealand's animals were brought from other lands.

From your study of evaluating information on pages 279–280, you probably recognize that the first sentence in each group is a fact. It can be proved to be true. The second sentence is an opinion. It is someone's belief or judgment. In other words, too few people to one person might be too many to someone else.

The third sentence is a **general statement.** A general statement is based on facts. It often contains words such as *many, most, generally,* or *usually.* Writers use general statements to summarize groups of facts and show relationships between them. A general statement tells what is true most of the time but not always.

To evaluate a general statement, try to find facts to support it. For example, you might read that deer, pigs, rabbits, cattle, and sheep came to New Zealand with the Europeans. This fact supports the statement that most of New Zealand's animals came from other lands. A general statement should be supported by several facts.

CHECKING YOUR SKILLS

Three of the sentences below are general statements. The other six sentences are specific facts that support the general statements. Identify each general statement and tell which two facts support it.

1. Aborigines memorized the location of water holes in the desert.

2. Most Polynesians were skilled seafarers.

3. Polynesians could find their way across the sea by following sun, moon, and stars.

4. Australian rock groups INXS, Men at Work, and Air Supply are popular in Australia and the United States.

5. Aborigines usually could survive well in their harsh environment.

6. Polynesian canoes often traveled thousands of miles.

7. Aborigines used throwing sticks called boomerangs to kill animals.

8. Young people in Australia and the United States generally enjoy the same kind of music and movies.

9. The movie "Crocodile Dundee" drew large crowds in Australia and the United States.

USING WORDS

Write the letter of the definition that matches each of the words below.

1. **bauxite**
2. **commonwealth**
3. **primary products**
4. **stations**
5. **unfavorable balance of trade**

a. Economic situation in which a country's imports exceed its exports

b. Group of states with common ties and interests united under one central government

c. Sheep or cattle ranches

d. Products of the land

e. Mineral from which aluminum is made

REVIEWING FACTS

1. How are the landforms and climate of Australia different from those of New Zealand?

2. Why do you think most large cities in Australia and New Zealand are located along the coasts?

3. How did the American Revolution contribute to the settlement of Australia and New Zealand?

4. Why is dependence on primary products dangerous for a country?

5. How has trade changed in Australia and New Zealand in the last 15 years?

THINKING CRITICALLY

1. Compare the growth of Australia and New Zealand with that of the United States. Think about the way the three countries were settled, the kinds of people who settled them, and the reasons why people were attracted to the countries. How are the governments similar? What are the people in each country concerned about?

2. What advantages might Australia gain by greatly increasing its population through immigration? What problems might arise?

3. How might life and culture in Australia and New Zealand change if large numbers of Asians immigrate there?

◯ PRACTICING SKILLS

General Statements Indicate whether each sentence below is a general statement or a specific fact. Tell which facts support each general statement.

1. Ranch and farm products account for 42 percent of Australia's export income.

2. Ninety-five percent of Australians are descended from the British.

3. Many Australians and New Zealanders are of British descent.

4. Twenty-nine percent of Australia's export earnings comes from minerals.

5. Most of Australia's export income comes from primary products.

6. Eighty-four percent of New Zealanders are of British descent.

CLOSE-UP

Farmers use a *shadoof,*
an ancient irrigation
method.

COMPARING ECONOMIC SYSTEMS

The production of goods and services depends on resources—natural resources and human resources, including work, or **labor.** However, there are not enough resources for people's increasing wants and needs. In all societies, people must decide how best to use their resources. All groups are different, but each must make the same important choices. What goods and services will it produce? How much will it produce? What resources will it use? How will it **distribute,** or share, resources and goods and services? Who will decide?

The way people produce and use goods and services is called an **economic system.** The word *economy* means "management of a household." Just as many families must manage their work and money, nations have economic systems to manage their resources and money.

Types of Economic Systems

There are different types of economic systems. One way to study economies is to identify the differences among **traditional economies, market economies,** and **command economies.** However, no nation has an economy that fits one type exactly. All economies are mixtures, and each one is different.

TRADITIONAL ECONOMIES A traditional economy stays the same over a long period of time. Everything is done as it was in the past. If parents are farmers, their children

470

grow up to be farmers. Families perform tasks in ways that have been passed from generation to generation. They spend most of their time raising food for themselves. They produce little surplus. Without a surplus to sell, people do not have enough money to buy better tools. They continue to work and produce as usual, unchanged from their past.

Most countries have had traditional economies at some time in their history. A few countries in Latin America, Africa, and Asia still have mainly traditional economies.

MARKET ECONOMIES In many modern countries there are a variety of goods and services from which to choose. In a market economy the people decide which goods and services to buy and sell. They make choices about how to spend their money. They can choose how they will earn their living. They are free to own property.

The market economy is also called a **free enterprise economy.** *Free enterprise* means that people have many choices about how to make and spend their money. The United States, Canada, and India are examples of countries with market, or free enterprise, economies.

Consumers and **producers** work together in a market economy. When people make goods or provide services, they are producers. When people spend money, they are consumers. Both consumers and producers influence what is produced in a market economy.

The demand for video equipment brings profits to this small business.

You are a consumer whenever you buy something. Suppose you buy a video game for $25. By buying it, you are showing a **demand** for it. You want the game. The price is right for you.

Suppose that many other people buy the same video game that you do. The **supply,** or the number of available games, runs out. Because it sold so many, the company will make more games.

The company will make more games because it wants a greater **profit.** There are many costs in making a product, such as the costs of labor and materials. Profit is the money left over after paying these costs. With their profits, producers can buy better equipment. They earn more money for themselves. They can improve their work and

471

their lives. Profit is an important goal in a free enterprise economy.

Now suppose the video game company makes a new supply of games. This time they raise the price to $35. The company thinks that it can make higher profits. Instead, fewer people buy the games. Many will not pay the higher prices. Demand for the video game drops.

In ways like these producers decide what and how much to produce. They also decide what price to charge. What products a consumer will purchase and for how much influence the producer. The price of a product is influenced also by what is available to sell. This process is called the **law of supply and demand.** In a market economy, prices depend on demand. They also depend on how large the supply is.

COMMAND ECONOMIES Command economies differ from market economies in many ways. In command economies the government owns almost all land and natural resources. It controls farms and factories. In other words, it *commands* the economy. Two countries with command economies are China and the Soviet Union.

Government leaders make most decisions in a command economy. They decide what will be produced. They set production goals for each factory and farm. The government decides what goods and services are most important. For example, many people may want to buy automobiles. The government may think it is more important to use steel and rubber for tractors. As a result, few consumers will be able to have cars.

When goods and services are sold, the government in a command economy controls the profits. It decides how much workers should earn and how much they must spend for what they need. The profits then go for more materials and machines. The government can use them to build new factories. In this way, leaders in command economies try to produce what they think people need. They believe that the government, not the individual, knows what is best for the people.

Trucks roll off of a Soviet production line.

Developing and Developed Economies

Every nation has different resources. Some nations are rich in **capital resources**—money, tools, machinery, factories, and knowledge. Some nations use their resources efficiently, that is, without waste. They can provide for most needs of their people. These nations have developed economies. Their farmers raise enough food for everyone. Many people work in modern industries or service jobs. Nearly all can read and write.

Other countries have economies that are still developing. Most of these are trying to change their traditional economies. Their people have been mainly farmers. Now these countries are developing modern industries to produce more goods and services. Some have changed to market economies. Others have changed to command economies.

CHINA'S ECONOMY With more than a billion people, China is the largest nation in the world. For centuries, most Chinese had small farms. They could grow barely enough food for themselves. If they did not own the land, they had to pay high rents. They often paid high taxes to the government.

After 1949 China's communist government wanted to change China into a command economy. Land was taken from landowners. The government made people move to large communes. Leaders believed that government-managed farms would be more efficient. Then, if enough food was produced, the Chinese could start new industries. Life would improve for everyone.

A command economy can develop quickly. The government controls all resources—labor, raw materials, and capital. It can move them when and where it wants to. Even so, progress in China was slow. Often there was little rain. The farms were managed poorly. People did not feel they were working for themselves. China's leaders continued to make changes. Farmers were given some land of their own. With better planning, crops improved. New industries arose in cities everywhere.

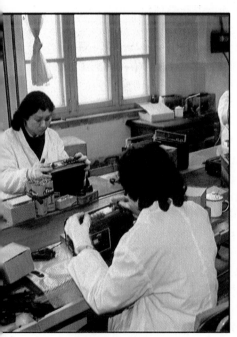

China's government commands industry. In this factory women assemble radios.

473

Today, China's developing economy meets its people's basic needs. China feeds its people. It produces machinery for its factories and farms. It is trading with other nations and asking them to supply new technology and ideas. China hopes that it can absorb these new ideas to develop an economy that is modern and yet entirely Chinese.

The use of pesticide is taught in southern India.

INDIA'S ECONOMY When India became independent in 1947, its leaders began to develop a market economy. India's task has not been easy. There are more than 700 million people in India. The land is poor and dry in many places. There is not enough food. Also, some people still value the old ways. It is difficult to persuade them to change their ideas.

With modern equipment and education, India is producing more food. People are slowly learning new farming methods. India is using some of its money to build new industries. Trade is bringing more money from other countries.

Solving India's problems will take time. Although changes are being made, India's continually growing population places heavy demands on its resources. The Indian people are learning new skills, however. Their work will produce more jobs and goods. Indians point to the successes of other market economies. India's developing economy is trying to improve life in India.

THE SOVIET UNION'S ECONOMY In 1917 the Soviet Union became the first communist country. Most of its people were poor, but the country had many resources. Today the Soviet Union has a developed command economy.

The Soviet economy grew quickly. Farmers were grouped on government lands. New factories began to make machinery. Leaders used the profits to build more factories. The nation soon produced more steel, tractors, and printing presses.

Many Soviet plans failed. The government often set goals that were too high. Factories and farms could not meet the goals. Often products were poorly made. The

Shoppers line up in a
Moscow department store.

People invest in
businesses by buying
shares through the New
York Stock Exchange.

country still does not produce all the food it needs. The government has to buy wheat from other countries, such as Canada and the United States.

The Soviet **gross national product** (GNP), its total amount of goods and services, is the second highest in the world. Only the GNP of the United States is higher. However, the Soviet Union does not yet produce enough goods for consumers. Thus, the **standard of living** in the Soviet Union remains lower than in most developed countries. Standard of living is a measure of how well people live. On the one hand, taxes and rents are low in the Soviet Union. Medical care and education are free. On the other hand, Soviet citizens often must stand in long lines to buy the few available goods. Housing is scarce and crowded.

The Soviets will need more technology and machinery for the future. They need to become more efficient. Soviet planners are now using some methods of market economies. They are rewarding workers with higher pay. Some factories and farms can use profits to buy their own equipment. Workers can make more decisions. With these changes, the Soviets hope to produce more goods.

THE ECONOMY OF THE UNITED STATES The United States has a highly developed market economy. In our system private citizens, not the government, own many of the capital resources that produce goods and services. These people decide what is produced and sold.

Americans have many choices in their market economy. It produces a wide variety of the goods and services people want. People can train for thousands of different jobs at schools and universities. Anyone who can raise money can start a business or share profits in one.

The American economy has grown because people **invest,** or put money, in business and industry. A type of business called a **corporation** can sell part of the ownership in itself to people who are willing to invest. The corporation uses the money to improve and expand. Improvements result in higher profits for the corporation and its investors. Satisfied customers continue to invest.

475

AVERAGE PER CAPITA INCOME IN DOLLARS	
United States	$12,482
Canada	10,610
Japan	9,774
Soviet Union	5,991
China	630
India	235

In a free enterprise system any number of companies can supply the same kinds of goods and services. For example, many different companies try to persuade consumers to buy their brands of televisions. This is called **competition.** Competition for profits influences companies to make better and less expensive goods. To attract the consumer, companies also must make their products efficiently. They need to use profits to replace outdated equipment and to build new factories. They reward good workers with higher wages. They know that other companies are doing the same thing.

The American economy keeps growing as it produces the goods and services people want. Producers earn profits and improve their businesses. Over the years Americans have produced more than any other country in the world. Its gross national product is the highest.

At the same time, Americans have a high standard of living. **Per capita income,** or average earnings per person, is another way to see how well Americans live. Compare the American per capita income to other incomes on the table above. What does this tell you about America's standard of living?

Although the United States has a market economy, the government does have a limited role. It makes laws to protect and manage scarce resources. It does not control the economy, however. The government, and its citizens, believe that the people do that best.

UNIT 4 REVIEW

WORDS TO REMEMBER

Number your paper from 1 to 10. Complete the sentences below with words from the following list.

archipelago	**dynasty**
boycott	**neutral**
caste	**raw materials**
civil service	**reincarnation**
commonwealth	**traditions**

1. India's _____ system separated people into classes that could not mix.

2. The Hindus' belief in _____ helped them fit into India's complex society.

3. Mahatma Gandhi led a _____ of British goods.

4. India avoids choosing sides between the Soviet Union and the United States to stay _____.

5. During China's history, rebellion often meant that a new _____ would come to rule.

6. Ancient Chinese had to pass an exam to enter the _____.

7. To solve their mutual problems, the Australian states formed a _____.

8. Japan attacked other Asian countries to get the _____ it needed for its industries.

9. One of the Minangkabau _____ is to name children after the mother's family.

10. The nation of Indonesia is made up of a chain of islands called an _____.

FOCUS ON MAIN IDEAS

1. Give examples of how mountains and seas have affected such things as trade and agriculture in Asian countries.

2. List three contributions from early Asian civilizations.

3. What role did Arab Muslims and Europeans play in the history of Asia?

4. Identify the Asian country in which each of the following traditions played a major part. Briefly describe the influence of each on the culture of the country.

   a. the philosophy of Confucius
   b. the bushido code
   c. the caste system

5. Why did the Chinese and Japanese close their countries to foreigners?

6. Name an Asian country where each of the following is a main religion:

   a. Islam   c. Hinduism
   b. Buddhism   d. Shinto

7. Why are large populations a problem for industrial development in Asia?

8. How does Japan's industrial growth compare to that of India and China?

9. How has communist fighting affected the development of Southeast Asia?

10. At one time India, Australia, and New Zealand were all a part of the British Empire. Compare and contrast the ways in which these three nations gained their independence.

Rudyard Kipling, a British writer who spent time in India, wrote in "The Ballad of East and West":

> Oh, East is East, and West is West, and never the twain shall meet . . .

What Kipling meant is that Eastern and Western cultures are very different. They have often conflicted. Imagine what it would be like to come in contact with someone from a culture different from your own. Write a dialogue for the first meeting between one of the following pairs of people.

a. Commodore Perry and the shogun
b. Marco Polo and Kublai Khan
c. Anna Leonowens and King Mongkut
d. Captain James Cook and an Aborigine

ACTIVITIES

1. **Research/Art** Chinese writing is very different from Western writing. Chinese characters represent ideas rather than sounds. In an encyclopedia or a Chinese dictionary, find examples of some Chinese characters. Draw four or five characters as carefully as you can and write the meaning of each one. You also might try to find and compare Japanese characters that represent the words you have drawn.

2. **Research/Current Events** Southeast Asia has suffered a long history of fighting, often involving other nations around the world. Find newspaper or magazine articles that discuss current conflicts in Southeast Asia. Find out who the current leaders are in Southeast Asian countries. Perhaps you can find pictures of these leaders. Which leaders are new? Which ones are the same as those mentioned in the text?

1. **Using a Cultural Map** Southeast Asia is home to many different groups of peoples, some of which are shown on the map below. Use the map to answer the questions.

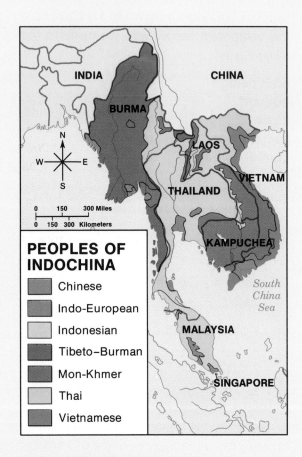

PEOPLES OF INDOCHINA

- Chinese
- Indo-European
- Indonesian
- Tibeto–Burman
- Mon-Khmer
- Thai
- Vietnamese

a. What do the seven colors on the map represent?
b. Which three groups shown make up the largest area of the Indochina peninsula?
c. Identify the two groups of people who share the country of Malaysia.
d. Name the four groups that share the border between the Indochina peninsula and China.
e. Which group occupies the smallest area in Indochina?

YOUR WORLD

MAKING A TIMELINE

1. Continue the illustrated timeline that you began in Unit 1. Notice that ancient civilizations in China and India occur near the beginning of the timeline. Choose other dates during Asia's history that show when major changes took place in the cultures of India, China, and Japan. For example, show when dynasties or governments changed, when new religions, philosophies, or foreign influences appeared, and when inventions or discoveries were made. For Southeast Asia, you might find out when those nations became independent or when some of them came under communist rule.

LEARNING ABOUT PEOPLE

2. When scientists or researchers explore cultures, they often choose a typical person or family in that culture to study. They prepare what is called a **case study,** which includes notes and comments based on their observations. Pretend you are a researcher preparing a case study. Choose one of the "cases" below to feature in your notebook on Cultures of the World. Write a description of a day in the life of the person you choose.
A Buddhist monk in Nepal
A Mongol herder
A Filipino fisherman
A Thai "fingernail" dancer
A rice paddy farmer in Taiwan
A Brahman priest in India

EXPRESSING IDEAS

3. Find and study examples of Chinese landscapes or Japanese scrolls. Paint a landscape that shows the type of land, vegetation, and animal life in your environment. Try to imitate the style used by Chinese or Japanese artists.

4. Research one of the following art forms and prepare an oral report or a demonstration for your class.
origami (Japanese paper folding)
cloisonné (enamel painting)
calligraphy
woodblock printing
silkscreening
flower arranging

SHARING CULTURE

5. What Asian foods have you eaten? Which ones might you like to try? Pick a country in Asia and write a menu showing what someone from that country might eat in a day. Describe how the dishes are prepared, served, and eaten.

6. The Asian diet is influenced in several ways. Geography makes fish and rice important foods. Soybeans and seaweed often are eaten because they are nutritious but inexpensive. Religious customs prevent some Asians from eating beef or other meats. Make a list of your favorite foods. Think about how geography, economics, and customs or traditions affect your diet.

Key Dates and Events

About A.D. 100–900
Height of Mayan Empire

1325
Aztecs discover site for their capital city

1438–1531
Height of Inca Empire

1492
Christopher Columbus lands on San Salvador

1500
Pedro Cabral discovers Brazil

1519
Hernando Cortés conquers Aztecs in Mexico

1532
Francisco Pizarro conquers Inca Empire

THE WESTERN HEMISPHERE, PAST AND PRESENT

From the ruins of ancient civilizations, we find evidence of how ancient peoples lived. Here, the ruins of Tikal offer such clues to an early civilization in the Western Hemisphere. Even though these civilizations have disappeared, their art, architecture, and customs influence the lives of their descendants today. In this way, their gifts enrich us all.

In this unit you will find out about the achievements of different peoples who came to live in the Western Hemisphere. You will read about life today in Brazil, Canada, and other Western Hemisphere nations.

1605	1822	1867	1889	1914	1982
Samuel de Champlain establishes first settlement in New France	Brazil gains independence from Portugal	Canada becomes a Confederation	Brazilian Empire becomes a Republic	Panama Canal completed	Canada gains control of its Constitution

GEOGRAPHY OF THE WESTERN HEMISPHERE

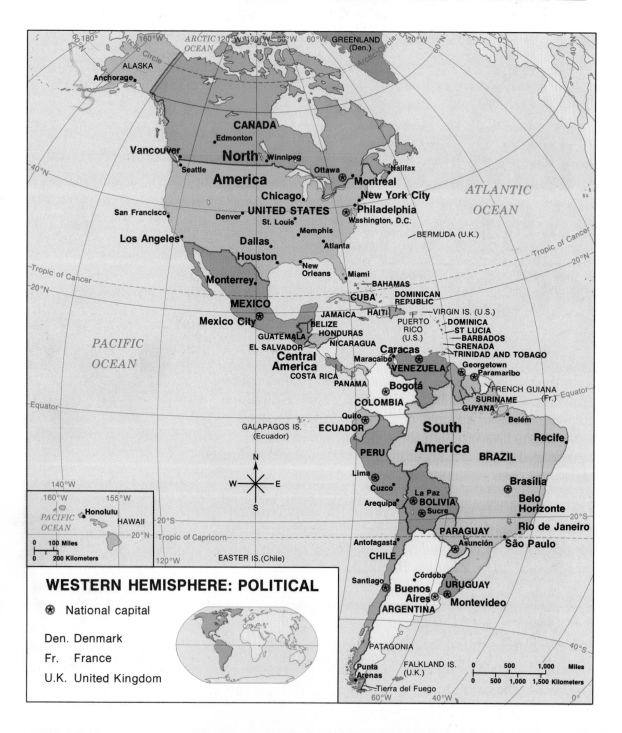

WESTERN HEMISPHERE: POLITICAL

⊛ National capital

Den. Denmark

Fr. France

U.K. United Kingdom

Location

The Western Hemisphere includes the continents of North America and South America. It also includes Greenland, the largest island in the world, and the many islands of the Caribbean (car•uh•BEE•uhn) Sea.

How would you like to journey the length of the Western Hemisphere? June and Greg Siple of Missoula, Montana, did just that—and on bicycles! They called their trip Hemistour because it was a tour of the Western Hemisphere.

The Siples began Hemistour in Anchorage, Alaska, on June 17, 1972. Two years, eight months, and nine days later, they arrived in Tierra del Fuego (tee•AIR•uh del foo•AY•goh), Argentina. Tierra del Fuego is not far from **Cape Horn,** the southernmost part of South America.

The Siples had traveled over 18,000 miles (28,960 km) on their journey. They were amazed by the contrasts they saw. They saw mountains, grassy plains, rain forests, and deserts. They experienced the hot summers and cold winters of the middle latitudes as well as the moist heat of the tropics.

After leaving Anchorage, the Siples bicycled south through Canada, the western United States, and Mexico. These three nations are the largest nations of North America. Of these, Canada is the largest in size. The United States has the greatest number of people—more than 236 million.

As the Siples continued south from Mexico, they entered Central America. Central America includes seven countries. They are Guatemala (gwah•tuh•MAH•luh), El Salvador, Panama, Costa Rica, Honduras, Nicaragua (nik•uh•RAHG•wuh), and Belize (buh•LEEZ).

Crossing the forested hills of tropical Central America, the Siples reached South America. The nations of South America are Argentina, Brazil, Chile, Colombia, Ecuador, Bolivia, Peru, Paraguay, Uruguay, Guyana, Suriname, and Venezuela. Also included is French Guiana, a department of France. The largest of these nations is Brazil. Brazil, with about 134 million people, also has the greatest population.

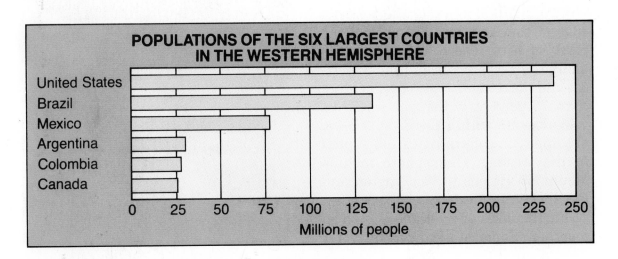

POPULATIONS OF THE SIX LARGEST COUNTRIES IN THE WESTERN HEMISPHERE

Millions of people

A narrow land bridge called the **Isthmus of Panama** connects North and South America. It also separates the Atlantic and Pacific oceans. For 400 years ships sailing from one ocean to another in the Western Hemisphere had to travel far south around Cape Horn. In 1914 the United States completed the **Panama Canal.** Today ships enter a series of **locks,** or gateways, to make the eight-hour trip between the two oceans.

The Land

If you look at a physical map of the Western Hemisphere, you will see that mountains extend over the whole length of the western part. In North America the largest of these mountains are the Rocky Mountains. In South America they are the Andes (AN•deez). The Andes are 4,500 miles (7,240 km) long, the longest mountain chain in the world. Mt. Aconcagua (ak•uhn•KAHG•wuh) in Argentina is the highest mountain in the Western Hemisphere, with an elevation of 22,830 feet (6,960 m).

The mountains along the western edge of the Americas are part of the **Ring of Fire.** The Ring of Fire runs along the western coast of the Americas and the eastern coast of Asia. More than 75 percent of the world's active volcanoes lie within the Ring of Fire. Volcanoes that have recently erupted in the Western Hemisphere include Mount St. Helens in Washington and El Chichón in Mexico.

Earthquakes and volcanoes often go together. Some of the world's worst earthquakes have occurred near the Ring of Fire. In 1976 an earthquake in Guatemala destroyed $700 million worth of property and resulted in the deaths of 23,000 people. In 1983 an earthquake severely damaged the California town of Coalinga.

Low mountains and highlands are found in the eastern parts of both Americas. In North America the Appalachian Mountains run in a north-south direction. In South America the highlands include the Brazilian Highlands and the Guiana Highlands.

The Western Hemisphere also features huge plains. In North America they include the interior plains of both Canada and the United States. In South America plains are in the Amazon Basin and in Paraguay and Argentina. The vast grassy plains of Argentina are called **pampas.** *Pampa* is taken from an Indian word meaning "plain."

Molten lava flows from the crater of Kilauea, one of Hawaii's active volcanoes.

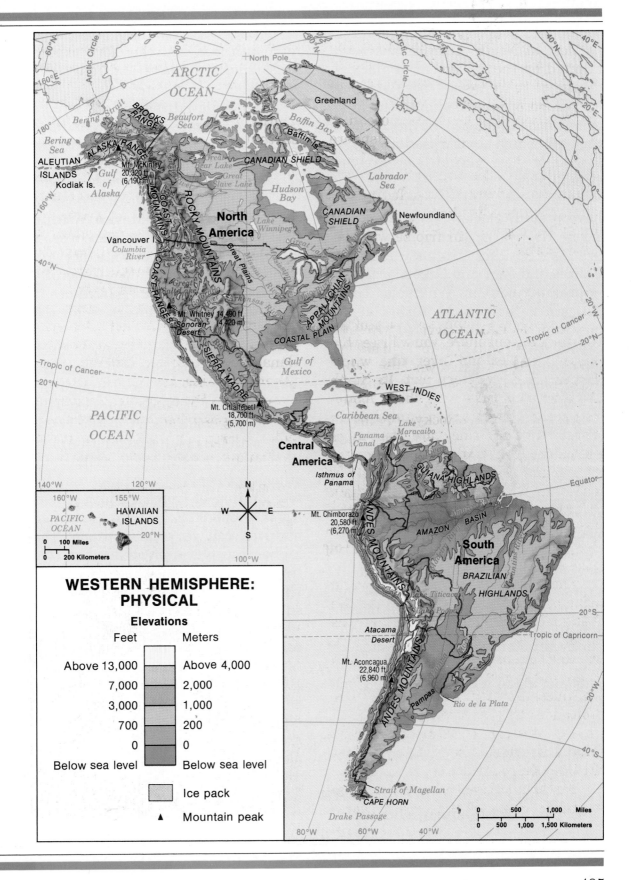

WESTERN HEMISPHERE: PHYSICAL

Elevations

Feet		Meters
Above 13,000		Above 4,000
7,000		2,000
3,000		1,000
700		200
0		0
Below sea level		Below sea level

Ice pack

▲ Mountain peak

ARCTIC OCEAN

North Pole

Greenland

Beaufort Sea

Baffin Bay

Baffin Is.

BROOKS RANGE

Bering Strait

Bering Sea

ALASKA RANGE

ALEUTIAN ISLANDS

Kodiak Is.

Gulf of Alaska

Mt. McKinley 20,320 ft. (6,190 m)

Great Bear Lake

CANADIAN SHIELD

Great Slave Lake

Hudson Bay

Labrador Sea

Newfoundland

CANADIAN SHIELD

Lake Winnipeg

North America

ROCKY MOUNTAINS

COAST MOUNTAINS

Vancouver I.

Columbia River

Great Plains

Great Lakes

APPALACHIAN MOUNTAINS

ATLANTIC OCEAN

Great Salt Lake

Colorado River

Arkansas River

Missouri River

Mississippi River

COASTAL RANGES

Mt. Whitney 14,490 ft. (4,420 m)

Sonoran Desert

COASTAL PLAIN

Tropic of Cancer

SIERRA MADRE

Rio Grande

Gulf of Mexico

Mt. Citlaltepetl 18,700 ft. (5,700 m)

WEST INDIES

Caribbean Sea

Lake Maracaibo

PACIFIC OCEAN

Central America

Panama Canal

Isthmus of Panama

GUIANA HIGHLANDS

Equator

Mt. Chimborazo 20,580 ft. (6,270 m)

ANDES MOUNTAINS

AMAZON BASIN

South America

BRAZILIAN HIGHLANDS

Lake Titicaca

Atacama Desert

Tropic of Capricorn

Mt. Aconcagua 22,840 ft. (6,960 m)

Pampas

Rio de la Plata

Strait of Magellan

CAPE HORN

Drake Passage

Arctic Circle

PACIFIC OCEAN

160°W

155°W

HAWAIIAN ISLANDS

20°N

0 100 Miles

0 200 Kilometers

N
W   E
S

0 500 1,000 Miles

0 500 1,000 1,500 Kilometers

485

Most of North America has been affected by the movement of glaciers during past ice ages. These glaciers carved, scraped, and shaped the land over which they passed. As they melted, they left behind thousands of lakes. The largest of these glacial lakes are the Great Lakes.

In contrast, South America did not have as many glaciers. Thus it has few lakes. Its two most important lakes are Lake Titicaca (tit·ih·KAHK·uh) in Bolivia and Peru and Lake Maracaibo (mar·uh·KY·boh) in Venezuela. Lake Titicaca is high in the Andes, at an elevation of 12,506 feet (3,812 m). Steamboats regularly carry passengers and freight across the lake. Lake Maracaibo is in the center of Venezuela's rich oil reserves.

Great river systems drain the continents of both North America and South America. In North America the largest river is the Mississippi, which drains much of the interior of the continent. The Mississippi, however, is not nearly so large as the Amazon River of South America. The Amazon River is the largest river in the world. It drains an area almost the size of the continental United States. At its mouth the Amazon discharges into the Atlantic Ocean 50 times as much water as the Nile River. The Amazon is navigable for 2,300 miles (3,700 km) from the sea.

The Climate

The climate of the Western Hemisphere varies according to latitude. A large part of North America lies in the high latitudes and therefore experiences short summers and long, cold winters.

The middle latitudes have a more moderate climate. These areas have cool to cold winters and warm to hot summers. It is in the middle latitudes of North America that most people live. The middle latitudes extend from southern Canada to Mexico. Within the middle latitudes, climate varies depending on ocean currents, prevailing winds, and mountains. Generally the climate of the middle latitudes is well suited for agriculture or for the raising of livestock.

In contrast to North America, much of South America has a tropical climate. The equator passes through the northern part of South America. This is near the widest part of the continent, with the result that South America has more tropical lowlands than any other continent. The average annual temperature of tropical South America is about 80°F (27° C). Elevation, however, can vary this pattern. The higher the elevation of land in the tropics, the cooler the climate becomes. High mountains on the equator have snow on their peaks all year.

Most of tropical South America receives at least 60 inches (152 cm) of rain a year. Average precipitation of 100 to 120 inches (254 to 305 cm) a year is common in the rain forests. This high precipitation occurs because the prevailing easterly winds pick up moisture from the Atlantic Ocean and drop it on the land.

In contrast, the west coast of Peru and Chile from 5°S to 30°S is one of the

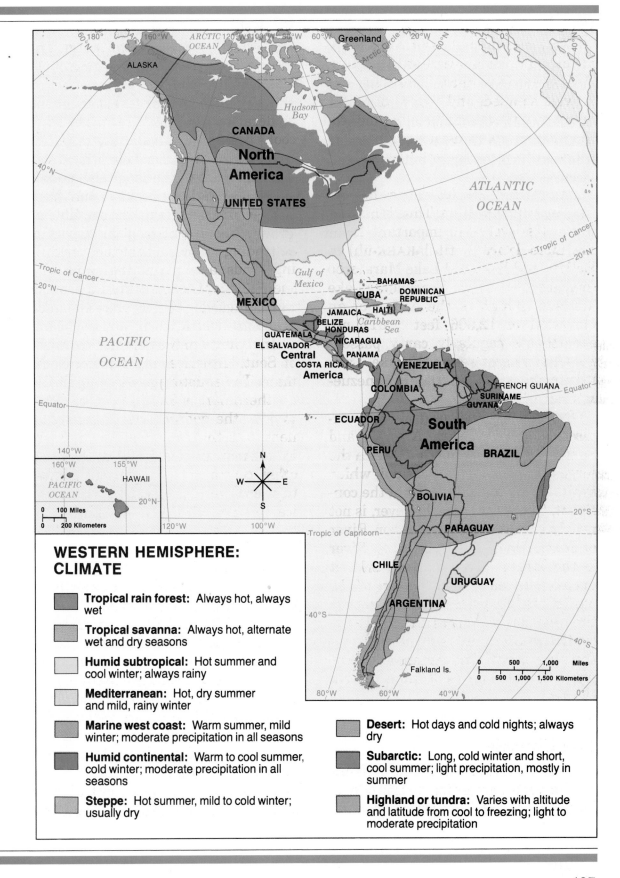

WESTERN HEMISPHERE: CLIMATE

Tropical rain forest: Always hot, always wet

Tropical savanna: Always hot, alternate wet and dry seasons

Humid subtropical: Hot summer and cool winter; always rainy

Mediterranean: Hot, dry summer and mild, rainy winter

Marine west coast: Warm summer, mild winter; moderate precipitation in all seasons

Humid continental: Warm to cool summer, cold winter; moderate precipitation in all seasons

Steppe: Hot summer, mild to cold winter; usually dry

Desert: Hot days and cold nights; always dry

Subarctic: Long, cold winter and short, cool summer; light precipitation, mostly in summer

Highland or tundra: Varies with altitude and latitude from cool to freezing; light to moderate precipitation

driest areas in the world. This is the Atacama (ah•tuh•KAH•muh) Desert. It is so dry because the moisture-bearing easterlies rarely cross the high Andes. A cold ocean current off shore adds little moisture to the clouds. As a result, the coast is often foggy, but rain rarely occurs.

At the middle latitudes of South America the prevailing winds are from the west and bring moisture from warmer waters in the Pacific. Therefore, southern Chile receives much moisture.

Resources

The resources of the Western Hemisphere are vast. They include good soil, forests, minerals, and water. The kind of resources in each region of the Western Hemisphere has an effect on the region's industrial development and the life of its people.

One of the most important resources of the Western Hemisphere is good soil. The best soil is found in the middle latitudes. In those areas of the Western Hemisphere farmers are able to grow a surplus of food for export to nations in other parts of the world.

The interior plains region of Canada and the United States is a major grain-producing region. Here the main crops are wheat, corn, and soybeans. Cotton, fruits, and vegetables are raised in abundance in many parts of North America.

Wheat fields cover much of the province of Alberta. Canada, larger in area than the United States, has about one-tenth its population.

Colombia's coffee crop, 816 metric tons each year, is the world's second largest. The entire crop is picked by hand.

The grassy regions of North America provide nutritious food for animals. Cattle and sheep are raised from southern Canada to northern Mexico.

In South America the best soil is found in Uruguay and Argentina. Cattle are raised on the pampas of Argentina and Paraguay. Argentina is the second-largest exporter of beef in the world. Farther south in Argentina, in the region of Patagonia, are large sheep ranches. Argentinian sheep are known for their meat and fine wool.

Most of the population of Chile lives in Chile's central valley. There farmers grow grains as well as grapes and other fruits. It is summer in South America when it is winter in North America. For that reason grapes from Chile can be found in many American grocery stores from December through May.

In tropical areas the soil is generally poor. Sometimes the soil is so poor that even large amounts of fertilizer do little to improve it.

Forests have long been one of the Western Hemisphere's most important resources. Pine trees in North America provide an important resource for making paper. Forests yield a variety of trees that are turned into lumber.

In South America the tropical forests produce hardwood trees. These are valued the world over for the beauty of their wood. Tropical fruit trees provide the world with supplies of bananas and cacao. Other important agricultural products from the tropics include coffee beans and sugar cane.

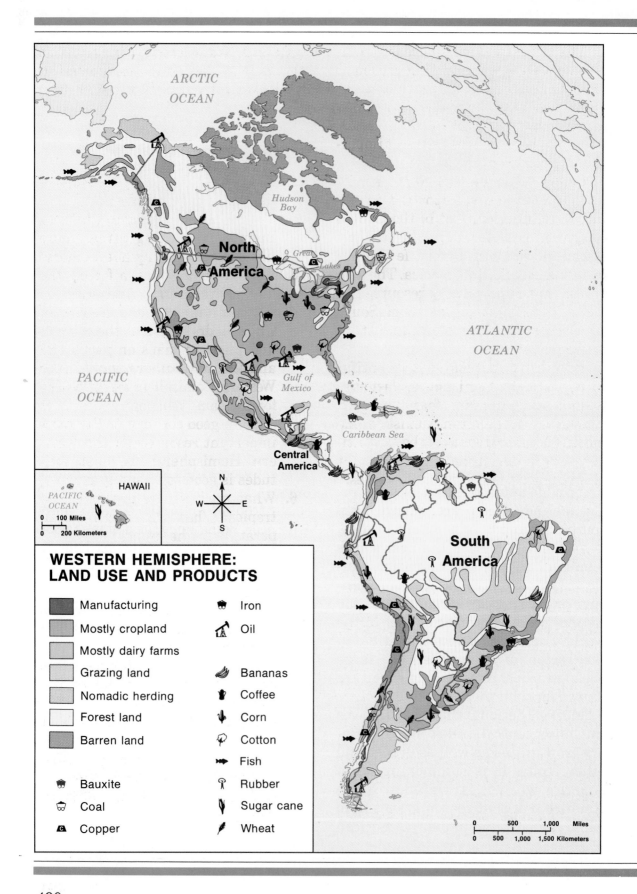

WESTERN HEMISPHERE: LAND USE AND PRODUCTS

Manufacturing

Mostly cropland

Mostly dairy farms

Grazing land

Nomadic herding

Forest land

Barren land

- Bauxite
- Coal
- Copper

- Iron
- Oil

- Bananas
- Coffee
- Corn
- Cotton
- Fish
- Rubber
- Sugar cane
- Wheat

ARCTIC OCEAN

Hudson Bay

North America

Great Lakes

ATLANTIC OCEAN

PACIFIC OCEAN

Gulf of Mexico

Caribbean Sea

Central America

South America

HAWAII

PACIFIC OCEAN

0   100 Miles
0   200 Kilometers

N
W   E
S

0   500   1,000   Miles
0   500 1,000   1,500 Kilometers

The Western Hemisphere is rich in minerals. Oil and natural gas are found in abundance on both continents. In North America, the United States and Mexico have large oil fields. In South America, Venezuela is the most important oil-producing nation.

Coal is abundant in North America. Coal has been important in the industrial development of the United States. Except for deposits recently discovered in Colombia, little coal has been found in South America. The lack of this important energy resource has made it difficult for parts of South America to achieve much industrial development.

Important metals are plentiful throughout the hemisphere. Vast supplies of iron ore are found in both Americas. Copper mines exist in the mountainous regions of both continents. Bolivians mine a large amount of tin. Mexico has many silver mines.

One of the most important resources of South America is bauxite. Other minerals in the Western Hemisphere include zinc, lead, chromium, and manganese. All these minerals are important to the modern industrial world. In addition, Colombia supplies 90 percent of the world's emeralds, green gemstones used in jewelry.

The water resources of the Western Hemisphere provide people with water for irrigation and for making electricity. Hydroelectric dams on rivers generate electricity for both home and industrial use. The United States ranks first in the world in the generation of hydroelectric power. Canada ranks third. Because South America has little coal, hydroelectric power has been particularly important to the industrial development of South American nations.

Geography Review

1. Name the three main divisions of the Western Hemisphere.
2. Are people in Santiago, Chile, or Buenos Aires, Argentina, more likely to feel earthquake tremors?
3. How have glaciers affected the landforms of North America?
4. Why is the Atacama Desert in Chile so dry? Look at the climate and physical maps on pages 485 and 487. What other regions in the Western Hemisphere might be dry for the same reasons?
5. Why is good soil one of the most important resources of the Western Hemisphere? In what latitudes is good soil usually found?
6. What products are grown in the tropics? What is the average temperature in the tropics?
7. Which is the most important oil-producing nation in South America?
8. Name a mineral resource that is found in North America but is rare in South America.
9. In what ways are water resources important to the people of the Western Hemisphere?
10. Using the maps on pages 487 and 490, compare and contrast the climate and products of the Mississippi Basin of North America with the Amazon Basin of South America.

Europeans Explore a New World

Focus

In 1492 a European explorer, Christopher Columbus, was trying to find a new route to India. When he sighted land after a long voyage, he thought he had succeeded. Instead, he had accidentally discovered the "New World."

The lands that Columbus found were not unsettled. People whom Europeans called Indians had developed civilizations there. Some had large empires. The riches of these empires attracted many European explorers. The explorers were followed by settlers. In time, European and Indian ways of life blended to form new cultures.

Look for these important words:

Key Words
- Mayas
- maize
- Aztecs
- Incas
- quipu

- llamas
- alpacas

People
- Pachacuti

Places
- Yucatán
- Lake Texcoco
- Tenochtitlán
- Cuzco

Look for answers to these questions:

1. What achievements in math and science were made by the Mayas?
2. How and where did the Aztecs build their capital?
3. How did a strong central government contribute to the success of the Inca Empire?

1. EARLY CIVILIZATIONS IN THE AMERICAS

Indian peoples have lived in North, Central, and South America from early times. These peoples and two other groups, Europeans and Africans, are the ancestors of most people in the Western Hemisphere today.

The native peoples of North, Central, and South America developed many kinds of cultures. Some lived simply, hunting and gathering the food they needed. Many others were farmers. Some Indians lived in small groups. Others, especially in Central and South America, formed large empires. They made striking achievements in science, government, and art.

The Mayas

The **Mayas** (MAH•yuhz) were the first great native civilization of Central America. They reached the height of their achievement between A.D. 100 and 900. They lived in the part of Central America called the **Yucatán** (yoo•kuh•TAN) peninsula. This land is mostly rain forest. Belize, southern Mexico, and part of Guatemala occupy it today.

Most of the Mayas were farmers. Their main crop was **maize** (MAYZ), which we call corn. They also grew beans, squash, peppers, and other vegetables. Flocks of turkeys added meat to their diet.

The Mayas built huge cities of stone. Each city had its own rulers. Large parts of the Mayan cities were devoted to religious worship. Temples rested atop tall pyramids. Stone masks 8 feet (2.4 m) high stood above the temple doors. The masks showed faces with narrow eyes, huge round noses, and feathered headdresses. These giant sculptures were painted in bright colors. The Mayas' love of art also showed in their pottery, feather decorations, and jade jewelry.

493

The Mayas associated the sun, moon, and other heavenly bodies with their gods. These religious beliefs caused the Mayas to become fine astronomers. Some Mayan buildings were both temples and places to observe the stars.

Mayan religion and astronomy also led them to invent a calendar. Their well-developed mathematics made their calendar far more accurate than those used in Europe at the time. The Mayan calendar could give correct dates for thousands of years into the past or the future. The Mayas also had a system of picture writing that is beginning to tell us more about their culture.

The Mayan civilization ended around A.D. 900. No one knows exactly why. The Mayas left their cities and never returned. The Mayan farmers, however, did not disappear. Many of their descendants still live in parts of Central America.

The Aztecs

The **Aztecs** of central and southern Mexico created one of the most powerful Indian civilizations in North America. They conquered much of the land that the Mayas had once ruled. The original homeland of the Aztecs may have been in northern Mexico. Around the twelfth century the Aztec people moved south into the Valley of Mexico. According to legend, their war god predicted that they would find a new home when they saw an eagle grasping a serpent in its mouth.

In 1325 the wandering Aztecs came to a marshy lake, **Lake Texcoco** (tes•KOH•koh), spread across the land.

During a period when the Mayas were ruled by the Aztecs and their allies, pyramids and temples were built at the ancient city of Chichén Itzá.

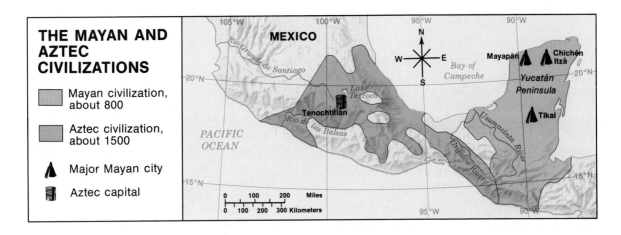

On an island in the center of the lake, the Aztec leaders saw the eagle with the snake in its beak as promised.

The Aztecs built a beautiful city on islands in the lake. They drove pillars into the soft earth and rested reed houses on them. They built four bridgelike roads across the marsh to connect the city with the mainland. They called their city **Tenochtitlán** (tay•noch•tee•TLAHN), which means "stone rising in water."

Aztec engineers built huge groups of temples and pyramids in Tenochtitlán. As Aztec power grew, priests began to make human sacrifices to the Aztec gods at the tops of the pyramids. Sometimes thousands of people, mostly war captives, were killed in single ceremonies.

Like the Mayas, the Aztecs had calendars and writing. They were wise in the use of plants as medicines. The Aztecs were also skilled metalworkers. Abundant gold and silver lay in their streams and mountains. The Aztecs made beautiful bells, earrings, and animal statues from these precious metals. When the Spanish came to Mexico, these treasures proved to be the Aztecs' downfall.

The Incas

The mountain range called the Andes curves like a backbone down the western side of South America. High in these snow-capped mountains, in the country of Peru, lies a city called **Cuzco** (KOOS•koh). Cuzco was the capital of another native civilization, that of the **Incas.**

In their own time, only the rulers of the empire were called Incas. Today we speak of their whole empire and its people as Incas. Descendants of the Incas live in Peru and Bolivia.

The Inca rulers claimed that they were children of the sun god. Legend says that they came to Cuzco around 1100. In 1438, under a strong king named **Pachacuti** (pah•chah•KYOO•tee), their power began to grow.

By the time Spanish explorers came to South America, the Inca emperors made no idle boast when they called their empire the "Four Quarters of the World." It stretched 2,500 miles (about 4,000 km) along the Andes, from southern Colombia far into Chile. It extended inland more than 300 miles (about 480 km) to include Bolivia and part of Argentina. It held about 7 million people.

To understand better the glory of the Inca empire, read what a young boy of Cuzco might have seen on a festival day at the height of the empire.

Day of the Sun

The chilly early morning was still dark, but already thousands of people thronged Cuzco's ceremonial square. They wore their finest clothes, cotton tunics and brightly dyed shawls of soft wool. On the edge of the crowd, Capac stared around him excitedly. Today the people of Cuzco would celebrate the "return of the sun."

The stone buildings of the Inca capital surrounded Capac, but he had eyes for only one: Coricancha (koh•rih• KAHN•chah), the House of Gold. He

Inca stonemasons reshaped a mountaintop to build Machu Picchu, a city whose ruins were long buried in the rain forest of Peru.

knew that inside this great temple, home of the sun god, the Inca was praying.

The broad strip of gold that rimmed the top of Coricancha's outer walls hinted at the beauty inside. Only the priests and priestesses of the sun and the royal family were allowed in the House of Gold. Yet Capac had heard rumors of the treasures it held. A great golden wall ran all through the building, people said. A huge disc of gold showed the sun's face. The temple's courtyard held a fantastic garden of plants and animals made from gold and silver.

Now the eastern horizon was growing lighter and lighter. Suddenly there was a gasp from thousands of throats. Capac shouted with the others as the first rays of dawn appeared. The sun was returning to its people!

A few moments later the huge doors of Coricancha opened. The Inca in all his splendor came out, carried in a litter. Capac and the others bowed to the ground.

A priest met the Inca's litter as it approached the center of the square. The priest and the Inca led the people in ceremonies to welcome the returning sun. Then the Inca went into his palace. Capac joined the crowd for a day full of parades and dancing.

Governing an Empire

The Inca rulers set up a powerful central government. The government's leaders had accurate records of everything in the empire. They knew how many men and women lived in each village, how old they were, and how much food their farms produced.

They knew how many workers could be called on to build a new temple or to fight in the army.

The Incas did not write down their records. They kept them by tying knots in colored strings called **quipu** (KEE•poo). In every Inca village one man was responsible for making quipu records for each ten families. The *quipu camayoc* (kahm•ah•YAHK), or rememberer, kept all the important records for the village. Copies were sent to the government in Cuzco. A royal storehouse contained thousands of these knotted strings.

The Incas held their empire together by constructing a system of wide, stone-paved roads. Across high mountain gorges where roads could not go, they built suspension bridges of rope cables. Some cables were as thick as a human body.

The Incas had neither horses nor wheeled vehicles. Instead, fleet-footed runners carried messages along the Inca roads. During their 15-day turns

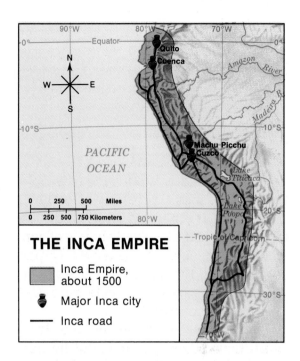

THE INCA EMPIRE

- Inca Empire, about 1500
- Major Inca city
- Inca road

Gold was highly prized by the Incas. From it they crafted ornamental birds and animals as well as utensils.

on duty, the runners lived in little houses beside the roads. One runner receiving a message would dash about 2 miles (3 km) to the next runner's house. The second runner continued on with the message as soon as it was received. This relay system could carry a message 150 miles (about 240 km) in a day. In time of war, soldiers could march along the roads very quickly, as well.

The people of the Inca empire were excellent farmers. They terraced the hillsides to keep the soil from washing away. Using irrigation and fertilizer, they raised abundant maize, potatoes, squash, and tropical fruits. The Incas were the first people known to cultivate the white potato.

The Inca people herded camellike animals called **llamas** (LAH•muhz) and **alpacas** (al•PAK•uhz). Inca women wove the coarse wool of the llamas and the finer wool of the alpacas into clothing. Llamas could carry fairly heavy loads.

497

Today as in Inca times, farmers terrace slopes of the Andes Mountains. Llamas, well-suited to the mountain air, are still used as pack animals.

When the animals died, the people used their hides and their meat.

Most of the food and clothing produced in Inca villages was given to the government. It was put in storehouses throughout the empire. Food from these storehouses fed the old, the crippled, and the helpless in each village. It fed the people of villages stricken by floods or earthquakes. It fed the conquering Inca armies. Because of this storehouse system, people almost never went hungry in the Inca Empire.

The Inca rulers expected work in return for the care they gave their people. At dawn on most days, a town crier climbed a high tower near each village and called out the orders of the day. Then the Inca people went to their tasks. Some built roads, temples, or bridges. Some went to the mines to extract gold or silver. Others toiled in palaces or forts. Most Incas worked together in the fields or guarded the llama and alpaca herds.

Were the Inca people happy with their carefully controlled lives? No one knows. We do know, however, that when a handful of Spanish invaders captured their king and took over their empire in 1532, few Incas resisted.

Reading Check

1. Why were the Mayas interested in astronomy?
2. In which North American country did the Aztecs settle?
3. Which precious metals were used by Aztec metalworkers?
4. How did the Incas keep important records in their empire?

Look for these important words:

Key Words
- compromise
- conquistadors

People
- Pedro Cabral
- Ferdinand Magellan
- Hernando Cortés
- Malinche
- Montezuma

- Francisco Pizarro
- Atahualpa

Places
- San Salvador
- Hispaniola

Look for answers to these questions:

1. Which European countries sent explorers to the Western Hemisphere?
2. How did Hernando Cortés conquer the Aztecs?
3. How did Francisco Pizarro conquer the Incas?
4. In what ways did Spanish conquerors change life in the Western Hemisphere?

2. CONQUERING A NEW WORLD

While Pachacuti's soldiers were setting up the Inca Empire, the countries of Europe also were expanding their horizons. Groups of Europeans had visited the Western Hemisphere long before the time of Columbus. Columbus, however, was the first to direct Europe's full attention to these faraway lands. His small fleet set sail on August 3, 1492. Columbus hoped to find a western route to the Far East.

On October 12, 1492, Columbus landed on a small island that he called **San Salvador** (SAN SAL•vuh•dawr). It was one of many islands in the Caribbean Sea, which lies between North and South America. Columbus was sure that he had come to the Indies, just as he had planned to do. For this reason he called the island's people Indians. Columbus never realized he had discovered a "new world," although other Europeans were soon to realize it.

The Explorers

Columbus received a hero's welcome when he, his crew, and six "Indian" captives returned to Spain in 1493. King Ferdinand and Queen Isabella quickly sent him back with 1,500 people and enough supplies to set up a colony on the large Caribbean island of **Hispaniola** (his•puhn•YOH•luh), which he also had discovered on his first trip.

Both Spain and Portugal wanted to protect their claims to the lands their sailors were exploring. They appealed to the Pope, who in those days made rulings in global affairs. In 1494, to keep peace between the two countries, the Pope suggested a **compromise.** A compromise is a solution that gives each side a part of its demands.

The Pope divided the still-unknown parts of the world between Spain and Portugal. Africa and the eastern lands

499

went to Portugal. Spain received most of the Western Hemisphere. The eastern bulge of South America fell within the lands given to Portugal, however.

In 1500 the king of Portugal ordered an explorer named **Pedro Cabral** to make a wide westward sweep before continuing around Africa. On his journey Cabral found the edge of the land later known as Brazil. As a result, the Portuguese settled Brazil, while most of the rest of Latin America was settled by the Spanish.

England, France, and other European nations also were sending ships into Atlantic waters at this time. Often they, too, were looking for a passage to the Far East. Rather than following the paths taken by Spain and Portugal, they sailed north. They were hoping to find a "Northwest Passage," a water route through North America to China and Japan. They did not find what they were looking for, because it does not exist, except through the frozen Arctic Ocean area. However, French and English explorers learned much about the eastern coast of North America.

European explorers had mapped the entire Atlantic coast of the Western Hemisphere by 1525. They had sighted

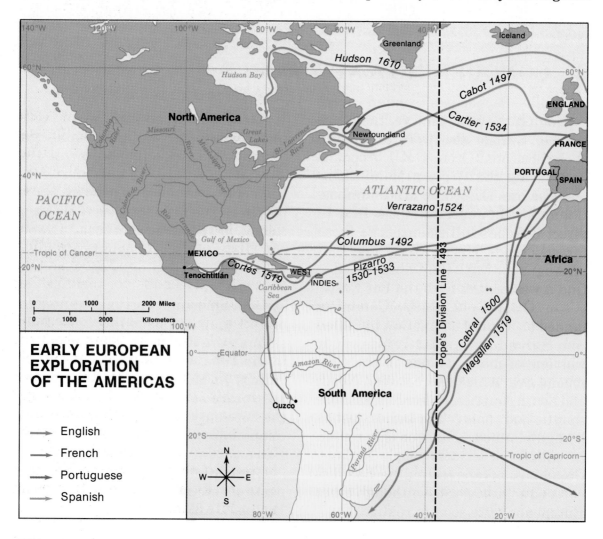

EARLY EUROPEAN EXPLORATION OF THE AMERICAS

→ English
→ French
→ Portuguese
→ Spanish

Doña Marina translates as Cortés and Montezuma exchange suspicious greetings. The Aztec ruler hoped that generous gifts would satisfy the Spanish.

the Pacific Ocean and had begun to explore the shores that it touched. Between 1519 and 1522 the ships of a daring Portuguese explorer named **Ferdinand Magellan** (muh•JEL•uhn) sailed all the way around the world.

The Conquistadors

Most of the men who came after the first explorers were the bold, treasure-seeking adventurers whom the Spanish called **conquistadors** (kahng•KEES•tuh•dawrz), or conquerors. The conquistadors wanted one thing above all else—gold.

In 1519 a black-bearded Spanish captain named **Hernando Cortés** (huhr•NAN•doh kawr•TEZ) set out to explore rumors of wealth in Mexico. He was one of the first and most famous conquistadors.

After Cortés arrived on the Yucatán, he greeted his translator. She was a woman named **Malinche** (muhl•IN•chee), who had been an Aztec princess before being captured and enslaved by the Mayas. She was one of 20 slaves whom the coastal Indians gave to the Spanish conquerors as a peace offering. She spoke both the Mayan and the Aztec languages. Cortés renamed her Doña Marina.

The Aztec ruler, **Montezuma** (mahn•tuh•ZOO•muh), heard about the arrival of Cortés. He could think of only one explanation for this tale of men with white skins. The chief Aztec god was Quetzalcoatl (ket•sahl•KWAHT•uhl), the "Plumed Serpent." Legend said that Quetzalcoatl would someday come to his people from across the sea. He would take the form of a man with a beard and white skin.

501

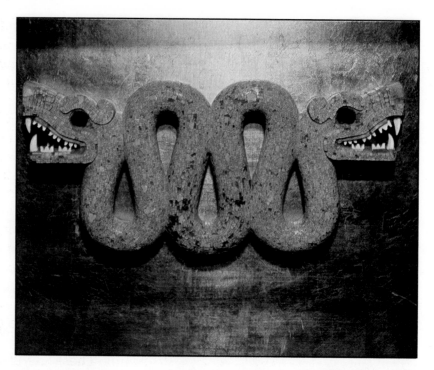

This ornament, a double-headed serpent made of turquoise and shell, was once worn by an Aztec priest. Montezuma sent it to Cortés as an offering of peace.

Montezuma thought that Cortés might be Quetzalcoatl. He ordered his representatives to present the "god" with gifts. They gave the Spaniards fabrics, foods, pottery, and gold. The beautiful golden jewelry and plates that the Aztecs gave Cortés sealed their fate. The Spaniards now more than ever wanted to see the source of all this wealth.

Cortés and his men marched to Tenochtitlán, the Aztec capital. There Montezuma greeted them warmly. The Aztec ruler and his people were awed and somewhat frightened by the Spaniards' horses and guns. They had never seen such things before.

Although they were at first treated as guests, the Spanish knew that the Aztecs would turn against them. To prevent the Aztecs from attacking, they held Montezuma as a hostage. Cortés used Montezuma to control the Indians and to make them bring payments of gold and other treasures.

Thinking that Montezuma was somehow cooperating with the Spanish, the Aztecs began to distrust their ruler. According to Spanish accounts, when Montezuma appeared before a rebellious crowd, the Indians hurled rocks at him. Three days later he lay dead from his wounds.

The Aztecs blamed Cortés for Montezuma's death. They wiped out almost all the Spanish soldiers in one terrible night. On June 30, 1520, many Spaniards drowned in Lake Texcoco as they tried to flee with their heavy stolen gold. Cortés, however, escaped. He returned the following year with more men. His army surrounded, captured, and finally burned Tenochtitlán.

Pizarro and the Incas

Another Spanish conquistador brought the great Inca civilization to an end. His name was **Francisco Pizarro** (frahn•SEES•koh puh•ZAHR•oh).

Unlike Cortés, Pizarro never learned to read and write.

Pizarro was a gray-bearded soldier when he came into Peru in 1532. Fortunately for him, he came at a time when the Inca empire was torn in two by civil war. The war was fought between two brothers named Huascar (WAHS·kahr) and **Atahualpa** (aht·uh·WAHL·puh). Both brothers claimed the Inca throne. After much fighting, Atahualpa killed his brother. The empire was weakened as a result of the civil war.

Atahualpa apparently saw no reason to hide from the white-skinned men who were looking for him. He sent messengers to bring Pizarro to him at a town called Cajamarca (kah·huh·MAHR·kuh). Pizarro staged a surprise attack during that meeting and quickly took the Inca prisoner.

Alarmed, Atahualpa tried to buy his freedom. "I will give you a large room filled with gold as high as I can reach if you release me," he said. The Spaniards agreed. Atahualpa kept his word, but Pizarro's men killed him anyway. They went on to capture Cuzco and the empire with amazing ease.

Many explorers and conquistadors came after Cortés and Pizarro. Chasing golden legends, they discovered vast new lands whose real riches—good water and rich soil—they never fully understood.

These first European visitors to the Western Hemisphere were often greedy and cruel. They destroyed much. Yet no one can deny their courage. They were willing to risk their lives to get what they wanted. The icy peaks of the Andes, the steaming rain forests of Central America, and the parched deserts of North America's Southwest did not stop them. As the conquistadors pursued their quest for gold and silver, they paved a path for others to follow. Their explorations made possible the colonization of these rich lands.

Pizarro, conqueror of the Incas, was later killed by others who envied his power.

Reading Check

1. Which two European countries sent explorers to Central and South America?
2. Why were the conquistadors interested in coming to the New World?
3. How did the Aztecs first react to the Spaniards who entered their capital?
4. What had weakened the Inca Empire just before Pizarro came?

COMPARING MAP PROJECTIONS

When Columbus sailed to the Western Hemisphere, he did not have accurate maps to help him. Most Europeans at that time knew about only three continents: Europe, Africa, and Asia.

When New World explorers made discoveries, they drew maps to record them. Mapmakers added the new places to their maps. As knowledge of the world increased, maps became more complete. Yet no map could represent the Earth exactly.

Maps are more skillfully drawn today, but they still have a problem common to those early maps. Since the Earth is a sphere, a flat map cannot show it exactly. Shapes and sizes of continents, distances, and directions are accurate only on a globe.

Mapmakers have developed different ways to show the round world on paper. These different views are called **projections.** Every map projection has some errors or **distortions,** however. This is because mapmakers must change the shape of the globe, splitting or stretching it to make it flat. When a small area of the Earth is shown, the distortion is not great. When the whole world is shown, some areas will be distorted more than others.

Different kinds of projections create different kinds of distortions. Some maps change the shape or size of the area shown. Some maps show distances greater or less than they actually are. A mapmaker chooses a projection depending on the purpose of the map. For example, in a map showing countries and cities, the mapmaker will use a projection that makes the shapes of most continents look correct.

Polar Projections

A **polar projection** shows the Northern or Southern hemisphere. The North or South pole is at the center of the map. The lines of latitude are circles that get larger the farther they are from the center. The lines of longitude are straight lines that extend from the center in all directions, like the spokes of a wheel.

Look at the land areas near the North Pole on the polar map. Like a globe, this map shows that the northern parts of North America, Europe, and Asia are close together. Now look at the outer edges. The shapes and actual distances become quite distorted.

This type of projection is useful mainly to airplane pilots. You may recall that the shortest distance between two points on the

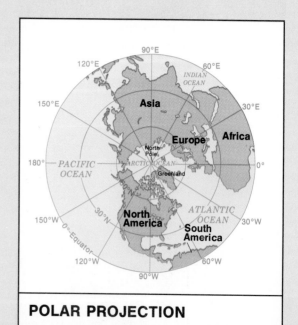

POLAR PROJECTION

globe is on a great circle. On a polar projection any straight line between two points is on a great circle. Using this projection, a pilot can find the shortest route between places.

Mercator Projections

One of the most common kinds of flat maps is the **Mercator projection.** It was named for its sixteenth-century inventor, Gerhardus Mercator (gair•HAHR•duhs mur•KAY•tuhr). Notice that the meridians on a Mercator projection are an equal distance apart. On a globe the meridians get closer as they near the poles, where they meet. The parallels on a Mercator projection get wider apart toward the poles. On a globe, all such lines of latitude are an equal distance apart.

Find the equator and latitude 30°N on the map. Notice how close together they are. Now find latitudes 30°N and 60°N. The distance between these lines is greater. Because of these changes, a Mercator projection shows most continents in about the right shape.

Notice, however, that the land near the poles looks larger than it really is. Mercator maps of large areas distort the size of some countries. Find Greenland on this map and on the polar projection. On which map does Greenland seem larger than Europe?

Because of this kind of distortion, the Mercator projection is not accurate for measuring long distances. It is most useful, however, for finding correct compass directions. Sailors since Mercator's time have used this kind of map to figure out their routes. Find the United States and France on the map. In what direction would you travel from the United States to France?

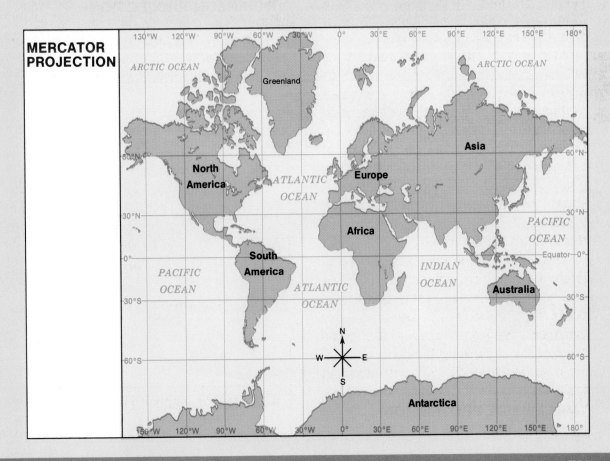

Equal-Area Projections

Some projections show the whole world in a shape that looks somewhat like a globe. The Prime Meridian and the equator divide the hemispheres so that their areas are equal. This type of map is called an **equal-area projection.** It is useful for comparing information about different parts of the world. The equal-area projection is often used to show world population, vegetation, and rainfall.

There are many different types of equal-area projections. Look at the **Mollweide** (mohl•WYD•uh) **projection** below.

On this map the parallels get closer together toward the poles. The meridians are evenly spaced and meet at the poles, as they do on a globe. Find North America on this map and on the Mercator projection. Notice that the shape of the continent becomes distorted at the sides of the Mollweide map.

Now find South America on this map and on the Mercator projection. The Mollweide map shows the size of South America more accurately. Which of these two maps shows the size of Africa more accurately?

The equal-area projection used in this text to show the whole world is called the **Robinson projection.** Look at the following illustration. How is the Robinson projection different from the Mollweide projection?

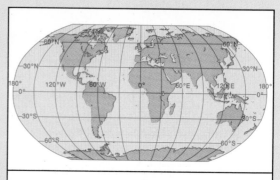

ROBINSON PROJECTION

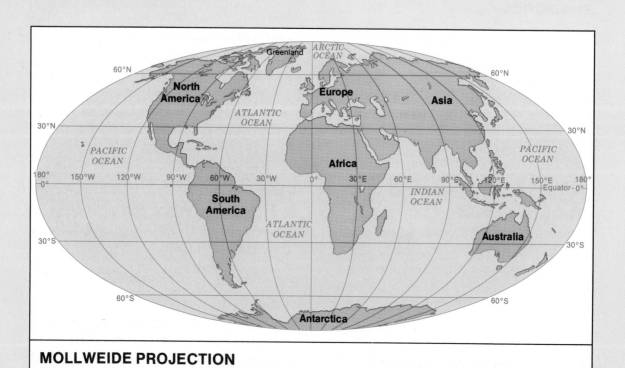

MOLLWEIDE PROJECTION

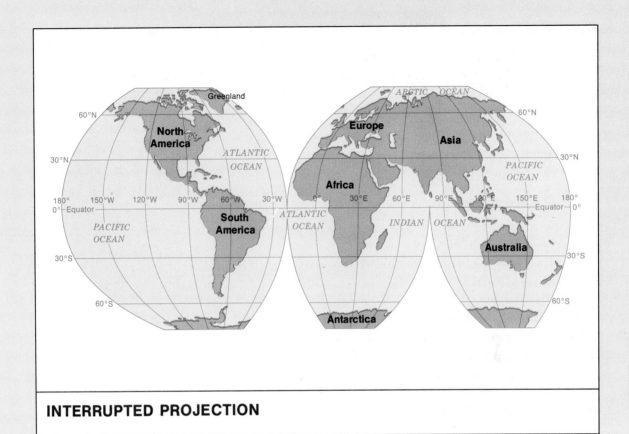

INTERRUPTED PROJECTION

Interrupted Projections

If you look at a globe closely, you will see that a map is pasted in pieces around it. An **interrupted projection** is like this kind of map. If you gathered together the tips of each part, it would form a shape much like a globe.

Look at the lines of latitude and longitude on the interrupted projection. The lines of latitude are evenly spaced, and the meridians meet at the poles, as they do on a globe. Because an interrupted projection is also an equal-area projection, the shapes and sizes of the continents are fairly accurate. Antarctica and the oceans are split, however. This makes it difficult to judge distances between some places. With the exception of travel maps, this projection can be used for a wide variety of maps.

CHECKING YOUR SKILLS

Use the maps in this lesson to answer these questions.

1. Look at North America on the Mercator and Mollweide projections. On which projection does it appear larger?

2. On which projections are the shapes of South America the most similar?

3. Which projection can help you find great circle routes? Which projection is best for finding a compass route?

4. Where is the equator on a polar projection?

5. On any map, find the latitude and longitude of the southern tip of South America. Is it at the same latitude and longitude on all the maps?

Look for these important words:

Key Words
- haciendas
- viceroys
- audiencias

- Creoles
- mestizos
- quinine
- malaria

Places
- Latin America
- Veracruz
- Porto Bello
- Lima

Look for answers to these questions:

1. How were farming and ranching carried out in Latin American countries?
2. How were government and trade controlled in the colonies?
3. Who were the Creoles? Why were they interested in independence?
4. How did contact with the Western Hemisphere affect Europeans?

3. COLONIAL LIFE IN LATIN AMERICA

The Western Hemisphere was under the control of Europe from about 1500 to 1800. People from different European countries settled in different parts of the Americas. As a result, the regions of the Western Hemisphere developed in different ways.

Mexico and Central and South America were settled mostly by people from Spain and Portugal. These lands still show many signs of Spanish and Portuguese culture. Because of their common heritage, Mexico and Central and South America are often grouped together under the name **Latin America.** *Latin* refers to the origin of the Spanish and Portuguese languages.

The English settled much of North America. Large French settlements in the northern part of the continent and Spanish settlements in the south were also important in North American history.

The English and French began coming to North America in large numbers around 1600. By that time the Spanish had already built more than 200 towns and many small settlements in Latin America. Towns and settlements also were thriving in the large Portuguese colony of Brazil.

The lure of rich farmland brought many people to Latin America. Early settlers set up big farms or plantations called **haciendas** (hah•see•EN•duhz). They raised tropical crops, such as sugar cane, cotton, coffee, cacao, and tobacco. Later, other settlers established cattle ranches in the grasslands of Argentina and Brazil.

Spanish and Portuguese landowners forced the Indians to work on their

Grist mill

Workers' houses

Blacksmith Stable Livestock

Corral

Storage

Spinning and weaving

Carpenter Pottery

Well

Kitchen and baths

Vegetable gardens

Canals

Priests' quarters

Patio

Main house

Church

Orchard

A SPANISH HACIENDA IN THE NEW WORLD

Throughout their history, Indians have traded goods and produce at markets like this one in Cuzco. Their method of weaving is 3,000 years old.

haciendas and ranches. Spanish law said that the landowners were supposed to educate and care for the Indians in return for this work. However, the landowners often did not keep their part of the bargain.

The hacienda owners soon found they needed more labor than the Indians could give. Therefore, they brought millions of African slaves to work on their plantations. The Africans proved to be skilled, hardy workers.

Government and Trade

The chief government officials in the Spanish colonies were **viceroys.** *Viceroy* means "one who takes the place of the king." The viceroys were chosen by the king of Spain. Each viceroy's huge territory was divided into smaller parts run by captains-general. Courts called **audiencias** (oh•dee•EN•see•uhz) also helped govern the colonies. Town councils made local decisions.

The rulers of Spain made sure they got the largest share of New World wealth. For example, one-fifth of all gold and silver went to the king. The Spanish kings also grew rich by controlling all trade in the colonies. The colonists were not supposed to trade with any other colonies or other European countries. Many colonists felt that these trade laws were unfair.

Spain sent two large fleets of ships to the New World each year. One fleet went to the Mexican city of **Veracruz** (ver•uh•KROOZ). The other went to **Porto Bello,** in Panama. The ships were laden with trade goods.

510

When word came that the Spanish fleet was on the way, traders from all over the colonies journeyed to meet them. They set up log booths on the town square and covered them with sailcloth. They sold hides, sugar, silver, spices, and jewels to the Spanish. They bought fine clothing, dishes, and other manufactured goods.

This giant trade fair lasted for over a month. When it was finished, the fleet sailed away. The traders loaded Spanish goods onto the backs of mules or into their own ships to take to eager buyers in distant colonial cities.

Social Life and Religion

A person's parents and place of birth determined his or her social class in colonial Latin America. People who came from Spain held the highest positions. They looked down on the **Creoles** (KREE•ohlz), people who had European parents but were born in the colonies. The Creoles owned land and were often wealthy. They could not take part in government, however. They filled their time with sports events, parties, and the theater.

Far below the Spanish-born and the Creoles were the people of mixed blood. People of European and Indian descent, **mestizos** (mes•TEE•zohz), were the most common kind of mixture. Mestizos and other people of mixed blood were usually poor. Yet, their lives were easier than those of the Indians and African slaves, who were at the very bottom of the social ladder.

Catholic missionaries accompanying the conquerors to Latin America gained tremendous influence. This cathedral was built over an Inca palace in 1654.

The Catholic religion was important to Spaniard, Creole, mestizo, and Indian alike. Priests came to the New World with the first explorers. They converted millions of Indians to Christianity. Most of the missionaries worked hard to care for the natives. Often they tried to stop Spanish landowners from mistreating these people.

The church was always the biggest building in a Spanish town. It was the center of social life for all the townspeople. Every important religious holiday brought parades, carnivals, and festivals. Priests also provided the only education for the townspeople.

Government, trade, and religion in Spanish colonies were wholly controlled by laws made in Spain. These laws were strictly enforced by representatives who were appointed in Spain. The majority of the people living in Spanish colonies had no voice in their government.

Moves Toward Independence

In 1700 Philip V, who was related to the kings of France, inherited the Spanish throne. He relaxed some of the strict laws that governed the colonies. Many colonists felt the changes were not enough. They had heard about new ideas of freedom spreading through Europe and North America. These ideas stated that all people had certain rights, including the right to participate in government.

The Creoles especially were interested in these new ideas. More and more they resented the governments across the sea. They were often both richer and better educated than the European-born nobles who ruled over them.

Simón Bolívar, a Creole, fought Spain for Latin American independence.

They wanted control over their land and their lives.

In the last quarter of the eighteenth century, the American and French revolutions showed the Latin American colonists that people could fight for their freedom and win. Following these examples, the Latin Americans began fighting for their independence around 1800. By 1825 revolutions had freed most Latin Americans from European rule.

By that time, however, the peoples of Europe and the Western Hemisphere had changed each other's lives forever. New foods, such as corn, potatoes, coffee, and chocolate, graced many European tables. **Quinine** (KWY•nyn), a medicine taken from the bark of South American cinchona (sin•KOH•nuh) trees, was used to help Europeans recover

512

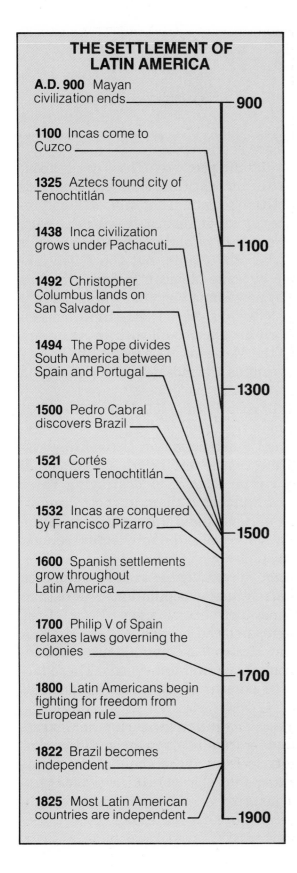

THE SETTLEMENT OF LATIN AMERICA

A.D. 900 Mayan civilization ends —— 900

1100 Incas come to Cuzco ——

1325 Aztecs found city of Tenochtitlán ——

1438 Inca civilization grows under Pachacuti —— 1100

1492 Christopher Columbus lands on San Salvador ——

1494 The Pope divides South America between Spain and Portugal —— 1300

1500 Pedro Cabral discovers Brazil ——

1521 Cortés conquers Tenochtitlán ——

1532 Incas are conquered by Francisco Pizarro —— 1500

1600 Spanish settlements grow throughout Latin America ——

1700 Philip V of Spain relaxes laws governing the colonies ——

1700

1800 Latin Americans begin fighting for freedom from European rule ——

1822 Brazil becomes independent ——

1825 Most Latin American countries are independent —— 1900

from the deadly fever called **malaria** (muh•LAYR•ee•uh).

The changes that the Europeans brought to the Western Hemisphere were both good and bad. The Europeans damaged or destroyed many Indian civilizations. They deliberately killed thousands of people. Smallpox and other European sicknesses killed millions more.

The Europeans built as well as destroyed, however. For example, Cortés built Mexico City on the ruins of Tenochtitlán. After Pizarro had captured Cuzco, he started a new city of his own: **Lima** (LEE•muh), the "City of Kings." Europeans introduced cattle, sheep, horses, and other useful livestock to the Western Hemisphere. They introduced iron tools and the wheel.

Indian, European, and African cultures have combined to make the Western Hemisphere what it is today. This is especially true of Latin America. Many Latin Americans, for example, speak both an Indian language and Spanish or Portuguese. Latin American music contains echoes of lively African rhythms, the flutes of the Andes, and stately court dances of Portugal and Spain.

Reading Check

1. Why are Mexico and Central and South America often called Latin America?
2. Which people were forced to work on the haciendas?
3. What was the center of social life for all of a town's people in colonial Latin America?
4. What changes did Europeans bring to Latin America?

513

Mexico City

"The city is a great domed tree, precious as a jade.... Beneath it the lords are sheltered."

A Nahuatl (NAH•waht•uhl) poet wrote these words about the ancient Aztec city of Tenochtitlán. Today, another city has risen in Tenochtitlán's place. That city, still as precious as a jade, is the capital of Mexico. It is Mexico City.

Mexico City is a mixture of old and new. Spanish is spoken by most of the inhabitants, but the Aztec language is still spoken by some Mexican Indians who live there. Mexicans enjoy plazas and airy courtyards that are similar to old Spanish designs. At the same time, modern buildings of Mexico City have been built with an eye toward the Aztec heritage of the Mexicans. As a result, the beauty and style of Aztec pyramids and mosaic murals have been preserved.

Even a ride on the recently completed subway system of Mexico City can be a reminder of the great Aztec civilization. While tunnel construction for the subway system was under way during the late 1960s, workers often encountered Aztec ruins. Instead of destroying these ancient finds, planners included them in their designs. Mexico City's many museums and universities help the city retain its reputation as one of the intellectual centers of the Western Hemisphere.

Mexico City is rapidly becoming the largest urban area in the world. It has an estimated population of more than 15 million people and continues to grow. Many of its industries also are growing and provide jobs for Mexican workers. Factories in Mexico City manufacture automobiles and trucks, appliances, and televisions. These factories supply up to 60 percent of the nation's industrial output.

Old and new Mexico City play a large part in Mexico's tourist industry. Visitors from all over the world land at Mexico City's airport to enjoy all of the sights, sounds and tastes that make this city one of the centers of Western culture.

Museum display—
Aztec calendar

Ruins in subway

University library

CHAPTER 17 REVIEW

USING WORDS

Explain the meaning of each of the words listed below. Then use each word in a complete sentence.

1. **alpacas**
2. **compromise**
3. **conquistadors**
4. **Creoles**
5. **haciendas**
6. **maize**
7. **mestizos**
8. **quinine**
9. **quipu**
10. **viceroys**

REVIEWING FACTS

1. Name three great Indian civilizations of Latin America.

2. What science was developed by the Mayas because of their religion?

3. What was done with the food and clothing that the Inca villages gave to the government?

4. How did the Pope keep peace between Spain and Portugal?

5. Why did Montezuma send Cortés gifts?

6. How was gold responsible in part for the fall of the Aztec and Inca empires?

7. How were Spanish colonies governed?

8. What influence did the Catholic religion have on Latin American colonies?

9. Which Latin American group was most interested in new ideas about freedom and equality? Why?

10. What cultures have combined to make up the Western Hemisphere?

THINKING CRITICALLY

1. Compare what you know about the early civilizations of the Eastern and Western hemispheres. How were the cultures of the ancient Sumerians and Egyptians similar to the cultures of the native Indian groups of Latin America? How were they different?

2. England, rather than Spain, was the main influence in North America. Think about the reasons for exploration, the discoveries that were made, and the ways in which colonies were organized. In what ways were European exploration and colonization in Latin America like exploration and colonization in North America? In what ways were they different?

◯ PRACTICING SKILLS

Projections   Number your paper from 1 to 4. Identify each map shown below as a polar, a Mercator, an equal-area, or an interrupted projection. Describe how each projection is most commonly used.

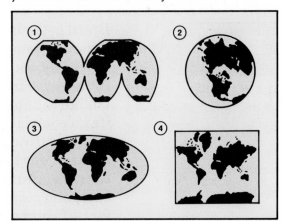

Brazil Moves Ahead

Focus

Brazil is the largest country in Latin America. It is different from other Latin American countries in several important ways. Most of the Europeans who settled in Brazil came from Portugal rather than from Spain. Unlike the Spanish American republics, Brazil gained its independence without having to fight for it.

Today, Brazil is a leader among Latin American nations. It is the most industrialized country in South America. Brazil has many problems to solve, but its energetic people and vast untapped resources offer hope for its future development.

516

Look for these important words:

Key Words
- sertão
- fazendas
- gauchos

- manioc
- hammocks

Places
- Great Escarpment

- Amazon Region
- Minas Gerais
- Brasília

Look for answers to these questions:

1. What are the five regions of Brazil?
2. How do land, climate, and resources differ among the regions?
3. What groups have contributed to the culture of Brazil?

1. THE GEOGRAPHY OF BRAZIL

Brazil is the giant of Latin America. It takes up almost half the continent of South America. It is the world's fifth-largest country. Only the Soviet Union, Canada, China, and the United States are larger. Brazil touches the borders of all the countries in South America except Chile and Ecuador.

Beautiful beaches and fertile farmland lie along Brazil's Atlantic coast. Just inland from the coast the land rises abruptly in a clifflike wall called the **Great Escarpment** (eh•SKAHRP•muhnt). Much of Brazil beyond the Great Escarpment is highland plateau or low hills.

Most of Brazil is in the tropics and has warm weather. The areas closest to the equator are hot and humid, averaging almost 80°F (27°C). Because of their elevation, however, the central highlands are usually not unpleasantly hot.

Heavy rainfall occurs in the northern and southern areas and along the coast. All areas receive some rainfall, with the average in most of Brazil being about 50 inches (127 cm) in a year.

Brazil is made up of 23 states and three territories. It can be divided into five large regions. Each region has different geography, climate, and resources.

The North

The North is Brazil's biggest region. Most of it is covered by thick rain forest. The world's largest river, the Amazon, flows through this part of Brazil. North Brazil is therefore often called the **Amazon Region.** The Amazon River is so wide in places that a person cannot see from one shore to the other. In some places the river is 300 feet (91 m) deep.

Very few people live in this hot, humid land. Here and there, small groups of Indians farm, gather fruit from the forest trees, or hunt animals with poison darts shot from blowguns.

517

Some Indian groups live along the Amazon. They gather products of the rain forest and ship them down the river. One important product is rubber, made from the sap of a tree that grows wild in the forest. Other products are fine woods, forest plants that can be made into medicines, and the tasty nuts called Brazil nuts.

The Northeast

Northeast Brazil is a land of contrasts. A strip of rich farmland lines the coast. This was the first part of Brazil to be settled by the Portuguese. The colonial capital city of Bahia (buh•HEE•uh), now called Salvador (SAL•vuh•dawr), is on the northeast coast. From this port Brazilians ship large quantities of tobacco, sugar, and cacao. From this region also comes the valuable wax from the leaves of the carnauba (kahr•NAW•buh) palm tree. Carnauba wax is used to make record albums, lipstick, and wood polish.

The inland part of the Northeast is a semiarid plain dotted with coarse grass and scrubby trees. Brazilians call this plain the **sertão** (sur•TOW), or wasteland. Drought often strikes the small farms of the *sertão*, causing crops and animals to die. Helping the people of the *sertão* has been a major goal of the Brazilian government.

The East

The East is perhaps the most beautiful part of Brazil. Green fields of sugar

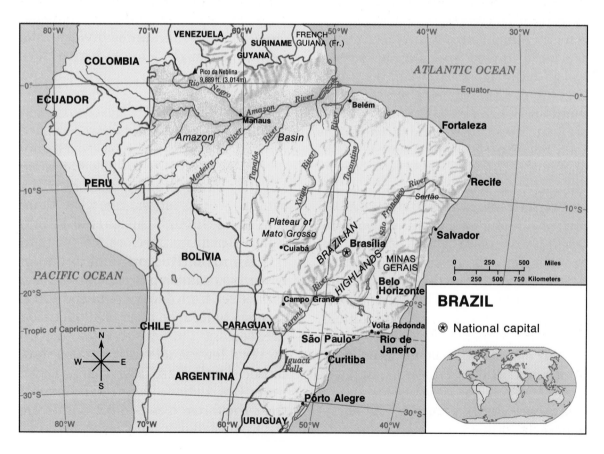

cane, coffee trees, and other farm crops cover much of it. The hills and white-sand beaches of Rio de Janeiro (REE•oh day zhuh•NAIR•oh), Brazil's second-largest city, attract visitors from all over the world.

The inland Eastern state of **Minas Gerais** (MEE•nuhs zheh•RYS), whose name means "general mines," is rich in minerals. Three hundred years ago the mines of Minas Gerais produced gold and diamonds. Today their main product is iron ore, less glamorous but just as important.

The Southeast

Southeast Brazil is the richest and most heavily populated part of the country. It contains Brazil's largest city, São Paulo (SOW POW•loo). More than 80 percent of Brazil's industrial output comes from the São Paulo area's busy factories.

Coffee, Brazil's biggest export crop, thrives in the red-purple soil of the Southeast. The coffee trees are grown on large plantations called **fazendas** (fah•ZEN•duhz). Workers care for the trees and pick the red coffee berries when they are ripe.

Other farms in the Southeast grow rice, corn, or grapes. Vast herds of cattle and sheep roam the South's grassland, tended by cowboys called **gauchos** (GOW•chohz).

The Central-West

The Central-West is the "Wild West" of Brazil. It had a gold rush, and it still has cattle and gauchos. About half of it is covered by forests. Most of the rest is grassland.

Gauchos who once freely roamed the pampas now work on large ranches.

The Brazilian government has encouraged more people to move to this thinly settled part of the country. In the late 1950s a new city, **Brasília** (bruh•ZIL•yuh), was built in the Central-West and was made the capital of Brazil. Today the Central-West is the fastest growing region of Brazil.

The People of Brazil

Half the people in South America live in Brazil. Even so, Brazil is thinly populated for its size. Nine out of every ten Brazilians live on one third of the country's land, the fertile strip along the coast. Most are jammed into Brazil's largest cities.

Today about 45 percent of Brazilian workers are farmers or ranchers. They grow rice, corn, beans, squash, and a starchy, edible root called **manioc** (MAN•ee•ahk). In addition to food they grow cash crops such as coffee, cotton, cacao, tobacco, soybeans, and sugar cane. Brazilian ranchers tend one of the largest livestock populations in the world.

519

Factories are important to Brazil, employing about one out of five of Brazil's workers. Millions of others have government or service jobs.

Most Brazilians are descended from one or more of three groups of people: Indians, Africans, and Europeans. Sixty-two percent of Brazil's people are descended from Europeans. Another 11 percent are of African descent. Most other Brazilians, except for a few hundred thousand Indians, are of mixed blood.

Each of these groups has made important contributions to the culture of Brazil. Indians taught Europeans how to live in the new land. They showed them how to grow and cook maize, manioc, and sweet potatoes. They taught them to use the comfortable sling beds called **hammocks.**

Indians living in the Amazon forests make up about 1 percent of Brazil's population.

Most Europeans who came to Brazil in its early days were from Portugal. Adventurers, settlers, and priests spread Portuguese culture, language, and religion throughout the country. Nearly all Brazilians still speak Portuguese and are Roman Catholics.

The late nineteenth and early twentieth centuries brought a new wave of European immigrants to Brazil. These immigrants included people from Germany, Italy, Poland, and Switzerland. In recent years, people from Japan, Syria, and Lebanon also have come to live in Brazil.

The Portuguese brought almost four million African slaves to Brazil. Often the Africans knew more about farming and mining in the tropics than the Indians or the Europeans did. Their work made the settlement of Brazil possible. The Africans left a deep imprint on Brazilian music, cooking, folklore, and art.

Indians, Europeans, and Africans mixed and married more freely in Brazil than in most other parts of the Western Hemisphere. As a result, many people in Brazil are descended from two or even all three of these groups. These very different kinds of people combined to make a new people, the Brazilians.

Reading Check

1. By what other name is the North of Brazil often called?
2. What is Brazil's biggest export crop? Where is it grown?
3. From which three groups of people are most Brazilians descended?
4. How did the Africans influence Brazil's settlement?

Look for these important words:

Key Words
- brazilwood
- bandeirantes
- illiterate

People
- Pedro I
- Pedro II
- Getulio Vargas
- Juscelino Kubitschek

Places
- Volta Redonda

Look for answers to these questions:

1. How did Brazil gain its independence?
2. What different kinds of government has Brazil had since its independence?
3. Why was Pedro II popular in Brazil? Why did he lose his popularity?
4. How did many Brazilians feel about Getulio Vargas? Why did they feel that way?

2. GROWTH OF A NATION

The Portuguese explorer Pedro Cabral discovered Brazil in 1500, and Portugal claimed this part of South America. It did not pay much attention to its huge new colony at first. The only valuable thing there seemed to be **brazilwood,** which was used to make a red dye. Brazilwood gave the colony its name.

Brazil's farmlands later attracted Portuguese settlers. They set up large sugar cane plantations on the country's northeastern coast. The settlers forced Indians and large numbers of African slaves to work on the plantations.

Meanwhile, small groups of men explored the backlands of Brazil. Because these adventurers often carried a flag or banner, they were called **bandeirantes** (ban•DEE•uh•rahn•tayz). Missionary priests and roving cattle herders also explored and settled the interior of Brazil.

An Independent Empire

Brazil's history began to change one day in 1808, when a small fleet of ships sailed into the harbor of Rio de Janeiro. The ships carried the Portuguese royal family. They were fleeing from the French emperor, Napoleon, who had invaded Portugal. Prince John of Portugal set up a new capital in Rio. He allowed free trade between Brazil and other countries for the first time. The Brazilians felt a new pride in their country.

Prince John became king of Portugal in 1816, but he preferred to remain in Brazil. In 1821 the Portuguese parliament insisted that John come back to Portugal. He reluctantly agreed,

521

leaving his son, **Pedro I,** behind to rule Brazil.

In 1822 the Portuguese government demanded that Prince Pedro also come home. Pedro refused. He knew that Brazilians were eager to break their colonial ties. He drew his sword and shouted, "Independence or death!" The joyful Brazilians crowned Pedro as their first emperor that same year.

In contrast to the republics of Spanish America, Brazil gained its independence peacefully. Portugal acknowledged the new empire without a fight in 1825.

Pedro I liked the Brazilians, but his ways of acting and ruling were Portuguese. He frequently ignored the Brazilian legislature. The Brazilians finally decided that Pedro's ties with Portugal were too close. The emperor, realizing he was unpopular, gave up the throne to his son, also named Pedro, in 1831. **Pedro II** at that time was just five years old.

Brazil changed its government peacefully when Pedro I, shown here, resigned.

Young Pedro was a serious, intelligent boy who loved to study. He once said, "If I were not emperor, I should like to have been a schoolteacher." The Brazilians let him take control of the country when he was only 15.

Pedro II was a wise and popular ruler. He chose the best people he could find for his government. He included people with different political views. He brought the parts of his sprawling country closer together by setting up telegraph lines, building railroads, and beginning steamer service on the rivers. He encouraged business and started Brazil on its way to becoming a modern nation.

After about 1870 the United States became Brazil's chief trading partner. Emperor Pedro strengthened the ties between these two important Western Hemisphere nations. He visited the United States Centennial Exposition in Philadelphia in 1876. He was fascinated by the many inventions he saw there, especially Alexander Graham Bell's telephone.

Emperor Pedro was troubled deeply by the problem of slavery. Slavery had been outlawed in most countries by the 1870s, but it was still allowed in Brazil. Many Brazilians, including the emperor, wanted to free Brazil's slaves. However, the powerful owners of the sugar and coffee plantations insisted that they needed slave workers.

Pedro tried to prepare his country for the changes that freeing its slaves would bring. He encouraged new workers to come to Brazil from Europe. He started factories so that Brazil's economy would not depend on plantations alone.

In 1888 Pedro's parliament passed the "Golden Law," which freed all slaves in Brazil. This law made the plantation owners angry with Emperor Pedro. They felt that he was trying to change Brazil too fast.

Other people felt that Pedro was not changing Brazil fast enough. During a long border war with Paraguay in the 1860s, Brazil had developed a powerful and professional army. The army leaders wanted to play a larger part in government than the emperor would allow.

A growing number of people in Brazil's cities were also impatient for change. They decided they did not want an empire at all. They wanted Brazil to be a republic, like most of the other countries in the Western Hemisphere.

In 1889 these groups forced Pedro II to give up his throne and leave Brazil. The emperor was sad to go, but he refused to fight his people. Once again Brazil made a major change in its government without bloodshed.

A New Republic

After Emperor Pedro left Brazil, the army leaders took over the government. They proclaimed Brazil to be a republic and wrote a constitution that was closely modeled on the Constitution of the United States.

There were important differences between Brazil and the United States, however. According to Brazil's constitution, people who were **illiterate** (ih•LIT•uhr•it), or unable to read and write, were not allowed to vote. Since most Brazilians were illiterate, this meant that only a small number of people could vote. Brazil had become a republic in name, but in fact most power remained in the hands of the plantation owners and the army.

The young Brazilian republic made rapid progress in the early twentieth century. It rebuilt Rio and other cities and opened many new factories. It also took part in world organizations, such as the League of Nations.

Brazil's development brought growing pains, however. The government printed so much money to spend on improvement projects that inflation resulted. Immigrants made the cities grow too fast. Many of the new arrivals crowded together in slums.

Brazil's coffee crop also grew too fast. By the 1920s "coffee was king." The Brazilian economy hovered near disaster whenever world coffee prices fell. The worst coffee crisis came when the Great Depression started in the United States in 1929. During the depression the demand for coffee dropped. Brazilian planters were left with so much unsold coffee that they had to burn it or dump it into the sea.

Vargas and After

Because of the unrest caused by the depression and other problems, army leaders took over Brazil's government again in 1930. They installed as president a man named **Getulio Vargas** (zheh•TOO•lyoo VAHR•guhs). Vargas kept control of Brazil's government for more than 15 years. Between 1937 and 1945 he did not allow elections or opposition parties. He ruled as a dictator.

In spite of this, many Brazilians liked Vargas. His economic programs helped Brazil survive the depression. Vargas helped the coffee planters, but

Brazil's steel production has increased greatly since the Volta Redonda steel mill was built. It was constructed with aid from the United States.

he also ordered them to begin growing other crops. He encouraged Brazilian industry by starting a big steel mill at **Volta Redonda,** near São Paulo. He built new railroads and improved air transportation.

Vargas passed many laws to help Brazilian workers. He guaranteed them fair salaries. He limited the number of hours they could be made to work. He brought education to more Brazilians.

Pressure from the army and the Brazilian people forced Vargas to allow free elections again in 1945. The people elected another leader, but in 1950 they returned Getulio Vargas to office for an additional four years. He had given them a sense of unity and national pride that they remembered.

Presidents since Vargas also have had ambitious plans for Brazil. In 1956, for example, President **Juscelino Kubitschek** (zhoo•seh•LEE•noo KOO•bih•chek) ordered the new capital city of Brasília to be built. His government also began building 11,000 miles

(17,699 km) of highways to connect all parts of the country with Brasília and each other.

In 1964 the military again took control of Brazil. Three generals, one after another, headed Brazil's government. They refused to allow elections and punished political protest. However, unhappiness with military rule led to the formation of new political parties and a demand for a presidential election. In January 1985 an election was held. For the first time in 21 years, Brazil had a democratic government.

Reading Check

1. What attracted Portuguese settlers to Brazil?
2. Why were plantation owners angry with Pedro II?
3. What caused the coffee crisis in Brazil?
4. What group has controlled Brazil's government for most of the past 100 years?

Look for these important words:

Key Words
- favelas

- gasohol
- LANDSAT

Places
- Iguacú Falls

Look for answers to these questions:

1. What important sides of today's Brazil are shown by Rio de Janeiro, São Paulo, and Brasília?
2. What new sources of energy is Brazil developing?
3. How is Brazil developing its land resources?

3. BRAZIL TODAY

Modern Brazil is a land of progress, but it also has problems. Both problems and progress show in the way Brazilians are developing their cities and their natural resources.

A Tale of Three Cities

Rio de Janeiro, São Paulo, and Brasília are three of Brazil's largest cities. Each shows important sides of today's Brazil.

Beautiful Rio de Janeiro was Brazil's capital for 200 years. It is a strong example of the country's heritage. Many of Rio's broad streets are named for important people in Brazilian history. Rio represents the traditions of the different cultures that influenced the development of Brazil. Every year these traditions are celebrated in Rio's world-famous carnival.

Rio also shows a problem that has haunted Brazil in the past and still plagues it today—the large gap between rich and poor. Wealthy Brazilians and tourists flock to the expensive hotels near Rio's beaches. Meanwhile, in the slums, or **favelas** (fah•VEL•ahz), in the hills behind the city, whole families live in one-room shacks.

São Paulo, the biggest manufacturing center in Latin America, is an example of Brazil's development as an industrial nation. Businesspeople from all over the world feel at home in São Paulo, with its skyscrapers and modern subway. São Paulo, however, also has that curse of industrial cities everywhere—smog.

Brasília, the nation's new capital, shows Brazil's hope for the future. This ultra-modern city, partly surrounded by an artificial lake, rises out of open land in Brazil's western wilderness. Appropriately for a city of the future, Brasília has the shape of an airplane. Striking government buildings fill the body of the plane. The wings are made up of giant apartment complexes called Superblocks. Each Superblock has a small park and stores as well as living space for its residents.

Brasília has few slums and no smog. Many people find this carefully planned city clean and beautiful. To others it

525

Wealth from the coffee trade sparked the growth of modern, industrial São Paulo.

Rio de Janeiro's crowded favelas overlook beautiful beaches and luxurious hotels.

seems inhuman and cold. They hope that Brazil, in reaching for the future, will not turn its back completely on the country's present and past.

Brazil's Search for Energy

Most of the oil Brazil uses for energy must be imported at great expense. The government oil agency, Petrobras, has found large oil fields, but production has been slow thus far.

Brazil's lack of oil has forced it to develop other sources of energy. For example, Brazil's rivers and waterfalls could give it huge amounts of hydroelectric power. To harness some of this power, Brazil has built the world's largest hydroelectric plant on the Paraná (par•uh•NAH) River between Paraguay and Brazil. Nearby are the raging **Iguacú** (ee•gwah•SOO) **Falls.**

Brazil also has become one of the first countries to use the automobile fuel called **gasohol** on a large scale. Gasohol is a mixture of gasoline and alcohol. Almost all the cars in Brazil—some six million of them—now run on gasohol or on pure alcohol. Brazil's former president uses an alcohol car.

Alcohol is a very useful fuel for Brazil because it can be made from plant waste. Sugar cane and other Brazilian farm crops produce millions of tons of plant waste each year. Brazil could grow additional "fuel crops" on some of its empty land.

Automobile experts are waiting eagerly to see the results of Brazil's experiment with gasohol. Such heavy use should answer many questions about this new fuel. It seems fitting that Brazil, which thinks of itself as the country of the future, should lead

This LANDSAT photograph compares land use on both sides of Brazil's Paraná River. Land west of the river is covered with scrubby woodlands and patches of savanna. Land to the east of the river is more highly developed. Coffee plantations, small towns, roads, and powerlines have affected the landscape.

the way in using what may be the fuel of the future.

Brazil's Resources

Brazil has vast amounts of undeveloped land, minerals, water power, and forests. The way Brazil uses these natural resources will have important effects on the country's future.

Brazilians have not always used their resources wisely. Brazilian farmers traditionally cleared land by cutting down the trees on it and burning them. They farmed the land until all its nutrients were gone. Then they moved to new ground, leaving behind barren fields. They had to move often, because most of Brazil's plantation crops used up soil nutrients quickly.

Today Brazilian farmers are using their land more productively. They use irrigation and fertilizer to put back soil nutrients. They plant a variety of crops in their fields. This new efficiency has helped Brazil become one of the major food exporters in the world.

Government programs to develop the unused parts of Brazil have caused unexpected problems. For example, workers cleared land in the Amazon Region to start farms. They found that the region's heavy rains washed away most of the soil's nutrients. With no forest plants to restore those nutrients, the soil quickly turned to barren sand.

New programs are being planned more carefully. Information from **LANDSAT,** an American space satellite, is helping Brazilians decide how to develop the remote parts of their country. LANDSAT shows what kinds of trees grow in different parts of the Amazon rain forest. It shows how well crops grow in different kinds of soil. By knowing more about their land before they try to change it, the Brazilians hope to avoid the mistakes of the past.

Brazil Today and Tomorrow

Some doubters have said that Brazil is on the edge of a wonderful future—and always will be. Most Brazilians,

527

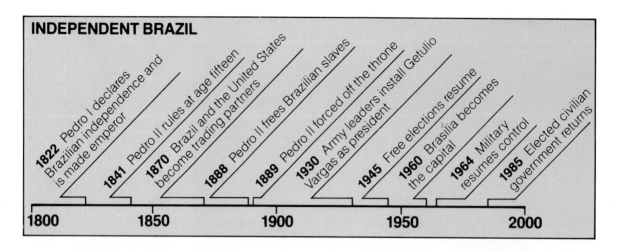

INDEPENDENT BRAZIL

1822 Pedro I declares Brazilian independence and is made emperor

1841 Pedro II rules at age fifteen

1870 Brazil and the United States become trading partners

1888 Pedro II frees Brazilian slaves

1889 Pedro II forced off the throne

1930 Army leaders install Getulio Vargas as president

1945 Free elections resume

1960 Brasília becomes the capital

1964 Military resumes control

1985 Elected civilian government returns

1800   1850   1900   1950   2000

however, are proud of their country's progress. They feel that Brazil will play an important part in the Western Hemisphere and the world.

Brazilians know that their country has major problems to overcome. Large numbers of Brazilians are poor, and about 25 percent are illiterate. Many parts of the country are almost empty, and poor transportation helps keep them that way. Brazil has huge debts and a high inflation rate. It depends too much on imported oil.

However, Brazilians have reason to hope. Brazil is Latin America's most industrialized nation. It sells cars, ships, cloth, machinery, and weapons all over the world. Manufactured goods now make up almost half of Brazil's exports. Also, Brazil has signed an economic agreement with Argentina that calls for increased trade and cooperation between the two countries. It is hoped that this pact will become the basis for a Latin American common market, similar to that of Western Europe.

Brazil is also developing space technology. It has launched successful space rockets, as well as its own satellites. Like LANDSAT, Brasilsat helps

in researching the wilderness areas of Brazil for mapmaking and possible cropland.

Brazil's land continues to be an important resource. Brazil is the world's largest coffee grower. It is among the world's leading growers of cacao, tobacco, cotton, sugar, soybeans, and livestock. Brazil is rich in minerals, too, including iron, manganese, chromium, bauxite, and rare metals.

The Brazilian people have shown their strength in the past. They gained their independence, freed their slaves, and changed the form of their government several times with little bloodshed. If Brazil can develop its resources wisely and treat its people fairly, the country's hopes for the future may come true.

Reading Check

1. Which city shows Brazil's hopes for the future?
2. Why is gasohol a good fuel for Brazilians to use?
3. In what way does LANDSAT help Brazilians?
4. List three examples of manufactured goods exported by Brazil.

Carnival

"Brazil, your magic spell is everywhere." So go the words of an old popular song. Nowhere in Brazil does the magic cast its spell more than in Rio de Janeiro at carnival time.

The word *carnival* roughly means "to take away meat." It relates to the Catholic practice of avoiding meat during Lent, the period before Easter. The Rio Carnival is held just before the beginning of Lent, usually in early February. The festivities of carnival time are a last celebration before the fasting begins.

Today, the Rio Carnival is one of the most amazing spectacles in the world. Lasting for four days, this spirited celebration of life includes parades of merrymakers in showy, fanciful, and exciting costumes. The goal of the Rio Carnival seems to be to wear the most eye-catching costume possible, and then to behave as if you *always* look like that.

Unlike carnivals in other countries throughout the world, the Rio Carnival is not just rides and favorite foods. The streets of Rio are packed with excitement and every kind of entertainment during carnival time. Bands playing metal drum instruments roam the streets while people dance the samba and other dances in time to the music. There are so many tambourines, it seems as if the whole city is a quivering charm bracelet. Open-air markets sell everything from oranges to monkeys. Traveling vendors shout *"Sanduiche! Guaraná!"* (SAND·weesh gwah·rah·NAH) to call attention to the snacks and surprises they have stored in their baskets.

Since tourism is a major industry in Brazil, carnival time is very important to the economy of Rio de Janeiro and the entire country. People of all ages travel from every part of the world to stay at Rio's luxurious hotels and take part in the excitement. This of course means that they will spend a great deal of money. That is another reason why the people of Rio are so joyful during carnival time.

Tambourine dance

Carnival magic

Glittering splendor

SKILLS FOR SUCCESS

SOLVING PROBLEMS AND MAKING DECISIONS

People make choices every day. When you awake, you choose what clothes to wear. You may choose what to eat for breakfast. Making choices is a relatively easy process. More important decisions, however, are made to solve problems.

Suppose you are about to go to a piano lesson. Just as you are leaving, you discover that your bicycle has a flat tire. You now have a problem. You must decide on a way to solve it. Here are some of the steps you might follow in solving a problem.

1. Identify the problem.

2. Identify ways to solve the problem.

3. Identify possible results of each solution.

4. Decide on a solution.

The problem you have to solve is how to get to your piano lesson when your bicycle has a flat tire. The next step is to find ways to solve the problem. You can fix the tire, or you can walk, borrow a bicycle, or stay home.

Which solution will you choose? Consider what can happen if you try each solution. If you walk or stop to fix the tire, you may be late. If you stay home, you will miss the practice you need. If your friend is home, he or she may lend you a bike. You probably can get to your lesson on time.

Now you are ready to decide on a solution. You choose the solution with the best chance of working. In this case, you would probably decide to borrow your friend's bike.

Usually, problems like this one can be solved quickly and easily. Some problems, however, require a great deal of thought.

For example, if you are deciding on a career, there are many things to consider. You must consider your talents, your interests, and the variety of possible careers. Often the solutions to such problems are not easy to see, or there may be many solutions from which to choose.

The process of solving complex problems is called **decision making.** Choosing a solution to a complex problem can be difficult. Here are steps you might follow.

1. Identify the problem.

2. Identify ways to solve the problem.

3. Identify results of each solution.

4. Rank the results. Put the best thing that could happen at the top of the list. Put the worst thing that could happen at the bottom of the list.

5. Decide which solutions are most likely to have the best result.

6. Decide which solutions are least likely to have a good result.

7. Decide on a solution.

Although you may not realize it, you often solve problems this way. Suppose you are deciding what to do after school. You want to play soccer with your friends. You have to write a book report, which is due in school on Monday. If you finish the report, you can go camping over the weekend. There is also a skating party you would like to attend. The following chart shows the ways you can solve this problem.

	Solutions			Results
	Thursday	**Friday**	**Weekend**	
1	Play soccer	Go to skating party	Write book report	Miss camping; book report is finished
2	Play soccer	Write book report	Go camping	Miss skating party; book report is finished
3	Write book report	Go to skating party	Go camping	Miss playing soccer; book report is finished

Now you must think about the results of each solution. Here is one way you might rank the results, from the most desirable to the least desirable.

Results

1. Go camping

2. Go to skating party

3. Play soccer

4. Do not play soccer

5. Do not go skating

6. Do not go camping

The best result is that you will be able to go camping. The worst is to have to miss weekend camping. Which solutions will allow you to go camping?

Look at the second solution again. If you choose this one, you will miss the skating party.

Now study the list of results. Skating is your second choice, and playing soccer is your third choice. You decide to write the book report today and go skating tomorrow. This solution will let you do two of the things you most want to do, go skating and camping.

Making Political Decisions

Governments try to solve problems that face their nations. These problems may be quite complex, since they can affect millions of people and their future. Here is one problem that the government of Brazil had to solve.

During the 1950s the leaders of Brazil were faced with a difficult problem. Government offices in the capital of Rio de Janeiro had become terribly overcrowded. The government needed to find more space so that its workers would be able to do their jobs. Almost no office space was available in Rio, and land was expensive there.

Brazil's leaders talked about building a new capital city in the Central-West, far from the crowded coasts. The leaders thought of reasons for and against this solution.

Actually, people in Brazil had been talking about a new capital for many years. There were good reasons for building it. Rio is one of the most crowded cities in the world. Building a new capital city would create the room the government workers needed. They would have better places to live and work. The new city also might bring more industry to an undeveloped region. This would mean new jobs and new wealth as the resources of the region were put to use.

Building continuously for four years, 60,000 people worked to create Brasília. More than one million people now live in Brazil's capital.

There also were some good reasons for *not* moving the capital. Building a new city would take years. It would be enormously expensive, especially since the site for the new capital was so wild and far from other cities. The Brazilians would have to build roads, since there were none in that part of Brazil. Airplanes would have to bring building supplies from the cities on the coast.

There were still other problems. Workers would need housing while they built the city. They would need food, medical care, and entertainment. Then, once the city was built, thousands of government workers would have to move away from their homes in Rio.

After weighing both sides of the question, the president and the legislature decided to go ahead with the plan. They felt confident that the problems could be solved. They gave the new capital the name *Brasília*. They hoped it would become one of the world's great capital cities.

CHECKING YOUR SKILLS

Follow the steps to solve each of the following problems. Compare your solutions with those of your classmates.

1. You must return the baseball glove that you borrowed from a friend, but somehow you have lost it.

   a. Identify the problem.
   b. Identify some solutions.
   c. Identify possible results.
   d. What would you do to solve the problem?

2. A school band wants to buy new uniforms and go on a trip. They cannot afford to do both.

   a. Identify the problem.
   b. Identify some solutions.
   c. Identify possible results.
   d. What would you do to solve the problem?

CHAPTER 18 REVIEW

USING WORDS

Replace each underlined definition with the correct word from the following list.

favelas   **gasohol**   **illiterate**
fazendas   **gauchos**

1. In the South of Brazil, workers on large plantations harvest Brazil's biggest export, coffee.

2. The South American cowboys rode across the pampas with their herds.

3. One goal of a successful democracy should be to decrease the number of its people who are unable to read and write.

4. Brazilians from rural areas have flocked to the cities, where many live crowded together in the surrounding slums.

5. Many automobiles in Brazil use a mixture of gasoline and alcohol for fuel.

REVIEWING FACTS

1. Which is Brazil's fastest-growing region?

2. What were some things that Indians taught European settlers in Brazil?

3. From what did Brazil get its name?

4. What event changed Brazilian history in 1808?

5. How did Brazil gain its independence? How was this different from the way other Latin American republics gained theirs from Spain?

6. What 3 groups disliked Pedro II? Why?

7. How was the new Brazilian republic different from the United States?

8. How did Getulio Vargas help Brazil?

9. What does Rio de Janeiro show you about Brazil's past and its present?

10. List three problems Brazil faces today and the ways Brazilians are trying to solve these problems.

THINKING CRITICALLY

1. Brazil continues to develop and improve connections within its vast country. Why do you think transportation systems are so important to Brazil? How do the land and climate of Brazil affect the development of transportation systems?

2. Brazil had good times and bad times under its military leaders. Why would Brazilians want to change from military rule to civilian rule? What are some dangers of military dictatorships?

PRACTICING SKILLS

Solving Problems Pick one of the following problems to solve. List the steps you would follow and decide on a solution.

1. Every morning just before school you deliver newspapers in your neighborhood. This morning you overslept.

2. You have just arrived at school. You realize that you left an assignment at home.

Canadians Develop a Vast Land

While the Spanish and Portuguese were exploring Latin America, people from France and England were building settlements in Canada, our northern neighbor in the Western Hemisphere. Later, Canadians united scattered colonies into a nation, explored a vast western wilderness, and developed their country into a modern industrial power.

Today, Canada has close ties with the United States. Those ties are geographic, political, and economic. Canada is our "good neighbor" in many ways.

Look for these important words:

Key Words
- muskegs
- provinces
- pulp

Places
- Canadian Shield
- Hudson Bay
- Ottawa

- St. Lawrence River
- St. Lawrence Seaway
- Yukon

Look for answers to these questions:

1. How do land and climate vary across Canada?
2. What resources are in each of Canada's four regions?
3. From what countries did Canada's people originally come?

1. THE GEOGRAPHY OF CANADA

Canada is the second-largest country in the world. Only the Soviet Union is larger. Canada takes up most of the northern part of North America, about two-fifths of the continent. It is bounded by the Pacific Ocean and Alaska on the west, the Arctic Ocean on the north, the Atlantic Ocean on the east, and the United States on the south.

The far east and west of Canada contain mountains. The low Appalachian Mountains of the eastern United States continue north into Canada. The much higher Rocky Mountains and the Coast Mountains run through western Canada.

The rocky land of the **Canadian Shield** makes up almost half of Canada. A shield is that part of a continent's surface where the rock is very old. The Canadian Shield is the oldest mass of rock in North America. It lies in the northern, central, and eastern parts of the country. In this region the soil is very thin. Farming is difficult as a result.

Much of the Canadian Shield was once covered by glaciers. The glaciers scoured deep gashes in the land and dropped huge boulders as they passed. Today much of the Canadian Shield is covered by thick forests, uncountable rivers and lakes, and numerous swamplike areas called **muskegs.** A large body of water, called **Hudson Bay,** cuts into the northeastern part of the Canadian Shield.

A country as large as Canada is affected by several types of climate. Mountains, oceans, and high latitudes contribute to its different climates. Most of southern Canada has warm summers and cold winters. The weather is milder in the ocean-facing areas. Northern Canada is cold almost all year.

Canada is divided into two territories and ten **provinces.** The provinces, which are self-governing and are similar to our states, are often placed in four regional groups. Each region contains resources that benefit Canada.

535

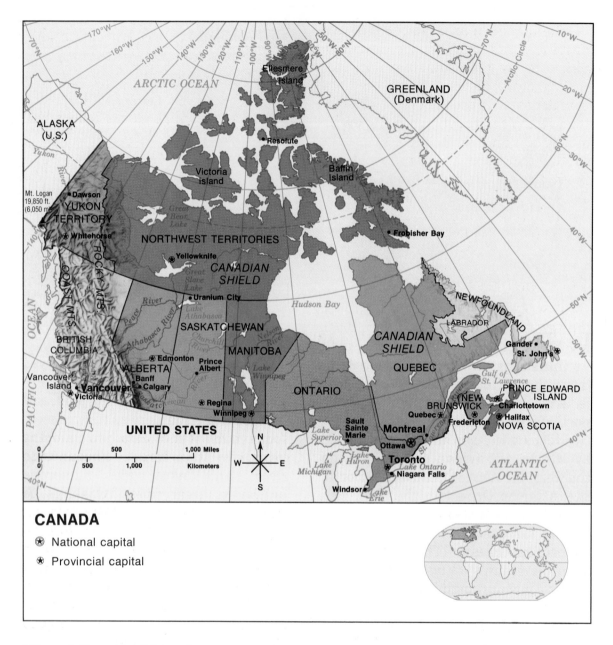

CANADA

⊛ National capital

⊛ Provincial capital

The Atlantic Provinces

The Atlantic Provinces are Nova Scotia (NOH•vuh SKOH•shuh), Newfoundland (NOO•fuhnd•luhnd), Prince Edward Island, and New Brunswick. Parts of Newfoundland and Nova Scotia are islands, separated from the mainland by narrow straits.

Fishing is important to the people of Nova Scotia and Newfoundland.

Lobsters, cod, and herring are caught there. Major ports are Halifax, Nova Scotia; St. John's, Newfoundland; and Saint John, New Brunswick.

Forests in Nova Scotia, Newfoundland, and New Brunswick provide wood for making **pulp.** Pulp is groundwood that is wet to make paper. Your daily newspaper might be printed on paper from Canada.

536

The northern areas of the Atlantic Provinces are part of the Canadian Shield. They have abundant minerals such as nickel and coal. There are huge iron deposits in the part of Newfoundland called Labrador (LAB•ruh•dawr).

Farms and orchards cover the southern part of the Atlantic Provinces. Prince Edward Island, Canada's smallest province, is called "The Garden Province." Fine potatoes, oats, and hay grow in its pleasant, fertile land.

The Central Provinces

The Central Provinces, Ontario (ahn•TAIR•ee•oh) and Quebec (kwi•BEK), are Canada's largest, richest, and most heavily populated provinces. More than 80 percent of Canada's manufacturing is done there, and more than 60 percent of Canada's people live there.

Most of Canada's big cities are in the Central Provinces. Canada's capital city, **Ottawa** (AHT•uh•wuh), is in Ontario. So is another large city, Toronto. Montreal (mahn•tree•AWL), in Quebec, is Canada's largest city. The industrial cities of this region have prospered partly because of the hydroelectric power provided by nearby bodies of water.

Four of the five Great Lakes lie on the border between the United States and Ontario. The **St. Lawrence River** connects the Great Lakes with the Atlantic Ocean. Ships can sail 2,342 miles (3,769 km) from the head of Lake Superior to the Atlantic Ocean. Between Montreal and Lake Ontario is the **St. Lawrence Seaway.** Locks and canals that bypass rapids in the river allow thousands of ships to use the St. Lawrence Seaway during the

The St. Lawrence Seaway was engineered by both Canada and the United States.

summer months of each year. During the winter the seaway is clogged with ice.

The northern parts of Ontario and Quebec, like the north of the Atlantic Provinces, are covered with forests. Canadian companies harvest trees from these forests for lumber, pulp, and paper. The southern parts of the Central Provinces, around the St. Lawrence and the Great Lakes, are good dairy land and farmland.

The Prairie Provinces

Alberta, Saskatchewan (sas•KATCH•uh•wahn), and Manitoba (man•ih•TOH•buh)—the three Prairie Provinces—are Canada's breadbasket. The southern parts of these provinces are much like the Great Plains of the United States. Fields of wheat cover the land as far as the eye can see. Southern Alberta also has large cattle ranches.

Much of Manitoba is dotted with rivers and lakes. People love to visit this land to hunt and fish. The mountain scenery around Banff, in Alberta, is equally popular.

Today the Prairie Provinces, especially Alberta, have a new source of wealth. Oil was discovered in northern Alberta in the 1940s. The Alberta oil fields now provide most of Canada's oil and natural gas. Canada also sells oil and gas to the United States. Because of its oil fields, Alberta has been Canada's fastest growing province.

North and West Canada

Most of Canada's far west is wild, beautiful land. British Columbia's two largest cities, Vancouver (van•KOO•ver) and Victoria, are in its southernmost part. Most of the rest of the province is covered by the jagged peaks of the Canadian Rockies and the lower Coast Range.

British Columbia's many forests supply its main industry, lumber. Some farming is done in the narrow valleys between the mountains. The ocean waters off British Columbia teem with fish, especially Pacific salmon.

Canada's two territories, the **Yukon** (YOO•kahn) and the Northwest Territories, lie to the north of British Columbia and the Prairie Provinces. Much of this northern land is half-frozen Arctic tundra. Oil, lead, zinc, gold, and uranium lie beneath the tundra. Many islands in the Arctic Ocean also belong to the Northwest Territories.

British Columbia is the major producer of lumber and wood products in Canada.

Vancouver's large, sheltered harbors are important to British Columbia's industry.

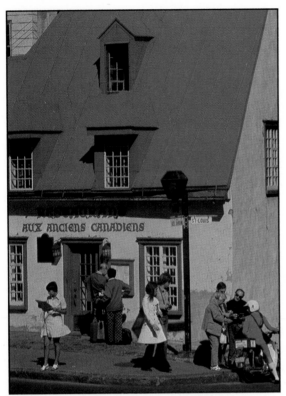

Tourists study the menu in French and English at the "Restaurant of Old Canada."

The People of Canada

Almost all of Canada's 25 million people are descended from Europeans. The largest number, about 62 percent, came originally from the British Isles. This figure includes people of British descent who lived in the United States before going to Canada. Canada's many British people reflect the country's long history as a British possession.

The second-largest number of Canadians, about 25 percent, are descended from French people. Canada was a French colony before it was a British one. Many of Canada's French-speaking people can trace their ancestry back to the farmers and fur trappers of that early French colony. Both French and English are official languages of Canada.

People from Germany, Italy, the part of the Soviet Union called the Ukraine (yoo•KRAYN), and other parts of Europe also live in Canada. Some came to the Prairie Provinces in the early years of this century. Others came to Canada's cities after World War II. All have contributed to Canada's culture.

Ninety percent of Canada's people live on 12 percent of its land, the part along the country's southern border. Many work in factories or have other jobs in Canada's large cities. Some are farmers in the Prairie Provinces. Others fish the waters of British Columbia or the Atlantic Provinces. Few Canadians live in the north of the country. Oil drilling, mining, and forestry are attracting more people to this area, however.

The Canadian people reflect the many cultures that have contributed to their nation. Many of them enjoy outdoor activities such as hiking and skiing. Large numbers are also fans of professional sports, especially ice hockey. Today's Canadians are an outgoing, energetic people who are proud of their country's important place in the modern world.

Reading Check

1. What rocky land makes up almost half of Canada?
2. How has an abundant water supply influenced the Central Provinces?
3. Why are the Prairie Provinces called the breadbasket of Canada? To what area of the United States do they compare?
4. From which two countries in Europe did the ancestors of most Canadians come?

The Arctic

A place as cold as the Arctic would seem to be a forbidding place to live. During the winter in the tundra, from November to February, the sun never shines at all. The temperature within the Arctic Circle sometimes sinks to −60°F (−51°C). Yet, the Arctic's 7 million square miles (18 million square km) of snow and ice and ocean are full of life and full of possibilities.

There are many different groups who live in the Arctic. Among them are 85,000 Inuits (IN•yuh•wuhts), or Eskimos, who live in Alaska, Greenland, Labrador, and in the Canadian Arctic. Another group of natives to the Arctic are the Laplanders, also called "Reindeer People." The people who live in the Arctic have found many clever ways to survive the harsh environment that has been their home for a thousand years.

The Arctic is a home not only for people but also for many kinds of plant and animal life. This frozen region produces diatoms and plankton. These extremely small growing plants and animals are food for krill, a tiny, lobsterlike creature. Krill in turn are food for many kinds of fish and birds as well as for seals, walruses, and whales. The Arctic is also the land of the fierce polar bear, whose favorite food is the seal.

Many other animals have adapted to life in the Arctic tundra. There are the huge caribou and musk oxen and the small arctic foxes and lemmings. There are ptarmigan (TAHR•mih•guhn), seagulls, snow owls, and snow geese. The coats of many of these birds and mammals turn white in winter to blend with the snow and hide them from preying enemies.

People have explored the Arctic to hunt for the valuable skins of its many animals. People have also explored the Arctic for its plentiful mineral deposits. In addition to rich oil and gas deposits, gold, copper, silver, zinc, coal, lead, iron, cobalt, and uranium have been found in the Arctic. In years to come, people may find better ways to live in the Arctic to take advantage of its resources.

Arctic Circle

Snow geese

Polar bear

Musk oxen

SKILLS FOR SUCCESS

USING TIME ZONES

The Earth is divided into 24 **time zones.** Time zones are needed because the sun does not shine on all the Earth at the same time. When the sun is rising at one place, it is setting half a world away. The Earth makes one complete spin, or **rotation,** during a day. Each of the 24 time zones represents a different hour of that day.

This map shows all 24 **standard time zones.** It shows that the time is the same for any area within a particular standard time zone. For example, when it is 7:00 A.M. in Quebec, Canada, it is the same time in Lima,

Peru. The map tells you what time it is in each zone when it is 12:00 noon at 0° longitude, the Prime Meridian.

Look at the times given at the top of the map. Notice as you read from left to right, or from west to east, that the time is one hour later in each zone. Do you know why? The Earth rotates in an easterly direction. The arrow at the bottom of the map indicates the direction of the Earth's rotation.

Now find the International Date Line at 180° longitude. When it is 12:00 noon at the Prime Meridian, it is 12:00 midnight along

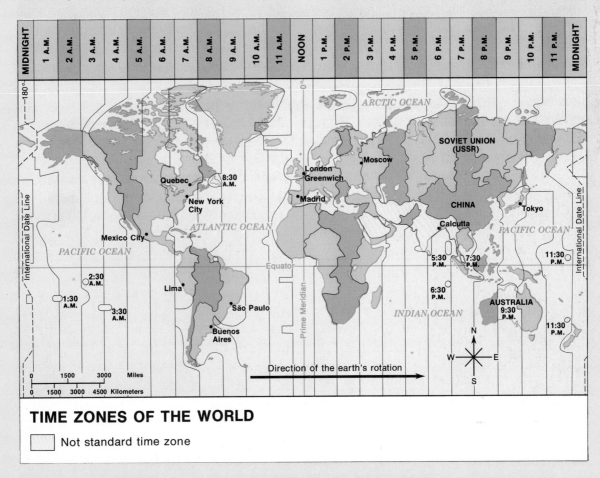

TIME ZONES OF THE WORLD

☐ Not standard time zone

the Date Line. The sun is on the other side of the Earth. As the Earth turns, a new day begins at the Date Line. Let's say it is Sunday morning in the United States. It is Sunday afternoon in Africa and Sunday evening in Asia. At the International Date Line, Monday morning is just about to begin.

Look at the 12:00 noon time zone. Notice that the top of the zone is colored green. It is 12:00 noon in these areas. Find Madrid in this zone. It is colored orange, like the zone to its right. Madrid is part of the 1:00 P.M. time zone, and so is most of Europe. The zone was made larger so people in Europe could use the same time.

Time zones also have been changed in other parts of the world. If they were not, some cities and continents might be divided in inconvenient ways. For example, most of China is in only one time zone. China's government prefers to have everyone on the same schedule.

Find the Soviet Union. Notice that it is in 11 time zones. However, the times are one hour ahead of other countries in the same zones. If the time zones were straight, Moscow would be in the 2:00 P.M. zone. The time in Moscow is actually 3:00 P.M.

Other areas of the world do not use standard time zones. Look at the yellow box in the map key. What does the key tell you about these zones? Find Australia on the map. Notice that central Australia is yellow. When it is 8:00 P.M. in western Australia, it is 9:30 P.M. in central Australia.

Figuring Time Differences

The map on the opposite page shows the time zones in the Western Hemisphere. Each time zone covers about 15 degrees of longitude. The United States covers about 60 degrees of longitude, so it lies in four time zones. Alaska and Hawaii lie in other time zones. Which time zone do you live in?

You can use this map to find the time in each zone. Imagine you are flying from Vancouver, Canada, to Caracas, Venezuela. You want to set your watch to the time in Caracas. First, find the two cities on the map. Next, count the number of time zones you will enter. Caracas is in the fourth time zone to the east of Vancouver. This means it is four hours later in Caracas. When it is 4:00 A.M. in Vancouver, it is 8:00 A.M. in Caracas. You would set your watch ahead four hours. On a trip from Caracas to Vancouver, you would set it back four hours.

If you know the time in one place, you can add or subtract to find the time in another place. For example, when it is 1:00 P.M. in Vancouver, it is 5:00 P.M. in Caracas: 1 + 4 = 5. When it is 12:00 noon in Caracas, what time is it in Vancouver?

CLOCKS AROUND THE WORLD

New York
7 A.M.

London
12 P.M.

Cairo
2 P.M.

Tokyo
9 P.M.

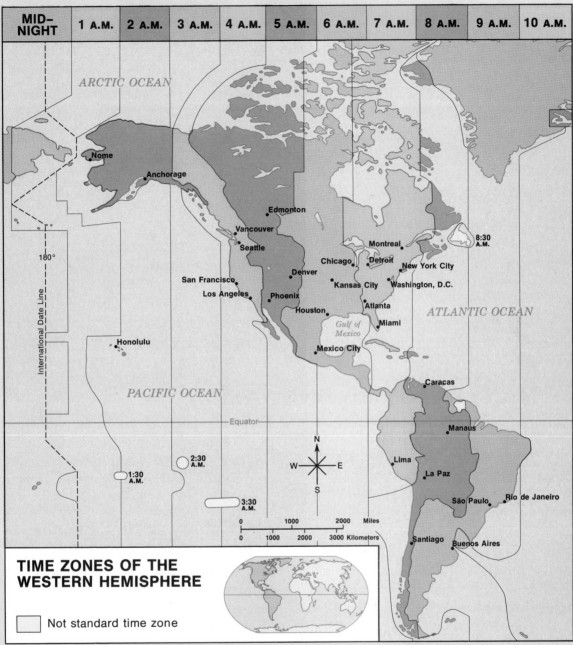

MID-NIGHT	1 A.M.	2 A.M.	3 A.M.	4 A.M.	5 A.M.	6 A.M.	7 A.M.	8 A.M.	9 A.M.	10 A.M.

ARCTIC OCEAN

Nome

Anchorage

Edmonton

Vancouver

Seattle

180°

Chicago · Detroit

Montreal

8:30 A.M.

San Francisco

Denver

New York City

Los Angeles

Phoenix

Kansas City

Washington, D.C.

International Date Line

Houston

Atlanta

ATLANTIC OCEAN

Gulf of Mexico

Miami

Honolulu

Mexico City

PACIFIC OCEAN

Caracas

Equator

Manaus

2:30 A.M.

1:30 A.M.

Lima

La Paz

3:30 A.M.

N
W   E
S

São Paulo   Rio de Janeiro

| 0 | 1000 | 2000 | Miles |
| 0 | 1000 | 2000 | 3000 Kilometers |

Santiago   Buenos Aires

TIME ZONES OF THE WESTERN HEMISPHERE

☐ Not standard time zone

CHECKING YOUR SKILLS

Use the time zone map of the Western Hemisphere to answer these questions.

1. You are flying from San Francisco, California, to Detroit, Michigan. Would you set your watch back or ahead?

2. How many standard time zones are in South America? in Canada?

3. You live in Chicago, Illinois, and you need to call someone in Honolulu, Hawaii. You want to call when it is daytime in Honolulu. Should you place the call at 6:00 P.M. Chicago time or at 8:00 A.M. Chicago time?

4. When it is 9:00 P.M. Tuesday in Nome, Alaska, what time is it in New York City? What day of the week is it?

Look for these important words:

Key Words
- Loyalists
- confederation
- dominion

People
- John Cabot
- Giovanni da Verrazano
- Jacques Cartier
- Samuel de Champlain
- Henry Hudson
- Sir Wilfrid Laurier

Places
- New France
- Port Royal
- Prince Rupert's Land

Look for answers to these questions:

1. Who were the early explorers and settlers of Canada?
2. How did Canada become a nation?
3. How was western Canada settled? How was it linked to the rest of the nation?
4. In what ways has Canada developed in the twentieth century?

2. MANY COLONIES, ONE NATION

Long before Europeans came to Canada, Indians hunted in the country's dense forests and paddled their canoes along its rivers and lakes. Inuits hunted seals and polar bears in Canada's far north. The first Europeans to visit Canada were the Vikings. They came across the Atlantic to Newfoundland around A.D. 1000. There they settled for a brief time. They did not set up permanent colonies, however.

About 500 years after the first Viking settlement, people representing England and France, the two European countries that were to be most important in Canadian history, came to Canada. An Italian named **John Cabot** claimed Newfoundland for England in 1497. **Giovanni da Verrazano** (joh•VAHN•nee dah vayr•rah•TSAH•noh), an Italian exploring for France, sailed up the eastern coast of North America as far as Nova Scotia in 1524. The French explorer **Jacques Cartier** (ZHAHK kahr•TYAY) discovered the St. Lawrence River in 1534.

The Colony of New France

Fishing vessels from England, France, Portugal, and other European countries visited Canada's Atlantic waters often in the sixteenth century. French traders sailed up the St. Lawrence River and bartered with Indians for the skins of foxes, beavers, and other furred animals. These skins brought high prices in Europe. French priests opened missions to convert the Indians to Christianity. None of these groups formed permanent settlements in Canada, however.

At the beginning of the seventeenth century, a company of traders

544

got permission from the king of France to control the fur trade. In return, they promised to establish a colony in the new land. The colony was to be called **New France.**

An explorer named **Samuel de Champlain** (sham•PLAYN), the "Father of New France," led the first colonists. In 1604 he started a settlement at **Port Royal,** in what is now Nova Scotia. This was the first permanent European settlement in North America north of Florida. Champlain also traveled up the St. Lawrence and founded the city of Quebec in 1608. Other settlements were made in New France later, but most of this land remained an untamed wilderness.

The English settled in Canada in the early seventeenth century. In 1610 a Scottish noble set up a colony called Nova Scotia, or "New Scotland," in eastern Canada. The English also set up villages in Newfoundland.

French fur traders as well as French colonists had English rivals. In 1670 King Charles II of England created the Hudson's Bay Company. He gave the company the right to all the fur trade in the land around this huge bay, which had been discovered by **Henry Hudson** in 1610.

Wars between France and England in Europe heightened the rivalry between French and English settlements in Canada. Often the people of these settlements attacked each other directly or through Indian allies. In 1763, following a European war of which the French and Indian War was a part, France and Great Britain signed the Treaty of Paris. The Treaty gave all of New France to Great Britain, and France's rule in Canada ended.

Eskimos who have paddled out to meet ships of the Hudson's Bay Company collect beads and knives in exchange for the beaver pelts they have brought.

The British in New France

Far more French people than British lived in Great Britain's new colony of Quebec, which had been New France. Great Britain already was having trouble with its original 13 colonies in North America. The British knew they would have to treat Quebec carefully to avoid still more trouble. In 1774, therefore, Great Britain passed the Quebec Act. It guaranteed French Canadians the right to keep their own laws and language and the Roman Catholic religion.

When the colonies that were to become the United States declared their independence from Great Britain in 1776, they invited the Canadian colonies to join them. The Canadians, however, refused. They felt that Great Britain, in the Quebec Act, had shown that it intended to govern them fairly. They were willing to remain part of Great Britain.

Some people in the 13 colonies took the side of Great Britain during the Revolutionary War. They were called **Loyalists.** Many Loyalists and their families fled to Canada. Some settled in Nova Scotia. Others went to a nearby area that became a new Canadian colony, New Brunswick.

Moving West

The Canadians turned their attention to the western half of their land during the nineteenth century. Most of this land was an almost empty area called **Prince Rupert's Land.** People who worked for the Hudson's Bay Company or other fur trading companies explored Rupert's Land in the hope of finding new sources of furs or other

wealth. They claimed the land, not for Canada or Great Britain, but for the fur companies.

Rivalry with the United States further caused Canada to look westward. The Revolutionary War and the War of 1812 left bad feelings between the two countries. The United States and Canada also claimed some of the same land in the Pacific Northwest. Canadians hoped that settlements in the west would strengthen their claims.

Canada Becomes a Nation

A growing number of people in the Canadian colonies felt that the colonies would have more power if they joined together. In 1867, after much argument, four colonies—Upper and Lower Canada (Ontario and Quebec), Nova Scotia, and New Brunswick—voted to form a **confederation,** or union. Each colony became a province in the confederation.

The colonists decided that their new country would have a prime minister and a parliament, just as Great Britain did. Canada would still be a British possession. Instead of being a colony, however, it would be a more independent possession called a **dominion.** The British Parliament gave the Canadians permission to set up their confederation by passing a law called the British North America Act.

The new confederation's first job was to link itself with the lands to the west. In 1869 the Canadian government bought Rupert's Land from the Hudson's Bay Company. In 1870 a new province, Manitoba, was created from the settled part of this land. British

Columbia voted to join the Canadian confederation in 1871. Now Canada could really live up to its national motto, "From Sea to Sea."

Canadians further united their sprawling country by building the Canadian Pacific Railroad. This railroad ran across high mountains and through forested wilderness to join eastern Canada with British Columbia and other western lands. It was completed in 1885.

Excitement swept through both Canada and the United States in 1897 when gold was discovered in the Yukon. Eager gold seekers poured into Canada. They climbed over snow-covered mountain passes with their supplies on their backs. They huddled in cabins beside icebound streams. A few "struck it rich." Many others died without finding gold. Some stayed to make new homes in the wild land.

Canada Comes of Age

As the twentieth century began, **Sir Wilfrid Laurier** (LAW•ree•ay), prime minister of Canada, announced enthusiastically, "The nineteenth century belonged to the United States. The twentieth century will belong to Canada!"

No wonder Laurier felt that way: Canadians were discovering that they had many natural resources that the world wanted. Deposits of nickel and other metals in British Columbia and the Canadian Shield, for example, proved as valuable as Yukon gold.

People also learned how to make paper from wood pulp at about that time. Canada's forests suddenly became very valuable. The prairie grasslands of southwestern Canada were excellent for wheat farming and ranching. They became the provinces of Saskatchewan and Alberta in 1905.

A hopeful family heads for the Yukon Territory with a gold pan topping their pile of belongings. About 33,000 gold seekers lived there in 1898.

Thousands of Canadians volunteered to fight against Germany during World War I. They fought and died in France and elsewhere. Their bravery brought strong national pride to many Canadians for the first time.

Like the United States and other countries, Canada suffered economic troubles during the 1930s. Many people lost their jobs. Drought brought hardship to the Prairie Provinces. The Canadian government had to find ways to aid its people. Money from new mineral discoveries in Ontario and Quebec helped make this possible.

Canada strengthened its defense ties with the United States during World War II and the postwar years. The two countries set up the Permanent Joint Defense Board in 1940. Defense cooperation led to the building of the Alaska Highway and U.S. naval and air bases in Canada. These added to the protection of the coasts of both countries during World War II. After the war, Canada and the United States worked together on radar and defense stations in the far north. These stations can warn both countries of a possible threat, such as Soviet missiles.

Economic ties bind the United States and Canada. The United States has replaced Great Britain as Canada's chief trading partner. American companies have invested money to help Canada develop its resources. Some have built factories in Canada.

Canadians worked hard to develop their country. They began industries to make automobiles and machinery and to produce iron, steel, and aluminum. They built some of the longest pipelines in the world to send oil and natural gas from Alberta to Montreal

The Trans-Canada Highway passes through a national park in the Canadian Rockies.

and California. In 1962 they opened the Trans-Canada Highway, which stretches 4,860 miles (7,820 km) from St. John's, Newfoundland, to Victoria, British Columbia. This great highway is one more sign that Canada has become a modern nation from sea to sea.

Reading Check

1. Who were the first Europeans to establish a permanent settlement in Canada?
2. How did Canada become a British colony?
3. What group of people fled from the United States to Canada during the Revolutionary War?
4. Why did the Canadian colonies form a confederation?

Look for these important words:

Key Words
- amendments
- premiers

- Charter of Rights and Freedoms

People
- Pierre Trudeau

Look for answers to these questions:

1. What problems does Alberta's oil present for Canada?
2. Why do the people of Quebec Province often disagree with the rest of Canada?
3. How did Canada gain control of its constitution?

3. CANADA TODAY

Canada today is a fully developed industrial nation. It has one of the highest standards of living in the world. It exports both raw materials and manufactured goods to the United States and other countries. Modern Canada faces certain problems, however. Some of these, such as unemployment and inflation, trouble many countries today. Other problems are part of Canada's special land and history.

The Problem of Oil

Canada's large supplies of oil and natural gas are valuable both to Canada and to other countries of the Western Hemisphere. Most of the oil and gas comes from the province of Alberta. New oil discoveries also have been made in the Northwest Territories and off the coasts of Newfoundland and Nova Scotia.

The Canadian government must answer some difficult questions as it plans the development of the country's oil resources. For example, which decisions about oil development should be made by the federal government? Which ones should be made by the provinces in which the oil is found? Who should get the profits?

Protecting the environment is another important concern. Heavy equipment can be brought to northern oil fields during only a few months of the year. Ice blocks the way the rest of the time. An oil well that goes out of control in this icy land might spout oil for months before it could be stopped.

Offshore wells in the North Atlantic present another problem. An oil spill there could kill millions of fish and harm the Newfoundland fishing industry. Canadians are finding ways to develop their oil resources safely.

The Question of Quebec

Ever since New France became a British colony, the government of Canada has had to deal with the problems of ruling over people with two cultures and two languages. These problems still divide Canada today, especially in the province of Quebec.

French Canadians are a minority in most parts of Canada. Yet, in Quebec they are a majority. Because most of the people in Quebec speak French, street signs in Montreal and other cities in Quebec are printed in both English and French.

At many times in Canada's history, the people of Quebec have disagreed with the British-dominated part of the country. Their opinions could not be ignored, for Quebec is a large and powerful province. It is rich in industry and natural resources that all of Canada needs. Some of Quebec's people feel that Quebec and the rest of Canada can never get along. They want Quebec to withdraw from the Canadian union and become a separate country.

Most people in Quebec would not want to go that far even if the Canadian government would let them. However, they feel very strongly that their rights to their own culture must be respected. The tension between the people of Canada's two main cultures is one of the greatest problems facing the country today.

Canada's New Constitution

The Canadian government is trying to strengthen Canada and solve the problems that its people face. One important thing it has done is gain control of the constitution that governs Canada.

Unlike many other nations, Canada never had a constitution of its own. The British North America Act set up rules for governing the country. All major **amendments,** or changes, to this

Queen Elizabeth, her husband Prince Philip, and Pierre Trudeau (right) smile for photographers while Canadians celebrate their newly arrived constitution.

550

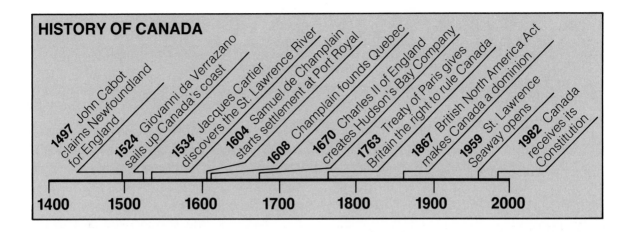

HISTORY OF CANADA

1497 John Cabot claims Newfoundland for England

1524 Giovanni da Verrazano sails up Canada's coast

1534 Jacques Cartier discovers the St. Lawrence River

1604 Samuel de Champlain starts settlement at Port Royal

1608 Champlain founds Quebec

1670 Charles II of England creates Hudson's Bay Company

1763 Treaty of Paris gives Britain the right to rule Canada

1867 British North America Act makes Canada a dominion

1959 St. Lawrence Seaway opens

1982 Canada receives its Constitution

1400　1500　1600　1700　1800　1900　2000

act had to be approved by the British Parliament. Although Canada was self-governing for many years, in some ways it was still tied to Great Britain.

In 1981 Canadian Prime Minister **Pierre Trudeau** (pee•AYR troo•DOH) met with the **premiers,** or government leaders, of the ten provinces to write a **Charter of Rights and Freedoms** to add to the British North America Act. The different premiers, representing the interests of their provinces, wanted different things. For a while it seemed that no agreement would be possible. However, the group finally worked out compromises that most of them could accept.

The Charter defines which powers belong to the federal government and which belong to the provinces. It gives rules for amending the constitution. It also guarantees the right of both French- and English-speaking Canadians to use their own language in government, courts, and schools.

In addition, the Charter guarantees certain rights to Canadian citizens. Most are the same rights given to United States citizens by the Bill of Rights and other amendments to our Constitution. The Charter makes it against the law to discriminate against anyone because of race, origin, religion, sex, age, or mental or physical disability.

The British Parliament approved the Charter and agreed to send the entire constitution to Canada. On April 17, 1982, with Queen Elizabeth II of Great Britain in attendance, Canada's amended constitution was officially recognized.

Now Canada's Parliament can change its constitution without asking Great Britain's permission. Canada has achieved full independence as a nation. As a member of the Commonwealth of Nations, however, Canada continues to recognize the British monarch as its ruler.

Reading Check

1. From where do most of Canada's oil and natural gas come?
2. In what province are French Canadians a large majority?
3. Before 1982 how were changes made in the rules that governed Canada?
4. In what way is the Charter of Rights and Freedoms similar to the American Bill of Rights?

SKILLS FOR SUCCESS

CONSERVING ENERGY

Canada and the United States are fortunate to have high standards of living, made possible in part by a wealth of resources. Many of these resources supply the energy necessary to run modern nations. We rely on fuel to power our factories, to heat our homes, to cook our food, and to operate cars and tractors. Almost everything we use requires energy from fuel to produce it. Our major energy sources today are oil, coal, natural gas, water power, and atomic, or **nuclear** (NOO•klee•uhr) **energy.**

Three of our most important energy sources, oil, natural gas, and coal, are called **nonrenewable** resources. Nonrenewable means that neither we nor nature can make more of them. When nonrenewable fuels are used up, we must find other sources of energy.

Some energy sources, however, are in more or less unlimited supply. They can be reused or remade, either by nature or by humans. For example, alcohol fuels are made from plants. Alcohol fuels are thus a **renewable** energy source, as are sun, wind, water, and certain special kinds of nuclear power. Wood is also considered a renewable energy source, though forests may be used up faster than they are replanted.

The Energy Problem

Look at the chart on the next page. In the mid 1980s oil supplies 41 percent of the world's energy. Some experts think that people will continue to use the same amount in the future. At that rate, the sources of oil we know about now will last for about 30 years. Before then, the nations of the world must develop energy sources that can replace oil. New energy sources must be fairly inexpensive so that we can afford to use them. They also must be safe so that they do not endanger our health.

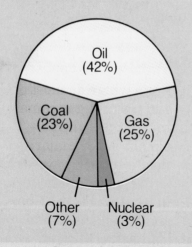

OUR ENERGY SOURCES

Oil (42%)
Coal (23%)
Gas (25%)
Other (7%)
Nuclear (3%)

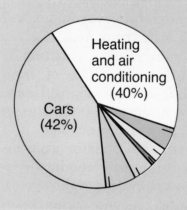

OUR ENERGY USES

Heating and air conditioning (40%)
Cars (42%)

WORLD ENERGY USE AND SUPPLY		
Fuel	Percent of Total Energy Use	Estimated Remaining Supply
Oil	41%	30 years
Coal	33%	200 years
Natural gas	22%	50 years

As we try to plan for our future energy needs, a number of choices face us. We can, for example, use more coal. The world's coal supply, at the present rate of use, can last for at least 200 years. It is a fairly inexpensive fuel. Coal, however, is not practical for some purposes, such as running cars. Where it is burned in large amounts, it can **pollute,** or dirty, the air. Special devices that effectively clean the smoke from coal are being tested, but they are expensive.

In time we may rely more on renewable energy sources. Each of these now presents certain problems, especially in terms of cost and safety. For example, **solar,** or sun, **power** is safe, but it requires expensive equipment, such as new roofs on houses.

Nuclear power supplies about 4 percent of the world's energy and could produce far more. However, the way it makes energy is complicated and possibly unsafe. A major concern is its use of uranium as fuel.

Uranium is a metal that is **radioactive.** Radioactive material gives off harmful rays, called **radiation,** that are extremely dangerous to humans. As they produce energy, nuclear power plants create radioactive waste material. It takes many years for nuclear wastes to become harmless. In the meantime, safe places must be found to store these wastes. Such concerns regarding nuclear energy sources have not yet been solved.

Solving the Energy Problem

Many people are working to solve the energy problem. They have already made some important progress. New methods help produce more oil from oil fields. New types of windmills are producing electricity. More discoveries probably will be made in the coming years.

Another solution to the energy problem is one in which everyone can participate—energy **conservation.** Conserving energy means using energy wisely. Conserving energy saves money. We can have more energy tomorrow if we use less energy today.

Finding Ways to Conserve Energy

Read the list of ways to conserve energy on page 554. See how many suggestions you already use or can start to use.

With about 75 plants, the United States is a chief producer of nuclear energy.

Water

- Use hot water only when necessary.
- Take short warm showers rather than hot baths.
- Use a dishwasher or clothes washer with full loads only.
- Wash clothes in warm or cold water if possible.

Heat/Air Conditioning

- Set the thermostat to 68°F (20°C) in the winter and 78°F (25.6°C) in the summer.
- Instead of turning up the heat, put on more clothing.
- Use comforters and blankets instead of electric blankets.
- Keep the fireplace damper closed when the fireplace is not being used.
- Close the shades or curtains to keep heat in or out.
- Open windows at night to cool the house.
- Use fans instead of air conditioners whenever possible.
- Turn off the heat or air conditioning when you are out.
- Ask your parents if your home is insulated and weatherproofed; in some parts of the country, power companies will help pay for insulating houses.

Electricity/Natural Gas

- Use hand-powered appliances rather than electric ones wherever possible.
- Use energy-efficient appliances, ones that use less power.
- Keep the refrigerator door closed as much as possible.
- Do not open the oven door while food is cooking.
- Let dishes or clothes air dry.
- Turn off the lights, the radio, or the television when you leave a room.

Gasoline

- Ride bikes, walk, or use public transportation instead of driving whenever possible.
- Plan to combine errands into as few trips as possible.

Careful Shopping

Another way to conserve energy is to buy only the things we really need. Then, we should use them as long as possible before buying new ones. Almost everything we use, whether clothing, sports equipment, or machinery, takes energy to make.

Many communities now have places where people can bring old newspapers, used bottles and cans, paper bags, and cardboard. These materials are **recycled,** or reused. You can further encourage recycling by buying recycled products. Recycling takes a little effort, but it can save energy and other valuable resources.

CHECKING YOUR SKILLS

1. Is wood a renewable or a nonrenewable source of energy? Why?

2. Look at the chart on page 553. What percentage of the world's energy came from coal? How long is the world supply of gas expected to last?

3. To conserve the most energy, should you use a clothesline or a gas or electric dryer to dry clothes? Why?

4. Look at the circle graphs on page 552. In what way do Americans use the most energy? What type of energy is consumed in the greatest quantity?

5. What are three ways that you can conserve energy?

CHAPTER 19 REVIEW

USING WORDS

Write the letter of the definition that matches each of the words below.

1. **amendments**   4. **premiers**
2. **confederation**   5. **provinces**
3. **dominion**

a. self-governing divisions of Canada
b. union of Canadian provinces
c. an independent possession of Great Britain
d. changes in laws
e. types of government leaders

REVIEWING FACTS

1. How did glaciers affect Canada?

2. Which two provinces are the largest, richest, and most populated in Canada?

3. What are the two official languages of Canada?

4. What attracted traders to New France?

5. Why did Canadians refuse to join American colonists against Britain?

6. What was the purpose of the British North America Act of 1867?

7. In what ways have Canada and the United States cooperated?

8. What are two major problems that face Canada today?

9. What rights are guaranteed in the Charter of Rights and Freedoms?

10. When did Canada gain independence?

THINKING CRITICALLY

1. Thousands of Canadians and Americans cross each other's border every year. How do you think such things as similar histories and language, abundant resources, and democratic governments have influenced the cooperation of the United States and Canada?

2. What problems can arise from having a single country with two major cultures, each with its own language? What might be done about these problems?

○ PRACTICING SKILLS

1. **Time Zones**   The United States, without Hawaii and Alaska, covers four time zones. On a sheet of paper label four columns as follows: "Eastern Standard Time (7 A.M.)," "Central Standard Time (6 A.M.)," "Mountain Standard Time (5 A.M.)," "Pacific Standard Time (4 A.M.)." Use the map on page 543 to find the following cities. Then write the name of each city under its appropriate time zone.

Kansas City	Denver
Seattle	Atlanta
Phoenix	Chicago
Houston	San Francisco

2. **Conserving Energy**   Make a list of all the things you use in a day that require some form of energy to operate. What forms of energy are used? Which energy sources are nonrenewable? How might you conserve your daily energy use?

CLOSE-UP

PROTECTING OUR ENVIRONMENT

It is 1969. You are an astronaut on the Apollo space flight returning from the moon. You see the Earth approach, a lovely blue ball laced with white clouds. As it slowly turns, the Earth seems to breathe, as if it were alive.

You may think your eyes are playing tricks. The truth is, you are seeing the Earth's **biosphere.** The biosphere, which means "circle of life," is a thin skin of water, soil, and air. The biosphere is home for all the living things on Earth.

556

LIFE IN THE BIOSPHERE

Snow and ice
Springtail
Mayfly
Jumping spider
Golden eagle
Tundra
Bighorn sheep
Evergreen forest
Grizzly bear
Dipper
Deciduous forest
Sparrow hawk
White-tailed deer
Rain forest
Spider monkey
Poisonous frog
Toucan
Coastal waters
Lobster
Haddock
Sea lion
Deep sea
Giant squid
Fin whale
Tuna

Like a living skin, the biosphere has different parts—oceans, rivers, air, forests, and soil. Yet all parts of the biosphere are connected. What happens in one part affects all the others. If one part of the biosphere does not work properly, nothing will be able to live.

At one time people thought the Earth could provide endless resources. Today, the Earth seems much smaller. There are many more people than in the past. In 1600 there were less than 500 million people. Today more than 4.8 billion people must find food, materials, and energy on the same planet. As the world's population expands, people find new ways to meet their growing needs. They change the courses of rivers and grow food on deserts. Using machines, factories, and power plants, people are producing more goods than ever before.

Producing food and shelter for all these people also is creating new problems. The Earth cannot replace some resources as fast as people use them. Forests that take centuries to grow can be chopped down in a few weeks. Soil that takes thousands of years to form can blow away after too much plowing. Other resources, like oil and coal, are nonrenewable. The Earth will take millions of years to produce them again. If these fuels are used up, they will be gone.

In the future people will still need clean air and water and good soil. Yet researchers say that pollution is threatening the Earth. As a result, the environment may not be able to meet people's future needs. Smoke from factories and cars is adding tons of waste matter to the air. Land and water are being polluted with wastes, such as plastics and chemicals. Some of these wastes do not **decay,** or break down. Others decay very slowly. Cities and factories must find safe ways to dispose of them. Wastes from nuclear power plants remain dangerous for thousands of years. Ways to store them safely must be found, too.

To help understand these problems, scientists called **ecologists** study living things and their environments. The word *ecology* is related to a word meaning "household." The Earth is the "household" for all living things. Ecologists know that living things depend on the Earth and on each other.

557

Mount St. Helens erupts.

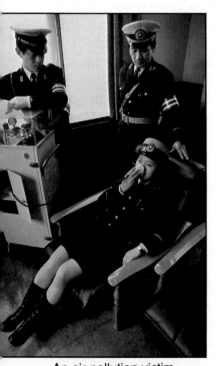

An air pollution victim receives oxygen.

Problems with Air

There has always been some natural air pollution. Forest fires begun by lightning fill the air with smoke. Erupting volcanoes, like Mount St. Helens in Washington, also throw smoke and ash into the air. Wind blows dust into blinding clouds. Nature could always wash the air clean with wind and rain, however.

Air pollution became a problem during the Industrial Revolution. People began to use coal to run machines and factories. By the 1950s black smoke hung over many cities and factory towns in Great Britain. Everyone could see and smell these "black fogs" and knew they were unhealthy. Many deaths were blamed on the bad air. In 1956 the British passed the Clean Air Act to restrict widespread burning of coal. Black fogs no longer occur.

Meanwhile, oil was becoming more widely used. Oil, like coal, produces energy as it burns. Fuel oil and some coal now power factories and heat homes. Automobiles and other vehicles use gasoline, a form of oil. When oil burns, it throws tiny particles and poisonous gases into the air. Most air pollution is caused by the millions of cars burning gasoline.

Unlike smoke from coal, gasoline pollution is hard to see. In some places pollution mixes with fog to form smog. A blanket of warm air above it holds smog in place. As time passes, the air grows worse. This occurs today in many large cities around the world. Smog alerts warn people that the elderly, children, and people with breathing problems should stay indoors. In Tokyo, traffic police sometimes need oxygen masks to help them breathe.

Some governments have passed laws to control air pollution. Like Great Britain, the United States has a Clean Air Act. These laws require factories and automobiles to use pollution-control equipment. Each year, however, air pollution increases around the world. More cars and factories burn more fuel. Winds carry the pollution away and scatter it. Lead from automobile exhaust has turned up in the distant snows of Greenland. No one knows how much pollution the Earth's air can take. Ecologists warn that the limit is not far off.

Problems with Water

People need clean water to live, but pollution also threatens the sources of our water. Cities use water to carry their sewage. They dump the waste water into rivers and oceans. Chemicals and other wastes from factories reach important water sources. Even some chemicals that are used to grow crops may pollute water. The chemicals drain into underground streams. Rain washes the chemicals into lakes and rivers and finally into the oceans.

All this pollution can harm water life. In a complex process, pollution in water chokes off oxygen. The water can no longer support living things. For example, most fish and plants in Lake Erie once died from lack of oxygen in the water.

Water pollution also threatens humans. It can poison drinking water and food. When chemical wastes containing mercury were dumped in Minamata Bay in the 1950s, Japanese who ate fish from the bay became poisoned. Fifty-two people died and many more were permanently damaged. Ecologists warn that some ocean fish may also contain harmful chemicals.

Many countries have taken steps to **reclaim,** or renew, their waters. The Thames River in England, like Lake Erie, became so polluted that its fish could not survive. Now, laws forbid factories and city sewage plants to dump wastes into the river. People also began to clean up Lake Erie's water. Today marine life is returning to both the Thames and Lake Erie.

Pollution of waters that nations use in common is still a serious problem. Sometimes, as the result of accidents at sea, ships spill thousands of gallons of oil. The oil then spreads to cover the water and beaches. Many nations fish the oceans. Oil spills destroy ocean plants and fish. A layer of oil on the water also prevents proper evaporation. This could greatly affect climate. With so much oil being transported in larger ships, shipping safety rules are stricter now. In this way it is hoped that accidents can be avoided. Nations must work together to keep the oceans clean.

The animal population suffers from an oil spill.

559

Coal is strip-mined in
southern Montana.

Small planes cover fields
with pesticide.

Problems on Land

Growing populations change the face of land. This growth has meant less land for wilderness. Some animals no longer exist or are few in number because their living space is gone. Buffalo that once roamed the Great Plains in large numbers are now found only in small herds on ranches or in parks and zoos. Wolves, tigers, and other animals have been forced into remote areas.

People change the land in other ways. Loggers cut trees for lumber. Miners strip away miles of soil to get at coal and other minerals. Farming, too, can change land. Erosion is an important cause of soil damage. The topsoil where all plants must grow is a very thin layer. It depends on trees and grass to hold it down. Modern farms usually have large open fields. Strong winds and heavy rain can carry away tons of this unprotected soil. Some ecologists say that topsoil is disappearing at an alarming rate worldwide.

Farmers have known about erosion for some time. There are a number of ways to prevent it. In some countries, for example, farmers plant crops on terraces along hillsides. This helps keep the soil from washing away. Farmers plant rows of trees around fields to break the winds.

Chemical pollution is creating other problems. Many crops, such as corn, wear out soil in one or two seasons. Scientists in the nineteenth century discovered how to make fertilizers out of chemicals. These fertilizers can be used to restore worn-out soil. They also learned that chemicals called pesticides could kill harmful pests.

Such attempts to improve farming can have harmful effects on the environment. By the 1960s bad side effects began to appear. As more chemicals were added every year, they built up in the soil. Rain then washed them into rivers. Some chemicals in pesticides, such as DDT, began to show up in fish and birds. These chemicals could eventually reach humans in their food.

It is in this way that people have learned the real lessons of ecology. Science has given people powerful tools to help them. Yet people cannot always foresee the effects of these tools on the land.

On Earth Day, Americans promote awareness of environmental concerns.

Bottles and cans are recycled at a community center.

What To Do

People worldwide know that pollution is dangerous. Yet the problems continue. Why does this happen?

A major reason is cost. People enjoy having automobiles and electrical conveniences. The energy sources they now use create pollution. Controlling pollution or developing other forms of energy is expensive. Every community would have to buy new equipment to produce energy. Homes and cars might have to be built differently. Many industries would have to invest in new equipment. The costs would be passed on to consumers as higher prices.

Many solutions might seem obvious. Everyone should use fewer resources. All nations should pass the same laws. It is hard for all to agree, however. Not all nations have equal wealth. Many poorer nations have just begun to build industries. Their use of chemicals and resources is increasing. They want the same good life that wealthy nations have had. For many people, too, most dangers seem to be far in the future. Given the choice, they tend to choose their own comfort today.

Some of the world's governments have taken an interest in the problems of protecting the environment. In the United States the **Environmental Protection Agency** (EPA) encourages laws to safeguard the environment. The EPA provides information to educate the public about the problems. The EPA also investigates threats to the environment.

Meanwhile, each person has the responsibility to use resources wisely. We know that there are many ways to protect our environment. We can conserve. We can pass laws. We can clean up or restore damaged parts of the environment.

Today we must plan the future carefully. In the United States, when new buildings, factories, or roads are proposed, studies are done. When new technology is developed, tests are made. Researchers **predict,** or try to guess, the future effects of these changes. In that way they can suggest ways to protect the environment. The biosphere can continue to "breathe."

561

WORDS TO REMEMBER

Number your paper from 1 to 10. Complete the sentences below with the words from the following lists.

amendments	haciendas
compromise	illiterate
confederation	mestizos
conquistadors	provinces
gauchos	viceroys

1. The Pope proposed a _____ to keep the peace between Spain and Portugal.

2. Spanish _____ in search of treasures in the New World destroyed early American civilizations.

3. Early settlers in Latin America raised tropical crops on their _____.

4. The king appointed _____ to govern the colonies.

5. _____ make up a large part of the Latin American population.

6. The _____ herd cattle in the grasslands of Brazil.

7. In the past, people who were _____ could not vote in Brazil.

8. To increase their power, Canadians formed a _____, which united four colonies.

9. Canada is divided into ten _____ and two territories.

10. The British Parliament approved the _____ that brought Canada its own constitution.

FOCUS ON MAIN IDEAS

1. Identify each of the following people:

   a. Atahualpa   d. Pizarro
   b. Montezuma   e. Malinche
   c. Cortés   f. Cabral

2. List the social classes of colonial Latin America in the order of their importance.

3. What role did the Spanish play in the government, trade, and religion of Latin American colonies?

4. How did the American and French revolutions affect Latin American colonies?

5. Identify the region of Brazil where each of the following is found. Name a resource associated with each.

   a. fazendas   c. Salvador
   b. Minas Gerais   d. rain forest

6. How was Brazil's history different from that of other Latin American nations?

7. What problems face Brazil as it changes from a farming economy to an industrial one? How can Brazilians solve their problems?

8. Name the four regions of Canada and a major resource found in each.

9. What influence did the French have on Canada in the past? How do French Canadians affect Canada today?

10. Describe how the British role in Canada's government changed as Canada went from a colony to a dominion to a fully independent nation.

THINK/WRITE

As we near the next century, it is more important than ever for the nations of the Western Hemisphere to cooperate with one another. Why is this interdependence so vital to our future? Write a paragraph giving three reasons for Western Hemisphere nations to get along.

ACTIVITIES

1. **Research/Art** Research one of the three great Indian civilizations of Latin America. With a group of classmates, draw a mural or make a diorama showing various parts of life in that civilization.

2. **Research/Biography** Choose one of the following people from Western Hemisphere history and prepare a short biography. Try to use direct quotes.

   a. Count Frontenac
   b. Tupac Amaru
   c. Pierre Radisson
   d. Pierre Toussaint L'Ouverture
   e. José de San Martín

3. **Reading/Current Events** Collect newspaper and magazine articles that tell about the relationship of the United States with any of our neighbors in this hemisphere. Place them in a class scrapbook.

● SKILLS REVIEW

1. **Making Decisions** Read the paragraphs and answer the questions.

   On March 13, 1968, rich oil deposits were discovered at Prudhoe Bay, Alaska. The problem was how to get the oil to other parts of the United States. An 800-mile (1,287-km) pipeline across Alaska to Valdez seemed the best solution. There, tankers could load and deliver the oil.

The idea for the trans-Alaska pipeline caused some disputes. The public land on which the pipeline would be built was being claimed by different groups. Other groups were concerned that changing the Alaskan landscape might damage the natural environment and threaten wildlife. These groups were particularly concerned about breaks in the pipes that would result in oil spills. Also, construction of a pipeline would be costly and difficult. Such problems as mountainous terrain, freezing temperatures, and earthquakes would have to be considered carefully.

In the early 1970s oil prices began to rise. Long lines formed at gas stations. People were dissatisfied with paying high prices for oil from other countries. In November 1973, Congress agreed to the construction of the pipeline. Land claims and environmental objections were settled. The pipeline was completed in 1977.

   a. What problem is being discussed in the first paragraphs?
   b. What solution was suggested?
   c. What kinds of problems did some groups of people think the pipeline might cause?
   d. If no pipeline had been built, what problems would people face?
   e. What did Congress decide?

2. **Using Time Zone Maps** Use the time zone maps and your skills lesson on pages 541–543 to answer these questions.

   a. About how many standard time zones are there in the world?
   b. If you fly from the West Coast of the United States to the East Coast, does the time get earlier or later?
   c. When it is 4 P.M. in San Francisco, what time is it in Hawaii?
   d. When it is 9 A.M. in Santiago, Chile, what time is it in São Paulo, Brazil?

YOUR WORLD

MAKING A TIMELINE

1. Complete the illustrated Timeline of the World that you began in Unit 1. As you add dates for key events in this unit, compare the histories of the Eastern and Western hemispheres.

LEARNING ABOUT PEOPLE

2. Today there are small Indian groups in remote areas of the Amazon Region and the Andes Mountains. Various Eskimo groups live in Canada and the Arctic. Research one of the native American groups listed below. Include information about the group in your Cultures of the World notebook. Discuss the ways in which the people of the group meet their needs in harsh environments.

   Aymara (Peru/Bolivia)
   Guarani (Brazil)
   Jivaro (Ecuador/Peru)
   Polar Eskimo (Greenland)
   Netsilik (Canadian Eskimo)

3. The gauchos of Argentina and Southeast Brazil are much like the "cowboys" of the American West. In the Northeast of Brazil there is another group of cattle herders with a unique lifestyle. They are called **vaqueros** (vuh•KAR•ohz). Find out about the gauchos and the vaqueros. Draw pictures showing how these groups live. Write captions that briefly explain some of the details in your pictures.

EXPRESSING IDEAS

Cultures throughout history have made and worn masks. Masks are examples of the art and crafts of the cultures who made them. Styles vary from real-appearing human and animal masks to greatly exaggerated and sometimes frightening masks.

4. In your library find pictures of a variety of masks. Then design a mask of your own. You might try constructing your mask from papier-mâché.

SHARING CULTURE

The names of towns, cities, mountains, and bodies of water often reflect the layers of history in an area. Such names may refer to Indians who lived there, or they may be Indian words. For example, Chichén Itzá, Mexico, was named by the Mayas. *Chi* means "mouths," *chen* means "wells," and Itza was the Mayan group who occupied the area. Names such as Hudson Bay recall famous explorers. Ciudad Bolívar, Venezuela, which means "Bolívar City," was named after a South American patriot.

5. Look at a map of your state. Make a list of names from the map that are like the examples given above. Find out where your community and others got their names. What names were taken from other languages or belonged to famous people? What can you tell about your state's history from these names?

CONCLUSION
A VIEW OF TOMORROW

What will the future be like?

Many people ask that question. Some even make their living predicting the needs, problems, and successes of the future. These experts are called **futurists** (FYOO•chuh•rists).

The challenges of the future are likely to be the same ones that people on Earth have always faced. Where is food to come from? How are we to get enough energy and other resources to meet our growing needs? How are we to get along with other people in the world? How are we to ensure justice and freedom for all?

There is also another challenge— taking care of our environment. People now have the power to destroy life on Earth. How do we protect the Earth for generations to come?

THE FUTURE IN THE PRESENT

It is hard to predict the future exactly, because technology can change very quickly. Think about life in the United States 100 years ago. Radio, television, automobiles, and airplanes had not been invented. Writers such as Jules Verne imagined that people might travel under the seas or go to the moon, but these ideas were science fiction. No one believed that such things would happen very soon.

Yet the future will not be totally different from the present. The seeds of the future lie in the present. In 1885 people might not have been able to predict the invention of radio, television, automobiles, airplanes, or computers. However, the groundwork for such achievements had already been laid. By then, people had begun to use electricity for the telegraph and telephone. Gasoline engines were being made. An Englishman named Charles Babbage had designed an adding machine that was the ancestor of the computer.

The achievements of the twentieth century were built on foundations laid by nineteenth-century scientists and thinkers. It should be possible, therefore, to get some idea of the twenty-first century by looking at today's science and technology.

Feeding the World

Today about 5 billion people live on Earth. By the year 2000 there are likely to be more than 6 billion people. By the year 2025 there may me 8 billion. Today millions of the world's people go hungry. What will happen when there are even more people? How can enough food be provided?

In recent years scientists have developed new kinds of food plants with high **yields.** Yield is the amount a plant produces. Wheat yields in the United States and Canada have doubled since 1970. In the 1960s new types of corn, rice, and wheat were planted in Southeast Asia, Africa, and India. The harvests from these crops were so much greater than before that people talked about a "Green Revolution."

The Green Revolution boosted food production, but it also presented new challenges. The new varieties of plants proved to be not as strong as older ones. The new plants needed large amounts of fertilizer and pesticides in order to grow well. Many farmers in poor countries could not afford to buy these chemicals.

Today, plant scientists are trying to develop high-yield plants that can fight off disease and grow in poor soil. "There is a need for crops that can adapt to the soil rather than having the soil conditioned to suit the crops," says one scientist.

Scientists are working on this problem in two ways. One way is **tissue culture.** Scientists culture, or grow, single cells from plants in their laboratories and study the cells for special traits. Some cells might grow well in salty water. Others might do well in extreme heat or cold. When the scientists find cells with desirable features, they cause them to develop into whole plants.

In a computer-age greenhouse, plants are grown under a variety of conditions. Electrical devices are attached to check their growth.

In the future, scientists may develop high-yield crops through **plant genetics** (juh•NET•iks). Genetics is the study of the complex way in which each living cell reproduces itself. Using the principles of plant genetics, scientists hope to change cells so that they develop into completely new plants. One of these plants may be the "pomato." Such a plant would grow potatoes on its roots and tomatoes on its branches!

Future Energy Sources

Finding sources of energy is a concern of the present and a challenge for the future. Some people's energy needs are as simple as wood for a cooking fire. In parts of Africa, Asia, and the Middle East, hills that were once wooded are now bare because people cut down the trees without replacing them. Today people in these parts of the world are helping to meet their future energy needs by planting trees. With careful management, the new forests should take care of the heating and cooking needs of people in these rural areas.

Many nations cannot become industrialized without more sources of energy. Energy, especially electrical energy, is important to today's technology. Think of a modern city. Elevators, lights, subways, telephones, televisions—all use electricity. A city that does not have electricity cannot function.

Petroleum is the major source of electricity in many countries. Petroleum also meets other needs. Imagine a city without oil and gasoline for automobiles, trucks, trains, and airplanes. Imagine your school or home without any plastic or synthetic products. The buttons on your clothes, the pen you write with, the soles of your shoes—all are likely to be synthetic. Most synthetic products are made from petroleum.

Petroleum is so important that it is hard to picture life without it. Supplies of petroleum are limited, however. For this reason, people have begun trying to conserve petroleum. From 1972 to 1982, Americans cut back their use of petroleum by 20 percent. Meanwhile, scientists are developing new sources of energy that may replace petroleum in the future.

Some countries have used nuclear energy to make electricity in recent years. However, the building of nuclear power plants has slowed because of their high cost and because of safety concerns. Wind is an old source of energy. It has been used for hundreds of years to run machinery. Machines powered by windmills have pumped water, ground grain, or sawed lumber. Today people are using wind power to make electricity. In California dozens of modern windmills have been set up on windy hilltops. In a year one windmill produces enough electricity to meet the needs of 25 homes.

The sun's rays also are being used to make electricity. The largest solar center receiver today is located near Barstow, California. It is called Solar One. Solar One has a field of mirrors that covers 20 acres (8 ha) of land. The mirrors focus the sun's rays on a "power tower." Water inside the tower is heated by the sunlight until it boils, making steam that drives generators. The amount of electricity produced by Solar One supplies the needs of 6,000 homes.

Much of our solar technology has developed because of the space program. **Solar cells** have helped to provide energy for people in space. Solar cells turn the sun's rays directly into

Solar One at Barstow, California, is shown here. Electric companies, the city of Los Angeles, and the United States government sponsored the project.

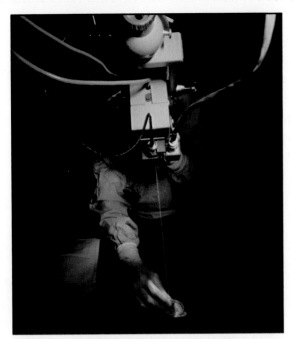

Here, a surgeon focuses a laser beam to remove an ear's unhealthy tissue.

For nuclear experiments, the Shiva laser produces heat as hot as the sun.

electricity. You may have seen solar-powered watches and calculators. These devices use solar cells.

So far, making electricity with solar cells is expensive. It is useful, however, in places that have no other sources of electricity. Developing countries can use solar cells to provide power for such things as water pumps and communication systems. Solar cells may even be used to power automobiles. In 1983 an Australian drove his solar-powered car 2,500 miles (2,673 km) across that continent.

Light Waves

Would you believe a camera that can take pictures through a curving tube? Until recently such a thing existed only in people's imaginations. Now it is real. It is part of a new technology that uses light waves. Controlled beams of light waves are called **laser** (LAY•zuhr) **beams.** Devices called lasers produce these beams.

The use of laser technology has just begun. Surgeons use some kinds of laser beams as "knives" in delicate operations. Other very hot laser beams weld metals together.

Laser beams also can carry information. The beams pass through cables made of special glass fibers bound together. Each fiber is thinner than a human hair. Pulses of laser light carry information along the fibers in a coded form, something like the dots and dashes of a telegraph signal. Most ground communication systems of the twenty-first century will use glass-fiber cables and laser beams.

Computers

Computers have brought great changes into our lives. Computers themselves also have changed greatly since their invention. The first electronic computer filled several rooms when it was built in 1946. Only the largest businesses could have computers at first. The machines were as expensive as they were huge.

All the information stored in one of those early giant computers now can be put on a "computer chip" about the size of a letter on this page. That tiny chip probably costs less than ten dollars. Such chips are the "brains" of most computers today.

Computers have become smaller, smarter, and cheaper each year. In 20 years, computer chips are likely to be so small that doctors will be able to put one inside a living cell. Computers will be so "smart" that information from a whole library could be stored on a single chip. They will be so cheap that almost every home in industrial nations will have a computer, just as most homes have television sets today.

Computers have made it possible for people to store and use great amounts of information. Our modern life depends on computers. With computers, people can figure out problems in a day that might otherwise take years.

A kind of computer called a **word processor** (PRAHS•es•uhr) has begun to replace typewriters. People type on word processors much as they do on typewriters. They then can use the word processors to change the order of paragraphs, replace words, or put lists into alphabetical order. Some word processors even let you know when you have misspelled a word!

Until recently, computers were used mostly by businesses. Today, however, computers are becoming common in

Many different kinds of jobs are made easier with the use of computers.

homes. There they are used both as tools and as sources of knowledge and entertainment.

Computers will make shopping at home possible. Suppose you want to buy canned tomatoes or a garden hose. You will give certain directions to your computer. Pictures of all kinds and sizes of canned tomatoes or garden hoses then will appear on the computer's screen. You will choose what you wish. Money to pay for the items will be taken from your bank account and the goods will be sent to you. This way of shopping is already being tested.

Robots

One kind of computer device is a **robot.** Robots are computer-controlled machines that try to imitate human movements and thinking processes.

Robots of today can imitate some of the ways people move. However, scientists say that it will be a long time, if ever, before robots will be able to imitate the way people think.

Robots are hard at work today in factories in such countries as Japan, West Germany, and the United States. Some of these factory robots have moving "arms" and TV-camera "eyes." Some are box-shaped and move around on wheels. Robots usually do such jobs as welding, sorting, putting on bolts, and carrying. Robots are especially useful for jobs that might be dangerous. A few robots that can do simple household tasks are now available. They are very expensive, however. In the future, household robots will be able to obey voice commands. These robots will be helpful to handicapped people. Such a robot may wash dishes, cook meals, and sweep floors. It may answer the telephone, turn on the television, and lock the door.

A robot arm does heavy welding in an Italian automobile factory.

Transportation

The airplane, the automobile and the truck rule the world of travel today. As we go into the twenty-first century, however, there probably will be new forms of transportation. Use of these new ways of going places is already beginning.

In some parts of the world, trains have now been built that work differently from the trains we know. They are called **maglev** (MAHG•lef) trains. *Maglev* stands for magnetic levitation. Maglev trains do not travel by moving wheels on tracks. Instead, they ride over a small cushion of air. They are lifted and pulled along by magnets. Such trains can reach speeds of more than 250 miles (402 km) an hour. In the twenty-first century, we may ride maglev trains instead of airplanes over distances of several hundred miles.

We probably will still have automobiles in the next century, but the automobiles may become more like moving robots. Today, some factory robots can follow electrified tracks in the floor. They have sensors that keep them from running into each other. This kind of technology may be on the streets in the twenty-first century. Cars may follow electrical "tracks" in the street. They will be able to avoid collisions with other cars. They may even be able to obey a spoken command: "Take me to Grove and 21st Street, please."

New Materials

Some of Earth's most common resources may be the important materials of the future. They are sand, clay, and chalk. **Silicon** (SIL•ih•kuhn) is a mineral found in sand. It is the most common mineral on Earth. Silicon can conduct electricity. It is used to make solar cells and computer chips. Silicon is so important for computers that the center of California's computer industry, near San Jose, is nicknamed "Silicon Valley."

People have made pots of clay mud since the beginning of human history. Objects of shaped and heated clay are called **ceramics** (suh•RAM•iks). Ceramics may play an important part in the technology of the future. Ceramics that are able to withstand tremendous heat and pressure now can be made. For instance, an American spacecraft called the space shuttle is covered with ceramic tiles. These tiles allow the shuttle to survive the immense heat of leaving and reentering the Earth's atmosphere. Another future use for ceramics may be in engines, which also must take heat and pressure. Japanese scientists have made a diesel engine that has ceramic instead of metal parts.

Clay mixed with chalk makes cement. Scientists are learning to use cement to make springs as strong as aluminum ones. In the future, cement may replace plastic in such common goods as plates and cups. Using less plastic will help conserve petroleum.

Space

Gerard K. O'Neill, a scientist interested in both space and the future, has called space "the high frontier." We have just started to explore space. In the last 25 years our knowledge of space has grown tremendously. We have learned how to launch people and spacecraft

The space shuttle Columbia climbs into space carrying experimental equipment.

into space and bring them back again. We have learned how to make materials that withstand the extreme temperatures and radiation of space. We have learned to help people live in space for weeks or months at a time. All of this knowledge of the high frontier is only the first step. In the twenty-first century, many people probably will live and work in space colonies.

Questions to Answer

1. In what two ways are scientists developing high-yield plants that fight off disease and can grow in poor soil?
2. What are controlled beams of light waves called? How are they used?
3. What work do most robots do today? How may they be used in the future?
4. How are maglev trains different from the trains we know?
5. How might cement be used in the twenty-first century?

IMAGINING THE NEXT CENTURY

A person born in 1900 was born before the Wright Brothers made the first successful airplane flight. When that person was 69, Americans walked on the moon. Think of the technological changes that person saw in a lifetime! You may see just as many changes—or perhaps more—during your lifetime.

It can be fun to predict the future based on what we know today. Try to picture your community in the twenty-first century. It may be covered by a huge plastic bubble. Within the bubble, the air is always a comfortable temperature, even though a blizzard may be howling outside.

As you enter your home, you hear: "Good evening. What would you like for dinner?" It will be your house computer speaking. The computer will be able to understand your speech.

"I'd like spaghetti, please," you say.

"Coming up," replies the computer. While you read or talk with your family, the computer orders your household robot to cook the meal. The robot will also set the table and tell you when dinner is ready.

Refrigerators may seem as old-fashioned in the twenty-first century as iceboxes do today. You may use a refrigerator because you like your milk cool rather than warm. You will not need a refrigerator to preserve foods, however. Milk, for instance, will be preserved by being sterilized at a very high temperature for a short time. It may then be packaged in a special plastic container. It may stay fresh for months, even years.

You may work at home in the next century. If you want to talk to other people in your business, you will call them on your picturephone. You can talk to several people at once, even if they are in different parts of the world. You may see each other as three-dimensional pictures, or **holograms** (HAHL•uh•grams), made by laser light. It will seem as if you are all in the same room.

To get around the city you may use a small electric car that acts like a wheeled robot. You will tell your car where you want to go. The car's computer will steer it along tracks in the road. Television "eyes" will keep your car from running into other cars.

Suppose you live in New York and want to visit a friend in Boston. You can make the trip in half an hour on a maglev train.

Space Colonies

In the next century you may not live on Earth itself. You may live in a space colony. Space colonies are one of the most exciting things to imagine in the twenty-first century. The purpose of space colonies will be much like that of the original American colonies. They will be sources of raw materials and energy for the mother country.

If you live in space, your colony probably will look like a wheel or a doughnut. It may look like a giant erector set, with new sections added to it as the need arises. The space colony will turn to give people a sense of gravity. Otherwise they would float

This future space colony is topped by a fan-shaped mirror which catches the sun's rays. Moon rocks covering it block harmful radiation.

instead of walk. The colony will have been built in space. Materials for the colony will have come from the moon or from tiny planets called **asteroids** (AS•tuh•roydz). Each space colony will grow its own food and recycle its water.

Part of the space colony may be a factory. We know from experiments that certain kinds of manufacturing work better in space. Some materials in computer chips are best made in space, for example. Minerals mined from asteroids may be used in some kinds of space manufacturing.

Electricity for the space colony will come from solar cells. Solar cells will also send electricity to Earth. People based on space stations may build platforms many miles long. These orbiting platforms will be covered with solar cells. The energy gathered by the cells will be beamed to Earth and then turned into electricity.

Your job in the space colony may be to help take care of the solar power satellite that sends energy to Earth. Your job may be to help grow and harvest food for the colony. If you are a scientist, you may spend your time studying the outer reaches of space to learn more about the universe.

Questions to Answer

1. What roles may computers and robots play in your home life in the twenty-first century?
2. What will be the purpose of space colonies?
3. What may be a major source of energy for Earth in the twenty-first century?

574

HUMAN SOCIETY IN THE TWENTY-FIRST CENTURY

It is fun to imagine life in the next century, a life full of new technology and achievements. But what will this new life mean for people?

Whatever changes technology may bring, we can be sure that people in the future will experience many of the same joys and sorrows as people today or 1,000 years ago. Literature and art show us that people of the past had feelings much like ours. They laughed and cried. They loved stories, songs, and games. They liked to make beautiful things to use and look at. In the future, too, people will find joy and meaning through the arts and through love of family and friends.

Many of people's needs will be the same, too. People have always had to find ways to feed, house, and clothe themselves and their families from limited resources. They have always tried to improve their lives. To do this, they thought about what they needed. Perhaps it was food. Perhaps it was water. Perhaps it was knowledge. To meet their needs, people worked out new ways of doing and making things. They learned about the stars, about mathematics, about writing. People will continue to have to find ways to meet basic needs in the future.

Even some ways of life will be the same in the next century. Not everyone will live in a world of high technology. From your study of the past you know that technology has never been the same at the same time all over the world. The Chinese, for example, learned to make beautiful bronzes while much of the world was still in the Stone Age. In the twenty-first century, too, there will be differences in technology. Some people will go on living much as their ancestors have—farming the land, herding reindeer, or fishing.

Avoiding War

The big problems that people have faced for thousands of years have not gone away. They include disasters such as fire, earthquake, flood, famine, and war. These problems most likely will still be present in the future.

The worst of these problems is war. War has been part of most human societies throughout history. Today, however, we face a new, far greater threat from war. This is the danger of nuclear war. We now have the power to

All over the world, people are asking governments to solve problems peacefully.

blow up our planet and poison its environment for thousands of years. A nuclear war could destroy all life on Earth—forever. People must find ways besides war to settle their conflicts.

Competition for scarce resources has often led to war in the past. Finding new supplies of resources may help us avoid war. If people can mine minerals from asteroids and the moon and get energy from the sun, they may not need to fight over resources on Earth.

Finding New Jobs

In today's industrial societies many people fear losing their jobs to robots and computers. One futurist agrees: "Human workers will go the way of the horse." He means that in the last century automobiles, trucks, and tractors replaced horses on roads and farms. Will computers and robots replace human workers?

"Nonsense!" say many. They point out that when automobiles replaced horses, new jobs were created. Today's technology also makes new jobs, they say. We need people to design, build, and fix computers. We need people to operate them.

The truth may lie between these two viewpoints. Computers and robots will be likely to take over many kinds of routine jobs. The people who lose jobs on an assembly line will not necessarily be able to get jobs fixing computers. Society will have to find new ways to give people meaningful work.

More than ever before, people will need skills to use the tools of the future. New jobs will demand that people have good reading and math skills. People will need these skills to use

Computer technology will offer new challenges to job seekers.

computers well, for example. The computers will not "do all the work" for their users. Owning a computer will not make someone a mathematician or engineer. Using a word processor will not make someone a good writer.

Technology

In today's world there is a mixture of old and new, big and small. There are small farms and huge farms, villages and cities, tiny businesses and huge corporations. People need advanced technology to run large cities or maintain complex communication and transportation systems. However, such technology may not be the best choice for the small town, the small farm, or the small business.

It is less costly to use horses on a small farm than to use tractors. It may be cheaper and easier to use an adding machine than a computer in a small store.

India has chosen to use advanced technology in a way particularly suited to its needs. It is a large country but has few electrical power lines. Most of its people do not have televisions. They have little knowledge of the outside world. They do things exactly as their parents did them.

To bring information and education to its people, India is using two items of technology: the satellite and the transistor radio. India has a communications satellite in space. It uses this satellite to beam radio broadcasts to the country. Villagers can hear these broadcasts on transistor radios. Such radios are cheap and easy to carry. Even one transistor radio in a village can bring new ideas to the village's people.

Developing nations are using the new solar and wind technology to make electricity. The electricity will be used to run irrigation pumps or factory machines. As these countries gain more energy, they will be able to increase their agricultural and manufacturing production. This in turn will allow them to improve their standard of living.

This radar dish is used to send and receive messages from space satellites.

Taking Care of Earth

Decisions about a new technology will have to take into account its effect on the environment as well as its cost in money. For example, the United States government decided not to allow passenger planes traveling faster than the speed of sound to use our air space. It made this decision because such planes cause environmental damage through noise. Their exhaust also may harm the upper atmosphere. Such decisions about the use of technology will continue to be made in the next century.

People of the twenty-first century will be very aware of the need to take care of Earth. Scientists will understand the delicate balances needed to maintain life on this planet. Satellites and new communication systems will help to keep people in touch with changes in Earth's environment.

People probably will have agreed to leave large parts of Earth in their natural state rather than developing them. This is because plants in some parts of the Earth, such as the tropical rain forests, produce much of the oxygen needed for life. Destroying these areas could mean destroying our source of life.

People also will want to preserve the natural environment because they find it beautiful. Contact with nature has always been important to human beings. As more people have found themselves working indoors, more have looked for recreation that would keep them in touch with nature and the Earth. In recent years backpacking and camping have become very popular in America. Running in the ocean surf, climbing a high mountain,

Oregon's Crater Lake National Park is one of the state's undisturbed natural areas. National parks are important to preserving the environment.

flying a kite, or picnicking by a lake are likely to be as important in the next century as they are today.

Scientists will be very important in making sure that people's technology and high use of energy do not harm Earth during the next century. They also may be able to protect Earth from other kinds of disasters. For example, suppose that Earth's temperature begins to cool and an Ice Age threatens life. Using new knowledge about Earth, scientists may be able to stop the Ice Age by warming up the high reaches of the atmosphere.

Scientists might save Earth in another way. Suppose that an asteroid is on a collision course with Earth. If an asteroid struck Earth, it could cause terrible damage. In the next century we may be able to use explosions in space to push the asteroid onto another course.

Justice and Freedom

People have always faced the problem of how to get along with one another and treat each other fairly. The oldest stories in the world deal with these questions: What is fair or just? What are the rights and duties of the individual? What is important to the survival of the group?

Each society has defined justice in its own way. People's ideas of justice have changed over time. We no longer think it is just to cut out a person's tongue for telling a lie, for example. Almost all societies have agreed, however, that justice is an ideal for which to strive. In the future, whether in a farming village in Europe or in a space station, people will still be working on the problem of getting along with each other and achieving justice.

Our society also has a long tradition of seeking freedom. Our heritage of freedom goes back thousands of years to the ideas of the Greeks. An ancient Greek might be bewildered by today's world, but he or she would not be surprised by our love of freedom.

Freedom, like justice, must be continually guarded. Future technology can create both opportunities and dangers for freedom. In some ways, technology can give people more freedom. It can relieve them of tiring or dangerous tasks. It can give them access to more information and to ideas of great thinkers.

At the same time, some technology offers new ways of controlling people. People in the next century could wear ankle bracelets that send out a signal, for example. A central computer will receive these signals and know where each person is at every moment. Do we want this kind of control? People will need clear ideas of what freedom is and how to preserve it when they make decisions for the future.

Seeking New Challenges

In every age and every place, people have looked for challenge. Think of the challenge the Egyptians faced when they built the pyramids. Think of the challenge the Europeans of the Middle Ages faced when they built soaring cathedrals. Imagine the challenge of translating the Rosetta Stone or inventing a better steam engine or a vehicle for space travel.

People will go on seeking challenges. They will look for new frontiers to explore. They will define problems and search for answers. People have always been this way and no doubt always will be.

A jet-powered backpack steered this astronaut alone through space in 1984.

You, too, probably want to seek challenges in your life. Your future can be very exciting. You will see and experience things that others can only imagine. You may live on a space station. You may climb Mount Everest. You may write and perform music. You may be elected as a lawmaker. You may be an ocean explorer. It is not too soon to think about your future, the world you would like to live in, and what you want to do to help make that world a reality.

Questions to Answer

1. What new threat do people face today that is greater than disasters people faced in the past?
2. How is the world of work likely to change in the future?
3. Why is the most advanced technology not always the best technology?
4. For what ideals will people still strive in the future?

REFERENCES

FACTS ABOUT THE WORLD

Nation and Capital	Population	Economy	Nation and Capital	Population	Economy
AFRICA					
Algeria Algiers	20,499,000	oil, gas, steel, fertilizers, plastics	Kenya Nairobi	18,784,000	tourism, hides, gems, cereals, cotton, gold
Angola Luanda	8,339,000	cotton goods, palm oil, diamonds, coffee, bananas	Lesotho Maseru	1,366,000	diamond polishing, grains, wool, mohair
Benin Porto-Novo	3,720,000	palm products, oil, peanuts, coffee	Liberia Monrovia	1,911,000	rice, cassava, iron, rubber, timber, gold
Botswana Gaborone	941,000	big game hunting, tourism, corn, coal	Libya Tripoli	3,356,000	carpets, textiles, oil, gas, fruits
Burkina Faso Ouagadougou	6,360,000	grains, manganese, gold, diamonds	Madagascar Antananarivo	9,400,000	vanilla, cloves, sugar, chromium, coffee
Burundi Bujumbura	4,114,000	coffee, cotton, tea, animal hides	Malawi Lilongwe	6,430,000	textiles, sugar, farm tools, peanuts, tea
Cameroon Yaounde	9,160,000	aluminum, palm products, cotton, tea, coffee	Mali Bamako	7,528,000	millet, rice, iron, bauxite, copper, peanuts, cotton
Cape Verde Praia	296,000	bananas, coffee, sugar cane, salt	Mauritania Nouakchott	1,407,000	grain, iron, dates, gypsum, ores
Central African Republic Bangui	2,442,000	textiles, diamonds, timber, minerals, cotton, coffee	Mauritius Port Louis	983,000	tourism, sugar cane, tea
Chad Ndjamena	4,405,000	cotton, uranium	Morocco Rabat	20,420,000	carpets, leather, oil, minerals, dates, tourism
Comoros Moroni	421,000	perfume, vanilla, fruits, coconut	Mozambique Maputo	12,615,000	cement, textiles, tea, cashews, cotton, coal
Congo Brazzaville	1,580,000	palm oil, cacao, oil, gas, coffee	Niger Niamey	5,686,000	peanuts, cotton, uranium
Djibouti Djibouti	220,000	salt, minerals	Nigeria Lagos	89,022,000	oil, gas, machinery, cacao, coal
Egypt Cairo	44,673,000	cotton, chemicals, steel, movies, oil	Rwanda Kigali	5,046,000	coffee, tea, tin, gold
Equatorial Guinea Malabo	304,000	cacao, coffee, bananas, timber	São Tomé and Principe São Tomé	97,000	cacao, coffee, fish, coconut products
Ethiopia Addis Ababa	33,680,000	coffee, cement, gold, platinum, copper, textiles	Senegal Dakar	6,316,000	food processing, fish, rice, phosphates, peanuts
Gabon Libreville	1,127,000	oil products, manganese, uranium, cacao, coffee	Seychelles Victoria	65,000	foods, cinnamon, vanilla, shark fins, coconuts
Gambia Banjul	696,000	tourism, peanuts, rice, fish	Sierra Leone Freetown	3,472,000	wood, diamonds, iron, bauxite, coffee, cacao
Ghana Accra	12,700,000	aluminum, cacao, gold, manganese	Somalia Mogadishu	5,269,000	incense, sugar, bananas, tin, iron
Guinea Conakry	5,177,000	bananas, pineapples, bauxite, diamonds, iron	South Africa Capetown/ Pretoria	25,591,000	steel, tires, motors, diamonds, uranium
Guinea-Bissau Bissau	810,000	peanuts, bauxite, cotton			
Ivory Coast Abidjan	7,920,000	coffee, cacao, gold, manganese, timber, rubber	Sudan Khartoum	20,564,000	gum arabic, cotton, sesame, chromium

Nation and Capital	Population	Economy	Nation and Capital	Population	Economy
Swaziland Mbabane	605,000	wood pulp, pineapples, asbestos, corn, iron	Uganda Kampala	12,630,000	coffee, cotton, tea, copper, cobalt
Tanzania Dar es Salaam	20,378,000	cotton, clothing, coffee, salt, gold, hides, diamonds	Zaire Kinshasa	30,148,000	cobalt, coffee, cotton, rice, copper, rubber
Togo Lome	2,747,000	textiles, shoes, yams, phosphates, coffee	Zambia Lusaka	5,680,000	corn, cobalt, ivory, rubber, manganese
Tunisia Tunis	6,840,000	textiles, oil, fruit, construction materials	Zimbabwe Harare	7,539,000	light industry, chemicals, clothing, chromium, sugar

ASIA

Nation and Capital	Population	Economy	Nation and Capital	Population	Economy
Afghanistan Kabul	16,348,000	carpets, copper, coal, cement, lead, wool	Lebanon Beirut	2,635,000	oil products, fruits, iron, olives, grapes, textiles
Bahrain Manama	371,000	oil products, aluminum, shipping	Malaysia Kuala Lumpur	15,264,000	rubber, pottery, fertilizers, tin, electronics, rice
Bangladesh Dacca	94,651,000	jute, cement, oil, fertilizers, rice	Maldives Male	168,000	fish, tourism, shells, coconuts, fruit
Bhutan Thimphu	1,160,000	cloth, rice, corn, yak products, wax, timber	Mongolia Ulan Bator	1,866,000	textiles, chemicals, cement, foods, coal
Brunei Bandar Seri Begawan	214,000	oil, rice, bananas, cassavas	Nepal Katmandu	15,033,000	hides, medicines, jute, tourism, grains, quartz
Burma Rangoon	35,680,000	rice, sugar cane, rubber, teakwood, gemstones	Oman Muscat	2,000,000	oil, wheat, fruits, vegetables, bananas
China Beijing	1,024,950,000	iron, steel, rice, cotton, plastics	Pakistan Islamabad	91,880,000	textiles, wheat, wool, iron ore, chemicals
Cyprus Nicosia	649,000	wine, clothing, grain, minerals	Philippines Manila	52,055,000	clothing, food, medicines, wood, rice, sugar
India New Delhi	732,256,000	textiles, cement, steel, rice, rubber, tea, spices	Qatar Doha	270,000	crude oil, petroleum products
Indonesia Jakarta	157,495,000	rice, coffee, sugar, tin, rubber, nickel, oil	Saudi Arabia Riyadh	10,421,000	oil, petroleum products, gas, dates, wheat
Iran Tehran	40,777,000	steel, cars, oil, carpets, chemicals	Singapore Singapore	2,529,000	shipbuilding, cloth, banking, electronics
Iraq Baghdad	14,110,000	oil refining, rice, textiles, hides, oil and gas, wool	Sri Lanka Colombo	15,606,000	plywood, tea, rice, ceramics, coconuts, rubber, paper
Israel Jerusalem	4,097,000	aircraft, textiles, electronics, munitions, citrus	Syria Damascus	9,606,000	oil, textiles, wheat, cement, brassware, wool, olives
Japan Tokyo	119,450,000	steel, motor vehicles, electronic equipment	Taiwan Taipei	18,733,000	textiles, electronics, glass, clothing, chemicals
Jordan Amman	3,247,000	textiles, cement, wheat, vegetables	Thailand Bangkok	50,588,000	rice, cars, textiles, electrical goods, wood, rubber
Kampuchea Phnom Penh	6,747,000	textiles, paper, plywood, rice, corn	Turkey Ankara	47,279,000	silk, steel, shoes, wheat, glassware, tobacco, cotton
Korea, North P'yongyang	19,185,000	minerals, textiles, fertilizers, grain	United Arab Emirates Abu Dhabi	1,206,000	oil, steel, shipping, pearls, vegetables, dates
Korea, South Seoul	39,951,000	electronics, ships, motor vehicles, rice, clothing	Vietnam Hanoi	57,020,000	food processing, rubber, machinery, rice, textiles
Kuwait Kuwait	1,672,000	oil, oil products, gas	Yemen Sana	7,162,000	textiles, salt, wheat
Laos Vientiane	4,033,000	wood products, rice, tin, tobacco, cotton, coffee	Yemen (P.D.R.) Aden	2,158,000	shipping, cotton, grains

Nation and Capital	Population	Economy	Nation and Capital	Population	Economy
AUSTRALIA AND OCEANIA					
Australia Canberra	15,379,000	wool, wheat, iron, electrical goods	Solomon Islands Honiara	244,000	fish canning, rice, coconuts, yams, cacao, palm oil
Fiji Suva	672,000	cement, shipping, sugar, tourism	Tonga Nuku'alofa	96,000	tourism, coconut products, livestock, fish
Kiribati Tarawa	60,000	coconut products, fish, bananas	Tuvalu Funafuti	7,000	coconut products
Nauru Yaren	8,000	phosphate mining, coconuts	Vanuatu Port Vila	128,000	fish, meat canning, tourism, coconuts, manganese
New Zealand Wellington	3,266,000	food processing, paper, steel, wool, timber	Western Samoa Apia	156,000	cacao, hardwoods, coconuts, fish, coffee
Papua New Guinea Port Moresby	3,239,000	coffee, coconuts, gold, copper, silver, cacao			
EUROPE AND THE SOVIET UNION					
Albania Tirane	2,752,000	chemicals, fertilizers, electrical cables, grain	Luxembourg Luxembourg	366,000	steel, tires, beer, roses, iron, wine
Andorra Andorra	42,000	tourism, sheep, commerce, services, tobacco products	Malta Valletta	329,000	textiles, tourism, potatoes, onions
Austria Vienna	7,549,000	steel, machines, cars, optical supplies, timber	Monaco Monaco	27,000	tourism, chemicals, plastics
Belgium Brussels	9,853,000	steel, glassware, chemicals, grains, diamond cutting	Netherlands Amsterdam	14,362,000	metals, tourism, oil refining, diamond cutting
Bulgaria Sofia	8,949,000	chemicals, machines, furs, leathers, wine	Norway Oslo	4,134,000	paper, shipbuilding, engineering, foods, timber
Czechoslovakia Prague	15,415,000	machines, oil products, iron, steel, glass, wheat	Poland Warsaw	36,745,000	shipbuilding, wood products, aircraft, metals
Denmark Copenhagen	5,112,000	furniture, machines, dairy products, textiles	Portugal Lisbon	10,099,000	textiles, pottery, ships, glassware, fish, cork
Finland Helsinki	4,868,000	machines, metal, ship-building, leather, timber	Romania Bucharest	22,600,000	steel, metals, machinery, textiles
France Paris	54,273,000	foods, chemicals, cars, wine, perfume, clothing	San Marino San Marino	22,000	postage stamps, tourism, woolens
Germany, East East Berlin	16,702,000	steel, chemicals, machinery, textiles, electrical products	Spain Madrid	37,746,000	machinery, textiles, shoes, cars, ships, olives, metals
Germany, West Bonn	61,421,000	steel, ships, cars, oil products, coal, chemicals, beer	Sweden Stockholm	8,331,000	steel, machinery, shipping, paper, autos, timber
			Switzerland Bern	6,423,000	machinery, banking and commerce, chocolate
Greece Athens	9,740,000	textiles, chemicals, wine, foods, fruits, olives	Turkey (European) Ankara	4,600,000	(See Asia.)
Hungary Budapest	10,679,000	iron, steel, grain, electronic supplies	United Kingdom London	56,377,000	shipbuilding, steel, metals, banking, cars, insurance
Iceland Reykjavik	238,000	fish products, aluminum, potatoes	USSR (Soviet Union) Moscow	275,000,000	steel, machinery, motor vehicles, cement, oil, chemicals, appliances
Ireland Dublin	3,508,000	cars, metal, grain, potatoes, textiles, tourism			
Italy Rome	56,742,000	steel, cars, shoes, machine tools, textiles, wine	Vatican City	830	postage stamps, tourism
Liechtenstein Vaduz	27,000	international banking, leather, machines, chemicals	Yugoslavia Belgrade	22,800,000	steel, chemicals, wood products

Nation and Capital	Population	Economy	Nation and Capital	Population	Economy
NORTH AND CENTRAL AMERICA					
Antigua and Barbuda St. John's	78,000	manufacturing, tourism	Haiti Port-au-Prince	5,054,000	rum, tourism, coffee, molasses
Bahamas Nassau	222,000	tourism, international banking, sugar	Honduras Tegucigalpa	4,276,000	clothing, bananas, coffee, sugar
Barbados Bridgetown	246,000	rum, tourism, sugar products	Jamaica Kingston	2,223,000	rum, bauxite, sugar cane, tourism, coffee
Belize Belmopan	158,000	sugar, fruit, fish	Mexico Mexico City	75,702,000	steel, chemicals, silver, electronics, oil, cotton
Canada Ottawa	25,128,000	vehicles, wheat, wood pulp, paper, livestock, fish	Nicaragua Managua	2,812,000	oil refining, cotton, yucca, bananas
Costa Rica San José	2,624,000	fiberglass, coffee, aluminum, roofing	Panama Panama City	2,134,000	international banking, bananas, mahogany
Cuba Havana	9,889,000	textiles, tobacco, wood products, sugar	St. Christopher-Nevis Basseterre	44,000	sugar, tourism
Dominica Roseau	74,000	bananas, citrus fruits, tourism, coconuts	St. Lucia Castries	126,000	tourism, bananas, coconuts
Dominican Republic Santo Domingo	5,962,000	sugar refining, cement, coffee, pharmaceuticals	St. Vincent and the Grenadines Kingstown	128,000	bananas, tourism, coconuts
El Salvador San Salvador	4,724,000	foods, textiles, petroleum products	Trinidad and Tobago Port-of-Spain	1,149,000	rum, oil products, cement, tourism
Grenada St. George's	113,000	rum, nutmeg, bananas, mace	United States Washington, D.C.	234,496,000	machinery, electronics, wheat, computers
Guatemala Guatemala City	8,161,000	sugar, coffee, tires, rare woods, textiles			
SOUTH AMERICA					
Argentina Buenos Aires	29,627,000	meat processing, cars, chemicals, grains	Guyana Georgetown	793,000	clothing, medicines, furniture
Bolivia La Paz/Sucre	5,883,000	tin mining, potatoes, sugar, chemicals, textiles	Paraguay Asunción	3,472,000	corn, wheat, cotton, beans, wood products
Brazil Brasília	131,305,000	coffee, steel, cars, chemicals, appliances	Peru Lima	18,707,000	fish, steel, cotton, sugar, copper, beans
Chile Santiago	11,486,000	copper, steel, wood, beans, grain, rice	Suriname Paramaribo	364,000	aluminum, rice, sugar, bauxite
Colombia Bogotá	27,663,000	chemicals, coffee, emeralds, tobacco	Uruguay Montevideo	2,947,000	meat, metals, oil products, textiles
Ecuador Quito	9,251,000	bananas, coffee, rice, beans, wood	Venezuela Caracas	16,400,000	steel, oil, iron textiles, coffee

THE WORLD: POLITICAL

—— National boundary

------ Disputed or undefined boundary

⊛ National capital

• Large city

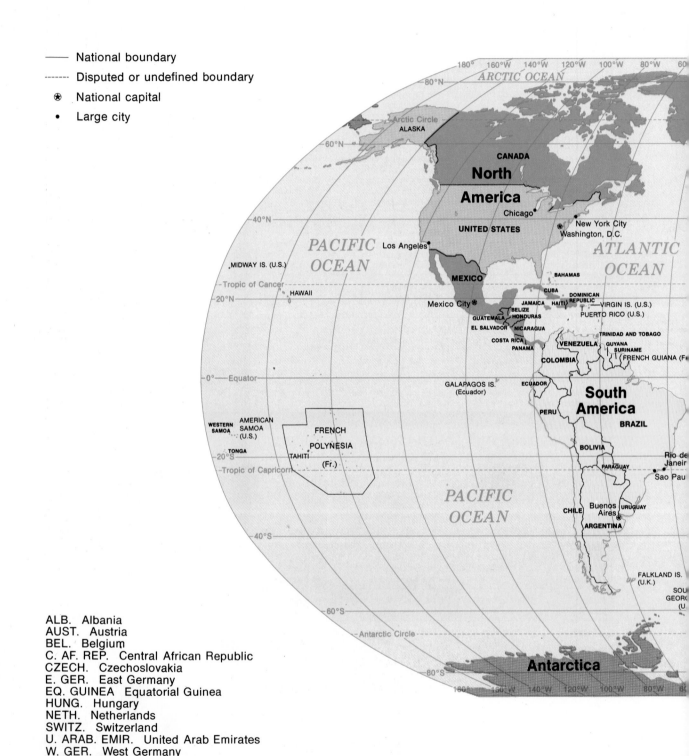

ALB. Albania
AUST. Austria
BEL. Belgium
C. AF. REP. Central African Republic
CZECH. Czechoslovakia
E. GER. East Germany
EQ. GUINEA Equatorial Guinea
HUNG. Hungary
NETH. Netherlands
SWITZ. Switzerland
U. ARAB. EMIR. United Arab Emirates
W. GER. West Germany
YEMEN (P.D.R.) People's Democratic
    Republic of Yemen
YUGO. Yugoslavia

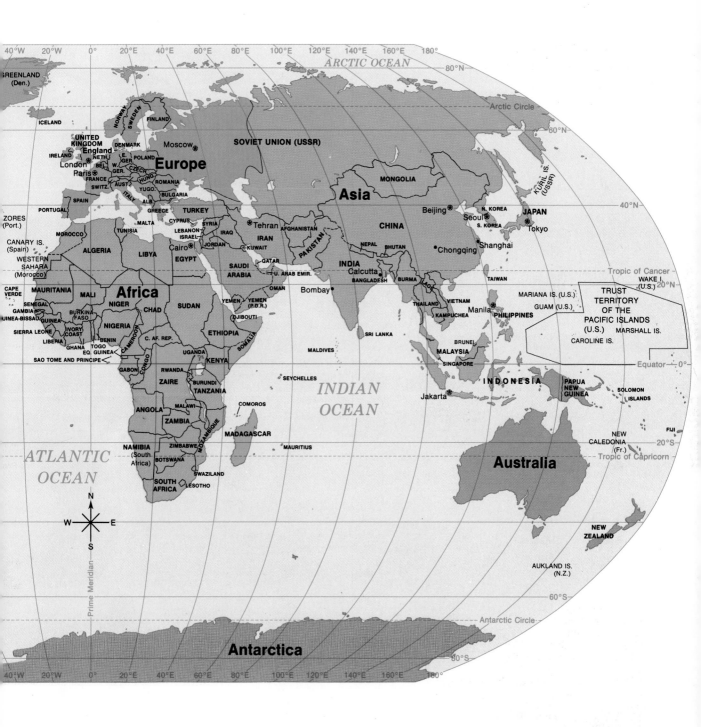

ARCTIC OCEAN

GREENLAND
(Den.)

Arctic Circle

80°N

60°N

ICELAND

NORWAY

SWEDEN

FINLAND

SOVIET UNION (USSR)

Moscow

UNITED
KINGDOM
England
IRELAND
London
Paris
FRANCE
SWITZ.
DENMARK
NETH.
BEL.
W.
GER.
E.
GER.
POLAND
CZECH
AUST.
HUNG.
YUGO.
ROMANIA
BULGARIA

Europe

Asia

MONGOLIA

40°N

PORTUGAL

SPAIN

ITALY

ALB.

GREECE

TURKEY

CYPRUS

LEBANON

ISRAEL

SYRIA

IRAQ

JORDAN

Tehran

IRAN

AFGHANISTAN

Beijing

N. KOREA

Seoul
S. KOREA

JAPAN

Tokyo

ZORES
(Port.)

MALTA

TUNISIA

CHINA

PAKISTAN

NEPAL

BHUTAN

Chongqing

Shanghai

MOROCCO

CANARY IS.
(Spain)

ALGERIA

LIBYA

EGYPT

Cairo

KUWAIT

QATAR

SAUDI
ARABIA

U. ARAB EMIR.

INDIA

Calcutta

BANGLADESH

BURMA

Tropic of Cancer

WAKE I.
(U.S.)
20°N

WESTERN
SAHARA
(Morocco)

TAIWAN

CAPE
VERDE

MAURITANIA

MALI

NIGER

CHAD

SUDAN

YEMEN

YEMEN
(P.D.R.)

OMAN

Bombay

THAILAND

VIETNAM

Africa

MARIANA IS. (U.S.)

GUAM (U.S.)

TRUST
TERRITORY
OF THE
PACIFIC ISLANDS
(U.S.)

MARSHALL IS.

SENEGAL
GAMBIA
GUINEA-BISSAU
GUINEA
SIERRA LEONE
LIBERIA

BURKINA
FASO

NIGERIA

DJIBOUTI

KAMPUCHEA

Manila

PHILIPPINES

IVORY
COAST

GHANA

TOGO

BENIN

EQ. GUINEA

CAMEROON

C. AF. REP.

ETHIOPIA

SOMALIA

SRI LANKA

CAROLINE IS.

SAO TOME AND PRINCIPE

GABON

CONGO

UGANDA

KENYA

MALDIVES

BRUNEI

MALAYSIA

SINGAPORE

Equator
0°

ZAIRE

RWANDA
BURUNDI

TANZANIA

SEYCHELLES

INDONESIA

PAPUA
NEW
GUINEA

SOLOMON
ISLANDS

Jakarta

INDIAN
OCEAN

ANGOLA

MALAWI

ZAMBIA

COMOROS

MADAGASCAR

FIJI

NEW
CALEDONIA
(Fr.)

20°S

Australia

ATLANTIC
OCEAN

NAMIBIA
(South
Africa)

ZIMBABWE

MOZAMBIQUE

BOTSWANA

MAURITIUS

Tropic of Capricorn

SWAZILAND

SOUTH
AFRICA

LESOTHO

NEW
ZEALAND

N
W E
S

AUKLAND IS.
(N.Z.)

Prime Meridian

60°S

Antarctic Circle

Antarctica

80°S

40°W 20°W 0° 20°E 40°E 60°E 80°E 100°E 120°E 140°E 160°E 180°

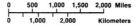

0   500   1,000 1,500 2,000 Miles

0   1,000   2,000   Kilometers

THE WORLD: ELEVATION

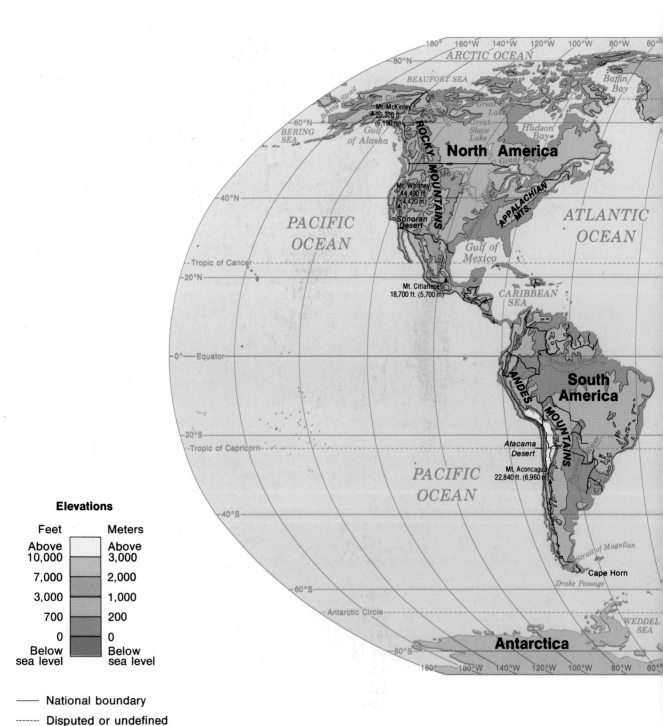

Elevations

Feet		Meters
Above 10,000		Above 3,000
7,000		2,000
3,000		1,000
700		200
0		0
Below sea level		Below sea level

—— National boundary

------ Disputed or undefined boundary

Ice pack

▲ Mountain peak

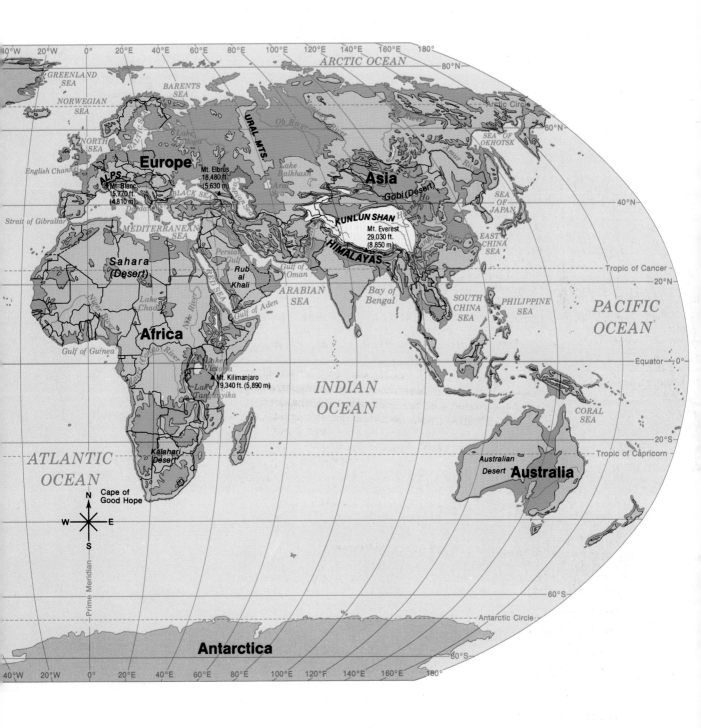

ARCTIC OCEAN

GREENLAND
SEA

NORWEGIAN
SEA

BARENTS
SEA

Arctic Circle

80°N

60°N

SEA OF
OKHOTSK

URAL MTS.

NORTH
SEA

English Channel

Europe

ALPS
Mt. Blanc
15,770 ft.
(4,810 m)

Mt. Elbrus
18,480 ft.
(5,630 m)

Lake
Ladoga

Lake
Balkhash

Aral
Sea

Asia

Gobi (Desert)

Ob River

Amur River

SEA
OF
JAPAN

40°N

BALTIC SEA

BLACK SEA

Caspian Sea

Danube

Strait of Gibraltar

MEDITERRANEAN
SEA

KUNLUN SHAN

Mt. Everest
29,030 ft.
(8,850 m)

EAST
CHINA
SEA

HIMALAYAS

Persian
Gulf

Rub
al
Khali

Gulf of
Oman

Tropic of Cancer

20°N

**Sahara
(Desert)**

RED SEA

Gulf of Aden

ARABIAN
SEA

Bay of
Bengal

SOUTH
CHINA
SEA

PHILIPPINE
SEA

**PACIFIC
OCEAN**

Lake
Chad

Niger River

Nile River

Huang Ho

Gulf of Guinea

Africa

Congo River

Lake
Victoria

Mt. Kilimanjaro
19,340 ft. (5,890 m)

Lake
Tanganyika

**INDIAN
OCEAN**

Equator 0°

CORAL
SEA

20°S

**ATLANTIC
OCEAN**

Kalahari
Desert

Australian
Desert

Australia

Tropic of Capricorn

Cape of
Good Hope

N
W E
S

60°S

Prime Meridian

Antarctic Circle

80°S

Antarctica

40°W   20°W   0°   20°E   40°E   60°E   80°E   100°E   120°F   140°E   160°E   180°

0   500   1,000   1,500   2,000   Miles

0   1,000   2,000   Kilometers

R9

NORTH AMERICA: PHYSICAL

Europe

Asia

ARCTIC   OCEAN

Bering Strait

Bering Sea

Beaufort Sea

Greenland Sea

Greenland

Arctic Circle

Baffin Bay

BROOKS RANGE

Yukon River

▲ Mt. McKinley
20,320 ft.
(6,194 m.)

Gulf of Alaska

▲ Mt. Logan
19,850 ft.
(6,050 m.)

Denmark Strait

Great Bear Lake

Great Slave Lake

Davis Strait

Mackenzie River

Labrador Sea

COAST MOUNTAINS

ROCKY

Hudson Strait

Hudson Bay

Canadian   Shield

Great   Plains

Lake Winnipeg

Columbia River

MOUNTAINS

Great Salt Lake

Lake Superior

Lake Huron

Gulf of St. Lawrence

St. Lawrence River

Bay of Fundy

Hudson River

Missouri River

Lake Michigan

Lake Erie

Lake Ontario

ATLANTIC

OCEAN

Great
Basin

▲ Mt. Whitney
14,494 ft.
(4,418 m.)

Death Valley
−282 ft.
(−86 m.)

▲ Pikes Peak
14,110 ft.
(4,301 m.)

Ohio   River

APPALACHIAN MTNS.

Ozark
Plateau

Mississippi River

Coastal

Plain

Gulf of California

Rio Grande

Tropic of Cancer

SIERRA

MADRE

SIERRA MADRE ORIENTAL

OCCIDENTAL

Gulf of Mexico

PACIFIC

OCEAN

Bay of
Campeche

▲ Citlaltépetl
18,700 ft. (5,700 m.)

Yucatán
Peninsula

Hispaniola

SIERRA MADRE
DEL SUR

Mosquito Coast

Caribbean

Sea

Panama Canal

Lake Nicaragua

Gulf of Panamá

South

America

━━━ International boundary

▲ Mountain peak

| 0 | 300 | 600 | Miles |
| 0 | 300 | 600 | 900 | Kilometers |

N
W   E
S

Equator

SOUTH AMERICA: PHYSICAL

Caribbean Sea

ATLANTIC

OCEAN

Lake Maracaibo

Orinoco River

Guiana

Highlands

Angel Falls

A N D E S

Pico da Neblina
9,889 ft. (3,014 m)

Amazon

Negro River

River

Equator

▲ Cotopaxi
19,347 ft.
(5,897 m)

Amazon

Basin

Mt. Huascarán
22,205 ft. (6,768 m)

A N D E S

M O U N T A I N S

Lake Titicaca

Mato Grosso

Plateau

Xingu River

Brazilian Highlands

São Francisco

PACIFIC

Atacama Desert

Chaco

Gran

Salado R

Paraguay River

Uruguay River

River

OCEAN

Tropic of Capricorn

P a m p a s

ATLANTIC

OCEAN

Mt. Aconcagua
22,840 ft. (6,960 m)
(highest point in S. America)

Negro R.

A N D E S

Valdés Peninsula
(lowest point in S. America)

International boundary

▲ Mountain peak

N
W · E
S

| Miles |
| 0   250   500 |
| 0 250 500 750   Kilometers |

Cape Horn
Drake Passage

R11

EUROPE: PHYSICAL

R12

— International boundary
▲ Mountain peak

Asia

Asia

Africa

URAL MOUNTAINS

Arctic Circle

Caspian Depression

Volga River

Caspian Sea

Mt. Elbrus 18,480 ft. (5,630 m)

Volga

River

White Sea

Lake Onega

Central Russian Highlands

Black Sea

Sea of Azov

European Plain

Lake Ladoga

Gulf of Finland

Great Salpausselkä Lake System

Gulf of Bothnia

Dneiper

Dneiper River

Don

Carpathian Mountains

Transylvanian Alps

Balkan Mts.

Rhodope Mtns.

Aegean Sea

Crete

North Cape

North Sea

Baltic Sea

Bay of Gdansk

Dneister River

Great Hungarian Plain

Mt. Olympus 9,570 ft. (2,917 m)

Lake Mälaren

Lake Vänern

Lake Vättern

Kattegat

Skagerrak

Elbe River

Oder River

Danube River

Dinaric Alps

Julian Alps

Grossglockner 12,470 ft. (3,800 m)

Adriatic Sea

Mt. Vesuvius 4,190 ft. (1,277 m)

Gulf of Táranto

Mt. Etna 10,902 ft. (3,323 m)

Jotunheimen Glittertind 8,110 ft. (2,472 m)

Harz Mtns.

BLACK FOREST

ALPS

Matterhorn 14,690 ft. (4,478 m)

Mt. Blanc 15,770 ft. (4,810 m)

French Alps

Apennines

Tyrrhenian Sea

Mediterranean Sea

Norwegian Sea

Rhine River

Po River

Corsica

Sardinia

NORTH SEA

Loch Ness

Firth of Forth

Ben Nevis 4,406 ft. (1,343 m)

HADRIAN'S WALL

Seine River

Balearic Is.

Iceland

ATLANTIC

Pennines

Irish Sea

Thames River

English Channel

Strait of Dover

Bay of Biscay

Pyrenees

Aneto Peak 11,168 ft. (3,404 m)

Cantabrian Mtns.

Sierra Morena

Mulhacén 11,407 ft. (3,477 m)

Strait of Gibraltar

Carrauntoohill 3,414 ft. (1,041 m)

OCEAN

N
W E
S

Tagus River

Ebro River

Miles
250   500
Kilometers
0   250   500   750

ASIA: PHYSICAL

Europe

Australia

ARCTIC OCEAN

PACIFIC OCEAN

INDIAN OCEAN

Africa

Bering Sea

Sea of Okhotsk

Kamchatka Peninsula

Chukchi Sea

East Siberian Sea

Laptev Sea

Kara Sea

Barents Sea

Central Siberian Plateau

SAYAN MTNS.

ALTAI SHAN

TIEN SHAN

Takla Makan

Gobi (Desert) DESERT OF CHINA

GREAT WALL OF CHINA

Godwin Austen
28,250 ft. (8,611 m)

KUNLUN SHAN

KARAKORAM

HINDU KUSH

HIMALAYAS

Mt. Everest
29,028 ft. (8,848 m)

Kanchenjunga
28,146 ft.
(8,579 m)

Communism Peak
24,590 ft. (7,495 m)

Khyber Pass

Thar Desert

Rann of Kutch

VINDHYA RA.

WESTERN GHATS

EASTERN GHATS

ARAKAN RA.

ANNAM RA.

Malay Peninsula

BARISAN MTNS.

Bay of Bengal

Arabian Sea

URAL MOUNTAINS

Aral Sea

Lake Balkhash

Ob River

Irtysh River

Karakum Desert

Caspian Sea

ELBURZ MTNS.

CAUCASUS

Mt. Ararat
16,946 ft.
(5,165 m)

KURDISTAN

ZAGROS MTNS.

TAURUS MTNS.

Syrian Desert

Negev Desert

Euphrates

Persian Gulf

Gulf of Oman

Strait of Hormuz

Al Hadidah
(meteor crater)

Rub' al-Khali

ASIR MTNS.

Red Sea

Gulf of Aden

Mediterranean Sea

Black Sea

Baltic Sea

Sea of Japan

Tsugaru Strait

Mt. Fuji
12,388 ft.
(3,776 m)

Inland Sea

Korea Strait

Yellow Sea

East China Sea

South China Sea

Philippine Sea

Gulf of Tonkin

Strait of Malacca

Sulu Sea

Celebes Sea

Java Sea

Banda Sea

Kolyma R.

Tropic of Cancer

Equator

Arctic Circle

Legend

— International boundary

--- Disputed boundary

▲ Mountain peak

Miles
0   500   1000
Kilometers
0   500   1000   1500

R13

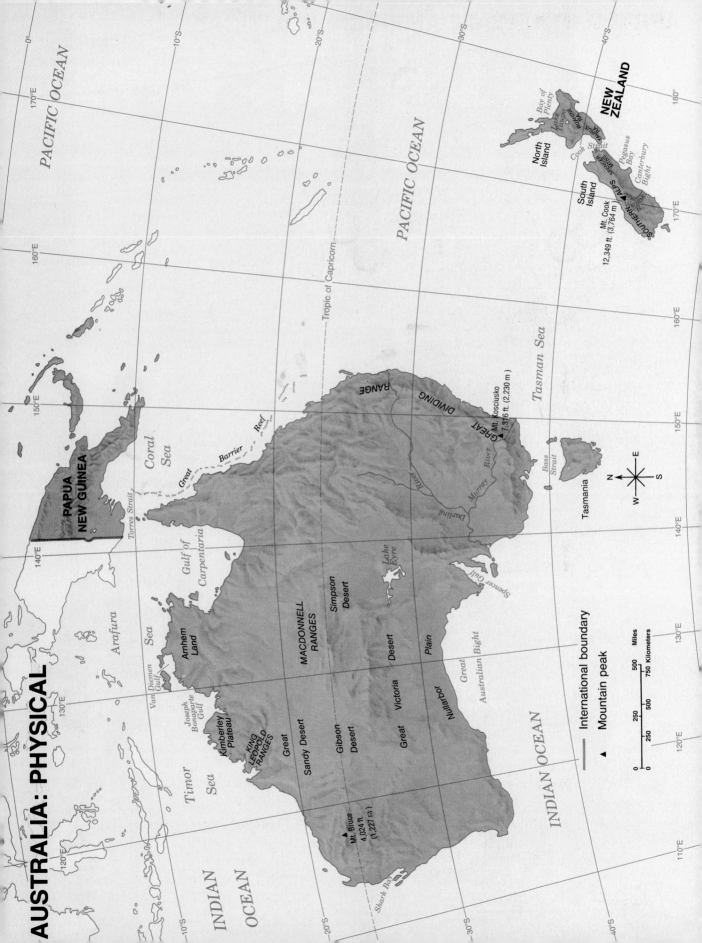

AUSTRALIA: PHYSICAL

PACIFIC OCEAN

INDIAN OCEAN

NEW ZEALAND

North Island

Bay of Plenty

Lake Taupo

Cook Strait

South Island

Mt. Cook
12,349 ft. (3,764 m)

SOUTHERN ALPS

Pegasus Bay

Canterbury Bight

Tasman Sea

PACIFIC OCEAN

Tropic of Capricorn

PAPUA NEW GUINEA

Coral Sea

Great Barrier Reef

Torres Strait

Gulf of Carpentaria

Arafura Sea

Timor Sea

Van Diemen Gulf

Arnhem Land

Joseph Bonaparte Gulf

Kimberley Plateau

KING LEOPOLD RANGES

Great Sandy Desert

Gibson Desert

Simpson Desert

MACDONNELL RANGES

Lake Eyre

Great Victoria Desert

Nullarbor Plain

Great Australian Bight

Spencer Gulf

Murray River

Darling River

GREAT DIVIDING RANGE

Mt. Kosciusko
7,316 ft. (2,230 m)

Bass Strait

Tasmania

Mt. Bruce
4,024 ft. (1,227 m)

Shark Bay

INDIAN OCEAN

N
E
S
W

—— International boundary
▲ Mountain peak

Miles
0   250   500
0   250   500   750 Kilometers

170°E
180°
170°E
160°E
160°E
150°E
150°E
140°E
140°E
130°E
130°E
120°E
120°E
110°E

10°S
20°S
30°S
40°S

UNITED STATES OF AMERICA: POLITICAL

CANADA

Winn

WASHINGTON
- Seattle
- Olympia ⊛
- Tacoma
- Spokane
- Portland
- Salem ⊛
- Corvallis
- Eugene ● Springfield

OREGON
- Lewiston
- Medford

IDAHO
- Boise ⊛
- Idaho Falls
- Pocatello

MONTANA
- Missoula
- Helena ⊛
- Great Falls
- Butte
- Billings

NORTH DAKOTA
- Bismarck

Gra
For

WYOMING
- Casper
- Laramie ● Cheyenne ⊛

SOUTH DAKOTA
- Rapid City
- Pierre

NEBRASKA
- North Platte
- Grand Island

CALIFORNIA
- Eureka
- Sacramento ⊛
- San Francisco
- Oakland
- San Jose
- Stockton
- Fresno
- Bakersfield
- Santa Barbara
- Los Angeles
- San Bernardino
- Long Beach
- San Diego

NEVADA
- Reno
- Carson City ⊛
- Las Vegas

UTAH
- Great Salt Lake
- Ogden
- Salt Lake City ⊛
- Provo

COLORADO
- Grand Junction
- Boulder
- Denver ⊛
- Colorado Springs
- Pueblo

KANSAS
- Sal
- Wichita

ARIZONA
- Phoenix ⊛
- Tucson

NEW MEXICO
- Santa Fe ⊛
- Albuquerque
- Roswell
- Las Cruces
- El Paso

OKLAHOMA
- Amarillo
- Oklahoma City
- Lawton
- Lubbock
- Fort Wo

TEXAS
- Austin ⊛
- San Antonio
- Corpus Christi
- Monterrey

PACIFIC OCEAN

MEXICO
- Ciudad Juarez
- Chihuahua

Gila River

Colorado River

Pecos River

Rio Grande

Brazos River

Platte River

Green River

Snake River

Columbia River

Sacramento River

45°N
40°N
35°N
30°N

105°W
100°W
120°W
115°W
110°W

SOVIET UNION

ARCTIC OCEAN

- Prudhoe Bay
- Arctic Circle

ALASKA
- Fairbanks
- Anchorage
- Juneau ⊛

CANADA

Yukon River

70°N
70°N
60°N

150°W
170°W
160°W
130°W

0 250 500 Miles
0 250 500 750 Kilometers

PACIFIC OCEAN

R16

Tropic of Cancer

PACIFIC OCEAN

- Kauai
- Oahu
- Honolulu ⊛
- Maui
- Hilo

HAWAII

160°W
155°W
22°N
25°N
20°N

0 100 200 Miles
0 100 200 300 Kilometers

UNITED STATES OF AMERICA: PHYSICAL

CANADA

105°W · 100°W

▲ Mt. Rainier
14,410 ft. (4,390 m)
▲ Mt. St. Helens
9,680 ft. (2,950 m)

Columbia Plateau

COAST RANGES

CASCADE RANGE

45°N

Fort Peck Missouri Lake

River

Yellowstone River

ROCKY
BITTERROOT RANGE

Snake River

TETON RANGE

MOUNTAINS

Lake Oahe

GREAT PLAINS

Cape Mendocino

40°N

INTERMOUNTAIN

Great Salt Lake

WASATCH RANGE

Continental

Divide

BLACK HILLS

North Platte River

SIERRA NEVADA

Lake Tahoe

Great Salt Lake Desert

Great Basin

Central Valley

San Joaquin River

Great Basin Desert

AREA

Green River

South Platte River

Platte River

COAST RANGES

Monterey Bay

Mt. Whitney
14,490 ft. (4,420 m) ▲

Death Valley

35°N

Colorado River

FRONT RANGE

Mt. Elbert
14,430 ft. (4,400 m)

▲ Pikes Peak
14,110 ft. (4,300 m)

PACIFIC OCEAN

Mojave Desert

Lake Mead

Grand Canyon

Painted Desert

Colorado Plateau

ROCKY

MOUNTAINS

Salton Sea

Sonoran Desert

Imperial Valley

Gila River

Divide

Continental

Canadian River

Llano Estacado

River

Brazos River

30°N

Gulf of California

Continental

Pecos River

Chihuahuan Desert

Edwards Plateau

Rio Grande

120°W · 115°W · 110°W

MEXICO

105°W

SIERRA MADRE

100°W

Alaska inset

SOVIET UNION

70°N

150°W

ARCTIC OCEAN

70°N

BROOKS RANGE

Arctic Circle

CANADA

Bering Strait

Yukon River

Mt. McKinley
20,320 ft. (6,190 m) ▲

ALASKA RANGE

60°N

170°W

Bering Sea

R18

Gulf of Alaska

250 · 500 Miles
250 · 500 · 750 Kilometers

ALEUTIAN ISLANDS

160°W

PACIFIC OCEAN

Hawaii inset

160°W

155°W

Tropic of Cancer

PACIFIC OCEAN

22°N

Kauai

Oahu

Molokai

Maui

Mauna Kea
13,800 ft. (4,210 m) ▲

Hawaii

20°N

0 · 100 · 200 Miles
0 · 100 · 200 · 300 Kilometers

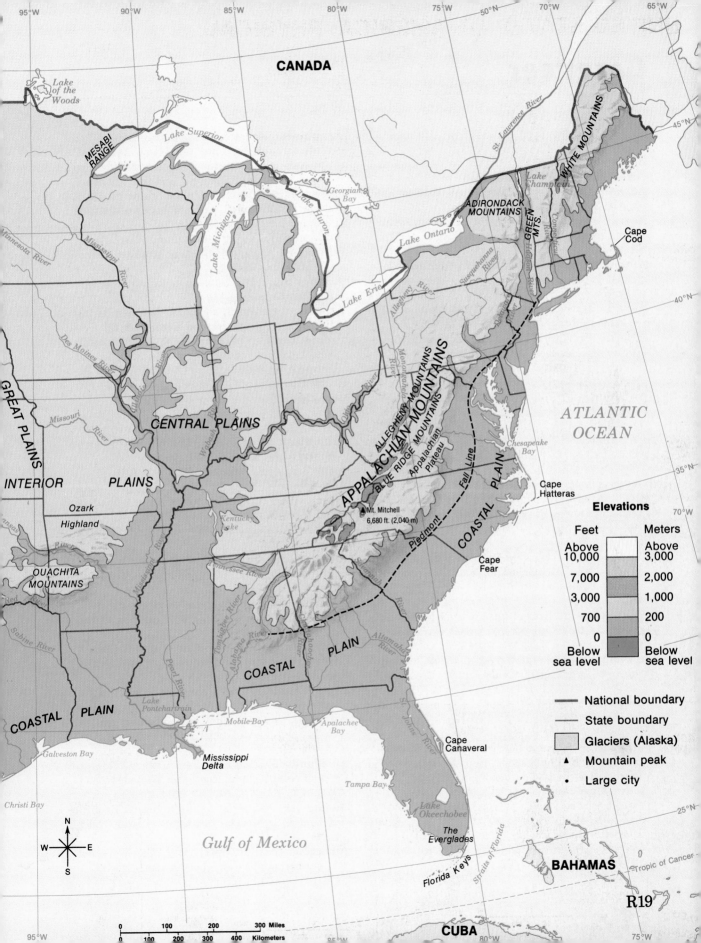

CANADA

Lake of the Woods

MESABI RANGE

Lake Superior

Georgian Bay

Lake Huron

Lake Michigan

Minnesota River

Mississippi River

Des Moines River

Missouri River

St. Lawrence River

WHITE MOUNTAINS

ADIRONDACK MOUNTAINS

Lake Champlain

GREEN MTS.

Connecticut River

Cape Cod

Lake Ontario

Lake Erie

Allegheny River

Susquehanna River

GREAT PLAINS

INTERIOR   PLAINS

CENTRAL PLAINS

Monongahela River

ALLEGHENY MOUNTAINS

APPALACHIAN MOUNTAINS

BLUE RIDGE MOUNTAINS

Appalachian Plateau

ATLANTIC OCEAN

Chesapeake Bay

Wabash River

Ozark Highland

Kentucky Lake

▲ Mt. Mitchell
6,680 ft. (2,040 m)

Fall Line

Cape Hatteras

Arkansas River

OUACHITA MOUNTAINS

Tennessee River

Piedmont

COASTAL PLAIN

Cape Fear

Red River

Mississippi River

Tombigbee River

Alabama River

Chattahoochee River

Altamaha River

COASTAL   PLAIN

Sabine River

Pearl River

Lake Pontchartrain

Mobile Bay

Apalachee Bay

St. Johns River

COASTAL   PLAIN

Galveston Bay

Mississippi Delta

Cape Canaveral

Christi Bay

Tampa Bay

Lake Okeechobee

The Everglades

Gulf of Mexico

BAHAMAS

Florida Keys

Straits of Florida

Tropic of Cancer

R19

CUBA

Elevations

Feet	Meters
Above 10,000	Above 3,000
7,000	2,000
3,000	1,000
700	200
0	0
Below sea level	Below sea level

━━━ National boundary

─── State boundary

▨ Glaciers (Alaska)

▲ Mountain peak

• Large city

N
W ◆ E
S

0   100   200   300 Miles
0 100 200 300 400 Kilometers

95°W 90°W 85°W 80°W 75°W 70°W 65°W

50°N 45°N 40°N 35°N 70°W 30°N 25°N

Gazetteer

A

Adelaide (35°S/139°E) Capital of Australian state of South Australia. (p. 448)

Adriatic Sea Arm of Mediterranean Sea between Italy and Balkan Peninsula. (p. 110)

Aegean Sea Island-dotted arm of Mediterranean Sea that separates Greece from Asia Minor. (p. 18)

Africa Second-largest continent on Earth; located in both Northern and Southern hemispheres. (p. 9)

Akkad Ancient city-state in Mesopotamia, north of Sumer on the Euphrates River. (p. 31)

Alberta Province of Canada; one of three Prairie Provinces; borders Northwest Territories, Saskatchewan, United States, and British Columbia. (p. 536)

Alexandria (31°N/30°E) Chief port and second-largest city in Egypt; located on Mediterranean Sea; founded by Alexander the Great about 332 B.C. (p. 81)

Alice Springs (23°S/134°E) City in the Northern Territory, Australia, located in almost the exact geographic center of the continent. (p. 448)

Alps Largest group of mountains in Europe; located in France, Switzerland, Italy, and Austria. (p. 111)

Amarna Former capital of Egypt under Akhenaton; located on the Nile River halfway between Thebes and Memphis; important documents found in ruins here tell about Amarna Age. (p. 48)

Amazon Basin Area drained by Amazon River; hot, humid climate; covered mostly by rain forest. (p. 485)

Amazon River Largest river in world; located in North Brazil; empties into Atlantic Ocean. (p. 485)

Amsterdam (52°N/5°E) Capital and largest city of the Netherlands; located in North Holland; connects with North Sea by canal. (p. 108)

Amur River River in northeastern Asia; formed by joining of Shilka and Argun Rivers; forms part of Manchuria-Russia border. (p. 332)

Andes Mountains Longest mountain chain in world; located along west coast of South America. (p. 484)

Antarctic Circle Line of latitude located at 66½°S; high-latitude region of Southern Hemisphere begins here. (p. 11)

Apennines Mountain range that runs north and south through the center of Italy. (p. 141)

Appalachian Mountains Range extending from Newfoundland, Canada, to northern Alabama; covers much of eastern United States. (p. 535)

Arabian Peninsula Located between the Red Sea and the Persian Gulf. (p. 20)

Arabian Sea Part of Indian Ocean; lies between India and Arabian Peninsula; southern boundary of Middle East. (p. 18)

Arafura Sea Sea between northern Australia and Indonesia. (p. 447)

Aragon Kingdom in northeastern Spain during the Middle Ages; stretched south from the Pyrenees; bordered by France, the Mediterranean Sea, Dominions of the Almohades, Castile, and Navarre. (p. 209)

Arctic Circle Line of latitude located at 66½°N. (p. 11)

Arctic Ocean Icy ocean north of Arctic Circle. (p. 9)

Arno River River in central Italy; flows through Florence into Ligurian Sea. (p. 142)

Asia Largest continent on Earth. (p. 9)

Asia Minor Peninsula at western end of Asia occupied by Turkey; located between Black Sea and Mediterranean Sea. (p. 117)

Assyria Ancient city-state in northern Mesopotamia. (p. 40)

Aswan Dam One of largest dams in the world; built on Nile River; stores enough water to last entire Nile Valley a full year. (p. 82)

Atacama Desert Located on west coast of Peru and Chile; one of driest areas in world. (p. 485)

Athens (38°N/24°E) City-state of ancient Greece; located near southeastern coast of Greece; capital of present-day Greece. (p. 122)

Atlas Mountains Low range of mountains located in northwestern Africa. (p. 259)

Attica Ancient region in southeastern part of Greek mainland, of which Athens was the chief city. (p. 118)

Auckland (37°S/174°E) Chief port and largest city of New Zealand; located on Waitemata and Manukau Harbors, North Island. (p. 452)

Audaghost (18°N/10°W) City in ancient Empire of Ghana; located on important African trade route. (p. 271)

Australia Smallest continent on Earth; located in southern and eastern hemispheres. (p. 9)

B

Babylon (33°N/44°E)   Ancient city-state in Mesopotamia; capital and chief city of Babylonia; located on Euphrates River. (p. 40)

Babylonia   Ancient kingdom in lower Euphrates Valley in southwestern Asia. (p. 40)

Baghdad (33°N/44°E)   Capital of Iraq; located on both sides of Tigris River. (p. 18)

Bali   Island in Indonesia; located east of Java, between Bali Sea and Indian Ocean. (p. 430)

Balkan Mountains   Range covering most of Balkan Peninsula. (p. 110)

Balkan Peninsula   Peninsula in southeastern Europe occupied by Greece, Bulgaria, Albania, European Turkey, and most of Yugoslavia. (p. 110)

Baltic Sea   One of three seas surrounding Scandinavian Peninsula; part of Atlantic Ocean. (p. 108)

Banff (51°N/115°W)   Resort town in Banff National Park; located near Lake Louise in southwestern Alberta, Canada. (p. 536)

Bangkok (14°N/100°E)   Capital of Thailand; located on Chao Phraya River. (p. 434)

Barents Sea   Part of Arctic Ocean; located north of Europe. (p. 108)

Bay of Bengal   Part of Indian Ocean; located off the coasts of India, Bangladesh, Burma, and the Malay Peninsula. (p. 330)

Beijing (40°N/116°E)   Capital of China; center of Chinese government, culture, and education. (p. 369)

Bering Sea   Part of north Pacific Ocean; located between Alaska and the Kamchatka Peninsula. (p. 330)

Berlin (53°N/2°W)   Former capital of Germany; now divided into West Berlin, part of West Germany, and East Berlin, capital of East Germany; located in East Germany. (p. 108)

Birmingham (53°N/2°W)   City in central England; important manufacturing and transportation center. (p. 216)

Black Sea   Sea between Middle East and Europe. (p. 18)

Bombay (19°N/73°E)   Second-largest city and port in India; located in western India on the Arabian Sea. (p. 351)

Borneo   Island in Malay Archipelago occupied by Malaysia, Indonesia, and Brunei; third-largest island in world. (p. 333)

Bosporus   Narrow strait between European and Asian Turkey; connects Sea of Marmara with Black Sea. (p. 20)

Botany Bay   Inlet of south Pacific Ocean; located at Sydney, Australia. (p. 456)

Brahmaputra River   One of three large rivers in plains of South Asia; flows through China, India, and Bangladesh. (p. 340)

Brasília (16°S/48°W)   Capital of Brazil built in late 1950s; located in Central-West region of Brazil. (p. 519)

Brazilian Highlands   Highland region in eastern Brazil. (p. 485)

Brisbane (27°S/153°E)   Capital of Queensland, Australia; located on north bank of Brisbane River. (p. 448)

British Columbia   Province of Canada; located on Pacific coast of Canada; borders on Yukon Territory, Northwest Territories, Alberta, and the United States. (p. 536)

British Isles   Two large islands occupied by the United Kingdom of Great Britain (England, Wales, and Scotland) and Northern Ireland, and by the Republic of Ireland. (p. 110)

Brussels (51°N/4½°E)   Capital of Belgium; located on Senne River; headquarters of NATO. (p. 108)

Byzantine Empire   Empire covering Greece, Balkan lands, and Asia Minor; center of Roman civilization after collapse of Roman Empire; lasted until 1453. (p. 152)

C

Cairo (30°N/31°E)   Capital of Egypt; located on right bank of Nile River; largest urban area in Middle East. (p. 18)

Calcutta (21°N/88°E)   Largest city and chief port in India; located on Hooghly River. (p. 351)

Canadian Shield   Oldest mass of rock in North America; located in north, central, and east Canada. (p. 535)

Canberra (35°S/150°E)   Capital of Australia; located in Australian Capital Territory in southeastern New South Wales on Molonglo River. (p. 460)

Canterbury Plain   Large area of flat land located on South Island, New Zealand. (p. 453)

Cape Horn   Southernmost part of South America. (p. 483)

Cape of Good Hope (34°S/19°E)   Cape on southwest coast of Africa. (p. 257)

Caribbean Sea   Part of Atlantic Ocean; bordered by Central America, South America, and the West Indies. (p. 485)

Carthage (37°N/10°E)   Ancient city-state in north Africa. (p. 144)

Caspian Sea   Inland salt lake between Europe and Asia; largest inland body of water in world. (p. 18)

Castile   Kingdom in central Spain during the

Middle Ages; bordered by León, Navarre, Aragon, and Dominions of the Almohades. (p. 201)

Caucasus Mountains Mountain range in southern Soviet Union separating Europe from Asia; located between Black and Caspian seas. (p. 110)

Cebu One of the largest islands in Philippines; located in central Philippines. (p. 431)

Celebes One of the islands of Indonesia; located in Malay Archipelago; also called Sulawesi. (p. 333)

Chang Jiang Longest river in Asia; flows from Plateau of Tibet into East China Sea; sometimes called Yangtze. (p. 333)

Chao Phraya River located in Thailand; flows into Gulf of Siam near Bangkok. (p. 430)

Chichén Itzá (21°N/88°W) Village in Yucatán State, Mexico; was an important center for Mayan civilization. (p. 494)

Christchurch (44°S/173°E) City in New Zealand; located on South Island. (p. 452)

Coast Mountains Range running through western Canada; located in British Columbia and Yukon Territory; continuation of Cascade Range in the United States. (p. 536)

Congo River *See* Zaire River.

Constantinople (41°N/29°E) Built by Emperor Constantine as capital of Roman Empire; located where city of Byzantium once stood; now Istanbul, Turkey. (p. 152)

Coober Pedy Town in Great Victoria Desert in South Australia; important for opal mines. (p. 450)

Coral Sea Part of Pacific Ocean; located between Queensland, Australia, on the west and New Hebrides and New Caledonia on the east. (p. 448)

Corinth (38°N/23°E) City-state of ancient Greece; located on Isthmus of Corinth. (p. 118)

Corsica French island located in Mediterranean Sea near Italy; birthplace of Napoleon. (p. 108)

Crete Large Greek island southeast of Balkan Peninsula; located in southern Aegean Sea where it joins the Mediterranean. (p. 118)

Cuzco (14°S/72°W) City located high in Andes Mountains in Peru; capital of Incan civilization. (p. 495)

D

Damascus (34°N/36°E) Capital of Syria; located on Barada River. (p. 18)

Danube River Second-longest river in Europe; flows from West Germany through Austria, Czechoslovakia, Hungary, Yugoslavia, Romania, Bulgaria, and the Soviet Union; empties into the Black Sea. (p. 110)

Dardanelles Narrow strait leading from Black Sea to Mediterranean Sea; formerly called Hellespont. (p. 87)

Darwin (12°S/131°E) Capital of Northern Territory, Australia. (p. 448)

Dead Sea (32°N/36°E) Salt lake located on Israel-Jordan border; lowest place in world at 1,299 feet (396 m) below sea level. (p. 20)

Deccan Plateau Area in south-central India; ringed by triangle of hills and mountains to north, east, and west. (p. 339)

Delhi (29°N/77°E) Third-largest city in India; located on Yamuna River. (p. 340)

Delphi (38°N/23°E) Town in Greece; located between Gulf of Corinth and Mt. Parnassus; site of famous oracle in ancient Greece. (p. 118)

Drakensberg Mountains Range located in the southeast of the Republic of South Africa. (p. 257)

Dunkirk (51°N/2°E) Seaport in northern France; located on the English Channel. (p. 227)

E

East China Sea Part of Pacific Ocean; located off east coast of China from Japan and South Korea in the north to Taiwan in the south. (p. 330)

Eastern Hemisphere Half of Earth east of Prime Meridian; includes Europe, Asia, Africa, and Australia. (p. 7)

Edinburgh (56°N/3°W) Capital of Scotland, located on south shore of Firth of Forth. (p. 108)

Elburz Mountains Range in northern Iran; runs west to east and parallels southern shore of Caspian Sea. (p. 20)

Ethiopian Highlands Mountainous region covering most of Ethiopia. (p. 259)

Euphrates River River in southwestern Asia; rises in mountains in eastern Turkey; flows through Syria and Iraq where it joins with Tigris River; continues as Shatt al Arab and empties into Persian Gulf. (p. 25)

Eurasia Name used to refer to the entire landmass of Europe and Asia. (p. 331)

Europe Second-smallest continent on Earth. (p. 9)

F

Fertile Crescent Region of Middle East shaped like a quarter moon; starts on eastern shore of Mediterranean Sea; curves around Syrian Desert and reaches south to Persian Gulf; rich food-growing area. (p. 25)

Flanders Formerly a small country along the

coast of the Low Countries on the North Sea; included parts of present-day France, Belgium, and the Netherlands. (p. 182)

Florence (44°N/11°E)   Renaissance city-state and now a city in Italy; located on Arno River. (p. 191)

G

Gambia River   Located in West Africa; rises in Fouta Djallon, Guinea; flows through Senegal and into Atlantic Ocean at Banjul. (p. 258)

Ganges River   Sacred river in India; rises in Himalayas; joins with Brahmaputra River and flows into Bay of Bengal. (p. 333)

Gao (16°N/0°)   Town located on Niger River; part of an important trade route for Saharan merchants. (p. 271)

Gaul   A rich province of the Roman Empire, which included most of present-day France. (p. 150)

Genoa (44°N/9°E)   Chief seaport of Italy; located on northwest coast at Gulf of Genoa. (p. 108)

Ghana   First great West African empire; founded by Soninkes in A.D. 700; located between Senegal and Upper Niger rivers; now refers to nation that was formerly Britain's Gold Coast Colony located next to Burkina Faso, Togo, Gulf of Guinea, and Ivory Coast. (p. 268)

Gilf Kebir Plateau   Area in southwestern Egypt; 3,000 to 7,000 feet (1,000 to 2,000 m) above sea level. (p. 66)

Giza (30°N/31°E)   City in Egypt; located on west bank of Nile; site of about 80 pyramids, including Great Pyramid. (p. 56)

Gobi Desert   Third-largest desert in world; largest desert in Asia; located in Mongolia and China. (p. 333)

Grand Canal   Located in eastern China; connects Chang Jiang with Huang He; links Beijing with Hangzhou; oldest canal in world still in use. (p. 378)

Great Barrier Reef   Largest deposit of coral in world; located off northeast coast of Queensland, Australia; 1,200 miles (1,950 km) long. (p. 448)

Great Dividing Range   Mountain ranges found in Queensland, New South Wales, and Victoria, Australia; located inland from Australia's east coast. (p. 448)

Great Escarpment   Clifflike wall found inland from Brazil's Atlantic coast. (p. 517)

Great Lakes   Located in central North America; largest group of freshwater lakes in world; form part of United States-Canada border. (p. 485)

Great Rift Valley   Site of some of Africa's lowest points; large valley extending 3,500 miles (5,600 km) north and south through East Africa. (p. 259)

Great Victoria Desert   Desert in South Australia and Western Australia. (p. 448)

Great Wall of China   Wall in northern China; 25 feet (8 m) high and more than 1,500 miles (2,414 km) from east to west; built from 214 B.C.–A.D. 1646 to protect China's civilization from outsiders. (p. 368)

Greenland   Largest island in world; belongs to Denmark; located off northeast coast of North America. (p. 482)

Greenwich (51.4°N/0°)   Location of Prime Meridian; sets standard for correct time throughout much of world; now a suburb of London, England. (p. 541)

Guangzhou (23°N/113°E)   Fourth-largest city in China; main port of south China; located in Xi Jiang delta. (p. 330)

Guiana Highlands   Highland area in northern South America; extends from eastern Venezuela to Brazil, Guyana, Surinam, and French Guiana. (p. 485)

Gulf of Guinea   Large inlet of Atlantic Ocean; located on west coast of Africa; borders Ghana, Togo, Benin, Nigeria, Cameroon, and Equatorial Guinea. (p. 259)

H

Hague, The (52°N/4°E)   Seat of government of the Netherlands; location of United Nations World Court. (p. 321)

Halifax (45°N/64°W)   Capital of Nova Scotia, Canada; important port on Atlantic Ocean. (p. 482)

Hamburg (54°N/10°E)   Town in West Germany; major port on the Elbe River; gave name to hamburgers. (p. 115)

Harappa (31°N/73°E)   Site of ancient Indian city in Indus Valley. (p. 343)

Himalaya Mountains   Highest mountain range in world; forms Nepal-Tibet border. (p. 333)

Hindu Kush   Mountain range in central Asia; joins the Himalayas to form a wall between the Indian Peninsula and the rest of Asia. (p. 339)

Hiroshima (34°N/132°E)   Industrial city in Japan; first atomic bomb dropped here on August 6, 1945. (p. 414)

Hispaniola   Island in the West Indies; located in Caribbean Sea between Cuba and Puerto Rico; now occupied by the countries of Haiti and the Dominican Republic. (p. 499)

Hobart (43°S/147°E)   Capital of Tasmania, Australia; located on Derwent River. (p. 448)

Hokkaido Northernmost of four main islands of Japan. (p. 396)

Holy Roman Empire Name for lands ruled by Charlemagne, then Otto the Great; included Germany, Italy, and the Low Countries. (p. 166)

Honshu Largest and most important of four main islands of Japan. (p. 395)

Horn of Africa Located on Somali Peninsula in East Africa; shaped like rhinoceros tusk. (p. 257)

Huang He Second-largest river in China; connected by the Grand Canal to the Chang Jiang; also called "China's Sorrow." (p. 333)

Hudson Bay Located in Canada; borders Northwest Territories, Manitoba, Ontario, and Quebec; reaches Atlantic Ocean through the Hudson Strait. (p. 535)

I

Iberian Peninsula Peninsula in southwestern Europe; occupied by Spain and Portugal. (p. 110)

Iguacú Falls Falls located on Iguacú River near point at which Iguacú joins Paraná River at Brazil-Paraguay border. (p. 526)

Indian Ocean Large body of water touching Africa, Asia, and Australia. (p. 9)

Indian Peninsula Located in South Asia; bordered by Arabian Sea, Indian Ocean, and Bay of Bengal; occupied by India, Pakistan, Nepal, Bhutan, and Bangladesh. (p. 333)

Indochina Peninsula Located in Southeast Asia; occupied by Burma, Thailand, Laos, Kampuchea, Vietnam, and Malaysia. (p. 333)

Indus River River in Asia; rises in southwestern Tibet, China; flows through Pakistan; empties into Arabian Sea. (p. 333)

International Date Line Line of longitude located at 180°; exactly opposite Prime Meridian (0°); place where each calendar day first begins. (p. 7)

Ionian Sea Part of Mediterranean Sea; located between Italy and Greece. (p. 118)

Irian Jaya Part of Indonesia; located in west Pacific Ocean on New Guinea, second-largest island in world. (p. 431)

Irrawaddy River River in central Burma; formed by joining of Mali and Nmai Rivers; empties into the Bay of Bengal near Rangoon. (p. 431)

Isthmus of Panama A narrow land bridge connecting North and South America; separates Atlantic and Pacific Oceans. (p. 484)

Italian Peninsula Middle peninsula of southern Europe; extends into Mediterranean Sea; shaped like high-heeled boot. (p. 109)

J

Jakarta (6°S/107°E) Capital of Indonesia; located on island of Java; found at mouth of Liwung River. (p. 437)

Java The most important of Indonesia's islands; located between Java Sea and Indian Ocean; 1,500 people per square mile (2.6 sq km) give it one of the highest population densities in the world. (p. 431)

Jenne (14°N/5°W) Town in central Mali, West Africa; center for law and study in fourteenth century. (p. 273)

Jericho (32°N/35°E) City just north of Dead Sea; oldest known city in world; destroyed and rebuilt many times; located in present-day Jordan. (p. 28)

Jerusalem (32°N/35°E) Capital of Israel; holy city for Jews, Christians, and Muslims; means "city of peace." (p. 62)

Jordan River Rises in Syria and ends in Sea of Galilee; forms Israel-Jordan border. (p. 83)

Jutland Peninsula between the North Sea and the Kattegat; occupied by Denmark. (p. 110)

K

Kalahari Desert Plateau and desert area of Botswana, in Southern Africa. (p. 259)

Kalimantan Province of Indonesia; located on island of Borneo. (p. 431)

Kano (12°N/9°E) City in central Nigeria; historic center for caravans; now important trade center located on railroad line. (p. 271)

Kanto Plain Coastal plain located between Tokyo and Yokohama, Japan. (p. 397)

Karnak (26°N/33°E) Village on east bank of Nile River in Egypt; during the Middle Kingdom, site of temples to honor Amon. (p. 48)

Khyber Pass Narrow pass through Hindu Kush; located on Afghanistan-Pakistan border. (p. 344)

Kilwa (10°S/40°W) Located on little island off coast of present-day Tanzania; one of richest Swahili trading cities. (p. 284)

Kobe (35°N/135°E) Sixth-largest city of Japan; located on southern coast of Honshu, Japan. (p. 396)

Krakow (50°N/20°E) City in Poland; located on Vistula River. (p. 108)

Kumbi (16°N/8°E) Former capital of the empire of Ghana; located on most important trade route in western Sahara. (p. 269)

Kyoto (35°N/136°E) City in western central Honshu, Japan; originally called Heian-kyo and served as the capital of Japan for more than 1,000 years. (p. 396)

Kyushu One of four major islands of Japan. (p. 396)

L

Labrador Part of Newfoundland, Canada; borders the Atlantic Ocean, Quebec, and the Hudson Strait. (p. 536)

Lake Chad Located in Central Africa; found where Nigeria, Niger, and Chad borders meet. (p. 259)

Lake Eyre Largest salt lake in Australia; lowest place on continent at 52 feet (16 m) below sea level. (p. 448)

Lake Maracaibo One of two most important lakes in South America; located in center of Venezuela's rich oil reserves; found at southern end of Gulf of Venezuela. (p. 485)

Lake Nasser Lake formed after building of Aswan High Dam; located in southern Egypt and northern Sudan. (p. 66)

Lake Tanganyika Lake located in Great Rift Valley in central Africa; found at Tanzania-Zaire border. (p. 259)

Lake Texcoco Dry lake in central Mexico; located east of Mexico City; site of Aztec city of Tenochtitlán. (p. 494)

Lake Titicaca One of two most important lakes in South America; located in Bolivia and Peru. (p. 485)

Lake Victoria Largest lake in Africa; located in Tanzania and Uganda; second-largest freshwater body in world. (p. 259)

Lancang Jiang River in southeastern Asia; rises in eastern Tibet; becomes the Mekong River and empties into South China Sea in southern Vietnam. (p. 368)

Le Havre (50°N/0°) Seaport city in northern France; located on the English Channel. (p. 108)

Lena River River in central Soviet Union; rises near Lake Baikal and flows north into Arctic Ocean. (p. 333)

Leningrad (60°N/30°E) Second-largest city in Soviet Union; located at east end of Gulf of Finland; formerly called St. Petersburg and was capital of Russia. (p. 108)

Leon Kingdom in northwestern Spain during the Middle Ages; bordered Portugal, the Atlantic Ocean, Castile, and Dominions of the Almohades. (p. 209)

Leyte One of the largest islands in the Philippines. (p. 440)

Lhasa (30°N/91°E) Capital of Tibet, region of China; located in lower plains of Plateau of Tibet on tributary of Brahmaputra River. (p. 368)

Libyan Desert Desert area in eastern Sahara Desert in North Africa; located in Libya, Egypt, and Sudan. (p. 259)

Lima (12°S/77°W) Capital of Peru; located on Rimac River; name means "City of Kings." (p. 513)

Limpopo River River in southeastern Africa; rises near Johannesburg; empties into Indian Ocean; also called Crocodile River. (p. 259)

Loire River Longest river in France; empties into Bay of Biscay. (p. 110)

London (51°N/0°) Capital of United Kingdom; located on both sides of Thames River. (p. 9)

Luanda (9°S/13°E) Capital of Angola; located on Bay of Bengo on west coast of Africa. (p. 256)

Luzon Most important island in the Philippines. (p. 431)

M

Macao (22°N/113°E) Portuguese colony near Guangzhou, China; important port on South China Sea. (p. 380)

Macedonia Region in center of Balkan Peninsula; includes parts of present-day Greece, Yugoslavia, and Bulgaria. (p. 129)

Madras (13°N/80°E) Fourth-largest city in India; main port on India's southeast coast. (p. 351)

Malay Peninsula Peninsula in Southeast Asia; Malaysia and parts of Thailand and Burma located here. (p. 431)

Mali Second great West African grassland empire and second-largest empire in the world in fourteenth century; located in sub-Saharan Africa; also refers to nation in West Africa next to Algeria, Niger, the Upper Volta, the Ivory Coast, Guinea, Senegal, and Mauritania. (p. 272)

Malindi (3°S/40°E) Seaport town in southeastern Kenya. (p. 285)

Manchuria Large region in northeastern China. (p. 380)

Manila (15°N/121°E) Capital of Philippines; located on island of Luzon; principal port and industrial center of Philippines. (p. 440)

Manitoba Settled part of Rupert's Land purchased in 1869 by Canadian government; province in central Canada; next to Hudson Bay, Ontario, Minnesota, North Dakota, Saskatchewan, and Northwest Territories. (p. 536)

Marathon Plain in east Attica, Greece; located northeast of Athens; site of Greek victory over Persians in 490 B.C. (p. 124)

Marseille (43°N/5°E) Chief seaport of France; located in southeastern France on Gulf of Lions. (p. 108)

Mecca (21°N/40°E) City in western Saudi Arabia; birthplace of Muhammad; holy city for Muslims. (p. 71)

Medina (24°N/40°E)   City in western Saudi Arabia; site where Muhammad and followers fled from Mecca. (p. 72)

Mediterranean Sea   Inland sea enclosed by Europe, Asia, and Africa; connects with Atlantic Ocean, Red Sea, and Black Sea. (p. 108)

Mekong River   One of chief rivers of southeast Asia; as Lancang Jiang, rises in Tibet and flows through China; as Mekong, flows through Laos, Thailand, Kampuchea, and Vietnam; empties into South China Sea. (p. 431)

Melbourne (38°S/145°E)   Capital of Victoria, Australia; located at north end of Port Phillip Bay. (p. 448)

Memphis (30°N/31°E)   Ancient city in Egypt near present-day Cairo; built by pharaoh Menes to be his capital. (p. 49)

Mesopotamia   Area between Tigris and Euphrates rivers; means "land between the rivers." (p. 25)

Mexico City (19°N/99°W)   Capital of Mexico; located on southern edge of Central Plateau; has an elevation of about 7,000 feet (2,134 m). (p. 9)

Milan (45°N/9°E)   Industrial and second-largest city in northern Italy; located in fertile plain of northern Italy between Adda and Ticino Rivers. (p. 108)

Minas Gerais   Inland state in eastern Brazil; important for minerals; name means "general mines." (p. 519)

Mindanao   Southernmost of four largest islands in the Philippines. (p. 431)

Mohenjo-Daro   Site of early Indian civilization on the Indus River; remains of city show use of written language, plumbing, bronze, silver, copper, and lead; located in present-day Pakistan. (p. 343)

Mombasa (4°S/40°E)   Second-largest city and chief port of Kenya; located on the mainland and on an island off the coast in the Indian Ocean. (p. 285)

Montreal (45½°N/73½°W)   Major port and largest city in Canada; located in Quebec on an island in the St. Lawrence River. (p. 537)

Moscow (56°N/38°E)   Capital and largest city of Soviet Union; important center of transportation. (p. 232)

Mt. Aconcagua (32°S/70°W)   Mountain in western Argentina; highest peak of Andes Range; highest peak in Western Hemisphere. (p. 485)

Mt. Elbrus   Peak in Caucasus Mountains; located in the Soviet Union; highest peak in Europe. (p. 110)

Mt. Everest (28°N/87°E)   Highest mountain in world; over 29,000 feet (8,850 m); located in Himalayas. (p. 333)

Mt. Fuji (35°N/138°E)   Sacred mountain in Honshu, Japan; highest peak in Japan. (p. 395)

Mt. Katherine (28°N/34°E)   Highest peak of Gebel Musa Mountains; located on Sinai Peninsula. (p. 66)

Mt. Kenya (0°/37°W)   Extinct volcano near equator; located in Kenya, Africa. (p. 259)

Mt. Kilimanjaro (4°S/38°W)   Mountain in northeastern Tanzania; highest point in Africa at 19,340 feet (5,894 m). (p. 257)

Mt. Olympus (35°N/33°E)   Highest mountain in Greece; in Greek mythology, home of gods and goddesses. (p. 118)

Mt. Sinai (29°N/34°E)   Mountain in Gebel Musa Range; located on southern Sinai Peninsula. (p. 66)

Murray River   Major river of Australia; rises in Victoria; flows into Encounter Bay through Lake Alexandrina. (p. 449)

Mycenae   Ruined city in Peloponnesus, Greece; one of the oldest cities of Greece. (p. 118)

N

Nagasaki (33°N/130°E)   Seaport city in southern Japan; second atomic bomb fell here on August 9, 1945. (p. 406)

Nagoya (35°N/137°E)   Major city in southern Honshu, Japan; located at head of Ise Bay. (p. 396)

Nairobi (1°S/37°E)   Capital of Kenya; located near British-built railway line. (p. 297)

Naples (40°N/14°E)   Third-largest city in Italy and major seaport in south; located on north side of Bay of Naples. (p. 108)

Nara (35°N/136°E)   City east of Osaka; site of oldest permanent capital of Japan, built in A.D. 710. (p. 403)

Navarre   Kingdom in northern Spain during the Middle Ages; bordered France, Aragon, and Castile. (p. 209)

New Brunswick   One of Atlantic Provinces in Canada; next to Quebec, Gulf of St. Lawrence, Northumberland Strait, Bay of Fundy, Maine, and Nova Scotia. (p. 536)

New Delhi (29°N/77°E)   Capital of India; located on Yamuna River. (p. 348)

Newfoundland   One of Atlantic Provinces in Canada; located on east coast of Canada and island in the Atlantic Ocean. (p. 536)

New Guinea   Island in Malay Archipelago; located in west Pacific Ocean, north of Australia; second-largest island in world; occupied by Indonesia and Papua New Guinea. (p. 431)

Niger River   River in West Africa; rises in Guinea near border with Sierra Leone; flows across West Africa into Nigeria; ends in Gulf of Guinea. (p. 259)

Nile River Longest river in world at over 4,000 miles (6,500 km); North Africa's most important river; White Nile in Uganda, and Blue Nile in Ethiopia; two rivers meet in Sudan to flow north into Mediterranean Sea. (p. 47)

Nineveh Ancient capital of Assyria; ruins located on Tigris River. (p. 40)

North China Plain One of four main inhabited areas in China; noted for pleasant, dry summers and high winds that carry clouds of dust from deserts to banks of Huang He. (p. 368)

Northern Hemisphere Northern half of Earth; region from equator to North Pole. (p. 7)

North Island Northernmost of the main islands of New Zealand. (p. 452)

North Pole Northernmost point on Earth; one of the two coldest places in the world. (p. 7)

North Sea Part of Atlantic Ocean; located east of Great Britain and west of Scandinavia. (p. 166)

Northwest Territories One of two territories in Canada; located in far north; small population. (p. 536)

Norwegian Sea Part of Atlantic Ocean; located between Iceland and Norway. (p. 108)

Nova Scotia One of Canada's Atlantic Provinces; located on the east coast of Canada. (p. 536)

Nubia Region in Nile Valley, Africa; includes Aswan, First Cataract, Sudan, Egypt, and Nubian Desert; conquered by Egyptians during Middle Kingdom. (p. 48)

Nubian Desert Desert area in northeast Sudan; located east of Nile River. (p. 259)

Nullarbor Plain Plain located along southwest coast of Australia; starts at east end of Great Australian Bight; ends in Western Australia; name means "no trees." (p. 458)

O

Ob River River in western Soviet Union; flows into Gulf of Ob; major transportation route in Siberia. (p. 333)

Olympia Plain in western Peloponnesus, Greece, on north bank of Alpheus River; site of first Olympic games to honor Zeus. (p. 118)

Ontario One of Canada's Central Provinces; located between Quebec and Manitoba; borders Hudson Bay, Great Lakes, and United States. (p. 536)

Orange River Located in Southern Africa; empties into Atlantic Ocean at Alexander Bay; forms South Africa-Namibia border. (p. 259)

Osaka (35°N/136°E) Seaport on northeast shore of Osaka Bay; third-largest city in Japan; major industrial center. (p. 396)

Ottawa (45°N/76°W) Capital of Canada; located in Ontario; found in the St. Lawrence Lowlands. (p. 537)

P

Padang (1°S/100°E) Seaport city on Sumatra, Indonesia. (p. 431)

Palestine Ancient part of Fertile Crescent on Mediterranean Sea; occupied by present-day Israel and the part of Jordan west of Jordan River; holy land of Jews, Christians, and Muslims. (p. 40)

Pamir Knot Region located where Pakistan, Afghanistan, China, and the Soviet Union meet; most of Asia's mountains are centered here; also called "roof of the world." (p. 331)

Panama Canal Canal across the Isthmus of Panama; connects the Atlantic and Pacific oceans. (p. 484)

Paraná River River in central South America; starts in Brazilian Highlands; flows through Brazil, Paraguay, and Argentina; empties into Rio de la Plata in Argentina. (p. 485)

Paris (49°N/2°E) Capital of France; located on both banks of Seine River. (p. 180)

Peloponnesus Peninsula region of southern Greece; connected to north by Isthmus of Corinth. (p. 117)

Persepolis (30°S/53°E) Ancient capital of Persia; built by Darius; located in present-day Iran. (p. 64)

Persia Previous name for present-day Iran; located in southwestern Asia; next to the Soviet Union, Caspian Sea, Afghanistan, Pakistan, the Gulf of Oman, the Persian Gulf, Iraq, and Turkey. (p. 41)

Persian Empire Ancient empire that included Egypt, Syria, Assyria, Mesopotamia, Babylonia, and Persia. (p. 63)

Persian Gulf Part of the Arabian Sea; connects with Gulf of Oman and Arabian Sea. (p. 87)

Perth (32°S/115°E) Capital of Western Australia; located on Swan River. (p. 448)

Phoenicia Ancient country in western Syria; located on narrow strip of land west of Lebanon Mountains. (p. 130)

Plateau of Iran Large area stretching from the Zagros Mountains to India; original home of Persians. (p. 20)

Plateau of Tibet Highest region in world; located in Tibet, China. (p. 426)

Prime Meridian   0° line of longitude that divides Earth into the Eastern and Western hemispheres. (p. 7)

Prince Edward Island   One of Canada's Atlantic Provinces; Canada's smallest province; also called "The Garden Province." (p. 536)

Prussia   One of many separate states that made up Germany from Middle Ages until late 1800s; located in present-day northern and central Germany. (p. 224)

Punjab   Region in northwestern India and Pakistan; former province of British India. (p. 341)

Pyrenees Mountains   Range that separates Iberian Peninsula from rest of Europe; forms France-Spain border. (p. 110)

Q

Qattara Depression   Low region in northern Egypt; lowest point is 440 feet (134 m) below sea level. (p. 66)

Quebec   One of Canada's Central Provinces; part of former colony called "New France." (p. 536)

Quelimane (18°S/36°E)   Town on Africa's southeastern coast; located on Quelimane River in Mozambique. (p. 283)

Quito (0°/79°W)   Capital of Ecuador; located on fertile plateau. (p. 482)

R

Red Sea   Water between Africa and the Middle East; connected with Mediterranean Sea by Suez Canal and with Arabian Sea by Gulf of Aden. (p. 18)

Republic of Venice (45°N/12°E)   City-state of Italy in Middle Ages and Renaissance; located in present-day Venice; seaport of 118 islands in Lagoon of Venice; found in northeastern Italy. (p. 192)

Rhine River   River in central Europe; begins in Switzerland; forms Liechtenstein-Austria border; flows into North Sea. (p. 110)

Rhodes   Greek island in southeastern Aegean Sea; near southwest coast of Turkey. (p. 118)

Rhone River   River in Switzerland and France; rises in Alps; empties into the Gulf of Lions in southern France. (p. 110)

Rio de Janeiro (23°S/43°W)   Second-largest city and former capital of Brazil; seaport on shore of Guanabara Bay. (p. 519)

Riyadh (25°N/47°E)   Capital of Saudi Arabia. (p. 79)

Rocky Mountains   Range that covers much of western North America; extends from Alaska through Canada and ends in New Mexico; moun-

tains divide rivers that flow east from those that flow west. (p. 485)

Rome (42°N/13°E)   Ancient city as well as present capital of Italy; located on both sides of Tiber River. (p. 108)

Rotorua (38°S/176°E)   City on North Island, New Zealand; located on Rotorua Lake. (p. 452)

Rotterdam (52°N/4°E)   Located in Netherlands on Rhine River; busiest port in world. (p. 108)

S

Sahara Desert   World's largest desert; covers northern third of Africa. (p. 259)

Sahel   Dry plain south of Sahara; extends across northern Africa. (p. 258)

St. Helena   British island in south Atlantic Ocean where Napoleon was sent after his defeat. (p. 222)

St. John (45°N/66°W)   Major port in southern New Brunswick, Canada; located on Bay of Fundy at mouth of St. John River. (p. 536)

St. John's (48°N/53°W)   Major port and capital of Newfoundland, Canada; located on Atlantic Ocean. (p. 536)

St. Lawrence River   Forms part of United States-Canada border; begins at Lake Ontario; flows into Atlantic Ocean. (p. 537)

Salamis (38°N/23°E)   Island in Saronic Gulf in eastern Greece; location of important sea battle between Greeks and Persians in 480 B.C. (p. 124)

Salvador (13°S/38°W)   Seaport in eastern Brazil; located on All Saints Bay; was called Bahia while Portuguese colonial capital. (p. 518)

Salween River   River in southeastern Asia; rises in Plateau of Tibet; empties into Gulf of Martaban in Burma. (p. 333)

Samar   One of the Philippine islands; landing place of Magellan in 1521. (p. 431)

São Paulo (24°S/47°W)   Largest city in Brazil; major industrial area; located on Tietê River. (p. 482)

Sardinia   Island in the Mediterranean Sea; located west of Italian Peninsula; part of Italy. (p. 108)

Saskatchewan   One of Prairie Provinces in Canada; next to Northwest Territories, Manitoba, North Dakota, Montana, and Alberta. (p. 536)

Scandinavian Peninsula   One of Europe's four large peninsulas; surrounded by Baltic, North, and Norwegian seas; occupied by Norway and Sweden. (p. 110)

Sea of Japan   Part of the western Pacific Ocean; located between Japan and the Soviet Union and Korean Peninsula. (p. 333)

Sea of Okhotsk   Part of Pacific Ocean; found off

coast of Soviet Union; located west of Kamchatka Peninsula. (p. 333)

Senegal River River in West Africa; rises in highlands of Guinea; empties into Atlantic Ocean in Senegal. (p. 259)

Shanghai (32°N/122°E) City with largest population in China; important port; Chang Jiang empties into East China Sea here. (p. 369)

Shatt al Arab estuary Place where Tigris and Euphrates Rivers flow into Persian Gulf; area of conflict between Iran and Iraq. (p. 90)

Shikoku Smallest of four major islands of Japan. (p. 333)

Siberia Largest region in Soviet Union; extends from Ural Mountains to Pacific Ocean in eastern Soviet Union. (p. 229)

Sichuan Basin High, hilly region in central China; about 2,000 feet (600 m) above sea level; fertile land and mild climate; name means "four rivers"; also called Red Basin. (p. 368)

Sicily Largest island in Mediterranean Sea; part of Italy; located southwest of Italy. (p. 108)

Sinai Peninsula Peninsula between Egypt and Israel; lies between Gulf of Suez and Gulf of Aqaba. (p. 51)

Singapore (1°N/104°E) Island nation and city off southern tip of Malay Peninsula; one of the world's major seaports; located on Singapore Strait. (p. 330)

Songhai Former West African grassland empire located along Niger River in central Sudan; included conquered lands belonging to Mali Empire. (p. 275)

South China Sea Part of Pacific Ocean; bordered by Taiwan, southeast China, Indochina, Malay Peninsula, Indonesia, and Philippines. (p. 330)

Southern Hemisphere Southern half of Earth; region from equator to South Pole. (p. 7)

South Island Largest island of New Zealand. (p. 452)

South Pole Southernmost point on Earth; one of the two coldest places in world. (p. 7)

Sparta (37°N/22°E) Ancient inland city-state in the Peloponnesus, Greece; present-day city located in southeastern Peloponnesus, Greece. (p. 122)

Strait of Gibraltar Narrow waterway between Africa and Europe; connects Mediterranean Sea with Atlantic Ocean. (p. 110)

Suez Canal Connects Mediterranean Sea with Red Sea; located on Isthmus of Suez in northeastern Africa; 100 miles (160 km) long; built from 1859 to 1869. (p. 87)

Sumatra Westernmost island of Indonesia; home of Minangkabaus. (p. 333)

Sumer Land in southern Mesopotamia; location

of world's first known civilization. (p. 29)

Sydney (34°S/151°E) Capital of New South Wales, Australia; located on Pacific Ocean; largest city and chief port of Australia. (p. 448)

Syrian Desert Large desert located in Saudi Arabia, Syria, Iraq, and Jordan. (p. 20)

T

Tasmania Australian state; island separated from southern coast of Victoria, Australia, by Tasman Sea; located in south Pacific Ocean. (p. 448)

Taurus Mountains Mountain chain in southern Turkey; runs parallel to coast of Mediterranean. (p. 20)

Tel Aviv (32°N/34½°E) Second-largest city and former capital of Israel; major manufacturing center; located on Mediterranean Sea. (p. 84)

Tenochtitlán (19°N/99°W) Located where present-day Mexico City stands; was capital of Aztec Empire; means "stone rising in water." (p. 495)

Thar Desert Also called Great Indian Desert; forms India's northwest border; located in India and Pakistan. (p. 339)

Thebes Capital of Egypt during Middle Kingdom; located along left bank of Nile River; site of Temple of Karnak. (p. 56)

Thermopylae (39°N/22°E) Narrow pass in eastern Greece; located between Mt. Oeta and Gulf of Maliakos; site of battle between Greeks and Persians in 480 B.C. (p. 118)

Tiber River River in central Italy; rises in Apennines; flows through Rome; empties into Tyrrhenian Sea. (p. 141)

Tibet Region in China; bordered by Sichuan, Yunnan, India, Nepal, Bhutan, and Sikkim; highest inhabited land on Earth; called Xizang in Chinese. (p. 330)

Tierra del Fuego Archipelago off southern South America; includes all islands south of the Strait of Magellan to Drake Passage. (p. 482)

Tigris River River in southeastern Turkey and Iraq; rises in Kurdistan Mountains; joins with Euphrates River to form Shatt al Arab. (p. 25)

Timbuktu (16°N/4°W) Town in Mali, Africa; located near Niger River; famous city and center of learning and culture in sixteenth century. (p. 273)

Tokyo (36°N/140°E) Capital of Japan; located on Tokyo Bay; found on island of Honshu. (p. 397)

Toronto (44°N/79°W) Capital of Ontario, Canada; located at northwestern end of Lake Ontario; second-largest city in Canada. (p. 536)

Tropic of Cancer Line of latitude at 23½°N. (p. 11)

Tropic of Capricorn Line of latitude at 23½°S; region between it and Tropic of Cancer called low latitudes or tropics; usually very warm. (p. 11)

Troy (40°N/26°E) Ancient city in northwestern Asia Minor; located south of Dardanelles; location of Trojan War described in Homer's *Iliad*; also called Ilium. (p. 118)

Turkish Empire Ancient empire with lands in Europe, Asia, and Africa; area included all lands surrounding eastern Mediterranean and parts of Soviet Union around Black Sea; after capture of Constantinople in 1453, called Ottoman Empire; collapsed after defeat in World War I. (p. 168)

Tyrrhenian Sea Part of Mediterranean Sea; located between Italy and Sicily, Sardinia, and Corsica. (p. 142)

U

Ukraine Republic in Soviet Union; next to Hungary, Czechoslovakia, Poland, and Black Sea. (p. 230)

Ur (31°N/47°E) Ancient city in Sumer; birthplace of Abraham, early leader of Hebrew people. (p. 31)

Ural Mountains Located in Soviet Union; form Europe-Asia border. (p. 110)

V

Vancouver (49°N/123°W) City in British Columbia, Canada; most important Pacific seaport in Canada. (p. 536)

Venice (45°N/12°E) Seaport city in northeastern Italy on the Adriatic Sea; made up of 118 islands in Lagoon of Venice. (p. 168)

Vichy (46°N/3°E) City in central France; located on Allier River; famous for spa and health resort; headquarters of French government during German occupation in World War II. (p. 227)

Victoria (48°N/123°W) Capital of British Columbia, Canada; located on southeastern Vancouver Island. (p. 536)

Victoria Falls (18°S/26°E) Located on Zambesi River at Zimbabwe-Zambia border; more water flows over these falls than over any other falls in Africa. (p. 259)

Vienna (48°N/16°E) Capital of Austria; located on Danube River. (p. 108)

Volga River Europe's longest river; located in Soviet Union; empties into Caspian Sea. (p. 110)

Volta Redonda (23°S/44°W) City in eastern Brazil; center of Brazil's steel industry. (p. 524)

Volta River River in Ghana, Africa; rises in Burkina Faso; flows into Bight of Benin. (p. 258)

W

Walata Ancient city in Ghana Empire, Africa; was located on important trade route near Timbuktu. (p. 271)

Warsaw (52°N/21°E) Capital of Poland; located on both banks of Vistula River. (p. 108)

Wellington (41°S/175°E) Capital of New Zealand; located on North Island in Cook Strait. (p. 452)

Western Hemisphere Half of Earth west of Prime Meridian; includes North and South America. (p. 7)

X

Xi Jiang River in southeastern China; flows into China Sea near Macao; Guangzhou found here. (p. 333)

Y

Yellow Sea Inlet of Pacific Ocean; between China and Korean Peninsula. (p. 333)

Yenisey River River in Soviet Union; begins where Bolshoi Yenisey and Maly Yenisey rivers join; ends in Arctic Ocean at Yenisey Bay; one of world's longest rivers. (p. 230)

Yokohama (35°N/139°E) Second-largest city and chief port of Japan; located in southeastern Honshu on Tokyo Bay. (p. 396)

Yucatán Peninsula Peninsula in southeastern Mexico and northern Central America; occupied by Mexico, Belize, and Guatemala; separates Gulf of Mexico from Caribbean Sea. (p. 493)

Yukon One of Canada's two territories; borders Arctic Ocean, Northwest Territories, British Columbia, and Alaska. (p. 538)

Z

Zagros Mountains Series of parallel mountain ranges in southern Iran; some found along and across Iran-Iraq border. (p. 20)

Zaire River One of the largest rivers in world; located in central Africa; formed by joining Luapula and Lualaba rivers. (p. 259)

Zambezi River River in Southern Africa; rises in Zambia; flows across Angola and Zambia; forms Zambia-Zimbabwe border; empties into Mozambique Channel at Chinde, Mozambique. (p. 259)

Zanzibar (6°S/40°E) City on Zanzibar Island, Africa; located off east coast of Africa; part of present-day Tanzania. (p. 290)

Glossary

This glossary contains important social studies words and their definitions. Each word is pronounced as it would be in a dictionary. When you see this mark ´ after a syllable, pronounce that syllable with more force than the other syllables. The page number at the end of the definition tells where to find the word in your book.

add, āce, câre, pälm; end, ēqual; it, īce; odd, ōpen, ôrder; tŏŏk, pōōl; up, bûrn; yōō as u in *fuse*; oil; pout; ə as a in *above*, e in *sicken*, i in *possible*, o in *melon*, u in *circus*; check; ring; thin; this; zh as in vision.

A

Aborigine (ab·ə·rij´ə·nē) A native of Australia. (p. 455)

acropolis (ə·krop´ə·lis) A walled fortress built on a hill. (p. 119)

A.D. (ā·dē) An abbreviation that is used to name the years after the birth of Christ. A.D. stands for *anno Domini,* a Latin phrase meaning "in the year of the Lord." (p. 42)

agora (ə·gor´ə) An open marketplace in ancient Greece. (p. 120)

agriculture (ag´rə·kul·chər) Farming. (p. 26)

alliance (ə·lī´əns) An agreement between countries, states, or people. (p. 195)

Allies (al´īz) The nations that fought together against the Central Powers in World War I and against the Axis Powers in World War II. (pp. 225, 227)

altitude (al´tə·tŏŏd) Height above sea level. (p. 12)

amendment (ə·mend´mənt) A change or correction, as of a law. (p. 550)

anthropologist (an·thrə·pol´ə·jist) A scientist who studies cultures. (p. 279)

apartheid (ə·pärt´hāt) A word meaning "apartness." The belief of the Afrikaners that the different races in Africa should have as little contact with each other as possible. (p. 308)

apprentice (ə·pren´tis) A young person who learns a trade from a master. (p. 184)

aqueduct (ak´wə·dukt) A structure for carrying water over a distance. (p. 150)

archaeologist (är·kē·ol´ə·jist) A scientist who studies cultures of the past by digging up and examining artifacts. (p. 97)

archipelago (är·kə·pel´ə·gō) A chain of islands. (p. 395)

architect (är´kə·tekt) A person who designs and plans buildings. (p. 55)

architecture (är´kə·tek·chər) Style, or special way, of building. (p. 134)

arid (ar´əd) Having a very dry climate. (p. 20)

aristocrat (ə·ris´tə·krat) A member of the noble class. (p. 218)

artifact (är´tə·fakt) A tool, article of clothing, or other object made and used by people. (p. 97)

assembly (ə·sem´blē) A lawmaking group. (p. 120)

astrolabe (as´trə·lāb) A navigational instrument developed by Islamic scientists. (p. 75)

atlas (at´ləs) A collection of maps. (p. 2)

atmosphere (at´məs·fir) The air that surrounds the Earth. (p. 3)

atoms (at´əmz) Tiny particles of which everything is made. (p. 131)

Axis Powers (ak´sis pou´ərz) The nations that fought against the Allies in World War II. (p. 227)

B

barter (bär´tər) To trade for goods without the use of money. (p. 267)

bauxite (bôk´sīt) The mineral from which aluminum is made. (p. 450)

bazaar (bə·zär´) Marketplace. (p. 81)

B.C. (bē·sē) An abbreviation that is used to name the years before the birth of Christ. B.C. stands for *before Christ.* (p. 42)

biosphere (bī´ō·sfir) A word meaning "circle of life." A thin skin of water, soil, and air in which life on Earth exists. (p. 556)

Bolsheviks (bōl´shə·vikz) Members of the political party in Russia that gained control late in 1917, becoming the Communist party in 1918. (p. 231)

boundaries (boun´drēz) Borders of nations, counties, or states. (p. 6)

boycott (boi´kot) To refuse to buy or use a product. (p. 355)

Buddhism (bōō´diz·əm) An Asian religion in which people seek friendship, knowledge, and peace of mind through meditation. (p. 346)

C

calligraphy (kə·lig′rə·fē) Artistic writing. (p. 75)

capital resources (kap′ə·təl ri·sôr′səz) Money, tools, machinery, factories, and knowledge of a country. (p. 473)

cartogram (kär′tə·gram) A special map used to show statistics geographically. (p. 316)

caste (kast) A class or group of people in Indian society. (p. 344)

cathedral (kə·thē′drəl) A large church. (p. 179)

cause and effect (kôz and i·fekt′) A cause is an action that leads to an event. The effect is the event brought about by an action. (p. 240)

census (sen′səs) A population count. (p. 154)

Central Powers (sen′trəl pou′ərz) The nations who fought against the Allied Powers in World War I. (p. 225)

chancellor (chan′slər) In some nations the head of government, or prime minister. (p. 226)

charter (chär′tər) 1. A document from a lord granting a town the right to self-government. (p. 181) 2. A constitution. (p. 319)

checks and balances (cheks and bal′ən·səz) A system of sharing power among branches of government. (p. 249)

chieftains (chēf′tənz) Leaders of a tribe. (p. 165)

chivalry (shiv′əl·rē) The rules of behavior followed by the knights of the Middle Ages. (p. 175)

Christianity (kris·chē·an′ə·tē) The religion taught by Jesus Christ and his followers that has become the major religion in Europe and the Western Hemisphere. (p. 71)

city-state (si′tē stāt) A city and the surrounding lands that it governs. (p. 30)

civilization (siv·ə·lə·zā′·shən) A society that has created a high level of culture, including the building of cities. (p. 1)

civil service (siv′əl sûr′vəs) A government system that selects officials on the basis of qualifications. (p. 377)

civil war (siv′əl wôr) War among opposing groups of citizens of the same country. (p. 148)

clan (klan) A group of related families. (p. 401)

class (klas) A group of people making up part of a society. (p. 36)

clergy (klûr′jē) Religious workers, such as ministers, monks, nuns, priests, and rabbis. (p. 177)

climate (klī′mət) The annual weather patterns of a place. (p. 10)

collective farms (kə·lek′tiv färmz) Small farms combined together into large units in order to increase food production. (p. 233)

comedy (kom′ə·dē) A play that tells a story in a humorous way and has a happy ending. (p. 133)

command economy (kə·mand′ i·kon′ə·mē) An economy controlled completely by the government. (p. 472)

commonwealth (kom′ən·welth) A group of states with common ties and interests. (p. 460)

commune (kom′yoon) A government-run farming or factory community in China with shared housing and work. (p. 386)

communism (kom′yə·niz·əm) A system in which the state controls the production and distribution of goods. (p. 230)

competition (kom·pə·ti′shən) The contest between different companies that provide the same goods or services. (p. 476)

compromise (kom′prə·mīz) A solution that gives each side a part of its demands. (p. 499)

confederation (kən·fed·ər·ā′shən) A union. (p. 546)

conquistadors (kon·kēs′tə·dôrz) Spanish explorers, or conquerors, who came to the New World in search of gold. (p. 501)

conservation (kon·sər·vā′shən) Saving; or the wise use of resources. (p. 553)

consul (kon′səl) A chief official of the Roman Republic. (p. 143)

consumer (kən·soo′mər) One who spends money for goods or services. (p. 471)

convent (kon′vent) A special community in which nuns live. (p. 177)

coral (kor′əl) A stony material formed by the skeletons of millions of tiny sea animals. (p. 448)

core (kôr) The center of the Earth. The inner core is made of iron and nickel. Surrounding it is an outer core of hot, liquid iron and nickel. (p. 4)

corporation (kôr·pə·rā′shən) A type of business in which people may invest money. (p. 475)

courier (koor′ē·ər) A person who carries messages. (p. 65)

Creoles (krē′ōlz) People who had European parents but were born in the Latin American colonies. (p. 511)

crop rotation (krop rō·tā′shən) A system of farming that helps the soil stay fertile by alternating the kinds of crops planted. (p. 215)

crusader (kroo·sā′dər) A Christian soldier who fought to free the Holy Land from Muslims in the Middle Ages. (p. 169)

crust (krust) The outermost layer of the Earth, made of a thin layer of rock. (p. 4)

culture (kul′chər) The customs and beliefs of a group of people. (p. 1)

cuneiform (kyoo·nē′ə·fôrm) Sumerian writing system made up of wedge-shaped marks. (p. 33)

current (kûr′ənt) The flow of water in a certain direction. (p. 12)

czar (zär) The king of pre-revolutionary Russia. (p. 231)

D

degree (di·grē′) A unit of measure used to describe lines of latitude and lines of longitude. (p. 7)

delta (del′tə) A deposit of rich soil at the mouth of a river. (p. 47)

demagogue (dem′ə·gog) A leader who appeals to people's feelings to gain power. (p. 128)

demand (də·mand′) In economics, the number of people who want to buy something. (p. 471)

democracy (di·mok′rə·sē) A government ruled by the people. (p. 124)

depression (di·presh′ən) 1. A low area, such as a valley or canyon. (p. 66) 2. A slowdown in business. (p. 226)

descendant (di·sen′dənt) A child or grandchild of an ancestor. (p. 303)

dhow (dou) A large, triangular-sailed boat. (p. 283)

dictator (dik′tā·tər) A leader who has total power. (p. 146)

dictatorship (dik·tā′tər·ship) A political system led by one powerful ruler, or dictator. (p. 245)

direct rule (di·rekt′ rōōl) A type of colonial government in which Europeans chose all officials. (p. 295)

disciples (di·sī′pəlz) Followers, as of Jesus. (p. 71)

distribute (dis·trib′yōōt) To hand out shares of resources, goods, or services. (p. 470)

divine right (də·vīn′ rīt) The belief that a king's authority to rule came from God. (p. 218)

division of labor (di·vizh′ən uv lā′bər) A way of dividing the work a society does into a variety of tasks to be performed by different individuals or groups. (p. 31)

domesticate (də·mes′tə·kāt) To tame or fit plants or animals to the needs of people. (p. 26)

dominion (də·min′yən) A member of the Commonwealth of Nations that governs itself, such as Canada. (p. 546)

dwarf rice (dwôrf rīs) A sturdy rice that grows quickly and produces a large crop. (p. 440)

dynasty (dī′nə·stē) A ruling family that passes control from one generation to the next. (p. 372)

E

ecologist (i·kol′ə·jist) A scientist who studies living things as they relate to their environment. (p. 557)

economic system (ek·ə·nom′ik sis′təm) The method a country uses to produce and use goods and services. (p. 470)

economy (i·kon′ə·mē) The way people use resources to meet their needs. (p. 1)

elevation (el·ə·vā′shən) Height of land above sea level. (p. 67)

empire (em′pīr) A group of different, sometimes widespread states, nations, or territories under a single ruler or government. (p. 39)

environment (in·vī′rən·mənt) Surroundings. (p. 8)

epic (ep′ik) A long story-poem. (p. 119)

erosion (ir·ō′zhən) The gradual wearing down of rock or earth by water, wind, or ice. (p. 4)

evaluate (i·val′yōō·āt) To judge the worth or truth of something. (p. 279)

executive (ig·zek′yə·tiv) The branch of government that manages and carries out the laws. (p. 249)

export (eks′pôrt) To send goods out of a country for sale. (p. 115)

extended family (ik·sten′dəd fam′ə·lē) A group of relatives who live together, including others besides parents and their children. (p. 358)

F

fable (fā′bəl) A short story, often about animals, that teaches a special lesson. (p. 133)

federal republic (fed′ər·əl ri·pub′lik) A political system formed by a union of states, where the national government decides matters that affect all of the states. (p. 247)

fellahin (fel·ə·hēn′) Egyptian peasant. (p. 81)

feudalism (fyōōd′əl·iz·əm) The system of loyalties and protections in the Middle Ages. (p. 171)

fief (fēf) A piece of land given to a vassal by a lord or king in return for military service. (p. 172)

fjords (fyôrdz) Narrow inlets of the sea between high, steep banks. (p. 111)

fraternity (frə·tûr′nə·tē) Brotherhood; unity. (p. 219)

free enterprise economy (frē en′tər·prīz i·kon′ə·mē) A market economy in which people can decide how to make and spend their money. (p. 471)

fundamentalist (fun·də·men′tə·list) One who wants a return to old ways of thinking, believing, or behaving. (p. 89)

G

gasohol (gas′ə·hôl) An automobile fuel made of a mixture of gasoline and alcohol. (p. 526)

gaucho (gou′chō) A cowboy of the South American plains. (p. 519)

gazetteer (gaz·ə·tir′) A geographic dictionary that includes the locations of places shown on maps in a text. (p. 2)

geography (jē·og′rə·fē) The study of the physical features, resources, climate, and people of the Earth. (p. 4)

gladiators (glad′ē·ā·tərz) In ancient Rome, trained fighters who fought with weapons against other men or wild animals for public entertainment. (p. 158)

Gothic (goth′ik) A style of architecture in the Middle Ages that used pointed arches and a new kind of roof support, leaving more wall space available for windows. (p. 180)

government (guv′ərn·mənt) The system or group that makes decisions and solves problems for the people in a city, state, or country. (p. 1)

graph (graf) A diagram for showing numbers. (p. 91)

gravity (grav′ə·tē) The force that holds objects to the Earth and keeps planets circling the sun. (p. 207)

great circle (grāt sûr′kəl) Any complete circle around a globe that divides it in half. (p. 443)

grid (grid) A pattern of crossing lines. (p. 8)

gross national product (grōs nash′ən·əl prod′əkt) The total amount of goods and services in a country. (p. 475)

guild (gild) A group organized by merchants and craft workers to protect members and set standards of quality. (p. 182)

H

hacienda (hä·sē·en′də) A big farm or plantation in Latin America. (p. 508)

haiku (hī′kōō) An unrhymed three-line Japanese poem that has seventeen syllables and is often about nature. (p. 408)

heir (âr) One who inherits possessions or social position following someone's death. (p. 203)

heliocentric (hē·lē·ə·sen′trik) Having the sun as the center. (p. 206)

heresy (her′ə·sē) The crime of denying the beliefs of the Church. (p. 199)

heritage (her′ə·tij) The ideas and customs of a people passed down through their history. (p. 239)

hieroglyphics (hī·rə·glif′iks) A writing system in which pictures or symbols stand for ideas, objects, or sounds. (p. 52)

Hinduism (hin′dōō·iz·əm) A religion, native to India, in which there is belief in many gods and in reincarnation. (p. 345)

historian (his·tôr′ē·ən) A person who studies and writes about the past. (p. 298)

history (his′tə·rē) Events that happened in the past. (p. 1)

humid (hyōō′mid) Having a moist, wet climate. (p. 430)

hydroelectric (hī·drō·i·lek′trik) Having to do with electricity produced by water power. (p. 310)

I

illiterate (i·lit′ər·ət) Unable to read or write. (p. 523)

imperialism (im·pir′ē·əl·iz·əm) The practice of building empires to protect trade. (p. 293)

import (im·port′) To bring in goods from another country for sale. (p. 115)

index (in′deks) An alphabetical list of the subjects in a book. (p. 2)

indirect rule (in′də·rekt rōōl) A type of colonial government which allowed some participation by local officials. (p. 295)

Industrial Revolution (in·dus′trē·əl rev·ə·lōō′shən) In the eighteenth century, the invention of new machines and the discovery of new sources of power in Great Britain that changed the way people worked, lived, and traveled. It soon spread from Great Britain to other parts of the world. (p. 213)

inflation (in·flā′shən) A constant increase in the price of goods and services. (p. 237)

invest (in·vest′) To put money into a business. (p. 475)

Islam (is·läm′) The religion of the Muslims, founded by Muhammad, in which there is only one god, called Allah. Islam is the major religion in the Middle East, northern Africa, and parts of Asia. (p. 71)

isolates (i′sə·lātz) Separates. (p. 265)

isthmus (is′məs) A narrow strip of land, with water on both sides, that connects two larger masses of land. (p. 117)

J

jade (jād) A hard precious stone, often in shades of green or in black, brown, white, or lavender. (p. 377)

journeyman (jûr′nē·mən) One who works at a trade while learning advanced skills of the trade. (p. 184)

Judaism (jōō′də·iz·əm) The religion of the Jews, taught by Moses and the Hebrew prophets. (p. 71)

judicial (jōō·dish′əl) The branch of government that decides if laws have been broken or if they are unfair. (p. 249)

justice (jus′tis) A judge. (p. 249)

K

kaiser (kī′zər) A king of Prussia. (p. 224)

knight (nīt) A trained, armored horseman who fought wars in the early Middle Ages. (p. 175)

L

labor (lā′bər) Work. (p. 470)

language family (lang′gwij fam′ə·lē) A group of similar languages. (p. 303)

law of supply and demand (lô uv sə·plī′ and di·mand′) A general rule stating that prices tend to go up when a product is scarce and tend to go down when a product is plentiful. (p. 472)

legend (le′jənd) A key on a map that explains its features. (p. 6)

legion (lē′jən) A unit of soldiers in the Roman army. (p. 150)

legislative (lej·is·lā′tiv) The branch of government that makes the laws. (p. 249)

lines of latitude (līnz uv lat′ə·tōod) The imaginary lines that go east and west around the Earth. See also *parallels*. (p. 7)

lines of longitude (līnz uv lon′jə·tōod) The imaginary lines running from the North Pole to the South Pole. See also *meridians*. (p. 7)

M

manor (man′ər) A large estate or farm belonging to a noble family. (p. 172)

mansa (man′sə) Title for an emperor in West Africa. (p. 272)

mantle (man′təl) The third layer of the Earth, between the core and crust. It is made of soft rock. (p. 4)

market economy (mär′kit i·kon′ə·mē) An economy in which people can decide how to make and spend their money; free enterprise. (p. 471)

martial law (mär′shəl lô) Rule by the military. (p. 442)

master (mas′tər) One who has learned a trade and produces fine work. (p. 184)

mercenary (mûr′sə·ner·ē) A soldier who fights for pay, not out of loyalty to a cause. (p. 195)

meridians (mə·rid′ē·ənz) The imaginary lines running from the North Pole to the South Pole. See also *lines of longitude*. (p. 7)

mestizos (mes·tē′zōz) People in Latin America of mixed European and Indian descent. (p. 511)

migrated (mī′grā·təd) Moved from one country or region to settle in another. (p. 78)

minarets (min·ə·retz′) Towers on top of a mosque. (p. 74)

missionary (mish′ən·er·ē) A person sent out to teach about religion. (p. 292)

moderate (mod′ər·it) Having a mild climate. (p. 12)

monarch (mon′ərk) A royal ruler; king or queen. (p. 203)

monasteries (mon′əs·ter·ēz) The village-like communities in which monks live. (p. 177)

monks (mungks) Male religious workers who live together in special communities called monasteries. (p. 177)

monopoly (mə·nop′ə·lē) Complete control or ownership. (p. 271)

monsoons (mon·sōōnz′) Seasonal winds in Asia that bring large amounts of rainfall. (p. 335)

mosque (mäsk) A sacred Muslim building. (p. 74)

mummies (mum′ēz) Dead bodies preserved by embalming them and wrapping them in cloth. (p. 50)

muskegs (mus′kegz) Swamplike areas. (p. 535)

myth (mith) A story, often passed by word of mouth, that usually told an adventure of a god or goddess. (p. 135)

N

nationalism (nash′ən·əl·iz·əm) Patriotic pride in one's country. (p. 225)

nation-state (nā′shən stāt) A country with a strong central government and usually a common history and culture. (p. 185)

natural resources (nach′ər·əl ri·sor′səz) Things in nature, such as forests, minerals, and water, that help people supply their needs. (p. 10)

Nazi (nät′sē) A political party led by Adolf Hitler that controlled Germany from 1933 to 1945. Also a member of that party. (p. 226)

neutral (nōō′trəl) Not taking sides. (p. 359)

noble (nō′bəl) A member of the wealthiest class of some societies. (p. 36)

nomads (nō′madz) People who move from place to place. (p. 26)

nonrenewable (non·ri·nōō′ə·bəl) Once used, not able to be replaced by humans or nature. (p. 552)

nonviolent action (non·vī′ə·lənt ak′shən) Seeking political change in a peaceful way. (p. 353)

nuclear energy (nōō′klē·ər en′ər·jē) Atomic energy. (p. 552)

nuns (nunz) Female religious workers who live together in special communities called convents. (p. 177)

O

oasis (ō·ā′səs) A fertile place in the desert. (p. 28)

oba (ō′bä) Title for a king in Benin. (p. 277)

obelisk (ob′ə·lisk) A square stone shaft that tapers to a top shaped like a pyramid. (p. 57)

obsidian (əb·sid′ē·ən) A black volcanic rock. (p. 28)

oligarchy (ol′ə·gär·kē) A political system which is controlled by a small and powerful group. (p. 246)

oral history (ôr′əl his′tə·rē) Ideas and records passed on through spoken language. (p. 97)

outback (out′bak) A remote, undeveloped area, especially in Australia. (p. 450)

P

paddies (pad′ēz) Flooded fields where rice grows. (p. 337)

page (pāj) In the Middle Ages, a young boy who carried messages and waited on a lord. (p. 175)

pampas (pam′pəz) Indian for "plains." The vast, grassy plains of Argentina. (p. 484)

papyrus (pə·pī′rəs) Reeds that grew in the Nile River, used to make paper. (p. 52)

parallels (par′ə·lelz) The imaginary lines running east and west on the Earth. See also *lines of latitude*. (p. 7)

parchment (pärch′mənt) A paperlike material made from sheepskin. (p. 178)

patrician (pə·trish′ən) A member of a noble family in ancient Rome. (p. 143)

patron (pā′trən) A rich person who pays artists and writers to produce their work. (p. 192)

peasants (pez′əntz) Poor people who live on and farm the land. (p. 55)

per capita income (pûr kap′ə·tə in′kəm) Average earnings per person. (p. 476)

periodicals (pir·ē·od′ə·kəlz) Newspapers or magazines issued at regular intervals. (p. 136)

perspective (pər·spek′tiv) The differences in the way things look when they are close to a person and when they are far away. (p. 193)

pesticide (pes′tə·sīd) A chemical used to kill insects. (p. 358)

pharaoh (fâ′rō) A ruler of ancient Egypt. (p. 49)

philosopher (fəl·os′ə·fər) A person who studies truth; "lover of wisdom." (p. 132)

pictograph (pik′tə·graf) A drawing or symbol used to represent a word in the Chinese language. (p. 373)

pilgrimage (pil′grə·mij) A visit to a holy place, such as the holy city of Mecca. (p. 272)

pinyin (pin′yin′) A system used to represent Chinese speech sounds with letters of the English alphabet. (p. 371)

plague (plāg) A widespread sickness that appeared in Europe in the 1340s. Also called the "Black Death." (p. 185)

plebeian (pli·bē′ən) A member of the common people in ancient Rome. (p. 143)

plunder (plun′dər) Goods taken by force. (p. 167)

policy (pol′ə·sē) Plan of action. (p. 308)

polis (päl′əs) In ancient Greece, a city-state consisting of a town and the farms and villages around it. (p. 120)

political system (pə·lit′ə·kəl sis′təm) The way a nation governs itself. (p. 243)

pollute (pə·lōōt′) To make dirty. (p. 553)

Pope (pōp) Leader of the Roman Catholic Church. (p. 166)

population density (pop·yə·lā′shən den′sə·tē) The number of people who live in a square mile or other measured area. (p. 114)

porcelain (pôr′sə·lin) A type of clay pottery. (p. 377)

precipitation (pri·sip·ə·tā′shən) The amount of moisture that falls to the Earth in the form of rain, snow, sleet, hail, dew, or fog. (p. 13)

prejudice (pre′jə·dis) A belief that is not supported by facts. (p. 293)

premier (prə·mir′) The government leader in a Canadian province. (p. 551)

prevailing winds (pri·vāl′ing windz) Winds that generally blow in one direction. (p. 420)

primary products (prī′mer·ē prod′əkts) Products of the land rather than of industry. (p. 465)

primary source (prī′mer·ē sôrs) Information source recorded at the time of the events being studied. (p. 298)

producer (prə·dōō′sər) A person who makes goods or provides services. (p. 471)

profit (prof′it) The money left over after paying the costs for making a product. (p. 471)

projection (prə·jek′shən) A view of the round world shown on a flat map. (p. 504)

protectorate (prə·tek′tər·it) A country protected and controlled by another country. (p. 441)

province (pro′vins) A self-governing region of Canada, similar to a state. (p. 535)

pulp (pulp) Ground wood that is wetted to make paper. (p. 536)

pygmy (pig′mē) A member of a group of small, light-brown-skinned people who live in Africa. A Greek word meaning "dwarf." (p. 304)

pyramid (pir′ə·mid) A stone structure with a flat base and four triangular-shaped sides meeting at the top; a tomb for a ruler of ancient Egypt. (p. 54)

Q

quota (kwō′tə) Required amount. (p. 389)

R

racism (rās′iz·əm) The belief that one person is better than another because of race. (p. 291)

radiation (rā·dē·ā′shən) Harmful rays given off by nuclear material. (p. 553)

rain forest (rān fôr′ist) A place with rain almost all year round, where trees and plants grow close together. (p. 260)

rajas (rä′jəz) Hindu princes. (p. 346)

raw materials (rô mə·tir′ē·əlz) Natural resources that can be made into useful products. (p. 431)

recycle (rē·sī′kəl) To reuse. (p. 554)

Reformation (ref·ər·mā′shən) The religious movement in the sixteenth century in Europe that began as an attempt to reform the Roman Catholic Church and ended with the founding of Protestantism. (p. 200)

refugee (ref′yōō·jē) A person who leaves his or her home to seek shelter and safety elsewhere. (p. 88)

reign (rān) The rule of a monarch. (p. 220)

reincarnation (rē·in·kär·nā′shən) The return of a soul to a new life after death. (p. 345)

Renaissance (ren′ə·säns) A period of reawakened interest in the arts, literature, science, and ideas between 1400 and 1600. A French word meaning "rebirth." (p. 190)

renewable (ri·nōō′ə·bəl) Able to be reused or remade by humans or nature. (p. 552)

republic (ri·pub′lik) A form of democratic government run by elected representatives. (p. 143)

Romanesque (rō·mən·esk′) An early Middle Ages style of architecture that grew out of Roman style and featured rounded arches and vaults. (p. 179)

rotation (rō·tā′shən) A complete spin of the Earth on its axis; one day. (p. 541)

S

samurai (sam′ər·ī) A Japanese warrior. (p. 405)

Sanskrit (san′skrit) The ancient, classical language of India that is the basis for many Indian languages today. (p. 344)

satyagraha (sə·tyä′grə·hə) A Sanskrit word meaning "truth force." A way to bring about change through peaceful methods. (p. 355)

savanna (sə·van′ə) A broad, grassy plain. (p. 258)

scale (skāl) A way of showing the number of miles or kilometers there are for each inch or centimeter on a map. (p. 6)

scarce (skārs) Not enough to meet demand. (p. 270)

scholar (sko′lər) A learned person. (p. 166)

science (sī′əns) Measurable knowledge gained through study and experiment. (p. 1)

scribe (skrīb) A person who writes. (p. 33)

scroll (skrōl) A roll of paper, made by gluing together several sheets. (p. 52)

seceded (si·sēd′id) Withdrew from a political union or association. (p. 310)

secondary source (sek′ən·der·ē sôrs) A description of past events, usually based on knowledge collected from several sources. (p. 300)

serf (sûrf) A person who lived and worked on land belonging to nobles or to the Church. (p. 172)

shahs (shäz) Kings of Iran. (p. 89)

sheikh (shāk) The chief or head of an Arab tribe or family. (p. 77)

Shinto (shin′tō) A religion of Japan in which nature, heroes, and ancestors are worshipped. A word meaning "way of the gods." (p. 401)

shogun (shō′gun) Japanese "leading general." (p. 404)

shrine (shrīn) A holy place. (p. 168)

silt (silt) Fine bits of rock and sand carried or deposited by water. (p. 48)

slash and burn (slash and bûrn) A farming method where trees are cut down and burned to prepare a field for planting. When the field no longer produces, it is abandoned for a new one. (p. 263)

slave (slāv) A person who was owned by another. (p. 36)

socialism (sō′shəl·iz·əm) A political idea that all means of production and distribution should be owned by the government or groups of workers. (p. 230)

society (sə·sī′ə·tē) A group of people bound by common laws and culture. (p. 1)

solar power (sō′lər pou′ər) Energy from the sun. (p. 553)

soviet (sō′vē·et) Any of various councils in the Soviet Union formed to run government, industry, and farms. The highest legislative body is the Supreme Soviet. (p. 232)

sphere (sfir) Globe or ball. (p. 3)

squire (skwīr) In the Middle Ages, a servant of a knight at the lord's court. (p. 175)

standard of living (stan′dərd uv liv′ing) A measure of how well people live. (p. 475)

standing army (stan′ding är′mē) A full-time army made up of paid professional soldiers. (p. 275)

stations (stā′shənz) Sheep and cattle ranches in Australia and New Zealand. (p. 448)

statistics (stə·tis′tiks) Facts presented as numbers. (p. 279)

steppes (steps) Semidry plains, which produce some grasses and thorny plants. (p. 19)

strait (strāt) A narrow water passage connecting two larger bodies of water. (p. 257)

stylus (stī'ləs) A pointed reed instrument used for writing on clay tablets. (p. 33)

subarctic (sub·ärk'tik) Having long, cold winters and cool summers. (p. 334)

subcontinent (sub·kon'tə·nənt) A large part of a continent. (p. 339)

sultan (sul'tən) The ruler of a Muslim country. (p. 349)

supply (sə·plī') The amount of something that is available for use or purchase. (p. 471)

surplus (sûr'plus) Extra supply. (p. 31)

Swahili (swä·hē'lē) A language of East Africa, used widely in African business and trade. Also used to describe the people and culture from that area. (p. 284)

T

taiga (tī'gə) The forest of northern Asia. (p. 331)

tariff (tar'əf) A tax on goods or services. (p. 271)

technology (tek·nol'ə·jē) The tools and skills used to build or create things. (p. 1)

telescope (tel'ə·skōp) An instrument that uses glass lenses to make distant objects appear nearer or larger. (p. 207)

terrace (ter'əs) To build steps or levels on a hillside to prevent erosion. (p. 396)

terrorism (ter'ər·iz·əm) The use of violence and killing by a group to force a government to meet its demands. (p. 89)

textiles (teks'tīlz) Woven fabrics. (p. 78)

timeline (tīm'līn) A diagram of a certain period of time with important events marked. (p. 42)

time zone (tīm zōn) A division of the Earth that represents an hour of the day. (p. 541)

totalitarianism (tō·tal·ə·târ'ē·ən·iz·əm) A political system in which the government controls everything, or has "total" authority over all aspects of human life. (p. 243)

tradition (trə·di'shən) A custom or belief passed from one generation to the next. (p. 418)

traditional economy (trə·dish'ən·əl i·kon'ə·mē) An economic system that stays the same over a long period of time. (p. 470)

tragedy (traj'ə·dē) A serious play which has a sad or disastrous ending. (p. 133)

transportation (trans·pər·tā'shən) The act of sending a person convicted of a crime to serve time in a distant colony. (p. 457)

tribune (trib'yoon) A Roman official elected by the plebeians. (p. 144)

tribute (trib'yoot) Regular, often annual, payments made by one nation to another as the result of having been conquered. (p. 64)

tropics (trop'iks) The low latitudes on the Earth, where climates in most places are warm all year. (p. 11)

tundra (tun'drə) Cold, treeless plain whose subsoil is permanently frozen. (p. 331)

typhoons (tī·foonz') Violent hurricanes in the western Pacific Ocean. (p. 400)

U

unemployment (un·əm·ploi'mənt) Lack of work. (p. 237)

unfavorable balance of trade (un·fā'vər·ə·bəl bal'əns uv trād) The situation that exists when the income from a country's exports is less than the cost of its imports. (p. 466)

untouchables (un·tuch'ə·bəlz) In India, people who are below all castes. The name came from the idea that others would be made dirty and impure from the touch of an untouchable. (p. 344)

V

vassal (vas'əl) In the Middle Ages, one who served a lord, often in exchange for land. (p. 172)

vegetation (vej·ə·tā'shən) The natural plant life of an area. (p. 15)

veld (velt) Broad, grassy plains in Southern Africa. *Veld* is Dutch for "field." (p. 258)

veto (vē'tō) To stop passage of a law. A Latin word meaning "I forbid." (p. 144)

viceroy (vīs'roi) The chief government official who ruled as the king's representative in a Spanish colony. (p. 510)

W

warlord (wôr'lôrd) A bandit chief in China. (p. 382)

Z

ziggurat (zig'ə·rat) An ancient Mesopotamian temple. (p. 31)

Index

Page references for illustrations are set in italics.

Cacao, 263, 296, 508, 518, 519

Caesar, Augustus (emperor of Rome), 148–149, 154, 167, *243*

Caesar, Julius (emperor of Rome), 146–147, *147*, 158

Caillie, Rene, 292

Cairo, Egypt, 75, 78, 81

Cajamarca, 503

Calcutta, India, 351, 356

Calendars, 494, 495
    Chinese, 372
    of Julius Caesar, 147
    structures used as, 99–100

California, 458, 548

Calligraphy, 75, *75*
    See also Writing

Call number, of books, 136

Cambodia
    See Kampuchea

Camels, 20, 77, *77*, 266, 268–269

Camp David Accords, 88

Canada, 237, 483, 517, 534
    as an industrial nation, 549
    boundaries of, 535
    capital of, 537
    climate of, 535
    constitution of, 550–551
    cultural problem, 549–550
    development of, 544–548
    economics, 548
    forests of, 536, 547
    geography of, 535–536, *536*, 537–538
    history of, *551*
    languages, official, 539
    Loyalists in, 546
    manufacturing, industry, 537, 539, 548, 549
    modern, 549–551
    oil, 538, 539, 540, 548, 549
    people of, 539
    population of, *483*, 537
    ports of, 536
    recreation, 539
    regions of, 535–538
    resources of, 547, 548, 550
    size of, 535
    in the twentieth century, 547–548
    and the U.S., 546, 548
    in World War I, 548

in World War II, 548

Canadian Arctic, 540

Canadian Pacific Railroad, 547

Canadian Rockies, 538

Canadian Shield, 535, 537, 547

Canals, 5, 29, *87*, 216, 337, 436, 537

Canberra, Australia, 460, *460*

Canterbury Plain, New Zealand, 453, *453*

Canton Delta
    See Guangzhou

Cape Horn, 483, 484

Capitol (U.S.), *247*

Caracol, Central America, 100, *100*

Card catalog, 137
    author, title, subject cards in, 137–138, *137–138*

Careers
    See names of careers

Caribbean Sea, 483, 499

Caribou, 540

Carnauba palm, 518

Carnival, in Rio, 525, 529, *529*

Cars, 528

Carter, Howard, 58, *59*, 60

Carter, Jimmy, 88, *88*, 388

Carthage, 144, 145

Cartier, Jacques, 544

Cartoons, political, 391, *391, 392*

Caspian Sea, 19, 64, 111, 150

Cassava, 296

Caste system, 344, 345, 347, 349, 359

Castle, *174*, 175

Cathedrals, 179–180, *179, 180, 511*

Catholic
    See Roman Catholic Church

Cattle, 27–28, 47, 117
    in Australia, 452, 453, 463, 464, *464*
    in Brazil, 519
    in Canada, 538
    and the Fulanis, 305
    in India, 349, *357*
    in New Zealand, 452, 453
    in South America, 508, 513

Caucasus Mountains, 19, 111

Cause and effect, 240

Cave paintings, 98

Cebu, 440

Celebes, 437

Census, 154

Central America
    countries of, 483
    early civilization in, 493–494
    settlement of, 508

Central Lowlands, Australia, 447, 450, 451

Central Powers, 225

Central Provinces, 537

Central-West Brazil, 519

Century, 43, 573

Ceramics, 572

Chain mail, 176

Chalk, 571, 572

Champlain, Samuel de, 545

Champollion, Jean Francois, 52

Chancellors, 226

Chandragupta Maurya (king of India), 346

Chang Jiang, 332, 367, 369, 370, 372

Chao Phraya River, 430, 434

Characters, Chinese, 373

Chariots, 40, *41*, 63, *142*, 158, *158*, 372

Charlemagne, 165–166, *166*, 167, 172, 178, 197

Charles II (king of England), 545

Charles V (Holy Roman Emperor), 199–200

Charter of Rights and Freedoms, 551

Charter, 181, 319

Chartres, France, 180, *180*

Checks and balances, 249

Chemicals, 557, 559, 560, 566

Chiang Kai-shek
    See Jiang Kai-shek

Chichén Itzá, *494*

Chieftains, 165

Children
    education of, in Saudi Arabia, 80
    during Industrial Revolution, 216, *217*
    on kibbutzim, 83
    in Sumer, 36, 37–38
    See also Boys; Girls

Children's Crusades, 169, *169*

Chile, 483, 486, 488, 495, 517

China, 239, 284, 331, 337,

347, 366, 367, *381*, 385, *389*, 413, 425, 428, 430, 435, 500, 517, 575
    ancient, 372–374, *374*, 375–376, *376*, 377
    as China Proper, 367
    coal in, 336
    economic system of, 473–474
    foreign influences on, 378–382
    geography of, 367–368, *368*, 369–370
    internal changes in, 383–389
    population distribution in, 9, 369

Chinese language, 371

Chivalry, 175

Chocolate, 512

Chou dynasty
    See Zhou dynasty

Christchurch, New Zealand, 453

Christian Church, in the Middle Ages, 177–180

Christianity, 71, 74, 85, 512
    Crusades and, 168–170
    in Germanic tribes, 165
    in Japan, 406
    origins of, 71
    in Roman Empire, 151–152

Chromium, 261, 491

Chung-Kuo, 372

Church of England, 203

Church of the Holy Sepulcher, 85, *85*

Churchill, Sir Winston, *234*

Cicero, 155, 198

Cinchona, 512

Circuses, Roman, 158

Circus Maximus, *149, 158*

Cities
    of Australia and New Zealand, 463
    of Europe, 115
    growth of, in Middle Ages, 181–186
    in Industrial Revolution, 216–217
    of Minoan civilization, 118
    See also City-states; Villages and towns

Citizens
    in Greece, 124, 134
    in Italian city-states, 191

Photographs

Key: T, Top; B, Bottom; L, Left; C, Center; R, Right.

Page 3, Historical Picture Service; 9, Loren McIntyre/Woodfin Camp and Assoc.; 16, H. Armstrong Roberts; 16, Inset, Leo De Wys; 19, Mike Schneps/The Image Bank West; 27, Granger Collection; 28, Rene Burri/Magnum Photos; 32, 33, Trustees of the British Museum; 34T, SCALA/Art Resource; 34B, University of Pennsylvania Museum; 35, Hirmer Fotorachiv Munchen; 37, Trustees of the British Museum; 39, Hirmer Fotoarchiv Munchen; 41, Trustees of the British Museum; 49, Jon Arnold/Werner Forman Archive; 50, Trustees of the British Museum; 51, SCALA/ Art Resource; 52, Trustees of the British Museum; 53T, 52B, SCALA/Art Resource; 55, SEF/Art Resource; 56, John G. Ross/Photo Researchers; 57L, Bearnday/Art Resource; 57R, Granger Collection; 58, Farrell Grehan/Photo Researchers; 59TL, Steven Meir Blau; 59TR, 59BL, Photri; 59BR, Erich Lessing/Magnum Photos; 60, George Holton/Photo Researchers; 63, Erich Lessing/Magnum Photos; 64, SEF/Art Resource; 73L, Werner Forman Archive; 73R, Karen Rantzman; 74, Mehmet Biber/Photo Researchers; 75, Granger Collection; 76, Jerry Cooke/Photo Researchers; 77, Charles Harbutt/Archive Pictures; 78, Fred Mayer/Woodfin Camp and Assoc.; 80, Rene Burri/Magnum Photos; 81, Bernard Pierre Wolfe/Photo Researchers; 82, Franke Keating/Photo Researchers; 83, Charles Harbutt/Archive Pictures; 84, Erich Lessing/Magnum Photos; 85T, Alan Reininger/Contact; 85C, George Rodger/ Magnum Photos; 85B, Richard Pasley/Stock, Boston; 87, Gerhardt Leibman/Photo Researchers; 88, SIPA-PRESS/Art Resource; 89, Olivier Robbot/Woodfin Camp and Assoc.; 90, SIPA-PRESS/Black Star; 98, Art Resource; 99, FOSCH/Art Resource; 100, David Alan Harvey/Woodfin Camp and Assoc.; 102, Lawrence Migdale; 106, Shostal Associates; 106, Inset, Art Resource; 111, Shostal Associates; 114L, Nik Wheeler/Black Star; 114R, D. Beal/Black Star; 115, William Hubbell/Woodfin Camp and Assoc.; 119, Art Resource; 123, Granger Collection; 125, Bettman Archive; 126, Courtesy of the Royal Ontario Museum, Toronto, Canada; 127, Steven Meir Blau; 128, 129, SCALA/Art Resource; 132, Dan McCoy/Black Star; 133, Constantine Manos/Magnum Photos; 135, All, Granger Collection; 138, HBJ Photo/Rodney Jones; 142, The Metropolitan Museum of Art/Rogers Fund, 1903; 145, 147, Granger Collection; 149, SCALA/Art Resource; 151, Granger Collection; 152, SCALA/Art Resource; 156, Peter Menzel/Stock, Boston; 157, Larry Mulvehill/Photo Researchers; 158, All, 159, All, SCALA /Art Resource; 160, 161, All, 162, HBJ Photo/Karen Rantzman; 166, Art Resource; 167, University Museum of National Antiquities, Oslo, Norway; 169, Historical Pictures Service, Chicago; 170, Art Resource; 174, Henry Clay Lindgren, Ph.D.; 176, Metropolitan Museum of Art, Rogers Fund, 1927; 178TL, Metropolitan Museum of Art, The Cloisters Collection, 1969; 178BR, Granger Collection; 179, Bettman Archive; 180, SCALA/Art Resource; 183, All, 184, Granger Collection; 186, Bettman Archive; 192, SEF/Art Resource; 193, SCALA/Art Resource; 194L, Cliche des Musees Nationaux, Paris, 194R, Art Resource; 195, Dr. Eugene A. Eisner/ Photo Researchers; 196, Bibliotheque Nationale; 197T, Bettman Archive; 199, SCALA/Art Resource; 200, Bettman Archive; 201, "ARXIU MAX"; 202, Granger Collection; 203, Art Resource; 204L, Bettman Archive; 204R, Lauros-Giraudon; 205, Granger Collection; 206, Bulloz; 215, 217, Granger Collection; 219, Bulloz; 220, Granger Collection; 221, Cliche des Musees Nationaux, Paris; 223T, Ian Berry/Magnum Photos; 223C, Photri; 223B, Wide World Photos; 225, Imperial War Museum; 226, Culver Pictures; 228, Wide World Photos; 229, Howard Sochurek/Woodfin Camp and Assoc.; 231, Granger Collection; 232, Jergen Bitsch/Black Star; 233, Frank Viner/UPI; 234, Granger Collection; 235, Chuck Fishmann/Woodfin Camp and Assoc.; 247, UPI; 238TL, Sepp Seitz/Woodfin Camp and Assoc.; 238TR, Gary Wolinsky/Stock, Boston; 238BL, Granger Collection; 238BR, Ingeborg Lipmann/Magnum Photos; 243, Robert Emmett Bright/Photo Researchers; 244, Tim Graham/ Sygma; 245, Jim Holland/Stock, Boston; 246T, Granger Collection; 246B, Burt Glinn/Magnum Photos; 247T, Richard Kalyar/Woodfin Camp and Assoc.; 247C, 247B, Granger Collection; 249, Andy Levin/Black Star; 250T, Owen Franklin/Stock, Boston; 250B, Wide World Photos; 254, Shostal Assoc.; 254, Inset, H. Armstrong Roberts; 258L, Victor Englebert/Photo Researchers; 258R, Paulo Koch/Photo Researchers; 261, John Elk III; 265, National Commission for Museum and Monument, Nigeria; 266, Larry Burrows, LIFE Magazine, 1966, Time, Inc.; 269, George Holton/Photo Researchers; 270, Victor Englebert/Photo Researchers; 273, The British Library; 274, Werner Forman Archive; 278, New York Public Library/The British Museum; 284, Morgan C. Cowin; 285, Granger Collection; 286, J. Bryan/Photo Researchers; 287, All, James A. Sugar/Black Star; 288, Bettman Archive; 289, New York Public Library; 291, Granger Collection; 293, Bettman Archive; 294, Photri; 299, Granger Collection; 304L, Nik Wheeler/Black Star; 304R, Alouise Boker/Photo Researchers; 305, Marc and Evelyne Bernheim/Woodfin Camp and Assoc.; 306, George Gerster/Photo Researchers; 308L, UPI/Bettmann Newsphotos; 308R, Bettmann Newsphotos; 309, Sygma; 310, Bruno Barbey/ Magnum Photos; 311, Photri; 312T, Fred Ward/Black Star; 312C, Jean Graumy/Magnum Photos; 312B, Fred Ward/Black Star; 314, Monkmeyer Press Photo; 319, George Holton/Photo Researchers; 320T, Lisl Steiner/Photo Researchers; 320B, Maggie Steber/Stock, Boston; 321T, United Nations; 321B, Burt Glinn/Magnum Photos; 322, All, UPI; 323, UNICEF; 324, Dominique Roger/UNESCO; 328, Irvin E. Newman/The Image Bank; 328, Inset, Art Resource; 332L, Peter Jackson/ Bruce Coleman, Inc.; 322R, M. Fantin/Photri; 335, David Austin/Black Star; 341L, George Gerster/Photo Researchers; 341R, Brian Brake/Photo Researchers; 342T, Bruno Barbey/Magnum Photos; 342C, Dan DeWilde; 342B, Jehangir Gazdai/Woodfin Camp and Assoc.; 344, Harry Groyaeri/Magnum Photos; 345, John Elk III/ Bruce Coleman, Inc.; 346, Bradley Smith/Photo Researchers; 347T, Roland Michaud/Woodfin Camp and Assoc.; 347B, Dan DeWilde; 348, Helen Marcus/Photo Researchers; 350, Metropolitan Museum of Art, Gift of Alexander Smith Cochran, 1913; 351, Roland and Sabrina Michaud/Woodfin Camp and Assoc.; 352, Art Resource; 354, Bettman Archive; 355, Wayne Miller/Magnum Photos; 357T, Eliha Blotnik/Woodfin Camp and Assoc.; 357B, Ira Kerschenbaum/Stock, Boston; 358T, Dan DeWilde; 358B, Marc and Evelyne Bernheim/Woodfin Camp and Assoc.; 359, Marilyn Silverstone/Magnum Photos; 360, Reuters/Bettman Newsphoto; 368, Elisa Leonelli/Bruce Coleman, Inc.; 369L, Bruno Barbey/Magnum Photos; 369R, A. Topping/Photo Researchers; 371T, Jackie Swenson; 371C, Leslie Wong/Contract; 371B, Lauren Freudmann/Woodfin Camp and Assoc.; 373, Columbia University; 374TL, Asian Art Museum of San Francisco; 374BR, Photri; 375, Art Resource; 377, Granger Collection; 379, Photri; 380, Granger Collection; 381, Trustees of the British Museum; 382, Owen/Black Star; 384, 385, Eastfoto; 386, Photri; 387TR, Eastfoto; 387BL, Paulo Koch/Photo Researchers; 388, Alan Zenuk/Black Star; 391, Steve Kelley; 392, Tribune Company Syndicate, Inc., Jeff MacNelly; 396, Brian Blake/Photo Researchers; 397T, Photri; 397BR, Art Resource; 398, Bob Glaze/Artstreet; 399, Bradley Smith/Gemini Smith; 400, Sotheby Parke-Bernet/Art Resource; 401, Roy King; 402, Henry Clay Lindgren/Photo Researchers; 403, Susan McCartney/Photo Researchers; 404, TIME, Inc., 1953; 405, Photri; 406, Werner Forman/San Francisco Museum of Asiatic Art; 407, Werner Forman/ Burke Collection; 408, /Werner Forman; 409, R. A. Vroom/Black Star; 410T, Dana Levy/Photo Researchers; 410C, Fred Ward/Black Star; 410B, Cleveland Museum of Art, The Norweb Collection; 412, Bettman Archive; 414, Stuart Cohen/Stock, Boston; 416, Photri; 417L, Adriano Heitmann/Archive Pictures; 417R, Fred Ward/Black Star; 418, Photo Researchers; 419, Rich Smolan/Contact; 426L, SCALA/Art Resource; 426R, Rene Burri/Magnum Photos; 427, Eve Arnold/Magnum Photos; 428, Jim Balog/Black Star; 429, SEF/Art Resource; 432, Dan Burstein/Contact; 433T, Robert Perron/Photo Researchers; 433C, Nik Wheeler/Black Star; 433B, Arthur Zich; 435L, Paolo Koch/Photo Researchers; 435R, Porterfield-Chickering/Photo Researchers; 436L, Susan McCarthey/Photo Researchers; 436R, John Launois/Black Star; 437L, David Alan Harvey/Woodfin Camp and Assoc.; 437R, Paul Fusco/ Magnum Photos; 438, All, Werner Forman Archive; 439, Frank Schrieber; 440, John Launois/Black Star; 441, J. Messerschmidt/Bruce Coleman, Inc.; 442, Leo De Wys, Inc.; 449, Al Grotell; 450, The Photo Source; 451, James Walshe/The Stock Market; 452, F. Prenzel/Earth Scenes; 453, Robert Frerck/Woodfin Camp and Assoc.; 454T, J. Cancalosi/Tom Stack and Assoc.; 454TC, G. R. Roberts, Nelson, N. Z.; 454BC, J. Cancalosi/Tom Stack and Assoc.; 454B, Robert Frerck/Odyssey Productions; 455, David C. Fritts/Earth Scenes; 456, Granger Collection; 457, 458, Culver Pictures; 459, Alexander Turnbull Library, Wellington; 460, G. R. Roberts Nelson, N. Z.; 463, Camaramann, Intl.; 464, Robert Frerck/Odyssey Productions; 465, Momatiuk-Eastcott/Woodfin Camp and Assoc.; 466, G. R. Roberts, Nelson, N. Z.; 470, R. G. Evert/Photo Researchers; 471, HBJ Photo/Karen Rantzman; 472, Tass/Sovfoto; 473, Larry Mulvehill/Photo Researchers; 474, Marc and Evelyne Bernheim/Woodfin Camp and Assoc.; 475T, Henry Clay Lindgren, Ph. D.; 475B, H. Armstrong Roberts; 480, H. Armstrong Roberts; 480, Inset, Museum of the American Indian; 488, Valan Photos; 489, Loren McIntyre/Woodfin Camp and Assoc.; 494, Kal Muller/Woodfin Camp and Assoc.; 496, Photri; 497, Werner Forman, Private Collection; 498, Loren McIntrye/Woodfin Camp and Assoc.; 502, Werner Forman, The British Museum; 503, Granger Collection; 510, Mel Wright/Art Resource; 511, Henry Clay Lindgren, Ph. D.; 512, Bettman Archive; 514T, John Flannery; 514C, Cary Wolinsky/Stock, Boston; 514B, Norman Tomalin/Bruce Coleman, Inc.; 519, Loren McIntyre/Woodfin Camp and Assoc.; 520, Victor Englebert/Black Star; 522, Granger Collection; 524, Ellis Herwig/Stock, Boston; 526T, Claus Meyer/Black Star; 526B, Carl Frank/Photo Researchers; 527, U. S. Geological Survey/EROS Data Center; 529T, Lawrence Migdale; 529C, Tom McHugh; 529B, Claus Meyer/Black Star; 532, SEF/Art Resource; 537, Erich Hartmann/Magnum Photos; 538L, John DeVisser/Art Resource; 538R, Douglas Kirkland; 539, Burt Glinn/Magnum Photos; 540T, Marcello Bertinelli; 540TC, Helen Williams/Photo Researchers; 540BC, Dan Guravich/Photo Researchers; 540B, Steven Krasemann; 545, Public Archives of Canada, Ottawa, Picture Division; 547, Bettman Archive; 548, Paolo Koch/Photo Researchers; 550, Jonathan Wenk/Black Star; 556, NASA; 558T, Roger Werth/Woodfin Camp and Assoc.; 558B, Eijii Miyazawa/Black Star; 559, J. Flannery/Black Star; 560T, Richard Kehrwald/Black Star; 560B, Junebug Clark/Photo Researchers; 561T, Doug Wilson, Black Star; 561B, Donald Dietz/Stock, Boston; 565, Photri; 567, Rene Burri/Magnum Photos; 568, Peter Menzel; 569L, A. Tsiaras/Photo Researchers; 569R, Douglas Kirkland/Contact; 570, Lawrence Migdale/Photo Researchers; 571, Peter Menzel; 572, Photri; 574, NASA; 575, Barbara Alper/Stock, Boston; 576, Bill Gallery/Stock, Boston; 577, HBJ Photo/Eric Arneson; 578, Photri; 579, NASA.

Covers: L, Dallas and John Heaton/After Image; C, Milt and Joan Mann/Cameramann International; T, Zefal H. Armstrong Roberts; B, H. Armstrong Roberts.

Illustrations

Walter Brooks: 30, 51, 172, 185. Kirchoff/Wohlberg, Chris Calle: 24, 46, 116, 140, 164. Kirchoff/Wohlberg, Bradley Clark: 212, 264, 282, 302, 338, 366, 424, 492, 516. Larry Hughston: 267. Intergraphics: 4, 5, 7, 11, 13, 42, 43, 44, 45, 48, 65, 91, 92, 93, 94, 104, 121, 134, 137, 143, 144, 157, 186, 188, 207, 239, 241, 248, 261, 279, 290, 297, 335, 360, 364, 370, 389, 416, 419, 444, 476, 482, 483, 513, 528, 531, 551, 553. Eric Joyner: 38, 120. Jang Ju-Yü: 373. Charles McBarron: 446. Stephanie Pershing: 155, 173, 509. Carla Simmons: 35, 97, 557. Kirchoff/Wohlberg, Arvis Stewart: 62. Kirchoff/Wohlberg, Jas Szygiel: 70, 190, 394, 534. Bill Walker: 136, 156, 187, 491. Nancy Warner: 214, 542.

Maps

R. R. Donnelley Cartographic Services: 6, 8, 9, 10, 12, 14, 15, 18, 20, 21, 22, 26, 31, 40, 63, 66, 67, 68, 72, 108, 110, 112, 113, 118, 130, 142, 150, 166, 168, 182, 192, 208, 209, 210, 216, 222, 227, 230, 256, 259, 260, 262, 271, 275, 285, 296, 315, 330, 333, 334, 336, 340, 344, 361, 362, 363, 368, 376, 396, 413, 421, 422, 431, 443, 448, 452, 478, 482, 485, 487, 490, 495, 497, 500, 504, 505, 506, 507, 518, 536, 541, 543, R6, R8, R10, R11, R12, R13, R14, R15, R16, R18.

8
9
0
E 1
F 2
G 3
H 4
I 5
J 6